The Heart of Europe

𝕁𝔹

Previous Books by J.P. Stern

Ernst Jünger: a Writer of Our Time

G.C. Lichtenberg: a Doctrine of Scattered Occasions

Re-interpretations: Seven Studies in Nineteenth-Century German Literature

Idylls and Realities: Studies in Nineteenth-Century German Literature

On Realism

Hitler: the Führer and the People

Nietzsche

A Study of Nietzsche

The World of Franz Kafka (editor)

Nietzsche on Tragedy (with M.S. Silk)

Landmarks of World Literature (general editor)

The Heart of Europe

Essays on Literature and Ideology

J.P. Stern

BLACKWELL
Oxford UK & Cambridge USA

The right of J.P. Stern to be identified as author of this work has been asserted in accordance with the Copyright, Designs and Patents Act 1988.
First published 1992

Blackwell Publishers
108 Cowley Road
Oxford OX4 1JF
UK

Three Cambridge Center
Cambridge, Massachusetts 02142
USA

A CIP catalogue record for this book is available from the British Library.

Library of Congress Cataloging in Publication Data
Stern, J.P. (Joseph Peter)
   The heart of Europe : essays on literature and ideology / J.P. Stern.
   p.   cm.
   Includes bibliographical references and index.
   ISBN 0-631-15849-9 (alk. paper) : ISBN 0-631-18473-2 (pbk.)
   1. German literature—20th century—History and criticism.
   2. German literature—Central Europe—History and criticism.
   3. Central Europe—Civilization.   4. Literature and society—Central Europe.   I. Title.
   PT405.S7426   1992
   830.9'0091—dc20   91-25266
                                                               CIP

Typeset in 10 on 11 pt Ehrhardt
by Photo·graphics, Honiton, Devon
Printed in Great Britain
This book is printed on acid-free paper.

In memoriam Erich Heller
Chomutov/Komotau (Bohemia), 27 March 1911 –
Evanston (Illinois), 5 November 1990

Contents

Introduction

1

There are no Central European patriots. 'Central Europe' is a notion we need but don't cherish. Once 'the old lands of Western Christendom', it is neither a geographical unit nor, after the dissolution of the Habsburg Empire, a political one. For the French and British tourists of the Victorian age the centre of Europe lay in Switzerland, Northern Italy and Bismarck's Germany. In the years between the two world wars that centre shifted further east, to include Czechoslovakia and Hungary. After the Yalta and Potsdam conferences and the westward shift of the Polish frontier in compensation for the territories annexed by Soviet Russia, 'Central Europe' has come to include the Polish People's Republic. It seems to be 'a concept with blurred edges'. 'But is a blurred concept a concept at all?' asks Wittgenstein (see essay 28)*, and he answers himself with another question: 'Is it indeed always an advantage to replace an indistinct picture by a sharp one?'

There is much that is tragic and much that is absurd about the recent history of this ill-defined territory, and often it is difficult to tell which is which. The Central European states that owed their existence and independence to the settlements of Versailles, Saint-Germain and Trianon bore the seeds of their own destruction. Take the Austrians' clamour for unification with Germany: it was certainly intensified by the propaganda campaign of Hitler's Third Reich after 1933, but the slogans of 'Deutsch-Österreich' go back to the party of Hitler's mentor, Georg von Schönerer, and they accompanied the birth of the first Austrian Republic in 1919. The 'successor states' founded after the dissolution of the Empire were by no means new creations: their new frontiers often coincided with their 'historic' frontiers both before and throughout the Habsburg era. But from their beginnings under the aegis of President Wilson's Fourteen Points of 1918, their statehood was flawed by a contradiction. They

---

* Bracketed essay-references are to essays in this volume.

were conceived as single-nation states equipped with all the outward trimmings of national sovereignty, and yet, contrary to the Wilsonian doctrine, the victorious Allies allowed them to include large German and Hungarian populations, that is, minorities with irredentist aspirations similar to, but more virulent than, those aspirations which had contributed to the breakup of the Habsburg Empire.

So there is a 'definition' of Central Europe after all: it includes all those European states created at the end of the Great War which, come the crunch, proved incapable of defending their independence. A major reason for that incapacity lay in the defection of their minorities. On the first occasion that offered itself, these minorities ceased to be loyal to the states in which their own national status had been either inadequately recognized or recognized too late. It was all too easy for Hitler's Germany to foster an atmosphere of violent discontent among fellow Germans beyond the borders of the Reich, thus making sure that no recognition of their national claims should ever be seen as adequate. What is special, and characteristically Central European, about every phase of this recent history is the part played by propaganda – by the politics of claims and demands of ideologies formulated and made effective with the help of the rhetoric of nationalism. 'The pen is mightier than the sword' and 'The truth will prevail' were the mottoes on which many of these claims were based: conceived as salves (or at least as consolation prizes) of the weak, such mottoes were proved disastrously wrong as soon as they were contested.

The rhetoric of nationalism was not a recent invention but had its origins in the old Empire; yet in its ever more insistent form it did become a new element in the history of international relations. It was the product of intellectuals, some of whom were self-seeking and hungry for power, while others, chief among them T. G. Masaryk, conceived their goals with great moral integrity. *Public Relations (PR)* itself, also known as *Kulturpolitik*, one of the vehicles of this propaganda, seems to have been an invention of the upper ranks of the much maligned Viennese civil service, though by no means the only one. But the sophisticated and by and large uncorrupt bureaucracies which administered the lands of the Austro-Hungarian Empire at a time 'when Britain was being governed by parish vestries and Justices of the Peace' did not survive the cataclysm of the Great War, whereas *PR* did. It is the successor states' Austrian inheritance.

After 1945, the arrival of Soviet Russia as the dominant power in Central Europe (for the first time in history) made it easy (as it had never been before) for Czechoslovakia and Poland to expel their 'foreign' minorities, even though most of those minorities had been inhabiting those lands for 1,000 years. Considering the atrocities the Germans of the Third Reich had committed in the years of occupation, the violence of the expulsions that followed in the first two years after the end of the war is not surprising. The fate suffered by the Jews of Central Europe was worse but resulted from similar passions. Their annihilation had been Hitler's and his party's major aim (essay 21).

There were few local difficulties about achieving this aim, for compared with the Jews of Italy and of western and northern Europe, the Jews of this region received very little succour from their Aryan fellow citizens during the German occupation; and after that was over anti-Semitism continued to make life hard for the few that were left. They too, like the expelled Germans, were the victims of the various nationalisms the Germans had humiliated while they were masters of continental Europe, for the Jews were regarded as members of a hostile, 'Germanizing' minority. There are times in the history of this region when one has to remind oneself that (to quote Marlow, Joseph Conrad's narrator) some of its inhabitants were . . . 'No, they were not inhuman. Well, you know, that was the worst of it – this suspicion of their not being inhuman.' Here, then, is a second definition of Central Europe: Auschwitz, Katyn and Dresden mark it as a zone of deadly hostilities, the very heart of darkness. And, strange though it may seem and discomforting as I have found it, some of the most revealing reports on what was done in that zone in our time come from deeply tainted and suspect sources.

As after 1918, the eventual settlement after 1945 was based on a contradiction, though this time there were no intellectuals of sufficient standing and moral integrity to advise the victorious Allies on the future of the region. The 'population transfers' of 1945–6 did not reach the degree of lawlessness and violence experienced under the German occupation, nor however were the expulsions compatible with the ethos of democratic government under the rule of law which these states professed and to which their dissidents would eventually appeal. Partly as a consequence of these forced mass migrations and partly because of fundamental and I think permanent changes in the ethos and conduct of successive (West) German governments over the last four-and-a-half decades of peace, there are now no irredentist populations and no serious minority problems in Central Europe. If there is a threat to the European peace, it will come from the nationalist aspirations of minorities further east and south.

The nations and tribes that inhabit this space with blurred edges have lived at daggers drawn with each other for many centuries, and some of their old hostility survives. And yet: there is a congruence about the peaceful revolutions which followed on Mikhail Gorbachev's accession to power in 1985 and proceeded according to an extraordinarily neat timetable through Poland, Hungary and Eastern Germany to Czechoslovakia, in a sequence of events in which Austria managed both not to take an active part and yet to play a crucial role. Now, one liberation didn't merely follow another, but each was triggered off and made possible by the example of its unloved neighbour. What this suggests is not only a series of psychological and social resemblances among the members of this family of states, but also, for the first time since the Middle Ages, at least the possibility of a common future based not on conquest and compulsion but on something like democratic free choice. Who would ever have thought that the opening of the Austrian border on the Neusiedlersee would cause a huge convoy of stinking Trabanten to set out from the German

North Sea ports, or that a Hungarian border guard would take a pregnant East German woman into his house so that his wife could assist at the birth? And so a third definition emerges, of Central Europe as the heir of the French Revolution, two hundred years and almost no violence after the event.

2

This is the background to most of the essays collected in this book. It is history seen in terms of wars and treaties and international politics, from the hilltops. 'Josef K.', the pseudonymous author of one of the many samizdat essays which circulated in Czechoslovakia in the 1980s, offers the view from below. It is not a flattering picture, nor is it meant to be. Central Europe (or 'central Europe', as the *Encyclopædia Britannica* coyly calls it) is seen by 'Josef K.' as 'a torso that is forever being eroded by the waves of history'. It is a region populated by Franz Kafka's anti-heroes, the K.s, at the mercy of events they have long since given up controlling, their energies taken up with foraging, their ingenuity employed in the service of creature comforts, their morality worsted in their collaborating as readily with the German National Socialists and their minions as with the communists whose Reich was Soviet Russia (for some of them the old adages 'ubi bene, ibi patria' and 'ex oriente lux' were conflated into 'ubi Lenin ibi Jerusalem' (essay 26)). In this view of the jumble of territories, history has given way to anecodote, tragedy to the grotesque. No great passions, creative or destructive, are at work in these grey-on-grey societies of modest little people. This ('Josef K.' concludes) is a landscape without great dramatic peaks; above it there hovers a smell of braised cabbage, stale beer and overripe melons.

The characteristic culture of Central Europe, which is the main concern of 'Josef K.', is literature – a literature which (by way of a paradox he doesn't explain) achieves its greatness and symbolic value throughout the Western world by faithfully and unsparingly evoking this dispiriting everyday. Enter Franz Kafka, whose main achievement and originality are seen to derive from his portrayal of this grey life under the aspect of bureaucracy. Kafka's novel *The Trial* (written in 1914) ends with the execution of its 'hero', Josef K., in a quarry which most Bohemian readers will identify with the Strahov quarry behind the Hradčany Castle–now Havel's castle (essay 24) – that towers over the city of Prague. With Josef K.'s execution 'ends the era of the state officials, and the era of the functionaries begins.' But both are 'little people', endowed with power from a source that remains mysterious to them. The difference between them lies in the different structures they serve. The official acts and hides 'under the blanket' of the power structure of the existing, tradition-bound state, whereas his successor, the functionary, owes his authority to his allegiance to a notional construct such as 'gesundes Volksempfinden' ('sound national feeling') or 'real existing socialism' – that is, to an ideology of the state to come, an ideology of promise. Western readers are bound to object that the way the pseudonymous 'Josef K.' interprets the realistic and prophetic aspects of the novel does not reveal all there is to Kafka's work. But then, its metaphysical and religious implications, all too readily fantasized by Western critics, are not so readily accessible to readers who are forced to live within the penumbra of a soul-destroying bureaucracy. By anchoring Kafka's fiction in 'real existing' institutions, interpretations such as that of 'Josef K.' remove the ground from under countless speculative extravaganzas: providing Kafka's writings with their human and historical substance, he reminds us that it isn't only its sorties into metaphysics that keep the work alive. Without their substantiation in the social, political and legal world, Kafka's writings would have suffered the same oblivion as most of what was written in his time and place.

Kafka is one of those writers who cause us to revise our notions of the borders between the literary, the documentary and the autobiographical aspects of a work of literature, and by doing so creates his own context. His achievement owes little to the ambience of the German-speaking and largely Jewish writers of Prague (essay 4): there is a search for the lurid and the sensational in the writings of many of his friends, which in most of his stories are kept at bay. His best readers were elsewhere. Among them was Bruno Schulz, a Polish Jewish writer and draughtsman who was born in 1892 (nine years after Kafka) and was murdered in 1942 by a Gestapo man in a street of his native town of Drohobycz in Galicia. (Is it worth speculating what Kafka's fate would have been had he not died in the summer of 1924? (essay 12).) Certainly, the influence of Kafka's stories (some of which Schulz translated) is discernible in Schulz's prose. The source of its inspiration, too, is what Kafka described as 'my dreamlike inner life,' and from his own inner life each author devised images and scenes that are particularly suited to the short prose forms. Above all, Schulz shares something of Kafka's true poetic gift: in his writing, too, words assume a life of their own – a life which only later turns out to be the life they were intended for. But there are also imporant differences. Kafka's imaginative uses of that inner life have more substance of the everyday than Schulz's, he orders his images and scenes by drawing more abundantly on his (and our) world of things and encounters, yet avoids explicit historical settings; whereas Schulz's small œuvre, while less tied to the actuality of the things and relationships we know, draws on and fictionalizes the particulars of history for its own ends. In one of his haunting fantasies the Polish author recaptures the fountainhead of the bureaucracy that ruled the Austro-Hungarian Empire:

> There is much to be said for the belief that Franz Joseph was at heart a powerful but sad demiurge. His narrow eyes, dull like tiny buttons embedded in triangular deltas of wrinkles, were not human eyes. His hairy face, with its milky white sideburns brushed back like those of Japanese demons, was the face of a glum old fox. Seen from a distance, from the height of a terrace at Schönbrunn, that face, owing to a certain firm arrangement of wrinkles, seemed to smile. From nearby that smile

unmasked itself as a grimace of bitterness and prosaic matter-of-factness, unrelieved by a spark of an idea. At the very moment when he appeared on the world stage in a general's green plumes, slightly hunched and saluting, his turquoise-blue coat reaching to the ground, the world had completed a happy epoch in its development. All set forms, having exhausted their content in endless metamorphoses, hung loosely upon things, half wilted, ready to flake off. The world was a chrysalis about to change violently, to breed in young, clashing and unheard-of colours, happily stretching all in sinews and joints. It was touch and go, and the map of the world, that patchwork sail of many colours, might, in sheer enthusiasm, float away on the air. Franz Joseph I felt this as a personal danger. His true element was a world held captive by prosy routine orders, by the pragmatism of boredom. The ambience of government offices and circulars filled his spirit. And, a strange thing, this dried-up, dull-witted old man, with nothing in the least engaging in him, succeeded in pulling the greater part of creation to his side. All the loyal and provident fathers of families felt threatened along with him, and breathed a sigh of relief when this powerful demon laid his weight upon everything and checked the world's upward flight. Franz Joseph ruled the world into squares like a sheet of paper, regulated its course with the help of patents, tied it up in procedural red tape, and insured it against derailment into things unforeseen, adventurous and entirely unpredictable.

Franz Joseph was no enemy of decent, godfearing pleasures. It was he who had thought up, under the spur of a certain anticipatory benevolence, the imperial-and-royal lottery for the people, Egyptian dreambooks, illustrated calendars, and the imperial-and-royal tobacco shops. He standardized the heavenly servants, dressed them in symbolic sky-blue uniforms and, dividing them into ranks and sections, he let these heavenly hosts loose upon the world, in the shape of postmen, conductors and tax collectors. The meanest of those heavenly messengers wore on his face a reflection of age-old wisdom borrowed from his creator, and a jovial, gracious smile framed by sideburns, even if, as a result of his extensive earthly wanderings, the messenger's feet reeked of sweat.

We are back again in the company of those put-upon, little people of the sketch by 'Josef K.' Their main spokesman is Jaroslav Hašek, the 'crass' Czech humorist who, in 1911, created 'the good soldier Švejk' (essay 7), an archetypal figure who needed the monstrous event of the Great War to emerge into the full light of history. The fact that Švejk or Kafka's K.s or Schulz's strange, shadowy figures are anything but conventional heroes must not mislead us, as it has misled many critics, especially Central European ones: none of these authors ever writes about 'the masses.' None of them is guilty of that contempt for the 'masses' which so many of their contemporaries – among them Oswald Spengler (essay 8) and Martin Heidegger (10), Hermann Broch and Elias Canetti (25) – place at the centre of their historical or philosophical constructs.

Shortly after the dissolution of the state the Habsburgs had created and failed to keep alive, the satirist Karl Kraus depicted these 'masses' with the full force of his mordant wit:

> Once, at a railway station near Vienna, I saw the face of Austria in a ticket-window. The shutter had been down for the last two hours, and a flock of 500 sheep-like Viennese were standing patiently in front of it. Nothing stirred until I used my walking-stick to get a reaction. Then the shutter went up, revealing an exceptionally undernourished face, a face such as I had never seen so sated with its own diabolical enjoyment. A bony finger also appeared, wagging to and fro, denying all hope to life before this gate of Hell. And I don't know, now, whether it was the finger or the expression or an actual voice calling out – I heard the words quite clearly – 'We're not going to sell no tickets!' ['Wird koane Koaten ausgeben!'] It was the signal for the Austrian revolution. The Viennese began to rage, groups formed, a reliable source announced that he was ready to lead everybody onto the platform through a little back door. When he had done so, the train arrived, and turned out to be so crowded that another 500 passengers made no difference; they got on without tickets, and from the mass of groaning bodies I could make out the voices of two revolutionaries: 'Up in front it's empty, but the guard told me to get in at the back,' and 'He told me to get in at the front, so I thought to myself it's bound to be empty at the back.' I saw no face, but it was Austria's.

Critics have sought to enhance Kraus's literary fame by presenting his writings as 'prophetic,' and so in some ways they are. Yet his satires, having a life of their own, lose neither their interest nor their vigour when we acknowledge our particular good fortune in having witnessed a series of revolutions of a very different kind, which Kraus's writings don't prophesy in any way. And much the same can be said about 'Josef K.'s' image of 'the torso that is forever being eroded by the wave of history.' It reflects, no doubt accurately, the awful inertia of Central European history in the 1970s and 1980s, but it does nothing to help us understand what ended it. The thesis this image supports is one which Hannah Arendt borrowed from Karl Kraus's mega-drama *The Last Days of Mankind* and in her report of the trial of Adolf Eichmann in Jerusalem named 'the banality of evil'. It is an unfortunate phrase. More than of braised cabbage, stale beer and overripe melons, the intellectual atmosphere of Central Europe reeked of the contempt expressed in that phrase; and contempt everywhere and always, except in the form of the figured contempt of satire, is a bad guide. True, mass murderers and other people who act from evil motives for evil ends often lead lacklustre, ordinary lives, like those who act from good motives for good ends. But to claim that this makes them or their deeds banal is sophisticated nonsense. The forces at work in the world of Central Europe were more dramatic and more powerful for good and evil than Arendt's phrase allows. What the argument from 'banality' cannot account for are not only the monstrous deeds of genocide (of the Gypsies (essay 15) as well as the Jews) which traumatized whole populations for many decades, but also the events of 1989 and 1990 (essays 22, 24) – the days and weeks of spontaneous, non-violent revolt without intellectual leadership or ideological directives. These were strange, unexpected events, unprecedented in recent histroy, yet I think there is no mystery why ideological explanations do not fit them. The one thing most ideologists of the Left and Right were agreed on, though for different reasons, was their contempt for 'the masses.'

3

In several of the essays that follow it has been my aim to present scenes from the life and literature of Central Europe in yet another perspective, under yet another definition: to see it as a region in the heart of Europe which was shaped by the conflicting forces of language consciousness. Here, language, being contested, provides the impetus to antagonisms and social change which in the nineteenth century were falsely ascribed to race:

> One evening six years ago [writes an English correspondent in 1990] I was sitting in a pub drinking beer with several sociologists from Budapest University. I was explaining to three of them some work in which I had been involved on youth culture in Czechoslovakia, East Germany and Hungary. One bearded man asked how I could begin to understand anything about Hungarian culture if I did not speak the language fluently. I replied that even without [the] language it is possible, through study and observation, to draw some conclusions about other cultures. He then denounced me publicly for daring to write anything about Hungary. The conversation was happily diverted for a few minues until I mentioned the name Košice. My bearded friend turned round at this point and smashed his beer glass down on the table. 'What did you say?', he roared at me, silencing the entire table.
> 'Košice,' I replied.
> 'And what is this "Košice"?' he continued, foaming at the mouth.
> I told him that it was a city in eastern Slovakia, as he very well knew.
> 'Oh,' he said, 'our English friend means Kassa but obviously finds Hungarian pronunciation difficult.'
> I continued to call it Košice, but for the remainder of the evening this man, who was about to become a doctor of sociology, glared at me as though I were sub-human.

Although somewhat unpropitious to scholarly or philosophical inquiry, this conversation points to the importance assumed in this region by questions of language – an importance they have nowhere else in modern Europe; nor, however, is it surprising that some of the most original and illuminating thinking about the status and diverse functions of language in experience come from this part of our world. It is here that Ludwig Wittgenstein's philosophical investigation originated, here that some of the pviotal insights of his work (essay 28) receive what, on the face of it, he gave little attention to – their concrete historical and political confirmations. The relationship of words to deeds (essay 3), the merits of the method of 'family resemblances' over categorical rules, and of designations with 'blurred edges' over procrustean notions of 'scientific' exactitude, the recognitions of meaning as determined by usage, or again our beguilement by the metaphors and images we use – these are some of the insights which are very directly related to the setting which the essays of this book present; and so, above all, is the function of language that is fundamental to these insights:

> 'So you are saying that human agreement decides what is true and what is false' – It is what human beings *say* that is true and false; and they agree in the *language* they use. That is not agreement in opinions but in form of life.

In this Central European setting violent and eventually bloody conflicts arose between societies committed to different languages and thus divided not merely by different 'opinions' about the social and political problems they had in common, but by different forms of life. Here a poet and grammarian – L'udevít Štúr – could straitjacket a dialect (of Central Slovakia) into a norma- tive grammar in order to try to magnify its differentiæ and thus substantiate its speakers' aspiration to linguistic and therefore national independence (first from the Hungarians, then from the Czechs) – one of several instances when the claim that languages cannot be 'the creation of grammarians' was undermined. Here, and here alone, it was a matter of pride not to know a language (first German or Hungarian, now Russian). This was, and often still is, not a matter of 'accents' determining social status within one national whole, of failing to get into the Foreign Office because you drop your aitches or intrude your *r*'s. Here the ability to roll and trill your *r*'s could become a matter of life or death (essay 4).

Different forms of life enshrined in different languages don't necessarily lead to conflicts. There have been times in the history of Central Europe when different languages and their interaction brought with them an enrichment of culture and of life itself; that the country's future would be so enriched was the hope of the Bohemian philosopher-priest Bernard Bolzano in the years before 1848 (essay 2). It was a vain hope. The date marks not only the débâcle of German liberalism, but the beginning of an era when the differences – in language and culture, in music and dress, in myth and custom – were cultivated, consciously and deliberately, until they reached the point of incompatibility. Of course, at no point was this a matter of 'language as such', of language out of context: nothing interesting ever is that. These forms of life became incompatible only when one linguistic community acquired the power to assert itself over another or, conversely, when one felt threatened by another. (This too is history, seen neither from the hilltops nor from below.) There is a strange irony about Wittgenstein's emphasis on the contexts, conventions and institutions which form a language and are formed by it, coming as it does from one who was apt to ignore conventions and felt alienated from and ill at ease with institutions of any kind. But this irony, too, belongs to the setting I have sought to re-create in these pages.

4

The pen is nothing, unless 'you can finish the sequel with the sword'. To emphasize the language wrangles of the region (as I have done here) is not to subscribe to the kind of Franco-American 'panlogism' or 'panliteralism' that has become fashionable of late. This is the doctrine which argues from the Hobbesian (or commonplace) view that 'Truth is of proposition only' or, in a more recent formulation, 'that there are no plain moral facts out there in the world, nor any truths independent of language', to the far from common-place view that 'it does not really matter whether "two and two is four" is true...[because] all that matters is that if you believe it, you can say it without getting hurt. In other words, what matters is your ability to talk to other people about what seems to you true, not what is in fact true.' To suggest (as I have done) that truth does not necessarily prevail is not to say that truth does not matter. No contemporary of ours should be so innocent of the facts of political life as to sanction accounts of the past that lay it open to such flagrant misinterpretations as were practised by totalitarian regimes, and continue to be practised in many parts of what we like to call 'our world'. The history of Central and Eastern Europe records many occasions when the pursuit of truth – of, for example, getting the past right – cannot be separated from the prohibition to hurt and to humiliate; when monstrous cruelty follows on, because it has been made possible by, falsehood and lies. A common name for such situations might be 'the Katyn syndrome'. In the face of that, the panlogistic idyll of life seen as an interweaving of metaphors in a non-referential language collapses. It was Nietzsche who, in all innocence, theorized that syndrome under the guise of 'critical history', by which he meant an account of the past fashioned by omissions of all that should not have hap-pened. But the motto of this kind of history, 'Thus I willed it, therefore it was', might be the inscription Kafka's torture machine tattoos on the body of its sacrificial victim. Inscriptions (in Kafka's *In the Penal Colony*, at all events) are more than inscriptions, and words (we might say) are more than words. And this is a lesson that Central Europe can teach many other places.

5

The essays that follow were collected at the end of an era, near the beginning of which, in 1948, there appeared a book with a very similar title, *From the Heart of Europe*. Its author, F. D. Matthieson, an eminent New England literary scholar and critic, was still able to write: 'I accept the Russian Revolution as the most progressive event of our century...'; and: 'Revolutions happen because conditions have become so insupportable that the pople are driven to right them by whatever violent means. But they also happen only when the people and their leaders possess a sufficiently defined goal which they hope to achieve, and the vitality and courage to drive towards it...'; and: 'The Russians, whatever their failures in practice so far, however short they may have fallen of some of Lenin's aims through the grim pressures of dictatorship, have not been deflected from the right of all to share in the common wealth.' Many would have found these articles of faith unacceptable when they were first published; today hardly anybody would think them anything but quaint. Whatever the long-term outcome of the events of 1989, the 'advance in social progress' for which Matthieson hoped was brought about not by violent revolutions but by spontaneous, non-ideological uprisings of remarkable moderation.

These essays are companion pieces to my more circumspect literary productions. Their agenda – episodes from the literature, politics and philosophy of the region – is embarassingly large. It has been my intention to let each topic choose its own approach. And so, since 'Theory is done only when there's nothing left to be done' (as Odo Marquard remarked), the theory behind these essays is that there is here no theory – neither 'Marxist' nor 'liberal ironist', neither 'receptionist' nor 'deconstructionist', neither 'critical' nor 'post-modern', nor any other. Written for the most part over the last twenty-five years, most of them have been revised (some quite radically) – only a few (those commemorating specific events) retain the form in which they were first published.

Putting these essays together was a matter of great pleasure, rather like meeting again old friends and finding that they are still on speaking-terms. They owe their presence inside a single volume to the friendly invitation of Stephan Chambers and to the editorial care of Alison Mudditt, both at Basil Blackwell, Wittgenstein's publishers; to them, and to Stephen Ryan, go my first words of thanks. I am grateful to the Fritz von Thyssen Foundation for support that enabled me to conclude the work of revision more expeditiously than I would otherwise have done. I have received much kind help from William Abbey, librarian of the Institute of Germanic Studies, University of London, and from the staff of the Cambridge University Library – to them too my warm thanks are due. To Mary-Kay Wilmers, who published several of these essays in the *London Review of Books*, I am indebted for helpful criticism; and so I am to three friends in Germany – Richard Humphrey, Gerhard Hufnagel and Karl Heinz Bohrer.

As on previous occasions, I wish my friend John Sugden to know how grateful I am for his criticism as well as for his determination to create order out of – well, less than order. To Sheila Stern I owe not only some of the best translations to be found in the book, but many other felicities from which it has profited, including its title. We have shared the sadness of losing the friend to whose memory this volume is dedicated.

Specific editorial acknowledgements as well as notes and references to the sources of quotations are to be found at the end of the book.

J. P. S.
St George's Day 1991

1

Literature and Ideology

The times are gone when we could happily accept that 'a political song is a horrid song', that only such plays as Schiller's *Wilhelm Tell* or certain aspects of *Wallenstein* have anything to do with politics, or that human relations can ever be purely private. After a long period of that ostensibly unpolitical literary history and scholarship that enjoyed its St Martin's summer in post-war Germany under the slogan of *werkimmanente Wissenschaft* ('uncommitted study', resembling the New Criticism in the English-speaking world), our time is one in which the interpretation of literature, if not literature itself, is becoming increasingly political and ideological. This means, first, the shifting into the foreground of those works of the past which convey a more or less explicit political message – a process which changes the literary canon in favour of some works hitherto reckoned to be of secondary value (I am thinking, for instance, of the political comedy of the *Vormärz*, the era leading up to the revolution of 1848). Secondly, it means that works (like those of the 'classical' period in German) from which it is impossible, or nearly so, to extract an overt political message are interpreted as having implicit political tendencies, and these nearly always of a conservative and repressive kind. And thirdly it means that works which show tendencies now considered undesirable are reinterpreted in such a way as to serve to confirm quite different political aims or poetic intentions, on occasion directly opposed to those of the original – I am thinking, for instance, of the fundamentally anti-political anarchism of *Dantons Tod* (sometimes seen as a song of praise of 'populist' values) or of Shakespeare's *Coriolanus*, the strikingly anti-plebeian tone of which offended the tender conscience of many German intellectuals until Bertolt Brecht rewrote it. Literary historians are familiar with similar practices in Germany from the 1920s and 1930s, that is, from a time when literature and criticism were supposed to be unpolitical; whereas in those days the reinterpretation proceeded from Left to Right, it is now usually the other way round. This development might be demonstrated by the history of the 'reception' of almost any author. An obvious and fairly recent example would be the treatment of Kleist's dramas, from the nationalist criticism of August Sauer and the heroic aestheticism of Friedrich Gundolf up to the present-day Marxist-inspired performances of them on the West German stage.

The fundamental question arises whether literature is bound in every case to contain an explicit or implicit political message; whether the political dimension is an *a priori* of literature. In looking for an answer we may begin by noting that, as a general rule, works of literature are by their nature datable, that is, they cannot help manifesting a specific linguistic constellation as part of the social and temporal dimension of their place of origin. Every work of literature has its *parole*. A glance at the first stanza of Matthias Claudius's 'Kriegslied' ('War-song') should make this clear:

> 'S ist Krieg! 's ist Krieg! O Gottes Engel wehre,
> Und rede Du darein!
> 'S ist leider Krieg – und ich begehre
> Nicht schuld daran zu sein!

('Tis war! 'Tis war! O be our ward, God's angel, / And speak thou to be heard! / 'Tis war, alas – and my desire / Is not to bear the guilt of it!)

Even if we were ignorant of the historical connection of the poem with the era of the Frederician wars, we could arrive at a date in the late eighteenth or early nineteenth century from the construction 'rede Du darein!', no longer in use and almost synonymous with the preceding 'wehre'; still more conclusive is the strong use of the little word 'leider', now merely a casual 'alas', a weak survival, which for Claudius has the power to express a full measure of 'lament, regret, distress' (as the word is defined in Adelung's Dictionary of 1796). So much for the specifically linguistic aspect of this poem's datability. Our argument could be rounded off by pointing to the political or (it comes to the same thing) ideological attitudes expressed in the poem; starting under the sign of civic passivity, timidity and resignation to the will of God, which form one important structure of the poem, the story of civic conformism and political backwardness (of the onset of what Marx would eventually call 'die deutsche Misere') could then be unfolded. The only doubt that remains is whether this is the right way to approach this particular poem; whether its specific mood and meaning can be communicated to the reader in this way. That meaning and mood are profoundly private, religious and anti-worldly. The moment we acknowledge this, the political analysis, without becoming entirely superfluous (for we may assume that all private concerns are interwoven in a dialectic with the public and the political), is none the less seen to be quite marginal to any critical commentary that could illuminate the poem. Admittedly such an analysis points to the occasion and some of the circumstances in which the poem originated, but the poem itself is barely touched by them.

My example is meant to show only that there are degrees of relevance, and therefore that there is a possibility of entirely irrelevant criticism; that while all criticism is necessarily 'aspectival', some aspects of a text are more important than others, and some are perfectly useless. (Uselessness and irrelevance of evidence are possibilities which professional critics and other persons interested in literature are reluctant to acknowledge, for in their heart of hearts they believe that every interpretation and thus every aspect of a text is 'bound to come in handy' in some way.) In other words, to recognize that language is a public or common medium (Nietzsche complains of its excessive 'commonness') and that it always bears some relation to the public sphere is by no means the same as to say that the detailed working out of this relationship necessarily assists the better understanding of any and every text. Ludwig Wittgenstein once remarked that the answer to the question whether a set of chessmen is carved out of oak or deal in no way affects or explains the rules of chess. Every hermeneutic, especially that of literary texts, remains inadequate as long as it contains no theory of the irrelevant. (Not that a panjandrum like H.-G. Gadamer has ever worried about this.) Thus an illumination of a work of literature by reference to its political and public dimension is only to be expected in cases where the work itself touches on or perceptibly suppresses political themes, and so in either case arouses the expectation of political solutions. This is not a tautology: the first and most obvious source of a legitimate literary expectation is not politico-ideological but literary form. As the competent speaker of a language expects from his collocutor a certain conformity in the observance of syntactic rules and semantic conventions, or else the express rejection of them in favour of new forms, so the good playgoer or reader expects that certain formal presuppositions with which he comes to the theatre or settles down to a novel will either be fulfilled or be replaced by others that will justify themselves on their own terms. What seems to me irreconcilable with the idea of literary effectiveness is the incidental or unintended disappointment of literary expectations; that is, their non-fulfilment by inadvertence.

The problem posed by literary expectation is particularly clear – or particularly crass – in the case of the writings of the German classicists. Thus in Goethe's *Götz von Berlichingen*, *Egmont* and *Die natürliche Tochter* there are situations, of fundamental importance for the action of the plays, which demand political solutions. (I mean solutions such as we find in Shakespeare at the point where Caesar is murdered or Prince Hal crowned; in Racine, where Titus renounces Bérénice; or in Sophocles, where the fatal dialectic between Antigone and the *raison d'état* is fully worked out and leads not only to Antigone's personal doom but also to the threat to Creon's rule.) In situations of this kind Goethe avoids the political solution, abandons the plane of dramatic and political action and replaces it by purely private episodes which lead on to a lyrical mood. Götz von Berlichingen's loyalty to the Emperor is unshakeable only because it is never shaken either by an actual confrontation with the Emperor or by a clear understanding of the real circumstances in the Empire. Goethe never allows Götz or Egmont an insight into the real conflict of their (very similar) situations – the conflict between personal glory and social responsibility; never allows either of them to arrive at a conscious decision, for any politically clear-sighted action is condemned in advance as unheroic politicking, not only by them but by the characterizations and the slant of each play. Neither Götz nor Egmont is conscious of responsibility for the popular movement he has brought into being. What they are really concerned with is not the political freedom germane to their task as popular leaders, but the purely personal freedom appropriate to their heroic or 'daemonic' personality; that is, they are concerned with 'freedom' in a situation in which we should expect 'liberty' to be the primary legitimate aim. And so there is nothing left for Egmont but the experience of that celebrated vision which substitutes dream symbolism for the real chance missed, and an erotic apotheosis for the political component of liberty.

It might now be asked why Goethe was apparently not capable of taking the political course of his plays to a rigorous conclusion and thus satisfying the *literary* expectation he himself had aroused – a question usually answered with an allusion to the historic conditions in which he worked. It is not his everyday personal interest, as expressed for instance in his conversations with visiting statesmen, that is at issue here, nor his creative intentions, as when he says, of *Die natürliche Tochter*, that 'it was designed to be a vessel in which I hoped to deposit, with due seriousness, all that I had written and thought during many a year about the French Revolution and its consequences.' But when, in a play as politically inspired as this, he contents himself with dark allusions to nameless powers and 'necessary unjust deeds', and sacrifices his heroine to those powers, then we may well see this as an indication that his imagination is constrained by the unpolitical and anti-political ideology of his time and place. The 'due seriousness' of his poetic creativeness is devoted to the private and personal sphere on the one hand and the cosmic and metaphysical on the other, but not as readily to what he himself called 'the middle altitude of life', the sphere of the social and political, from which certain fundamental decisions proceed which affect our daily lives. (Nietzsche too, with his notorious lack of positive concern with social and institutional questions, is in a similar predicament.)

'It were easier to turn the wind round or stop it blowing than to imprison the minds [*die Gesinnungen*] of men,' says Lichtenberg: there is nothing impenetrable about the limitation imposed on people and poets by the ideology of their time. The tremendous lyrical (and partly irrelevant) last act of *Egmont* contains not only the bewildering apotheosis of the dream of freedom, but also the dialogue between Egmont and Ferdinand, the son of his arch-enemy Alba, in which Egmont becomes aware of the meaning of his own impending sacrificial death: his existence and something of his message of freedom will survive him as an effective national example and future political message. It goes against the grain for Goethe to draw these conclusions, rooted in the theme of this play – 'political' still means for him, as it did in *Werther*, something of unpleasant shrewdness and prudence – and yet Egmont's last words to the people are more than empty rhetoric.

A recurring pattern emerges. The ideology or, to use Lichtenberg's more modest expression, the 'system of convictions' *(Gesinnungensystem)* of an age is not *a priori* limiting. On the contrary: in their initial stages, before they have petrified into clichés, the convictions of an age form the very staple of its literature. They come to impose themselves as a system of intellectual bondage on a literary work or on a man's imagination in any of its forms when they become embattled in dogma (the stage which Goethe recognized and warned against, 'lest it should arm itself into rigidity'). Only then does a writer's intellectual and affective horizon become restrictive, but even then it is not absolutely limiting. It may be forced open, transcended, and this may lead to new insights and creative solutions, which will not however be characterized by the same conviction and stylistic assurance as were the thoughts and motives that were part of the system when it was novel.

An example from the late nineteenth century is Theodor Fontane, who occupies himself again and again with the question of who wields power in Wilhelmine Germany. He never comes nearer to it than in *Der Stechlin*, his last novel, in the words addressed by the young Countess von Barby to Pastor Lorenzen:

> You used the word 'Regime'. Who is this Regime? A person or a thing? Is it the old machine inherited from past times, with its clockwork clattering away automatically, or is it the fellow who stands at the machine [Bismarck]? Or again, is it rather a particular limited multiplicity that tries to determine and direct the hand of the man at the machine?

The subject of *Der Stechlin*, once chosen, makes questions of this kind inevitable: it seems that, as a German of the post-1870 era, Fontane cannot avoid posing them; and it is certain that, as a novelist, he was content to ask them. Should he have committed himself to an answer? In the 1920s and 1930s his lack of 'commitment' was taken to be proof of his reactionary conformism, after 1945 of his democratic liberal outlook ...

Nietzsche, and the ideology prevailing in German literature in the first half of the twentieth century, offer a further example, which moreover has the advantage of being almost immediately accessible to us. From his first work, *The Birth of Tragedy* (1872), to the very last notes made in the months and weeks before his breakdown in January 1889, Nietzsche embarked on numerous attempts to confront his existential morality of values – that is, his philosophy of evaluations and judgements – with an aesthetic, non-judging, playful attitude to the world. The motto of this aesthetic attitude is to be the sentence that occurs three times in *The Birth of Tragedy* – 'Only as an aesthetic phenomenon are the world and existence eternally justified' – yet his attempts to elaborate this aesthetic attitude all fail. His lack of consequentiality, here at all events, is notorious. It may be objected that the systematization of his existential morality of values, that is, the elaboration of a philosophy of 'the will to power', also remains fragmentary. But from the surviving fragments we may clearly see what such a moral system would have been like and why it suffered an internal collapse. Nietzsche's notes for a comprehensive aesthetics or metaphysic of play, on the other hand (which extend from his earliest Basle lectures on the pre-Socratics to the last jottings of the *Nachlass*), are so rudimentary, so fragmentary, that we are justified in assuming that to complete and work them out in full would have been a task beyond the creative gift that characterizes his philosophical imagination – beyond his historical horizon. Like Egmont's vision of freedom, Nietzsche's aestheticizing of the world remains a dream framed by a realistic scenario.

It is hardly possible to overestimate Nietzsche's influence on German literature and ideology in the first half of the twentieth century: Gottfried Benn, Rilke and Brecht dedicate poems to him; Stefan George writes unconvincing disclaimers and Thomas Mann critical essays about his influence; a whole spectrum of writers bear witness to the overwhelming attraction of his thought. What our century inherits from Nietzsche, however, is not an aesthetic theodicy, but in the first instance his moral philosophy, by which I mean his philosophy of moral and existential strenuousness and sacrifice; that ideology which in *Zarathustra* is given the name of 'the Spirit of Heaviness'. (Nietzsche himself notes the self-referential irony of the phrase.)

In all the phases of his philosophical career, brief as it was, Nietzsche vows allegiance to this philosophy. The way he comes to formulate 'the most difficult ideal of the philosopher', his insistence on truths which are true only by being 'in the highest degree harmful and dangerous' to the very existence of man, the value he sees as inherent in insights which offer the greatest possible resistance to man's cognitive powers and his instinct of self-preservation alike, his refutations of any possible harmony between true insight and comfort – all these components of his philosophy of strenuousness and sacrifice have been assembled and considered at length by me in another context. Here I wish merely to assert that they are the constitutive elements of the ideology which Nietzsche bequeathed to our century. Thomas Mann's *Doctor Faustus* and its central theme, the ineluctable costliness of 'authentic' artistic experience, is the most obvious example of the way the Nietzschean heritage is applied and thematized in the era that follows his death in 1900. Hardly less obvious (to choose another example) is the peculiar dichotomy from which Hermann Hesse's *Glass-Bead Game* (a precise analogue, in Hesse's œuvre, to Mann's *Doctor Faustus*) is built – 'the Game' versus 'Reality'. This dichotomy comes to a head in that peculiar confession of the novel's hero when he resigns from his magisterial office in order to choose what he calls 'the Absolute' (*das Unbedingte*) as the aim of his life, and equates 'reality' not only with 'risk, weightiness and danger', but even more emphatically with 'deprivation and suffering'. Of this concept of 'reality' it has been well said that it ceases to be a concept, that it merely generates an appearance of understanding and befogs thought. This attack is well-founded; but unfortunately it does not ask why this non-concept is so flourishing in the *parole* of our century. One hardly thinks Shakespeare as being short of the words he really needed, yet the word 'reality' does not occur in his works. To the writers of the post-Nietzschean era it seems indispensable. For all its ambiguity, for all its fuzziness and squidlike amorphousness, it is impossible to banish it from the vocabulary and the ideology of that age.

Reversing the meaning of a seventeenth-century sonnet, I have called it the ideology of the 'dear purchase'. Every important work of German literature in the first half of the twentieth century places the redemption and justification of man at its centre. No doubt this is a wholly unorthodox valuation, and yet this 'redemption', which is unthinkable without Nietzsche's critical anti-religious reflections and his 'philosophy of strenuousness', stands in a partly antagonistic, partly dependent, partly parodic relationship to the traditional Christian values and concepts. The redemption and justification which we encounter in that literature is attempting to break through the dualism of world and transcendence, of the here and now and the beyond, and often it is in the no man's land between the finite and the infinite that the just attainable or finally unattainable act of redemption or justification takes place. Every major German writer of the time forms his work from the experience of a redemption or a valuation of man which is only to be obtained at the highest price; the highest price that the author, and also the hero whose fate is described, is capable of paying. We encounter fictional situations in which this exaction is still further heightened, where more is demanded of the characters than they can possibly pay. And finally we come to the most radical of all conceivable situations, in which the impossibility of paying the price as such is the very token and confirmation of the redemptive or justificatory act and its validity – the more impossible, the truer, more authentic, more 'real'.

Turning the argument around, we see that the age is one in which all easy, flowing solutions and liberations are suspect; in this ideology all values that are to be had at a lesser price are suspected to be or rejected as 'unreal' and invalid. And it is significant that many lesser German authors of the time either ignore this theme or, if they do take account of it, fail to acknowledge its scope or to exhaust its profundity, or else evade it by undertaking traditional and less costly bargains.

In the poetry, drama and prose of the age this exacting theme is not confined to characterization and plot, but also manifests itself in the style and attitude towards language which these works display. It seems that the time is past when 'the language of the market-place' and the language of poetry were mutually comprehensible, and when a linguistic consensus informed literature. 'Nothing but misunderstandings' might well be the motto of Hofmannsthal's finest comedy, *Der Schwierige (Will He? – Won't He?* might be a translation of its title). Fear of misinterpretation and an acute feeling for the inadequacy of linguistic formulation go hand in hand with an extraordinary virtuosity in the realm of language; and we can see that this linguistic creativeness (sometimes acrobatic in its allusiveness and originality) is nothing other than the linguistic correlative to the exacting theme itself.

Here I must interrupt this description of the period from the perspective of its literary history in order to avert a possible suspicion that may have arisen in the reader's mind: that I am using the word 'ideology' in some special, merely literary sense, and trivializing it by depriving it of its political denotation. Again *Doctor Faustus* is our seminal text. The allegorical relation between its hero, Adrian Leverkühn, and Germany, stressed by Thomas Mann himself, mainly through his locum tenens Serenus Zeitblom, is an indication of the interlocking of art and politics. This allegory leads to conclusions which neither the novelist nor his worthy narrator was intending and of which they would not approve, for seen from the perspective of the 'dear purchase' the story of the Third Reich takes on a new and in no sense less terrifying meaning: is the central allegory of the novel, or rather the reader's interpretation of it, to be interrupted before the final justification and salvation of Leverkühn through his striving after 'the difficult' – and, if so, where? – or is there some other way to prevent such an interpretation from yielding a certainly unintentional justification of National Socialism?

All this is mentioned here to show that we are not concerned with some merely neutral system of thought, indifferent to questions of power, but with ideology in the accepted sense of the word, ideology as a means toward the attaining, stabilizing and maintaining of political power in the world. There is no space here for more than the assertion that this *Gesinnungensystem*, this ideology of exaction, characteristic of a whole period at least in respect of its salient features, is by no means a purely literary matter but also typifies and determines politics and all its means, including the language of which politics availed itself in Germany in the era under discussion. There is abundant evidence to demonstrate that the inherent attraction, indeed the lure, of National Socialism would be inexplicable were it not that its system of values possesses certain striking 'family resemblances' with the ideology of the 'dear purchase' and with the theme of the inconceivably, even mortally difficult salvation and justification at the regime's centre. The usual reply to this claim (which I have endeavoured to give grounds for elsewhere) is that it applies only to certain phases and aspects of National Socialist propaganda, and that in any event we know this propaganda was full of lies. Such a reply fails, however, to explain why it was precisely that vocabulary of the wager requiring every kind of sacrifice, that language of '*Gemeinschaft*' and '*Not*' (the language of a community formed by a common need, real and imagined, and requiring ever-new emergencies for its survival as a community), which the regime made use of from the beginning and more and more exclusively as time went on, and from which the language of National Socialism drew its stock of metaphors.

At this point a warning is necessary. The fact that the National Socialists availed themselves of the 'dear purchase' ideology and that it was indispensable to their evil ends does not necessarily imply that there was anything evil about it in its literary uses; nor was it necessarily restrictive in its initial stages, where it is conveyed to us as a major literary theme and with the passionate serious-ness of a new discovery about the being of man in the world. The works which are informed by it belong among the major German contributions to world literature. Yet the moment of some of German literature's greatest achievements is also the moment when we can see the theme impose itself on the imagination as an intellectual bondage – though even then it can never be the monolithic scheme which political propaganda and counter-propaganda would make of it.

Ideology – always a skeletal statement, related to political conduct no more closely than is a cookery book to cooking – connotes not an identity but a family resemblance of ideas within one period. The phrase 'family resemblance' I take from Wittgenstein's critique of the traditional language of universals. Phenomena which seem to us to have something in common are referred to and subsumed, since Aristotle, under a single conceptual heading, one common denominator. Inherent in this method is the danger of the 'contemptuous attitude towards the particular case' – a kind of totalitarianism, if not of perception, at least of description. How can we avoid this totalitarianism? All great generalizing laws are suspect, says Lichtenberg: 'They give me no joy ... : at close quarters none of it is true.' In most cases, says Wittgenstein, things 'commonly subsume[d] under a general term' are in fact very different. Thus we may think, for example, of the various particular attitudes and convictions collectively subsumed under the heading of 'ideology': in reality such phenomena 'form a *family*, the members of which have family likenesses. Some of them have the same nose, others the same eyebrows and others again the same way of walking; and these likenesses overlap.'

It is at this point that literature (by which I mean anything that is a cut above the hackwork of party stooges) parts company with a totalitarian regime, which is sustained by the assertion that its ideology is not a matter of family resemblances at all, but of a 'total', monolithic *Weltanschauung*. Now, it is true that the more ramshackle the ideology, the more emphatic its self-assertion. But whatever may be its sources (and intellectual cogency is not among them), the strength and staying power of a totalitarian regime's ideology are such that its traces are recognizable in writers who happen to be uninterested in politics and indifferent to party allegiance; and when we observe its presence even in actual opponents of the regime (here too Thomas Mann and his *Doctor Faustus* are the type of many others) this kinship resemblance of ideologically related ideas which apparently suspends moral contradictions gives our argument the deceptive form of a paradox which must be resolved.

This is the question we are trying to answer: if the prevailing mental attitude of an age is really so comprehensive and all-determining, even to stylistic nuances, as is here, if not demonstrated, at any rate asserted; if scenes and moods, whether in literature or outside it, in political or daily practice, can be so closely identified with an ideology and thus determined and restricted by it; if finally, as was said at the beginning, we draw all the consequences from the fact that literature (and every other form of cultural life) is datable, what then becomes of the possibility of opposition and protest, what (not to mince matters) happens in that case to human freedom? That it exists and is no

chimera we know from our daily experience, in particular from our capacity
to consider and arrive at decisions, and to convert them into actions; but we
also know it by way of hindsight, for the very possibility of historicizing the
politics, literature or thought of the past (including the judgement, 'They
could do no other than . . .') implies some degree of liberation from the
present. To know one kind of past is to know that it was not of another kind.
Any attempt either to describe or to explain the Third Reich in any detail at
all is to show that life in that society, as in every other, was made up of
numerous individual decisions, and this in turn is to show a society which
might have chosen to live differently; historical theories which operate with
notions of 'catastrophe', 'fate' and 'preordainment' find themselves short of
material with which to demonstrate the difference between the natural and
the human, a difference which those who hold such theories do not usually
regard as chimeric.

How then is our practical experience of the possibility of decisions and of
freedom to be reconciled with the recognition (without which there would be
no historical continuity in literature, ideas or institutions) that men belong to
their time and that no man can jump over his own shadow? We need a model
to embody and perhaps explain the possibility of nonconformism in the face
of the ideological dominant; moreover, this is to be a functional nonconformism, not mere caprice.

One of the metaphors we have used here will help us on: I am thinking of
the phrase (almost a cliché) 'the language of National Socialism', in which the
literal meaning of 'language' is not sharply divided from the metaphorical.
What is it that enables us to regard such a 'language' (which, as we can easily
discern, is not really a self-contained and entire language at all) as a conceptual
unity and to subject it to examination? Whether we are acquainted with it or
not, it is the theory of language of Ferdinand de Saussure, the basis of modern
linguistics. Fundamental to Saussure's theory is his postulate (illustrated by
means of a good many philological details) that the connection between a
linguistic sign (for example, a word) and the thing signified is arbitrary or
conventional. This Hobbesian postulate is significantly different from the
German traditional view of language, implicit in Herder's, Hegel's and Heidegger's philosophies. However, it need not concern us here beyond saying that
on it are based the two cardinal distinctions with which Saussure operates
throughout. (Both of them are not physical facts, but working hypotheses or
'methodological fictions'.)

First (and central to our argument) is his distinction between the concept
of *langue*, a system of signs coextensive with the whole potential, the totality
of a natural language, and the concept of *parole*, which refers to that part of
a natural language which is activated at a particular moment by an individual
speaker.

There are several ways of paraphrasing Saussure's distinction: actualization
of linguistic phenomena within a system of rules and potentials, or again *praxis*
within theory – these and other formulations are not sanctioned by Saussure

himself yet they are faithful to his basic idea and show something of its far-reaching significance. Nor is it doing violence to it if (for the sake of the present argument) we disregard Saussure's own insistence that *parole* denotes a strictly individual use of language and apply the distinction to the linguistic usage of a *group* defined in social, geographical, professional or some other terms. What must not be abandoned is the part-within-a-whole relationship.

Equally important (though ancillary to our argument) is Saussure's second distinction, between the study of a language as an inquiry into its state at any one time (a synchronic study – the horizontal cross-section of a tree that reveals its history in a single, momentary view), and the study of that language as an inquiry into its history (a diachronic study – the following of a tree's development at various stages of its life); and this is a particularly clear-headed piece of the argument, seeing how common, in Saussure's day and ours, in linguistics and elsewhere, is the habit of confusing what a thing is with how it came to be what it is.

There is no need to demonstrate at length the usefulness of the *langue–parole* distinction: most modern linguistics is based on it, including Chomsky's distinction between linguistic 'competence' and 'performance'; and Roland Barthes' notion of *écriture* is an extended application of it to literary history. The question that concerns us here is that of the relationship between the two concepts. Clearly, some relationship there must be and, equally clearly, it cannot be simply cumulative. As a first step towards establishing such a relationship we may note that both *langue* and *parole* are aspects of language which may be examined both synchronically and diachronically. Now, it seems self-evident that a large number of individual *paroles* considered synchronically can never make up the totality of *langue*. (The totality of a natural language is not simply the sum total of the linguistic usages of its speakers; when Shakespeare or Dickens arrives on the scene something new happens to that language, which, nevertheless, continues to be English.) If there is to be a connection, it can only be effected on a diachronic view of *parole*. The connectedness of the two phenomena (as opposed to the working-hypothesis separation with which we began) becomes manifest in the recognition that *parole*, viewed diachronically, is capable of expanding in the direction of *langue*, to the point where the one – actualization – comes close to becoming coextensive with or growing into the other – the full theoretical potential of a natural language. But what, on that hypothesis, is left of the initial distinction? The concept of *parole*, critics have argued, is neither useful nor 'scientifically' respectable since it obviously depends on an arbitrary definition of what is meant by 'synchronicity' or 'a particular moment' in the life of an individual speaker. Yet this 'uncertainty factor' ('how *long* is "a particular moment"?'), far from undermining Saussure's theory, reveals its usefulness as analogy. Within linguistics, this 'uncertainty factor' points to the living, developing, protean nature of language; while in our search for a model which would clarify the function of ideology in its relationship with literature this 'factor' confirms the relevance of the *langue–parole* distinction. Precisely because *parole* turns out to be a concept with blurred edges ('Is it indeed always an advantage to replace an indistinct picture by a sharp one?'), it turns out to be what is needed for our purpose.

Now we are in a position to return to our main topic: here is the model we needed to characterize the relationship between an individual and his age, or rather between the ideologically determined outlook of an individual or a group of individuals and the full potential – the mental and experiential horizon – of an age.

Of course we speak the *parole* that belongs to our age and no other. Of course we see and evaluate the past that the modern world has taught us to see. Certainly 'man is doomed to the state of *seeing his own system* everywhere he looks', as Lichtenberg observed. But neither our speech nor our seeing is determined once and for all. Every living organ of experience and thus every living language changes and develops. Just as, on the diachronic view, it is a condition of their connectedness that *parole* should be capable of expanding in the direction of *langue* without yet ceasing to display those features which characterize it as belonging to that particular *langue* and to no other, so an individual outlook is capable of transcending its own ideologically determined limitations in the direction of a fuller consciousness (it would be absurd to speak, as the Marxists do, of a 'total' one), without yet ceasing to show its membership of a particular era and no other; and nowhere is this more patently and abundantly true than in that area of experience where the dialogue between the individual self and the age to which it belongs is at its most conscious and articulate: the area of literature. The condition of such transcending, however, is not the synchronic view – consciousness as a state, as an aesthetic phenomenon – but the diachronic – the self-understanding of consciousness as a historical phenomenon, capable of growth and not fearful of change. In this sense, then, it should no longer be paradoxical to claim that 'the language [= *parole*] of National Socialism' belongs to the same age and displays at least some of the same features – significant features – as the writings of the major German poets and novelists of the age, though only the poets and novelists attempt to transcend the limitations of their *parole*, only they strive for a fuller consciousness.

Parole and *langue* never overlap completely, nor do ideological and potential consciousness. Conversely, liberation from the embrace of ideology can never be complete or definitive. (Works of literature are always datable.) Through one feature or another the products of the mind always remain bound to the style of their time, indeed it is they that exemplify that style. Nietzsche made fun of 'the Spirit of Heaviness' and yet could not avoid continually boasting of his extreme mental exertion, and making a virtue, not only in his letters but also in the main stream of his philosophizing, of the dreadful loneliness which was the price of it. Part of the inheritance he left us is that the first half of our century became a time in which unselfconscious ease was difficult to achieve. Stefan George's striving for grace and *élan* embarrasses us. There is little or none of this striving in Trakl's dark poetry or in the grand poetic cycles of Rilke's maturity. How unintentionally comic it seems to us when Hofmannsthal concludes a heavy and amorphous tragedy with a miraculous peace-bearing infant king! Can we imagine Ernst Jünger's 'Worker' dancing? And yet Thomas Mann redeems the promise of a life in the funny story of *Felix Krull*, his con-man's memoirs, in which Nietzsche's projected aesthetic justification of man is parodied and fictionalized; many of the poems Rilke wrote in the last four years of his life, after the completion of the *Duino Elegies* in February 1922, are filled with a lightness of touch and a grace of poetic expression that do not so much overcome the ideology of the 'dear purchase' to which the great cycles were devoted (each overcoming is an exertion), as seem rather to have forgotten all about it. And Bertolt Brecht confesses in his poem 'To Posterity':

> Dabei wissen wir doch:
> Auch der Haß gegen die Niedrigkeit
> Verzerrt die Züge.
> Auch der Zorn über das Unrecht
> Macht die Stimme heiser. Ach wir
> Die wir den Boden bereiten wollten für Freundlichkeit
> Konnten selber nicht freundlich sein.

(And yet we know / Hatred, even of meanness, / Contorts our features. / Anger, even against injustice, / Makes the voice hoarse. Oh, we / Who wanted to prepare the ground for friendliness / Could not ourselves be friendly.)

It would have been hard to foresee the author of these lines in the Bert Brecht of the early 1930s, preoccupied with ideological aridities. However much of a party henchman he could be when it seemed necessary, in poems such as these he speaks not as an ideologue but as a free man; as the exemplar of one who, in the second half of his life as a writer, discovers a language that was not available to him in the first half. His death (in 1956) and those of his great literary contemporaries brought to an end an age that believed more than any other in the determining power of ideology, furthered the dominance of ideology by this belief, and yet – at least in the case of some of its creative minds – succeeded in breaking through this dominance.

Whatever is, in one generation, thematically marginal and only realized with great effort, becomes, in the succeeding generation, less problematic and more easily accessible, and can be made use of with less exertion. A new style comes into being. In a popular German novel of the late 1960s (a work of decent sentiments though no great originality), a habitually intimidated son describes his father:

> Him – what a performance he made out of sitting there, wrapped in deep significance. I detest this overweening manner of sitting, I fear this silence that pretends to importance, I hate this laconic solemnity, the

eye transfixed in that far-off gaze and the gesture that is hard to describe, and I fear, I fear our habit of listening inwardly and dispensing with words.

(Even a major German novel written before 1945 would be bound to mention 'silence', 'that far-off gaze' or 'the gesture that is hard to describe' with bated breath.) It seems as though the author of that scene had actually read and was taking issue with the following passage from the last of Nietzsche's *Untimely Meditations*:

> When on that May day in 1872 the foundation-stone had been laid on the hill at Bayreuth in drenching rain and under a dark sky, Wagner drove back to the town with a few of us. He was silent and was all the time gazing into himself with a look which no one word could possibly describe.

This is a passage that is characteristic in every detail, and to the point of parody, of the prose and scale of values of the ideological age, but from which it would scarcely be gathered that this silent man with the deep introspective glance, this paragon of inwardness, was capable of behaviour that would make a mountebank look respectable. We can certainly find headlong attacks on 'the Spirit of Heaviness' in Nietzsche's later books – passages of exhortation to laughter and in praise of the light touch – but not the attitude of that (less than outstanding) novel of the 1960s, its combination of unemphatic irony and discretion:

> And I ask myself why our people can see more deeply and more penetratingly in the evening than in the daytime, and why they are so totally absorbed in the pursuit of a task undertaken. The wordless lust for food, the self-righteousness, the talk of ancient folklore which they prefer to going for a swim: these too I question . . .

and in this almost entirely unsentimental form an attitude to the preceding age is developed which is new – that is, critical and different. The superior status and greater depth of wordless experience (in which Nietzsche believed) are part of that very ideology which no longer holds sway.

Certainly the analogy I have chosen, between the structure of language and the structure of ideology, is not accidental. It is indicative of the fact that the rules of linguistic activity are such that they relate it to other cultural activities; for language does not (as most nineteenth-century writers believed) only describe the world, without at the same time forming a part of it, it does not stand separate in some chimeric relationship to 'life'.

Our argument confirms the fact that language and ideology are both forms of life. The transcendence involved within the *parole–langue* relationship (viewed diachronically) functions as a paradigm. A similarly structured relationship can be found between any text and its critique, between any experience and its subsequent account, and in respect of every procedure (not necessarily narrative) that historicizes an event. The attainment of any new perception, any new knowledge (including such knowledge as literature offers), is only possible from the vantage point of a wider view – a view beyond the frontiers of the old. One might be tempted to continue the pattern, albeit in a speculative, metaphysical vein, by tracing the expansion or growth of *langue* (seen diachronically) into that totality of linguistic systems which Saussure calls *langage*. And beyond that? All these are merely ways of suggesting that what Saussure got hold of looks like the empirical end of an archetypal movement within human experience, a leapfrog pattern not confined to the sphere of language; and from that one might venture two further guesses: that most of what Saussure has to say is capable of translation into non-linguistic terms, and that whatever is really interesting in linguistic thinking contains the possibility of a translation beyond the linguistic. Perhaps the *parole–langue* relationship provides a model, too, of the relationship in all that 'now we see through a glass, darkly; but then face to face.'

Sentimental theories of alienation will not get us very far: every wider view and every fuller consciousness – that is, every extension of knowledge – implies an estrangement from the familiar, a relative alienation. A true view of the past is no less attainable for being disturbing. To affirm that the dominance of ideology is absolute is to render the past inaccessible. To render the past inaccessible in order to hide its crimes (as the Marxists have done, and the National Socialists would have done had they had more time) is to perpetuate those crimes, to annihilate the dead once more. These are forms of solipsism of which Hitler and Stalin are the representative figures.

It is no homage to the past and its victims to say of it that it is indescribable or inexplicable. But can it then really be said that the period here described is the past, that it has now come to an end and can thus be historicized – known as history and experienced as such? This much at least seems certain: the proposed relativization of the concept of ideology, the Wittgensteinian theory of family resemblances, the dissolving of the polarity between world and language, the suspicion with which we regard the antics of the 'embattled personality' – all these belong to a new style of thinking, a new *Gesinnungen-system*.

And so, finally, the question may be asked whether the model I have sketched here of the relationship between literature and ideology can also be of use in other periods, or whether it only applies to the nineteenth and twentieth centuries, that is, to an epoch in which the concept of ideology was invented and became modish, and which believed in ideological determination. 'And I saw too', St Augustine writes, 'that all things are fit and proper not only to their places, but also to their times.' Every work of literature – this was our point of departure – is essentially datable (if not always with the same accuracy), not only according to its historical content, but also by its language and style; and this (as we have seen) throws light on a variety of connections between literary works of art and other ways in which human societies express themselves. Are there alternative solutions to this relationship, more appropriate to other, 'non-ideological' ages? Were there such ages, or were they merely less articulate about their beliefs? But is not this articulateness itself part of the ideological system of an age? However we answer these questions, the hypothesis that literature might be completely independent of the contemporary state of the language and ideology (and thus independent of society, whose manifestations they are) must surely seem to us today as absurd as its opposite, the hypothesis of the necessary determination of man, his language and his literature as well as his every thought process, by the prevalent ideology of the time.

1977 (1989)

2

Bolzano's Bohemia

1

From the end of the eighteenth century an especially close, complex and ultimately disastrous interrelationship developed in Central Europe between language consciousness and nationality. In this region, nation and natural borders have not often coincided for very long; and in this age, greater value was ascribed to political notions of 'natural' or 'organic' being than to politics based on tradition and agreement bureaucratically enforced. Here linguistic borders are endowed with the strong feelings that go with national borders, national consciousness is identified with language consciousness.

This interaction between language and nationality became an important determining factor in the attitudes of the various Slavonic peoples to the Austrian, later Austro-Hungarian, Empire. Nowhere were the effects of this interaction so strongly marked as in the ancient Kingdom of Bohemia and Moravia, which, as the westernmost Slavonic country, came most directly under the influence of German culture, that is, of the Enlightenment in its last phase, and of early Romanticism. Here Herder's ideas of nature and history, language and nationality, fell on particularly fertile ground, yet their reception was hedged in by a strong 'anxiety of influence'. There can be no doubt that the resistance against German culture derived its arguments from German Romantic nationalism, and so did the cultivation of a Czech national consciousness, yet Herder's disciples in Bohemia were apt to misinterpret important parts of his work for their own ends.

Herder's *Ideas Toward a Philosophy of the History of Mankind* (1784–91) take as their premise the historical *donnée* of his age: in the absence of any kind of political unity, it is the German language as the medium of German culture by which the conception of Germanness is characterized. However, Herder is no less concerned that his philosophy of history should be focused not on 'language' but on 'the languages of the world'. On this point the *Ideas* (book 9) are quite unambiguous: it is by virtue of their manifold variety that different languages are capable of representing human thoughts, feelings and 'images of the eye' in their full variety, and thus contributing to a 'history of mankind'. To do this, the various nations with their various languages must be acknowledged as equal in value and standing, for 'the general medium of language makes human beings inwardly more equal than is shown by their outward appearance'. And Herder continues: 'The finest attempt at a history and manifold characteristic of the human understanding and heart would therefore be a *philosophical comparison of languages*; for into each of them the understanding of a people and its character are engraved.' Thus languages are seen as media or means of expression, they function as representations or descriptions of things or ideas or feelings given previously, perhaps in some non-verbal form. But beyond this descriptive or (as modern linguists would call it) 'referential' function of a language, its 'performative' function is acknowledged ('the general medium of language *makes* human beings inwardly more equal'). Thus a language is seen under two aspects, as manifesting two functions: it describes, and refers to, what is already given (say, in the history of a nation), but at the same time a language constitutes, and is asserted as, the basic condition of a people or a state, and as such it contributes to a present or future attainment of that people's political goals. Herder's views may thus be seen as prior applications of Wittgenstein's well-known *aperçus*: 'to imagine a language means to imagine a form of life', and: 'Words are also deeds'.

But what happens to Herder's theory of language in a country in which two languages are used? The postulate of the equal value of languages (and thus of peoples) becomes problematic when, for historical or administrative or power-political reasons, one language takes precedence over the other, and when the political dominance of one language leads to the suppression of the other. And it is at such a time of pressure and counter-pressure, and of the radical polarization of the two national groups which follows, that Herder's identity of nation and language becomes the focus of an aggressive nationalism. The nationalisms which now emerge are not confined to the sphere of politics, but are laced into a vicious circle of social immobility and economic deprivation. The Marxist doctrine of the two-class society, which has lost its relevance in present-day Western societies, is confirmed by the situation in early nineteenth-century Bohemia, albeit in an unexpected form: as the industrial prosperity of the country grows, so does the inequality that obtains between the language of power and the language of vassals, that is, between German and Czech. And language assumes its dual function: it becomes the expression of the resentments, and one of the sources, of social and economic inequality which nationalism is ready to exploit.

The most influential among the mediators of Herder's ideas in the Kingdom of Bohemia and Moravia was Josef Jungmann (1773–1847), writer, translator, philologist and author of the first large Czech–German dictionary (1835–9). When invited to join the preparatory committee of the Frankfurt parliament (the *Vorparlament*) in March 1848, Jungmann, the poet Ján Kollár (a Slovak writing in Czech) and a group of other like-minded intellectuals reacted by composing the first Czech national programme, in which Herder's 'Ideas' were radicalized into a novel ideology. These are its main points.

(1)   A sharp distinction is set up in order to separate the concepts of Nation and State. The Nation alone is the bearer of a (mystical?) national character, its life continues even though the statehood of which it was once constitutive has been destroyed. The State (the Austrian Empire) which has usurped its place comes to be seen as a transient artefact, external and hostile to the life of the Nation.

(2)   The Nation is personalized: it has, and is identical with, a character that is identical with language. The Nation, in this context, means above all the peasantry, the artisan and lower middle classes and, of particular importance for Bohemia and Moravia, the teachers, popular educators, journalists and writers. The emotions which will inform the bitter linguistic quarrels of the 100 years after 1848 (and which will end only with the expulsions of the German Bohemians in 1945–7) are already contained in this postulate of an identity of language and nation. Language is moralized, the enemy as Jungmann sees them are not only the Germans, but also the alienated Czechs who, by denying their native tongue, deny their nationhood. (Now, 'Fremdwörter', 'linguistic contaminations', 'cizí slova' are condemned as unpatriotic, in both languages deviations from standard phonemes are derided, and Czech is inundated with often absurd neologisms.)

(3)   Like 'das Volk', 'národ' (the Nation) is seen as given by nature itself, as an 'organic' entity. Neither loyalty nor civil duties bind the Nation to a state 'artificially' constructed from several nations – a state, moreover, that owes its existence to a national defeat (the Battle on the White Mountain in 1620). The Nation is seen in a positivist perspective as a 'natural' community that has its origin in a mixture of legend and history, requiring no further moral legitimation (either from a divinity or through a dispensation from the Enlightenment concept of humanity as a whole): the Nation manifests all values in and by its very nature. It is at this point that Franz Grillparzer's famous prophesy of 1849 becomes relevant: 'The path of modern culture runs from humanity through nationality to bestiality'; though it must be added that, while the nationalisms in the Bohemian lands were harsh and occasionally violent, they were not murderous.

(4)   Only a quantitative difference divides family from nation and nation from related tribes. While the older Panslavism of the Bohemian Enlightenment represented by the abbé Josef Dobrovský (1753–1829) and his generation was founded on cultural affinities and a common Slavonic mythology, its modern descendant invokes the political conception of a national racial family. Culture is politicized, *Kulturpolitik* comes into being: proclamations of a Slavonic tribal

unity are intended to strengthen the national consciousness of a *small* Slavonic nation (and the syndrome of 'smallness' wil accompany Czech national life almost to the present day).

This, broadly speaking, was the programme of the Slavonic Congress which the Czech nationalists convened in Prague in 1848. But in the Kingdom of Bohemia and Moravia of the *Vormärz* the Herder–Jungmann ideology was not the only solution on offer to the contending parties.

2

Pater Bernard Bolzano (1781–1848) was a professor of philosophy and religion at the (then entirely German) University of Prague, priest and mathematician, theoretician of science and philosopher of the Enlightenment in its last phase, prolific author of social tracts and devotional writings. Bolzano has entered literary history through Adalbert Stifter's portrait of him in his novella 'Kalkstein' (1853), through Ferdinand von Saar's story 'Innocens' (1865) and through Hermann Hesse's *Glass-Bead Game* (1943). Stifter portrays a life epitomized by frugality, selflessness, and charity; von Saar's priest is involved in a love-affair that ends in renunciation; only Hesse makes the attempt to encompass Bolzano's lifelong philosophical concerns, by fictionalizing Bolzano's search for the logical foundation of all sciences into 'a game with the entire content and all the values of our culture'.

Bolzano has become famous in the history of philosophy as one of the founders of mathematical logic (as a predecessor of Franz Brentano and especially of Gottlob Frege); he wrote no systematic work on the subject of language and nationality. But although his numerous writings on the social problems of his age do not amount to a national programme, they yet contain a highly positive alternative to both Jungmann's and the German Bohemians' nationalist ideologies. Had the influence of Bolzano's humanism been greater, the history of Central Europe of the last 150 years would indeed have been different.

Born in Prague into a family of German-speaking merchants who had recently immigrated from Northern Italy, Bolzano was no Sudeten German, but (the exact opposite of that emotive term) a Bohemian; and the word 'böhmisch' was intended to contain the solution by which he hoped to pacify the parties contending for domination in the country whose future he viewed with foreboding.*

---

* 'Böhmisch', in Bolzano's and the subsequent use of it to the end of the Empire, included both the German- and Czech-speaking inhabitants of the Kingdom, but was regarded as a taboo word by the Czechs; while *their* language has no word that relates etymologically to Tacitus's 'Bohemia', which they refer to as 'Čechy', 'tschechisch' in Bolzano's day seems to have been used only as the name of a mythical barbaric tribe – and if, to all this, we add that 'the Germans' are, for the Czechs, 'Němci', the barbaric 'dumb ones', we begin to see how tribal antagonisms come

Bolzano's place in the history of mathematics is assured by his contributions to the theory of numbers and to the probability calculus. His starting-point in these studies as well as in his writings on the foundations of mathematics seems to have been his conviction that 'the philosophy of mathematics, which aims to do no more than to discover the objective ground of that which we already know with the greatest certainty and concreteness, has almost no other use than as an exercise in thinking'; but it may well be that in this very modest assessment of what was obviously his favourite intellectual pursuit he is deferring to the clerical authorities, who were apt to suspect heterodoxy in independent thinking of any kind. Edmund Husserl (a Moravian compatriot of his) says that in 'the theory of elements . . . Bolzano's work far surpasses everything else world literature has to offer as a systematic exposition of logic'; and the Oxford logician and Frege biographer Michael Dummett calls him 'the great-grandfather of analytical philosophy' and the first philosopher who succeeded in 'firmly separating logic as well as theories of ideas and meaning from psychology'. The relevance of some of these investigations to my theme will be considered towards the end of these remarks. When assessing the originality of Bolzano's work, we must see him not merely as 'Bohemia's greatest thinker' (which is what the philosopher and historian Jan Patočka (1907–77) has called him) but also as *the first philosopher* in a country 'whose history of philosophy seems at times to turn into a history of the reasons for the non-existence of philosophy'.

Bolzano was an immensely popular preacher (his weekly sermons drew as many as 1,000 listeners) and a most conscientious teacher. His heavy pastoral and university duties were the main reason why many of his philosophical projects remained unfinished, and it was only when he was dismissed from his professorship that he found the time to devote himself to them completely. Accused of preaching revolutionary and heretical views and of exercising a subversive influence on his students, he was subjected to a pre-trial investigation lasting six years (1819–25), in the course of which he was threatened with unfrocking. These were anxious years, yet they enabled him to complete the four volumes of his *Wissenschaftslehre* (1837), of which he himself says that it is 'a massive book' which needs only to be read in extracts.

One of the major aims of this *Theory of Science* is to refute Kant's critical metaphysics of 'das Ding an sich' ('the thing in itself'), and to replace it by a theory of absolute 'propositions in themselves' or 'truths in themselves'. Disappointed in his hopes of finding anyone to review his *magnum opus*, he wrote his own résumé of its argument:

> Bolzano abolishes Kant's entire antithesis between a sensible and an intelligible world by asserting that time and space are by no means mere forms of our sense perception, but ideas in which things in themselves

---

to be confirmed and strengthened by national designations, how the very giving of names becomes a hostile act.

are placed, regardless of the manner in which they are perceived. He proves this by determining the difference between concept and perception more accurately [than Kant had done] and by setting up certain explanations concerning time and space. He goes still further and seeks to prove that the Kantian claim that we cannot judge supersensory things synthetically is bound to lead to a contradiction; likewise, that the manner in which this sage intended to explain the origin of our synthetic judgements concerning the objects of mathematics and physics from the construction of [our] perception of time and space is untenable ...

In such arguments Kantian critical terms are used in the service of pre-critical metaphysics; similarly, in his definition of philosophy he appeals to the ethos of the Christian Enlightenment:

> Philosophy is the science of the objective connection of all those truths to the last causes of which we seek to penetrate, in order thus to become better and wiser.

Although Bolzano's work is a mixture of the timely and untimely, and although his anti-Kantian arguments were considered outmoded by some of his contemporary critics, his inquiries into the connection between logic and mathematics prepared the ground for the analytical philosophy of our own time. There is a formal connection between these inquiries and his religious and social ideas, though whether he himself was aware of it must remain an open question. However that may be, the clerical and imperial authorities – Rome and Vienna – seem to have found no difficulty in discovering such a connection, and roundly condemned all his teaching, including his sermons and his seminars as well as his Utopia *Of the Best Possible State* (1831, first printed in 1932). This may not have surprised him. Where one nation oppresses another (he wrote), there 'a spirit of calumniation and denunciation prevails'. And yet it was not a Bohemian, but a Viennese court physician who denounced him to the Emperor Francis II by quoting from one of his devotional tracts of 1813:

> May it please Your Majesty to read only the passage on page 99, for there it is said: 'A time will come when the thousandfold hierarchies and divisions among men, which cause so much evil, will be reduced to their proper bounds, when everyone will treat his neighbour as brother should treat brother! A time will come when constitutions will be introduced which are no longer open to such terrible abuse as are our present constitutions'

– a time when wars will be condemned as 'we nowadays condemn duelling', and when nobody will be honoured and praised for amassing as many worldly goods as would suffice to abolish the poverty of thousands.
Significantly, Bolzano's support in Prague came mainly from the Czech

middle classes, and from Count Leo Thun, a friend of the Czech patriotic cause, whereas Bolzano's German fellow-countrymen *(deutschböhmisch)* regarded him as a turncoat and renegade. They sought to prevent the publication of his writings; after his death they set up a commission to prove that he was not really 'a German'; and they took no part in the hundredth anniversary celebrations of his birth in 1881. The Czechs, on the other hand, saw in him (in 1914) a true Bohemian patriot and 'the founder of the Czech National Revival'. In 1882, Thomas Garrigue Masaryk came to Prague as the first professor to teach philosophy in the Czech part of the recently divided university. It is one of the sad ironies of Central European history that he seems never to have taken notice of Bolzano's patriotic and socially conscious writings. Perhaps Masaryk's lack of interest is to be explained by his recent conversion to Protestantism, and by his turning away from 'German metaphysics' in favour of the philosophies of Hume and Locke. Masaryk's sharp criticisms of Czech chauvinism made him deeply unpopular throughout almost the entire political spectrum, yet he accepted the nationalist mystique that was founded in Jungmann's doctrine of the identity of nation and language. When, in 1939, the Czech University of Prague was dissolved, its 'return to the Reich' was celebrated by the Reich Minister of Education, Bernhard Rust: his address on that occasion, in which he expressly distanced 'the culture' of the Third Reich from Bolzano and his humanist heritage, takes the *deutschböhmisch* attitude of the previous 100 years to its logical conclusion. What could the new masters of the old Kingdom have made of Bolzano's teaching – the epitome of liberalism and tolerance? 'Precisely the circumstance that we are a nation made up of unequal components [Bolzano had written] – precisely this circumstance would, if only we succeeded in suppressing the national party spirit that results from it, raise us up and make of us one of the happiest nations of Europe.'

Bolzano's reflections on the problems of nationalism in Bohemia and Moravia were no less than revolutionary. He contrasts Jungmann's 'national pride' with his own 'Landespatriotismus', while his conception of a 'double mother tongue' is intended to lay the foundation of the unity of both 'national tribes'. Again and again he proclaims the equal right of both nations to the worldly goods of the Kingdom, which he regards as potentially the richest country of the Monarchy and of Europe. He commends education as providing the only means to unmask the rhetoric of 'the rich and landed classes', and thus 'to end the bashful and undemanding attitude of the poor': 'Does not the entire Czech-speaking part of our nation live in a pitiable condition of poverty and oppression? And, most scandalous of all, is it not those who are German or belong to the Germans who have been appointed everywhere as their superiors?'

As a member of the Royal Bohemian Society of the Sciences in Prague, Bolzano befriended the country's first great historian, František Palacký (1798–1876); their relationship shows that the time for Bolzano's admonitions and warnings was over. In the years leading up to 1848 no radical polarization between the two nations occurred, yet there was no conciliation either. Palacký, the son of a Calvinist village schoolmaster from Moravia, rose swiftly (and not without help from aristocratic ladies) from an indigent background to a position of great academic and political eminence – one of the first commoners of the Kingdom to do so. What brought Bolzano and Palacký together was their fervent patriotism as well as their critical attitude to Vienna; yet whereas Bolzano was intent on the revival of Bohemian culture as part of his Christian appeal for justice, Palacký's attitude was increasingly political.

When Palacký began work on his *magnum opus*, his *History of Bohemia* (1836–67), its first version written in German and planned in five volumes, Bolzano acted as his adviser and 'gentle censor'. Yet the first volumes of the *History*, which appeared in Bolzano's lifetime, must have deeply disturbed him. Palacký's was the first medieval history of Bohemia written from an emphatically Czech perspective. It was also the first history of the country worked from primary sources, which is what makes for the vividness of its narrative of events. But somewhat disconnected from this narrative are passages of historical generalization, amounting to a reprise of Jungmann's 'spirit of the Czech Nation' – the ideology which Bolzano had rejected as the seedbed of modern nationalism. Palacký's moving account of John Hus's trial and execution in 1415 and his friend Jerome of Prague's similar fate a year later (written with Bolzano's assistance) is followed by chapters on 'The Hussite Wars'. Czech history is presented as the continuous progress of 'the Nation's Spirit' in an unbroken libertarian and egalitarian tradition: the Hussite movement in particular is seen as a part of 'the unending task of the Nation on behalf of humanity as a whole'. Another part of this vision is the apparently unchanging and unending Czech–German 'contest and conflict' seen as 'the red thread stretching for 1,000 years through Bohemian history'. Some social and material background to life in medieval Bohemia is provided, but obviously Palacký's concern is with higher matters. And so we read a good deal about the spiritual unity of the Nation and its 'old-Slavonic democratic spirit', its national pride, its fight for personal liberty and an indigenous culture; the Hussite movement especially, seen as an amalgam of national consciousness with Christian conscience, becomes the new nationalism's historical paradigm. A retrospective view suggests that what came to be called Palacký's 'philosophy of Czech history' is a revamping of early-fifteenth-century Czech history for mid-nineteenth-century political ends. Though it was at all times strongly opposed, first by German historians, then by some of the best Czech historians, this 'philosophy' was soon to provide the basis of Masaryk's politics and, with Masaryk's authority behind it, would dominate the historiography of the Czech establishment to the end of the first Czechoslovak Republic and beyond. If Palacký's text became canonical, and has remained so to the present day, this is not because its account of the Hussite era is true, but because, being accepted as true, it 'made history'. For such a (positively Nietzschean) 'use of history' Bolzano had no understanding.

In spite of his well-known hostility to the German Confederation, Palacký was invited to take part in the preparatory *Vorparlament* in Frankfurt; as 'a Bohemian of the Slavonic tribe' he refused the invitation, perhaps with Bolzano's approval. But when, as a gesture of protest, a Slavonic Congress was convened in Prague – against Palacký's wishes but under his chairmanship – this proved to be the gravest disappointment of Bolzano's last years, and (as Palacký's granddaughter notes in her biography of Bolzano) it brought their friendship to an end. Palacký's *Programme and Outline of a Constitution for the Federal State of Austria*, which appeared in the year following Bolzano's death, contains proposals for constitutional reforms intended to safeguard Bohemia against German expansionism. At the same time Palacký adhered to the cause of cultural Panslavism, at first rejecting the politicization of Czech–Russian relations – 'Imagine Austria dissolved into a large number of big and small republics! What an excellent foundation for a Russian universal monarchy that would provide!' – but then he changed his mind and advocated contacts with Russia as a counterweight to Austria's increasing dependence on Germany, which (he believed) would weaken the Monarchy and lead to an *Anschluss*. (Palacký's notorious changes of mind have themselves become a part of Czech history.)

However inconsistent Viennese policy in the Crown Lands of Bohemia and Moravia may have been, the national aspirations Palacký and his friends voiced were never strong enough to bring about major changes or lasting reforms in the institutional life of the country. Instead, there took place that radical politicization of culture of which Palacký's history is an early example. In poetry, in the study of the old literature (including the notorious forgeries of fourteenth-century epics which Palacký never ceased to regard as genuine), in the writings of grammarians and linguistic purists, in operas, in novels and in the popular theatre and journalism – in all these a strong patriotic vein was struck; and again it is the sheer literariness – a kind of proto-*PR* – of the national revival that is so marked, and that has remained one of the determining factors of Czech national life to this day.

Bolzano warns against this development in his own way, the way of a German-speaking Enlightened philosopher and priest with deep sympathies for the other side. He attacks the Czech–German language barrier above all in terms of its social consequences. He complains that all higher education in Bohemia is available only to the German and German-speaking inhabitants. He describes the oppressive poverty of the Czech peasants, artisans and labouring classes, and their servile attitude to the German officials responsible for their wretched condition, comparing those officials to the Egyptian 'bloodsuckers and taskmasters . . . who made the lives of the children of Israel bitter with hard bondage' (Exodus 1: 8–14). There are many such poignant pleas in his sermons and occasional writings. All the same, many Czech intellectuals outside the circle of his pupils and friends remained suspicious of his conciliatory attitude, which they interpreted as a gesture coming from a position of German cultural superiority. There are no indications that he fully understood the intensity of these feelings.

A few months before his death Bolzano writes to a friend:

> But the worst is this: we shoot nobody nor do we flog anybody to death.
> But we lock up thousands in dark holes and chain them to labour that
> ruins their health, until through hunger and cold, through sorrow and
> wretched heartbreak they sink so low that no human skill can save them
> from a horrible death! And so a curse upon our civic constitution
> whatever its name may be, whether it is an absolute monarchy or
> constitutional state, whether it is a republic or an aristocracy or whatever
> it may call itself!

And in a sermon of 1818: 'The socialist constitution upon earth is the most
effective constitution of all', because it alone is founded on an equality of life
chances and upon equal rights of happiness for all. It must be a rare event
for a Catholic priest to speak approvingly of Jeremy Bentham and to invoke
his doctrine of eudemonism: 'Not Kant's categorical imperative, but the
advancement of the common welfare of all is the highest moral law'.

From Bolzano's several refutations of the categorical imperative speaks the
Catholic pastor's dislike of a Protestant moral rigorism. He criticized Kant's
determination of 'the state of mind' that may accompany the fulfilment of 'the
good intention' (not, as in Kant, 'the good will'). The moral value of an act
(Bolzano argues, as Schiller had done before him) should not be diminished
because the act is done with a feeling of pleasure or satisfaction – the pleasure
which accompanies not indeed the fulfilment of the Kantian moral law, but
'the advancement of the common welfare of all'. The kindly thought behind
Bolzano's argument is not in doubt. But by being made to serve the eudemonic
ideal in a world seen as the world of the common weal and thus of the felicity
of all, his imperative no longer legitimates moral acts merely formally, but
proceeds to determine their content as well. For Kant all actions are good in
so far as their 'maxim' or guideline can be raised to a commonly binding law,
a law which is constituted by virtue of those acts alone; whereas for Bolzano
such acts are preceded by the *a priori* of a reasonable Leibnizian world, and
they become moral by freely complying with that postulate: acts are good
because and in so far as they conform with a world programmed for felicity.
In other words: Kant's law is constituted by the maxim of acts whose value
lies in the means and in nothing beyond those means; whereas in Bolzano's
law the means serve the end – the attainment of felicity – and are subordinated
to that end. Ultimately, his concern is for a Christian ethic that is to be given
a secularized categorical foundation. In his own terminology this means that
the 'real' or possible world of felicity is one of the 'truths in themselves' which
constitute a part of 'the highest moral law'. (This, incidentally, is the 'gentle
law' of which Stifter speaks in his preface to *Bunte Steine*, cautiously avoiding
any mention of Bolzano's name.) As we shall see, the form of Bolzano's
argument – the subordination of the means to an end – has analogies in other
parts of his work.

The possible is the real inasmuch as both are logically possible, and the predicate 'Es gibt . . . ' ('There is . . . ') applies to existence and non-existence alike (*Wissenschaftslehre* §182). Thus 'there is' a Leibnizian world of felicity for all, regardless of whether anyone has ever lived in it, and it is our moral duty to bring it into being, however incompletely. Bolzano perceives very clearly that an understanding of the question of bilingualism in Bohemia and of the antagonisms which arise from it leads to an understanding of social changes and to practical proposals of reform, ultimately to a world of felicity. But in making these practical proposals he no longer considers the language question to be relevant. On the contrary: in the quest for equality and justice (he writes) language differences are 'the least essential' part of the problem. And this is a conclusion he can hardly avoid, for he sees in language always merely a means, a designation of things, truths, ideas and facts (*Wissenschaftslehre* §285). In this way a theory is implied which would relate language to a non-linguistic sphere of 'truths in themselves', but such a theory is never worked out, for his interest is confined to speech as a medium of communication, and does not extend to language as a major philosophical topic (let alone an issue in ontology). His 'ontological commitment' is to 'propositions and ideas in themselves', regardless of their verbal formulations. The possibility of such propositions being dependent on, or modified by, language is not considered. The content of the lectures on language which he gave in the last years of his life is not known, the manuscripts are lost.

3

Bolzano's deep and moving concern with the social and economic state of the Empire is reflected in the number of charities he helped to found, it speaks to us from his lectures and sermons, it is present in his letters and in his occasional writings. Among the institutions he founded and helped to maintain was the Sorbian seminary in the Saxon town of Bautzen; among the social causes pleaded in his sermons was the wretched state of the Jews of Bohemia (which Bolzano's chief modern editor and biographer, Eduard Winter, fails to mention). 'The Jewish question', writes the author of a recent study of *The Political and Social Views of Bernard Bolzano*, 'was understood by the priest and philosopher not as a religious or national problem, but solely as a social matter'. In his sermon of 2 February 1809 Bolzano attacks the attitude of contemporary society to the Jews, condemning anti-Semitism 'not only among the Christian rabble, but also among educated and distinguished people in our Bohemia.' Christian society reproaches the Jews with the faults and vices which it taught them in the first place. He describes the appalling material conditions under which they have lived for centuries, lists the legal constraints which force them to concentrate on trade and finance. He speaks of Jewish illiteracy, ascribing superstition and lack of education among the Jews to their being banned from all public schools (at a time when 95 per cent of all

Bohemian and Moravian children of school age were said to be literate), but he also praises their industry, their moderation, their gratitude and eagerness to learn ... These observations may not strike us as profound, but in the climate in which he made them they were regarded as philo-Semitic sentimentalities, and they made him unpopular among the Czechs and the Bohemian Germans alike; while his warnings against the enforced conversion of Jews and their 'culpable self-persuasion' cannot have pleased the clerical authorities either. A generation later, Masaryk was prepared to risk his entire political career by conducting the defence of a Jewish pedlar accused of the ritual murder of a Christian girl – again one is bound to ask whether he knew of Bolzano's pleas for equal rights for the Jews and against the obscurantism they encountered. Whether Masaryk recognized the connection between the rising tide of national phobias, including anti-Semitism, and the linguistic chauvinism Bolzano had attacked, is less certain.

Bolzano was anything but a revolutionary. The friendly but ascetic narrow face with its shining eyes, as it appears in contemporary portraits, the tenor of his sermons and letters, the reports of his many friends – all speak of a life lived in great humility and charity, a life accompanied by long periods of ill health borne with much patience (from childhood he suffered tubercular hæmorrhages). It was a saintly life, resembling at least partly Stifter's characterization of him in 'Kalkstein', one of his best-known stories. But all this must not mislead us, as it seems to have misled Stifter: Bolzano was no timid conformist, but an *anima candida et fortis*. He remained faithful to the Church in his own fashion, as did all his disciples, with the exception of the most gifted of them, the revolutionary journalist and poet Karel Havlíček Borovský. Neither Bolzano's social criticism nor his independence of mind ever put him in danger of his life, and in this respect the comparison with John Hus, which was made by both his friends and his detractors, is certainly exaggerated; though without the protection of the young Archbishop of Prague, Alois Josef von Schrenck, he might well have suffered the fate of at least one of his disciples, who spent four years in detention while awaiting trial, and was never rehabilitated. Living in an atmosphere of threats and intrigues, Bolzano never retracted any of his views, never hesitated to offer a challenge to the authorities – clerical, imperial and national – who conspired and plotted against him. He resembled John Hus not in his fate but in his manner, which was gentle, courteous, insistently rational and utterly resolute.

4

Returning to our comparison between Bolzano's enlightened views and the Herder–Jungmann postulate of an identity of nation and language, we are bound to ask why the importance of a substantial part of this thesis escaped him.

Bolzano has often been called 'Bohemia's Leibniz', a name which alludes to his logical atomism and its foundation in Leibniz's monadic theory, to his doctrine of a world designed for universal felicity, and to the views of the pre-critical Enlightenment, which Bolzano found in Christian Wolff, Leibniz's chief popularizer. He was at home in four or five intellectual disciplines: in theology and a modified Catholic moral doctrine; in mathematics and its logical foundations; in the metaphysical inquiry into 'truths in themselves'; and in the political ethics of nationalism or, as he himself called it, 'ultra-patriotism'. The question arises whether these apparently disparate pursuits are in any way related – whether (in Wittgenstein's terminology) there is a family resemblance that connects them; and if so, how it is to be formulated.

We may begin with mathematics, which Bolzano sees as a system of numbers that exist within our perception of space and time, but which (as he argues against Kant) are in no way dependent on the forms of our perception. The signs we use in arithmetic and geometry to designate 'real numbers' have merely a secondary significance, much as (to use a modern analogy) in a statistical inquiry we use diagrams and graphs in order to present the result with greater clarity, yet such diagrams remain ancillary and exchangeable means. This turns out to be a faulty analogy, yet at the point at which it goes wrong it becomes useful as an example of the concrete, lateral thinking that does not seem to be available to Bolzano but is characteristic of Wittgenstein, in, for example, his *Remarks on the Foundations of Mathematics*:

> If you have a proof pattern [for example, a complicated mathematical calculation] that cannot be taken in at a single glance, and by a change in notation [for example, by means of two lines in a coordinate system] you turn it into one that can, then you are producing proof where there was none before.

Assuming a function analogous to the function of language in its performative mode, the notation ceases to be exchangeable, the result is fully dependent on it. (This is the kind of lateral thinking practised by Lichtenberg.)

In our search for resemblances between the various parts of Bolzano's writings we next recall what was said about his subordination of means to an end in his reflections on an 'imperative of the common weal'. The same is true of those absolute or objective 'truths in themselves' for which he sought at all times to provide a secure foundation. These truths 'exist' even though they may not appear in any actual written or spoken propositions, that is, even if no 'real' signs correspond to them. The reasoning behind this central tenet of Bolzano's philosophy may be retraced in non-technical terms: his 'ontological commitment' to these 'truths in themselves' is no heavier than the commitment of, say, a mathematician who speaks about an undiscovered formula that will generate all prime numbers, and Bolzano merely extends this argument by the claim that such a formula is a 'proposition in itself' and not a proposition thought by somebody; he is committed to no more than is a man who says that there are truths which are not yet known. In other words: the formulation of such truths does not matter to their existence.

Furthermore, the same applies to Bolzano's religious views. All our statements about God and the heavenly kingdom are images, the literalness of our expressions of transcendence is first relativized and then rejected:

> ... people take the teachings of religion in their literal sense, they understand literally what is meant to be merely a picture. To the untutored, who do not notice this figurativeness, such an illusion does no harm; indeed, it might even be pernicious for them to be told openly that here nothing is said about *the thing in itself* ... Is it possible to think of God other than figuratively? What is thus more natural than that we should gradually confuse the pictures in which we think of him with God himself? Is it to be wondered at that there were at all times people who exaggerated this? ...
> Do I need to tell you, my friends, that the name of the heavenly kingdom is to be understood as meaning nothing other than what is also known as the kingdom of God on earth; that is, nothing other than a gradual dissemination of such teaching and arrangements among people as will enable them to gain wisdom, virtue and happiness, whereby the states which they have founded among themselves should come more and more to represent *the picture* of an empire ruled by God himself? [my italics]

The conviction that we are mistaken in ascribing absolute truth to mere pictures provides the ground on which Bolzano's liberal and ecumenical attitude in matters of faith is based. And so, finally, we come to his ethical view of politics. Here above all his conviction is operative that the fact that people speak different languages is 'the least essential' thing of all. Does this mean that essentiality is to be ascribed to other, presumably non-linguistic modes of experience – to considerations which relate not only to the 'truths in themselves', but perhaps also to social and economic motives? However that may be, the fact that language is involved in every conceivable aspect of our experience is not considered.

How then are all these inquiries related? Some occasional remarks of Bolzano's are written at the conjunction of philosophy and history characteristic of Czech and indeed of Central European philosophizing. This is the kind of thinking we found in Palacký, and it would predominate in the writings of Masaryk and a host of their followers, when they wrote on such topics as 'the philosophy of Czech history', 'the spirit of Russia', or 'the philosophy of democracy' and the like. Such investigations are apt to be questionable as history, and unilluminating as philosophy. There is very little of this kind of thinking in Bolzano. The internal resemblances in his thinking lie elsewhere, in the methodological premise of his work.

In all the (clearly very diverse) inquiries I have mentioned, signs are invariably reduced to unimportant means. Language is seen as purely referential and informative, a system constituted by our 'capacity of signification' (Kant's term is 'Bezeichnungsvermögen'). The chief virtue of such a system is paraphrase, and (as my readers have no doubt noticed) paraphrase is the chief characteristic of Bolzano's style. What is omitted from this view is the feedback of language from signification to the signified, from description to the thing or state described – as in Herder's and the Romantics' inference from national language to nation. This omission represents one of the blank spots in the ideology of the Enlightenment, which offers no account of the great variety of things we can do with words. The intensity of the Romantic apotheosis of *das Volk* together with its new system of values was bound to escape Bolzano – this was the *Pathos* that would dominate the next 100 years of Czech and Central European history. This omission is all the more surprising since Bolzano (in contrast to Frege, and to the young Wittgenstein) had a very clear understanding of the social function of language; but because he failed to provide a theoretical foundation for them, his insights do not go beyond the practical concerns of daily life. He sought to solve the problem of the two languages in social and economic terms, which he hoped would lead to moral and spiritual improvement. But the subsequent history of Bohemia as well of most other parts of Central Europe has taught us that the economic motive need not be decisive; that the appeal to a threatened language consciousness can be politically effective even when it entails social and economic deprivations; that nationalism is stronger than Marxism. Languages – the two languages of Bohemia – are indeed what Wittgenstein calls them: 'forms of life'. The common humanity to which Bolzano appealed lies behind this insight, buried beneath the antagonisms of two nations once united by their common roots in one soil.

Austrian philosophy – or, to be precise, philosophy in Austria – has often been described as a line of railway stations on the Austrian *Südbahn*: from Bolzano to Brentano, from Brentano to Meinong and Husserl, last stop Wittgenstein. Here too we must look, not for a common denominator, but for the resemblances of a philosophical family. There is such a resemblance between the questions which Bolzano left unanswered and those taken up by Wittgenstein – on a foundation of ideas which Bolzano bequeathed to modern analytical philosophy. His work is the first element of the context which will be examined in the concluding essay of this book.

1989

3

'Words are also Deeds'

1

The evidence that will help to foreground language consciousness, the subject of these observations (and a topic merely implied in Pater Bolzano's attacks on early-nineteenth-century German and Czech chauvinism), is bound to be eclectic and to some extent speculative – in other words, methodologically unsound; and this is bound to be so even if the topic is narrowed down to its Austrian form. The reasons why writers, and people generally, think about language are as often as not implicit in what they say, and they are likely to differ; yet these reasons are bound to affect the view of language that emerges as the result of such thinking, and with it the politics of language. However, even though the observations that follow are incomplete, reflecting an individual choice of texts, they are intended to show the development of an idea. Although we are concerned with a mode of thinking that is to be found everywhere in the Western world, it is the *Pathos* that is Central European.

It is hard to know where to begin. Perhaps best with the assertion from which the Bolzano essay proceeded, that from the days of the Baroque and of Leibniz's and Herder's defences of the German language – the period covered by Eric Blackall's study *The Emergence of German as a Literary Language* – a special and complex interrelationship developed between the German language and national consciousness, an interrelationship which is quite unparalleled in respect of the major languages west of the Rhine. Furthermore, this interrelationship became profoundly influential in Central Europe, especially among Austria's eastern neighbours and Slavonic subject nations. As a consequence, from 1848 onward, a special moral fervour and political passion accompanied most of the language-conscious arguments with which I shall be concerned here. These matters lie on the borderline of literature, and it will not surprise us that a grim political undertone accompanies some, though by no means all, of the contributions to our topic.

2

It certainly accompanies the first of our documents, a letter from Josef Weinheber to Will Vesper, written on New Year's Eve 1938, which sets the scene for our discussion. Neither of the two poets could be described as a great authority on the history of the German language, nor was the atmosphere in which the letter was written – nine months after the incorporation of Austria into Greater Germany and three months after the Munich agreement – likely to foster a spirit of scholarly detachment. Born in Vienna in 1892, Weinheber had spent the first forty years of his life as a humble civil servant, unable to make a living from his abundant poetic production and failing to get much recognition from the public of the First Austrian Republic. All this changed at the *Anschluss*, when he was honoured as Austria's greatest poet, and made much of in university and National Socialist circles, on the strength of a few *völkisch* odes and a poem to Hitler; he took his life in Vienna at the approach of the Soviet tanks in May 1945. My reason for quoting from Weinheber's letter to the senior German (as opposed to Austrian) National Socialist Party poet, Will Vesper, is that here is language consciousness which reveals in a singlularly direct way the grim undertone I mentioned. Evaluating his own poetic achievement, Weinheber sees it beset by a special difficulty – the difficulty of 'thinking in *two* languages, in Viennese and High German':

> Viennese lost its claim to linguistic and thus to actual harmony ... at the point, around 1800, when the German classics [Lessing, Goethe and Schiller] sealed the victory of High German. The Emperor Francis I's resignation of the Holy Roman Crown was nothing but the visible, albeit unconscious, expression of the fact that the Imperial dialect had been reduced to the idiom of a clan. We Austrians have no classics (Grillparzer [1791–1872, Austria's greatest dramatist] wasn't one), and Nestroy [1801–62, its greatest comedy writer], who was one, came half a century too late. He could do no more than confront Viennese with High German, which in those days still sounded very alien and affected, achieving his comic effects from a linguistic tension, which is the work of a genius, precisely because its roots lie in language. Shortly after that begins the domination of the Jews. Since the Jew has no language of his own (the claim that Hebrew is his language is a troglodytic mistake), he clung to High German ... – this was our misfortune – to the High German of the newspapers. We Viennese (excluding myself!) heard the Jew talk 'posh' and were quite overcome with awe. Our tragic guilt – like all guilt, all error, all suffering – is ultimately a matter of language.

As for the political undertone, it is made up of that mixture of unhappiness, infamy and uneasy collaboration with which we are familiar from the statements of numerous Austrian writers throughout the 1930s and 1940s, before and

during the *Anschluss*, and which Weinheber himself movingly recaptures in a
poem of 1942:

> Vielleicht, daß einer spät,
> wenn all dies lang vorbei,
> das Schreckliche versteht,
> die Folter und den Schrei –
>
> und wie ich gut gewollt
> und wie ich bös getan;
> der Furcht, der Reu gezollt
> und wieder neuem Wahn –
>
> und wie ich endlich ganz
> dem Nichts verfallen bin
> und der geheime Kranz
> mir sank dahin . . .

(Perhaps one day / when all this is long past / someone will understand
the terrible thing it was – / will understand the torture and the cry //
and how I meant well / and how I did wrong / how I paid tribute to
fear and repentance / and again to new acts of madness, // and how at
last I succumbed to Nothingness / and my secret garland withered away
. . .)

The poem is one of many examples which are bound to bewilder readers
'when all this is long past': a singularly clear testimony from a troubled and
tainted source. However, our business is with Weinheber's letter to Will
Vesper. Much of what it contains is the staple substance of Karl Kraus's
polemics and satires. The exaltation of Nestroy at the expense of Grillparzer,
the tie-up of anti-Semitism with an attack on the rule of the Press (a general
Austrian topos since 1848), the emphatic identification of linguistic with
'factual' (*tatsächlich*) harmony, the claim that great poetry is rooted 'in language'
in some special way in which, by implication, minor poetry is not, the use of
'troglodytisch' as a term of abuse, and finally the immense, heedless exaggeration of the linguistic aspect of experience ('all guilt, all error, all suffering) –
all these prove that Weinheber had been and remained, in his opinions and
preoccupations (though not, alas, in his prose style), a faithful reader of the
satirical periodical *Die Fackel (The Torch)*, whose last number had appeared in
February 1936, four months before Kraus's death.

The historical statement contained in Weinheber's letter, outlining the
defeat of what he calls 'the Imperial dialect' by High German, is not to be
found in the pages of *Die Fackel*. It must be read as a tribute to the new
masters of Austria by a poet who had very little reason to regret the departure
of the old ones, hoping to improve his literary standing as well as his appalling

material circumstances as a result of the change – let him that will cast the first stone at him. More important from our point of view, this 'victory of High German' is offered as an explanation of the chief weakness of Weinheber's poetry as he himself saw it. His weakness – most clearly betrayed in some of his odes in *Adel und Untergang* (1934) – is, like Grillparzer's weakness, an excessive solemnity of tone and an excessive weightiness of diction derived, in Weinheber's case, not from Weimar classicism but from Hölderlin, Rilke, and Stefan George at his most vatic and arid. Yet (as Weinheber himself knew) here also lies his strength, for his most characteristic achievement – like, in a different poetic sphere, Nestroy's – is to be found in those poems which issued from his concern with that very medium to which he attributes his difficulties. The autobiographical poem from which I have already quoted contains lines which illustrate my point. These lines are hesitant, enigmatic, even unclear, and as such they are perfectly expressive of the deep, unhappy puzzlement of one who fears that his 'name was writ in water':

> Was will die Zeit von mir? Ward mir Gebühr?
> Geehrt hat mich die Macht, doch nicht gefragt.
> So schließt sich nimmer das Geschwür.
> Und alles, was ich sprach, bleibt ungesagt.

(What does the age want of me? Did I receive my due? / Honoured was I by the mighty, but not asked. / The sore remains unhealed for ever / And unsaid all that I spoke.)

However, it was not in these solemnities that Weinheber achieved that which he desired above all things, even above success – a valid poetic diction – but in a creative acknowledgement and articulation of his experience of language as a deeply problematic form of life; and these – acknowledgement and articulation – he finds where Kraus found them before him, in Johann Nestroy.

3

Nestroy's strength, which Weinheber envied, was not simply that of a dialect poet, let alone a 'regional' writer (*Hoamatdichter*). Part of it derives, as Weinheber points out, from his discovery – Nestroy had predecessors, but none who brought this particular art to such perfection – that the juxtaposition of High German and Viennese could, in and by itself, be a source of superb humour. (Among the many absurdities uttered by many solemn Austrian critics is the assertion that Nestroy's 'word-creations were never an end in themselves'.) Nestroy's wordplay is not just a clever trick, but a whole bag of clever tricks, all of them dependent on his highly developed language consciousness.

Of course (to paraphrase Wittgenstein's gibe against those who would have
'pure beauty, unadulterated by anything beautiful'), one cannot have 'pure'
comedy, unadulterated by anything comic: the comedy Nestroy has created
plays with situations and characters – but over and above that it is a comedy
of language. Which is as much as to say that in a historical predicament in
which his own language has been squeezed to the margins of literary respectability (as indeed its 'heroes' have been squeezed to the margins of social
respectability) – in that threatened state, Nestroy has created a comedy which
is as nearly a pure play with words as comedy is ever likely to be. Embodying
the conflict between high and low (language or society) – a conflict both
hopeless and comic, comic in its hopelessness – language in Nestroy is the
dominant form of life.

Here each word game is part of a scene in which the anchorman is the
dialect expression, and against it Nestroy plays off a piece of High German,
or a bit of learned mythological bric-à-brac, or a philosophical abstraction –
or simply the expression itself looked at in a different way. I need hardly say
that, since these are conceits which depend on affinities of sound and idiomatic
association characteristic of one language (the Austrian or rather Viennese
dialect), they are untranslatable into another (as, to choose a notorious example,
almost any translator would find when trying to render Hamlet's question to
Ophelia, 'Do you think I meant country matters?' and as Thornton Wilder
found when adapting one of Nestroy's comedies to the idiom of Yonkersville).
All that can be done here is to assert Nestroy's supreme success in this comic
mode. The source of such word games is an acute language consciousness;
and this, at its most characteristic, is joined by authorial self-consciousness.
Thus, a poor devil of a lawyer's clerk soliloquizes on the dreary routine of
copying unfair contracts in his fair hand, making his chore tolerable by punning
his way from the deadly boring business before him to an imaginary world of
opulent living and unattainable comforts: a world – like his author's – created
entirely by his verbal imagination.

The emphasis in a discussion of such ploys of Nestroy's must always be on
single verbal elements of his comedies, for in these, rather than in dramatic
continuities, lies his most distinctive achievement. But this emphasis on the
atoms of language is bound to be repeated throughout our entire discussion.
We find it in the classical statement of a poet's linguistic doubt, Hofmannsthal's
famous *Letter of Lord Chandos*, in Fritz Mauthner's language critique, in
Wittgenstein's *Tractatus* and its inquiry into the pictorial (*abbildend*) function
of language, and in Kraus's verbal polemics as well as in the 'Language
Lessons' (*Sprachlehre*) of the last few years of *Die Fackel* – everywhere the
focus is on single words, phrases, or at most *Sätze*, individual propositions.

Why does Nestroy play on language? I have already given one very simple
explanation: his love of wordplay is a source – his chief source – of humour
and fun. In this respect Nestroy differs radically from Kraus, his great admirer,
for whom wordplay was almost invariably a source of satire and thus a means
toward certain moral or ethical ends. (And considered as a satirist, Nestroy is

less effective than Kraus.) However, besides the motivation of wordplay as play, we can, I think, see something else. This is how penpusher Federl begins his monologue: 'All you have to have is a lively imagination – but it's got to be damned lively – and then all's right with the world,' and with this Federl, and with him Nestroy and his fellow punsters and language-conscious writers, all give a novel form to an old discovery. I mean the discovery that the imagination at work in the world of words acts in a consoling, conciliatory and compensatory manner; and that to an extent that varies from author to author the world of words offers assurances, comforts and occasionally the power which the world of things and people, of social and political relations and politics, does not yield. (The world of words is, as we shall see at the end of this essay, more than a world of words.) This, again and again, is Kraus's theme, for instance in the poem 'Bekenntnis':

> Ich bin nur einer von den Epigonen
> die in dem alten Haus der Sprache wohnen.
>
> Doch hab' ich drin mein eigenes Erleben
> ich breche aus und ich zerstöre Theben.
>
> Komm' ich auch nach den alten Meistern, später,
> so räch' ich blutig das Geschick der Väter.
>
> Von Rache sprech' ich, will die Sprache rächen
> an allen jenen, die die Sprache sprechen.

(I am no more than one of the epigonoi / living in the ancient house of language. // Yet the life I live therein is still my own / I break out and destroy Thebes. // Though I come after the masters of old, later, / yet bloodily I revenge the ancestral fate. // I speak of revenge, and to revenge language / on all those who speak it is my will.)

Indeed, it seems that the more hostile, disenchanting and chaotic the world of politics and social discontent, the more insistent the preoccupation with what Kraus called 'The Magic of Language', the more intense the feeling that (to quote from one of W. B. Yeats's poems) 'words alone are certain good.'

4

Wordplay is to be seen as an aspect of language consciousness, as a source of humour, and as a compensatory activity in the face of all manner of personal and social deprivations. This predicament was experienced most acutely and exploited most thoroughly by those writers whose deprivations were felt most keenly – those writers who not only were made to experience their social, political and racial situation first as radically problematic, then as existentially threatened, and finally as a matter of life or death, but had their right to possession of the very language of their creativeness challenged: I mean the German-writing Jews of the Austro-Hungarian Empire. Their situation was summed up in an unusually frank and accurate way in the autobiography of Fritz Mauthner (1849–1923), journalist, philosopher and founding father of the Viennese school of language criticism:

> Much would have to be said about the special circumstances which intensified one's interest in a psychology of language to a passion. From my earliest youth this interest was very strong in me – indeed, I don't understand how a Jew who was born in one of the Slavonic lands of the Austrian Empire could avoid being drawn to the study of language. In those days [the 1860s] he learned to understand three languages all at once: German as the language of the civil service, of culture, poetry and polite society; Czech as the language of the peasants and servant girls, and as the historical language of the glorious Kingdom of Bohemia; a little Hebrew as the holy language of the Old Testament and as the basis of Jewish-German jargon [*Mauscheldeutsch*] which he heard not only from the Jewish hawkers, but occasionally also from quite well-dressed Jewish businessmen of his society, and even from his relatives ... Moreover, the mixture of quite dissimilar languages in the common Czech-German jargon [*Kuchelböhmisch*; Mauthner might have mentioned the equally despised *Wasserpolnisch*] was bound to draw the child's attention to certain linguistic laws.

The Swiss critic Walter Muschg used parts of this quotation to describe what he took to be Franz Kafka's language problem, and the Austrian critic Hans Weigel took it over from Muschg to characterize Kraus; but they didn't look at it closely enough.

Mauthner here accepts and unquestioningly shares the value judgement of his non-Jewish environment, and so did almost all the writers I have mentioned. They all regarded linguistic contaminations as despicable and evil, and, as often as not, a legitimate source of malicious jokes. (This is the value judgement we encountered in Weinheber's letter to Will Vesper.) But, of course, there is nothing self-evident about these value judgements, and one cannot readily think of them outside the particular political climate of the declining Austro-Hungarian Empire. Did the Norman courtiers who came over with William feel that the contaminated French which the London plebs and court purveyors spoke in contact with them was despicable? Yet without that 'Frensh ... / After the scole of Stratford-atte-Bowe' there would have been no Chaucer nor his affectionate portrait of the prioress who speaks it, and no Shakespeare either. However much they may have denied it, Mauthner's, Kraus's and in due course Weinheber's hostile evaluations were inseparable from the virulent nationalism which was at its most uncompromising in those areas of Bohemia and Moravia where nationhood of both kinds, Czech and German, was felt to be most threatened. Only Kafka – for instance in his address of welcome to the Yiddish players in Prague – shows some sympathetic understanding of Yiddish and of the situation in which it was born.

But there is a second, no less important corollary to Mauthner's autobiographical observation. The situation he describes may well be specifically Jewish in its intensity, but *mutatis mutandis* it applies beyond the reach of any racial criteria – it is, in this respect too, an Austrian problem. There are Jewish writers – Joseph Roth is an obvious example, Arthur Schnitzler is another – who experienced no such anxieties and qualms and were stimulated by no such linguistic curiosity as are described in Mauthner's autobiography, and whose work shows none of those language-conscious preoccupations which for Weinheber, following Kraus, constitute the essence of great poetry. And there are non-Jewish writers who felt these qualms and searchings and uncertainties every bit as acutely. The poet Rainer Maria Rilke is one of them. In a remarkably candid letter to the Prague Germanist August Sauer (11 January 1914), he looks anxiously back on the linguistic predicament of his childhood; and the description Rilke gives of it is strikingly similar not only to that of Weinheber (whose origins place him on the same side of the racial divide) but also to Mauthner's (on the opposite side). Rilke writes that just as there is no Austrian national idea to embrace and unify the countries of the Monarchy, so Austria has failed to develop a valid language of its own – a deprivation which he feels more and more poignantly as the years go by. Instead, the heritage of a poet born in Prague is no better than 'verbal refuse' (*verdorbene Sprachabfälle*), a hotchpotch made up of incompatible linguistic bits and pieces and contained within 'the deteriorating margins of language'. So disabling is this predicament, Rilke concludes, that it taints even what is most valuable to a poet – the memory of the earliest and most tender experiences of childhood, making him turn his back on them in shame.

Kafka's observations about the German word 'Mutter' and the feelings of inappropriateness and coldness which, he says, a Prague-German-Jewish child experiences in using that word, are written from the Jewish side of the racial divide, but they reveal the same problematic, not to say traumatic, attitude toward the language of childhood. This is particularly ironical, seeing with what quasi-religious solemnity the word 'Ursprung' ('origins') is endowed by this generation of poets and literary men – a generation that was after many strange gods, of which 'language' was one. However, the point at issue is that each of these writers – first Mauthner, then Kraus, Rilke and Kafka – made use of a different aspect of his linguistic unease, turned a different strand of his language consciousness to good account.

Surprisingly enough (for Rilke is often seen as politically uninformed), the letter of Rilke's from which I have quoted opens with an interesting and valid political insight of the kind expressed by many patriotic Czech writers throughout the nineteenth century: it is Rilke's view that in the course of more than 100 years the idea of Austria and its statehood had failed to 'penetrate' into 'the constituent parts' of the State. The literary argument that follows, though no less perceptive, is really incomplete in the same way as was Weinheber's, for in his anxiety to dissociate himself from his Prague origins, Rilke fails to recognize one of the sources of his own poetry. He fails to see that to the extent that his own linguistic ideals and the linguistic creativeness in which they are embodied strain away from the common linguistic norms of the society that surrounds him and toward a wholly individual mode of expression, these ideals and creativeness are the offspring of the problematic linguistic situation of his origins, and hence of the kind of language-conscious preoccupation which by implication he deplores. When he too complains that Austria (and the German minority of Prague) has no uncorrupted language of its own, he is, in fact, describing the grounds of his own linguistic inventiveness, the conditions under which (to quote from a letter written eight years later – 17 March 1922 – a month after the completion of the *Duino Elegies*) 'the task of the poet and his craft' should be accomplished. 'The hardest part of this task', he writes there, 'arises from the poet's strange obligation to distance his words radically and essentially from the words of mere social intercourse and communication. *No* word in the poem (I mean words like "und", "der", "die", "das") is *identical* with a word of similar sound in common use or in a dictionary.' It is not surprising that Rilke's view is identical with the opening of Karl Kraus's essay 'Die Sprache', often regarded as the most magisterial and self-consciously formal of his pronouncements on language, in which Kraus argues that there is no overlap between 'language as poetic creation' and 'language as communication', and that all attempts to unite and subsume both in a single, undivided body of knowledge are bound to fail. And it is no less significant that the most general philosophical amplification of this language view of Rilke's and Kraus's is expressed in Wittgenstein's proposition: 'The sense of the world must lie outside the world ... In the world [Rilke would say: In the world of social intercourse and communication; Kraus would say: In the world of journalism and mere information] everything is as it is and everything happens as it does happen. *In* it there is no value [*In* it there is no artistic, poetic value, both Rilke and Kraus would say] and if there were, it would be of no value.' Poetry, satirical prose and philosophy are inspired by the view that, whenever they are true to themselves, they are concerned with a sense or value of the world which does not reside in the world.

I must leave to one side the question of how meaningful this language view of Rilke's (and Kraus's) really is – it obviously leads to the idea of a private language, which is refuted at length in Wittgenstein's later work – though it is relevant to observe that even very peculiar and obviously inadequate theories of language can turn out to be perfectly compatible with the highest literary and poetic achievements. (The surprising analogy is with fictions which are unimpaired by being based on demonstrably wrong views of the physical universe.) And this precisely is the case here: such total alienation from the common use of words as Rilke proposes may be a practical impossibility, but the need for it was the theoretical starting-point from which Rilke's language consciousness and hence his creativeness proceeded – moreover, the need arose from the feeling of linguistic impoverishment shared by all the other writers I have mentioned. And this was Kafka's condition too.

Kafka *or* Rilke. It is fascinating to observe how from one common or at least profoundly similar linguistic ground there emerge two totally dissimilar literary œuvres – dissimilar, above all, in their linguistic dimension. Rilke's essential medium is poetry; Kafka's sole medium is prose: two different kinds of literary creativeness face a profoundly similar experience of linguistic (and, incidentally, also social) deprivation. Rilke (accepting 'the poet's strange obligation') hides the experience by building it into the very foundations of his poetry and imposing on it his complex and vertiginous metaphoric structures – structures which remind one of nothing so much as of those 'ladders, / long since – where ground never was – just quiveringly / propped against each other' of the Fifth Duino Elegy ('ihre / längst, wo Boden nie war, nur an einander / lehnenden Leitern'). He writes – in the crucial places of his poetry, but in his letters no less – like one who has only just come to the language and finds in it – in words like 'könntens', 'auf gestilltem / Teppich', 'Es wäre ein Platz, den wir nicht wissen', 'und dorten, / auf unsäglichem Teppich', to quote from a single stanza of that Fifth Elegy – a series of partly new meanings: new, partly unfamiliar yet perforce cognate with the words we know ('suppose they could', 'on the quietened / carpet', 'Suppose there's a place we know nothing about', 'and there / on some indescribable carpet'). He writes like a foreigner, but one the effect of whose words depends on deliberate rather than inadvertent (conscious rather than uninformed) departures from the linguistic norm of 'mere social intercourse and communication'. There is in Rilke's poetry an absolute determination to see the thing through, however idiosyncratic or grammatically odd it may be – a sort of heedless will to a personal poetic form and language (and the same is to be seen in his use of traditional metres).

In all this 'poetic heartwork' – in the poetry whose sources lie in language consciousness – he had a faithful disciple and continuator in Paul Celan. A different set of languages (German, Romanian, Ukrainian and French) and linguistic doubts is accompanied by a similar dislike of the 'contaminated' medium, a similar heedless immersion in German, which is, for Rilke, the language of the dreary *Bürger* – for Celan, the language of the deadly enemy – yet the inalienable mother tongue for both. It is no diminution of Celan's immense originality to recognize his poetry for what it is – a radicalization of the Rilkean mode of creativeness.

Kafka's attitude, on the other hand (whose life Celan re-enacted under some of the conditions Kafka foresaw), is the reverse of Rilke's. He remains faithful to the original experience of social and linguistic deprivation: he stays utterly close to it and the grey-on-grey metaphors it dictates. These he then uses to the full, with a minimum of linguistic creativeness as Rilke or Kraus would understand the term, but of course with a quite different creativeness of his own: by tying the grey-on-grey metaphors of everyday into his scenes and actions, rather as Picasso and Juan Gris stuck bits of newspaper and the odd label or advertisement into their still lifes. For Rilke the personal idiom is of the essence of poetry; to Kafka, in his humility, it is likely to appear as an unwarranted intrusion, a manifestation of the *moi haïssable*. Yet the initial consciousness of linguistic inadequacy and deprivation, as well as the initial hesitancy and uncertainty *vis-à-vis* German German, is much the same in both.

All this leads me to reiterate a point which should now appear as less paradoxical than it may have done at the beginning of this essay. What is being presented here is a middle ground of literary creation. Irrespective of the various personal dilemmas and deprivations which lie at its origins, and irrespective too of the overall language views and practices to which they lead, this language consciousness is an immensely fertile literary preoccupation and theme, inseparable from some of the major achievements of Austrian and German Central-European literature in this century.

5

What, then, are the overall views of language which this consciousness yields? Let me state them in their extreme form. On the one hand there is language as an absolutely reliable moral indicator of life, acting as an infallible witness to all that happens in the world, part of a pre-established and perhaps even mystical harmony between words and action; this is the main inspiration of Kraus's work, but it is shared to some extent and at some points in their works by Rilke and Weinheber. On the other hand there is Mauthner's philosophical language critique and its literary descendants. These arrive at the opposite conclusion, arguing that language is metaphorical and therefore inaccurate (a central tenet, it should be added, of Nietzsche's fragmentary language theory), and that the inherent propensity of language toward abstraction, generalization and reification makes it an unreliable and uncontrollable instrument for all forms of communication, including the crudest and most readily verifiable, let alone those that are more subtle and more valuable. Mauthner's argument, in other words, leads in a discursive and analytical way to that position of apparently total language scepticism with which we are familiar from Hofmannsthal's Chandos letter and which in turn is closely related to the radical conclusions of Wittgenstein's *Tractatus*. Certainly, Mauthner as well as Hugo von Hofmannsthal would have agreed with that passage in *The Man Without Qualities* where Robert Musil considers language as one of the ways in which 'the practical realist' (*der Wirklichkeitsmensch*) satisfies his unending restlessness and compensates for his inability to commit himself absolutely to his experience of the world; where Musil considers language as the source of the inauthenticity of modern man:

It seems that reality is something the worthy, practical realist can never wholly love or take seriously. As a child he crawls under the table of his parents' living room when they're not at home, in order by this brilliantly simple trick to make it into a place of adventure; as a boy he longs for a watch of his own; as the young man with a gold watch he longs for the woman to go with it; and as a man with a watch and wife he hankers after promotion; and when he's been lucky enough to fulfil this little circle of wishes and is calmly swinging to and fro in it like a pendulum, yet it seems that his store of unsatisfied dreams has not diminished at all. For when he aspires to greater heights he resorts to simile. Apparently because snow is at times disagreeable to him, he compares it to a woman's gleaming breasts, and as soon as his wife's breasts begin to bore him, he compares them to gleaming snow; he'd be horrified if one day he and his little turtledove suddenly had horny doves' bills to coo with or if her lips turned to corals – but poetically it excites him. He is capable of turning anything into everything – snow into skin, skin into blossoms, blossoms into sugar, sugar into powder, and powder back into a little flurry of snow – for all that apparently matters to him is to make things into what they are not, which is doubtless proof that he cannot stand being anywhere for long, wherever he happens to be.

It is difficult to think of a more glaring contradiction than that between language as a reliable moral guide and omnipotent source of life on the one hand (with occasional, quite gratuitous allusions to the biblical Logos thrown in), and, on the other, language as a manifestation of man's incapacity, his failure to be reliably at home in a world permeated by such an unreliable medium – his failure, it seems, *because* it is an interpreted world. Yet the two views turn out to be compatible, and Rilke's poetic concern is to make them so. Thus, in the Ninth Duino Elegy he proclaims man's chief task in our time and identifies it with the poet's task:

> *Hier* ist des *Säglichen* Zeit, *hier* seine Heimat.
> Sprich und bekenn. Mehr als je
> fallen die Dinge dahin, die erlebbaren, denn,
> was sie verdrängend ersetzt, ist ein Tun ohne Bild.

(*Here* is the time of the *Sayable, here* is its home. / Speak and proclaim. More than ever / the things we can live are falling away, for / that which ousts and replaces them is an imageless act.)

This is language in its sphere of omnipotence. Yet man's ultimate destiny, 'under the stars', which is here and not quite here, is described as indescribable (*unsäglich*): 'Preise dem Engel die Welt, nicht die unsägliche' (Praise *this* world to the Angel, not the unsayable); and again, at the conclusion of the Tenth Elegy, man's ultimate destiny peters out into wordlessness, a last silence –

> Einsam steigt er dahin, in die Berge des Ur-leids.
> Und nicht einmal sein Schritt klingt aus dem tonlosen Los.

(Solitary he climbs the Mountains of Primal Pain. / And not even his step resounds from the soundless fate.)

– language announcing its own failure and in the announcement transcending it. Perhaps, after all, seeing that ' . . . Lebendige machen / alle den Fehler, daß sie zu stark unterscheiden' ('the living all / make the error of drawing too sharp distinctions') (First Elegy), the words which avoid this error do lead from omnipotence to the renunciation of all power, from Rilke's *here* to an ineffable *there*.

Language all-powerful in its very impotence – is that not what Hofmannsthal shows in his greatest comedy, *Der Schwierige*? On the face of it the play presents the failure of communication (surely the finest subject for comedy in our age) and the indecency and indelicacy of words – but it is only the indecency of the wrong words that is (and can ever be) demonstrated. The rest is silence? Not at all. The silences in the play are shown to be what silences always are – an indispensable part of our use of words.

6

The language consciousness that has here been described is not a mere biographical quirk nor is it a topic shrouded in provincial or historical obscurity. On the contrary: from its place on the borderlines between literature, philosophy and political ideology, it provides much of the empirical basis of the philosophy of language in our time. A major inquiry of that philosophy concerns the place of language in experience, and our last point takes up this problem in its most concrete form, though here again our approach and evidence will be mainly literary.

Samuel Beckett once observed that literature is the one human activity which can draw achievement even from a proclamation of its failure. This is what Rilke does, for instance, by treating the word 'unsäglich' as if it were a simple descriptive adjective, indicative of a particular and, as it were, positive quality; or again by saying, in the Eighth Elegy, 'Immer ist es Welt / und niemals Nirgend ohne Nicht' ('Always there is world / and never a Nowhere without No'), he intimates some sort of absolute space and traces out the contour it shows in our world. Putting things into words is presented as the very symbol and pattern of what is irrefutable in human experience:

> ... Sind wir vielleicht *hier*, um zu sagen: Haus,
> Brücke, Brunnen, Tor, Krug, Obstbaum, Fenster, –
> höchstens: Säule, Turm ... aber zu *sagen*, verstehs,

oh zu sagen *so*, wie selber die Dinge niemals
innig meinten zu sein.

(Are we perhaps *here* just for saying: House, / Bridge, Fountain, Gate,
Jug, Fruit Tree, Window – / possibly: Pillar, Tower? . . . but for *saying*,
remember, / oh, for *such* saying as never the things themselves / hoped
so intensely to be.)

Naming becomes, in the Ninth Elegy, the paradigm of human creativeness.
But no sooner has it been raised to this solitary eminence than it sports
an extravagant metaphysic, according to which things named and poetically
described assume a greater reality than 'Tun ohne Bild' (imageless act); and
in the Tenth Elegy we read that reality begins where our common world ends
– 'gleich dahinter, ists *wirklich*' ('just behind them, it's real!'). It may be said
quite generally that most (though perhaps not all) of the language-conscious
thinking of the era with which we have been concerned was based on a
dichotomy between language and reality in one form or another. Now, whenever this thinking issues in poetry, this dichotomy becomes, if not logically
tenable, at least a valid metaphor for an important contemporary state of mind.
In critical and philosophical arguments, however, it is demonstrably absurd.
When a critic asserts that 'language cannot express what is most real', or when
a language critic like Mauthner argues that 'because language is only a
convention, like a rule or a game . . . it is neither going to grasp nor alter the
real world', the need to show up the absurdity of such statements becomes
imperative.

Again it is the language consciousness of the age, reaching its apogee in
the work of Kraus, which comes to our aid. It is obvious that his writings,
which are both satirical and didactic (in the sense that Swift's writings are
both satirical and didactic), cannot rest on a dichotomy which would place
language in total separation from 'reality'. Moreover, from a certain point
onward Kraus's work becomes an explicit refutation of the spurious dichotomy.

Kraus believes in a sort of panlogism. This view is often esoterically
expressed, yet in certain of its aspects it turns out to be anything but remote
from his everyday world and ours. Kraus's expression of it is neither theoretical
nor systematic, but is offered as a challenge to the reader through a series of
polemical attacks and satirical exaggerations. One such attack, in which all the
threads of Kraus's satire are drawn together, was written in November 1914;
its occasion was the outbreak of the Great War. The passage begins with a
refutation of the obvious, commonplace view of the Press:

What is the Press? Only a messenger? One who also importunes us with
his message? Torments us with his impressions? Insists on adding to the
fact he brings us his conception of it? One who, through the details of
the details of reports of moods, or through his perceptions about the
observations of details and the endless repetitions of all this, tortures us
to a state of frenzy? *Is* the Press a messenger?

At this point Kraus breaks off the rhetorical crescendo and thrusts before us a bold equation: a piece of information is not (*we* might wish to say: is not only) a set of words but an event; a speech is not just a speech but a piece of life:

> No: it is the event. Is it discourse? No, it is life. It not only claims that the true events are its news about the events, it also brings about the uncanny identity that makes it come to seem that deeds are first reported and then done – and often too it brings about the condition in which war reporters may not watch [warlike events] but warriors become reporters. Thus it is that I don't mind being told that I am forever exaggerating the importance of the Press. It is no mere messenger – how could a messenger demand so much and get it too? – it is the event itself.

And from this recognition issues the immense generalization to which Kraus (like Kierkegaard before him) returns again and again – the modern confusion of means and ends and the moral consequences of that confusion:

> Once again a mere instrument has got the better of us. We have set the man whose job it is to report the conflagration and whose role in the State should be the humblest, above the world, above the conflagration and above our house, above the fact and above our imagination. But, eager and disappointed, like Cleopatra we should beat the messenger for bringing the message. As he announces the hated wedding and embellishes his report, so she makes him responsible for it.

There is thus an antecedent for this modern scandal among the creations of those few master poets who survive Kraus's scrutiny:

> *Cleopatra:* Ram thou thy fruitful tidings in mine ears,
> That long time have been barren . . .
> The most infectious pestilence upon thee . . .
> What say you? Hence
> (*Strikes him again*)
> Horrible villain! or I'll spurn thine eyes
> Like balls before me; I'll unhair thy head:
> (*She hales him up and down.*)
> Thou shalt be whipp'd with wire, and stew'd in brine,
> Smarting in lingering pickle.
> *Messenger:*   Gracious madam,
> I that do bring the news made not the match.

And connected with that illicit substitution of means for ends is the second major insight of Kraus's moral-linguistic vision – his understanding that the modern inflation of words and images entails that poverty of the imagination in which he sees, if not (as elsewhere) the full cause of war, yet the occasion of it: 'But the reporter contracts the marriage, burns down the house and makes the horror story which he invents come true. With many years' practice he has reduced mankind to such poverty of the imagination as to make it possible for man to wage a war of destruction against himself.' I need not dwell on the obvious – that this passage states, albeit in a radically exaggerated, satirical form, a fact of modern life, a predicament which is still with us and (with television added since Kraus's time) almost as far from a satisfactory solution as it was in 1914. But the importance of this passage for the central theme of these observations is somewhat different. For this is one of the places in Kraus's strange œuvre – and it is probably the first of such places – where a direct attack is launched on the language–reality dichotomy, and a true account of the multiple function of words is presented.

From Plato's *Cratylus* onward, that dichotomy had always been a particularly unconvincing piece of philosophical speculation. After all, what possible meaning can we ever attach to a notion called 'reality' that would exclude words? What spoken or written word is not part of our world? What statements can we ever make that do not connote, involve, inhere in, or become modified by actions? Language, Kraus is saying, is description and is one of the things described, repository and source of experience. It is word and deed – it is itself a form of life:

And to imagine a language means to imagine a form of life.

'So you are saying that human agreement decides what is true and what is false?' – It is what human beings *say* that is true and false; and they agree in the *language* they use. That is not agreement in opinions but in form of life.

And words can be wrung from us, – like a cry. Words can be *hard* to say: such, for example, as are used to effect a renunciation, or to confess a weakness. (Words are also deeds.)

But these statements – the importance of which can hardly be exaggerated since they mark the end of an exclusively referential view of language, and with that the end of the language–reality dichotomy – come not from Kraus but from Wittgenstein, and not from the *Tractatus* of 1922 but from the first part of the *Philosophical Investigations*, concluded in 1945.

With these statements and their manifold implications we reach the high philosophical point of the linguistic thinking I have outlined. No doubt these insights were anticipated intuitively by poets from Novalis onward. But as parts of the new theoretical thinking about language, they contain a wholly new key to an understanding of a vast range of things, including politics, historical studies, and other forms of social life that Wittgenstein himself was not interested in. Together with that small number of literary works which may survive our century and which happen to make up half the canon of modern German literature, these insights of language consciousness, begotten by a generation that died a bitter death in lands now changed beyond recall, constitute in their own strange way a living heritage of the Austro–Hungarian past.

1980

4

On Prague German Literature

1

In the late autumn of 1947 in Göttingen, where I was working on my Cambridge thesis, the news reached me that some Prague German friends of my parents had been expelled from our common homeland and settled near Stuttgart. The mail being unreliable, I set off to visit them, to see if I could be of any help. All I knew about their life in the Protectorate of Bohemia and Moravia was that Oskar N., a Sudeten German bank employee, had refused to give way to pressure from the Office of the Reich Protector to divorce his Jewish wife. Despite this, shortly after the end of the war, the couple had been 'repatriated' – that is, forcibly transported to a Württemberg village where they were total strangers. I was taken as far as Stuttgart by some wartime RAF friends. The bus from Stuttgart was full of people in white woollen knee-length socks, at the sight of whom I couldn't help wondering if this well-meant visit was more than I could cope with; but then I was also curious to know how Hanne N. – who had no time for folklore in any guise – would be reacting to the Aryan rustics who now surrounded her. (These racial labels will doubtless arouse the disapproval of some of my readers, but I am afraid they belong to my theme. These people called themselves Aryan and hence they *were* Aryans; they called Hanne Jewish and hence she was just that, even if all she understood by this name was that it made her an outlaw. I shall come back to this later.)

It was a sad reunion. Oskar N. had died shortly after their arrival. Hanne had no relatives left, and few friends – I was the first visitor to remind her of her native city. On a walk through the village that was now her home, she talked about her homesickness for beautiful Prague, about these 'impossible Germans' among whom she felt such a stranger, whereas the Czechs . . . – I interrupted her. I was rather surprised that she seemed to miss the Czechs; and I asked why, as a native of Prague, she had never taken the trouble to learn their language. At a pinch she had been able to discuss a few things with the charlady; she could sing the Czech national anthem, 'Kde domov můj?'; she wasn't quite so sure of the Slovak national anthem, which she preferred to hum; and that was about as far as it went.

'Don't you really understand why I miss Prague so much?' she said. 'I'm not talking about the war years, when the Germans were there, and you just didn't dare set foot in the street. You couldn't talk to *them* in any case. But all those wonderful years *before* the war! When you went out of the house there was always a risk you'd meet someone who'd turn a bit nasty on you for speaking German. He'd say "Zatracená Němka!" ["damned German woman"].'

'And you *miss* that?' I asked.

'Oh yes, that's just the way things were. Don't you understand? The bit of excitement – that was what being at home meant.'

It was a long time before I understood her. By her interest in things alien, Hanne N. was really making an issue of what Coleridge calls 'alterity' – a concept about which a fair amount of fuss is being made in present-day literary theory. Most Prague German writers would scarcely have known any more Czech than Hanne did; many of them had a similar ambivalent feeling for Bohemia, their homeland, and, like her, derived excitement and stimulation from their precarious national status. For all of them, the alien world began outside their front door; it was mainly hostile, often interesting, at once dangerous and enticing. Nearly everyone who expatiates on Kafka's or Rilke's biography stresses the writer's national, social and racial isolation, and speaks of a threefold ghetto (though in Rilke's case the racial issue has presented certain interpretative difficulties, as when the Austrian Germanist Josef Nadler, pupil of the Bohemian Germanist August Sauer, lauded the mysteries of Rilke's Jewishness in one edition of his literary history and Aryanized him in the next). What is mentioned less often is that this very milieu, in its partial foreignness, was at once oppressive *and* stimulating, debilitating *and* inspiring – in short, rich in thematic material.

Even more than that of Czech-speaking Prague, the culture of the Prague Germans in the first four decades of this century was a literary culture. Neither money nor noble birth nor politics, but literature – 'my writing' as Kafka repeatedly calls it – secured acceptance in this society. Of the 500,000 inhabitants that Prague counted at the turn of the century, 30,000 named German as their mother tongue, and, of these, two-thirds were of Jewish descent. Jürgen Serke's book, with its striking but inaccurate title *Böhmische Dörfer* (*Bohemian Villages* – inaccurate because he is chiefly concerned with the literature of Prague), contains roughly fifty literary biographies of writers who can be classed as Prague Germans; this thoroughly middle-class society was permeated with literature through and through. One of its chroniclers has compiled the portrait of an archetypal Prague German writer, who never put pen to paper again from the moment he left Prague and its coffee-houses.

This society lasted for scarcely four decades, and when it came to an end in the years 1939–46 the community of Czechs and Germans – the Bohemian symbiosis, which went back nearly 1,000 years – ended with it. A feature of the history of Bohemia, ever since the time of the Luxemburg king Charles IV (reigned 1342–78), was that all political, social and religious conflicts inside the 'Bohemian citadel' were accompanied by bitter conflicts between the two nationalities and national languages – the linguistic quarrel not merely articulating the political strife, but also nurturing it. Both sides – Czechs and Germans – repudiated each other's language as alien. Language became a weapon in the arsenal of power politics; literature was viewed as an expression of cultural politics, even though this politicizing was by no means always intended – and often, indeed, was hardly understood as such – by the writers themselves. But to all this it must be added that the relationship between the two languages and literatures was thoroughly lop-sided.

'Feindschaft / ist uns das Nächste' – 'Enmity / Is what is closest to us' – says Rilke in the Fourth Duino Elegy. In the current debate about the concept of 'alterity', a point usually overlooked is how easily the interest in the foreign can be seen – and repudiated – as a betrayal of one's own kind, and how such an interest usually only exists where the foreign is neither feared as a threat to the familiar nor despised as inferior to it. In Bohemia both these obstacles were present. Thus, the Czechs, on their side, especially after 1848, were ever more averse and resistant to the foreignness all around them, thinking of their immediate neighbours (in their public utterances at least) as hostile – their obvious targets being the German language, the influence of Vienna, and the Jewish element which they associated with the German. Where Czech artists and their public did take a creative interest in things foreign, it was directed towards distant countries – France and the West on the one hand, and on the other the mythologized Slav fraternity (which included Russia but not the neighbouring Poles). In the prolific work of the greatest Czech literary critic, František Xaver Šalda, there is one solitary mention of Franz Kafka – namely, as a virtually unknown Prague German, 'with whom the French are very much preoccupied at present [1934]'. On the German side too, at least until the turn of the century, the literary interest in the other nation was slight; the reason in this case being not fear of the foreign influence but disdain, and its concomitant, sentimentality. True, Rilke's early volume of poetry *Larenopfer* (1896) mentions the names of a few contemporary Czech poets, yet 'the lay of the Bohemian folk' – which the young poet, apparently unafraid of bathos, finds 'touching' – records sentiments proper to the era of the *Vormärz*. Even the generation of Franz Werfel (who was born in 1890) and his friend Johannes Urzidil had a somewhat condescending affection for the old-world Romantic folk ethos of the Czechs – at a time when the Czechs possessed their Realists (Neruda, Hálek, Čapek-Chod), their Parnassians (Vrchlický, Sládek) and their Symbolists (Březina, Sova). As, over the period from 1848 to the turn of the century, tolerance in political life in Bohemia and Moravia steadily declined, the literary contact between the Czech and German languages became correspondingly more tenuous. It was only after 1900 that the German side began to show a certain interest in Czech literature, which was made available through a series of excellent translations with critical introductions, almost entirely the work of German-Jewish authors.

The history of the Bohemian and Moravian Jews, from their expulsion by Maria Theresa in 1744–5 up to the execution of the Czechoslovak Communist Party Secretary-General Rudolf Slánský in 1952, has recently been set out, comprehensively and vividly, in Wilma Iggers' splendid collection of documents. Here I shall do no more than briefly comment on the very short yet astonishing history of their literary activity.

Again we return to the beginning of the nineteenth century (1809), when Pater Bernard Bolzano condemned anti-Semitism 'not only among the Christian rabble, but also among educated and distinguished people in our Bohemia' (by which he meant both nationalities), and blamed the Christians for the illiteracy of the rural Jewish population. What Bolzano did not foresee was the extraordinary development among the Bohemian and Moravian Jews in the second half of the century. What had happened in the eighty years that saw the rise of the Jews? The path taken by the Jewish population in these decades led them out of the ghetto and the small village congregation, out of the relative security of the orthodox way of life, and into the risk-laden world of commerce, into agriculture, entrepreneurial cosmopolitanism and the learned professions. Among the descendants of those Jewish families whose 'appalling lack of education' Bolzano deplored, we find, scarcely half a century later, men such as Fritz Mauthner, Edmund Husserl, Sigmund Freud, Gustav Mahler and Karl Kraus.

2

The rank people occupy in modern society, Talcott Parsons writes, is determined in two ways. On the one hand, they possess the status ascribed to them by friends and enemies; on the other, they stand on what they have achieved or acquired by their own merits. When a social group loses out in the competition for acquired status, it compensates for this by the good name which it carries – which has been ascribed to it – and by the bad name it ascribes to others. The distinguishing feature of radical nationalism in all its forms, and of 'racial' theories, is that, on the basis of ascribed characteristics, entire human groups are excluded from the political struggle, from economic activity, from the very life of the nation, from life itself.

The Jews we are speaking of hardly held the political or socio-economic power to determine their own status – their worldly well-being – let alone that of their Aryan neighbours, by ascription. What they were, they were by their own efforts, that is, the status they had they had achieved or acquired by their own merits. And as their relation to the synagogue and the religious community grew progressively weaker, eventually they were Jews only in name. But what does 'only in name' mean? Names are not 'natural', they are bestowed, ascribed. The choice of ascribed names may be arbitrary, it may stem from power-political or social interests, or it may result from the exercise of the literary imagination. In cultures as deeply involved in language consciousness as were those of the Dual Monarchy, the bestowing of names – denoting and assessing what a person is – was of existential importance. Naming – language – was indeed a form of life.

Inasmuch as others treated them as Jews – in 1920 Kafka heard (and never forgot) the phrase 'prašivé plemeno' ('mangy race') in the streets of Prague – they had in important respects to view themselves as Jews, whether they liked it or not. They would have liked to be Jewish Bohemians, but to those around them they were Bohemian Jews. Only in imagination, for example in literature, did they have the freedom to create a world that was not determined by the ascriptions of others.

What Talcott Parsons doesn't say is that ascription is not identical with the giving of power, that it is nothing – mere empty words – without the possession of power; mere empty words, or literature. Of course, literature didn't give them the power they lacked in the social and political world. What it gave them were images of that power, which misled them into thinking that power itself might not, after all, be worth having, that being the makers of images would make them acceptable. In all this they weren't necessarily different from their Aryan fellow writers – as long as things went reasonably well. It was when the institutions which kept the peace began to founder that, having nothing else but literature to appeal to, they discovered that they were different.

Did they really have nothing else to appeal to? Surely being German writers was enough. German was the language that had led these generations out of the ghetto, it was the language of their economic and social rise; for the intellectuals and writers of the last Habsburg years, the German language was the bearer of a culture from which they expected paradise on earth. Poetry was the coinage in which they paid their tribute: it seems as if the power released by the celebration of the German language carried the poems they wrote beyond their sad and often tragic themes to unexpected affirmations – affirmations which the 'real' Germans regarded as importunate.

The more problematic their allegiance to their ancient religious institutions, the more they succumbed to the anachronistic delusion of viewing the Germans as the nation of Herder, Schiller and Goethe, of Kant, Schopenhauer and Nietzsche – the delusion of seeing in the Germans what they themselves had once been, the nation of the written word, of books and of learning. They were loyal to the Monarchy, regarded themselves as good Austrians, and as such were a thorn in the side of the Czechs. For, while the most active and talented of Czech intellectuals took less and less interest in the Austrian (later Austro-Hungarian) state, and felt it more and more to be the oppressor of their national aspirations, this very state was venerated by its Jewish citizens as the guarantor of their rights, as their protector.

There is no need to stress the irony of this identification between Jewish and German. The Bohemian Germans – who only much later called them-

selves 'Sudeten Germans' – considered that they alone were the true bearers
of German culture in Bohemia and Moravia; they despised and resisted the
Jews as parasitical assimilators of a literature and learning to which they (the
Jews) had no right. Hence the unenviable situation in which the literary,
intellectual elite of the Bohemian Jews found themselves: the Czechs resisted
them as Germanizing enemies, the Germans disowned them as embarrassing
aliens and upstarts. Their Germanness found little recognition, their identification with *deutscher Geist* was spurned as infamous and ludicrous.

Many years later the poet and novelist Johannes Urzidil (himself neither a
Jew nor a Sudeten German but 'ein Deutschböhme', a Bohemian German,
the son of an anti-Czech and anti-Semitic father married first to a Czech and
then to a Jewish lady) looked back on their situation from his exile in New
York. 'The Prague Germans and the Prague Jews were the trustees and
guardians of what we must call the classic German language', Urzidil wrote,
and, singling out the 'tenor' (*Sprachakzent*) of this language, praised it for
being enriched by 'the magnetic field of Czech' and by 'the force emanating
from Hebraic sources'. I doubt whether many Prague authors saw their
medium in that way, but I am certain that what Urzidil is talking about is a
chimera. The German Jewish authors of Prague were ridiculed precisely
because a few of them took on themselves the role of trustees and guardians
– a somewhat unrealistic role in any context, which implied a linguistic
conservatism, a retreat to the language of Weimar classicism, such as Karl
Kraus preached (but didn't practise), and which in turn led to a kind of
linguistic petrifaction or misapplied formality – a prose of awkward, angular
turns, such as characterizes the English ideolect of post-Imperial India. And
as for the Czech and Hebraic influences Urzidil mentions, they, far from
being felt as an enhancement, were the subject of countless hostile jokes.
Unlike English, German is a homogeneous language, derived from a single
group of tribal dialects – so much so that one of its features is an inbuilt
structural intolerance of foreign linguistic influences, born of the fear that
they will affect Germanic syntax, vocabulary and idiom. At the same time,
resistance to foreign influences is also determined by the given contemporary
political constellation. (Incidentally, Czech is in much the same position,
especially in its rejection of 'Germanisms'.) Thus, when Urzidil speaks of 'the
magnetic field of Czech' and of 'the force emanating from Hebraic sources',
and does so in an era of radical nationalism, what he is describing and
commending is precisely the sort of language that most Prague writers, including Rilke and Kafka, the greatest of them, were anxiously trying to leave
behind, restricting its literary uses to satire. Unlike Urzidil, his friend Franz
Kafka trusts an image to tell the truth as he sees it. In a letter to Max Brod
of June 1921 he writes: 'Most of those who began writing in German wanted
to be rid of their Jewishness – that's what they wanted, but with their little
hind legs they were stuck in the Jewishness of their fathers, and their front
legs could find nothing to hold on to [*keinen freien Boden*].' (The phrase 'keinen
freien Boden', literally, 'no free ground', is idiomatic German and, *pace* Zionist

interpreters, has nothing to do with Palestine.) As so often with Kafka, the image has a force that takes it beyond the sphere of autobiography: ceasing to be a mere personal complaint, it becomes a piece of literature, to be used again in the last chapter of *The Trial*: '"I won't need much more strength, I shall use all I have"', Josef K. thinks as he is being taken to his execution; and: 'He thought of the flies trying with their broken little legs to get away from the lime twig.' Kafka is not Josef K., but Josef K.'s creator. It is his creativity that takes him from the lime twig to the free ground of literature.

3

Aliens and upstarts: at the turn of the century, that was no longer how the Jews of Bohemia and Moravia experienced everyday life, and yet it is how their existence was transfixed in the daily press and in literature. For instance in one of the scenes of a three-part essay by Šalda – and again one has to say that the scene is more typical of the public voice of its time of writing (1904) than it is of its author. The first sketch in this triptych depicts a poor Moravian Slovak peasant girl on a pilgrimage. As a study in naïve piety, it carries about as much conviction as Franz Werfel's portrait of Bernadette Soubirous, the difference being that Šalda's essay did not become a best-seller. The third sketch is about an unemployed proletarian with tuberculosis. In the middle sketch a house with bare, unadorned walls and small barred windows in an unnamed provincial town is described, recalling the fortified house of the Jew Abdias in Adalbert Stifter's story of that name. Everything about this house is turned inwards – outside is the enemy. Next to the narrow ground-floor entrance there is a little sign with the announcement, in Czech, 'Brandy and other spirits served here.' But coming from the first floor voices are heard singing excerpts from *Tristan* and *Die Meistersinger*; here (we are told) the lyrical poems of Gerhart Hauptmann and Hugo von Hofmannsthal are recited; the weak, derivative verses composed here will be printed in expensive private editions in Dresden and Leipzig; tomorrow the members of the younger generation in the house will be moving to Vienna . . . To be sure, this is something of a caricature: not all the Jews were sellers of brandy; my own grandfathers were both farmers – in 1921, 44 per cent of all Bohemian and Moravian tenant farmers were of Jewish descent. Yet Šalda's sketch does contain a partial truth.

The historical explanation with which Šalda underpins his genre picture is simple enough. Everything – the piety of the peasant girl, the exploitative morals of the Jewish innkeeper with his debtors' slate, the wise, bitter resignation of the unemployed workman – all these clichés are explained as the effect of fate and its anonymous forces. The girl and the workman, who will never emerge from their poverty and servitude, are victims of these anonymous demonic forces, as is the Jew, who will go on prospering in a milieu that can never be his own. But then (as Šalda does not say), it is only those who are or feel powerless who invoke the workings of anonymous powers.

And this brings me to my central theme. What I take to be crucial in Šalda's scene is not its anti-Semitic component, but the example it provides of the literary practice of spiritualizing or demonizing the foreign. Foreignness – whether German, Jewish or Czech – is made available to literature through the medium of the demonic. By demonization I mean the problematic attempt to go beyond the pragmatic and hence partial motivation of actions and explanation of events – the attempt to transfigure actions and events by invoking 'total' or absolute metaphysical values or powers. Many writers in many countries feel this urge; few are able to turn it into convincing fiction. More than any other factor (it seems to me), this process of demonization determines Prague German literature. Of course, modern German literature as a whole abounds in scenes which shift from a realistic plane to a metaphysical intensification or heightening of 'reality' – from the Schopenhauer chapter in Thomas Mann's *Buddenbrooks*, through Kafka, to Hermann Hesse's *Glass-Bead Game* and Mann's *Doctor Faustus*, and, in poetry, from the early Stefan George, through Georg Trakl and Rilke, to Gottfried Benn. Yet Prague German literature performs this metaphysical heightening in its own way – with a penchant for the demonic which at times (more often than elsewhere in modern German writing) degenerates into a sort of tragic kitsch, mostly in the shape of the Gothic novel.

This leaning towards the demonic is characteristic of a literature which on the one hand lacked the social *données* of European Realism (those which form the basis of, for instance, Theodor Fontane's narrative art), but on the other hand was unable to draw upon the mythology of a national awakening, such as inspired the Czechs with its watchwords of the 'young nation' and the 'Slavonic dove' – on the contrary, it degenerated into such clichés as the Wandering Jew or the immortal desert people, the wanderers in the wilderness. The literary sources of the demonic are all too readily found in E. T. A. Hoffmann and Mrs Radcliffe, in the mephistophelean element in Balzac, in Villiers de l'Isle-Adam and Eugène Sue and above all in Edgar Allan Poe. On the indebtedness of Kafka's work to this tradition, too much rather than too little has been said. His stories are unimaginable without their Prague origins; yet they owe their significance and greatness to the bridling of the demonic and diminution of the sensational. This is not a case of the much-discussed 'anxiety of influence'; it is the creation of original contexts, the *avoidance* of influence, that testifies to his genius. 'Mother Prague [*matička Praha*] has claws', he writes, and he struggles against them – if not always successfully.

As examples of this demonization, I shall confine myself to two well-known legendary subjects taken from a single historical context. The first, which links the sixteenth century to the technological dreams and dystopia of the twentieth, is the Golem legend in its numerous versions. The best known of them is by

Gustav Meyrink, who was not a Jew and, though he lived in Prague, was not a native of the city either. Meyrink's 'fantastic novel' *Der Golem* (more fantasy than novel), which appeared in 1915, takes from the cabbala the story of the robot-like servant that Rabbi Löw has created for himself ('and yet it never turned into a real human being,' we are told, 'and Golem only breathed a torpid, half-conscious vegetable life'), and combines it with Buddhist and ancient Egyptian elements and elements of the psychology of dreams. In the novel's extravagant mode of narration, it is the sexual component of demonization that is stressed above all – as is shown by the titles of the loose succession of chapters ('Ghosts', 'Light', 'Distress', 'Fear', 'Desire', 'Woman', 'Ruse', 'Anguish'). Golem appears, 'strains to take shape', out of a tarot card. For a whole night he 'crouched in the corner and stared across at me with my own face'. Eventually, he 'grew smaller and smaller, and at dawn he crept back into his tarot card; then I stood up, went across to him and put him in my pocket'. In this motif of the double, Meyrink's Manichaean narrative finds its climax. All this takes place in an atmosphere of decay, of moral and material corruption, which seems contrived, too heavily laid on: gloomy courtyards, barred dungeons and secret underground passages, 'vaults . . . hung with old iron clutter, broken tools, rusty stirrups and skates and all sorts of decrepit objects'. But in this part of the world, it seems, nothing is too heavily laid on, as by another sleight-of-hand the divisions of time and space are blurred, and we are among the nightmare paraphernalia of the old-iron market of the German concentration camp of Łódź, where a bunch of rusty keys is offered for sale though they no longer fit any conceivable locks.

Alfred Kubin too takes the stereotyped demonic Prague as the scene of action for his dystopia *Die andere Seite* (*The Other Side*), and names his magical, mysterious hero Patera after a head waiter who was known throughout the city. Kubin is mainly known as an important graphic artist and lithographer; he wrote this novel, his sole literary work, probably six years before *Der Golem*, but it was conceived in close contact with Meyrink. Like Meyrink's novel, Kubin's fantastic juxtaposition of two worlds (one old and corrupt, the other a Brave New World) is distinctly (and unintentionally) loose in form. The weak thread of the plot, and arbitrariness in the characterization, detract from the unity of the story; its ending is anticipated by importing into the fiction the visit to Prague of Thomas Alva Edison, of which Kafka also wrote. Kafka's early sketch of the city's coat of arms contains in its last paragraph a vignette of the catastrophe with which Kubin's story ends: 'Everything that this city has produced in the way of legends and songs is filled with the yearning for a day which is prophesied, when the city will be crushed by a giant fist with five blows in quick succession. That is why the city has the fist in its coat of arms.'

What of the Czechs? All these evocations of the city's ancient demons (including the prophecy of Libussa, the city's foundress, to which Kafka seems to be alluding) were, of course, familiar to them, but they reminded them of their dark past at a time when they looked forward to a bright new national future. They too, like the Germans, are a nation that has changed its historical identity more than once this century.

In Rudolf II of Habsburg, the 'emperor with a mystagogue's beard and bags under his eyes' as Egon Erwin Kisch (a German Jewish Communist journalist and joker) calls him, the city possesses another figure from old Prague whose legendary stature has retained its literary interest down to our own century. Perhaps many German and Jewish authors saw a reflection of themselves in the figure of this emperor (reigned 1577–1611) – imposing, picturesque, morbidly sensitive and spurning all politics in his state of powerlessness. Everything about him is of interest to literature, furnishes literary themes: his scientific investigations, mixing astronomy with astrology, chemistry with alchemy, his mixture of religion and superstition; his love of art and capricious patronage of it (the Milanese painter Arcimboldo was his guest for years); and, not least, his special interest in the Jews, who advanced him money for his costly collections of art treasures and tasteless curiosities – all this is combined with Rudolf's great service to Prague, which he made the site of his residence and the seat of imperial government.

What I have listed as the personal attributes of the phlegmatic emperor can virtually serve as a synopsis of one of the many collections of stories about Rudolf's era – Leo Perutz's *Nachts unter der steinernen Brücke* (*Under the Stone Bridge at Night* – that is, Charles Bridge). This book too calls itself 'a novel of old Prague', although it consists of eleven novellas and an epilogue, with the action taking place in the three decades between 1589 and 1621 (the year of the execution of the rebellious Bohemian nobility). These stories have a unified setting in the ambience of Prague Castle, of the Kleinseite (the 'Little Quarter') and of the Josefstadt ghetto. The Emperor's love for the young wife of the old and rich Mordechai Meisl, Esther, 'whose beauty passed all bounds' – a love that hovers between dream and reality – forms a leitmotiv which recurs three times and is not helped by its recalling Hofmannsthal's *Das Erlebnis des Marschalls von Bassompierre*. When Rabbi Löw refuses to assist the Emperor in his sinful courtship, the Emperor threatens to expel all Jews from his kingdom:

Then the Chief Rabbi went and planted a rose-bush and rosemary on the bank of the Moldau under the stone bridge, hidden from the eyes of men. And he spoke the magic words over both. Then a red rose blossomed on the rose-bush, and the rosemary flowers reached out towards it and nestled against it. And each night the Emperor's soul flew into the rose, and the soul of the Jewess flew into the rosemary. And night after night, the Emperor dreamt that he was holding his beloved, the beautiful Jewess, in his embrace; and night after night, Esther the wife of Mordechai Meisl dreamt that she lay in the Emperor's arms.

Eros 'breaks the barbs' of foreignness in the Emperor's love for the beautiful Jewess; Eros disarms the angry Christian overlord who, as it happens, is up to his ears in debt to the rich Meisl. It is hard to say which part of this wishful dream – the erotic or the financial – is more embarrassing. However, the individual anecdotes expanded into novellas, reminiscent of Dutch genre paintings, often display wit and nearly always avoid that aura of the demonic which attaches to the emperor figure. Although the book appeared only in 1953, it was probably begun in the 1920s. A noticeable feature of it (common to most of these authors and also, incidentally, to Robert Musil) is that all of the lower class and comic characters have Czech names and nearly all of the Czech names denote lower-class characters (many of whom resemble the good soldier Švejk).

4

'I'll tell you what, Max, burn your own stuff instead!' Thus Morris Rosenfeld (scarcely a legendary figure himself) admonished his friend Max Brod during an encounter, of a somewhat apocryphal nature, in the Prague Zeltnergasse, after Kafka's death and in allusion to Kafka's testamentary request. The suggestion, which does seem a little hyper-critical, surely doesn't apply to Brod's novel *Tycho Brahes Weg zu Gott* (*Tycho Brahe's Way to God*, 1916). As far as I can see, this is the only work of Prague German literature which Šalda considers worthy of a critical examination. Šalda's essay (written in 1919?) begins with much the same aggressively nationalistic argument which was to be formulated a decade later, from the German viewpoint, by Josef Nadler:

> In Prague there is no German literature even though there are some German literati, just as there are in Budapest – or were until recently – with the same right and by the same accident. For literature is something different from, and more than, a group of writers, however numerous; it is a higher entity which in the law that governs its life corresponds to the national whole, much as blossom is formed by the tree that bears it. For the Germans in Prague there can be no such correspondence; it is not here that their tree grows with its roots reaching back into the dark depth of the centuries, into the forgotten soil of the deeds of State and Nation – these Germans are not the nation bound uniquely and by destiny to this land. Yet precisely because they constitute an exotic element here, many German writers succeed in capturing the particular external character of Prague – the personality of Prague as a European city, viewed from the standpoint of a cultured tourist and pleasure-seeker.

However, Max Brod's Tycho Brahe novel (this is the crux of Šalda's review) constitutes an exception: it is 'the novel of a soul – a Jewish soul – in exile'.

At first sight this description seems surprising. The famous Rabbi Löw (here, incidentally, called 'Löwe') appears in a secondary role, as one of the Emperor's advisers. The two main characters of the novel are the exiled Danish aristocrat Tycho Brahe and his pupil Johannes Kepler, a worthy Styrian with wife and children and the placid conscience of a positivist. But the reader soon notices that the roles of the two astronomers are conceived according to the polarity of Jewish and Christian character types, as shaped by the clichés of the last 2,000 years. Tycho is the brooding Faust-Ahasuerus type with obscurely mystical aspirations, at once sceptical and superstitious, in search of God, despairing of ever finding him, yet convinced that this very despair marks him as one of the elect. Kepler by contrast is the cool, self-assured, well-balanced scientist, who knows how to separate astronomy from astrology, religion from superstition, who cares neither for the philosophers' stone nor for the metaphysical mystery of the world, who is concerned with nothing more and nothing less than the exact understanding of what is, the cognition of the real world, objectivity. Tycho is the eternal stranger and outcast who, in his West Bohemian castle and then at the Prague court, must needs surround himself with books, instruments and riches in order to feel at home in the alien world of exile; whereas Kepler (though he too is in a foreign land) travels light, is not tormented by suspicions, and soon feels at home everywhere. The air is thick with philo-Semitic and anti-Semitic clichés, without the term 'Jewish' being mentioned. Of course, what takes place here is mainly the decking-out in period costume of an interesting theme from the history of ideas: myth versus science, the Middle Ages versus the modern age. Yet what this opposition of 'two intellectualities, radically different in kind', brings to mind is nothing so much as the sorry state of the German historical novel in the twentieth century, with its mixing of ideology and histrionics *à la* Döblin or Kolbenheyer. The characters don't actually swear by the Mass and by God's Body, and so forth, but there is no lack of *walterscottisant* jesters in the shape of dwarf hybrids ('half dog, half man'), and sentences like, 'Nonplussed, the squire stopped in his tracks, but in a trice he had unsheathed his naked sword!'

Šalda shows more sympathy for Max Brod's intended meaning. He sees *Tycho Brahe's Way to God*, 'thanks to its symbolic, fateful power, as a Jewish novel . . . whose essence is a tormenting and tormented yearning for redemption. And this archetypal Jewish quality', he concludes, 'constitutes the beauty of Max Brod's novel and is, ultimately, very close and very understandable to the true Czech mind.' It may not be out of place to reflect that half a century later, in the Protectorate of Bohemia and Moravia, little of this understanding closeness could be detected.

5

The Czech historical novel, since Alois Jirásek at the end of the nineteenth century, constantly returns to the tragic central themes of the nation's history

– to the Thirty Years' War, the defeat at the White Mountain and the conflict between Bohemian Protestantism and the Counter-Reformation (presented most tellingly in Jaroslav Durych's Wallenstein trilogy *Bloudění* (*Wanderings*) of 1928). The Prague German writers on the other hand, especially the Jews among them, adhered loyally to Austrian themes and the Habsburg past. This is the historical context of an ambitious, and politically and psychologically revealing, *biographie romancée* (whose subject is the Archduke Franz Ferdinand) which appeared at the end of the First Czechoslovak Republic: *Der Thronfolger* (*Heir to the Throne*) by Ludwig Winder. Here again we find passages revelling in emotional excess and occasionally foundering in false pathos. But Winder knows how to solve the central stylistic problem of a historical novel with ideological overtones. The appeal to demonic powers carries conviction as long as it is conveyed to the reader not on the author's own authority but through the consciousness of the hero – that is, in *style indirect libre*. Take Franz Ferdinand's invocation of the mythical-poetic figure Rudolf II:

> He [Franz Ferdinand] wanted to create order, he wanted to be the man of order. But impatient and unrestrained as he was, he dimly felt that his own heart and brain and thinking were out of joint. Within him was the chaos which had lured his ancestor, the fantastic Emperor Rudolf II, into dangerous experiments with alchemy. The world was dark and dangerous, filled with poisonous substances, pregnant with hatred and enmity.

(Jaroslav Hašek saw the heir-apparent somewhat differently: he is mentioned as one of the three Ferdinands on whom the good soldier Švejk meditates at the start of his adventurous journey through the Great War – namely, the fat one, 'what used to chase those old bags in his summer residence'.)

If historical reconstruction is saved from false pathos by *style indirect libre*, the psychological and ideological congruence of author and hero is the point at which the most significant modern German historical novel – *Die vierzig Tage des Musa Dagh* (*The Forty Days of Musa Dagh*), by Franz Werfel, a former inhabitant of Prague – becomes deeply problematic. This is the famous heroic saga, celebrated in many countries (and becoming a best-seller on the American market), of the Armenian resistance against the Young Turks in the Antioch foothills in 1915. It may be less well known that the events of the early 1930s in Germany caused Werfel deliberately to transform this resistance in its final phase into a model for European Jewry. The remarkable thing about the last chapters, in which Werfel realizes this aim, is not so much the fate of the hero, Gabriel Bagradian, as the blood-and-soil rhetoric in which these chapters are couched, and the hero's readiness for the sacrifice – senseless and pointless in spite of the biblical accoutrements – to which he believes himself summoned. For what this scenario amounts to is the author's apparently unwitting identification with the rhetoric and ideology which came to power in 1933 and which it was his intention to challenge in these very chapters.

6

Prague German writers, Aryan and Jewish, travelled the same route from the 'alterity' of the foreign to its demonization; but then, almost overnight, their paths divided. It turned out that the Aryan Germans didn't (as Kafka said of himself) 'consist of literature and nothing else', for theirs was the power: the power to convert disdain and dislike into political anti-Semitism, and hence into decisions of life and death. What was there left to say, once the politics of raving nationalism had caught up with the horror stories of the past and made many of them look like scenes from penny-dreadfuls?

One of the last products of this literature, written when all was over bar the mourning, is Hans-Günter Adler's story *Eine Reise* (*A Journey*, 1962). This journey takes the small Jewish family of old Dr Leopold Lustig from their home town to a concentration camp, which is barely described – we may identify the fictitious place-names in the novel as standing for Prague, Theresienstadt and Aussig on the Elbe (or, of course, Praha, Terezín and Ústí nad Labem). 'Those that had once been human beings were made of wax, yet they were still alive', we read; 'they live even though it is prohibited.' They, these people, live off refuse, are refuse, become refuse. (Incidentally 'refuse culture' – 'odpadková kultura' – is the term by which Šalda at the turn of the century had described the culture of the Jews in rural Bohemia.) The alien force which kills human beings in Adler's story is too much part of the daily routine of this place of death to be demonized: at the end point of this literature which neither Germans nor Czechs would acknowledge, demonization gives way to the creation of a strange, inhuman silence. For the narrator or author to identify himself with any recognizable ideology (as Werfel did) would be unthinkable. Where these skeletons live, there are neither politics nor social structures – only houses crammed with dying human beings. Here neither reasons nor causes are given; no explanations of any kind. And yet – something like a story, a narrative, is constructed from the semblance of continuity, a work of art which yet recalls a child's way of story-telling. I can think of no more succinct way of showing this wholly original narrative approach than by quoting an anecdote from the diary of an author on the opposite side, noted at the very time of the events recorded by Adler in his story. In his *Strahlungen* (*Radiations*), Ernst Jünger writes:

> Kirchhorst, 26 November 1943. Perpetua visited little Grethe, who has been attacked and nearly killed by a ram. The boy was playing with his brother near where it was grazing, and was knocked down by the animal, probably because he was wearing a red jacket. Every time he tried to get up again the ram grew more furious, smashed both his collar-bones

and battered his head, which swelled up so as to be unrecognizable. His brother ran into the village and fetched help. He could hear how the boy kept on trying to pacify his horned opponent by saying 'Ram, I'm a good boy' whenever he raised himself up.

(Here only the word 'Gegner' – 'opponent' – strikes a false note, though a characteristic one.)

A somewhat different kind of narrative is used by Adler in *A Journey* to present all those human beings who aren't qualified as 'former', who crop up on the periphery of the story and disappear again, make plans, pursue ambitions, have tables and chairs and more or less permanent domiciles, hush up their past and look forward to a future. One member of Dr Lustig's family survives. Yet he is no more able to relate to that periphery than are the countless dead: all that can be told is wrested from the silence at the story's centre.

7

And then it was all over. Most retrospective fiction written in the Federal Republic about the war and the Protectorate of Bohemia and Moravia is irenic, conciliatory and occasionally full of contrition, but not all of it: among the German survivors of the First Czechoslovak Republic who finished up in the West, the *et tu quoque* note – 'The Czechs did this because the Germans did that because the Czechs had done the other' – is common enough.

Josef Mühlberger (1903–85), the most prolific of his generation of Sudeten German authors, was the co-editor of the periodical *Witiko* (1928–31), in which stories by Kafka and Werfel were published, author of several studies of Czech and German literary history, and translator from the Czech. In 1937 Mühlberger was banned in Hitler's Germany for his pains; early in the war he joined the German Army; and in 1946 he was expelled from Bohemia. In the 1930s he had been one of the few Prague German writers who had tried to bridge the gulf between the conflicting nationalisms. Yet in the best-known of his many postwar books of fiction, *Der Galgen im Weinberg* (*The Gallows in the Vineyard*, 1960), a collection of stories based on episodes from his wartime experience, the conciliatory intention recedes behind the sophisticated fatalism of the age – the demonology which generalizes evil-doing and guilt as the inevitable predicament of mankind: 'It was neither the Germans nor the Czechs who turned our world into a plague-pit, but human beings in whom something has devoured humanity.' What this 'something' is, we aren't told. Instead, the story of Cain and Abel is dragged in, to provide the narrator with the only explanation of evil we are given; the reports on the expulsions of the Sudeten Germans between May 1945 and September 1946 are written from his point of view.

Set partly in Prague and partly in Theresienstadt (the concentration camp of Adler's story *A Journey*, which in 1945 was converted into a camp for Sudeten Germans awaiting expulsion), the main novella of Mühlberger's book takes us back to the beginning of this essay and throws a piercing light on my theme. For Hanna N., the language conflict was a stimulus and a living source of interest; in 'The Gallows in the Vineyard' the narrator's young son is murdered because the book that is discovered on him during a body-search has the word 'Prag' rather than 'Praha' in its title.

The little book which the boy had picked up while re-burying the corpses from a Jewish mass grave is Eduard Mörike's 'Mozart auf der Reise nach Prag' (1855), known to every German schoolchild. And Mörike's Swabian origins, Mozart's habits of composition, his irreverence and genius – all these are cultural landmarks familiar to every German-speaking reader of Mühlberger's story. The contrast he builds up, between Mörike's rococo Bohemia and the Bohemia which in May 1945 emerged from the most demoralizing years in its history, could hardly be greater or more obvious. Every detail of the final scene, in what was once Maria Theresa's fortress, contributes to the novella's affective power: the father's characterization of the boy as 'tall, blond, a magnificent human being'; evocations of the dead Jewish prisoner's love of German literature, of this quintessentially German story; the narrator's religiose celebration of Mozart's and Mörike's genius; the Czech guard's murderous boots, symbols and instruments of barbarous vengefulness; and, focusing all these narrative elements, the unfathomable absurdity of a contested syllable, which, like many of the things significant in the region's language consciousness, stands as a deadly symbol of conflicting forms of life. Yet in the end the reader is bound to ask: is all this literature or nationalist propaganda?

The story is unlikely to be literally true, yet I have no doubt that what it fictionalizes – throws into relief – are events similar to those that actually happened. To be sure, the story's sententious appeals to 'fate', the self-exculpation these appeals imply and its nationalist tenor are hard to take; they seem incompatible with one's literary expectations. And who knows in what circumstances – as victim or literary avenger? – the author may have acquired the detailed, 'authentic' knowledge of the atrocities here recorded? Who knows how he came to be acquainted with those who suffered and those who inflicted the suffering? Hard to fend off, such questions undoubtedly make the author, his narrative as well as his intention, suspect. And yet: what these questions point to is a moral ambiguity that clings to some of the most revealing literature in our age, an ambiguity that we share with the author. For the truth is that our deepest knowledge of life and death under the sway of the ideologies comes from tainted sources.

The story of the German literature of Prague is now concluded. What it proves is that, in an age of radical, embattled nationalisms, the pen is not mightier than the sword. In such an age, 'alterity' – the status of 'the other', the stranger's form of life – ceases to be a positive theme and inspiration;

instead, it comes to oppress and impoverish the creative imagination, to narrow the range and impair the quality of the language available to it.

Now freedom and peace reign in the 'Bohemian citadel', though a patriot of the First Republic can only regret that the price which the citizens of that conflict-torn country have had to pay for this peace has turned out to be so very high. Three elements – a Czech, a German and a Jewish element – contributed, albeit in different degrees, to the country's culture. Will the one that has survived be able to make good the loss of the others?

1991

5

The Education of the Master Race

1

The junketings that accompanied the Robert Musil centenary in 1980 were celebrated in an ahistorical Never Never Land. With very few exceptions, critics have concentrated on the formal aspects of Musil's work, its use of irony, satire, indirection and *erlebte Rede*, 'psycho-narration' and the like; or again, they have prosed about such devices as aphorism, fragment, *Essayismus* and philosophical reflection in an œuvre whose status remains uncertain, without enquiring whether that uncertainty, and the use of those devices, might not be related to the historical circumstances in which Musil's books were written and to which they relate. And so it is hardly surprising that while the literary conventions employed or challenged in Musil's fictions have been assiduously scrutinized, the social and political conventions which constitute their historicity have been taken for granted and consequently ignored. Of course, criticism can't do everything, and all criticism is aspectival. But validity in criticism depends on the critic's choosing the right aspect of the work; which is as much as to say that the critic's choice must be dictated, not by fashion or preconceived method, but by the work itself. Aspects of a literary work of art are not scientific domains but fields of inquiry with blurred, sketchy margins. Yet even though, from these margins, other fields and other possibilities of interpretation are visible, the inquiry at the centre is distinct enough.

The historical aspect of Musil's *Young Törless* – by which I mean, not the biographical details relating to its composition, but those of its elements which raised particular social and political expectations in the minds of the public for which it was written – is manifestly present in the work: Musil chose as the location of his first novel the military academy at Mährisch-Weisskirchen (= Hranice, referred to in the novel as 'W'), where, at the turn of the century, the scions of the German-speaking aristocracy and the upper ranks of the civil service were educated. What is relevant from the historical point of view I propose to adopt is not that Musil was drawing on his own nightmare recollections of that institution, but that in making that choice he was invoking those social and political connotations of 'W' which were recognized and responded to by his 'implied readers'. To recover the novel's early meaning is to insist that here at all events a historical reading is more than a mere option; to ignore it is to distort the novel's overall meaning and in the process to ascribe to the novel certain values which a truer reading will not yield. Where the historicity of the object – the novel in question – forms a continuity with the historical consciousness of the subject – the critical interpreter – obvious risks of anachronism arise. The need to avoid them may add to the interest of the inquiry.

2

First published in 1906, this novel was the opening move in the battle with recalcitrant narrative form which Musil fought throughout his life. Törless, its hero, is a first portrayal of Ulrich, the 'Man Without Qualities' of Musil's *magnum opus*, which he began writing in 1905 and left unfinished at his death in exile and great poverty in Geneva in 1942.

The book is called *Die Verwirrungen des Zöglings Törless*. 'Zögling' is a slightly old-fashioned and rather formal word meaning 'scholar' or 'boarder' at an educational establishment; it has strong overtones of the Austrian military and civil service establishment; it is upper class and closely connected with Church and Court. 'Verwirrungen' are dark confusions, chaotic states of mind. The word has no immediate moral connotations. Since the novel is cast in the narrative imperfect of an episode that is finished and done with, 'Verwirrungen' suggests the possibility that what was confused has been superseded by a state of adult clarity. The word is used several times throughout the novel; and at the end, when Törless (we are not given his first name) looks back on the turmoil he has caused, the embarrassments and the mental conflicts he has undergone ('But what were these things?'), we read in the report of his stream of conscious and half-conscious thoughts that, 'He had no time to think about it now and brood over the events. All he felt was a passionate longing to escape from this confused, whirling state of things ... (p. 171).'

The historicity of Musil's first book (unlike the historicity of his later novel) has to be pieced together from a mere handful of indications. The location is given in the first sequence of the book: 'A small station on the railroad that leads to Russia', at the 'outer edge' of Central Europe; and the subsequent description is permeated by indications of remoteness, alienness, of an inhospitable and outlandish atmosphere. We are placed at the point where the outposts of Occidental (that is, German) culture meet the mysterious Slavonic East – this is the feeling that is to be communicated in the opening sections of the book. The events into which we are drawn are confined to a dominant German-speaking class, soon to call itself 'das deutsche Herrenvolk', and eventually to form the spearhead of the German/Austrian *Drang nach Osten* –

we are within 100 kilometres of Treblinka and Auschwitz. Living in a sea of
Slav (Moravian) labourers and peasants, the German elite group depends on
them materially and sexually, but through the sexual link insecurity is carried
into its ranks.

In the buildings of an ancient monastery, 'a famous boarding school' has
been established. The young gentlemen of the Academy carry the light swords
of future officers and civil servants; the rural Slav proletariat live in the stews
and are dirty, drunken, foul-mouthed and darkly threatening. Contact with
them is seen as a contamination, yet life inside the citadel of learning, too, is
heavy with sensuality, disaffection and vice. The school was put there (we are
told) 'doubtless in order to safeguard the young generation, in its years of
awakening, from the corrupting influence of the big cities' (p. 12). Thereupon
we are introduced to Törless, aged sixteen, and von Reiting, his senior by two
years. They are walking back from the railway station, where they have just
been seeing off their parents and receiving their blessings and pocket money.
Predictably, their first port of call on their way back to school is an inn which
also serves as a whore-house. Equally predictably, the peasant woman they
meet on their way and the prostitute into whose room we follow Törless and
his companion are coarse and licentious, and Slavonic. The visit is remembered
later on in the story but not followed up in any direct way – Božena, the
prostitute, is introduced partly as an object of Törless's awakening sexuality,
partly (her coarseness being contrasted with recollections of his refined mother)
in order to indicate the chaos and divisions in Törless's mind.

But are we justified in drawing those – latter-day – nationalist implications
from the novel? After all, the main explicit ethnic indications we are given are
the German names of the three main characters, the geographical setting (the
mention of Russia in the first sentence) and the names of Božena and (later)
Basini. To speak of a German elite and a Slav rural proletariat may therefore
seem like an historicizing indiscretion – the sort of gratuitous hindsight that
is typical of interpreters with a historical or political axe to grind. And so it
is – a hindsight occasioned by certain similarities of the novel with an outlook
whose most virulent manifestations did not occur until a decade later. But it
is not only hindsight. What confirms our reading is the contemporary topicality
of the novel, the fact that it is only one of a whole series of prose works
embodying, in a variety of fictional forms and disguises, the theme of German
superiority and the Slav–German conflict. Arthur Schnitzler, Rilke, Kafka and
Franz Werfel, as well as Joseph Roth, 'Roda-Roda' and Felix Salten, are
among those who explored this topos within the context of Austrian *fin-de-
siècle* literature and sub-literature. Paradoxically, the historicity of *Young Törless*
is confirmed most strikingly by a work which critics have almost invariably
placed beyond concrete location and historical time: Kafka's novel *The Castle*
(written in 1922) shows the same sort of topography and, associated with it,
the same distribution of power and social status. However, there is a difference.
With Kafka, who does not give his characters or his locations recognizable
national names, the specific – as opposed to a general – historical reading is

irrelevant; with Musil, who has no qualms about giving such recognizable names, the relevance of such a reading is manifest. To give the action and location of *Young Törless* their national dimension and all that it connotes is thus to give them the meaning they had for Musil's first readers and contemporary fellow authors. Our interpretation of the novel is confirmed by its reception: history in the work coincides with the work in history.

3

In outlining the events of the novel we may as well be guided by Musil's own indication of how he saw his undertaking. Some ten years later (1913) he looks back on his first work and defends it against the critics' accusation that it is lacking in action and plot and even perhaps in individual characterization, and that he is a poor story-teller: 'The reality one is describing is always only a pretext', he writes. Because action and plot are constantly encroached upon by Törless's fantasies, as well as by his and the narrator's comments on these fantasies, they don't have the status they would have in a realistic novel. Only Törless's eventual repudiation of what is happening around him – an indispensable part of his journey out of the 'confusion' – is realistic. This is the programme we must keep in mind when outlining the events of the novel.

The events of the novel's 'reality', then, all take place inside the boarding school. Reiting (a tyrant who loves manipulating others in order, so he says, to train himself for life in the adult world) and Beineberg (a sadist with an interest in Indian mysticism) observe the boy Basini (pretty, effeminate and weak) stealing money from the other boys' lockers in order to pay off a debt to Reiting. Beineberg and Reiting decide not to report Basini to the school authorities, and instead to use their knowledge of his felony in order to blackmail him. Törless, who is curious, bemused and expectant, avidly yet uneasily waiting for some act of 'terrible animal sensuality' to happen, is initiated into their plan and takes part in its execution.

The acts of torture and buggery to which Basini is subjected take place in a secret room, draped in red flag cloth and furnished with whips, lamps and a revolver – a hide-out which Beineberg and Reiting have discovered under the rafters of one of the old monastic buildings in which the school is housed. While Beineberg and Reiting confine their treatment of the hapless Basini to physical torture, Törless is increasingly sickened by such acts and takes his pleasure – or at least follows his bent – in torturing Basini mentally, by insisting on having the boy describe to him as minutely as he can what is being done to him and what his reactions are. This verbal voyeurism is chief among Törless's conflicting character traits.

During a brief school vacation (one hesitates to call it anything so straightforward and Anglo-Saxon as 'half-term break') Törless and Basini are left alone in the school, and Basini (mainly, one gathers, as an act of self-defence and in the hope of getting him on his side) seduces Törless. At this stage Törless's reaction is shown to be simply sexual. In the absence of Beineberg and Reiting, both the sadistic and voyeuristic elements in Törless recede behind the gratification of a pent-up sexual urge; the homosexual nature of the act is incidental, determined merely by the circumstances in which it occurs.

The events of the story come to a head when Basini, unable to bear things any longer, decides to denounce his tormentors. As soon as the Headmaster starts the investigation, Törless runs away to a neighbouring town, though it is made clear that he has not been denounced. Beineberg and Reiting convince the school authorities that in beating up Basini (whose body is heavily bruised) they merely gave vent to their righteous indignation when they discovered that he was a thief. Basini is expelled, and Törless, on being made to return, tries in a confused and incoherent way to explain his involvement in the affair. His address to the assembled staff is largely unintelligible to them because it is cast in the allusive language of his interior monologue. Törless is not being accused of any misdemeanour and is not trying to excuse himself. The confusion of his account derives from his attempts to convey to the Headmaster and the other masters present the apparently mystical state of mind he was in when he joined Beineberg and Reiting in the persecution of Basini. It is made clear that the mysticism at issue is not to be seen as a religious experience, but as a necessary supersession of reason by the irrational. The irrational, we are told, is at the root of the world; any experience of the world that fails to take issue with it is inadequate. The Headmaster, however, takes Törless's confused account of his involvement to be indicative of great sensitivity and mental stress, and the story ends with Törless's being allowed to withdraw from the school in order to follow a course of private education likely to be more appropriate to his distraught state of mind.

It should be clear from this brief account that any resemblance to Kipling's *Stalky & Co.* is purely superficial, if only because (worse luck) Musil's story has not a funny line in it; what humour there is comes from the presentation of the Headmaster and the clergyman who teaches divinity, as well as the maths master, as simpletons who are not only wrong about Törless's true motives (whatever *they* may be), but also pompous and heavy-handed in their misapprehension. But if conventional public-school stories fail to provide an appropriate parallel, the powerful autobiographical element which pervades the book relates it not only to the actual episodes taken from Musil's own life in the military academy, but also, above all, to the mental states he himself experienced there. The portrait is that of a budding intellectual with strong aesthetic leanings and moments of 'an almost poetic inspiration' (p. 184), who, it is suggested, may eventually turn out to be a writer. But what sort of a writer? A carefully composed letter the boy writes to his parents, a set of notes in which he is attempting to find words for the 'unsayable', a secret diary – these signs have led numerous critics to interpret the book as a portrait of the artist as a young man. Perhaps so – but this only raises the question of what kind of writer Musil really was. What is claimed for Törless throughout the book is the aesthete's attitude and privileges; and although it is a moot point whether Törless's creator was – then or thereafter – aware of the difference, 'the aesthetic' is not, after all, the same as the artistically creative.

4

'The work of art', Musil writes in his diary, *c*.1919, 'is not like a single curved line, but like a line that is drawn with ever fresh starts. It is not continuous, but contains cracks [*Sprünge*] which remain below the threshold of observation or irradiate its [the work's] specific character.' The language of order, coherence and continuity is thus seen to be inadequate, to be at odds with the true nature of experience. And in saying this we are not only characterizing Musil's view of language and therefore the way he writes in this novel, we are at the same time approaching one of the novel's main preoccupations. Both in reporting the content of his consciousness and in reproducing his encounters with the school authorities and his school companions, Törless is shown to be struggling to find words with which to convey the confused experiences within – struggling and failing. Language, in the form of his introspection and inner discourse, is presented in the narrative as a dark medium, discontinuous, mere lungings at uncertain targets; here 'each venture / Is a new beginning, a raid on the inarticulate / With shabby equipment always deteriorating / In the general mess of imprecision of feeling'.

The inadequacy of language for conveying the kind of inner experiences young Törless undergoes becomes a theme of the novel. It is hard to know how seriously to take it. In the present context this talk about 'the limits of language' seems hardly more than the fasionable patter of the age, rather like the 'inability to communicate' which became the excuse for illiteracy half a century later. However, what is implied in that thematization – implied and in no way criticized – is a view of language as a system of labels or names for things which are in themselves wordless, silent. The novel is thus grounded in a dichotomy, with language on one side and experience or (to use the novel's own terminology) *Wirklichkeit*, 'reality', on the other; or again, language, being confined to the process of naming and describing things, and apparently incapable of truly explaining them, is felt, and presented, as being somehow 'unreal' (*unwirklich*), or at least as less real than events, or experiences, or feelings. This is not the place to show the inadequacy and incoherence of this kind of metaphysics. (In a diary note I quoted earlier Musil said that he had used 'reality' as 'a pretext for the presentation of inner states', and therefore as meaning the opposite of what it means here.) My point is that the authorial reliance on the language–'reality' dichotomy leads to a curious escalation of what is felt and said to be 'real'; so that 'reality' comes to consist of what is felt and said to be 'indescribable' (*unsagbar* and similar words occur throughout the text), and is apt to be confined to the marginal, the sensational and the catastrophic, to that which results in an overturning of the ordered and the orderly; and this became common practice for a whole generation of novelists.

'Reality', in its antithesis to language, means significant, weighty experience, and such experience is said to be found only on the margins of the ordinary world; hence Musil's frequent insistence on *Grenzsituationen, Grenzfälle, Grenzwerte* – marginal situations, marginal cases and marginal values. Hence, too, the significance of the secret red room. While most of the action of the novel takes places in the school, a domain deliberately separated from the everyday world, the revelations (such as they are) or – to use a word given a certain vogue by Joyce's Stephen Dedalus – the secular 'epiphanies' Törless experiences, or (to use yet a third fashionable term) his 'privileged moments', come to him at a double remove from the ordinary world, in that star chamber in which Basini is tortured and abused. Similarly, in Thomas Mann's *Magic Mountain* and Kafka's novel *The Trial* (to choose two out of a very large number of examples), insight and revelation, an understanding of existential truth (however enigmatic and inconclusive), come to the heroes of those novels in *Grenzsituationen*, in such exceptional locations and marginal planes of experience. 'Reality', in the sense which it is given in these marginal situations (and in the sense in which T. S. Eliot uses the word when he says, 'Human kind / Cannot bear very much reality'), is where there is no 'reality' in the sense of the ordinary and everyday world, where the everyday is worthless. And this rudimentary ideology provides a key to a good deal that is characteristic and significant in German literature in the first half of this century; and literature, in this respect, becomes a harbinger of politics.

The core of the book before us, then, lies not in its actions and events but (in Musil's own characterization) in 'the coming closer to the feelings and stirrings of the mind . . . of the single case' which the fiction is designed to make representative. These are 'die Verwirrungen', the inward dream-like adventures of a confused adolescent mind. And just as the words which describe this state of mind are searched for with great difficulty and said to be fundamentally arbitrary and imprecise, lungings in the dark, so the outward events, too, which set the search in train and which are presented with no other purpose in mind than to provide the occasion for and the way into these searchings – so these events too are presented as arbitrary. We shall have to see whether we as readers of the novel can really accept them as such. But first, we must try to indicate the nature of these 'feelings and stirrings of the mind', the nature of what it is that Törless is said to be seeking.

5

Törless is intent on understanding other minds not on their own terms and for their sake, but only to the extent that they should enable him to understand and grasp the content of his own mind; the understanding he is seeking is solipsistic. Other minds and the world itself are there only as the objects of

a series of avowedly arbitrary experiments, *actes* not altogether *gratuits*, designed
to reveal a mind that is a puzzle and a problem to itself, a mind that appears
to have no other puzzles and problems save those that are parts of its inscape.
The world that is presented as the object of such an inquiry is made up of
radical discontinuities. Let me enumerate some of them. The acts of extreme,
sordid cruelty in which Törless takes part are juxtaposed to a mind of extreme
fastidiousness and sensitivity; Törless's radical estrangement from all around
him is juxtaposed to the utmost intimacy and surrender of the sexual act; the
extreme closeness to the sentient self of events when experienced is juxtaposed
to the radical distancing of the events when formulated; his willingness to
share in the sadistic acts of tyranny and total domination over another is
juxtaposed to moments of complete indifference and aloofness – personal
aloofness from the events that are happening in his presence in the red
chamber, and indifference to the consequences of those actions; and exacting
attempts at a rational account of his psychic life are juxtaposed to mystical
intimations. The deep confusion Törless experiences in refusing to contem-
plate any possible link between his mother and the prostitute Božena, and
between himself and the thief Basini, is a further indication of the duality of
the world he inhabits. All these things he experiences as 'cracks' or 'breaks'
(*Sprünge*), juxtapositions without connecting links. For all these extremes of
hot and cold no authorial synthesis is offered. Törless *is* each of these in turn
(we have here an opening on to Musil's later work, the portrait of a hero 'with
indeterminate qualities'). True, the novel contains, with only the weakest traces
of irony, a brief observation to the effect that, 'Later, when he had got over
his adolescent experiences, Törless became a young man whose mind was
both subtle and sensitive . . . one of those aesthetically inclined intellectuals
. . . [whose] needs were acutely and singlemindedly focused on an aesthetic-
intellectual approach' to everything around him, especially to moral problems
(pp. 148–9). But this attempt at a synthesis (the eventual result of the contest
between the warring extremes of which Törless's confusions' are composed)
is confined to that inadvertent observation; neither the actions and events of
the novel nor the reported stream of conscious and half-conscious thoughts
pertaining to those actions and events contribute to it.

Alongside attempts at describing these extremes in analytical language, a
good many highly charged images are used. Some of them offer immediate
illumination: the path to Božena's house at the beginning of the novel leads
through a dark and sinister wood, but at the end this wood is seen to be a
mere 'dusty tangle of willows and alders'. But then again Musil takes recourse
to a sort of 'naturalistic fallacy', offering to convey darkness by darkness, and
leaving us with the impression that the clearer these images are, the less
appropriate they are for the purpose of conveying the unclarity that
encompasses the novel's central theme, Törless's 'confusions'.

These devices are at their most effective when, as in the torture scene, an
incongruity is achieved between imagery and scene. Basini is hit by Beineberg
('now, across his upper lip, mouth and chin, slowly, drops of blood were

making a red wriggling line, like a worm' (p. 95)), and Törless compounds Basini's debasement by ordering him to confess: 'Go on, say you're a thief.' As soon as he has said this, Törless is sickened by the scene – he recognizes it as a caricature of the illumination he is seeking, and withdraws his mind from it. There follows an instant act of self-absorption: Törless goes back in his mind to a thought he had during a maths lesson, when he found himself puzzled by the meaning and function of the square root of -1. It had been demonstrated to the class that the square of any number can have a square root; but now he is told that the square root of -1 is not a 'real' number, but that it may nevertheless be needed in certain mathematical operations in order to make possible (or, as Törless puts it, to 'connect') a calculation cast in 'rational' numbers, numbers designating tangible quantities like metres or pounds. In the 'real' calculation (Törless infers) there is a break which only the 'unreal' can bridge. This contrasting of 'the real' and 'the unreal' is seen by him as an illustration of the juxtaposing of maximum precision (calculation with 'real' numbers) and maximum arbitrariness (calculation with imaginary or 'unreal' numbers); and this in turn serves as an analogy of all the other juxtapositions of extremes, the totality of which is Törless's mind.

It is the sadist, Beineberg, who explains, imitating the voice of the divinity master:

> You see an apple – that's light waves and the action of the eye and so forth – and you stretch out your hand to steal it – that's the muscles and the nerves that set them in action – but between these two there lies something else that makes one emanate from the other, and that's the immortal soul, which in doing so has committed sin'. (p. 98)

The fact that Beineberg the sadist has produced this explanation has the same significance as the fact that Törless's recollection of these matters of high intellectual abstraction is occasioned by a scene of degradation and sordid violence; both are intended to illustrate the puzzle itself.

Of course, within the context devised by the narrator, Beineberg's explanation is given in a vein of mockery – that's precisely the sort of thing the divinity master would say; and for good measure one part of it is repeated at the end (during the Headmaster's investigation) in the most deflating terms by the clergyman himself. In the course of the novel all specifically religious connotations of the clergyman's parable and Beineberg's parody of it – all that is said in Christian terms about sin and the immortal soul – are denied both explicitly and by implication: throughout, we are moving in an era that lies in the shadow of 'the death of God'. Nevertheless, the analogy which Beineberg offers does provide a valid account of Törless's 'confusions'; and though by implication all such religious meaning is denied also to the analogy from the discontinuity of imaginary numbers, this is not intended to affect the metaphysical meaning, and validity, of that analogy:

experience *is* to be seen as discontinuous, toppling over from one extreme to its opposite, from (for instance) the extreme of rationality and scientific accuracy to its opposite, irrationalism and arbitrariness; and (we are meant to infer) if even mathematics hides such 'mystical' contradictions at its core, how hopeless must be all attempts designed to keep contradictions and thus the irrational out of more mundane and scientifically indeterminable areas of experience.

The strenuousness of this search for 'the mystical' receives in the novel a good deal of positive emphasis, yet at no point is there even a hint that this is mere ersatz mysticism. On the contrary: seeing it as a sign of Törless's protest against the incomprehension and insensitivity of the adult world, the author presents these mystical lucubrations as signs of his hero's authenticity.

Equally problematic is the narrator's attitude to the moral implications of Törless's search for a way out of his 'confusions'. Inevitably, a good deal of our account so far has been cast in terms connoting extreme cruelty, sadism, squalid violence – terms heavily loaded with moral values. Musil tries to avoid such terms. He resorts to them only once or twice, briefly, and then they are overshadowed by expressions of disapproval of a predominantly aesthetic kind, summed up in the word 'Ekel' – 'disgust'. And (we read), as soon as 'this disgust and a certain indistinct, hidden fear' are roused in Törless, 'the subtle voluptuousness that lay in his acts of degradation became ever rarer' (pp. 151–2). To the extent, then, that disapproval of the torture scenes is shown at all, it is because, at some point or other, they disgust Törless; and they disgust him because they do not fufill the promise they offered: they promised erotic gratification and looked like leading towards insight into the duality of things, but when he recognizes that they are brought about by agents whom he despises – he despises Reiting and Reineberg no less than Basini, with whom at least he could assuage his sexual desire – they turn out (in his mind) to lead only to the feeble beginnings of insight. Musil is thus caught in the same cleft stick as his young hero: in spite of the declared narrative intention to treat action, plot and even the psychology of individual characters as arbitrary, the fact that they are what they are turns out to be an indispensable part of conveying those 'feelings and stirrings of the mind' in the bearing they have on morality. Moral judgements, in the novel, are not an option.

6

We are, as I have said, moving within the shadow cast by 'the death of God'. And in this era, Nietzsche also wrote, 'Everything is possible, everything is permitted.' This is the moral space in which the events of the novel are enacted. When Törless tells his two companions that he is bored by the whole conspiracy and will no longer take part in it (the boredom being a mask for the 'disgust' and the 'indistinct, hidden fear' he felt), Reiting threatens to subject him to the same treatment as that meted out to Basini. Törless repeats his decision to quit:

> 'I'm not going to have any more to do with it. I am sick of the whole thing.'
> 'All of a sudden?' [Reiting retorts]
> 'Yes, all of a sudden. Before, I was searching for something behind it all ...' Why did this keep on forcing itself back into his mind ...?!
> 'Aha, second sight!'

Again, although this is said by Reiting mockingly, the words are an appropriate lead into Törless's searchings and confusions:

> 'Yes [he replies]. But now I can see only one thing – how vulgar and brutal you and Beineberg are.'
> 'But you shall also see Basini eating dirt', Reiting sneered.
> 'I'm not interested any more.'
> 'But you certainly used to be!'
> 'I've already told you: only as long as Basini's state of mind was a riddle to me.'
> 'And now?'
> 'Now I don't know anything about riddles. Everything happens: that's all the wisdom there is'. (p. 167)

'Everything is possible, everything is permitted', wrote Nietzsche; and, Musil/Törless adds, 'Everything happens: that's all the wisdom there is.'

I don't know whether there are literary genres that can bypass all moral considerations, but I very much doubt whether it is possible to write an amoral novel. It is in the nature of the writing and reading of novels (at least to the extent that they are about human beings, and perhaps even when they are not) that they cannot fail to give rise to questions of good and evil, however defined. Here they never become an explicit part of the novel, and, even when they occur in it, always in conjunction with an aesthetic judgement of disapproval, such considerations are unsustained and incidental. And the reason for this defectiveness – whether we see it as a defective presentation of a moral censure or of an aesthetic-moral distaste – is simple. It lies in the solipsism in which the novel is meant to be cast: all that happens is presented as happening ultimately in terms of Törless's mind, and at no point is the effect on other minds seriously considered.

Beineberg and Reiting are presented as bullies (there is an obvious moral-aesthetic judgement in that), but their main function is to provide Törless with a spectacle in which he also becomes an agent, and which is to offer him opportunities for gratification and insight – for the gratification of insight.

Basini's baseness – Italian names, in the Austrian stereotype of 'Katzelmacher', connote cowardice and treachery – is not confined to Törless's view of him; it is, astonishingly, the author himself, through the narrator, who speaks of Basini's 'moral inferiority and stupidity' (p. 67). Hence neither Törless nor his creator has any compunction in treating him as a mere object, a means to Törless's end. This is made abundantly clear in that brief and inadvertent page of recollection when, in the course of describing the kind of aesthetically minded intellectual Törless became in later years, the narrator tells us that Törless 'never felt remorse for what had happened at that [earlier] time' (p. 148). Through these experiences, we are told, he became 'one of those people who regard the things that make demands only on their moral rectitude with the utmost indifference'. And when asked whether, looking back on this episode of his adolescence, he did not after all have a feeling of shame,

> he answered, with a smile, 'Of course, I don't deny that it was a degrading affair. And why not? The degradation passed off. And yet it left something behind – that small admixture of poison which is needed to rid the soul of its over-confident, complacent healthiness, and to give it instead a sort of health that is more acute, and subtler, and more understanding.' (p. 149)

(The argument is pure Nietzsche.) And lovers too, the not-so-young Törless goes on to ruminate, share such journeys 'through all the circles of hell' – the tone of the recollection has suddenly changed – 'and just as such lovers go that way together, so I at that time went through all those things, but on my own.'

However, Törless's memory is playing him false: he was not alone and could not have been alone. And it is no irrelevant insight – though it is a judgement not contained in the text of the novel – to say, emphatically, that what was done to Basini at all events cannot be described as a 'small admixture of poison', as a homeopathic cure against 'over-confident complacent healthiness'. If ever one looks for a recipe of how to ruin a schoolboy for life, it is given, unintentionally but surely, in the fate of Basini.

True, Basini's later life is not the narrator's concern. All the same, any reader who is not prepared to take the novel's 'aesthetic' values uncritically will be looking either for the barest acknowledgement that the boy has been maimed for life or for reasons why he should not draw this obvious conclusion. But to make even that bare statement, or mention those reasons, the novelist would have had to acknowledge that here is a situation in which experience – the psychic consequences of torture – is continuous; and to do that, he – the novelist – would have had to go back on his narrative scheme of 'breaks', that is, of psychic discontinuities. There is an analogy from mathematics which illustrates Musil's difficulty more appropriately than anything to do with the square root of −1: it is the difficulty mathematicians have in devising series of numbers that are genuinely random.

7

If, then, the novel is not (and cannot be) amoral, what sort of a moral scheme does it show forth? The morality in terms of which Törless's 'confusions' are to be justified is put into words in three passages, each time by a different character. And again it must be added that, whether or not these passages represent the author's own beliefs, they are not subjected to any criticism; rather, the author gives the impression of one who has got his central character into a complicated mess and is quite pleased – in a suitably serious way, of course – that he has found a way of getting him out of it, without bothering too much about its relevance.

(1)   Early in the novel Beineberg explains his interest in Basini. Having expounded an obscure bit of some Indian mystical claptrap – a recipe for bending the external world, including other people, to his will, even if it means destroying it in the process – Beineberg concludes his harangue:

> 'Well, you can see what my interest is. The impulse I have to let Basini off comes from outside me and arises from base motives. You can obey it if you like. For me it's a prejudice, and I have to cut myself loose from it as from everything else that would distract me from my inner ways. The very fact that I find it hard to torture Basini – I mean, to humiliate him, to debase him, to cast him away from me – is good. It requires a sacrifice. It will have a purifying effect . . .' (pp. 79–80)

(2)   Immediately before the seduction scene Basini reports to the avid Törless how he was abused and tortured by Reiting:

> 'First of all he gives me long talks about my soul. He says I've sullied it, but as it were only the outermost forecourt of it. In relation to the innermost, he says, this doesn't matter at all, it's only external. But one must kill it. In that way sinners have turned into saints. So from a higher point of view sin isn't so bad: only one must take it to its extreme point, so that it breaks off of its own accord'. (p. 135)

(3)   And here, finally, is Törless himself, becoming conscious of what distinguishes him from his two companions:

> He believed that he could see no trace of shame in them. He did not think that they suffered as he knew he did. The crown of thorns that his tormenting conscience set on his brow seemed to be missing from

theirs . . . He knew that he would debase himself again, but he gave it a new meaning. The uglier and unworthier everything was that Basini offered him, the greater was the contrast with that feeling of suffering sensibility which would set in afterwards. (p. 147)

From a whole variety of sources, including a notorious speech by Heinrich Himmler of October 1943, we know that arguments of this kind were propagated among the SS and believed by some of them. Elisabeth Stopp, in her illuminating essay on *Young Törless*, says that Musil himself (presumably in his later diaries) had 'a mediumistic premonition of the SS officers who run concentration camps'. The parallel is certainly there in the novel (though not the premonition). After all, nowhere is there a statement to dissociate it from this ethos; nowhere is it said or shown that Törless's development, his journey through his confusions and out of them, is the worse for having been achieved in this way, or that it could have been achieved in any other way. There is even less warning in this portrayal with which Musil opens his literary career than there is in Kafka's novels, which are full of similar parallels. And by 'warning' I have in mind nothing more explicit than the narrator's acknow- ledgement (such as Kafka provides at the end of *The Trial*) that there might be occasions when the interests of his story are best served by calling evil by its proper name.

Again the question of anachronism arises. Insight into the full political implications of the 'mystical' attitude, or of those 'aesthetic' values, could not have been available to Musil any more than insight into all the political consequences of Josef K.'s or K.'s attitudes to power could have been to Kafka. And if Musil, and Kafka, had confined their novels to the portraiture of individual psyches, the relationship between private conduct and its political significance need have been no more than one of remote connection. But schools, courts of law and castles are institutions, and, in novels as heavily institutionalized in their settings as theirs, the social and political implications are anything but remote, and any critical account that lays some claim to validity – any aspectival account that intimates some measure of completeness – is bound to take issue with such implications. The social ramifications of what is given in the private sphere form a continuity with the moral ones: neither can be avoided except by an act of omission; morality is not an option.

8

Let me recapitulate the three passages I have quoted. Humiliation entails sacrifice, we read, though (given the ambiguity of the German word 'Opfer' which means both 'sacrifice' and 'victim') whose sacrifice is intended we are not told. And we also read: sinfulness must be taken to its extreme point, and then it will turn into sainthood. And finally, in terms of explicit blasphemy:

the 'crown of thorns' of tormenting conscience is a proof of a suffering aesthetic sensibility, 'eine leidende Feinheit'.

Young Törless stands at the threshold of modern German literature. All these ideas – mutations of Christian beliefs and precepts – constitute the moral horizon of the novel. And they are also central to that literature, the major theme of which is the search for redemption, validation and an encompassing meaning of life, which are invariably said to be attainable only at the margins of experience. It is the hardness and harshness, the difficulty in the way of attaining the goal, and indeed on occasion its radical unattainability that are offered, in this literature, as a proof of the value of the goal. The greater the sacrifice, the greater the need to commit oneself to acts that once used to be called 'sins', the harsher the torment of conscience – the finer, the subtler the experience and its validation. What this early novel contains is an unalloyed, uncritical – indeed, crude – version of the ethos, soon to become an ideology, of the literature of the subsequent age.

To say this is not to say that Robert Musil was some sort of proto-Nazi, any more than that the majority of latter-day critics of the novel, with less excuse than he had for failing to see its moral and political implications, are to be seen as some sort of *NS-Sympathisanten*. (Musil was a difficult, tetchy and honourable man; when Hitler assumed power in Germany, he went into exile, although he was neither a Jew nor in the least politically involved.) History in literary criticism is irrelevant if it does not throw light on the text, illuminating its excellences and flaws. And so here too our concern must be not with the novel's wrong politics, but with its lack of perceptiveness, disclosed by the historical view; or (to put it bluntly) with the authorial failure to make out the sinister but coherent whole that looms up behind the solipsistic self, the self on its indiscriminate quest for that romantically discontinuous experience that goes by the name of 'Erlebnis'.

But history tells us that there is experience which is continuous. National Socialism, the dominant ideology and political practice of the subsequent era, was not an isolated phenomenon that came down suddenly, like a thunderbolt from a blue sky. It arose out of an existing, as yet non-dominant ethos, representing its absolute radicalization. We have noted some of the components of this existing ethos. The exaltation of a catastrophic notion of 'reality' as the goal and of calculated sadistic acts as the test of authentic experience, the wholly uncritical emphasis on the 'irrational', the 'indescribable' and the ersatz-mystical – all these represent an ethos which was by no means exlcusively German or Austrian, though in due course it would appear at its most concentrated in the literature of those countries. Its literary manifestations at the beginning of Musil's literary career remained relatively harmless, because they did not attain any social or political embodiment. What prevented their translation into ideology and practical politics was partly the institutional inertia that was the political order of their day, and partly their status as fictions, poetry, literature, in a society that was still capable of distinguishing literature from politics, fiction from fact, though less and less so as time went by.

National Socialism, on the other hand, was the wholly nihilistic and destructive consummation of this ethos, born at the point where social anarchy made possible the translation of novels into ideology and into practical politics; fiction into fact.

Musil's fragmentary masterpiece, *The Man Without Qualities*, was begun the year before *Young Törless* was published. Its relation to the book before us is a matter of radical transposition into another key. Ulrich too (unlike Törless, he has no surname) is seeking enlightenment and a way out of his unclarities, and he too is immensely determinable, a receptacle rather than a fully formed character, experimenting with experience. But two radical changes – transpositions – occur: the experience with which Ulrich experiments is his own; and other people are involved in it on equal terms – they are not reduced to being mere means to his end. Moreover, the entire scenario of *The Man Without Qualities* – Ulrich and the curious world of Vienna 1913 around him – is itself heavily historicized, and suffused with the light of radical irony. Ulrich calls himself a 'possibilitarian' – one who, while seeking, like Törless, some profound mystical 'reality' behind all things, is content to see the world around him ironically, as a provisional abode on the way to the mystery, a spectrum of changing hues and mere possibilities. The transposition of the search into a new key confronted Musil with formal narrative problems which some critics (including this critic) think he failed to solve. However that may be, to see *Young Törless* as a first step on the road to *The Man Without Qualities* is only partly valid. One can see little in the early novel which would point to that transposition, little that would modify that spirit of clammy passion, heaviness and ritual sacrifice which informs Musil's first published work.

1983

6

The Ideas of 1914

Long before the English began worrying about their national identity, the Germans fought a war to assert theirs – or so many German intellectuals felt in August 1914. Thomas Mann's contribution to this eruption of nationalist self-consciousness was delivered in a series of essays written over the following four years, and it is among the strangest things he ever wrote. Not the least paradox of this exacting, ambitious and deeply ironical work is the fact that when it was first published, as *Betrachtungen eines Unpolitischen (Reflections of a Nonpolitical Man)*, in the month of Germany's defeat, the causes and attitudes so strenuously defended in its pages seemed to the German population at large all but discredited: and Mann's own rejection of most of them was soon to follow. Whatever his motives in writing these essays, there was nothing expedient about his publishing them.

By the time Mann, aged thirty-nine, wrote the first of these essays he was among his country's most highly regarded authors. After *Death in Venice* (1912), his most recent success, he had begun work on *The Magic Mountain*, and this was now put aside, 'for the duration'. Two events of very unequal importance unloosed the floodgates of this current of dialectical argument, special pleas, invective and self-revelation: the outbreak of the war, on the one hand, and his bitter personal and literary quarrel with his Francophile and politically committed elder brother Heinrich, on the other. Given the violent lurch toward war of the entire Wilhelmine establishment in the summer of 1914, Thomas Mann's part in the nationalist stampede is not all that surprising. Yet the irony of his own belated fervour was not lost on him: throughout the book he keeps on asking himself 'what the devil' *he*, the author of *Buddenbrooks* – one of German literature's finest contributions to the Western tradition of the realist novel – is doing among all those far from 'unpolitical' literati whom 'the sacred requirements of Germany's hour of need' had turned into anti-Western nationalists.

Alas, composing these lucubrations on the theme of 'des Volkes höchste Not' did little for Thomas Mann's temper:

He could still project an aura of kindness [writes Golo Mann, the third of his six children], but for the most part we experienced only silence, sternness, nervousness, or anger. I can remember all too well certain scenes at mealtimes, outbreaks of rage and brutality that were directed at my brother Klaus [Golo's senior by three years] but brought tears to my own eyes. If a person cannot always be *very* nice to those around him when he is devoting himself exclusively to his creative work, how much more difficult must it be when he is struggling day after day with the *Reflections* . . . , in which the sinking of the British ship *Lusitania* with twelve hundred civilian passengers on board is actually approved, to name just one of the book's grimmest features! This 'examination of conscience ', a duty imposed by the war, as he understood it, placed a heavy burden on the author himself, affording him none of the (admittedly somewhat uncertain) pleasure he had derived from the novels he had temporarily abandoned . . .

The public or national purpose of the book was to define and defend Germany as the land of music and philosophy, of *Geist* and of authoritarian government – of what Mann calls 'culture' – against 'the West', with its rationalism, its French revolutionary ideas and its belief in inevitable progress through technology – what Mann calls 'civilization'. Meanwhile, at a personal level, yet equally publicized, the aim was to define and defend its author's stance in relation to these two ideologically-loaded views of the German and European destiny. The tug-of-war between 'culture' and 'civilization', which Mann takes over from the conservative ideologists of the Wilhelmine Empire, is symptomatic of the dualistic manner that pervades the book. For many years, some would say since the Reformation, the obsessive play with antitheses was part of the German intellectual kit. So much so that at the end of the eighteenth century G. C. Lichtenberg in his *Waste-Books* conducted a series of aphoristic sorties against 'the *infamous* TWO in the world', singling out 'certain of our authors who, once they've given their subject-matter a good thump, declare that it naturally falls into two parts' and spend the rest of their time playing one off against the other. Such insights are lost on the less than mercurial author of the *Reflections*. Instead of trying to soften the antagonisms of the war situation, he deliberately intensifies them. The inveterate habit of dichotomizing everything on the cultural and political horizon prevails: the 'individualistic' masses, which are seen as 'democratic', are played off against *das Volk*, a concept which is said to be aristocratic; 'music' and 'philosophy', endowed with proper German gravity, are opposed to the shallow 'politics' of Western meliorism; 'power' is opposed to 'mind', and Heinrich Mann the irresponsible *Zivilisationsliterat* is thumped on the head by the nationally-committed Brother Thomas with his 'German-*bürgerlich*-artistic' conscience.

Explaining and slightly fudging his own pre-war attitude, Thomas Mann writes: 'A good part of my patriotism came and comes from the comparison of the German-tragic concept of events with the forensic-moral concept of our enemies' (as though tragedy excluded the moral view), and then adds: 'But did I not also see in this turn of the century a turn of my own personal life and of all our lives?' Here is the fatal slither from the national to the personal, from the political to the literary, that makes the book such embarrassing reading. He anticipates our embarrassment, and a few sentences later writes: 'What shook me and shamed me was the incongruity between my personal rank and the roaring display of world history that marked the crisis of my forty years.' What that admission (and countless others like it) subtly suggests – that somehow the 'incongruity' is beyond his control – is spelled out in the next sentence: 'No doubt it is fate to be placed so in time that a change in personal life comes together with a change in the times.' No doubt it is. But the Saint Sebastian posture he adopts in 'bearing witness' to these changes is not a matter of fate but a matter of choice – of literary choice. The book – he says so more than once – needs an apologia: this fatalism is meant to provide it.

Reflections of a Nonpolitical Man has often been attacked for its politics. It is, in its way, a conservative manifesto. Yet, as T. J. Reed has observed in *Thomas Mann: the Uses of Tradition*, there is an air of unreality in Mann's account of the issues involved – he is not in the least interested in the process by which political decisions are reached or enacted. 'Democratic politics' is condemned for lacking 'metaphysical dignity' – terms which make one wonder whether he was ever interested enough to find out what politics means in practice. The gulf between his own supposedly 'non-political' concerns and the European bloodshed is to be bridged by irony: and irony, in Mann's case, invariably involves lashings of authorial self-consciousness. Yet the 'incongruity' (some might call it indecency) of placing his own literary predicament on a par in terms of interest, importance and seriousness with the political situation – the incongruity of this 'symbolism' – doesn't, after all, strike him with sufficient force. The collapse of civilized values at the outbreak of the war was almost complete. Yet there were a very few German writers who saw 'service for the fatherland with pen in hand' for the abomination it was. Thomas Mann was not among them.

Instead, he creates a scenario of huge historical and cultural abstractions which he intersperses with anecdotes, brilliant insights and countless quotations from half a dozen literatures (as though his motto were 'I quote, therefore I am'); and this view of *Deutschtum*, of 'what it is to be German', he hopes will entertain us while he manoeuvres us across the book's fundamental flaw, the flaw inherent in placing literary representativeness – prose which is instinct with literary, that is, the novelist's devices – within a political context. Most of the time, however, the device works. We read the book not as fiction but as document, though what it documents is the fiction-like ambiguity of its attitudes. With Mann's whole œuvre before us we can see *Reflections* as one of his many attempts to grapple the single self to history, and to do this by means of a prose style which makes his own case of that relationship explicitly representative. The attempt will be repeated: first in *The Magic Mountain* (1924), where the two opposing sides – *Zivilisationsliterat* versus committed upholder of spiritual values – will be subjected to yet more irony and given a more directly fictional status in the figures of the humanist Signor Settembrini and the Jewish Jesuit Leo Naphta; and finally in *Doctor Faustus* (1947).

In these contexts – that is, in fictional achievements that are wholly free from the destructive fervour of serving a warlike cause – the confrontation reflected on in the book assumes a different function. It becomes part of a legitimate concern for a national culture and identity that must co-exist – and does today co-exist – with other national cultures and identities, without which Europe would be the less.

How do *we* see this wartime miscellany of pleas and accusations? Again and again Mann takes pride in comparing the effort their composition cost him with the effort of his country at war, again and again the strenuousness of both undertakings is commended as the supremely 'German' virtue. ('Around the house he wore a grey jacket,' reports Golo Mann, 'a sort of Russian soldier's tunic – *litevka* – which he called his "service jacket".') Seeing that the author sets up his literary emporium at a safe distance from the battle – a *vivandière's* enterprise seems more honourable – it can hardly be regarded as a heroic value. In any event, this elevation of the difficulties of composition to existential heights is part of a value scheme that hasn't worn too well. There was too much strenuousness, most of it 'beyond good and evil', in the decades that followed for us to believe in it as uncritically as Thomas Mann does in this book.

The merit of the book lies elsewhere. To anyone interested in the intellectual history of Germany not only up to the end of the Great War but beyond it, to the coming of Hitler, the book yields some of the most profound and illuminating insights into that history ever formulated. It has been called prophetic. It certainly prefigured developments, if only because it influenced them. Its very irony and uneasy alternation between the private and the public left the book defenceless against its exploitation by that 'conservative revolution' which prepared the way for the collapse of both 'civilization' and 'culture' during the events that led to Hitler's accession to power in January 1933; and the failure of the officers' plot of July 1944 sealed the fate of the old conservatism as Mann had interpreted it.

The political scene in Germany has now changed beyond recognition, yet something of the book's *Problematik* remains. The virulent nationalism of 'the ideas of 1914' is too heavily discredited to amount to a serious force in Germany today. But there are other issues, passionately disputed in this book, which are very much alive there in two more or less current controversies: controversies which are usually seen – mistakenly, I believe – as German contributions to an international movement. The first is the students' rebellion in the name of the 'ideas of 1968'. To see that turmoil exclusively as a violent reaction of the New (or whatever) Left to imperialism of one kind or another, to West German capitalism and to right-wing attempts to keep a few old National Socialist Party hacks in clover, is to ignore the deeply romantic nature of the rebellion. Its protest was directed, not only against the American military undertaking in Vietnam, but also against American empiricism invading the sociology seminars of the German universities; against Western positivism and 'functionalism' threatening to oust German holistic and deductive theories of society; against Anglo-Saxon analytical language philosophy (which Herbert Marcuse accused of 'academic sado-masochism', 'self-humiliation and self-denunciation') threatening to invalidate German ontological thinking. Marcuse's disciples of '68 are the schoolmasters, university teachers and civil servants of today. They certainly don't share, and would be embarrassed by, Mann's chauvinism. Yet their way of arguing that Germany is no longer nationalistic, that the country is deeply and irreversibly committed to a 'Western' sense of values – the very manner in which such arguments are conducted – is distinctly German, and valuable precisely because it is distinct.

'Could it be that German nationalism was part of the Marxist resurgence?' Johan Galtung asks in his *Structure, Culture and Intellectual Style* (1981). I am sure it was. Yet for all its spasms of violence, its silly extremism and absurdities galore, this nationalism has sometimes sought its legitimation in the defence of modes of thinking that are eminently worth preserving, and not for the sake of Germany only. And that, after all, was Thomas Mann's mission too.

Then secondly, there are the Greens. Their hostility to parliamentary politics, and their questioning of the value and meaning of technology and its apparently inevitable progress, have their direct counterpart in the *Reflections*. Although Germany's Green Party is pro-European and vaguely socialist in its programme, its anti-political and anti-American outlook springs from the same unease with modern civilization as does Thomas Mann's book; the old Tolstoy is patron saint to both. Again it may be said that such radical anti-modernism has been used – for instance, by Heidegger – and might be used again, as part of an anti-humanist and anti-democratic ideology. Such dangers are endemic in all 'alternative' philosophies. But we find ourselves in a situation in which we can afford intellectual risks better than we can afford intellectual stagnation. To bring Mann's critique up to date while avoiding his self-regarding devices would be a task worth undertaking. But I know of nobody writing in Germany today who has the self-confidence, the imagination and the wit of this 'non-political man'.

1986

7

War and the Comic Muse

1

The bright idea from which Jaroslav Hašek's masterpiece developed happens to be clearly identifiable. On his somewhat unsteady way into the matrimonial bed after a night out, Hašek wrote the following pencilled note – the date is probably June 1911: 'An idiot in the [army] company. He had himself examined [to testify] that he is capable of conducting himself like a proper soldier.'

From this enigmatically phrased idea there emerges a picaresque novel, *The Good Soldier Švejk and his Fortunes in the World War*, first published in instalments from 1921 till 1923, a novel constructed on the principle of 'one damn' thing after another'. Its hero is one Josef Švejk, in civilian life a dog-seller and -fancier, resident in a working-class district of Prague and operating on the margins of the law. The novel begins with the assassination of the Archduke Franz Ferdinand, and the hero gets called up soon after the declaration of war in August 1914. It was planned in four volumes, of which a little over three had been completed at Hašek's death in 1923, at the age of almost forty – its continuation by one of Hašek's friends is a let-down. The sequence of the main story is determined by Private Josef Švejk's journey to the war, his various adventures on the way there (including his arrest as a Russian spy) and his disastrous doings in Hungary and Slovakia, and behind the Galician front line east of Lwów. Most of his time is spent as a batman to First Lieutenant Lukáš, a professional officer and 'decent Czech' who is serving in an army and in a war he secretly regards as hostile to his nation's interests. The war and the bureaucratic machinery set up to keep it going are presented as corrupt and unjust, senseless and doomed to defeat, yet quite inescapable, this inescapability being shown by the fact that however often Švejk 'gets lost' on his perambulations through Southern Bohemia, he always ends up at his battalion, 'for all roads lead to the war'. The Great War dominates each man's life – at least its outward circumstances and events – and the movements of war give what shape there is to the novel as a whole.

The world that fills out this mosaic is constructed on a peculiar principle of verbal and factual associations, and the language represents a very rich and original retracing of the Czech vernacular, differentiated less according to class than according to the level of education of each speaker. There is something characteristically Czech in the way that cultural differences are reflected in each man's grammar, his choice of words and even his syntax (and this is one of the many obstacles in the way of the English translator). That these are differences in education rather than social class becomes clear when we compare the merely unslangy and precise language of First Lieutenant Lukáš with the choice and involuted expatiations of the company cook, Jurajda; the former is a professional officer in the Imperial Army while the latter has a university degree and is described as an occultist and metaphysician by profession. Or again, there is the case of the infamous Lieutenant Dub (like Hašek's father, Dub is a secondary schoolmaster in civilian life, but I have heard it said that he is also modelled on a well-known Czech linguist). Here verbal precision and pedantry are used to a political-satirical end, for Dub's pretentious utterances are filled with the clichés of Austrian, that is anti-Czech, war propaganda.

However, contrary to our expectations (and to the claims of Czech literary criticism), Hašek's imitation of the vernacular does not descend to the level of naturalism; phonetic transcriptions are neither consistently used nor very close, and, as in Dickens or Kipling, are of a most conventional kind. As the late Sir Cecil Parrott, Hašek's devoted English translator, pointed out, Švejk speaks throughout '*common* [vernacular] Czech' (*obecná čeština*), an ideolect somewhere between slang and the literary or bookish language, which has no equivalent in English. Hašek's language, on the other hand, is set off with surprisingly formal grammatical constructions, and consequently retains a good deal of dignity. An example of this effective formality is Hašek's use of present participles: 'And so, mounting the stairs . . . for his police examination, Švejk bore his cross to the summit of Golgotha, knowing nothing of his martyrdom' (p. 19).

What is meant to be funny about phrases like 'mounting the stairs' or 'knowing nothing of his martyrdom'? The formal point is that such participles would not occur in a naturalistically rendered Czech narrative at all. The English reader must imagine a language, highly inflected in all its parts, whose untutored speakers wage a war of attrition against its more elaborate inflections; and the present participles with their agreements of gender and number are among the first grammatical forms that are worsted by its speakers, or worst them in turn. When Hašek introduces such forms, therefore, his basic intention is satirical; and this effect is heightened when (as happens surprisingly often) a New Testament reference is added.

But such passages are not only satirical, for these formal grammatical turns and the many references to Christ both have a peculiarly ambivalent – that is, partly serious – effect. When Švejk, on leaving the maddened Dub, mutters to himself, 'A little while and ye shall not see me: and again a little while and ye shall see me' (John 16:16), the sentence leaves the reader bewildered and even strangely moved – moved, that is, to ask what connection there might be between the passion of Christ and the journey of the good soldier Švejk (p. 568).

At this point a reassurance may be in order: I am not trying to make a Christian allegory of the novel. And let me add that even the one man in the book who is described as 'one of those few who still believed in the Lord' (p. 695), Padre Martinec, is shown up as both feeble and corrupt (though not ill-intentioned). But I do suggest that these New Testament references are far from being only satirical, that they belong to a hidden positive image of the central character.

2

The political intention behind the satire is obvious enough throughout: it is anti-Austrian and anti-Hungarian, patriotic Czech and anti-militarist. (On one occasion though (p. 361), Švejk does magnanimously remark, 'There's many a Hungarian what can't help being Hungarian.') Decent Czechs are shown to oppose, sabotage or ridicule the Austrian war effort, but the end towards which they are doing this is not shown. Hašek does not condemn war as such; indeed, the campaigns of the Czech legions in Russia, directed against the Austrian and German armies, found his approval. He believes in the possibility of a just war. What he condemns, through his book, is *this* war, in which Czech regiments were forced to fight on the wrong side.

The several groups of men who are linked by Švejk's pilgrimage are all more or less at the mercy of a war machine to whose aims they are more or less indifferent or hostile. Various cogs in this machine – imbecile staff officers and generals, corrupt military priests and judges, foolish aristocratic ladies masquerading as nurses, the chief cog, the ancient Emperor Franz Joseph and his advisers – all these are drawn into the satire, but they are rarely (p. 486) presented in that white heat of indignation and never with that exploitation of verbal ambiguities which we find in Karl Kraus's contemporary *Die letzten Tage der Menschheit*. In the third book, Švejk explains to Lt. Lukáš why he stole a hen for his (Lukáš's) dinner:

> 'Beg leave to report sir,' Švejk said pleasantly, 'there must definitely be a mistake somewhere. When I got your order to scrounge something good, I started thinking what might be best. Behind the station you couldn't get a thing, only horsemeat salami and some dried donkey steaks. Beg leave to report sir, I pondered everything very carefully.' (p. 548)

Now, this last phrase is a well-known quotation from Franz Joseph's *Manifesto to my Peoples* of August 1914, 'Ich habe alles reiflich erwogen.' But the satire is quite unemphatic; no issue is made of the phrase.

The satirical vein is patent throughout, and occasionally it degenerates into unfunny abuse (p. 77). The satire is derived from absurd situations, not from corrupt language, and it is not absolute satire. By this I mean that it is essential to Hašek's scheme that Švejk, the medium through whom the corruption is satirized, should remain in constant contact with, and be tolerated by, the world around him. Throughout, Švejk's patter finds ready listeners, high and low; and the fact that he is not immediately interrupted by his superiors and brutally disposed of is, within Hašek's scheme of things, just on the borderline of the credible (as it would not have been in Hitler's war). Hašek of course operates with an immense poetic licence. Yet the licence gains its foothold in our credence because the satire is not all black, because the condemnation it implies is not absolute: Švejk belongs to the world that encompasses him, and occasionally he can even change a bit of that world for the better. The situation is not unlike that of Gandhi and the British Raj. Like Gandhi's disobedience campaign, Švejk's obedience campaign works and is effective because each side proceeds according to rules recognized by the other. Where there are no such rules – as in the German occupation of Bohemia and Moravia in 1939–45 – Švejk would either go to the gallows or become a collaborator.

Similarly, Hašek's social concern is undogmatic and unemphatic: 'ordinary people' – mainly the private soldiers – are right; the lower-middle and upper classes – Germanizing officers, Austrians and Jews – are usually in the wrong; and one can easily tell in whose company one is. Unsurprisingly, recent critics have seen signs of anti-Semitism in such figures as the medical officer, Dr Grünstein (a notorious lickspittle) or the chaplain, Feldkurat Katz (who hocks the portable field altar). Writing after 1945, they see here prefigurations of the horrors to come; whereas Hašek is serenely undiscriminating in his pet hatreds, rather like the Red Indian Chief from Oklahoma who remarked, 'Racial prejudice is a terrible thing . . . It really is. It's a terrible thing to treat a decent, loyal Indian like a nigger, kike, wop or spic.' The 'social message' of Hašek's novel is hilariously at odds with the tenets of Socialist Realism, which has not, of course, prevented its votaries from claiming the novel for their own. He upholds a private integrity in the face of bureaucratic intrusion, and implicitly recommends behaviour which, from the point of view of the organization against which Švejk defends himself, can only be described as asocial and anarchic.

<h1 style="text-align:center">3</h1>

The most interesting question the novel raises is neither political nor social nor psychological, but stricly literary. It concerns the 'simplicity', 'honesty', 'wide-eyed naïvety' and 'goodness of heart' of its hero, which are asserted in numerous passages. Is he (to put it in the hallowed terminology of the British Army) 'plain bloody hopeless' or is he 'hopeless with intent'? Is the consistent way in which he responds to the world at war part of a private strategy? Is that strategy conscious? Occasional remarks of the author's suggest that the character of 'congenital idiot' and 'certified moron' is a deliberate ruse. Yet these suggestions aren't accompanied by any disclosures of what the Good Soldier 'really is', and so they appear to be inadvertent and remain isolated from the rest of the narrative, in which the character's ambivalence is faithfully preserved; as when, hospitalized but suspected of malingering, he is examined (not for the first time) by a group of army doctors:

> The members of the commission . . . were remarkedly divided in their conclusions about Švejk.
> Half of them insisted that Švejk was 'ein blöder Kerl' [an idiot], while the other half insisted that he was a scoundrel who was trying to make fun of the army. (p. 76)

Nor can Lt. Lukáš, friendly but endlessly exasperated by Švejk's antics, make up his mind: ' "I am convinced, Švejk," the lieutenant put in [on discovering that one of the suitcases Švejk was meant to look after has been stolen, a mishap Švejk feels compelled to accompany with a lengthy explanation of what 'undoubtedly' happens in railway stations, as well as a reminiscence about 'a certain young lady who was robbed of a pram and a baby girl in swaddling clothes . . .'], "I am convinced, Švejk, that one day you really will come to a bad end. I still don't know whether you're just pretending to be a mule or whether you were born one" ' (p. 219). This opacity of motive becomes something like Švejk's personal device; which explains why the reader is left with the impression that there is a secret at the core of Švejk's character. This secret is shared by no one, not even by Officer Cadet Marek, the nearest thing we get to a self-portrait of the author. Considering that all the figures in the book are seen in relation to the hero and hardly at all independently, Hašek's lack of psychological disclosure regarding his hero appears at first surprising. Each man's relation to Švejk determines his place on Hašek's implied moral scale, which stretches from 'decent patriotic' to 'corrupt pro-Austrian' (which, incidentally, is worse than 'Prussian'), yet none shares the secret of Švejk's integrity. You may take it whichever way you like: if Švejk is taken as 'plain bloody hopeless', then clearly he confides in everybody; if as 'hopeless with intent', then he confides in nobody at all, not even in those who appear to wish him well. Not that he always behaves in the same way. His more outrageous idiocies are committed in contact with his superiors; whereas with his fellow soldiers he shows a great deal of sound common sense, and on one occasion, when he forces a hapless orderly to complain of the vile treatment he had received at the hands of the monstrous Lt. Dub, Švejk is shown as serious and almost angry. Significantly, this is the only time when he not only represents the integrity of the private individual but actively defends it. Yet all these different and appropriate responses spring from a single, undivided mind – or, at least, from a mind whose divisions are not disclosed.

In other words, Hašek does not portray a man who knows one thing and does another, as Cervantes does in Sancho Panza. *Don Quixote* is one of the few books actually mentioned by the author (p. 162), but the connection between the two novels, taken for granted by many critics, is far from obvious. To set it up, one would have to endow Švejk with a combination of Sancho's practical astuteness (which derives from a cunning that Švejk does not display) and the Don's naïvety and candour (which lead to disasters that the Good Soldier does not encounter). Occasionally, the hero's guilelessness reminds us of Prince Myshkin's, but Hašek doesn't of course probe into the recesses of his hero's consciousness in the manner of Dostoevsky in *The Idiot*. The kind of psychological unmasking that Dostoevsky achieves – one thinks of the revealing scene between Myshkin and Madame Yepanchin on the subject of humility – has no parallel in Hašek's novel. What he stresses is Švejk's candour. The comic muse operates, as always, with a licence. But here it is the licence not to explore, to stop short of disclosure, to leave the hero's mind, and the huge joke of which the mind is a part, unanalysed. And seeing that Hašek himself was a natural storyteller and the least literary of writers, forever engaging in elaborate practical jokes, which started with the purpose of undermining the Austrian police state and ended up (as great jokes always do) oblivious of their ultimate purpose – in brief, seeing that Hašek himself was a 'natural', the incurious comic muse with which he operates is not likely to be part of a conscious design – though, conscious or not, the ploy at the centre of the book is a literary one. Author and hero alike seem to share a naïve, or at least an unexplored consciousness. The result is a comic inspiration unique in twentieth-century literature, though comparable with that of P. G. Wodehouse.

4

Not honesty, but a peculiar kind of lunatic vacancy – the vacancy of a sleepwalker – informs the conduct of the good soldier Švejk. But though Hašek's inspiration is naïve, it has its literary antecedent, in a conflation of the Fat Boy and Sam Weller, two figures from *The Posthumous Papers of the Pickwick Club*, the least organized and most popular of Dickens's novels. (Nor is there any reasonable doubt about this source; in 1917 Hašek wrote a sketch entitled 'The Club of the Czech Pickwickians.') The first of these figures, the Fat Boy, is the highly defatigable servant of Mr Wardle of Dingley Dell. His demeanour as he comes upon Mr Tupman kissing the maiden aunt, is the pattern of Švejk's characteristic attitude:

There was the fat boy, perfectly motionless, with his large circular eyes staring into the arbour, but without the slightest expression on his face that the most expert physiognomist could have referred to astonishment, curiosity, or any other known passion that agitates the human breast.

Mr Tupman gazed on the fat boy, and the fat boy stared at him; and the longer Mr Tupman observed the utter vacancy of the fat boy's countenance, the more convinced he became that he either did not know, or did not understand, anything that had been going forward. Under this impression, he said with great firmness, –

'What do you want here, Sir?'

'Supper's ready, Sir,' was the prompt reply.

'Have you just come here, Sir?' inquired Mr Tupman, with a piercing look.

'Just,' replied the fat boy.

Mr Tupman looked at him very hard again; but there was not a wink in his eye, or a curve in his face. (ch. 8)

Once the amorous pair have departed, Dickens abandons the device and tells us that the Fat Boy has observed everything and will in due course profit from his knowledge. Not so Hašek. Placing his hero in a more precarious situation, he is obliged to preserve 'the utter vacancy of [his] fat boy's countenance'. Only this device preserves Švejk's candour and integrity, and makes them effective in his encounters with others, above all with Lt. Lukáš.

It is in the nature of Hašek's narrative method that the unity of his novel must remain haphazard. The only noticeable development occurs in Švejk's relationship with Lukáš, who, as one example of Švejk's 'lunacy' or 'idiocy' follows another, comes to acknowledge and, against his better judgement, to respect, not indeed his cunning but his almost physical integrity. Once more Hašek is secretive – in spite of Lukáš's growing fondness for Švejk, the question whether Lukáš understands him is never clearly answered. But, all the same, a difference for the better is wrought in Lukáš's character as he comes to accept and even to respect, if not to know, the 'certified idiot' and his serenely disastrous antics.

Hašek's great admirer, Bertolt Brecht, understood something of this curious enigma. Švejk does not represent a positive ideology (Brecht writes in a diary note of 27 May 1943), he cannot be made into a 'cunning and scheming saboteur', for he is 'merely the opportunist of the tiny opportunities that are left open to him'. 'His wisdom', Brecht continues, 'is subversive. His indestructibility makes him the inexhaustible object of abuse and at the same time a source of liberation.' What Brecht fails to see is that Švejk's invulnerability is tied to a privileged occasion, and that it is an aspect of his undivided mind. His own play, *Schweyk in the Second World War* (1941–3), fails precisely because he does not follow up his insight into Švejk's character. Transferring the situation to Prague under the German occupation, Brecht proceeds by modifying both sides of the conflict. First, he unscrambles the enigma of Švejk's integrity. The Good Soldier is now shown as a small-scale operator, wholly conscious of his ruses, purposefully working against the Germans. This involves a complete loss of that very special innocent humour which is the glory of Hašek's Švejk. On the other side of the conflict are the SS-men and Gestapo officials, and they are presented as gullible and stupid beyond the limits of our credence. If names like 'the SS' and 'Gestapo' have a meaning for us, then that meaning is lost the moment the members of these organizations are shown as the victims of 'Schweyk's' not-very-clever ruses; and the Epilogue of Brecht's play, the encounter between 'Schweyk' and Hitler, is hardly more than slapstick comedy. The result of all this is disenchantment on the one hand and trivialization on the other – German humour at its grimmest. Brecht's 'Schweyk' is not very funny, and his opponents are not very convincing. Hašek's realism, we can see from Brecht's failure, is tied to a very specific situation, in which a double accommodation – the Gandhi catch – is possible; it is only in this situation that the funny enigma works.

The main narrative device Hašek uses to give substance to this enigma is association. The peculiar associative principle on which Švejk's never-ending anecdotal patter is constructed derives from Sam Weller, Mr Pickwick's amiable servant and companion. Sam Weller is introduced to us cleaning boots at the White Hart Inn (ch. 10); when the chambermaid asks him to hurry up because 'Number twenty-two wants his boots', Sam replies (*inter alia*): '"Who's number twenty-two, that's to put all the others out? No, no; reg'lar rotation, as Jack Ketch said, ven he tied the men up. Sorry to keep you a waitin', Sir, but I'll attend to you directly."' And *The Pickwick Papers* abounds with examples of Sam's characteristic ploy of commenting on any situation by means of an anecdote of doubtful relevance, thus:

> 'Business first, pleasure arterwards, as King Richard the Third said ven he stabbed t'other king in the Tower, afore he smothered the babbies.' (ch. 25)

> 'Don't say nothin' wotever about it, Ma'am,' replied Sam. 'I only assisted natur', Ma'am; as the doctor said to the boy's mother, arter he'd bled him to death.' (ch. 47)

> 'Wery sorry to 'casion any personal inconwenience, Ma'am, as the housebreaker said to the old lady when he put her on the fire' ... (ch. 26)

In both cases – Sam Weller's and Josef Švejk's – such anecdotes derive their humour from their partial or defective relevance to the matter in hand. The 'As' in 'As so-and-so said when he did such-and-such' is almost entirely a spoof. Yet there is a little more to it than that. For one thing, this anecdotal incontinence removes the anonymity of Sam's servant status and establishes him as a character in his own right. Furthermore, it gives substance to the contrast between the highly susceptible Mr Pickwick and his wholly imperturbable servant. Things aren't really so bad, Sam Weller seems to be saying through these anecdotes, for the last time something like this happened it turned out all right. Where Sam Weller is imperturbable, Švejk is also invulnerable. His endless anecdotes too are funny because they are partially or defectively relevant to the situation at hand. But of course, Švejk's anecdotes occur in situations a good deal more hostile than most of those that Mr Pickwick and Sam Weller have to encounter, hence their function is somewhat more complex.

Hašek's novel opens with a conversation concerning the assassination of the heir presumptive to the Habsburg throne, which leads to the declaration of war in August 1914:

> 'So they've killed our Ferdinand,' said the charwoman to Mr Švejk . . .
> 'Which Ferdinand, Mrs Müller?' asked Švejk, continuing to massage his knees. 'I know two Ferdinands . . .' (pp. 3–4)

What happens here and throughout the book is (to put the matter briefly and obscurely) an exploration of the possible, as opposed to the relevant, data of a situation. Thus, the mention of one Ferdinand brings up the mention of all the Ferdinands Švejk knows, then of all he knows about that particular Ferdinand (who, as we have already seen, 'used to chase those old bags in his summer residence'); the mention of the Archduke's murder with a revolver in a car in Sarajevo brings up the mention of all that Švejk knows about cars and about Bosnia, of his experiences with explosive weapons and (relating to the Archduke Ferdinand's corpulence) of the necessary size of targets, and so on. Two other works come to mind in which such a procedure – the full exploiting of all the possible rather than meaningful implications of a situation – is adopted: Laurence Sterne's *Tristram Shandy*, and the work of Hašek's contemporary and distant acquaintance, Franz Kafka. Which is the relevant parallel? On the face of it, it is the Shandean philosophy of composition, 'My pen guides me, I guide not it', a philosophy issuing in that enigmatic thing called 'pure humour'. Yet the mention of Kafka is not wholly misleading: for not only does Švejk's associative procedure guy the actual (as Sterne guyed Locke's 'association of ideas' arguments); like Kafka, Hašek through Švejk disrupts and makes nonsense of the actual. But whereas Kafka's aim is to show a firmly embattled outside world in contact with which his 'heroes' disintegrate, Hašek's aim is exactly the opposite: it is the outside world that becomes nonsensical, and it is the unexplored integrity of his hero that grows in assurance and strength. Thus, in that fabulous discussion about His Highness the Archduke Franz Ferdinand, Švejk makes nonsense of the actual – here it is the public sphere – by exploring it in terms of his own purely personal range of experience. To be precise, the other Ferdinands that Švejk goes on about are wholly irrelevant to the Sarajevo murder; to be more precise, the Sarajevo murder is wholly irrelevant to Švejk. To be precise, his patter is meaningless; to be more precise still, this patter is the most meaningful protection of his person and integrity available to him against the meaninglessness of history. Švejk is thus the very opposite of the 'existential' and 'alienated' hero: he renders the hostile world harmless by domesticating it and making it familiar.

5

We have now traced two stages of the associative device. First, in the essentially harmless situations of Dickens's Pickwick characters, the emphasis was on the discrete and accidental nature of the patter. In Hašek we find a second stage: the relevance of anecdotes to situations is still tenuous, always oblique, but it is certainly more firmly established than in Dickens. Perhaps it is not too outrageously Hegelian to say that here meaningless irrelevance itself becomes meaningful and relevant as a part of Švejk's unconscious self-protection in a hostile world. And here now is the third stage:

> 'They're trying to kill me,' Yossarian [said] calmly.
> 'No one's trying to kill you,' Clevinger cried.
> 'Then why are they shooting at me?' Yossarian asked.
> 'They're shooting at *everyone*,' Clevinger answered. 'They're trying to kill everyone.'
> 'And what difference does that make?' . . .
> 'Who's they?' [Clevinger] wanted to know. 'Who, specifically, do you think is trying to murder you?'
> 'Every one of them,' Yossarian told him.
> 'Every one of whom?'
> 'Every one of whom do you think?'
> 'I haven't any idea.'
> 'Then how do you know they aren't?'
> 'Because . . .' Clevinger spluttered, and turned speechless with frustration. (ch. 2, p. 17)

This is one of the many variations on the central ploy, turn and conceit of Joseph Heller's *Catch-22*, its pivotal paradox, the catch to which all other catches are related.

The novel describes the life of an American bomber squadron on an island in the Mediterranean towards the end of 1944. Like Hašek, Heller focuses on the war through the medium of an anti-heroic hero, Captain John Yossarian, a bombardier, aged twenty-eight. Both writers establish their theme by means of anecdote and expatiation in such a way that the conventional distinction between foreground and background disappears. In both cases the central theme is the preservation (in Heller's novel also the development) of the integrity of a private individual against, but also in full contact with, the all-but-overwhelming pressures of a world at war. Both novels proceed from firmly realistic bases to the heights of humorous and satirical exaggeration –

their humour is never disconnected from their realism. And both do this by way of a peculiar logic which is at once both a joke and an illumination of the logic of 'ordinary' life.

Let it be said straightaway that some major aspects of Heller's novel have no parallel in Hašek's, that *Catch-22* is, above all, a much more highly-wrought work. The good soldier Švejk is, I believe, the only genuine popular creation of modern European literature: popular in the sense of immediately appealing to unliterary and relatively unsophisticated readers; popular in the sense of being the modelled on them; and popular in the sense of being the product of an unliterary and naïve creative imagination. Heller's *Catch-22* is popular only in the first sense (a fact I was able to verify in the course of a lengthy discussion about the book with a forest ranger in the Rocky Mountains). The creative imagination behind its mode of composition and organization is anything but unliterary and naïve. It has a symbolical God (Major – de Coverley (ch. 13)), a devil who puts his eye out (the lewd old man in Rome (ch. 23, p. 253)) and an avenging angel (Nately's whore (ch. 33)). It has a complex time-scale and a structure of leitmotifs and carefully wrought repetitions and parallels, and its verbal texture varies and is carefully modified according to its narrative situations – and all these devices give it the highly sophisticated form of a post-Joycean novel.

The obvious direct influences of Hašek's work on Heller's seem to occur where the conflict between the military machine and the private person is presented in its crassest and most absurd form. As for instance in the figure of Lieutenant, then Colonel, then General Scheisskopf (ch. 29, p. 333), who, like Lt. Dub, is mad about parades, and when he cannot get his squadron to parade finds equal satisfaction in circulating notices cancelling parades which had never been announced in the first place. Similarly, the scene in which the two squadron majors – Cathcart and Korn – confer on whether to court-martial Yossarian because he did a second bomb run on a bridge over the Po at Ferrara, causing the loss of another aircraft, or award him a medal for bravery and promote him to a captaincy (in the event they decide on the latter course (ch. 13, p. 143)) could readily find its place in *The Good Soldier Švejk*. Again the affinities are clear in the lethal double-talk between superior officer and enlisted man:

Lieutenant Dub stared in rage at the serene countenance of the good soldier Švejk and asked him furiously: 'Do you know me?'

'Yes, sir, I know you.'

Lieutenant Dub rolled his eyes and stamped his foot: 'Let me tell you, you don't know me yet.'

Švejk again replied, with the serene calm of someone making a

'I *want* someone to tell me,' Lieutenant Scheisskopf beseeched them all prayerfully. 'If any of it is my fault, I *want* to be told.'

'He *wants* someone to tell him,' Clevinger said.

'He wants everyone to keep still, idiot,' Yossarian answered.

'Didn't you hear him?' Clevinger argued.

report: 'Beg to report, sir, I know you. You're from our march battalion, sir.'

'You don't know me yet!' Lieutenant Dub shouted again. 'You may know me from my good side, but just wait till you know me from my bad side. I can be vicious, don't think I can't, I can make a man wish he hadn't been born. Now do you know me or don't you?'

'I do know you sir.'

'I tell you for a last time you don't know me, you jackass . . .'
(p. 526)

'I heard him.' Yossarian replied. 'I heard him say very loudly and very distinctly that he wants every one of us to keep our mouths shut if we know what's good for us.'

'I won't punish you,' Lieutenant Scheisskopf swore.

'He says he won't punish me,' said Clevinger.

'He'll castrate you,' said Yossarian.

'I swear I won't punish you,' said Lieutenant Scheisskopf, 'I'll be grateful to the man who tells me the truth.'

'He'll hate you,' said Yossarian. 'To his dying day he'll hate you.'
(ch. 8, pp. 70–1)

The literal response is a man's only way of parrying the assault of the military machine, and occasionally he can even return the attack; a man's own words are his only refuge and far from indomitable strength:

The chief medical officer came up close to Švejk. 'I'd like to know what you're thinking about now, you bloated seacow!'

'Beg to report, sir, I don't think at all.'

'Himmeldonnerwetter!' bellowed a member of the commission, clanking his sword, 'So he doesn't think at all! Why don't you think, you Siamese elephant?'

'Beg to report, sir, I don't think because soldiers on duty are forbidden to. Years ago, when I was in the 91st, our captain always used to tell us: "A soldier mustn't think. His superior officers do all his thinking for him. As soon as a soldier begins to think, he's no longer a soldier but a dirty, lousy civilian. Thinking doesn't get you anywhere . . ."'

The colonel sat down and settled back, calm and cagey suddenly, and ingratiatingly polite.

'What did you mean,' he inquired slowly, 'when you said we couldn't punish you?'

'When, sir?' [asked Clevinger.]

'I'm asking the questions. You're answering them.'

'Yes, sir. I . . .'

'Did you think we brought you here to ask questions and for me to answer them?'

'No, sir. I . . .'

'What did we bring you here for?'

'To answer questions.'

'You're goddam right,' roared the colonel. 'Now suppose you start answering some before I break your goddam head. Just what the hell did you mean, you bastard,

'Shut your mug!' the chairman of the commission interrupted Švejk furiously, 'We know all about you. The fellow thinks he'll be taken for a genuine idiot. You're not an idiot, Švejk, you're cunning, you're foxy, you're a scoundrel, you're a hooligan, the scum of the earth, do you understand ...?'

'Beg to report, sir, I understand, sir.'

'I've already told you to shut your trap. Did you hear?'

'Beg to report, sir, I heard that I must shut my trap.'

'Himmelherrgott, then shut it! When I've given you orders, you know very well we don't want any of your lip.' (p. 76)

when you said we couldn't punish you?'

'I don't think I ever made that statement, sir.'

'Will you speak up, please? I couldn't hear you.'

'Yes, sir. I ...'

'Will you speak up, please? He couldn't hear you.'

. . .

'Yes, sir. I said that I didn't say that you couldn't punish me.'

'Just what the hell are you talking about?'

'I'm answering your question, sir.'

'What question?'

'"Just what the hell did you mean, you bastard, when you said we couldn't punish you?"' said the corporal who could take shorthand, reading from his steno pad.

'All right,' said the colonel. 'Just what the hell *did* you mean?' . . . (ch. 8, pp. 78–9).

6

As these parallels show, the same logic operates in both novels. To compare them is a little like comparing one of those primitive biplanes that were flown in the Great War with the supersonic jets of our age, in which a machinery of considerable complexity and sophistication hides inside a smoothly streamlined fuselage, an exterior that is as efficient as it is deceptively simple; and *Catch-22*, once the reader begins to make consistent sense of its slick and exquisite humour, is a complex, in some ways difficult book. Yet the streamlined jet is part of a development which begins with the invention of the flying machine. For what those spindly biplanes have in common with our jets is the crazy principle that makes it possible for an object heavier than air to keep flying, and it is this principle at work in both novels that I wish to describe.

Both novels are based on the premise that war is meaningless, or, to be exact, they portray war to the extent that it is meaningless. They avoid all questions relating to the consequences of victory or defeat, that is, any political questions. (In the situation Heller develops, anyone who is against Hitler is apt to be suspected of engaging in un-American activities (ch. 4, p. 35).) Švejk was drafted against his will and Yossarian volunteered for flying duties. But at the point at which we first encounter them they are both concerned with one thing and one thing only: the protection of the threatened self against the accidents of war, against violent death. Unlike Barbusse, Remarque and Arnold Zweig, our two authors raise no social protest against the war they are in. Unlike David Jones and Hans Carossa, they do not accept death in war either with stoic resignation or as a fulfilment of a man's destiny. Unlike T. E. Lawrence and Ernst Jünger, they don't attempt to show a cause that would justify the war. They regard violent death not as glorious but as unnatural, as the opposite of a normal, rational occurrence. It follows from this premise that, while the social organizations which aim at the prosecution of war and thus at the efficient inflicting of violent death have, *qua* social organizations, the *appearance* of normality and rationality, they are, seen from outside the sphere of their own (abnormal) purposes, the opposite of normal and rational.

By a stroke of genius Heller realizes this parody of rationality in the unsparing image of the soldier in white (ch. 17). He is the reality behind the Unknown Soldier of patriotic rhetoric: a shape in a field-hospital bed, wholly covered in bandages, existing only as a thing, an anonymous 'middleman' between two jars through which runs a clear liquid: 'When the jar on the floor was full, the jar feeding his elbow was empty, and the two were simply switched quickly so that stuff could drip back into him' (ch. 17, p. 174). And the charming Texan's attempts to make friendly conversation with that anonymous shape (ch. 1, pp. 10–11) and the nurses' meticulous polishing of its jars and tubes (ch. 17, p. 173), as well as the other patients' refusal to believe that there is a man inside the bandages at all, are the responses of various kinds of 'normal' rationality to the absurdity of violent death. More than that: the soldier in white is the novel's most perfect and most terrible single embodiment of the idea of self-containedness, and it is against this idea and its implications that Yossarian defends his threatened self.

Whereas Hašek allows for areas of more or less harmless humour, Heller is relentless in exploring the all-encompassing absurdity. His Major Major becomes a major through the sole agency of an IBM computer (ch. 9, p. 88), and is no better or worse a squadron commander than any of his fellow officers, who may have been less adventitiously appointed. And it hardly surprises us, in the context of this relentless exploration of the absurd, that the only man who has any real power is not a general or a colonel but ex-Private First Class Wintergreen (ch. 10). The colonels and generals of Hašek's novel, too, are imbeciles, but on the whole they know how to run their wars. Both novels have a good deal to say about religion as it is institutionalized by the military chaplains, and show that the moment the chaplains cease to be hypocrites they cease to have a positive function in the warlike organization: Heller's Anabaptist chaplain puts up some resistance to the military machine (ch. 36, p. 396); and it is the good soldier Švejk who offers spiritual comfort to the padre who visits him in the cell (pp. 698). In both cases there is only one enemy: 'anybody who's going to get you killed, no matter *which* side he's on' (ch. 12, p. 127).

The speaker is Yossarian, and it is in Heller's novel that the absurdity is drawn to its furthest and most radical conclusions. The narrative structure by means of which the basic logic is elaborated may be complex, but the sentiment it expresses is simple enough. Yossarian will never 'go gentle into that good night'; his friend Clevinger, 'the dope' who does, is doomed (ch. 12, p. 127). Yossarian never ceases to be outraged by the astounding fact that men, surrounded as they are by an inexhaustible variety of diseases, from amyotrophic lateral sclerosis through clap and Ewing's tumour to Wisconsin shingles (ch. 17, p. 177), should be seriously intent on adding to the means of their destruction. But since that is the case, and in the light of this undoubted fact, a number of events which otherwise might seem unacceptable become not only acceptable but patterns of normalcy. When men ditch their aircraft they cannot inflate their Mae Wests because the carbon-dioxide capsules have been stolen to make ice-cream sodas in the officers' mess (ch. 28, p. 316); first-aid kits are rifled for morphine syrettes, which are replaced by a 'note that said: "What's good for M&M Enterprises is good for the country. Milo Minderbinder"' (ch. 41, p. 446); Captain Milo Minderbinder – Yossarian's friend, and boss of a huge black-market empire that stretches across the whole of wartime Europe – consummates the logic of war by contracting his mythical Syndicate ('What's Good for the Syndicate is Good for the Country')

> with the American military authorities to bomb the German-held highway bridge at Orvieto and with the German military authorities to defend the highway bridge at Orvieto with anti-aircraft fire against his own attack. His fee for attacking the bridge for America was the total cost of the operation plus six per cent and his fee from Germany for defending the bridge was the same cost-plus-six agreement augmented by a merit bonus of a thousand dollars for every American plane he shot down. The consummation of these deals represented an important victory for private enterprise, he pointed out, since the armies of both countries were socialized institutions. Once the contracts were signed, there seemed to be no point in using the resources of the syndicate to bomb and defend the bridge, inasmuch as both governments had ample men and material right there to do so and were perfectly happy to contribute them, and in the end Milo realized a fantastic profit from both halves of his project for doing nothing more than signing his name twice. (ch. 24, p. 261)

Such absurd happenings carefully avoid any suggestion of the supernatural. They are first mentioned quite casually ('Milo was away, too, in Smyrna for the fig harvest' (ch. 2, p. 21)), in contexts to which they have no immediate relevance. And only when they have been thus insinuated into the unsuspecting reader's mind are they described in a detailed narrative (ch. 24), which moves from the plausible and possible to the unlikely and the absurd.

Is there no regard (we are sure to ask) for the fact that the Second World War, in which Heller's (highly autobiographical) novel is placed, was assuredly the most justifiable war in recent history? The novel contains a number of deliberate anachronisms – chief among them are the IBM machines and the daily and even hourly signing of the loyalty oath by all flying members of the squadron – and it avoids all questions of war aims. Its realism is a means to an end. Heller uses the Second World War in order to show the impact of war – any war – on the privacy of a human being. (Significantly, the novel was written during the Korean War, reached its immense popularity during the Vietnam conflict and seems to be tailor-made in respect of the Gulf War.) It gives no account of, and offers no comment on, the freedom-loving and tyranny-hating consciousness of the combatants. ('Who is Spain?', 'Why is Hitler?', 'When is right?' are the questions they ask during an educational session which Yossarian attends in order 'to find out why so many people were working so hard to kill him' (ch. 4, p. 35).) That this positive conscious-ness existed need not here be argued. But war, like every other human activity that is purposefully pursued, is apt to become a self-contained activity. Side by side with the men who fought and fight for a goal, and even inside a part of their minds, there existed and exists a barely human machinery concerned with war as an end in itself. To this machinery Heller addresses himself; against it his hero defends his life – not his life only, but his soul too; and in terms of this machinery the basic syllogism – the Catch itself – makes perfect sense.

So powerful is the peculiar logic of the self-contained activity that it confuses and plays havoc with the ordinary thinking of all who come into contact with it. Time and again people's rational guesses about a future course of events turn out to be wildly wrong; or again, while clearly intending one thing they unresistingly drift into doing its opposite. Thus Major Major is determined not to take Yossarian's side in the dispute over how many missions the squadron should fly, he is quite clear that 'one thing he could not say was that there was nothing he could do' to make the commanding officer (Colonel Korn) reduce the number of missions, because:

> To say there was nothing he could do would suggest he *would* do something if he could and imply the existence of an error or injustice in Colonel Korn's policy. Colonel Korn had been most explicit about that. He must never say there was nothing he could do.
> 'I'm sorry,' he said, 'But there's nothing I can do' (ch. 9).

This short-circuiting of the normal nexus between intention and action, as well as the anticipatory device which Heller uses to gain our credence for the more *outré* episodes, works also in respect of the novel as a whole. It catches its reader by insinuating as self-evident a logic which, by the time he sees it for what it really is, has played havoc with his customary notions of 'the meaning of war'.

Other writers have told the story of the conflict between the individual and the military machine. Heller himself has claimed Louis-Ferdinand Céline's *Voyage to the End of the Night* as his main literary inspiration; and he rated it (in an illuminating conversation) as a more important influence than *The Good Soldier Švejk*, which he regarded as 'just a funny book – a Polish novel or something, isn't it?' It is certainly true that, in its first 100 pages or so, Céline's novel is concerned with much the same conflict. But there is in that violent onslaught on the modern world practically no trace of the liberating humour that informs at least a part of every chapter of Heller's novel; and the distinction of *Catch-22* lies precisely in its treating the basic catch and its implications humorously. Nevertheless, there are strands of the utmost seriousness, and they run through the whole work. The violent deaths of many of Yossarian's comrades – particularly the death of his gunner, 'Snowden of yesteryear' – echo from the early chapters (ch. 4, p. 35) all the way to the end (ch. 41). In the narrative that culminates in the 'grim secret' that Snowden 'spilled' in the long hour of his death (ch. 41, pp. 446–50), Heller proves beyond any doubt that he is capable of rendering tragic emotions to the full, that his humour is not an evasion.

Death is a serious matter, and was so even before the Existentialists came on the scene. ('As a matter of fact it makes no difference' as Švejk observes on seeing a corporal spiked on a points-lever, 'whether his guts come out of his belly for His Imperial Majesty here or there. He did his duty all the same' (p. 486).) But death is also, as the Dionysian revellers learned, an absurdity, and it is the privilege of the Apolline comic muse to present its absurdity in a humorous light. Humour (one is tempted to say: all humour) involves an exaggeration. But is also involves a privileged occasion – the freedom, that is, to push to its extreme conclusion a situation we know to be partial and incomplete. Heller presents war as a self-contained activity (which we know to be only a partial truth), and at the same time exaggerates the implications of that activity. His achievement lies in the dovetailing of these two narrative elements, in convincing us that exaggeration, and incompleteness treated as completeness, form an integrated whole: and Hašek, too, though less purposefully, is concerned with the same peculiar enterprise. For the comic treatment of war no apology is needed: humour is too serious to be fobbed off with trivialities for its subject-matter.

At this point we may return to the essential affinity of our two novels. Given that war, as a self-contained pursuit, is an unnatural and irrational activity, it follows that the two heroes, Švejk and Yossarian, being bent on self-protection and survival, must adopt a conduct that has, in that context, the appearance of being irrational or, as Heller puts it, 'crazy':

There was only one catch and that was Catch-22, which specified that a concern for one's own safety in the face of dangers that were real and immediate was the process of a rational mind. Orr was crazy and could be grounded. All he had to do was ask; and as soon as he did, he would no longer be crazy and would have to fly more missions. Orr would be crazy to fly more missions and sane if he didn't, but if he was sane he had to fly them. If he flew them he was crazy and didn't have to; but if he didn't want to he was sane and had to. Yossarian was moved very deeply by the absolute simplicity of this clause of Catch-22 and let out a respectful whistle.

'That's some catch, that Catch-22,' he observed.

'It's the best there is,' Doc Daneeka agreed. (ch. 5, p. 47)

With that in mind we may now recall the soldier in the army company who asked to have himself examined to testify that he is able to conduct himself as a proper soldier. If he asks to be examined, he is bound to be thought crazy; and if he is crazy, he cannot conduct himself as a proper soldier and cannot be sent to the front line, to which he can only be sent if he conducts himself as a proper soldier: this is Hašek's equivalent of Catch-22. The difference lies in the fact that Švejk's psyche remains undisclosed – why should he ask to be examined? – and the ploy seems to work without a catch to it:

> The colonel summed up the results of his observations in a brief question which he addressed to the sergeant-major from the orderly-room: 'Idiot?'
>
> Whereupon the colonel saw the mouth belonging to the good-natured countenance open before him.
>
> 'Beg to report, sir, yes, idiot,' replied Švejk on behalf of the sergeant-major. (p. 309)

But the result of the encounter between the private self, consciously or otherwise bent on self-protection, and the military machinery – in other words, the encounter between reason and the irrational – works in the same way. For now along comes the military organization and cuts the tangle by the simple device of ordering each man into combat. To this each man responds in three ways: by mild sabotage, by feigning sickness and by feigning insanity. All three ploys work in the same way – that is, irrationally towards a rational end. A howitzer or an intercom that functions well really functions ill, and all you have to do is fiddle with it a bit so that it stops functioning and thus enables you to return to base. For both Hašek and Heller, a hospital is a haven of life, the world outside is contaminated with death; the doctor's function is to make you so ill inside that you become well enough to quit, but to be well enough to be outside is to be ill enough to die. And the 'crazy' ploy works the same way.

7

We can now narrow down the principle of self-protection at work in both novels. The Italian island of Pianosa where Heller's novel is set encompasses the whole world at war in the same way as does the Bohemian, Hungarian and Polish countryside of Hašek's; and the domination of each life by war is equally powerful. Yet each hero retains the charm and the enigma of an essentially private person – Švejk unconsciously and passively, Yossarian aggressively and by means of conscious stratagems. We know a little about Švejk's background. Twice we are told that his brother is a 'professor,' which is meant to explain why some of the stories he tells are so complicated. In civilian life he dealt in stolen and rejuvenated mongrels, but when he explains that he faked pedigrees, painted fancy spots on mangy dogs and cleaned their teeth with emery-paper in order to please his customers, we accept the explanation without demur – to impute to him purely pecuniary motives would not fit his character. About Yossarian's background we know nothing. His name – an Assyrian stem with an Armenian ending, and an echo of the name of Jesus – is designed to give away nothing; the name symbolizes his total rootlessness and detachment. Švejk's name is a philological enigma.* The Good Soldier's only amorous adventure, with one of Lt. Lukáš's mistresses, is put in his way by mere chance, and his purpose in visiting the military brothel is to rescue one of his superior officers. Yossarian sleeps with every likely woman (and some unlikely ones) and falls in love half-a-dozen times, once because he hasn't fallen in love (ch. 13, p. 137). And when one of his mistresses explains that she cannot marry him, because she is no longer a virgin and she would certainly not wish to marry a man who is crazy enough to wish to marry a woman he knows not to be a virgin (ch. 16, p. 162), we are back again inside the logic of the Catch. ('What a whore, she won't let me sleep with her!' is the enraged comment on the obverse situation that Švejk hears just before being arrested for espionage (p. 235).) But Yossarian's

---

* Unlike most Czech surnames, 'Švejk' does not derive from a meaningful root; whether the name exists independently I do not know, though it is said to be listed in an old Prague telephone directory as 'Švejk, J., úředník' (= civil servant). Its pronunciation is suggested in the spelling of Grete Reiner's German translation, *Die Abenteuer des guten Soldaten Schwejk während des Weltkrieges* (Prague, 1926), and by Brecht's quaint 'Schweyk'; the English spelling 'Schweik' in Paul Selver's translation (1930) is something of a compromise. The semantic value of the name is comparable to some uses of 'ain't' in contemporary literature. It turns on the dipthong (ει), which occurs mainly in colloquial Czech ('hovorová' or 'obecná čeština'), where it replaces the 'correct' form 'ý', especially in masculine adjecrival endings ('dobrej' for 'dobrý'). It might thus be reasonable to infer that Hašek chose or made up the name in order to intimate, as it were onomatopoeically, the comfortably popular *Czech* ambience of his hero. However, there is a disconcerting catch to this attractive theory: 'Schweik' (in this and related spellings) is listed as a common *German* surname in M. Gottschald, *Deutsche Namenkunde* (Berlin, 1945), p. 531, and in J.-K. Brechenmacher, *Etymologisches Wb. der deutschen Familiennamen*, 2nd edn., vol. II (Limburg, 1963) p. 578.

promiscuity, which has all the signs of wartime sex in the shadow of doom, is qualified by the fact that he gives away nothing of himself, that he remains inviolate. His 'crazy' character is informed by an exquisite balance between sentient openness and protective integrity. The private person remains inviolate, but not (as in Ernst Jünger and Hemingway) as an embattled toughtimer, not at the expense of his capacity to communicate with others. Švejk communicates freely with everyone around him by virtue of his equanimity and disarming good humour. Yossarian's need for communication and his capacity for feeling are established through a contrast which yields some of the most moving passages in the novel. His true antagonist is the lead navigator, 'good old Aarfy', the insensitive, unimaginative, unheeding man with a constant grin on his face. In Yossarian's moments of agony, when he is roaring with pain and the fear of death (ch. 26, p. 297), good old Aarfy notices nothing, he simply doesn't hear him. Situations like these make it unnecessary for Heller to engage in a close psychological exploration of Yossarian's mind. Nor does the psychologist who is detailed to analyse Yossarian's obsession get very far (but then, in both books, the psychologists are the servants, at once clever and crazy, of the military machine):

> '. . . Would you like a cigarette?' He smiled when Yossarian declined. 'Just why do you think,' he asked knowingly, 'that you have such a strong aversion to accepting a cigarette from me?'
> 'I put one out a second ago. It's still smoldering in your ash tray.'
> Major Sanderson chuckled. 'That's a very ingenious explanation. But I suppose we'll soon discover the true reason.' (ch. 27, p. 304)

And the 'analysis' continues, inexorably, to the borders of the logic of the Catch:

> '. . . You're immature. You've been unable to adjust to the idea of war.'
> 'Yes, sir.'
> 'You have a morbid aversion to dying. You probably resent the fact that you're at war and might get your head blown off any second.'
> 'I more than resent it, sir. I'm absolutely incensed.'
> 'You have deep-seated survival anxieties. And you don't like bigots, bullies, snobs or hypocrites. Subconciously there are many people you hate.'
> 'Consciously, sir, consciously,' Yossarian corrected in an effort to help. 'I hate them consciously.' (ch. 27, p. 312)

The balance that informs Yossarian's character has its exact parallel in the balance that informs Heller's book: the hero's self-protection and the book's humour are subtly matched by his sentient nature and the book's ability to give expression to the horrors of war.

The private person remains inviolate. '"Which Ferdinand . . . ?" asked Švejk, continuing to massage his knees. "*I* know two Ferdinands . . . "'; and '"They're trying to kill *me*," Yossarian [said] calmly.' My emphasis, in recalling these two openings, is on the two pronouns, 'I' and 'me'. It is, when one thinks of it, an absurd emphasis. A more or less civilized world is about to enter on a war of unprecedented ferocity and horror, and a funny, slightly corpulent fellow with rheumatic knees and a two-days' stubble on his chin talks about the Ferdinands he knows. And another war, against one of the most monstrous tryrannies the world has ever known, is to be won, and another funny fellow, broad-shouldered and handsome and given to appearing in public without any clothes on, complains of being shot at. 'I' and 'me': no egomaniacal self-assertion speaks from these words. No salvaging of any sublime spiritual values occurs. Bare survival even remains precarious, far from certain. And yet what the two pronouns – the two novels – intimate is something more than survival at all costs. (Yossarian is given a chance of that, and rejects it (ch. 42).) What they intimate is human freedom. A freedom which is hedged in on all sides, heavily qualified, but to us as readers all the more valuable because it is so heavily, so realistically qualified. The condition of this freedom is not barren detachment or alienation, but the sentience and essential integrity of the self in the onslaught of history.

8

The reception of *The Good Soldier Švejk* is a fascinating lesson in the relationship between literature and politics. Of course, the *haute* and somewhat pompous *bourgeoisie* of the First Czechoslovak Republic was incensed by it, regarded it now as subversive, now as pornographic, and took as little notice of it as it could. And while the Prague *Cercle linguistique*, famous for its concern with all sorts of out-of-the-way literary matters, totally ignored it (as it ignored the writings of Hašek's Prague contemporaries, Kafka and Rilke), the most influential Czech academic critic of the time, Arne Novák, disposed of the book quite simply by damning its hero. But when Novák describes Švejk as 'a typical clown and coward, idiot and sybarite, cynic and common scoundrel [who] denies not only the war but also the State, manly honour, heroism and patriotism', he seems to have forgotten that he and his fellow citizens of the new republic were the beneficiaries of what might be called Švejk's 'Catch-22+', seeing that the moment Švejk becomes an Austrian coward he becomes a Czech national hero. The other major Czech critic of the time, F. X. Šalda (whom we have met in an earlier essay), is almost equally sure in his put-down: 'Since you cannot speak of any consciousness or purposefulness in Švejk, he is for that reason poetically not so great and considerable as his admirers would have us believe.'

Then came the communists, who, in their anxiety to be 'of the people', decided to make Hašek a posthumous member of the Socialist Realist club.

The communist critic and poet Julius Fučík, who was tortured and executed by the Germans in 1941, tried his best; and to read his two essays on *The Good Soldier Švejk*, one written in 1928, the other in 1939, is a strangely moving experience in the art of political accommodation in desperate circumstances. The purpose of Fučík's essays is to appropriate the book's immense popular acclaim for his party, and to do this by validating it in Marxist terms – in the face of the popular understanding of it as a picaresque celebration of private and anarchic values. In the first essay, 'War against Švejk' (1928), Fučík was true to the book and hostile to its message: 'Švejk is an essentially non-revolutionary character, because he lacks the power and above all the conscious intention to do away with the political apparatus [of the Austro-Hungarian Empire] by means of direct action.' By 1939, when the political situation had tragically changed, Fučík had decided to enlist the Good Soldier in the struggle against the German enemy: he therefore endowed him with at least a potential revolutionary mentality. In the sentences Fučík now writes we notice that ambiguity – that peculiar conflation of the present with the future tense characteristic of the Slavonic verb system – where what *is* the case almost imperceptibly slips into what *should be* the case, and present unpleasant truths recede behind future hopes. (Ernst Bloch – see below – practised the same ploy but without having any excuse from the grammar of *his* language.) 'Švejk's development', Fučík writes in the dark days of 1939, 'which recalls Hašek's development, is only just moving toward a full consciousness, and you really feel that at a given moment Švejk will become serious ... and then, when things get tough, he will seriously and purposefully get down to the business of fighting.' Will he? Did Fučík really feel this? What he is expressing – it is this that makes the later essay so moving – is a despairing exhortation to his fellow-countrymen, not a plausible reading of the book. And finally come the Post-Modernists (among them the egregious Milan Kundera) who praise the book as an anti-Hegelian and anti-Marxist manifesto announcing the End of History.

The common denominator to all these misprisions is the critics' inability or unwillingness to envisage that great literature may have questionable effects on its readers and (as Plato argues in book 10 of *The Republic*) occasionally disastrous consequences. Occasionally: here certainly it is the case that the more attractive the figure of its hero, the more of a national stereotype he will become, and the more devastating his influence on the morale of the nation in its hour of need.

That Švejk is a national stereotype, like John Bull, Uncle Sam, Marianne, the Nibelungen and 'der dumme Michel' cannot be doubted. But do national stereotypes matter? It's not that they are likely to determine the political conduct of a society; but what possible evidence is there that they even mould it, that they matter politically? The popularity of Hašek's book is attested by the vocabulary (name, abstract noun, verb, adjective) that has sprouted from its hero's name: 'švejkovina' (on the analogy of 'oblomovshchina') has conno-

tations of cunning and scrounging, of cutting corners and choosing an easy
way out, of talking oneself out of a difficulty and then lying low. In other
words, while its readers may be able to preserve in their minds the ambiguity
which (as I have argued) lies at the heart of the novel ('plain bloody hopeless'
or 'hopeless with intent'), there is no ambiguity about the meaning of the
name as it enters the common language – the language and the political life
of the nation. Literary subtleties don't survive the crude 'either/or' of politics.
Thus a Czech dictionary, quoting from a newspaper of the late 1940s: '"Švejk-
ism" has become a concept which characterizes the passive form of Czech
resistance against the superior power'; and again: 'It is often said that during
the [German] occupation we used "švejkovina" to defend ourselves.' And
there are historians of 'the Bohemian citadel' who have traced this 'Švejkian'
attitude of conformism, moral laxity and unheroic 'realism' back to the defeat
of the Protestant Czech estates on the White Mountain in 1620, see it as
characteristic of 'the leeward life of the nation' under the Habsburgs throughout the next three centuries, and offer it as an explanation for a host of more
recent events: the Munich surrender of 1938, the relative weakness of the
Czech resistance throughout the Second World War, the passivity of the
country's liberal majority during the communist *coup d'état* of February 1948
and the four decades of subservience to Moscow, including first the Slánský
trials of 1952 and then the suppression of the 'Prague Spring' and another
capitulation in the summer of 1968. Seen in this cheerless perspective, the
'velvet revolution' of November 1989, too, appears as a spontaneous but
prudently delayed reaction to a series of events initiated in Moscow, Gdynia
and Warsaw, Budapest and (who'd have thought it?) Dresden, Leipzig and
East Berlin.
   None of this amounts to hard-and-fast evidence of the book's political
consequences, and each of these moments is compounded of many causes.
But there is the close family resemblance between the thinking and acting
conveyed in *The Good Soldier Švejk* and those moments of the country's
history I mentioned – a resemblance and hence a self-recognition which in
turn explains both the book's repudiation by some of its critics and its
immense popularity, and legitimates its representativeness: it is this resemblance that has spilled over into a cause-and-effect relationship. The weaker
and the more threatened the social and political institutions of a people,
the more it seeks to replace them by myth, which in modern Europe means
by its literature. Through its textualization, the funny mimetic tale records
and transfixes a type of behaviour whose paradigm lies outside literature,
and in certain historical circumstances (such as the death-throes of the
Austro-Hungarian Empire or of the First Czechoslovak Republic, or the
years of the German occupation, or again the endless years of the Soviet
hegemony) the mimesis itself becomes a political influence. (That those
circumstances are themselves in part the consequences of the mimesis of
an earlier phase complicates the argument by a further twist, but most
reflecting on historical causes is apt to do that.) In this sense, Jaroslav

Hašek's masterpiece is a politically effective historical document and a fiction alike: deeply depressing as one; exhilarating the way only great literature can be as the other. Even though the borderline between the two is unstable, there is no call to confuse them.

1968 (1991)

8

The Rise and Fall of Random Persons

1

My present purpose is to describe, and show some implications of, two kinds of knowledge of the past, which may roughly be called Nietzschean and Hegelian respectively. For the liberal imagination (to use Lionel Trilling's phrase for a disposition of mind worth preserving) these two kinds of knowledge are bound to have a very different appeal; yet I hope to show that both offer powerful illuminations of our common past, our *Europe des patries*.

Since it is now unfashionable and often thought retrograde to emphasize the ethnic origin of almost anything, including science and research, in view of some fairly massive discouragements a generation ago, preoccupation with unmistakably German thought of that era may require an apologia. Hence this comparison of two very different but complementary books, Oswald Spengler's *Decline of the West* and Erich Auerbach's *Mimesis: the Representation of Reality in Western Literature*: the recognition that both are the fruits of German scholarship, learning and speculation may contribute to such an apologia. But why call these books unmistakably German?

Friedrich Schiller's inaugural lecture at the University of Jena on the meaning and uses of universal history, delivered in May 1789, is famous for its attack on professional studies conducted with a view to earning a living and for his enthusiastic advocacy of the pursuit of learning for its own sake. The study of world history, he told his audience, belongs to the latter approach; *its* method alone deserves to be called 'philosophical'. While the bread-and-butter approach must emphasize the divisions and delimitation of its material, he continued, the 'philosophical point of view' entails above all synthesis and meaningful coherence – the rounded picture. Aiming at a 'harmonious whole', the universal historian may have to 'create' the harmony and 'implant it in the order of things'. True, 'the whole' that Spengler creates is anything but harmonious, while the political ends he pursues would certainly have qualified for Schiller's scornful rejection; but even so, Schiller's argument helps us to locate our inquiry. What places these two books within a German tradition –

albeit a tradition founded by Giambattista Vico – is not only their 'philosophical spirit', with its strong element of synthesis, but the fact that they display these qualities as *historical* writings.

2

Common to both books is what most historians – general and literary – would regard as their enormous scope: out of a multitude of colourful, occasionally lurid details energetically (and almost always accurately) recorded, their authors present large, panoramic views, and they give expression to strongly contrasting 'world feelings' ('Weltgefühle' – to use a favourite term of Spengler's), in the one case tragic, in the other realistic.

Each of these books appeared after a war that ended in a German defeat, Spengler's in 1918 (volume I) and 1922 (volume II); Auerbach's in 1949. This fact of defeat heightened Spengler's childhood traumas into a feeling of anxiety and universal decline, which he calls 'Weltangst'. Auerbach's reaction was quite different. He concludes his epilogue, written at the end of the Second World War, with words of hope: 'May my investigation contribute to bringing together again those whose love for our western history has serenely persevered' (p. 518).

To what extent are the themes and goals of both books comparable? Spengler's book is animated by the enormous ambition to portray the whole history and the entire cultural life of mankind in one categorical schema of eight cultures delimited in time and space, to investigate and evaluate them 'morphologically', and to draw a prophetic conclusion from his global inquiry. Auerbach, on the other hand, limits himself in his twenty chapters to a chronologically ordered investigation of a sequence of about sixty texts, beginning with the return of Odysseus to Ithaca and the story of Abraham and Isaac from the twenty-second chapter of Genesis, and concluding with Virginia Woolf's *To the Lighthouse* (1927) and with some remarks on Marcel Proust's novel; he writes the history of literary realism.

These two works share neither a common style nor a common structure. Spengler's *magnum opus* is conceived in a sharply authoritarian spirit; it is peremptory, dramatic and at times prophetic in tone; it is concerned to establish exclusions and delimitations; it is sometimes provocative in its literary manner; and it bristles with animosity and with a highly intellectual type of German nationalistic sentiment – a nationalism, however, of a paradoxical kind.

Auerbach does not assert, he recounts: liberal in its disposition and good-tempered in its tone, now and again gently ironic, his book seeks out points of connection and transition; suspicious of all rigid categories, he replaces them with penetratingly accurate analyses and interpretations of specific textual passages; and he portrays Europe, together with an aspect of the Near East, from the viewpoint of its literature as a Romance philologist reads and understands it, making it live once more for the reader.

Something of the different tempers of the two books may be gleaned from the maxims that guide them. Spengler repeatedly quotes an old favourite of Schopenhauer's, 'Fata volentem ducunt, trahunt nolentem' ('The fates guide him who would be guided by them, him who resists them they drag along'); in the worldly-wise fatalism expressed in these words the question of the nature and origin of those *fata* is left open. The humanist Auerbach, on the other hand, chooses the opening line of Andrew Marvell's 'To His Coy Mistress': 'Had we but world enough and time', the motto of every realism, literary or pragmatic, that ever was; which says that you have to cut your coat according to your cloth; fate and fatalism are mentioned only when they appear in his chosen texts.

And yet, even in their contrasting 'world feelings', these two books belong to one world, a world portrayed for us by Thomas Mann in *The Magic Mountain* (1924), with this contrast immortalized in the figures of Naphta and Settembrini.

Oswald Spengler was born in 1880, the son of a post-office official, into a lower-middle-class family, whose atmosphere of quarrelling and bitter hatred is reminiscent of the family dramas of Ludwig Anzengruber or of a Carl Sternheim comedy. After his mother's death, having secured his inheritance, Spengler immediately abandoned his hated duties as a teacher in a Hamburg *Gymnasium* and moved to Munich. There, struggling along in penury and often on the breadline, in lodgings a good deal poorer than A. Hitler's, seated in a chair placed on top of a table in order to keep warm, he wrote his book and doggedly, with an astonishing effort of the will, brought it to completion. He craved for success. Yet when success eventually came – massively and in every form – he felt cheated: like Naphta he is motivated by the very pattern of that *ressentiment* of which Nietzsche wrote.

Erich Auerbach – the Settembrini of our comparison – was born in 1892 into a wealthy upper-middle-class family (one of his Marxist critics, afraid that we might miss the point, speaks of 'Jewish Berlin *Finanzbourgeoisie*'). He studied first law and then Romance philology, was relieved of his position as *Dozent* at Marburg because of his Jewish origins; wrote his book in Istanbul, where he taught until 1947, and died in Yale ten years later. In the epilogue to his book he tells us, briefly but not without a certain satisfaction, that 'it is quite possible that the book owes its existence' to the 'lack of a rich and specialized library' (p. 518), which was not to be found at the time in Istanbul; for otherwise, he suggests, he might never have ventured to tackle such an enormous theme – a theme which, when viewed from the Spenglerian perspective, appears to be minuscule.

The Spengler–Auerbach dualism could be developed further. Thus one might contrast the Spenglerian sense of catastrophe with the entirely literary spirit of Auerbach, the Dionysian with the Apolline, the Spenglerian hedgehog with the Auerbachian fox; or again (to point to a parallelism which Spengler himself employs (II, 234–6)) one could see this contrast in terms of the tragic-religious world view of Dostoevsky as against the epic-secular mode of Tolstoy. At this point, though, this dualistic game becomes imprecise and misleading, and I had better turn to my real theme. Before doing that, a last general comment: although I personally prefer reading Auerbach to reading Spengler, I don't doubt that Spengler's book, for all its rebarbativeness, is incomparably the more influential of the two.

What both works have in common above all is their burning interest in the West. Auerbach's subtitle is 'the representation of reality in Western literature'; in Spengler this interest is evident from the title itself – his is the story leading to 'the decline of the West', a story in which continuity and discontinuity alike are placed in the service of an explicitly total view.

3

The object of Spengler's investigation and theoretical construct – of his knowledge and his fiction – is world history: in his own words, 'the world as history'. He sees this history not in the traditional manner as a continuous development of humanity through the three stages represented by Antiquity, the Middle Ages and the Modern Age, but, in scornful opposition to this scheme, as a discontinuous series of eight sharply delimited cultures, a succession of eight 'morphologically similar cultural organisms': Egypt, Babylon, India, China, 'Apollonian Antiquity', 'Magian-Arabic culture', 'Mexican culture' and 'the Faustian West'.

These eight cultural organisms run their course completely independently of one another (the only contact between them is entropic). Like the Egyptian pyramids, like the Leibnizean monads, these cultures are windowless; that is to say, there is no possibility of a reciprocal influence being exerted between the organisms, indeed there is not even the possibility of a reciprocal under-standing – the basic constitution of any one of these cultural organisms is fundamentally incommunicable, incomprehensible to the members of a temporally and spatially adjacent organism. Spengler gives these organisms the form (and, in metaphorical terms, the content) of Goethean 'Urphänomene'.

To the late-Wilhelmine public for whom Spengler was writing the appeal to Goethe was soundly patriotic and reassuring, not to say anodyne; we are bound to look at it in a more critical light.

In Goethe's scientific writings these *Urphänomene* are archetypal constructs situated halfway between observable phenomena and ideas; they represent one of the great syntheses of his philosophy of nature. Yet when applied to the human sphere, for Goethe believed in the fundamental unity of man and nature, these *Urphänomene* raised problems of morality and of the freedom of the will – difficulties which he sought to solve, not discursively, in the context of his scientific inquiries, but in some of his poetry and fiction, above all in his novel *Elective Affinities*. Spengler pays lip-service to these poetic and novelistic solutions, but he is untroubled by such doubts: in his scheme of things the moral problems entailed by his method are not allowed to arise. Taking his cue from Goethe's botanical studies, he sets up a rigid analogy between plant life and the life of 'cultured organisms', with the express purpose of demonstrating (or, as he would claim, proving) the 'organically' or 'morphologically' determined nature of 'the world as history'.

However, the way in which Spengler treats these 'cultural organisms' is influenced throughout and all but determined by aesthetic considerations. In so far as such aesthetic considerations have no direct bearing upon my theme I shall disregard them here; thus I shall have nothing to say about those remarkable art-historical and art-critical aspects of his work upon which Spengler deploys his great literary talent and rhetorical skills. Indeed, so powerful are the aesthetic insights he communicates that many readers have ignored the philosophical scheme and ideological substance of the work for the illuminations it yields as a *musée imaginaire* of the world's paintings, sculpture and architecture.

What is important for my purpose in this aestheticizing of 'the world as history' is the fact that it causes Spengler's interest to be focused only on the great individuals – on those who in his view are responsible, though in a peculiarly impersonal way, for the particular 'morphological' composition of the cultures in question, and who bring out and express the form specific to each. Concomitant to this is Spengler's belief that the bulk of mankind play no independent, let alone determining, role in the history of any particular culture; they exist only as background, mere stage décor or 'extras', or at most as the purely passive chorus of the old men and women in Greek tragedy. He is hardly concerned with what Auerbach calls 'random everyday persons' (p. 458), raised out of the sphere of anonymity; these, in Spengler's history, appear only as an object of contempt. In this he radicalizes Nietzsche's habit of 'unmasking' as illusory the claim that there is any positive connection between the great creative individual and the society that encompasses him.

Spengler does not offer any reasons why his analogical application of Goethe's morphology should be considered relevant or valid. To the question, 'What evidence is there that should convince us that certain insights and conclusions which Goethe reached on the basis of his study of plants are also valid for the history of man in his world?', we receive no real answer, for (as Spengler insists) his historical insights are to be evaluated not according to whether they are true, but according to whether they are 'deep and therefore fortunately unpopular', or shallow and therefore popular, for their unpopularity will prove his freedom from, and stance beyond, the ideas of his day.

Although Spengler argues against a Eurocentric history, it has to be said that his remarks on the Chinese, Indian and 'Mexican' or Aztec cultures are not very abundant, and his picture of ancient Egyptian culture is limited for the most part to a few 'symbols' (even though, in the second volume, on which he worked toward and after the end of the Great War, this sketch was amplified

by drawing on the results of the most recent archaeological investigations).
His treatment of the last three cultures is quite different: 'Apolline culture'
(the expression derives from Nietzsche, whose influence is at work both
generally and in innumerable details of Spengler's overall construction), which
includes Greece and Rome; 'Magian-Arabic culture', which embraces the
cultures of Judaea, Byzantium, early Christianity and the whole world of Islam
(here we find remarks which seem far more instructive today than they could
have been in the 1920s); and finally 'Faustian culture', which extends from
the Gothic Middle Ages, through the Renaissance, Baroque and Enlightenment, all the way to our own age – into that era of the West's decline, which
Spengler foresees as occupying the 'first centuries' of the third millennium.

Each of these organisms is subject to the same morphological development:
these cultures (as Spengler puts it) are all structured in a 'completely homologous' way. Each manifests the same sequence of forms; within these homologous developments we can see at work the law to which each of the organisms
in turn is subject. The process unfolds in three stages:

(1)   It begins with the 'original soul-like condition of eternal childlike
humanity' (I, 142 ff.). A cultural organism is *born* when 'a great soul' awakens.
In this moment of its awakening this soul takes on the individual form and
identity proper to it from the world into which it is born – a form arises out
of the chaotically amorphous, 'a temporally and spatially limited phenomenon
separates itself off from the unlimited and infinite.'

(2)   A cultural organism *blossoms* in the soil of a precisely delimited landscape
and remains deeply rooted in it, resisting all transmission or adaptation, like
a full-grown plant.

(3)   A cultural organism *dies* when the great soul which dwells within it and
defines it has realized the sum of all its attainable possibilities in the form of
peoples, languages, religions, arts, political structures and sciences. At the end
of this process the cultural organism returns to its original condition, the chaos
from which it sprang.

Here again Spengler appeals to the Goethean idea that all of the forms and
possibilities of life proper to an organism are contained in its original state,
its seed. But for Spengler the life of a cultural organism consists in a passionate
inner struggle – a movement in which the primary idea of the culture in
question asserts itself against the chaos working upon it from outside, against
the chaos of the next culture awaiting the moment of *its* birth. And this
passionate struggle against the outside, against the external enemies of the
cultural organism, has its counterpart inside the organism – the external
enemies have their inner fifth column which threatens the life of the culture
with chaos and subversion. All this occurs not as the result of any individual
decisions or of a free choice made by everyday people, nor even through the

decisions of the great heroic figures, who are great because they are the positive embodiment of their age, but 'strictly scientifically' ('streng wissenschaftlich', an expression which Spengler employs almost superstitiously), as the unfolding of a law which is not accessible or intelligible to the culture in question – a law which is really understood by one man only, a man whose name – though for reasons of modesty this is not frequently mentioned – is Oswald Spengler. And again, the appeal to the all-validating authority of Goethe is less important than the *sous-texte*, the hidden meaning of Spengler's argument: this passionate struggle of the nascent culture against the forces of chaos outside we recognize as a thinly disguised metaphor for the political struggle for self-realization, recognition and domination characteristic of German nationalism after the turn of the century.

I spoke of Spengler's aestheticization of all world events. This is reinforced by means of a further analogy when he compares the life struggle of a cultural organism to the work of an artist. Just as the artist struggles to embody his idea against the resistance of his material on the one hand and against the chaos which is said to surround it on the other, so also a given culture (which the artist embodies in his work) is said to stand in a 'deeply symbolic relationship' to the substance, to the place and time, through which that culture struggles toward fulfilment. Spengler's paradigm is Michelangelo:

> For Phidias marble is the cosmic substance which yearns for form . . .
> For Michelangelo marble was the foe to be subdued, the prison out of which he must deliver his idea

– and the comparison Spengler now chooses is not meant as a metaphor or analogy but as a literal parallel –

> as Siegfried delivered Brunhilde . . . Michelangelo did not assimilate [the rough block] from every aspect to the intended form [as the Greek sculptors are said to have done], but attacked it with a passionate frontal attack, hewing into it as though into space, cutting away material layer by layer, and driving deeper and deeper until his form emerged . . . There is no clearer expression of *Weltangst* in the face of Death as the completion of becoming – no clearer expression of the will to exorcise Death by means of vibrant form. (I, 352)

Michelangelo is *the* 'Faustian' artist at work, and for the cultural epoch he represents no other form of artistic activity than 'the Faustian' is considered.

The cultural organism moves into its final, decadent phase at the historical moment when the living idea from which the organism draws nourishment has reached its complete fulfilment – when all the possibilities inherent in the organism have been exhausted. At that moment, which Spengler sees as having been reached by the Faustian culture in the nineteenth century, the culture rigidifies, its force wanes and it turns into a 'civilization'. In this form the decadent culture may continue to live on for some time. The dying tree with its enormous decaying form overshadows the new, young culture which is about to arise, and impedes its coming to life: a process for which Spengler introduces the concept of the illusory form, or 'pseudomorphosis'. This is the way civilizations like those of Egypt, Byzantium and the Mandarin era have stifled new cultures like the Apolline or the Magian-Arabic. Here is one of many highly rhetorical formulations which describe this process in its terminal stage:

> This – the inward and outward fulfilment, the finality, that awaits every living Culture – is the purport of all the historic declines, amongst them that decline of the Classical which we know so well and fully, and another decline, our own, entirely comparable to it in course and duration, which will occupy the first centuries of the coming millennium but is heralded already and is to be felt in and around us today – the decline of the West. (I, 143)

Elsewhere he draws the moral-political consequences of this forecast:

> Whoever does not understand that this outcome is necessary and not susceptible to modification, that our choice is between willing *this* and willing nothing at all, between being in love with *this* destiny or despairing of the future and of life itself; he who cannot feel the grandeur that lies in the realization of powerful [technical] intelligences, in *this* energy of natures hard as steel, in *these* battles fought with the coldest and most abstract means; whoever is obsessed with the idealism of the provincial and would pursue the ways of life of past ages – he must forgo all desire to comprehend history, to live through history, and indeed to make history. (I, 51)

If we now ask what may be the meaning of this entire process, the answer is yet another aesthetic concept, that of 'sublime purposelessness' (*erhabene Zwecklosigkeit*) (I, 28). All of Spengler's parallelisms come under this characterization of a 'purposelessness' which is 'sublime' only because it is imposing and because it subsumes all world history and worldly experience.

Spengler's synthesis of the last of his cycles will illustrate his procedure. The cycle of the Faustian culture begins with the 'dawn of Romanesque culture and the Gothic', and is initially impeded in coming to a new life by the pseudomorphosis of the Renaissance – the Renaissance is seen here as a futile attempt to resuscitate and keep alive the culture of Apolline Greece. From this dawn, the argument leads us on through centuries of German music and philosophy to the era of the modern metropolitan civilization of New York, which is portrayed as the era of decadence and decline of Faustian values. The individual phenomena of the Faustian culture, which die out as it turns into a civilization, are not connected logically, let alone causally, but through associations and contrasts, metaphors and metonymies. Thus Apolline culture is characterized by the phenomenon of the human body – 'soma' – and the 'eternal moment', the 'nunc stans' – whereas Faustian culture is composed of *Urphänomene* called 'soul' and 'transience'; Apolline culture uses number as the means of calculating the proportions of the concrete physical body – whether this body be human, natural or cosmic – whereas Faustian culture applies number in a purely abstract manner as a self-contained symbol, exemplified in Leibniz's infinitesimal calculus; Apolline art-forms attain their highest achievement in sculpture and relief, whereas Faustian art-forms are characterized by perspective and oil painting; the classical temple, modelled on the harmony of the human body, is contrasted with the 'forest infinity' of Faustian Gothic and with the fugue-like treatment of space intended to reflect infinity; the Apolline representation of the body in the archetypal, more-than-individual nude is 'homologous' with the Faustian psychologising of the individual in the novel; ancient tragedy is defined by external circumstances and fate, whereas its Faustian counterpart is the tragedy of individual character; the finite cosmos of Greek natural science is contrasted with the infinite universe of Faustian striving; the sunlit proximity and intimacy of the Greek world are contrasted with a universe whose constitutive features are the symbols of night, distance and solitude; the *pastoso* Greek music of the lyre and flute is contrasted with polyphonic music . . .

What do we make of this astonishing panorama of analogies, parallels and metaphors? Though frequently irritated by the exaggerations – the sheer overkill – of Spengler's mega-arguments, again and again the reluctant reader is sharply drawn up by a sudden recognition that this is very far from being all fantasy and fabrication, that substantial and unexpectedly illuminating insights do emerge out of this boundlessness – insights which point up our knowledge of the past as well as our understanding of important aspects of the present. Distortion – a sort of late-summer madness of historiography – goes hand in hand with illumination.

Spengler's ambition, however, goes beyond this. A guiding motif I have already hinted at emerges from this pattern of contrasts. A culture which is called Faustian and whose basic concepts or symbols are given as soul, transience, infinity, extension and the will to power and whose full realization bears the names of Leibniz, Bach, Beethoven and Goethe's *Faust II* – such a culture is conceived fundamentally as a German phenomenon. But at the same time history becomes for Spengler a means of invoking and articulating a 'world feeling', and the world feeling which finds expression in Faustian culture he calls 'Weltangst' – a deep and traumatic anxiety and fear of the world as the harbinger of death. In this way he becomes a late spokesman of that cultural pessimism which was fashionable among the intellectuals of the Wilhelmine era and with which, both before and during the Great War, they sought at once defensively and aggressively to preserve the spiritual particularity and integrity of Germany against 'the West' and the ideas of the French Revolution.

However, this Spenglerian nationalism is a highly paradoxical thing. On the one hand we read: Western culture is entering upon its process of decline, and Germany is part of the West. Germany must therefore relinquish the values of its own Faustian culture, which are now without particular meaning and purpose, and it must resolutely accomplish the next historical phase, that of technological civilization – Germany must now assert itself in the sphere of the new scientific discoveries. On the other hand: Germany is different, it is played off against the West and the rest of Europe. It can and must preserve its own Faustian values and inwardness, and in this way ensure its continued life and power. At this point, Spengler abandons his cultural relativism and is silent on the subject of pseudomorphosis. Like Spengler himself, Germany turns out to be the exception to the set of historical laws he has drawn up: now the future is said to belong to the German engineer and natural scientist who will preserve the German Faustian feeling of infinity and *Weltangst*, a world feeling grounded in the knowledge of the 'sublime purposelessness' of the whole process.

4

I turn now to the second part of my comparative sketch.

Auerbach's book, in contrast to Spengler's, traces the course of a single cultural development. The history of mimesis as Auerbach depicts it in his twenty chapters is the history of an expanding literary vocabulary, an increasingly rich treasure-house of literary forms, and this expansion involves not only an artistic enlargement but also an existential enrichment; new experiences seek out and find new forms. Western literature as Auerbach views it is the correlative of the Western experience: what he describes is the closely-wrought chain of what we have come to call literary narratives.

The broad premises on which the book is based are not as self-evident today as they were when it was published, so I shall start by enumerating them:

1   life in the world is a serious business and, for that reason, on the whole worth living;
2   life is, on the whole, recordable, a possible, worthy and adequate subject-matter of literature;
3   literature is worth reading and, on the whole, makes the world a better place to live in;
4   the works of literature are not self-generated agglutinations of words but have authors, often known and occasionally unknown; and the relationship between author and work can be one of mutual illumination;
5   a critic can be methodical without boring his readers with methodology; and
6   in some literary texts there are words which are so arranged that they

watch the text watching itself, but in all literary texts there are words which refer to things in the world. (I mention this referential premise last because it is the last thing it would have occurred to Auerbach to doubt.)

All this makes *Mimesis* not necessarily an optimistic book but certainly an immensely humane and cheerful one. It need not surprise us that, since the sort of 'sour kitsch' that prevails in some literary circles in Germany denies some or all of these premises, the book has been and continues to be ignored there; and the reasons why it is falling into neglect in this country may be similar.

Auerbach's procedure is analytical: the book begins with a stylistic examination of an episode in the *Odyssey* (book XIX), the story of the scar on Odysseus' thigh, by which the nurse Eurycleia recognizes him on his return to Ithaca; and the style of this is contrasted with 'an equally ancient and equally epic style from a different world of forms' (p. 5), the account, in Genesis 22, of the abandoned sacrifice of Isaac by Abraham. In his next chapter, three passages are contrasted: a scurrilous characterization given by Petronius of a fashionable society hostess at a banquet (used by Fellini in his *Satyricon* film); the account of a revolt among the Germanic legions from book I of Tacitus's *Annals*; and the arrest of Jesus, and Peter's denial of him, taken from Mark 14: 42–53, 66–72. Auerbach emphasizes the sheer variety of his sources, yet some elements from each are taken up in successive chapters; the analyses which give coherence to his book are cumulative.

In chapter 3, from which I will illustrate his procedure, a cluster of four analyses are added to the chain. The first is a passage from Ammianus Marcellinus, a high-ranking army officer and historian who, reporting on events between 353 and 378 AD, gives a vivid account of the unsuccessful revolt of the Roman *plebs*, egged on by a ruffian called Petrus Valvemerus. Ammianus's narrative is remarkable for its violence, sensuality and touches of sadism; its dominant note is not a realism of description so much as a dark frenzy set off by glaring colours. The high point is reached when Petrus is strung up, his hands bound behind his back, and 'flayed until his sides were harrowed open', while the mob, 'darting venomous glances like snakes', quickly flee, abandoning their leader to his fate. The narrator offers no motive for the revolt apart from insubordination and effrontery; the revolt is presented as a senseless attempt to indulge in brute force – even 'the scarcity of wine' as a possible reason for discontent is merely 'alleged'. All this is couched in a high rhetorical style that has its roots in Tacitus, but here expands into unbridled violence. The detailed reconstruction of the devices used by the narrator to achieve this complex effect, amounting to a 'mixture of rhetorical devices of the most sophisticated sort coupled with a glaring and boldly distorted realism', shows that they are used to reflect accurately the historical situation of the Roman upper-class intellectual in the last phase of the Empire. Here and there in this passage from Ammianus we are reminded of Kafka (this is the only time his name is mentioned in Auerbach's book), but there is here also an element of 'senseless silliness' (*Albernheit*) which has no parallel in Kafka.

The second passage exhibited in this chapter, from Apuleius's *Metamorphoses* (after 175 AD), displays the same violence and senselessness ('fear, lust and silliness') as the first, in a story as trivial as any in Petronius, in which the narrator, shopping for fish in the market, ends up losing both his money and his purchase through the gratuitous intervention of a friend, the aedile in charge of the market police. The episode, which ends messily, with the fish being trodden to pulp on the pavement of the market-place by order of the law, seems designed as a malicious and pointless practical joke. Auerbach's purpose is to show that the same 'progressive undermining of the classical separation of styles' and the same distortion of ordinary events into the gruesome and grotesque as found in the Ammianus passage may, as here, serve very different ends.

For now, in the third of these exemplary analyses, we leave *belles-lettres* and are taken through a hortatory epistle by St Jerome, one of the Latin Church Fathers at the end of the fourth century and beginning of the fifth. The gratuitous senselessness of the first two texts gives way to a tale of Christian morality. Jerome's letter tells of a woman of noble descent who has died and whose surviving husband, Pammachius, decides to sell all he has, including the rich jewellery and clothes she wore, and use the money to bring comfort to the poor. Extreme riches and extreme poverty are the two poles of the homiletic tale: the money from selling the 'shining gems ... silken robes interwoven with threads of gold ... luxuries' goes on the sustenance of the blind, on the support of a beggar with mutilated feet, on food for another, 'whose swollen belly is pregnant with his own death ... In them [the bereaved husband] cares for Christ, in their squalor he is washed white ... Other husbands scatter on their wives' graves violets, roses, lilies and purple flowers, and these offerings console the grief of their hearts. Our Pammachius sprinkles the balsam of mercy upon the sacred ashes and venerable bones.' The 'baroque' extremity of the contrasting descriptions (the 'shining gems ...' as against the afflicted beggars) is matched by the extremity of the moral exaction.

And so Auerbach sets the scene for that famous passage in the *Confessions* (book 6, chapter 8) where St Augustine tells how Alypius, a friend of his youth, 'being utterly opposed to and detesting gladiatorial spectacles', is seduced by his fellow students to attend one of these gory shows. Again violence, frenetic bloodlust and the magic of a raging crowd are evoked. Dragged into the amphitheatre by his fellow students, Alypius has shut his eyes, only the roar of the crowd reaches him – but it proves too much: 'Supposing himself strong enough to despise whatever he saw and to conquer it, he opened his eyes. He was struck in the soul by a wound graver than the gladiator in his body, whose fall had caused the roar. The shouting entered by his ears and forced open his eyes. Thereby it was the means of wounding and striking to the ground a mind still more bold than strong, and the weaker for the reason that he had presumed on himself when he should have relied on you [Lord].' Losing his self-possession in the intoxicating spectacle, 'he looked, he yelled, he was on fire, he took the madness home with him so that it urged him to return not only with those by whom he had originally been drawn there, but even more than them, taking others with him. Nevertheless,' Augustine concludes, 'from all you delivered him [Lord] by your most powerful and merciful hand, and you taught him to put his confidence not in himself but in you. But that was much later.' In the outcome of this episode – Alypius's conversion – the repentance of Peter after his denial of Christ and the conversion of Paul on the road to Damascus are re-enacted. Augustine's rhetorical devices – above all the Catilinarian parataxis and parallel clauses – create a mixture of styles which serves to embody an intense psychological struggle; but that struggle in turn is subordinated to the homiletic purpose, the representation of Christian doctrine in its relevance to the salvation of random persons in the worldly world. Christ himself (Auerbach returns to Peter's denial of him) comes not as a hero or king, but as a human being of the lowest social station, and Christ's passion, when he was 'treated as a low criminal ... mocked, spat upon, whipped and nailed to the cross, ... engenders a new, elevated style, which does not scorn everyday life and which absorbs the sensorially realistic, even the ugly, the undignified, the physically base.' Or, Auerbach adds, 'if you prefer to put it the other way round – a new *sermo humilis* is born, a low style such as would properly be applicable only to comedy, but which now reaches far beyond its original domain and touches on the deepest and highest, the sublime and the eternal.' The address to the reader here is not arbitrary, for in the alternative formulation not only the rhetorical terms but also the secular values are reversed. Auerbach traces the history of realism; moreover, he does so in the realist mode.

Throughout the book we encounter a remarkable paradox. His literary interest, his three kinds of analysis – historical, psychological and stylistic, including his preoccupation with *Stilmischungen* and literary genres – all these are worldly, 'immanent' investigations, and even where he reports on religious matters he does so by reverting to human relations within finite, worldly situations; yet we come away from reading his book with a very clear impression of man's spiritual dimension. This, we can see, is Auerbach's main theme: the more fully 'the serious representation of everyday reality' is achieved, the more broadly conceived the social setting from which literature generally and then the prose novel in particular choose their characters, the more consistent will be the realism which represents this constantly expanding world of themes. And the role and status of the Gospels in this history – in this development – of literature are clear: it is through the Gospels as accounts of the life of Jesus that quite ordinary people (people who in worldly terms are in no way distinguished) appear in the domain of serious literature for the first time; and this human worth, which is attributed to them in the Gospels, will not be lost, even in periods of waning belief or of unbelief.

5

Oswald Spengler too gives a place in his 'world as history' to Jesus 'the son of man', 'the redeemer sent into the depths'. Here at all events Spengler is consistent in his cultural relativism: living at the close of the Magian-Arabic cultural cycle, Jesus is for him the lonely and isolated prophet of his own solipsistic vision. Jesus's prophetic teaching (we are told) does not extend beyond his own culture, the religious feeling that survives him is a pseudo-morphosis. The significant moment singled out in the drama that Spengler's rhetoric conveys is the confrontation of two cultures:

> But when Jesus was taken before Pilate, the world of facts and *the world of truths stood face to face in immediate and implacable hostility*. It is a scene appallingly distinct and overwhelming in its symbolism, such as the world's history had never before and has never since looked on . . . In the famous question of the Roman Procurator, 'What is truth?' – the one sentence that is race-pure in the whole New Testament – lies *the entire meaning of history*, the exclusive validity of the deed, the prestige of the State and of war and blood . . . (II, 262)

('Das einzige Wort im Neuen Testament, das Rasse hat' takes up a remark from Nietzsche's *Anti-Christ*, where Pontius Pilate is described as the only true gentleman in a book full of plebeians.)

Spengler's way with quotations is very different from Auerbach's: on the basis of a single fertile insight an unlimited total view is asserted. Christ's words, 'My kingdom is not of this world' (John 18:36), are turned into a maxim of Spengler's morphological approach, which insists everywhere on separation, exclusion and segregation, denying every possibility of communication. The Christian message of salvation (as in Christ's words to the thief on the cross) is ignored. The message Spengler takes from the Gospels is the incompatibility of the two kingdoms, the absolute duality of darkness and light. On this Manichaean view of Christianity an absolute separation of politics and religion, of Church and State, of facts (that is *Realpolitik*) and truth is set up:

> No faith has yet altered the world and no fact can ever refute a faith. There is no bridge between directional Time [time directed by worldly goals] and Eternity, between the *course* of history and the *existence* of a divine order in the structure of which the word 'providence' describes the highest form of causality. *This is the final meaning of the moment in which Jesus and Pilate confronted one another.* (II, 263)

('Gerichtete Zeit', 'directional Time', is a chilling pun, for it also means 'time that has been executed', the death of Time).

Auerbach's conception of the human-Christian, his embedding of the spiritual in the human and worldly and his conception of history as development are incompatible with Spengler's 'religion in the supersensory sphere', religion seen as hostile to life in the world. And the new 'mixed style' that Auerbach traces back to the combination of *humilitas* and *sublimitas* (the terms come from St Augustine's commentaries), that is eventually seen as the direct forebear of modern Western realism – this new style bestows dignity and value on those random persons who play the role of extras in the crowd scenes of Spengler's 'world as history'.

This is one fundamental difference which our comparison yields. There is another. To the question of how these two books achieve their inner coherence and continuity, we receive for each a fundamentally different answer. Where Spengler relies on his organic-morphological method, Auerbach brings into play the concept of *figura* which he derives from Patristic rhetoric: 'Figural interpretation' (other writers speak of 'typology') 'establishes a connection between two events or persons in such a way that the first signifies not only itself but also the second, while the second involves or fulfils the first . . . The two poles of a figure are separated in time, but both are contained in the flowing stream which is historical time' (p. 75). True, the method cannot be applied directly to post-medieval literature. Yet it remains relevant to most of the modern literature that makes up the canon of Auerbach's book, at least in so far as it is populated by those 'everyday persons' who have inherited the value implied in the singling out of any figure, historical or fictional, for figural interpretation; and it is no accident that Auerbach's least successful critical studies are concerned with writings which call that inherited value into question. Any reader who cares to remember what the recent European past was like in places where 'ordinary people' ceased to have any value, will feel some sympathy for his limitation.

There is an inevitable element of contingency in Auerbach's method: *what* is singled out as a *figura* or as a representative text will depend upon an initial intuition – the critic's eye for what will turn out to be suitable – and on the persuasiveness and convincingness he is able to muster in presenting his choices – but then, the rhetoric of convincing insights is the very pattern of literary criticism, the bread-and-butter of the critical vocation. Spengler's procedure is very different. He too draws abundantly on metaphors and analogies for conviction. But whereas Auerbach's comparisons are in the service of the individual texts he analyses, Spengler's 'homologies' are in the service of his over-all scheme. There can be no doubt that Spengler opens up for us astonishing and illuminating perspectives, but each one of his insights is subordinated to the act of will manifest in the 'method'; and that, though he calls it 'strictly scientific', is not just contingent but again and again merely arbitrary. The history he writes contains elements of abstract fiction; his aim – at first merely implied, then gradually rising to the level of a *weltanschaulich* creed, and ending in the second volume with a prophetic *fortissimo* – issues in a politically effective myth, among the most powerful of his time.

The result of our comparison turns out to be surprising, indeed paradoxical. Whereas Auerbach pursues his technical investigations to the point where they contribute to moral insights into the history – that is, the development – of Western mankind, Spengler on his immense canvas uses moral insights (together with political, social, religious, scientific and aesthetic insights) as elements in a synchronic, panoramic view. Whereas Auerbach's study moves from aesthetic considerations toward a sequence – a true *nacheinander* – of diachronic illuminations of the being of man, Spengler aestheticizes – not finally, but each time anew – the 'world as history' as a 'morphology of man' made up of the forms of life. Thus Spengler, though his investigations are as varied and all-encompassing as he can make them, ends up with a mere *nebeneinander* in which each picture offers a more partial view of man than do the scenes from Auerbach's much more restricted history. And this difference takes us finally to their fundamentally different visions – the one humanistic, the other naturalistic – of the being of man. For Auerbach, men and women seek their fulfilment as free creatures in a world made meaningful by the actuality, and then the fading memory, of the Christian tradition. For Spengler, their fulfilment is identical with their nature, man is wholly and inexorably a part of the natural (the 'strictly scientific', determinable) world; here the only transcendence that is not relativized is that of the superior, universal understanding of one observer – Spengler, that supposedly detached observer, is his own god.

Where then is the truth to be found? In Auerbach or in Spengler; in Settembrini or Naphta? In the precise insights of the inspired philologist, in his literary history that is patiently built up from individual syntactic, lexical, stylistic and historical investigations? Or in the hard, sometimes hysterical and often only arbitrarily grounded constructions of Spengler? In the one who has 'a pragmatic faith in our spontaneous ability, based on our own experience, to understand one another', or in the other, who asserts that there are no windows from one culture to another? In the one who loves literature for its humanity, or in the other, who is in love with everything catastrophic, everything that separates peoples and people, to whom the charm of the lives and adventures of random persons means nothing and whose style of thinking and writing proclaims that will to power which Nietzsche described?

The obvious answer is that Auerbach in his depiction on the smaller canvas is the more accurate and truthful of the two. Why then is Spengler's book the more influential? His accuracy, indeed his truthfulness, is of a different kind. His work is not only descriptive but also, as he himself repeatedly claims, an attempt (he of course calls it the first attempt) to determine history in advance (I, 3), and that in a double sense: to see what will be, and to bring about what must be. Thus not only is the book a series of descriptions, but it also expresses political intentions, intentions which, together with the intentions of others, came to exert an influence on the course of history itself. Intentions become descriptions; descriptions in turn serve intentions. Of course, his predictions have not been fulfilled and his intentions have been overtaken by that course of history to which he so often appeals. Intent on writing a history of the world, he has done what was only marginally within Auerbach's scope: all but unwittingly Spengler has given us a portrait of his own time. It is this twofold achievement that makes his the more problematic and the more important of the two books.

It is no thanks to Spengler that the predicaments in which we find ourselves are different from anything he predicted. And yet, since an understanding of our situation is for us a matter of great urgency, we must not ignore any evidence concerning how it came about. Although the sources of historical insight are bound to be grounded in a national culture, the understanding which they yield can today be no longer particularist or nationalist – which is why we need both books.

1985

9

Freud by a Freudian

1

Professor Peter Gay is an eminent American cultural historian of German origin, an enthusiastic convert to Freudian doctrine and an honorary member of the American Psychoanalytical Association – you can't, as a warmly sympathetic biographer of Freud, do better than that. The sheer amount of biographical and psychoanalytical detail that has gone into the making of his *Freud: a Life for Our Time* is, as far as I can see, unparalleled in the literature of its subject; and so are the care and informed intelligence with which this stupendous mass of facts, conjectures and speculations has been sifted, as well as the attractive, good-humoured and unstrenuous way in which most of it has been presented. The book could have been shorter: some of the bitter quarrels fought out in Freud's circle of disciples, some of the tales of defection and betrayal, and some of the inconclusive arguments relating both to the most controversial of Freud's publications and to his personal attitudes are written out at greater length than seems necessary, and some quotations don't improve by being repeated. But even where similar insights are presented more than once, the *longueurs* seem to have been caused, not by a loss of narrative control, but by a scrupulous regard for fairness – fairness, one need hardly add, to Freud rather than to his adversaries.

In one sense, the subtitle of the book is justified. Gay has been able to use a great deal more material than did Ernest Jones when he wrote his three-volume *Sigmund Freud: Life and Work* (1954–7). And as long as the guardians of Freud's archives continue to exercise their censorship (which, now that scarcely any of the participants in this story are still alive, seems indefensible), this is bound to remain the definitive biography. In the bibliographical essays appended to each chapter Gay has indicated what the nature of the material still being withheld is likely to be, and how it may affect his own conclusions. (Thus one may infer from the evidence hinted at that Freud's own sex life, which, it had seemed, came to an end when he was not quite forty-four years of age, may turn out to have been less impoverished.) Gay is scrupulous in

141

his affection, claiming to have preferred reasonable and probable conjectures to scandalously improbable ones. By and large, this is a remarkably accomplished and rounded portrait of one of the last Central European intellectuals, and (famous last words?) it seems unlikely that any future disclosures will greatly alter our view of its faithfulness.

2

The early part of the book adds little to previous studies. Surprisingly, Freud's early childhood in Moravia (1856–9) is given almost no historical setting, nor are we told much about the first few years after the family's move to Vienna. Unsurprisingly – for this is, after all, a Freud biography by a Freudian – the boy's glimpse of his naked mother, conveyed by Freud in a letter to Wilhelm Fliess in Berlin in decorous Latin, figures more fully than does the account of the family's social situation. To be sure, there are some dutiful pages of background (together with a daunting bibliography) on Vienna in the brief era of liberalism and the subsequent reactionary era under Karl Lueger, the city's celebrated mayor (whom Hitler admired). But except for his account of life in the city during the Austrian *Anschluss* of 1938, which is exemplary, Gay's picture of Vienna is less convincing than his evocations of Freud's visits to the Berlin of Isherwood's days. Repeatedly, Gay asks why Freud, who was forever declaring his dislike of Vienna, nevertheless continued to live there for nearly eighty years, and why even after the *Anschluss* he was most reluctant to leave. The only answer we get is provided by that old stand-by called 'ambivalence'; a more generous reading of Carl Schorske's *Fin-de-Siècle Vienna* (1980), or indeed of Robert Musil's *Man without Qualities*, might have yielded a more abundant answer. (When he did leave Vienna, Freud was asked to sign a statement to the effect that he had not been ill-treated. He not only signed, but added the comment, 'I can recommend the Gestapo most highly to everyone.') On the other hand, Freud's warm if critical admiration of England (which he shared, incidentally, with members of the Viennese Jockey Club), his remarkable command of English and his consistently affectionate and trustful relationship with Ernest Jones (the Welshman who went about in a sort of honorary yarmulka), as well as his conventional dislike of America, are dealt with at great length.

The story of Freud's friendship with the Berlin ENT specialist Wilhelm Fliess, which ended in 1902 with a quarrel over a question of originality, sets the pattern for a series of similar rows throughout Freud's life. Gay's subtle account shows how many diverse elements were involved in this relationship. The closest mutual consultation in the treatment of patients, some of it with disastrous results for those patients; repeated and, as it turned out, temporary acquiescence in Fliess's fantastic diagnoses and cures; Freud's almost unreserved reports on the progress of his own self-analysis together with his theoretical speculations at a time when most of the tenets of psychoanalysis were maturing in his mind, not to mention his use of Fliess as a sort of 'analytical' guinea-pig – all these are aspects of a collaborative enterprise unique in Freud's life. This was the collaboration of as-if-equals. It foundered on Freud's assertion of independence and originality, his will to power. Gay presents the final quarrel as a focal point of feelings of guilt and Oedipal aggression. A non-analytical way to see it would be as the first of the numerous occasions marking Freud's indifference to the common-sense distinction between criticism and betrayal. None of his other emotional and intellectual relationships was ever as close; and though his hatred of those who 'betrayed' him in later years was no less implacable, and though at one time or another his 'enemies' came to include most of his disciples, no other break in his life – not even that with Jung – was as influential in his development. German intellectual discourse in the early twentieth century is not renowned for its irenic ways, but only the anathematizing of the German Marxists by their Muscovite enemies throughout the 1930s can compare for sheer harshness with Freud's reactions to his 'enemies'.

In the course of their last quarrel Fliess charged Freud with 'reading his own thoughts into other people', a charge which Freud rejected as an accusation that 'renders all my efforts valueless' (7 August 1901). Gay does not deny the subjectivity, or at least the subjective origin, of Freud's insights. On the contrary: his major theme throughout this book is 'the continuous traffic in Freud's mind between private feelings and scientific generalizations – a traffic that reduced neither the intensity of his feelings nor their relevance to science' (p. 470); and this, Gay argues, is as true of Freud's large-scale panoramas of universal history as it is of his contributions to individual psychology. Thus Gay writes of *Totem and Taboo* (1913), Freud's unrestrained speculation on primordial patricide as the origin of religion: 'To uncover [religion's] foundations in a prehistoric murder allowed [Freud] to combine his long-standing, pugilistic atheism with his new-found detestation of Jung' (p. 331). However infelicitous Gay's adversarial metaphors and admiration of the 'pugilist' in Freud, there can be no doubt of his candour. The adventitiousness of biographical events which cause changes in the content of the doctrine is to be made good in scientific terms: Gay sees the practice of converting contingencies (for example, 'private feelings') into laws of the mind as the basic move of Freud's new science.

In the evolution of Freud's thought we may discern three strands of public writings. The first, which provides the structure of the first half of Gay's book, consists of the case-histories, from Freud's beginnings with the hypnosis of hysterics onward. These derive partly from his analyses of actual patients and partly from literary fictions: 'Little Hans' and his wee-wee maker, 'The Wolf Man', 'The Rat Man' – titles that recall the Grimm brothers' fairy-tales. Written up by Freud with a surprising lack of ordinary sympathy, the case-histories represent his primary empirical material. The second strand is made up of his main theoretical writings, from his first book, on aphasia (1891), through *Studies in Hysteria* (with the physiologist Josef Breuer) (1895) to his first major independent work, *The Interpretation of Dreams* (1899), and thence to the writings of his maturity. These essays and treatises, which include his lectures and his textbooks on analytical practice, continued to be based on case-histories, but fanned out into ever more comprehensive theories. In the third strand, the immensely influential writings of Freud's last two decades, the material itself becomes yet more speculative, deriving from and in turn interpreting historical and aesthetic interpretations, anthropology, politics and the history of religion. These are three different kinds of writing and demand three different kinds of reading.

Whatever status and credence we give to Freud's work, it is unique in the history of ideas. There is no other *Weltanschauung* whose founder's authority was strong enough to ensure that the evolution of his thoughts remained all but identical with the history of the movement he founded, at least during his lifetime. Freud's authority derived primarily from a rhetoric which emphasizes the hardness of his chosen task, the strenuousness of his work: 'Traumarbeit' and 'Fehlleistung' are two of Freud's characteristic neologisms; in the *Introductory Lectures* (1917) he prides himself on the decades of work that have gone into the making of his theory (*schwere Arbeitsleistung*, and again, repeatedly *schwere, intensive und vertiefte Arbeit*), and offers this as proof of the superiority of analysis over hypnosis, 'which is all too easy' (*geringfügige Arbeitsleistung*); and in a passage in *The Interpretation of Dreams* he complains of the exhausting labour that compels him to 'rummage in human filth'. Gay doesn't quote any of these passages, but he shares their ideology: 'Every dream', he writes, 'is a piece of work, and hard work at that' (p. 113); and again, 'the sexual drive in its mature form is an achievement' (p. 148) (it is hardly what Max Weber meant by *Leistungsethos*). These assertions of arduousness, which give him a sort of Stakhanovite authority, seem to be present in all of Freud's writings, but they are by no means peculiar to him. They are the characteristic attitudes of German intellectuals of Freud's time. But 'when the cat's away . . . ?' A reading 'for our time', it seems to me, will have to look at each of those strands I have enumerated from a different perspective.

3

What are the elements of this immense and immensely influential enterprise that Gay's book enables us to see? First, and most obviously, there is Freud's intellectual energy and imagination, his untiring, strenuous search for ever more comprehensive and detailed accounts of areas of mental life: a search building on, and claiming authority for, insights already charted or asserted in his earlier writings, and seeking out ever wider implications in the culture of the West. However varied the material upon which this quest draws, it is almost always pathological; the occasions when someone is described as basking in the assurance of his mother's unproblematic love are not very frequent. The only way that Freud can make the whole of our mental life available to analysis is by abolishing any categorical distinction between mental health and mental illnesss, and thus incidentally making of the notion of normality a mere subterfuge and of the notion of spirituality an illusion. Gay mentions several occasions when Freud saw himself as a *conquistador*. This gigantic conquest emanated from a self that conformed, in the name of 'the Reality Principle', to all or almost all the social norms of its time and place (Gay never tires of telling us about the good liberal bourgeois paterfamilias with his three-course dinner, *Rindfleisch* and all). Yet it was a self which, in its creative mode, challenged and shocked some – that is, the most private – of those norms; which, unprecedentedly, displayed some of its own wounds as part of the evidence for the validity of its claims; which considered social institutions exclusively in terms of the individual psyche; a self, finally, which was in some important respects philosophically incurious. The motives of therapy and cure, and of emotional liberation, are present in this quest; so are the motives of securing a respectable social standing, material security and fame. But it is the *conquistador* of knowledge, with his yen to know not certainly but totally, to know not with the assurance of independent evidence but with the prospect of further knowledge, wider relevance, a still more comprehensive grasp – it is he who is the hero of the book, his cool passion and awful wrath. It is a piece of supreme irony not often remarked on that in his interpretation of Oedipus Freud has a great deal to say about the hero's sexual desires, but almost nothing about his equally strong desire to know the truth.

The young Freud himself speaks of his intense scientific curiosity and 'greed for knowledge' (p. 25); at a later stage he will diagnose 'the roots of scientific investigation' as being grounded in 'children's sexual curiosity' (p. 531). Yet if the source of this discovery is not to fade out in mere tautology (sexuality becoming both the source and object of such discovery), the desire for knowledge – or rather for a total, 'scientific' account of the psychic world – will have to be explained in some different way. For instance, by Nietzsche's 'unmasking' (or, to use a later jargon, 'deconstructing') that desire as a form of the will to power. In one of the essays in a book I have already mentioned, *Fin-de-Siècle Vienna*, Carl Schorske speaks of Freud's 'wish to bring political authority to heel' by celebrating 'in fantasy' – that is, in Freud's analysis of the dreams of those in power – 'a victory over politics'. In other words, psychoanalysis becomes the bone of consolation of the political underdog. But after this promising opening Schorske has to exaggerate Freud's concern with politics in order to make his argument stick, and Gay is, I think, justified in calling the bulk of the essay 'eccentric'. In fact, Freud's politics are hardly ever more than the 'politics' of the psychoanalytical movement (except for that dream in which he whistled a revolutionary aria from *The Marriage of Figaro* in the presence of a haughty aristocrat (p. 111)). He really was, to all intents and purposes, what Thomas Mann claimed to be: an unpolitical man.

Unlike Hobbes or Plato or Aristotle (Gay compares him to all three), Freud shows no informed interest whatever in social institutions. His observations on the danger of 'the psychological misery of the masses', which, Freud claims, leads to the 'identification of the members' of those masses 'with each other' and thus 'makes the emergence of leaders difficult', are a case in point. In the Germany of his time the opposite was true. As I have argued elsewhere: 'For 1930, the year when the *Führerindividualität* won 11.4 million votes, Freud's observations on the state of the world that surrounded him strike one as less than perceptive.'

He was as incurious about his Jewish background as he was about other social matters. Gay makes much of Freud's Jewishness, and praises him for his courageous stand as a declared 'atheist Jew'. It is not Freud's courage that is in question, though. If 'atheist Jew' is to be more than an oxymoron, a secular age offers nothing to prevent this Jewishness from being reduced to a racial phenomenon – that is, to qualities ascribed by Gentiles to Jews: a process described and analysed by Jean-Paul Sartre in his brilliant *Portrait of the Anti-Semite*. Rejecting the Jewish religion as well as Jewish nationality, Freud writes to the B'nai B'rith fraternity: 'But enough else remained to make the attraction of Judaism and of Jews so irresistible, many emotional powers, all the mightier the less they let themselves be grasped in words ' (p. 601). Here is that notorious appeal to the ineffable in the Jewish character which is basic to racial theory, whether philo- or anti-Semitic; but there is something irresistibly Viennese about this far from taciturn author's appeal to the indescribable. In Freud's writings such appeals are rare enough for Gay to conclude that 'these shadowy intimations obscure as much as they clarify': they 'scarcely constitute a rational analysis'. Rational analysis in this context would have to be social analysis, but this is an area in which Freudian analysis yields little insight.

4

Freud's quest is for an individual psychology of total, systematic knowledge. Gay doesn't comment on the fact that the bulk of Freud's mature work coincides with the publication of a whole series of all-about-everything books. Among these embattled mega-opuses, with their Faustian intellectual imperialism, are Otto Weininger's *Sex and Character* (1903) (briefly mentioned by Gay), Houston Stewart Chamberlain's *Foundations of the Nineteenth Century* (1899), Spengler's *Decline of the West* (1918 and 1922), Ludwig Klages's *Spirit as Adversary of the Soul* (1929–33) and Alfred Rosenberg's *Myth of the Twentieth Century* (1930). However ill-assorted the company may be, all these are intended as 'strictly scientific' attempts at asserting an authorial self by offering a total account of the human condition; and this is true even of works like Klages's, which systematically attacks all conceptualizing by 'the mind' or 'the intellect' because it invalidates authentic experience (*Erleben*), and thus life itself. Whatever their respective value, none of these undertakings, except Spengler's, has aroused much interest outside the German-speaking world. If we read Freud as a member of this warring club of 'universalists', the question

arises why his account has been 'universally' acclaimed, why he has had a
huge following and a continuous influence on our modes and mores, on our
appraisal of others and on our self-esteem, while the other works are all but
forgotten. It cannot be because of the scientific value of his theories, which
don't stand up to any of the criteria scientists employ in relation to their
discoveries; nor does Freud set up any alternative criteria of his own. In the
absence of statistics we don't even know whether the number of successful
analyses is larger than the number of botched ones, or how many patients
under analysis committed suicide. The reason for the Freudian success story,
or at least a substantial part of it, lies in the claim to scientific exactitude
rather than in the validation of that claim – in its validation (as I have argued
in a previous essay) by the rhetoric of persuasion. We should look for this
rhetoric in the 'mixture of genres' which (in Erich Auerbach's *Mimesis*) marks
each new stage in the history of Western realist literature.

Freud's mixture of discursive modes includes generalization and a high
degree of abstraction, mythology and telling anecdote, irony and feigned
hesitations, appeals now to authority, now to sweet reasonableness and common
sense. He has a superb command of the essay form, and uses the essay, with
its urbane opening and aphoristic closure – rather than the open-ended chapter
– in constructing his books. His wide reading of fiction and of the landmark
works of cultural history supplies him with a rich store of conventional but
effective metaphors and analogies. He has a felicitous, uncluttered way of
conveying abstruse information. And above all he has a singularly effective
way of reifying and making concrete the vocabulary of inward states – though
it must be added that the more readily his terminology is accepted and becomes
common usage, the more quickly it deteriorates into jargon. This armoury of
rhetoric is applied with great assurance and accuracy to a particularly vulnerable area of the modern experience. In Central Europe, at all events, among
Gentile and Jewish intellectuals alike, the end of the ages of faith in a divine
purpose is followed by an age in search of the meaning of life. Freud does
not offer to supply such a meaning. Pronouncements like 'the aim of all life
is death' are not designed to do that. On the contrary, what he proposes are
specific therapies, designed (among other things) to cure people of their desire
for any wholesale metaphysical or religious legitimation. What he offers as
their highest hope is 'to relieve the person from the tensions which his needs
create in him' (with *her* he is less concerned); or, as Kafka writes at the end
of his 'Letter' to his father, a hope 'for something so close to the truth that
it will bring a little peace to both of us and may make living and dying a little
easier'. But just as Kafka's end purpose was literary illumination rather than
conciliation, so was Freud's end purpose an intellectual quest he called
'Wissenschaft' rather than a therapeutic concern.

It is not clear how much importance Gay attaches to Freud's rhetoric. His
few observations on the subject, as he takes it up in his discussion of the
standard English translation of Freud's work, are not helpful. He rightly rejects
as 'cranky' Bruno Bettelheim's claim that this translation is wholly misleading,

and that its use of 'rebarbative' Greek and Latin terms ruins Freud's 'concern with man's soul' (p. 741). But Gay's own, less severe criticism is based on the mistaken belief that Freud used 'ordinary, highly suggestive German words'. Freud's numerous neologisms were not 'plain German' when he invented them, though they have very nearly become that. He creates his own technical vocabulary by exploiting the unique facility the language has for forming new compounds and creating abstract collective nouns and reified verbal forms, while yet retaining the appearance of 'plain German'. Here, too, the claim to *Wissenschaft* is upheld, and criticism of the terminology is disarmed by an implicit appeal to the natural language.

5

One of my reasons for speaking of Freud's lack of philosophical curiosity is that, focusing his criticism on the sexual mores of his society, he never questions some of the fundamental preconceptions with which that society, and he as a member of it, operate. Thus, the dichotomy of science versus myth, or fact versus fiction, in terms of which he formulated his view of the psyche and his guidelines of analytical practice, is never challenged. On the contrary: all that Freud does whenever methodological wrangles arise is to charge his 'enemies' inside the analytical movement and outside it – Adler and Jung especially – with disregarding the 'reality' of science and making up obscurantist mystical and mythopoeic stories instead. He is equally uncritical and dogmatic in his contradictory uses of 'reality' – an indeterminate 'principle' which sometimes excludes the entire psyche, sometimes only dreams, sometimes only illusions, and of which one cannot even say with any assurance, as one can of almost any politician's 'reality', that its connotations are unpleasant. That adherence to the celebrated 'Reality Principle' is likely to encourage craven conformity with the status quo is the sort of obvious political thought that seems never to have occurred to him.

So close is Gay's empathy with his hero that he fully shares these preconceptions: yet a reading of Freud 'for our time' might profit from a critical awareness of them. There are signs that the fact-versus-fiction dichotomy in its unqualified, uncritical form is ceasing to be a part of our accepted view of things. Recent developments in historical studies and literary criticism are among the signs of this change. The way Freud's writings are being read is not so much concerned with upholding or questioning their 'scientific' nature as with understanding their rhetoric. The American philosopher Richard Rorty is among those who have eloquently advocated this change in our reading habits. In his book *Contingency, Irony and Solidarity* (1989), he offers such a new reading.

Rorty opens his argument with a quotation from Freud's essay on Leonardo da Vinci:

If one considers chance to be unworthy of determining our fate, that is simply a relapse into the pious view of the universe which Leonardo himself was on the way to overcoming when he wrote that the sun does not move . . . We are all too ready to forget that everything to do with our lives is chance, from our origin out of the meeting of spermatozoon and ovum onwards . . . We all still show too little respect for Nature, which (in the obscure words of Leonardo which recall Hamlet's lines) 'is full of countless causes [*ragioni*] that never enter experience'.

Every one of us human beings corresponds to one of the countless experiments in which these *ragioni* of nature force their way into experience.

Gay uses part of the same quotation to argue that 'neither Freud's "chance", nor his "freedom", is a random manifestation of spontaneity.' Gay reads Freud as taking this notion of 'chance' as a radical challenge, an invitation to construct a system in which 'every event, no matter how accidental its appearance, is as it were a knot in intertwined causal threads' (p. 119). Even though, Gay continues, these threads 'are too remote in origin, large in number and complex in their interaction to be readily sorted out', it is the purpose of Freud's 'scientific' psychology to connect them causally as parts of 'the lawfulness of mind'.

Rorty's argument moves in the opposite direction. He takes the *aperçu* that 'everything to do with our lives is chance' as the motto for a sketch of the psyche which aims, not to define general laws, but to describe very particular reactions; not to eliminate episodes of contingent behaviour, but to recapture them in words; not to designate general traits and essential aspects of the human condition, but to tell illuminating human stories. His proposal is not to read Freud's 'facts' as 'fiction', but to make that and numerous other 'fundamental' distinctions contingent upon concrete individual situations and their describability in language.

What thus emerges from Rorty's account is a singularly literary Freud. However, the literariness of Freud's œuvre is to be seen, not as a quality attached to a genre called 'literature' (as opposed to a genre called 'science'), but as a particularly appropriate and felicitous use of language:

[T]here is no way to force Freud into a Platonic mould by treating him as a moral philosopher who supplies universal criteria for goodness or rightness or true happiness. His *only* utility lies in his ability to turn us away from the universal to the concrete, from the attempt to find necessary truths, uneliminable beliefs, to the idiosyncratic contingencies of our individual pasts, to the blind impress our behavings bear.

A less extreme view, that it is only false 'universals' that we have to guard against, is not mentioned – there are, Rorty believes, no valid criteria to distinguish false from true ones.

Is Rorty's reading plausible, convincing, possible? Freud himself, of course, is quite explicit in his insistence on the 'scientific', fact-versus-fiction view of the world, and on psychoanalysis as the embodiment of that view: that is, on the reading Gay offers. It is here that the distinction I proposed earlier should be helpful. The first of three strands of Freud's public writings I mentioned, the case-histories, fits the literary view of language and world Rorty proposes. As for the other strands, in which the role of contingency diminishes as the legitimation through system envelops more and more of our experience, to the point where rationality itself emerges as the enemy of contingency – these are outside Rorty's revision of Freud. The core of Gay's procedure is to describe Freud's act of incorporating 'events' in his 'personal life' into his doctrine, together with the particular urgency which these events had for him. Freud's strenuous search for laws and universally valid rules intended to validate this incorporation is a more powerful motive, in our world too, than Rorty is willing to admit (his remark that 'the sciences . . . have . . . receded into the background of our cultural life' strikes me as even more whimsical than the self-described ironist could have intended). In mentioning Freud's frequent exhortations 'to return to' the particular – to see particular situations and options as similar to or different from past actions or events – Rorty is describing the procedure of almost any respectable scientist of Freud's day and our own day too, and, ignoring its purpose, the formulation of scientific laws. In all this, Rorty seems surprisingly unconcerned about the precariousness of the borderline between contingency (one of his buzz words) and adventitiousness (one of his strongest terms of opprobrium). He misunderstands Wittgenstein's notion of 'concepts with blurred edges': to say that there may be more than one criterion for distinguishing between fact and fiction, science and myth, or contingency and arbitrary whim, is not to say that there is no difference between them. (There was no need to wait for Wittgenstein to formulate the obvious: '[T]hough no man can draw a stroke between the confines of day and night,' wrote Edmund Burke, 'yet light and darkness are upon the whole tolerably distinguishable.')

When (in a letter of 22 May 1922) Freud praised the Viennese playwright and novelist Arthur Schnitzler for arriving 'by way of intuition' at psychological insights which he, Freud, had had 'to discover through arduous labour', he was appealing to the difference between an artist's creativeness and a scientist's research work, a difference which Rorty thinks is no longer important or even (for those who view differences and distinctions ironically) valid. Well – it was valid for Freud. And (whether or not he was mistaken in never abandoning the hopes he first expressed in 'A Project for a Scientific Psychology' of 1895) a characterization of Freud's work which takes no account of his frequent appeals to the scientific ethos, nor of his wish that his work should be seen as a contribution to scientific materialism, is misleading.

The panliteralism or panaestheticism developed in the course of Rorty's book is as unconcerned with historical accuracy as with any other form of truth. The meanings which are said to be relevant to 'our world' and its *Zeitgeist* are stretched to the point where every conceivable kind of 'redescription' of the past is validated; so that, when it comes to interpreting past events or texts, anything goes. Here it must be enough simply to assert that to get the past right (as Gay, as Freud's biographer, does) is better than to fail to get it right (as the mythopoeist does). The Viennese *savant* whom Peter Gay celebrates with so much accurate affection did create 'a new language' and 'a set of new metaphors', which we have seen harden into clichés and technicalities so quickly that it is as difficult to recapture anything of their freshness and originality as it is with any technical language. But what he hoped to discover was a new science of the psyche, with its laws and systematic consistency. If, as I believe, he failed to do that, it isn't much good rejoining, 'Ah – but look what metaphors and myths he gave us to play with.'

1988 (1991)

10

Inauthenticity: Theory and Practice

1

Martin Heidegger was born in 1889 in Messkirch, a small town in the Black Forest with a strong minority of Old Catholics, the son of a cooper and salaried verger; he died at the age of eighty-seven, having lived during four successive German states – the Kaiserreich, the Weimar Republic, Hitler's Third Reich and, after an interregnum of three blank years, the Federal Republic. Hugo Ott's *Martin Heidegger: Toward his Biography* (1988) provides a vivid account of the youth and schooling of a poor Roman Catholic scholarship boy; it becomes clear that, but for an asthmatic heart-condition, Heidegger would have taken Holy Orders. Heidegger at all times emphasized his spiritual kinship with fellow Swabians like Hegel, Hölderlin and Johann Peter Hebel (a writer of enchanting Alemannic folk-tales). He saw himself as a contributor to this tribal lineage, and associated his writings with it; his biographer reports on this powerful rural mystique, and is (as far as I know) the first author to do so fairly and soberly. (To call Heidegger 'a Schwarzwald redneck', as a philosopher from Virginia has done, does not suggest much local knowledge.)

Of all those clerical, academic and political institutions which Heidegger, in the course of his life, succeeded in dominating or failed to put to his use, the first and most important was the Church. Heidegger's Catholic background remained a determining force in his thinking even after he explicitly and vindictively repudiated it; indeed, of much of his writing it may be said that it is part of a theology without a God. This background helps to account for Heidegger's truly immense learning, but it also remained what Heidegger in a private letter called 'a thorn in the flesh' – the challenge against which he was determined to assert himself and his philosophical vision after he left the Church in 1919. Four years later, his Marburg colleague and Germany's foremost Protestant theologian, Rudolf Bultmann, considered Heidegger to be one of the best Luther scholars in the country.

Ott's very full account of Heidegger's involvement with National Socialism makes it abundantly clear that he was neither a reluctant fellow traveller nor a non-political scholar, a naïve victim of hideous political events. Heidegger became rector of Freiburg University on 22 April 1933. When he assumed office, he did not do so with the greatest reluctance and under pressure from a previous rector (as he claimed in his memoir, 'Facts and Thoughts' of 1945, and in his replies to the university commission which examined his activities later that year). He contrived his election after having ousted his immediate predecessor (who held the office for a few days only), and as the nominee of the Prussian Ministry of Culture acting on the advice of the National Socialist members of the Freiburg University Senate. On the back page of the programme for the celebration of his 'unanimous' election (27 May 1933) appears the text of the 'Horst Wessel Song' and the new rector's instruction that the right hand should be raised at the singing of the fourth stanza of this, the 'Party anthem'. His inaugural address ends with an enthusiastic tribute to the nation's power and its resoluteness in embracing its new destiny 'in all its glory and greatness', for (he quotes from Plato's *Republic* 497d), 'All that is great stands in the storm', which other translators from the Greek render less dramatically: 'All great things are precarious.'

On 1 May 1933 Heidegger officially joined the National Socialist Party, with great ceremony and with the ambition of becoming the *Führer* of the whole German university system. The precise nature of the reforms by which he hoped to bring about 'the spiritual renewal of all life' is not clear. What is clear is his intention of exacting the same loyalties and unquestioning obedience in respect of his decisions and decrees that Hitler exacted from the German state and throughout most of German society. This is the authority he asserts in the second most notorious of his proclamations as rector, his Leipzig declaration of loyalty, whose demand that Hitler be supported was publicized 'worldwide' a day before the National Referendum of 12 November 1933. (At this referendum, 95 per cent of the electorate voted in approval of Hitler's decision to take Germany out of the League of Nations, and of his economic policies aimed at full employment; in addition, 92 per cent voted for the unitary Party list for the new Reichstag.) No other single proclamation can have had so great an effect at that moment on German intellectual life; no other was so skilful in politicizing the 'metaphysical nation' into craven conformity with the new regime.

The question of Heidegger's academic and political standing is inseparable from that of his relationships with his teachers and friends, which appear to have been consistently self-seeking, vindictive, and occasionally perfidious. This is especially true of his dealings with the aged Edmund Husserl, to whom he owed his first university appointment (at Freiburg) and his first Chair (at Marburg), and whom he succeeded as professor of philosophy on returning to Freiburg in October 1927, after the publication of *Being and Time* in February of that year. After the National Socialists' rise to power in 1933, Heidegger went to great lengths to collect evidence of some of his colleagues' pacifist and 'un-German' past in order to discredit them in the eyes of the Party and of influential civil servants, obsequiously retracting his accusations when he found that, for some expedient reason or other, they were being overruled or ignored. Even the polemics he conducted in his regular university lectures – as in his vicious attacks on the wholly defenceless Catholic philosopher Theodor Haecker – had a political edge. But then, it becomes abundantly clear that very few professors, scholars or students mentioned in Ott's book – Rudolf Bultmann is a shining exception – took a stand against the denunciation, backbiting and time-serving which prevailed in the German universities of the Third Reich.

Ott illustrates Heidegger's political activities in colourful detail, in a chapter called (appropriately, as we shall see) 'The peculiar search for hardness and weightiness'. In one of the few hilarious episodes recorded in the biography, Heidegger – a small man in carefully-designed peasant gear with, in later years, something of an embonpoint – is presented as the founder and leader of a National Socialist summer camp in which military training was to be combined with political and philosophical indoctrination, and which quickly collapsed in a welter of intrigue.

We have reached one of the points of complete incoherence between Heidegger's life and a major aspect of his philosophy. Among the most impressive passages of *Being and Time* is the analysis of 'das Existential des Man', by which he means that aspect of our being in the world and with other people which is constitutive of inauthentic conduct, conduct legitimated by an appeal to 'the average' or 'the everyday', and summed up in such phrases as 'one does', or 'they say' or 'it is thought that'. Beginning with a re-creation of the condition of inauthenticity (which I quote below, p. 308), the passage continues:

> Togetherness as such constitutes [*besorgt*] the average. *The average* is the pattern [*Vorzeichnung*] of all that can and may be ventured, it watches over every exception that asserts itself. Every kind of priority is silently suppressed. Overnight, everything original is instantly glossed over as long since familiar. Everything that has been fought for becomes readily available. Every mystery loses its power. This care of the average discloses once more the essential tendency of being in the world [*Dasein*], which we call the levelling-out of all possibilities of Being [*Sein*].

The simple fact is that the philosopher who has analysed inauthenticity more profoundly than any other, and given it its place not as an adventitious psychological phenomenon but as part of an ontological analysis of man's being, his *Dasein*, was among its most astute practitioners.

The attitude prevailing in the German universities of Heidegger's day is not usually to be found prevailing in the academic institutions of free societies. Backbiting and toadying are not unknown in professional circles the world over, but there everything was done with an eye to political power and under the watchful eye of the secret police; to which, in the particular situation Heidegger exploited, a philosophical legitimation was added. Any explanation of Heidegger's conformism would have to begin with his frequently proclaimed conviction that he and he alone knows the right questions to ask about the nature of Being, the right paths to take towards that supreme 'ontic' goal; that he is the first philosopher since the pre-Socratics to convey this truth, or at least to go along the paths to that truth; and that any criticism of his views amounts to an offence against the disclosure of Being, something resembling sacrilege. Hence his apparent assurance that questions involving lesser considerations – such as those of morality, loyalty, common decency and simple truthfulness – must be subordinated to his 'ontological' message; and hence, too, the apparently boundless vindictiveness towards those who dared to oppose his decrees and decisions. This attitude of assurance is what Karl Jaspers singled out in December 1945, when, on being asked whether he would recommend Heidegger's reinstatement as an academic teacher, he called Heidegger's '*Denkungsart* in its essence unfree, dictatorial, *communikationslos*', adding that he regarded this 'mode of thinking' as 'more important than the content' of Heidegger's 'political judgement'. The distinction is misleading. It was precisely Heidegger's astonishing political judgement that Hitler's National Socialism offered Germany (and Europe generally) the only chance of being saved from destruction by technology, and thus of keeping open the questioning, the 'mode of thinking', that really matters. The most direct public statement of the politics which sustained this 'ontological' belief is contained in the Leipzig proclamation of loyalty I have already mentioned. This was Heidegger's contribution to a pamphlet which a number of rectors of German universities (though by no means all) sent to their colleagues throughout the country on the eve of Hitler's plebiscite.

The style of the pamphlet is an amalgam of Heidegger's own terminology of 'Sein', 'Dasein', 'Vorhandensein' with the National Socialist adaptations of the Nietzschean terminology of the Will. The 'German Rectors' Declaration of Loyalty' begins by stressing the uniqueness and momentousness of this act of 'choice' or 'election' ('Wahl' covers both) which the Führer, who asks nothing for himself, is allowing the German people. What he expects is an 'absolute', that is, an all-or-nothing, decision, which will determine the nation's being or not-being. This decision will arise from 'the primordial demand of all Being' which, governed by 'the law of honour', sets the limits to what a nation may be expected to put up with. (While in other contexts *Sein*, or, after the war, the high camp of *Seyn*, has the status of a divinity, here it stands under an apparently self-evident 'law of honour'.) It is 'the labour of the estates' (like Hitler, Heidegger is anxious to avoid the term 'classes', because of its Marxist connotations) which guarantees the nation its rootedness in the soil, whereas the State is 'the reality of the nation in the active sphere of all the essential forces of the being of man'. By leaving the League of Nations, Hitler has not turned his back on the community of nations; on the contrary, this step, by which the Germans have assumed responsibility for themselves, has placed the country under 'the essential law of Being'. The will to a true national community is the enemy of any wishy-washy world-fraternity of nations no less than that of the blind rule of tyranny. Invoking the nation's will is not a return to barbarism. It amounts to a rejection of all vacuous negotiating and all hidden business-deals. It is not the irruption of lawlessness or the denial of a spiritual (*geistig*) nation's creativeness, or indeed a break with its historical tradition. The nation's willing is the awakening of its youth, which has been 'purged and is growing back into its roots'. This youth's political will (*der Wille zum Staat*) will lend hardness and strength to the nation and inspire it with the awe that is due to all authentic work. Through its act of choice the nation wins back 'the truth of its will to be' (*der Daseinswille des Volkes*); for 'truth is the revealing [*Offenbarkeit*, Heidegger just about avoids the biblical term '*Offenbarung*'] of all that makes a nature sure, lucid, and strong in its actions and in its search for knowledge'. The will to knowledge contains the entitlement to knowledge (*Wissensanspruch*) and determines the limits within which 'genuine inquiry and research have their ground and must prove their worth'. The science that arises in this way is bound into the necessity of responsible national (*völkisch*) being. Only *Wissenschaft* thus grounded is capable of clearly grasping things and of leading to decisive actions. There follows an attack on thinking that has lost all contact with the soil and with the sources of power (no names are mentioned), and a paean to what I presume Heidegger sees as his own philosophical undertaking: 'The primordial courage either to grow or to founder in the encounters with *Seiendes* (by which he here means the recalcitrance of things in the world) is the innermost motive of the questioning appropriate to a *völkisch* science.' And the declaration ends, 'No one may stay away on the day this will manifests itself. Heil Hitler!'

A threefold intention informs this ambitious document: to lobby the country's academic staff on Hitler's behalf; to claim a place of power for the German university as the faithful purveyor of the heroic ideology which the intellectuals of 'the Movement' have constructed from Hitler's rhetoric; and to give notice that Hitler's victory will ensure a return to the question of Being – the question which Heidegger alone is asking with the full seriousness it demands. I doubt whether anything Georg Lukács wrote in his Stalinist days was as damaging to continental intellectuals as this manifesto, in which one and the same style serves both politics and philosophy: at its salient points it is couched in the diction which its audience readily recognized as the diction of *Being and Time*. The rhetoric urges the identity between Heidegger's ontology and Hitler's politics while at the same time offering itself – in the language of power and command – as a pattern and example of this identity.

2

The most marked aspect of Heidegger's rhetoric is his adaptations, adjustments and reversals of the meanings of common German words, manipulations which seem expressly designed to make paraphrase difficult and translation into another language all but impossible. Is this then a style of wilful obscurity? Or it it to be justified as some sort of poetry of concepts, yet another variety of *Gedankenlyrik*? The relentless fragmenting and etymologizing of words seems ruinous to any conceivable notion of poetry. If the style is often inseparable from the philosophical substance, this is because Heidegger is convinced that certain pivotal forms of the German language are like those of Greek in that they do not describe and analyse Being, but rather are themselves re-enactments of it. Certain changes in etymology mark the turning-points in the history of *Sein*: changes in the history of *Sein* are made meaningful to us by changes in the etymology of its lexis, which are proved to be neither conventional nor fortuitous but necessary by being legitimated in the history of *Sein* . . . This belief (which Plato guys in *Symposium* 185c: 'When Pausanias paused – you see the kind of tricks we catch from our philologists') and the arguments derived from it are offered as proof of the legitimacy of the philosopher's questioning, and as a confirmation of the fact that all our authentic questioning of *Dasein* takes place within *Sein* and is encompassed by it. You the reader are to be shamed into admitting that to look for evidence in support of what all these grand words might mean is unworthy of the ontological venture.

Something like an angelic hierarchy will illustrate this scheme: from the summit of *Sein* (a sort of divinity) we descend to earthly and worldly *Dasein* and hence to *Seiendes*, the things and entities that are in the world. The false, inauthentic, 'scientific' view of language is to think of it as a convenience – a giving of handy names to things that exist or have been thought out independently of it; all that this kind of language does is to provide information (or scientific data and arguments leading to quantification) which is designed to satisfy the amassing of more and more things, and mere curiosity. (Here is one of the openings of Heidegger's attack on technology.) The true function of language is as 'the House of Being' – the place where *Seiendes* (being which constitutes our existence) is truly itself and whence it emerges into *Dasein*. Endlessly repeated, the claim that it is not man but language that speaks is as it were the key that unlocks the door of this 'House of Being', the magic password that allows the etymological exploitation of language, the squeezing of its syllables for the last drop of meaning. Arbitrariness seems to reign supreme, and yet: the historicizing and domiciling of the facts and fictions of language is a way of living and dealing with the unhappy 'errors' – 'die Irre' – of history.*

---

* 'Die Irre' is as good a word as any to illustrate Heidegger's method. In his use of it a number of more or less distinct meanings are conflated: (1) as a noun it is used by Goethe, Schiller and Klopstock as a metaphor for 'a maze or labyrinth'; (2) as such it derives from an older transitive verb, 'irren', while Luther uses it in translating 2 Samuel 7:10, 'daß mein Volk nicht mehr in der Irre gehe', in the sense of 'hindering one from attaining a goal'; (3) intransitively (= 'errare') it is 'to lose one's way', and so – this is the most common present use – 'to make a mistake'; (4) but at the same time, and returning to (1), the clinical meaning, again common today, of 'mental disturbance, madness'. It is to Heidegger's purpose that these meanings overlap, for instance in a world like 'Irrlicht', 'will-o'-the-wisp'. It is even more to his purpose that all these

A fuller consideration of Heidegger's style would amount to a retracing of his philosophical vision, though of course there are points where, to one side of the style, the postulates of this philosophical venture can be adequately paraphrased. But even then there are difficulties. These arise partly because the density of Heidegger's arguments – we might call it his philosophical patience – varies unpredictably, being often replaced by invective, indignation and scorn, or, again, by image, the grand vision or the evocation of a mood; yet partly these difficulties seem to be created not by the grand ontological task but by his contempt for the language of 'the everyday', and the high-and-mighty diction conceals his kinship with the bad temper of the age. The writings of contemporaries of his such as Carl Schmitt and Ernst Bertram, but also of major literary figures like Ernst Jünger and Gottfried Benn (not to mention Heidegger's imitators and 'philosophers of the Movement', licensed mountebanks with whom he was not ashamed to associate), mediate between the mysteries of the Sage of Todtnauberg and that part of the ruling ideology which emphasized the need for sacrifice, the 'clear hardness' of the struggle ahead, the value of intensity and 'resoluteness'. Of all those thousands of intellectuals who only did 'what one does', said 'what one says' and thought 'what is thought', he alone devised a language which under its eccentricity came to conceal their and his conformism. And yet, the language that 'spoke' to him does more than that. Heidegger's word-for-word and syllable-for-syllable translation and exegesis of the first chorus from the *Antigone* (verses 332–75) is a poem 'in its own right' – a profound poem which flows almost imperceptibly into its own exegesis. I think there are good reasons why we should welcome the breaking-down of the border between 'philosophy' and 'poetry', yet here such a move seems always to be accompanied by the breaking-down of the border between sublimity and contempt for the human.

3

The skill with which Heidegger manœuvred himself as rector into various positions of great authority is bound to make one doubt whether his 'ontic' belief was genuine; or, since questions of belief are notoriously difficult to answer, whether there was not at times an element of mental disturbance in this assertion of a self that is always right, always on the way to the 'unhidden' truth. However that may be, he did not last long in his high office. His decision to resign after twelve months had to do partly with the opposition of

---

words stand for misprisions which have either no moral connotations at all or only those of the vaguest, most indeterminate kind. The specific Heideggerian twist comes when the word – we are back at the noun, 'die Irre' – is identified with 'history' and made co-extensive with it, challenging our view of history as a realm for which we might be expected to bear moral responsibility, and presenting it in something like Nietzschean terms, as an extra-moral realm in which 'the tragic' is enacted. See, e.g., *Einführung in die Metaphysik* (*Introduction to Metaphysics*), §52.

courageous colleagues, and partly with his failure to initiate the reforms for which he claimed to have sought the office in the first place. But he also ran into intrigues from 'philosophers of Being' in the government office presided over by Alfred Rosenberg, author of *The Myth of the Twentieth Century*. They launched an attack on him in the Party press, which included the accusation that he was 'leader of a Jewish clique'. This of course was malicious nonsense. But in fact, as Ott points out, Heidegger's anti-Semitism was not as radical as other writers have made out, and it was certainly not racial; though Ott also observes that whenever Heidegger acted on behalf of a Jewish colleague, he did so (as 'one generally did' in German university circles) with the aim of protecting the name of German learning against critics of the regime abroad.

Heidegger mentions the massacre of Hitler's myrmidons in the course of the Röhm putsch of 30 June 1934 as the occasion of his break with the Party, though he remained a paying member of it to the end of the Third Reich. He dates his disillusionment with National Socialism as the end of 1933, though he only resigned as rector on 23 April 1934 (not, as he later claimed, in February of that year), continuing in his office as professor of philosophy until he was dismissed in 1946 by a tribunal set up in 1945 by the French occupation forces. His resignation from the office of rector (he later said) was caused by his discovery that the actual National Socialist Party and thus the government of Germany had betrayed the ideals of the revolution which brought Hitler to power, and if he was merely mistaken in his assessment of those ideals, then clearly he had little to apologize for or to retract. This notion of a *Privatnationalsozialismus* (as Ott calls it) was no more than an expedient fantasy. That Heidegger's break with the Party and its ideology cannot have been as radical as he claimed is shown by a remark he made in the course of a lecture on ethics he gave in the summer of 1935. Attacking the contemporary 'Philosophy of Value', Heidegger likens it to 'what is nowadays touted as the philosophy of National Socialism, but [this] has not the least thing in common with the truth and greatness of National Socialism' – a phrase he altered in 1953 to read: but this 'has not the least thing in common with the truth and greatness of the movement (to wit with the encounter between technology on a planetary scale and modern man)'.

When *did* Heidegger reject National Socialism? Since most of his wartime lectures remain inaccessible (an interdict *sine die* was placed by the philosopher's family on parts of the archives at Marbach), not even Ott can date his change of mind reliably. Ott's account of his post-war activities and proclamations includes what may well be Heidegger's only reference to the Jewish genocide, in a letter to Herbert Marcuse, one of his former pupils. Marcuse's reproaches are justified (Heidegger writes in January 1948): he can only add that 'instead of "Jews"' Marcuse's letter 'ought to say "East Germans"', and then it is equally valid in respect of one of the Allies, with the difference that the crimes perpetrated by the Russians have received worldwide publicity whereas the bloody terror of the Nazis was actually kept secret from the German people'. But by that time Sartre and others saw to it that biographical disclosures should not stand in the way of a rehabilitation if not of the philosopher then certainly of his 'existentialism', even though Heidegger had long since rejected that label. The decree that forced him to retire from his Chair was rescinded in 1950, when he was granted the status of emeritus and his teaching rights were reinstated. It seems that the University Senate had little choice in the matter. Enthusiastic audiences had welcomed Heidegger's return to the rostrum well before that time; a lecture at the Bavarian Academy brought him the greatest acclaim of his entire career; his mountain hut in the village of Todtnauberg in the Black Forest, visited by Paul Celan in 1967, became something of a place of pilgrimage; and when, finally, a Russian philosopher wrote to him that in the Soviet Union, too, his reading of Hölderlin's 'lament for the absent gods' was being accepted as a valid reading, meaning interpretation, of the modern age, the murky past seemed forgotten, the rehabilitation complete. He died on 26 May 1976 and was buried, according to his wish, in the churchyard next to St. Martin's in his native Messkirch. The immense productivity of the post-war years remained unimpaired almost to the end.

4

Does Heidegger's biography matter? Why not say that 'one of the century's most original thinkers happened to be a pretty nasty character', and leave it at that? Or one might add that 'he was the sort of man who could betray his ... colleagues for the sake of his own ambition, and then manage to forget what he had done', and leave it at *that*? Indeed, the ironist whom I have mentioned before goes one step further, with the additional nonchalant claim that 'as a philosopher of our public life, as a commentator on twentieth century technology and politics, [Heidegger] is resentful, petty, squint-eyed, obsessive ... and cruel', which I take to mean that his politics are trivial. Do we need the biography in order to understand the philosophy?

In contrast to the writings of, say, Kant or Hegel, Heidegger's work does not constitute a unitary body of thought. We must certainly give central importance to the question to which he himself repeatedly returns – 'Do we in our time have an answer to the question of what we really mean by "being"? – though we must take equally seriously both his insistence that what is important is asking the question, and his harsh criticism of the false assurance of anyone who expects a simple, definitive answer. But even if we reject 'the question of Being' as meaningless and point to the forty pages (in the *Introduction to Metaphysics*) of grammatical and etymological by-play on the verb 'sein' and the roots from which its various forms derive as evidence of its arbitrariness, we still cannot fail to recognize that the diverse perspectives of thought, experience and speculative hypothesis from which the question is asked, and the intensity and resourcefulness of the asking, reveal insights into our condition which are unparalleled in our time. These insights concern care, *praxis*, conscience, anxiety, death, historicity, the subject–object relation which philosophers since Descartes have postulated, and our 'being-there' in the world (*Dasein*), of which 'understanding' (*Daseinsverständnis*) is an integral part. And there is a *prima facie* case for some of these insights to be examined without recourse to biography.

This is what another American, Hubert Dreyfus, does in his recent discussion of 'Husserl, Heidegger and Modern Existentialism' in Bryan Magee's *Great Philosophers*. He begins by outlining Heidegger's claim that the relation of thinking subject to thought object does not adequately describe our most common relation to things. What Dreyfus calls our 'everyday masterful, practical know-how', our 'everyday coping', proceeds by dispensing with 'mental states like desiring, believing, following a rule, and so on, and thus with' – what Husserl called – 'their intentional content'. (This incidentally is the point at which Husserl became convinced that Heidegger had travestied his 'phenomenological' analysis.) Dreyfus goes on to describe the way Heidegger's concept of knowing how to practise a particular skill presupposes our familiarity with the world in which we are placed, presupposes all of our *Dasein*. But his 'knowing how' proceeds without need of rational choices, let alone of the kind of thinking that has led philosophers to their doubts concerning the existence of the external world. By emphasizing the habitual, unthinking disposition in which we take things and our use of them for granted, Heidegger relegates our conscious, reflective activity to situations in which our skills don't work because things go wrong, or to theoretical or scientific thinking, or again to an unsettling (*unheimlich*) search for a meaning to give to our existence, a 'meaning of life'. The search for a final, definitive meaning of life is inauthentic, but so is avoiding or giving up the search – the uncanny, unsettling (the Romantics would have said, demonic) nature of the search, that alone provides the ground of authentic *Dasein*.

Dreyfus then identifies Heidegger's 'turn': it occurred (according to this interpretation) when Heidegger introduced the historical dimension into the process he had been describing. Thus the present is the time when rational choices become efficient choices, and efficiency, in our historical situation, is identified with technology, whose aim is the pursuit of contingent ends for no other reason than that they are technologically interesting and technically attainable. All meaning, for Heidegger, is contained in our *Dasein*, but if nowadays our *Dasein* (including our understanding of it) is determined by technology, all meaning is destroyed by nihilism. How is this vicious circle to be broken?

Heidegger considers two ways out. Dreyfus outlines one of these ways, which Heidegger calls *Gelassenheit*, and which Dreyfus interprets nicely as the appreciation of 'non-efficient practices' and 'the saving power of insignificant things' – whether Heidegger would have recognized Dreyfus's colourful Californian illustrations of this laid-back condition is another question. But what he doesn't say is that Heidegger's celebration of *désinvolture* is the second (and much later) of his proposed solutions.

The first led to the political disaster Ott's book describes: it is Heidegger's briefly held but loudly proclaimed belief in National Socialism as the political system which relegates (or will relegate) technology to its proper sphere, renders the social sphere authentic, and thus opens the way to authentic *Dasein* in our time. If this system is seen as vouchsafing the return to 'the simple questioning of the essence of Being', so that what you have to do is give 'the Movement' your allegiance and support, then, clearly, an examination of Heidegger's politics (a part of his biography) and their place in his philosophy becomes inevitable. For, given what was known of National Socialism even then (given what he could not have failed to know of it, except through self-deception), the idea that it might produce a haven of authentic *Dasein* strikes one as both ludicrous and monstrous; though it has to be added that this political way out of the vicious circle of technology and inauthenticity does not invalidate the earlier phenomenological arguments of *Being and Time*.

If there is anything like a coherent explanation of this aberration, it must begin with Heidegger's conception of conscience. Conscience (for the philosopher of *Being and Time*) is the voice of 'care', and 'care' belongs to the very structure of man's *Dasein*. It is the call that bids him fulfil his own potentiality against, and in isolation from, 'the everyday self'. It is the wholly private voice, never the voice of communal experience, never the inward reminder of an external command, yet it is not 'subjective' either, because it is the voice of *Dasein* itself. The social being of man – 'Mitdasein', togetherness – amounts to 'forfeiture of the self to the world', and 'forfeiture' means 'absorption in togetherness in so far as togetherness is guided by chatter, idle curiosity and ambiguity'. (The flaw in Heidegger's conception of conscience is not solipsism, which denies the independent existence of others, but the egoism that interprets considerateness – the consideration of others – as a forfeiting or betrayal of the self.) But if this was Heidegger's view of the social being of man when he wrote *Being and Time*, how did he accommodate this view when he joined the togetherness of the Party six years later?

In 1933 a different *Mitdasein* is born, one that receives its metaphysical sanction from his philosophy and in turn validates the philosophy by being the realization of Being in time. When, in his wartime Nietzsche lectures, Heidegger proclaims that the single person 'as such and always' stands in a metaphysical relationship to others – a relationship (he adds) which is only accessible via a metaphysical understanding of Being, and which thus ceases to be a social relationship – he is in effect drawing the philosophical implications of his political commitment. And no matter if he was aware of the criminal character of the regime (which set up its first concentration camps within months of coming to power): the misprisions which govern *all* history – 'die Irre der Geschichte' – render all considerations of good and evil irrelevant. If 'our nation' is 'the metaphysical nation', gripped in 'the great double lock between Russia and America' (the double lock of technology gone mad on one side, and social organization ungrounded in Being on the other), then participation in the *Volksgemeinschaft* is justified by the nation's heroic fight for its 'return to the question of Being', from which the rest of Europe has defected. And, for good measure: 'The Leader himself and alone *is* the present and future German reality and its law.' Italicizing the 'ontic' verb. Heidegger is making sure that there is no doubt about the metaphysical legitimation of the Führer's – and thus also of his own – mission. And if, finally, guilt is involved in this participation, so be it: all *Dasein* is involved in guilt.

5

The truth is that politics and the political are a full mode of Heidegger's philosophy, present in various degrees of explicitness throughout. It is not the case that one can detach the political pronouncements from the rest of the *oeuvre* and disregard them as adventitious. The anti-scientific and anti-technological bias expressed in the early sections of *Being and Time* corresponds very accurately to the conservative *völkisch* ideals of the 1920s; the rehabilitation of the notion of togetherness conforms to the events of 1933; in his lectures of 1940 Heidegger gloats over the defeat of France, seeing it (as did numerous German journalists) as a warning sign of how a nation may turn out to be inadequate to its own philosophical (here: Cartesian) vision; the lectures on Nietzsche, and especially those on 'the Will to Power', from which he derives the 'epochal Will to Willing', are to be seen as Heidegger doing his bit for the war effort; and so are the later comments on the 'metaphysically necessary . . . idea of race' and on the dire consequences for the future of any nation of ignoring 'the principle of instituting racial breeding'.

   To sum up: it is some of the pivotal terms of Heidegger's philosophical system itself that are involved in politics (if, that is, we stretch the term 'politics' to cover what happens in the public life of a totalitarian society). These terms include 'history', 'guilt' and 'freedom'. Man's fullest encounter with Being brings him face to face with what is least familiar, most remote and 'most uncanny'. The *polis* is the site where this occurs, where human creativeness (other than the poet's) takes on the violence which is its innermost characteristic, where human greatness manifests itself in 'the excessive act' performed by men (*die Gewalttätigen*) as the agents of 'the uncanny' (*das Unheimliche*), and where each man is committed by his being (his *Dasein*) to guilt-and-error (*die Irre*). Here everything is permitted except indecision and halfheartedness (*Halbheiten*), for everything that *is*, is ensconced in 'the history of Being' (*seinsgeschichtlich*). In the face of that you can do nothing. You cannot slow things down in their inevitable 'onto-historical' course – you can either hasten them on or (after 1945) 'you let them be'. And Heidegger's notion of 'freedom', too, changes with each 'onto-historical' phase.

There is nothing fortuitous in the relationship of Being (in Heidegger's analysis of it) with historical – that is his own – time and its politics; and I hope that this sketch of what amounts to Heidegger's ontological ideology is supported by enough evidence to pass muster as accurate. With perhaps less assurance I would like to go a step further, and reinterpret Heidegger's political conduct – both its philosophical legitimation and its practice – as a violent and at times heedless attempt to find, almost invent, concrete manifestations for the high speculative abstractions of his ontology, to consider his *œuvre* on the analogy of a poet's or dramatist's search for what one of his contemporaries called 'objective correlatives', Plato 'enargeia' and Quintilian 'evidentia'. All that these terms offer are analogies, suggestions that his search for concreteness is not confined to the aesthetic. In a later essay (23) I shall try to show how this longing was assuaged among the Germans of Heidegger's generation by that intense endeavour which led them to the 'economic miracle' and the advances in industrial technology which supported it. This of course is not the domain in which Heidegger looks for his version of *enargeia*, or if he does, it is with a kind of epochal sadism, to hasten the completion of the modern age's self-destructive process. To one side of all philosophical considerations, like thousands and millions of other Germans, he chooses the Führer and *das Volk*, becuse they are *there, im Dasein*, the *données* of the 'onto-historical' process. The attitude I am describing is conveyed by Thomas Mann in *Doctor Faustus* through his narrator, Serenus Zeitblom, who reports on the patter of the intellectuals of 1919 as they rehearse their future roles in the 'nationalist revolution' which they fear and welcome at one and the same time:

'It is coming, it is coming, and when it is here it will find us rising to the occasion. It is interesting, it is even good, simply by virtue of being the coming thing, and to recognize it is achievement and satisfaction enough. It is certainly not our business to do anything against it.'

Long lists of names could be strung together of those who sought and 'erred' and thought they found true 'concreteness' in 'the Movement' that took them out of themselves and their isolation, though many of these men had the courage to quit the search and at least privately oppose (if not actively resist) the regime in whose *enargeia* they for a time believed. Heidegger doesn't seem to have had much of that courage, remaining more or less loyal to the Party to the end. Perhaps this is the reason why his report of what it was like to have been there, at the centre of guilt-and-error, at the dispensing of 'the uncanny', is so revealing. Once again we must end on a discordant note, confessing that profound and lasting insights may spring from tainted sources.

6

Much of Heidegger's energy in the last three decades of his life was devoted to philosophical reflections arising from the poetry of his fellow-Swabian Friedrich Hölderlin, in whom he saw above all a precursor of his own concern with pre-Socratic Greece. Among the great Hölderlin poems he did not subject to his 'interpretation' is 'Mein Eigentum' ('My Possessions') of 1799, a magnificent – and magnificently moderate – ode in praise of the things that tie a man to this earth; in praise of the husbandman who is safe and sure in the possession of home and hearth, field and orchard. And (my quotation begins at the sixth stanza) he is contrasted with the poet, the man without possessions, who has only one wish that the gods may grant him:

Beglückt, wer, ruhig liebend ein frommes Weib,
  Am eignen Herd in rühmlicher Heimat lebt,
    Es leuchtet über festem Boden
      Schöner dem sicheren Mann sein Himmel.

Denn, wie die Pflanze, wurzelt auf eignem Grund
  Sie nicht, verglüht die Seele des Sterblichen,
    Der mit dem Tageslichte nur, ein
      Armer auf heiliger Erde wandelt.

Zu mächtig ach! ihr himmlischen Höhen zieht
  Ihr mich empor, bei Stürmen, am heitern Tag
    Fühl ich verzehrend euch im Busen
      Wechseln, ihr wandelnden Götterkräfte.

Doch heute laß mich stille den trauten Pfad
  Zum Haine gehn, dem golden die Wipfel schmückt
    Sein sterbend Laub, und kränzt auch mir die
      Stirne, ihr holden Erinnerungen!

Und daß mir auch, zu retten mein sterblich Herz,
  Wie andern eine bleibende Stätte sei,
    Und heimatlos die Seele mir nicht
      Über das Leben hinweg sich sehne,

Sei du, Gesang, mein freundlich Asyl! sei du
  Beglückender! mit sorgender Liebe mir
    Gepflegt, der Garten, wo ich, wandelnd
      Unter den Blüten, den immerjungen,

In sichrer Einfalt wohne, wenn draußen mir
  Mit ihren Wellen allen die mächtge Zeit
    Die Wandelbare fern rauscht und die
      Stillere Sonne mein Wirken fördert.

Ihr segnet gütig über den Sterblichen
  Ihr Himmelskräfte! jedem sein Eigentum,

O segnet meines auch und daß zu
Frühe die Parze den Traum nicht ende.

(Blest is he who, calmly loving a pious wife, / Lives proud of his homeland beside his own hearth. / In his security this man sees his heaven / More brightly glow above the firm ground he treads. // For like the plant that is not rooted in / Its own soil, the soul of that mortal wilts / Who wanders with daylight only, a / Pauper astray on our Earth, the hallowed. // Too strongly alas! you heavenly heights, you pull / Me upward: when storms rage or on a calm day / I feel you, ravaging me, deep in my breast / Restless, you mutable powers of the gods. // Today, though, I'll quietly walk the familiar path / To the grove whose tree-tops are crowned with gold / By its dying leaves, and my brow too / Garland with gold, dear recollections! // And so that, to keep safe my mortal heart, / I may have, like others, a place of abode / And that my soul may not, homeless, / Impatiently flee this life in its longing // Be thou, my song, my friendly haven! be thou, / Giver of happiness, carefully, lovingly, / Tended by me, the garden where walking / Among the blossoms that are always young // I may live safely and in simplicity, while outside / With all its waves, great Time in its changes / Roars far away, and the / Gentler sun ripens my works. // You heavenly powers, your blessing falls / Kindly on each man's possessions, / Oh bless mine too, and let the / Fates not end my dream too soon.)

This is the great and deeply honourable expression of that longing (in a Europe of fatherlands we may call it a characteristically German longing) of which Heidegger's politicization of philosophy is a less than honourable version. Yet there are aspects of his philosophical venture to which this poem is relevant.

1989 (1990)

11

Günter Grass's Uniqueness

With the deaths of Thomas Mann in 1955 and of Bertolt Brecht and Gottfried Benn in 1956, a major era in the history of German literature comes to an end. These three are not only the greatest German writers of their age, they are also its witnesses. Each of them worked in a different genre: Thomas Mann in the convoluted, periodic and partly essayistic prose of his novels, Bert Brecht in the drama and narrative poetry of social dialectics, Benn in the lyrical poetry of radical Modernism. Each went through a different political development and reacted differently to the ruling political ideology. Yet the questions they ask have a family likeness; and the answers they offer remind us forcibly that theirs was an age of terror.

Any author whose literary gifts and moral disposition lead him towards this contemporary turmoil and who tries to come to terms with it creatively, with the best that is in him, is bound to have to face very special formal and compositional problems. These problems are likely to be different for a writer like Günter Grass, who faces the same world at one remove, reporting on the way the dead buried their dead. This is our first premise. The other is that, quite irrespective of that era, the German novel at its most characteristic has not been renowned for its contributions to the 'Great Tradition' of European Realism, which dominated French, English and Russian prose literature throughout the nineteenth and well into the twentieth century. Realism as we know it from Stendhal, Dickens and Tolstoy onwards entered German literature relatively late in the day and has been powerfully challenged by other modes of writing: Thomas Mann's very last work, for example, the unfinished *Confessions of Felix Krull, Confidence Man* of 1954, is a picaresque novel whose main narrative devices are a direct challenge to the verisimilitude of realistic fiction.

Chief among the literary and cultural patterns of Thomas Mann's novels had been the classical German *Bildungsroman*, the novel of initiation and development, in the course of which a young hero is led from adolescent self-absorption and egocentricity on the margins of the social world through a variety of instructive experiences – often a mixture of the erotic and the aesthetic – to a state of adulthood and responsibility at the centre of contemporary society. True, Thomas Mann's use of the *Bildungsroman* and its main theme had never been unambiguous and unproblematic, had always been informed – or undermined – by a spirit of irony; in *Felix Krull* this is radicalized to a point of fantasy and farce.

The pattern from which *Felix Krull* evolves is the picaresque novel, which, in German literature, goes back to the seventeenth century – 1668 to be precise, when Hans Jakob Christoffel von Grimmelshausen published his *Adventures of Simplicius Simplicissimus*, a novel which, in sharp contrast to the contemporary courtly novel, is set among soldiers, actors, servants, beggars, robbers and whores. There are characters exemplifying the Christian virtues, but the notion of moral and spiritual development recedes behind a rich and colourful series of adventures on the pattern of 'one damn thing after another'. Purposeful teleology gives way to the rule of fortune, spiritual uplift goes hang, cunning for the sake of mere survival is the order of the day, and, when salvation does come, it comes in as untoward and unmotivated a manner as do the temptations of the flesh and of the Devil. All this, as we shall see, is grist to Günter Grass's mill. The *pícaro* he will create from some of the elements of the traditional rogue novel is as radical a response to Thomas Mann's genteel Felix Krull as Krull is to Grimmelshausen's Simplicius. Very strong affinities of atmosphere connect the Germany of the Thirty Years' War, which Grimmelshausen portrayed, with the Germany of the 1930s and 1940s, which is the obsessive concern of Grass's 'Danzig Trilogy'. These are affinities which are not encompassed by Mann's imagination, or by the imagination of many writers of Mann's generation apart from Brecht.

Günter Grass was born in 1927 in a suburb of the Free City of Danzig, then under the protection of the League of Nations, and, like Charles Dickens, Jan Neruda, James Joyce, Theodor Fontane and Grass's acknowledged exemplar Alfred Döblin, he places a major city of marked character at the centre of his creative imagination. Grass's best work so far is given over, again and again, to its evocation: a very special piety ties him to the streets and places of Danzig, its beaches, its inhabitants and their desperate, murderous national conflicts. For even more than the London, Dublin, Berlin and Prague of the authors I have mentioned, Grass's Danzig is an intensely political city: the place, from the twelfth century onwards, where Prussia and Poland, the Knights of the Teutonic Order and Polish patriots, Germans and Slavs encountered each other in fierce rivalry. In 1933, when Hitler was appointed Chancellor of Germany, Danzig was experiencing growing unemployment, a deterioration of its maritime trade and an upsurge of nationalism; and the people of the deeply divided city elected a senate with a National Socialist majority and the local Party Gauleiter as its president.

To paraphrase a sentence of Brecht's Galileo, happy is the country that has no land frontiers. With the conflict of Ulster in the forefront of our minds, we now find it less difficult to imagine the protracted bitterness and violence of the Polish–German relationship that is epitomized in the history of Danzig

– the intensity of the passions, the internecine strife of centuries, which come to a head and lead directly to the outbreak of the Second World War in the first days of September 1939, and to the city's death in the last week of that war. The rhythms of the threnody which the narrator-hero of *The Tin Drum* chants for the city illustrate that special *pietas loci* which informs Grass's novel, and give us a first idea of the innovatory energy of his prose:

After that we seldom emerged from our hole. The Russians were said to be in Zigankenberg, Pietzgendorf, and on the outskirts of Schidlitz. There was no doubt that they occupied the heights, for they were firing straight down into the city. Inner City and Outer City, Old City, New City and Old New City, Lower City and Spice City – what had taken seven hundred years to build burned down in three days. Yet this was not the first fire to descend on the city of Danzig. For centuries Pomeranians, Brandenburgers, Teutonic Knights, Poles, Swedes, and a second time Swedes, Frenchmen, Prussians, and Russians, even Saxons, had made history by deciding every five years that the city of Danzig was worth burning. And now it was Russians, Poles, Germans, and Englishmen all at once who were burning the city's Gothic bricks for the hundredth time. Hook Street, Long Street, and Broad Street, Big Weaver Street and Little Weaver Street were in flames; Tobias Street, Hound Street, Old City Ditch, Outer City Ditch, the ramparts and Long Bridge, all were in flames. Built of wood, Crane Gate made a particularly fine blaze. In Breechesmaker Street, the fire had itself measured for several pairs of extra-loud breeches. The Church of St Mary was burning inside and outside, festive light effects could be seen through its ogival windows. What bells had not been evacuated from St Catherine, St John, St Brigit, Saints Barbara, Elisabeth, Peter, and Paul, from Trinity and Corpus Christi, melted in their belfries and dripped away without pomp or ceremony. In the Big Mill red wheat was milled. Butcher Street smelled of burnt Sunday roast. The Municipal Theatre was giving a première, a one-act play entitled 'The Firebug's Dream'. The fathers decided to raise the firemen's wages retroactively after the fire. Holy Ghost Street was burning in the name of the Holy Ghost. Joyously, the Franciscan Monastery blazed in the name of St Francis, who had loved fire and sung hymns to it. Our Lady Street burned for Father and Son at once. Needless to say the Lumber Market, Coal Market and Haymarket burned to the ground. In Baker Street the ovens burned, and the bread and rolls with them. In Milk Pitcher Street the milk boiled over. Only the West Prussian Fire Insurance Building, for purely symbolic reasons, refused to burn down. (pp. 389–90)

The fate of the city and its surrounding countryside becomes for a boy born of a German father and a Cashubian (Slav) mother, a part of his intimate personal history. As a member of the German lower-middle classes, which

were particularly receptive to the new racist and nationalist ideas, at the age
of ten he entered the 'Jungvolk', from which he was promoted to the Hitler-
Jugend, joining a tank regiment as a gunner when he was barely seventeen.
When, at the end of the war, on being wounded, he was taken prisoner of
war by the Americans, he still felt, as he says, 'that our war was all right'.
Then came the shock of a guided tour through the concentration camp at
Dachau and the gradual realization 'of what unbelievable crimes had been
done in the name of my ... generation and ... what guilt, knowingly and
unknowingly, our people had brought upon themselves'.

Here, then, are the elements present in this exacting setting: lower-middle-
class life with its hybrid linguistic milieu and its charged atmosphere of rival
nationalisms, with a small Jewish minority the butt of both sides, and a strong
and highly ritualized religious tradition – in Grass's case, Roman Catholic;
the smells and shapes of a small grocery store, the Party – its ideological
slogans, colourful ritual and sordid practices; school life, swimming in the
Baltic Sea; the war in its last, hopeless stages; and the true face of the regime
disclosed at last. On his release from the American POW camp, aged nineteen,
Grass did not go back to school but found himself a job as an apprentice
miner in a potassium mine near Hildesheim, listening during the breaks for
salami sandwiches to the last echoes of the political quarrels that had begun
long ago, in the Weimar Republic, and in which embittered communists and
disillusioned and resentful National Socialists together ganged up on 'the dry-
as-dust' SPD, who 'taught me how to live without an ideology'. Grass's
activism and his allegiance to the SPD date from those early post-war days
before the German economic miracle, and this allegiance was later strengthened by his friendship with Willy Brandt. When, in December 1970, Brandt
as German chancellor went to kneel before the monument to the dead of the
Polish resistance in Warsaw (a gesture that appalled the nationalists on the far
Right), Grass was among those who accompanied him. Yet he acknowledges, in
his major works, the need to separate his fiction, not from politics, but from
political advocacy. A strong political concern goes through his novels; a deep,
mature and tolerant understanding for the predicament of the little man at
the mercy of huge political forces. But his understanding goes further, beyond
this sort of tolerance, to major satirical sorties against the trimmers and fellow-
travellers and profiteers, culminating in that very special grotesque presentation
of the horrors of war, and of totalitarian regimes, which yields the most
remarkable passages of his prose so far (1981) and is his outstanding contribution to post-war German literature. The tolerance that informs his portraits
of the lower-middle classes must not obscure the fact that he is not content,
as many of his contemporary fellow-writers in Germany still are, to present
the predicament of the individual man as though it were caused by a stroke
of fate: it is part of his purpose to show the political sources and consequences
of that predicament.

After two years of mining, Grass became an apprentice in a monumental
mason's workshop in Düsseldorf, and then, after a brief period in a jazz band,

he won a scholarship to study drawing and sculpture at the academies of Düsseldorf and Berlin. He is a gifted draughtsman, and has produced some fine illustrations and the stunning designs for the dust jackets of his books. These were the years he went, penniless, on a series of extensive hitch-hikes through Italy and France. It was in the course of these journeys that he seems to have moved, quite imperceptibly, from drawing and sculpture to writing, and from huge and impracticable epic effusions to prose-poems, and thence to a highly rhythmic and rich, metaphor-studded prose. To this day, the early plans of his novels tend at first to be set out either like blueprints in multi-coloured graphs or in the form of brief, usually unrhymed poems.

Both the interest in the visual arts and the unfussy, easy way in which he moves from genre to genre – creating pictorial patterns and shapes in his literary fictions and complex literary allusions in his drawings – all this ease of transition between different kinds of creativeness is reflected in his prose. Not only that. These transitions have their parallel in the movement of his novels from the present to the past and back again, from the historical to the political and from the concrete to the abstract; and in the disconcerting and apparently arbitrary way in which he is apt to slip from the first- to the third-person narrative, from the point of view of one character to that of another, as though all men, even in their solitude, even in their moments of murderous enmity, were yet unable to deny the fact that they are made of one flesh, consubstantial, and as though the world of things, too, were solid yet not inanimate, part of and an extension of the living substantiality of men. And all this, which I present here as though it were an abstruse, excogitated aesthetic doctrine, is of course nothing of the sort: it is, for him, a literary practice, extensively reflected on, which enables him to match and make his vision of the world. He was seventeen and a half when the war ended in May 1945. The compulsion exerted on him comes, not from the events of the past, but from a recollection of those events. In Grass's early novels it was converted into a prose which turns out to be the first major source of liberation from an unmanageable literary past that post-war German literature had known.

The past as time and life irretrievably lost, and the past in the light of the present; the Grand Guignol of history and the actuality of its politics; the complex relationship of Eros and food, and the special place of the disgusting and the sentimental in the recesses, the oubliettes, of consciousness; the religious and the blasphemous, the pious and the obscene; things, animals and men, concrete objects and conceptual abstractions – all these parts of an acute sense of life are set out in Grass's prose; not, however, in some ghastly Hegelian dialectic of antitheses and radical contradictions, but in continuities and prismatic, rainbow patterns.

More than one critic has called Grass a humanist. I am not sure the word has much meaning left. He is one in the sense that there is no human experience too odd, too alien, to be made a part of one of his prismatic patterns. But he seems, as the author of certain substantial fictions, too diverse, too uncompromisingly interested in the fate of these fictions and in the process that gives rise to them – in short, too free – to be classifiable under any 'ism' or ideology. Literature is made of many different brews and dispositions, in freedom and in bondage, by the most doctrinaire no less successfully than by the least attached. But in his time and place – our assessment has the wisdom of hindsight – in that moment of defeat and dishonour, of shame and the posturing that tried to hide the shame, in that moment when the past could be neither forgotten (though it was denied) nor allowed to paralyse the present, a man without ideology was what was wanted, and Grass was and has remained such a man. I mean here not Grass the political man and responsible *Bürger* of what has become one of Europe's exemplary democracies, but Grass the author of the most passionately contended books in post-war German literature, books which were attacked, not just on moral grounds (like *Ulysses* or *Lady Chatterley's Lover*), but also on political and patriotic grounds (like the works of Sinyavsky and Daniel) – the author of 'The Danzig Trilogy'.

The trilogy consists of *The Tin Drum* (1959), the novella *Cat and Mouse* (1961) and *The Dog Years* (1963). What the three works have in common is, above all, the locale and the historico-political theme of Danzig at war. It is as if 'the Hellish Bruegel', his attention caught by the intricate pattern of one of his own landscapes with figures, had decided to devote two further panels to the subject: one small, exploring a single detail, the other on a larger and less intimate scale than the original picture.

In the first work, *The Tin Drum*, Oskar Matzerath – inmate of a mental hospital, which he describes, rather more euphemistically, as 'eine Heil- und Pflegeanstalt', a sanatorium and nursing home – is writing his memoirs. The time covered takes us from the bizarre scene when his mother was conceived under her Cashubian mother's fourfold skirts in a potato field at harvest time in 1899, through Oskar's own birth in 1924, through his arrest and hospitalization twenty-eight years later, in 1952, when (with the help of Bruno, his warden) he begins writing his memoirs, to his thirtieth birthday and the conclusion of his manuscript in 1954.

Narrative coherence in *The Tin Drum* is achieved by a complex but relatively unified point of view, the 'I-he' narration of Oskar Matzerath. In the novella *Cat and Mouse* – an adventure story of wartime adolescence, an offshoot of one of the episodes of the first novel – the point of view remains that of a single narrator, Pilenz, but because it is a confessional tale, involving a sequence of schoolboy jealousies and betrayals, the reliability of Pilenz as first-person narrator is constantly undercut. The truth of his narration remains as uncertain as does the character of the problematic hero and object of Pilenz's betrayal, 'the great Mahlke' himself. German *Novellen* are built around a single momentous event. Here the event is Mahlke's theft of one of Germany's highest military decorations, the Knight's Cross of the Iron Cross. The possession of it every German schoolboy's dream, a coveted toy and status symbol loaded with immense mystical, patriotic and sexual connotations, that Knight's Cross serves, in an almost physical sense, as the means of Mahlke's desperate self-defence and arrogant self-assertion (as the tin drum does for

Oskar Matzerath); and its ambivalent function – it commemorates the Knights of the Teutonic Order, yet it is a creation of Hitler's – corresponds to the narrator's unreliability and unstable point of view.

Finally, and again emerging from the episodic material of *The Tin Drum*, there is the mammoth undertaking of *The Dog Years*. This is the story of (among a great many other things) the friendship between Walter Matern, the son of a German miller from the Danzig hinterland, and the half-Jewish Eddi Amsel, alias Haseloff, alias Brauxell (in several different spellings). The account of three decades – from 1925 to the mid-1950s – is presented by various 'authors' including a whole post-war collective of them in the pay of the now baptized Amsel-Brauchsel, the artist-entrepreneur-manufacturer of Art Deco scarecrows, who (like most other characters in the novel) is in pursuit of a past he hopes he will never catch up with.

The coherence of *The Dog Years* is provided neither by the action nor by its characters: the discontinuous narrative, especially in the last section of the book, is a part of its programme – one might almost say of its ideology. The action is frozen into metaphors and images, which provide such unity as the book possesses. To say this, though, is liable to lead to a misunderstanding. Critics who point to the importance of images in novels often argue as though the patterns these images form were patterns in the book and nowhere else. This use of images is called 'non-referential' – I think nonsensically. The genealogy of black dogs, from which the book takes its title and which is reiterated throughout –

> Pawel ... had brought Perkun with him from Lithuania and on request exhibited a kind of pedigree, which made it clear to whom it may concern that Perkun's grandmother on her father's side had been a Lithuanian, Russian or Polish she-wolf. And Perkun begat Senta; and Senta whelped Harras; and Harras [covered Thekla von Schüddelkau] and begat Prinz; and Prinz made history [because Prinz was given to the beloved Führer and Chancellor of Greater Germany for his birthday and, being the Führer's favourite dog, was shown in the newsreels ...] (p. 15)

– this genealogical list, for all its symbolical overtones, is made up of the sequence of generations of actual SS black dogs and is the emblem of a historical experience. Similarly, the ontological blatherer with totalitarian collywobbles and attacks of authenticitis of the cervical membrane called Martin Heidegger is an identifiable caricature of the philosopher of that name; and the mountain made of human bones which lies between the outskirts of the city and the lunatic asylum at Stutthof, which everybody sees and nobody has seen, which everybody smells and nobody knows anything about – that mountain, expressed in Heideggerian gobbledegook, is 'being that has come into unconcealment' and 'the ontological disposition toward the annihilating nothingness of German history'.

There is no end to the strings of bizarre images which create the unity of the book. They all raise the same question: why is there no continuous action; why the *bizarrerie?* For an answer to this central question of Grass's early work, we had better return to his first and most accessible novel, *The Tin Drum.*

Here, certainly, there is something like a central character, depicted with a modicum of psychological coherence – a coherence which is undercut, but not fatally, by that opening confessional statement made in the haven of a lunatic asylum. Oskar Matzerath is presented – and presents himself – in a series of unstable and unnervingly ambiguous relationships with the people and events around him, mainly as the victim but occasionally as the victimizer in a bizarre world, a 'world turned upside down'. As a new-born baby, he is certain that his entry into the world will be disastrous – not because it is *his* entry, but because it is the world. (The heroes of the classical *Bildungsroman* similarly hesitate over whether to enter the social world or to remain safely hidden in the caul of their solipsistic imagination, but similarly, too, we read in one of Grass's favourite novels: 'My Tristram's misfortunes began nine months before ever he came into the world'.) And when Oskar's wish to return to the womb is not fulfilled (the midwife – I mean Oskar's midwife, but it could be Tristram Shandy's – having done the irreversible and cut the umbilical cord), Oskar does the next best thing: at the age of three he wills himself to stop growing, throwing himself through the trapdoor into the cellar to provide the adults with an acceptable explanation for his failure to grow. End of *Entwicklung* with a vengeance.

What this fairy-tale of outrageous absurdity is designed to suggest is the central insight of the novel, that there is no other way than this of coping with, and making sense of, the hideous events and encounters of the adult world, and also that this is really no way either, because, by becoming a freak with every *appearance* of a gravely retarded development, Oskar is liable to fall victim to the state-controlled euthanasia which the National Socialist regime practised in order to implement its racial policy: it is only the collapse of the postal service at the end of the war (when even the Prussian bureaucracy ceased to function) that prevents father Matzerath's letter, in which he consents to the eugenic killing of Oskar, from reaching what is so quaintly called the Reich Ministry of Health. And this world, in which Oskar wills himself to stop growing, still pays lip-service to the classical Weimar values of spiritual growth and development that had been central to the ideology of the *Bildungs-* or *Entwicklungsroman.*

These assaults on the reader's sensibilities dominate every part of the novel. Oskar has a mother who dies, hideously, of a surfeit of fried lampreys and eels, some of which, we are told, may have been the descendants of those Baltic eels that may have eaten her Polish father, assuming, what is never entirely certain, that he was drowned and didn't disappear in the United States. Her death, like so many deaths in the novel, is the sign of a botched life. And Oskar has two fathers: an elegant Polish one, who is his mother's lover, and a German one, the hefty grocer Matzerath, with whom he will eventually share a mistress. Jan Bronski, the Pole, is involved in 'the famous battle for the Polish post office' at the outbreak of the war, the later part of which he spends playing a difficult game of three-handed skat – difficult because one of the players, the janitor Kobyella, is wounded, and has to be propped up against, and then tied to, a basket full of blood-stained letters (surmounted by a dying man) to prevent him showing his hand, and eventually dies in the course of it. At the end of the battle, Bronski is executed with thirty or so other Poles, in the courtyard of the post office, 'with arms upraised and hands folded behind their necks . . . [they] were thirsty and having their pictures taken for the newsreels'. In Jan Bronski's 'upraised hands he held a few skat cards and with one hand – holding the queen of hearts, I think – he waved to Oskar, his departing son', (pp. 245–6). At the graveside of Matzerath, his other father, in 1945, Oskar wills himself to grow again, ready to assume the responsibilities of an adult, but after another three years, in the course of which he has merely succeeded in growing a hump, he decides (shades of Uncle Toby) that the sickbed in the asylum is the only safe haven and worthwhile goal, after all.

A child with an adult mind, a freak who combines the insights, feelings and sexuality of an adult with the guile and the scot-free licence of a child, Oskar has only two means of making an impact on the adult world: one is his drum, or rather series of drums, made of tin, the sides painted with red and white triangles, the colours of the Polish Army. (I recollect a string of grey stallions of the Polish cavalry, a couple of tall red-and-white drums slung from each, parading on a brilliant Sunday morning in August 1939 along the cobbled street of a little town in Polish Silesia, less than thirty miles away from the German frontier, less than three weeks away from their doom.) The tin drum is the instrument of Oskar's art and self-expression, and it is his defence – with it, he can both disrupt political meetings and entertain Wehrmacht audiences – and it is the means of his brief flights of freedom: all-powerful and compelling at one moment, useless in competing even with the noise of carpet-beating the next; an instrument of pure, disinterested *l'art-pour-l'art* at one point, a source of cheap and meretricious entertainment at another.

In the course of defending his drum from seizure by his exasperated family, Oskar discovers a second means of disrupting the adult world: his capacity to aim his voice at any glass area that is visible to him and to sing it to bits. And this talent, too, is used ambivalently, now as the desperate protest of a child that is being unspeakably maltreated by other children, now as a manifestation of aesthetic decadence and manneristic art: during his stay in German-occupied Paris, Oskar devises an art-historical scheme for his act according to which he systematically destroys items of glassware covering the history of glass from Louis XIV to Art Nouveau. The intermittent identifications of author with hero are as grotesque – and as outrageously explicit – as all the other ploys.

There are a good many story-lines one might follow through the novel, but a better way of conveying not only its extraordinary achievement, but also the formal difficulties that lay in the way of that achievement, is to concentrate on a single episode. Before doing that, though, the most obvious objection to the novel (and indeed to *The Dog Years* too) must be faced.

The reader may have gained the impression that here is a fictional monster – or a monster fiction – of six or seven hundred pages where anything goes – heedless fantasy let loose on unresistant material, with no discernible unifying meaning or coherence of any kind. Or else he may suspect that, German fictions being notorious for their high-flown metaphysical messages, the critic will now pull the rabbit out of the hat and demonstrate the transcendental meaning of it all.

There is (as far as I can see) no such transcendental meaning or message, and yet the novel is much more than a series of self-indulgent or author-indulgent images and random episodes. Its meaning is to be wrested from its compositional difficulties, and they in turn may best be approached from the perspective of another great favourite of Grass's, Melville's *Moby Dick*. In the very deeps of that other monster creation you may stumble across a rumination in which the narrator anticipates the charge of self-indulgence and of excessive preoccupation with the customs and the bits and pieces of the whaling craft: 'So ignorant are most landsmen of some of the plainest and most palpable wonders of the world, that without some hints [!] touching the plain facts, historical or otherwise, of the fishery, they might scout at Moby Dick as a monstrous fable, or still worse and more detestable, a hideous and intolerable allegory'. Grass is in a similar predicament. The story he is writing is deeply, irreversibly steeped in the history of its time – or rather, not in that history, but in the crude and gory facts of the past from which such a history will have to be fashioned. These facts are notorious for offering the utmost resistance to interpretation of whatever kind. This is both the experience of readers of a different generation or culture and the understanding which Grass himself has of his national past and which he shares with his own generation of readers. Yet his impulse to write a historical fiction is clearly every bit as strong as the impulse to understand and come honourably to terms with that impossible past: in the creative act the two are to be united.

The work, therefore, is threatened by two difficulties. One is the danger of creating a sequence in which one 'monstrous fable' follows another and the whole ends up as little more than an incoherent set of metaphors gone wild. The other, 'still worse and more detestable', is the danger that the impossible past gets swallowed up by 'a hideous and intolerable allegory'.

Again and again, we are likely to return to the question: can the unspeakable obscenity that called itself the Third Reich be fictionalized at all? Clearly, such an undertaking will require a certain imaginative freedom from the past – a freedom which was not available to Thomas Mann and his contemporaries, and which many critics may not be willing to grant. Yet 'unspeakable' is itself a descriptive adjective and a legitimate part of the critic's vocabulary; and it is one thing to say (as some critics have said) that the novel cannot be interpreted, that it is incapable of yielding a meaning, and another to say that its meaning is hedged in with meaninglessness, with the grave difficulty of making sense of apparently senseless horror. True, we cannot interpret the story that is told in its fantastic episodes in simple, unambiguous terms, but this isn't due to some degeneracy of its author's sensibilities (as was predictably claimed by his indignant right-wing critics), but, on the contrary, to the immense compositional difficulty he was bound to face when devising the underlying strategy of his novel. For what this writing aims to convey is the paradox that the daily practice and horrors of the Third Reich went on side by side with the daily practice and horrors of the ordinary world, that these things were and are and always have been a part of the human situation, and that this knowledge – I mean that monstrosities are human and that mankind is monstrous – must be grasped to the full, undiminished by the lethargy that comes from repetition and familiarity, and without allowing the thing made familiar to breed contempt, to destroy both the feeling of outrage and the capacity for interpretation, the capacity for giving a fictional account of it all. What Grass's novel in its own blasphemous way aims to convey is the paradox (whose supreme illustration is the death of Christ) that everything is ordinary and everything is special.

The two dangers that beset the work may now be restated: it is threatened by either a demonization of its material or a trivialization of it. There is the risk that the metaphors, set out to convey the terrible, 'unspeakable' evil, will turn out to be of an intolerable obscurity, incomprehensibly transcending all mundane experience – which is what, in *The Dog Years*, Grass satirizes in the oracular utterances of Martin Heidegger. And there is the opposite risk – of the story slopping over into a mood of ghastly tolerance, a mood in which we are asked to accept every infamy as part of the human condition, for no better reason than that (as the great Hegel observed in one of his less great moments) in the night all cows are black, boys will be boys, men will be men and that's how it's always been. These are the two dangers attending Grass's prose. They are reflected in his readers' occasional reactions – a sudden switching over from blank incomprehension to bored *déjà vu*.

But of course, at its best – as in 'Faith, Hope and Love', the last chapter of the first book of *The Tin Drum* – the narrative emerges from the shadow of those twin dangers with supreme success. The heading from 1 Corinthians 13:13 provides the chapter with its leitmotiv. It begins in fairy-tale fashion, with a phrase that will be repeated throughout the chapter: 'There was once a musician; his name was Meyn and he played the trumpet too beautifully for words' (p. 198). Meyn has been a friend of Oskar's, and of Oskar's friend Herbert, at whose funeral he blows the trumpet, as always when he is drunk, too beautifully for words. But Meyn is also a Storm Trooper, a member of the SA, a psychotic who, when sober and deeply disturbed, tries to kill his four cats and bury them in his dustbin, but 'because the cats were not all-the-way dead, they gave him away'. And so the SA man Meyn was expelled from the party 'for inhuman cruelty to animals' and 'conduct unbecoming a Storm Trooper' even though 'on the night of 8 November [1938 – actually, the night of 9th], which later became known as Crystal Night, he helped set fire to the Langfuhr Synagogue in Michaelisweg. Even his meritorious activity the following morning, when a number of stores, carefully designated in advance, were closed down for the good of the nation' could not halt his expulsion from the Mounted SA (p. 201). Later, Meyn joins the Home Guard, which later still becomes part of the SS.

This 8th of November is also the day when Oskar goes to visit his friend and chief supplier of red-and-white tin drums, the toyshop owner Sigismund Markus. He finds the shop full of SA men, in uniforms like Meyn's, but 'Meyn was not there; just as the ones who were there were not somewhere else' (this is the phraseology of post-war alibis). The shop is full of excrement (this connects with a lengthy disquisition on the colour of brown, which is also the colour of the Party) and:

> The toy merchant sat behind his desk. As usual he had on sleeve protectors over his dark-grey everyday jacket. Dandruff on his shoulders showed that his scalp was in bad shape. One of the SA men with puppets on his fingers poked him with Kasperl's wooden grandmother, but Markus was beyond being spoken to, beyond being hurt or humiliated. Before him on the desk stood an empty water glass; the sound of his crashing shop-window had made him thirsty no doubt. (p. 202)

The detail of the dandruff is no more grotesque than the spectacle of the men letting down their trousers or the picture of the dead man.

Oskar leaves the shop, and, outside, 'some pious ladies and strikingly ugly young girls' were handing out religious tracts 'under a banner with an inscription quoted from the thirteenth chapter of the First Epistle to the Corinthians. "Faith . . . hope . . . love," Oskar read and played with the three words as a juggler plays with bottles':

> Leichtgläubig, Hoffmannstropfen, Liebesperlen, Gutehoffnungshütte, Liebfrauenmilch, Gläubigversammlung, Glaubst du, daß es morgen regnen wird? Ein ganzes leichtgläubiges Volk glaubte an den Weihnachtsmann. Aber der Weihnachtsmann war in Wirklichkeit der Gasmann. Ich glaube, daß es nach Nüssen riecht und nach Mandeln . . .

The sequence is by definition untranslatable, but this is how the punning on the three saintly virtues may be conveyed:

> 'Faith . . . hope . . . love,' Oskar read . . .: faith healer, Old Faithful, faithless hope, hope chest, Cape of Good Hope, hopeless love, Love's Labour's Lost, six love. An entire credulous nation believed, there's faith for you, in Santa Claus. But Santa Claus was really the gasman. I believe

– such is my faith – that it smells of walnuts and almonds. But it smelled of gas. Soon, so they said, 'twill be the first Sunday of Advent. And the first, second, third, and fourth Sundays of Advent were turned on like gas cocks, to produce a credible smell of walnuts and almonds, so that all those who liked to crack nuts could take comfort and believe:

He's coming, He's coming. Who is coming? The Christ child, the Saviour? Or is it the heavenly gasman with the gas meter under his arm, that always goes ticktock? And he said: I am the Saviour of this world, without me you can't cook. And he was not too demanding, he offered special rates, turned on the freshly polished gas cocks, and let the Holy Ghost pour forth, so the dove, or squab, might be cooked. And handed out walnuts and almonds which were promptly cracked, and they too poured forth spirit and gas. (p. 203)

This is the horrendous side by side with, but undiminished by, the practices of the ordinary world.

'Ask my pen', says Tristram Shandy, when questioned about the design of his strange book: 'Ask my pen; it governs me; I govern not it.' What is being undertaken in Grass's equally strange book is something very new but also, going back to Laurence Sterne, very old. However different the moods of the two novels, they both disdain narrative order and live by extravagant metaphor, word games, situational games and the detailed working out of bizarre images. *Tristram Shandy* is certainly a humorous novel, but so, in parts, is *The Tin Drum*; where the humour of the one shades off into sentimentality, the other veers into tragi-comedy; and where *Tristram Shandy* is concerned to problematize arguments based on causality and replace them by arguments drawn out of a welter of associations of ideas, so *The Tin Drum* throws causality to the winds and replaces it – not so much by associations of ideas as by verbal associations; egging the reader on to react with indignation to the substitution. *The Tin Drum*'s humour and its seriousness are not polarized in some inhuman Hegelian dialectic: they are made continuous with each other, as the everyday and the monstrous are continuous in our experience.

Conventional critical terminology, which moves within the squirrel's cage of symbols and allegories, won't quite do. Oskar isn't the symbol of anything, just as Uncle Toby or Corporal Trim aren't the symbols of anything. Oskar is what he is, a freak, because freaks alone (according to the logic the author compels us to accept) can be brought into some sort of meaningful relationship with this world – and that relationship is one of metaphors and puns, and of the pseudo-logic that is built from metaphors and puns. The word game on 'faith, hope and love', on the spirit (*pneuma*) and gas, Santa Claus and the holy gasman, may suggest elements of satire (German love of Christmas, the Church's comforting concern for the spiritual weal of everyone except those who were gassed, Hitler's role as self-appointed Saviour, and so on), but the satirical element is subsidiary to the main undertaking of the novel, which is to match an almost unbelievable, inexplicable past with almost unbelievable and inexplicable metaphors, and thus to derive, from this matching, a modicum of meaning without reducing its tragic affect and without explaining it away. And it is an added grace that all this is done without succumbing to that ghastly tendency (characteristic of post-Nietzschean Germany) to justify and vindicate everything by adverting to a 'tragic view of life'.

There are traces and analogies of a Christian concern in the novel. At their most obvious, these traces are to be seen in the negative religiousness of blasphemy, such as the exegesis of 'faith, hope and love', or the repeated scenes of Oskar Matzerath's imitation of the Christ child. It is as if blasphemy were the only form of socialized religiousness available to blasphemous times. But there are also analogies pointing to a religious meaning. The precarious stylistic balance I mentioned, between the obscurity of demonization and the triviality of 'all's grist to the human mill', involving a full acknowledgement of the horrors of the past which the creative conscience prevents from turning either into complacent tolerance or into annihilating despair – this balance is surely seen at its clearest within such a framework as is provided by St Augustine's exhortation, often quoted 'with particular relish and sadness' by Samuel Beckett: 'Do not despair, one of the thieves was saved; do not presume, one of the thieves was damned'. If, in post-war German literature, other literary ways were devised of coming to terms with that past, without presumption and without despair, I have failed to notice them. So far, Grass's achievement is unique.

1981

12

The Matljary Diary*

In the High Tatra Mountains above M., 28 October 1944 Anniversary of the
Founding of the Republic. The sixth under German occupation, and we pray
it may be the last. We'd been promised reinforcements today, waited all day,
at last they came. What a crew – worse than useless. As far as I can tell they
are Prague coffee-house Jews, the lot of them. They all speak Czech – *of
sorts*(!). It does seem to have taken them a long time to discover their patriotic
vein . . . Heavens, what specimens! You only have to look at them to see they
don't know one end of a rifle from the other – a game of chess or rummy
seems to be the only kind of exercise they're used to. Still, now they've come
to join us, we must make some use of them. Better late than never, I suppose.

29 October They all turn out to be university graduates, of course, except the
one who was chef at the Hotel Paříž. We put him in charge of the cookhouse
straightaway, and I must say you certainly can tell the difference. What are
we going to do with the rest, I wonder? Most of them are lawyers – what else!
– but there is a real doctor among them, too, and he'll come in handy soon;
we've been without an MD so far. Among the lawyers there is one, Dr F. K.,
they all seem to look up to – very quiet, though.

30 October As I expected, the language question is proving troublesome and
is aggravating our relations with the new lot that arrived two days ago. It's
bad enough their talking nothing but German among themselves – they also
organize reading groups and read German poems and stories to each other,
and our chaps are furious. You can hardly blame them – after all, we're here
to *fight* the Germans, not to fill our minds with their nebulous Teutonic
poetry! I had to say something to Dr K. about it, simply because he seems to
be the most sensible one among them – also he seems to be fairly old, though
he doesn't *look* old at all – and he said he well understood why we were angry

---

* Franz Kafka stayed in a sanatorium in the mountain village of Matljary in Slovakia from
December 1920 until August 1921; he died in June 1924.

and he hoped we would bear with them. He then added that some people could not live without literature – people who hadn't much else in life, so to speak – and he thought that as long as these reading sessions didn't interfere with people's ordinary duties, we should let it pass. Fair enough, I suppose.

Somebody said Dr K. isn't really a lawyer at all but an author. *In German*, of course.

31 October This rumour about Dr K. being an author turns out to be a lot of nonsense, as I expected. I asked him point blank and he admitted that he has hardly published anything. How can you call yourself a writer if all you've done is a few stories about animals and that sort of thing? (We read some La Fontaine at school, the year before the Germans closed all our secondary schools, but that was *in verse*.) In fact, he worked in an industrial insurance office – bilking the workers of their rightful insurance money, I don't doubt. Still – he doesn't *look* like a capitalist hyena to me. As a matter of fact everybody seems to like him – I mean our chaps too – and since he is not very strong, everybody offers to help him, with the lugging of provisions etc. (They're none of them very strong, this 'Anniversary Crew', as we call them, worse luck! You don't grow muscles by moving pawns across the chess-board ...)

I've noticed he doesn't even keep a diary, though he seems interested in the fact that I do.

1 November 1944 There is no doubt that Dr K. is proving a useful addition to the camp. It turns out that he knows the region well – seems to have spent several months in hospital in Matljary; and even though it's *years* ago (well before I was born, I believe), he seems to remember the region quite accurately. Of course, we have our Slovak liaison men who come over from the next camp and know the mountains like the back of their hand, but they're not always around. Besides, Slovaks are a bit funny, as we know to our cost – look at what happened in '38 and '39, when they left the sinking ship and set up a state of their own, with Hitler's blessing. And whatever you may think of this new lot – though they're not exactly a heroic breed, *they* won't go over to the Germans, that's for sure! Poor devils, most of their relations are in German camps anyway.

2 November Shared the late watch with F. K. I asked him how he came to join us. At first it sounded like the usual story. Says he was in his lodgings in Prague one morning, still in bed, when a couple of uniformed men came into his room to arrest him. Sicherheitsdienst, I imagine – he couldn't remember their insignia (typical!), only that their uniforms were black and had pockets everywhere. He says he asked them their names(!), as if that was likely to cut any ice with the SD, and told them that they had no right to be in his lodgings, and that he had done nothing wrong, nothing that could give them the right to arrest him. He seemed at first to think it was all a joke – one of the men looked familiar, like one of the porters from his insurance office. It was a most peculiar story – I asked him whether he had forgotten about the German occupation. He said no, he remembered it all right, but that it took him some time before he realized that they really had come to take him away. Apparently he thought it had all happened before, though the way he said it I couldn't make out whether in reality or merely in his imagination. (He does seem to be a writer after all, lots of imagination and a bit slow on the uptake, I suspect.)

3 November First lot of snow. We spent the day improving the bivouac, sawing and piling up firewood. The sun came out at about noon and I got everybody out of their tents to do some exercises. I wonder how we're going to survive when the real winter weather comes, with this new lot to look after!

4 November F. K. told me that once he realized these two men had come to arrest him, he made up his mind to try to get away. 'Not like the last time,' he said (?). He quite simply pretended he had to go into the next room to get dressed and somehow managed to slip out of the house by the back stairs – a miracle he got away with it. After that he made his way into the Slovak mountains with the help of our underground network, the usual story.

'Not like the last time.' I couldn't make out what he meant by that, and so I asked him. It seems he was referring to a story he had written years before, which also began with a man being arrested. But in the story the man more or less accepted his fate, and although he was left at liberty, he actually started looking for the court of law that would be prepared to try him. Like a mouse looking for the cat that will eat it up! It sounded a most peculiar story, and I told Dr K. so. After all, he himself had said the man was innocent, that somebody had been spreading lies about him. I got a bit worked up about this – it seemed like a complete non sequitur – I had actually forgotten that what we were talking about was only a story. What could be more absurd, when you think of it, than arguing about a piece of fiction that wasn't even *published*, for God's sake! In *our* situation, with the German line in the Ukraine collapsing, and the Germans retreating westward and likely to run into us any day!

Yet I can't help feeling that this peculiar story *is* connected with our situation. And so, when he said, 'You're quite right, it was only a story, and not a very clear one at that' – I didn't want to hurt him and so didn't rub it in that the thing hadn't ever appeared in print – when he said *that*, I felt that I had somehow missed the point, and that he had really meant to say something quite different.

Then I remembered his saying that some people just couldn't live without literature – people who hadn't much else in life, I suppose – and I said I could see how important it was to him, even though it was only a story he had written ages ago. He smiled – I don't want to sound soppy over this, but he has a beautiful smile, gentle and intelligent and not a bit superior.

'Perhaps the only kind of fiction that should be written is the kind that life catches up with, don't you think?' he said. I replied that I hadn't given much thought to such things (which wasn't quite true), and that all I could think about right now was getting a chance to fight the Germans. But obviously, as far as that story of his was concerned life had not just caught up with it but had proved that the story was all *wrong*: the man should surely have resisted his arrest (not just asked those two SD thugs for their papers), he should not have let them mess him about endlessly but told them where they got off, instead of hanging about and even looking for a court that would be prepared to try him etc.

'Perhaps that's why I never published that story,' he replied – but again I had the feeling that somehow I had missed the point.

As I write this, it occurs to me that this story of the man's arrest wasn't really any *more* peculiar than Dr K.'s own arrest, or the reason why we're all here, too.

5 November The weather has improved. Surprise, surprise – most of our 'Anniversary Crew' turn out to be total civilians – somehow or other they managed to avoid conscription during the Republic and the only time they've ever seen a rifle being fired was in the fairground! God's mercy on us all, what *are* we going to do with them?

6 November I talked to F. K. about that queer story again, trying to get him to say why the man was being harassed, what he had done etc., making what I thought was a very obvious point: 'The truth is that a man cannot be guilty simply because he is what he is.'

'As you say, that is the truth. Unfortunately some stories get written by authors who just don't see the shortest way to the truth.' There was a note of irony in his voice, but I felt I would not give in.

'No, no – only a god can condemn a man for what he is. A god, or the Germans.'

He did give me a look of surprise then – I've noticed he seems to be surprised at the most obvious things people say.

7 November I'm doing rifle drill with them, but not firing practice. We have no ammunition to spare, and besides, we don't want to announce our presence prematurely! We are waiting for the Russian breakthrough, that's the time for letting the Germans know we're here.

So I spent most of the day explaining how to strip our good old Czech Bren-gun, clear stoppages, assemble ammo belts and feed them into the machine-gun, etc. I watched Dr K. It really is ridiculous – he has an extraordinary admiration for anyone who can strip the gun efficiently (seems to think it's a miracle to be able to do it in under a minute, the Sergeant-Major does it in 45 seconds flat!) – yet he himself is not in the least clumsy, though you can see from the careful way he picks up the parts that he is not used to handling machinery of any kind.

I said something like that to him, and he grinned with pleasure. 'I'm sure

you've never come across a less soldierly person than I am. I sometimes think
all this is happening on another planet from the one I used to live on, sending
occasional missives to the earth. A writer's imagination is unpredictable,
especially in its weaknesses. But, you know, I have many reasons to be glad
I am here, many reasons to be grateful.'

Several of the new lot are in a funk about being asked to handle the gun,
full of lousy excuses – why, one of the lawyers actually said they ought to be
regarded as 'non-belligerent partisans', I ask you. I told them in no uncertain
terms that nobody asked them to join us in the first place, but since they were
here they'd better jolly well do as they're told.

Dr. K. has *not* asked for any special privileges. All the same, I don't think
it's right for *him* to have to go through all this bull. I wonder why. I mean
why I think so.

I wish I could read some of his stuff, even though it is in German. It
appears that a lot of it was burned. By the Germans? Nobody seems to be
sure.

Incidentally, I don't like the way he admires everybody and everything.
Sometimes I think he behaves like some snivelling old Jew, trying to make up
to me.

8 November Truly, I've never had such weird conversations in all my life.
Today it occurred to me that perhaps he really is a very important writer. I'm
sure I can't think why I suddenly had this thought, but I felt I had to find out
more about it. I tried to draw him out in various ways, like asking whether he
had written a great deal more than he actually published, whether he was a
perfectionist, what literary movement he admired, who were his favourite
authors, and who influenced him most. In the end I got a bit embarrassed –
I could see that he thought all these were pretty silly questions but was too
polite to say so. Finally his very silence made me blurt it out: 'Are you a very
important writer?' I asked and, as though that question wasn't weird enough,
I added, 'You're really a sort of king among writers, aren't you?'

'You have said it,' he replied, and for a brief moment his smile became
almost a grin. 'A secret king, though.'

9 November It's ten days since F. joined us, and somehow the atmosphere in
the camp has changed. There is much less shouting and cursing and ordering
people pointlessly about – it's as though everybody had become more gentle,
more considerate.

F's smile is gentle, not a bit superior, yet there is something strange and
chilling about it. Like a gleam from a treasure trove far away.

10 November Went over to the other side of the camp (some brilliant wit calls
it 'our Kosher Reservation', I'm sick and tired of these 'jokes'), to listen to
K. reading one of his stories. It turned out to be a grotesque tale about a
singing mouse called Josephine. It did *not* remind me either of Aesop or of
La Fontaine, nor indeed of anything else I've ever read.

It seemed to be mainly about the relationship between this prima donna mouse and her audience – and yet the precise nature of that relationship remained unclear. Was this mouse, Josephine, meant to need her public, the mouse nation, in order to perform her ridiculous singing act, or was it the public that was supposed to need *her* and her singing, so that they could feel as one nation and in that way stand up to any danger or threat from the enemy, whoever *that* was? One couldn't even make out whether her singing was meant to be any good! Half the time the narrator (?!) was saying that it was much the same sort of whistling noise that any mouse can produce, and perhaps not even as good as that, yet the other half he was saying that it was quite unique and something very special.

Anyhow, why on earth write about a *mouse*, when all he's *really* doing is writing about himself, his own writing?! As if *that* was something so very special! . . . But perhaps it is?

Incidentally, I noted quite a few of our chaps among the audience, they seemed to have come over for the reading. I was glad about that – I must confess I did feel a bit embarrassed to be there on my own.

It was quite dark when he started, the air was thick with smoke. I thought once or twice he found it hard to breathe.

Later. Embarrassed about my embarrassment, really.

11 November Told the Sergeant-Major that there are plenty of jobs for Dr K. to do without his having to mess about with Bren guns and getting his fingers filthy and septic. To my surprise the SM instantly agreed. Dr K., on the other hand, said he wouldn't have it. He said he disapproved of 'Josephine'(!), with her constant petitions for recognition and for exemption from the ordinary chores of the mouse folk – it was part of her ridiculousness. (I hadn't told him I thought she was ridiculous.) He said he really wanted to be treated like everybody else and to go through with everything the others have to do. I was very glad he reacted in this way, but didn't tell him so. On coming back to my tent in the evening I found an envelope with a note from him:

> You think practical work is too coarse for me – that I am in some sense too good for it and should leave it to others. I too used to think this – used to think that not being very good at practical things was really a proof that I was good at my writing, at expressing my admiration of those who are good at practical things. The circumstances of my life – of all our lives, and mine too – were very different then. I could only admire what I was excluded from, what was done by others. I could accept that exclusion and even rejoice in it – or rather, not rejoice in it but lament it and from that lament – or perhaps it was no more than an endless complaint – draw the substance of my writing. Describing life among other people, I was describing a life determined by other people. In that way I came to have an exaggerated expectation of what happened on the other, the practical side of the world.

Things are different now, so different that I look on my own writings and on my own past life as on the life and writings of a stranger. I have never been so involved as I am here and now with you all. Perhaps this is why I can no longer describe this piece of world, except to say that I am *not* too good for it.

He seems to have an eerie capacity for answering my questions before I've had a chance to put them.

12 November He lent me a copy of the 'Josephine' story, but I must confess that reading it didn't make things much clearer. It seems to me that everything that is said about the mouse, about her singing and her relationship to her nation-public, is contradicted and cancelled out by its opposite, so that in the end the reader doesn't know where he stands.

'Do you mean it is as if you hadn't read the story at all?' he asked.

No, I said, it was much more confusing. After all, when La Fontaine writes about a beast or a bird, a clear message emerges – about the need for cunning or wariness, or the importance of prudence.

'The importance of prudence – my father had a very clear message about that, and about many other virtues. I think that's why I so admired him. I even admired him because he believed that all my 'writing' was arrant nonsense and a waste of time. Can you think of anything funnier than my trying to convince him of the opposite? Knowing all the time that the only thing that might possibly convince him would be my publisher's account books in fifty years' time?'

I remembered his saying that some people have only literature to make sense of their lives, and so I asked, 'You admired him for being contemptuous of what mattered to you most?'

'I admired his assurance, and I also knew that there wasn't enough of it for both of us. Of course, I could *describe* him and his immense power, and I knew he could do anything in the world except *that*, but as to having a message – any message – for other people, how could I presume?'

'It sounds like mock modesty to me.' I was suddenly afraid of having hurt him by saying that, and I realized that the last thing I wanted to do was to hurt him.

'Perhaps it is. But not because I secretly think I have a message, but because my real purpose, which is quite different, is not at all modest: to present a piece of the world, raised on a shield. Of course, it isn't the whole world, and I can't hold it up for very long.'

'You say your purpose is not really modest, yet you hide it behind a metaphor which seems to be deliberately trivial.' And I read out to him that passage in the 'Josephine' story where he writes: 'To crack a nut is certainly not an art, therefore no one would dare to call together an audience and crack nuts in front of them by way of entertainment. But if someone nevertheless does so and succeeds in his intention, then it does cease to be a matter of mere nutcracking. Or rather, it is a matter of cracking nuts, but it becomes apparent that we have overlooked this art because it was well within our powers, and that this new cracker of nuts was the first person to show us its real nature; and it might then be even more effective if he were a little less good at cracking nuts than the majority of us.'

'Perhaps it's only by arousing the reader's irritation that metaphors come into their own. Besides, when one raises the world or a part of it on a shield, one raises it only a little distance into the air. Yet it isn't like not having raised it at all.'

'You keep on speaking about the world. Do you mean our world? Frankly, I don't recognize any of it.' This wasn't really true – he was right about his metaphors being profoundly irritating.

'Don't you really? Perhaps you're just impatient, and are looking for superficial resemblances. I only describe what I see.'

'But why this game of hide-and-seek?'

'You must ask a higher authority. I only describe what I see.'

It sounded like a brush-off.

13 November Most of our supplies are stored in a fairly roomy cave in the rocks at the eastern end of the camp, and the CO has given strict orders that nobody is allowed there except on duty. As F. K.'s hoarseness, or whatever it is, has been getting worse, I asked the Adjutant whether we couldn't rig up a bed for him in there, quite close to the entrance, so he'd have some protection from the weather (which is no better than what you'd expect in the High Tatra at this time of the year). To my surprise the A. said he'd already got the SM to organize some extra blankets and a proper camp-bed. Of course, K. refused, and had to be *ordered* to kip down there. 'It'll be even more confusing than out here, among you,' he said.

14 November Another note from F. K.:

You are sure to have noticed how hopeless I am at talking to people – I think my bad throat must be a confirmation of my incompetence. Yet writing letters is even worse: the misunderstanding and mistakes which fill my life were all carefully prepared in the letters I have written. But I do like writing letters which aren't real letters but only envelopes for stories, like this one:

The three stages. There was a writer who was least unhappy, or so he thought, when he lived alone. And although he took little notice of the world, he discovered that in what he wrote he could foretell the future. When he wrote of war, war came upon the country, and when he wrote of pestilence, pestilence came, though not always in the form in which he had described it. He was not a stupid man, and he saw that all he was ever able to foretell were disasters, but it took him a very long time to see that. He was not a bad man, and he also saw how eager people were to make all that he foretold come true, but that too took him a long time to see. And when he wrote that the material world was real enough, but that it was only the evil in the spiritual world, his mind was divided between being pleased that what he had written turned out to be so splendidly true, and being frightened. Seeing at last how things were, he couldn't make up his mind whether to continue writing, which was all he knew, or to give it up, which seemed like giving up his life; and this hesitation made him very unhappy. This was the first stage of his life.

Then came the war and the pestilence he foretold, and he found that, whether he liked it or not, he could no longer live on his own. But as soon as he came to live with other people, partly in order to help them in the war he had foretold, but largely because he needed them for his own protection, he found he couldn't write another word. There was peace of mind, he felt at first, in this silence, but it was a peace of mind he couldn't distinguish from emptiness. That was the second stage.

Now he realized that what he had to look for was the pure power of description, the art of writing without foreknowledge or intent. That, he thought, would be the third stage. He liked the sound of those words – the third stage. But everything in his world had always gone in pairs – good or evil, spiritual or material, here or there – and so there is not much hope that he will ever reach that third stage.

15 November With every day that passes F.'s cough, hoarseness and breathlessness are getting worse. It's no good putting him on patrol duty.   His face is permanently set in a smile of apology.

The MD examined him at length and sounds very pessimistic.

There are signs – mainly intelligence gathered by our chaps when they last went down into M. village – that the German line to the east of us is at last beginning to break. Like some terrible ice floes, about to start their drift westward. It seems doubtful whether we can keep F. here much longer – the fighting may start any day.

16 November F. gave me his copy of the 'Josephine' story – for safe-keeping, he said. By chance I came across these lines – they seemed to jump out at me from the typed page:

'The threats that hang over us make us quieter and more modest, and more amenable to Josephine's imperiousness; we're glad to assemble and crowd together, especially as the cause of it is to one side of our tormenting preoccupation; it is as if, in great haste – for haste is essential, Josephine too often forgets that – we were drinking together a loving cup before battle.'

How terrifying a single sentence can be.

17 November The MD went down to Matljary after dusk. Apparently he knows one of the doctors at the local hospital (this is where years ago F. spent some months as a patient). He got the doctor to promise to find a bed for F. if things get worse. The MD has asked me to talk to F. about it.

18 November From the pass above the camp where we keep a permanent patrol you can look down into the Matljary valley, and with field glasses you can make out the village. F. insisted on coming up with me – it's a climb of ten minutes and I thought he would never make it. He picked out the village with my glasses and then identified the hospital. I thought it was the right moment to break the MD's verdict to him, but found my throat so dry with excitement that I couldn't say anything. As I was trying to get the words out, he said, 'Whatever happens, you must promise me not to put me into that hospital. What I saw there was much worse than an execution, yes, even than any form of torture. Surely, we ourselves haven't invented the tortures but have learned them from diseases – no man dares to torture the way they do.'

I didn't understand. He explained that during his time there he met a man who was dying of a throat disease. In the end the man couldn't talk at all and just wrote messages on slips of paper to the people who sat at his bedside. 'I've remembered what it said on those slips,' F. said, 'they were perfect sentences:

"I'd especially like you to take care of the peonies because they are so fragile.

And move the lilacs into the sun.

To think that once I could simply venture a large swallow of water.

Ask whether there is good mineral water, just out of curiosity.

Please see that the peonies don't touch the bottom of the vase. That's why they have to be kept in bowls.

Mineral water – once for fun I could

A little water; these bits of pills stick in the mucus like splinters of glass.

How trying I am to all of you; it's crazy.

A lake doesn't flow into anything, you know.

See the lilacs, fresher than morning.

You'll have to warn the girl about the glass; she sometimes comes in barefoot.

By now we have come a long way from the day in the tavern garden when we

But now enough flowers for the time being.

Show me the columbine; too bright to stand with the others.

Scarlet hawthorn is too hidden, too much in the dark.

More of the water. Fruit

Yesterday evening a late bee drank the lilac water dry.

Cut at a steep slant; then they can touch the floor.

Put your hand on my forehead for a moment to give me courage".'

I wondered how he came to remember these disconnected sentences and asked him whether he thought they were symbolical or had some special literary value.

'Forgive me, I embarrassed you,' he said; and, 'You didn't really mean to ask those questions.' And then, after another pause: 'But you are quite right. They are what I am looking for – pure description.'

19 November The first Very light signals from our neighbouring partisan battalion came early this morning, announcing German troops crossing the north-eastern mountain ridge. We were in readiness all day.

20 November Our first day of action. How can a single day bring victory and defeat?

At 8 a.m. we received a signal: an isolated infantry detachment is entering the Matljary valley. It was a brilliantly sunny November day, the beech woods were ablaze with colours. We slithered down the mountain-side with our Bren-gun carrier on patches of fresh snow, and found a good ambush directly above the road, only a few yards of which were visible from where we were. No sooner had we got our two guns in position than the first German soldiers appeared in the roadway below us: a fairly bedraggled lot. We waited till there was quite a sizeable crowd on our section of the road and then let go. Complete panic and decimation, no attempt to shoot back, they didn't even try to find out where the firing came from. They lost some twenty men – after our first burst of fire a number managed to hide in nearby houses. We would have liked to leave our ambush and get in among them, but as soon as movement on the road stopped, the CO ordered us to pull out and we came away without a single loss. It was my first action, and of course I was terrified that I might fail (helping to feed in the ammunition belts) – but elated when I didn't; it was all over in a few minutes.

We were all immensely bucked; clambering back to camp, I was thinking of the words I would use to describe it to F. He had stayed behind with four others. Before leaving we had told them to mount a guard of two on the opposite side of the camp, the wooded part at the end of a steep little path that leads up from the valley to the west of us. We didn't really think there was any danger from that side.

They were all dead. How the Germans came to discover that path – how many they were, whether they got detached from the rest and lost their way – we shall never know. The guards had undoubtedly put up a fight – one could see that from the positions of the bodies, and their magazines were empty. What had happened to the others wasn't clear. F. had been shot through the forehead, he was slumped over the last remaining Bren-gun. The Germans had taken most of our food stores, and had tried to set fire to the camp, but only in a half-hearted way. They had taken the ammunition belts but left the gun in position, with F. spread-eagled over it. The barrel was clean, but it seemed that he had tried to fire it. We shall never know for certain. I think he would have wanted to fire it. Not from any hatred or warlike feeling – as he himself once said, he was the least soldierly person you can imagine. But he did, in the end, make his choice, he wanted to be involved. 'Not like last time,' he had said.

21 November We buried them this morning on the eastern pass, close to the spot where F. had looked down into the valley with my field glasses. One of our chaps, a carpenter, made two crosses and three stars of David from the sweet-smelling wood of the mountain pine. No names.

The CO spoke at some length, first on the 'no difference of race or creed' line, then on 'death to the fascists', the word 'German' was never mentioned. Every inch the professional officer.

Our friendship was so short – sometimes it seems as if it had never been. Like a gentle ghost passing in our midst. Strange: since it happened I have hardly thought about his writing – only about the man. Would he have liked that?

The Sergeant-Major talked about him on the way back from the pass. He said there was something special about him – everybody seems to have felt that. I wonder what it was. Perhaps a kind of grace, a way of making us feel that there is something special about each of us. The SM would have understood that, but I didn't say anything.

1980

13

The White Rose

In memoriam Franz Hoffmann

1

Slowly, fragment by fragment, the complexity of wartime Germany emerges from behind the single, simple fact of defeat. Memoirs, ante-dated conversions and blustering apologias; scraps of paper, insignificant notes preserved by the hit-or-miss chance of a bomb; records of mass-murders, signed and countersigned, complete with receipted bills for ammunition used; the pure heartbreak of farewell letters and last notes, endless declarations of love of life; diaries, written secretly in anguished nights of solitude, full of a spiritual illumination that fades by the light of day; diaries, scribbled furtively in the hothouse rankness of the Führer's own armour-plated express, in air-raid shelters and in the officers' mess off the Boulevard Haussmann . . . all these are the sources of 'history'; for our age, conscious of its own copy value, is nothing if not well documented. And yet, the feel of it eludes us.

The crowd of red-faced men you saw last summer, piling into a gigantic perspex-covered bus outside Rheims cathedral: where were they ten years ago? A newsvendor on crutches, sorting his papers and weighing them down with rusty bits of shrapnel in the kiosk by the Munich Frauenkirche: what was he doing, twelve . . . fourteen years ago . . . ? That placid, slow-spoken porter who opens the door for you, shows you round the university lecture-rooms: who is he, who was he fifteen years ago? And the men: where are they all, the cheering masses of the newsreels, forests of spread-eagle-crowned standards, wheeling columns of boots and breeches and sashed shirts – all gone? Some things remain. They don't 'make history'; but they are still there, unchanged, for you to consider. Take the students – German students, metaphysic-inflated. How remote is life, you feel, the real situation, the living coarseness of actual events, from their talk, from these shadowgraphs of good intentions labelled 'Peace Eternal'! How 'real' is it, all that they talk about . . . ?

2

Hans Scholl was one of these students. He was born on 22 September 1918, in a small town at the foot of the Alps, where his father was a municipal clerk. Each step in the father's career was accompanied by a move of the whole family: Swabia, a little town in Württemberg (where Hans Scholl's sister Sophie was born on 5 May 1921), Ulm on the Danube, where after the war Herr Scholl was Burgomaster. Five children, small towns, middle-class worries in times of inflation – all this is true to type, an unremarkable background, it might be Leamington Spa except for the landscape. The Germans (they used to say) are full of Romantic nonsense: mountains and sunsets and Nature with an extra-large capital. It was the predicament of Hans Scholl's generation that some of its best members never settled down to the life in the big cities, to the prowl of the political animal in his statutory cage.

For the father, nominally Protestant, freethinking and liberal in outlook, the year 1933 meant the end of his public career: nothing dramatic, merely a recognition – immediately acted on – that the state which now came into being was not a state he could serve – hundreds of others acted in a like manner, hundreds of thousands did not. For the mother, a lay deaconess before her marriage, the year 1933 produced but a turning-in upon the family, an anxious gathering-in of the loved ones. But the son was to be typical, truly representative of his world. For when, after 1933, the youth movements of all political parties and religious denominations were disbanded, and their members pushed into the Hitler-Jugend, he did not hesitate to do what was asked of him. He belonged. For the first eighteen years of his life, before he took the decision that was to give a final shape to his mind and to his deeds, he belonged to his world and did what his world asked of him. For was it not noble and good, almost all of it: the rambles in the countryside; life in the mountain solitudes; campfires and ancient songs; flags and the oath of allegiance; immediate, palpable responsibility; the rights of a true leader and his duties to his comrades? Assuaged to the full were the longings which the Romantics had bequeathed to their century and the next. But then: is the need felt only where it is so readily supplied? Does the youth of Birmingham not feel what the *Jugend* of Ulm feels? Is it only the Germans who have a *Jugend*? There is less readiness, at any rate, to let the youth of Birmingham have its own way, its own 'laws'; there are fewer concessions perhaps and certainly less *Natur*; the 'autonomy' of youth, *Jugend* as a thing-and-end-in-itself, has little meaning for the councillors of Stepney or the magistrates of Cardiff Docks.

The day-to-day life of the Hitler-Jugend, their ritual and their customs were not, after all, so very different from earlier youth movements, those inspired by Romanticism, socialism, nature worship or the Christian denominations. True, the boys had all to be 'Aryan'; true, the new ritual was more formal, there was more regimentation. But the immediate, concrete life of

platoon and company, which is all that Hans Scholl knew at first, was remote
from the over-all political purpose of the Party. True, they were not Christian.
But what they believed in, *Natur*, was there, at hand, lived in and communed
with and tangible: discovered by Goethe, theorized over by Schiller, exalted
by the Romantics, preached by Nietzsche. A being not coldly remote but full
of the life of the seasons, not grimy like the towns but ever renewing itself,
'real', and free from the moralities and dogma, from the sordid practicalities,
of adult living in the world. Seventeenth-century chorales sung through the
mist at sun-rise from a mountain top, and the ritual of names – Bach and
Buxtehude, Franck and Schütz – forming a perfect continuity with the past.
As for the present, that was enshrined in the emblems of loyalty and self-
sacrifice. The innate generosity of the young, which time and the experience
of life among chimney-stacks and cement playgrounds have not blighted, this
generosity expanded in the mountains and by the rivers, it was tended and
blossomed forth in the 'Movement' that bore the evil name. And even though
Hans Scholl's father saw that all these – mountain climbs and country rambles,
ritual, oath and sacred loyalty – were no more than the means to an end he
abhorred, the boy did not. The boy believed only what he saw, and all that
he saw was good. Rumours there were, of persecutions and murders, of the
burning of books and of concentration camps, yet the rumours were unreal,
shadows cast by that adult world which they – the little groups and companies
– would one day sally forth to change, to reform, to make generous and young.
These things would assuredly come to pass, for he, Hans Scholl, led his little
group in good faith; they had sworn on the flag he held aslant before them
to be loyal and true, to honour their pledge and be brave.

Here is one of their songs:

> Schließ Aug und Ohr für eine Weil
> vor dem Getös der Zeit.
> Du heilst es nicht und hast kein Heil,
> als bis dein Herz sich weiht ...
> Die Stunde kommt, da man dich braucht,
> dann sei du ganz bereit,
> und in das Feuer, das verraucht,
> wirf dich als letzten Scheit!

(It is not the worst feature of modern English that it defies a serious rendering
of this bathetic trash: 'Close eyes and ears for a little while/ to the turmoil of
this age./ The age and you will not be cured/ Until you consecrate/ your
heart ... And when the hour comes/ that needs you, be prepared/ to fuel
with your own true self/ the sacrificial flames.')

Starry-eyed, Hans Scholl carried his unit's flag to the Party rally at Nuremberg, but when he returned home he no longer believed. For the first time
he had seen the unifying purpose. He had seen his own little group merge in
the common purpose of the Party whose tributaries they were, and it appeared

evil: a use merely, not an end, and a corruption of the good faith. What he experienced was no sudden conversion, no dramatic renunciation as yet, merely a first and halting reading of the signs that his father had been showing him, patiently, for several years. All he felt (as yet) was the threat to the self, to individuality – the pressure, the vulgarity and the brashness, the regimentation that was becoming intolerable. At this turning-point of his consciousness he ceased to be typical, representative; yet he would never be an outsider. Leaving the Hitler-Jugend was a struggle and a break, yet it was not a break with like-minded friends. And devoted and loving friends he would always have. Minute new groups, *Jungenschaften* of informal and laconic and deliberately unconforming young men, sprang up in Germany in the late 1930s, in this town and that, continuing the tradition of societies which the Party had banned. Was he, in joining such a company of like-minded friends, postponing his farewell to adolescence, to his own youth? But, then, he never did say farewell. If to grow up means to accept the world's coins and weights and measures, to come to terms with and make the best of and to conform to, then he never did grow up.

But the world around him gave him no respite. In the year of Munich, in the year of the first large Jewish massacres and of Hitler's consolidation of power, the sceptical little groups were broken up and Hans Scholl found himself for the first time in gaol. He came out after a few weeks, clearer in his mind than before and determined that he would not compromise, that he could not be of the world yet must live in it. He decided to become a doctor, and for a time there was only the family and his studies. Again (and now events began to move more quickly) he lived the typical life of his age: he served in the Labour Corps and, at the outbreak of war, was drafted into the army; he studied medicine, first in Göttingen and then in Munich, and joined the Army Medical Corps and served as an orderly sergeant; he took part in the campaign in France, returned to Munich on temporary leave of absence to continue his studies, rejoined his battalion on the Russian Front, and was once again given leave for further examinations and studies at Munich. He now saw and lived amidst some of the horrors of that New Order to which he had once given his generous allegiance; they were no longer rumours and chimeras but concrete reality, no less than a sunrise in the Alps had once been. Not only did he hear of concentration camps: he met Jewish prisoners in their hundreds, he met the starving and humiliated *one*, working on a railway embankment in Poland, who scorned the bar of chocolate he offered her. Not only did he hear of the secret police: his father was arrested for making a casual remark about Hitler and sentenced to imprisonment. Not only did he hear of the government's racial policy: an army comrade returned to his company in Russia whose own child had been diagnosed as congenitally insane and killed, with several hundred others, by a detachment of the SS. Not only did he hear of debauchery in the party: back in Munich, he attended an address by the local Gauleiter in the students' union in which promiscuity was encouraged on racial grounds, to make up for military losses. Not only

did he hear of the bombing of German towns: he met the crazed young
mother who wandered through the streets of the city, lugging her dead child
in a suitcase. These were the things that formed his mind.

Yet not these things alone. In the early autumn of 1941 he met in Munich
an old man, Carl Muth, editor of the Catholic periodical *Hochland*. Their
friendship began in a practical way (at least, one of his biographers describes
it as 'praktisch') – the young medical student was asked to arrange and
catalogue Muth's large library. Handling books, reading them, discussing them
– all this was not remote from the world outside, for the war and the strife
were not forgotten, they were focused in his growing mind. His mentor's
outlook was bound to determine what he read: Plato, the last four Socratic
dialogues on the commitment to morality in the face of death; he read Kant,
Schiller's panegyrics on freedom, Goethe's *Des Epimenides Erwachen*. Gently
and step by step, Muth and his friend the Catholic theologian and humanist
Theodor Haecker (whose work had been publicly ridiculed by the rector of
Freiburg University, Martin Heidegger) led Hans to examine the situation of
the Church in the terrible world around them. 'It is the German Catholics
who live in a ghetto', said Muth. And Haecker in his *Diaries* rejoiced in the
poverty, the oppression even, of a Church which has its being in the world
not in order to flatter the mighty but to save the humble. What these old men
showed to their young friend was the fabric of the Invisible Universal Church,
dogmatic but not narrow, orthodox but tolerant, unprepossessed and uncompromising – the spiritual fabric of the Church in the soul of the believer. But
Haecker also wrote at this time:

> The Catholic Church is very far from having recognized, let alone
> absorbed into her teaching, those treasures of knowledge – especially of
> things temporal – which have been amassed by men who stood outside
> the Church, men who loved Christ with all their heart ... Catholic
> theologicans have been very lukewarm towards men like Kierkegaard
> ... They don't see the lustre of bullion under the heretical dust – they
> only see the dust. What a pity ...

For Muth and Haecker and for their friends it was a time for personal
decisions. The stately ship of the Church, richly equipped with the treasures
of the ages, might not be able to ride it out, 'for there arose a great storm of
wind, and the waves beat into the ship, so that it was now full'. So, they
reasoned, it was the small vessels that counted now, the little boats with no
more on board than a few accoutrements, their bare necessaries. From time
to time sustenance came from the Catholic Hierarchy. In the letter-box one
morning Hans Scholl found the text of the sermons of Clemens August von
Galen, Bishop of Münster, clandestinely reprinted and circulated among many
people; Galen's forthright denunciation of the teachings and practice of the Party
(20 July 1941) deeply impressed Hans Scholl as an overt sign of internal
opposition. Indeed, long before this, Cardinal Faulhaber, Archbishop of Munich

and bearer of the Iron Cross First Class, in his Advent Sermons of 1934, had summed up the Christian view of Party doctrine in the memorable sentence, 'It is not by *German* blood that we are redeemed.' Anti-Semitism, the doctrine of Germanic values, the new paganism and its Germanic nature cult – all these Faulhaber's sermons and writings had exposed and attacked on many occasions since that Advent. But there had been no excommunication of Party members. The Church had withdrawn from politics; it continued to uphold, in spite of many infringements and under protest, the terms of the Concordat of July 1933. In his address of 2 June 1945, Pope Pius XII explained and defended his predecessor's policy:

> As long as the last glimmer of hope had not disappeared that the [National Socialist] Movement might take on a different and less pernicious direction – either through the intervention of its more moderate adherents or through the effective resistance of the opposing section of the German nation – so long did the Church do what was in her power to stem the tide of those destructive and violent doctrines ... Not that the Church had ever entertained any extravagant hopes, not that she wished the signing of the Concordat to imply an approval of the teaching and aims of National Socialism ...

But (he continued) the Church had, through the Concordat, secured 'various advantages' – above all the freedom of worship – which the Hierarchy would not jeopardize. For the rest, it was the groups of like-minded friends that counted, that kept the faith alive. And what informed and gave life to these groups was not narrow orthodoxy or the assertion of dogmatic differences, but the present threat to all things Christian and humane.

How much did Hans Scholl accept of the Christian teaching, how far would he be led by the guides of his little Academe? The Protestant, liberal-minded father and the devout mother had sown the seeds of conviction and piety in his mind; the precepts of Socrates and St Augustine, and of Kant's ethical doctrine, took root there. What would come of it all? This much was certain: he would never withdraw from living in the world around him, he would never deny that it was also *his* world. But as he lived and saw, and as he nourished that outraged compassion which sustained him, so his active self – joyful and troubled – grew within him; and so did his decision: he would be true to himself and to his friends.

3

For indeed he had friends. There was no harshness, no moral rigour, no cold marks of suffering in his mind, but warm-hearted affection and impulsive friendliness. At times a deep melancholy seized him: at times, past and present experiences and fears merged into terrifying nightmares. In his diary he writes of a dream he had:

> A very high railway-bridge stretching across the valley. Without hesitation I walked towards it, a quick glance into the depths below gave me a slight feeling of vertigo. Nevertheless I walked on bravely. Suddenly I knew: you must cross this bridge, even if it should cost your life. Now the iron structure under my feet began suddenly to slump forward, it grew steeper and steeper, soon it was hanging vertically above the abyss ... Calmly and with a firm hold I mounted from rung to rung; it was all so easy, I was a competent climber. The only thing that seemed difficult was how to escape the men who were waiting at the end of this fantastic ladder to arrest me ...

These nightmares were the price he had to pay for his strength, for the comfort he gave to others, for the courage which he shared with them.

During the early years of the war he met three students who were to remain with him to the end: Alexander Schmorell, Christoph Probst and Willy Graf.

How different they were ... The serious, exquisitely regular and italianate face of Hans Scholl, firmly featured and full of power, his finely shaped nose and dark, blazing eyes under a domed brow and rich dark hair; and Alexander Schmorell's – lean, fine-drawn and quixotic, a funny sort of face on a slim boyish neck with upturned nose and prominent cheek-bones. Alexander Schmorell's father was a German-Russian doctor, and the boy was born in Orenburg on the Ural River on 17 September 1917; his Russian mother, daughter of an Orthodox priest, died in a typhoid epidemic while he was still a child. In 1921, his father fled to Germany and later married a German; by then Russia cannot have meant more to the boy than a distant memory and the old nurse who had come away with them. Yet unlike Hans Scholl he never felt himself wholly German. Reading the memoirs and listening to the reminiscences of his friends, we are inclined to think that Schmorell's aloofness was a little self-conscious. How he clung to his dead mother's memory, to the old nurse's tales of Russia! Keeping himself remote from his German step-mother, from the Germany to which his father had brought him, he was dreamy and fanciful in his moods and his jokes, his sculpture and his reading. Best of all he loved his horse, a ride along the Isar River. During his compulsory military service he volunteered for a mounted artillery observation company; in 1938 he took part in the occupation of Austria and then, after the Munich agreement, of the Sudeten region of Bohemia. During the first year of the war he served as a medical orderly in France, in early 1940 he met Hans Scholl for the first time, in the pre-medical course at Munich University, and early in 1941 joined Hans's company in Russia. On horseback he celebrated his return to 'Mother Russia', like a dream come true. He fell in love again; he had never been out of love. Not, it may be, with anything very tangible, not with Bolshevism or the Russian state, but with Mother

Russia. (Later he tried to put into words this naïve, romantic, fundamentally German notion of salvation from the east.) His own inward light was different from, perhaps a little less steady than, the moral vision that illuminated Hans Scholl's thinking. When, in 1941, they met at Professor Kurt Huber's lectures on Leibniz, Alexander Schmorell seems to have recognized the clarity of that vision, to have decided that he would accept Hans Scholl's guidance.

Christoph Probst, born on 6 November 1919, Schmorell's closest school friend, though entirely German, had an upbringing which was a little similar in its rootlessness; he too grew up nurtured on dreams and longings. His parents were divorced, the father, an Oriental scholar with an interest in Eastern religions, lived a secluded life in the Bavarian Alps. For many years Christoph Probst and his sister divided their time between their parents and boarding-schools in the Alps. He married very young, at barely twenty-one, and, on joining the Luftwaffe, was given leave of absence to study medicine at Innsbruck University. The mountains, the starry sky and such philosophizing as might yield some large, encompassing principle behind all Nature were Probst's preoccupations. But above all he was lonely and hungry for love. As a child he had dressed up one day in rags and begged in the street from passers-by; and not so very many years later, in his last letter to his mother and sister, he wrote: 'Don't ever forget that life is nothing but a growing in love and a preparation for eternity.' He too, like Alex Schmorell, knew the emotional deprivations of childhood which Hans Scholl had never experienced; he too had always been a little different, set apart from his contemporaries. He was weighed down with responsibility for a wife and two little sons, and yet he never belonged to the world in the unambiguous way in which Hans Scholl had once belonged to it. He too, the memory of his dead father before him, drew on Hans Scholl's strength and affection, to find his own strength and to find himself.

The fourth, similar and different, was Willy Graf, born in the Saar on 2 January 1918. He alone among these friends had enjoyed a strict religious upbringing; he had belonged to a Catholic youth group, and had been arrested as its leader at the same time as Hans Scholl. In 1939 Graf joined the army as a medical orderly. He did not meet Hans Scholl and the others until the summer of 1942. More serious and withdrawn than the rest, it was he who brought mature, clearly formulated religious ideas into their evening conversations:

> To become a Christian [he writes in one of his letters], that is the most difficult thing of all, and only in death can we grow a little towards that goal ... Christianity is really a much harder and more uncertain way of life, you know, full of strenuous effort and strains and ever new obstacles on the way to achieving it.

What distinguishes Willy Graf from all his friends is the conviction, expressed in his letters, that an unbridgeable gulf separates the world from Christianity, that the spiritual and the worldly worlds are for ever different and distinct, that Christian values are unrealizable here and now, that only death brings us a little closer to them, that (in Job's words to God) 'My thoughts are not your thoughts.' Again we are reminded of Kierkegaard, and of Haecker's regret that the Church had ignored his teaching. When we read that Willy Graf's deepest wish was eventually to become a theologian, we recognize that his purpose was to solve the problem of how Christian faith is possible *in* the world, how such a disjunction between the spiritual and the worldly might be *lived*. Perhaps it was in death that he solved his problem.

The fifth of this group was Kurt Huber, professor extraordinary of musicology and philosophy in the University of Munich. Kurt Huber was born on 25 October 1893, in Chur (in Switzerland), the son of the headmaster of a private school; he studied music and philosophy at various universities, mainly Berlin, and though in 1920 he was admitted as a *Dozent* at Munich he was never appointed to a full Chair. As a child he had contracted infantile paralysis, and though he sought with great will-power to overcome his physical debility, he remained partly paralysed. He was married in 1928 and had two children, but for many years his position as an unpaid *Dozent* remained difficult and insecure. His most important work was done in the history and analysis of European folk-songs, and he was internationally known as one of the finest scholars in that field. His study of folk-music led him to the theoretical work of the Romantics and to the philosophy of Schelling, Fichte and Hegel. He published little, but, although shy and retiring and physically handicapped, he was an inspiring teacher, one to whom students of many countries came for instruction and advice. Early in the war he applied for a permanent post in the University and was told, 'We will only appoint professors who can also be officers.' When, in conversations with his students, he appealed to the moral law as the only true guide to action, he was consciously invoking a German moral tradition, a mode of German thought, which the government of his country had betrayed; the State itself he came to see not as the true bearer of this morality (as Fichte had claimed), but as the bearer of corruption, the source of evil. 'For this warning', he wrote, 'I stake my life.'

It was Sophie Scholl, Hans Scholl's younger sister, who brought Professor Huber to the meetings of the little group. Three years younger than her brother Hans, she had remained within the family fold longer than he, yet in the end she too was drawn into the orbit of the State; she was drafted into the Labour Corps, then for work in a factory:

> This doesn't really make me unhappy [she wrote in a letter], because I still want to suffer and endure (no, that's not the right word, I mean that I want to be more directly involved in) this age in which we live. You see, sympathy is often so difficult, it often becomes a cliché, when your own body doesn't directly feel the pain.

Both the motivation and the words in which it is expressed could be those of Simone Weil.

And then, in May 1942, she arrived in Munich at her brother's lodgings, intending to study biology and philosophy. Her first days there were the happiest of her life. In her letters it is her mother's piety that speaks most strongly. Sophie Scholl adored her brother – his gaiety, his clear mind, the passionateness of his convictions. Together they went to the house of Carl Muth; together they met their friends and planned the future.

In her diary for 1942 she tells of a dream she had, containing as precise an indication as only a dream can of what she felt about the world in which she lived. In it she goes for a walk with her closest friends – her brother Hans and Alex Schmorell. A dark landscape under a clouded sky. Hans speaks, and he says he has so convincing a proof of the existence of God that he can actually demonstrate His effect upon the world. The air is the proof. The air in the world is used up by millions and millions of men, Hans says, men would have to suffocate if God didn't very now and then blow a mouthful of His breath down into the world – 'otherwise the air would be so bad, so bad, they would all die of it . . .' 'This is how He does it,' says Hans, taking a deep breath and blowing, blowing hard. The column of his breath was blue, so blue, rising higher and higher, until it had swept away all the dark clouds in the sky. And all the sky was now sheer blue.

4

These then are the six members of the conspiracy that took its name from a novel popular in the 1930s, a novel with a Mexican setting written by the pseudonymous writer B. Traven. The thoughts of the group, the White Rose, are expressed in six broadsheets. The first four of these – their language influenced by Muth and Haecker – were composed by Hans Scholl and Alexander Schmorell in the summer of 1942; Professor Huber was involved in the composition of the fifth, in January 1943, and the sixth, in February, was written by him alone.

The harsh winter of 1942–3, the winter of Stalingrad, was the time they chose, their lodgings and a painter friend's studio were the hideouts where they wrote their messages of defiance and printed them in their thousands, on a small hand-press. In trunks and parcels and rucksacks they carried them into the grimy, war-stained towns of Germany and Austria, the towns whose names call to you, gaily, from holiday-posters: to Cologne and Innsbruck, to Essen and Vienna, to Nuremberg and Hanover, to the Saar; in Hamburg, Freiburg and the Saar similar groups were formed. In the dead of night they left their parcels in stations and deserted waiting-rooms, showered their papers into the wind in alleyways and dark thoroughfares, scattered them outside cinemas and in snow-covered public parks and in the streets of Munich. The threat of death attended their every excursion, their every pacific sortie into the alien town, at 5 o'clock on a winter morning, misty and raw and bleak, the icy wind hurtling in from the Alps, the streets deserted. The sirens had stopped now, stucco façades were crumbling, there were piles of rubble along the pavements, the street was full of silence and hostility. Here, like the city's good angels, they walked. They could do no other, then and there, nor change places with any living man or woman.

5

It is not easy to speak about their own past to people of Hans Scholl's generation in Germany today; the main impression they convey is one of complexity, even tortuousness. How complex, you feel, were the issues they had to solve, each inescapably alone! Of course, many of them disapproved of Hitler, were horrified by his criminal regime – and yet, how could they not obey the clarion-call of German patriotism, the call of their own country at war? Add, to this dilemma, the fashionable conceit of *fortiter peccare*, the 'death wish' sophistries, the intellectual baseness of a 'belief' in 'History', add 'Nietzsche' and 'Spengler' and the ragtag and bobtail of geopoliticians, neo-heathens, 'bio-centralists', 'neo-Christians'; add 'race' and 'clan' and 'soil' and 'blood'.

The young members of the White Rose, on the other hand, experienced no such complexities, no collision of loyalties. The war and the regime that wages it are evil, they wrote in their broadsheets. The war must be stopped, the regime overthrown:

> *Sabotage* armament works and war factories. *Sabotage* all meetings, assemblies and demonstrations organized by the National Socialist Party. *Obstruct* the smooth running of the war machine – a machine that is working for a war whose sole aim is the salvaging and preserving of the National Socialist Party and of its dictatorship. *Sabotage* all work in the sciences and all intellectual effort which effectively assists the prosecution of the war – in the universities, technical colleges, laboratories, research institutes and technical offices . . .

It was Hans Scholl who, inspiring the others with the strength of his conviction, knew well what to appeal to in the minds of his contemporaries:

> Nothing is less worthy of a cultured nation [he wrote in their language], than that it should allow itself to be 'governed' by an irresponsible caucus of tycoons who are at the mercy of their lowest instincts. If the German nation is so corrupted in its innermost core that it gives up, without lifting a finger, in reckless reliance upon dubious 'historical laws', the highest good that man possesses and that raises him above the beasts – the freedom of his will – if the German nation is ready to surrender a man's freedom to direct the course of history by his own reasonable

decisions, if the Germans are so completely lacking in individuality and have become a mindless and cowardly herd, then – oh then, indeed, they deserve extinction.

Individualism and personal freedom is the message of the White Rose. In long quotations the ideas of Schiller and Goethe, Kant and Fichte are invoked, their hallowed names set up as guides to a true German conception of freedom. The moral tradition to which the broadsheets appeal is that of German Idealism. And because this tradition tends to merge individual morality with a metaphysical notion, 'das Volk', it has the appearance of being non-political; but in actual fact it makes for bad political theory and worse politics.

In political terms the message of the broadsheets is ineffectual. The generalized and abstract nature of their political remarks, their naïvety and amateurishness ('All ideal forms of government are Utopian, but ... A State must grow and mature like a human being ... The family is as old as the race and from it ... We do not wish to compare the various possible forms of government ... Every man has a claim to ... It is God's Will that man ...') make one impatient with the political content of these pages of printed paper for which at least six people imperilled their lives. Yet it is precisely in its avowedly non-political character that Hans Scholl's and his friends' action is so 'German', so representative of his generation of German intellectuals, whose best thoughts were traditionally 'unpolitisch': concerned with personal and individual freedom only, indeed mainly with freedom of thought, in love with absolutes, leaving the detailed, concrete, day-to-day political arrangements to 'the politicians'.

The freedom of the spirit which German Idealism upholds has its historical foundation in Luther's doctrine of Christian freedom ('Wherefore does harm come to the soul, the body being imprisoned, sick and weak, hungry, thirsty and suffering that which it desires not?'), but in invoking this freedom Idealism cannot lay claim to the supernatural sanction which alone makes Luther's doctrine meaningful. It is compatible with this notion of freedom that the German intellectuals had shown themselves ready to render unto Caesar that which is Caesar's, even though they had their doubts about the God in whose service alone the demand is justified. To which Fichte adds that there is really no difference between the two, since Caesar – the Nation-State – is the true upholder of the moral good. But what if, as a matter of plain fact, it isn't? Here the political doctrine of German Idealism peters out. In his doctrine of the Categorical Imperative, Kant (and Kant only) speaks quite clearly: the moment the State encroaches upon the individual's pursuit of morality, it is the Moral Law that must be obeyed and not the State. And it is here that the members of the White Rose unlike their fellow intellectuals, take up the doctrine and act on it. But what Kant speaks of is only indirectly related to men's political and social experience.

It is not vicious nationalism that is the bane of Idealist political thought, but its remoteness from actual political conditions and its consequent

helplessness in the face of them. Twice in the broadsheets before us the name
of Fichte is invoked – a name associated outside Germany with rabid nationalism
and state worship. Yet the nationalist tone of the Fichte prose-poem which
Professor Kurt Huber quotes is no more than at best a local and particular
setting for noble sentiments, at worst a metaphysical plaster-cast; while the poem
itself is a simple exhortation to an individualistic, non-political morality:

> Und handeln sollst du so, als hinge
> Von dir und deinem Tun allein
> Das Schicksal ab der deutschen Dinge,
> Und die Verantwortung wär' dein . . .

(And you shall act as though/ The fate of all things German/ Were to
depend on you/ And were yours to answer for.)

The language used is nationalist, yet the sphere the poem describes is private.
The 'Deutschtum' (which never was on land or sea) that Fichte invokes is to
Professor Huber not a political reality at all; it has of course no recognizable
connection with the country which at that moment was at war with the world.
It is a metaphysical dream, unrealized in the there-and-then, an exquisite
abstract idea, of which Fichte had written in 1813: 'It is the Germans who
are called upon to realize the Eternal Empire in the world. In them the Empire
is to issue forth from a fully developed moral freedom and not the other way
about.' In the same vein, Professor Huber writes in 1943:

> A return to clear, moral foundations and to the rule of law in the State,
> a return to the mutual trust of man in man, this is not illegal, but on
> the contrary, a restoration of legality. In the terms of the Kantian
> Categorical Imperative I have asked myself what would happen if the
> subjective precept of my action were to become a general law. To this
> there is only one answer: then order, security and mutual trust would
> return into our state, into our political life.

But politics is concerned with maintaining a non-catastrophic distribution of
power such as might not be at the mercy of a 'mutual trust of man in man'.
Professor Huber's statement, though moving as an expression of personal
faith, does little or nothing to help bring about the sort of state which, although
not absolutely good, might at least have the merit of making the pursuit of
private morality a matter of personal conscience, not of life and death.

Here, it seems, lay the political task of the White Rose. It would be improper
to underestimate the difficulties, overwhelming in every respect, that they had
to face, but it is not their success which is here at issue. Having perceived
that, contrary to Fichte's expectations, the German state had utterly failed as
the guardian of morality, Professor Huber might have asked: what should men

do in the face of this failure, not individually and in the privacy of their own consciences, but as political beings, as the members of a society whose existing arrangements are to be replaced by others? In other words, we might have expected him not only morally to oppose but also politically to resist the National Socialist regime. But neither he nor his friends seem to have recognized at all clearly that the broadsheet campaign itself was necessarily also a political act, and that the give and take of association with other groups and other views and definite programmes would be necessary for success. Professor Huber goes out of his way explicitly to repudiate all 'organization', and he wishes to appeal, *in 1943*, 'by the simple word, not to an act of violence but to an ethical understanding'. ('I am not concerned with success in the real world,' Fichte wrote in 1813, 'but with insight and clarity.') But how, without 'organization', they could ever have 'stopped the war' is as difficult to imagine as what they would have done had they succeeded in stopping it. 'Federalism ... a Southern German democratic league ... the liberation of Germany from the Prusso-Bolshevik hegemony ...' are the names of some of their plans. None of these notions sounds more fantastic than (for instance) Count von Stauffenberg's plans for a government of hieratic syndicalism, or the proposal of Carl Goerdeler, Lord Mayor of Leipzig, of a return to the post-Munich (1938) frontiers. But the 'politics' of it all is utterly lacking – there is no suggestion of how any of it might be actually brought about. When we read that Hans Scholl was anxious to impress upon his friends the need for an 'education in politics', we may conclude that he at any rate was aware of this deficiency; and so, it seems, was Sophie Scholl – she (one of her friends writes) had acquired a very concrete and practical attitude to social problems, perhaps also to the question of political representation, during her time as a factory hand. And Professor Huber? He undoubtedly placed his convictions in the service of the action, but his convictions remained those of a patriotic German in a situation in which the appeal to patriotism was discredited. The only disagreement among the members of the White Rose we know about concerns a passage Professor Huber wished to include in the sixth (last) broadsheet: once the revolution gets under way (Huber had written), the students 'must place themselves totally at the disposal' of the German Army, whose 'magnificent achievements' had been misused by Hitler and the National Socialist Party for their own, criminal ends. Unlike Professor Huber, Hans Scholl had seen that army in action, and insisted on the sentence being removed before the leaflet was cyclostyled.

Did Kurt Huber ever unravel the muddle of misplaced absolutes, or see the defectiveness of Idealism's claim to be a non-political doctrine? By making 'the People' or 'the State' or 'the Human Race' absolute, Idealism does not remove the notion – or itself – from the sphere of politics. It merely encourages an *a priori* attitude in the light of which actual political questions appear trivial, unworthy of the philosopher's consideration. An absolute notion of 'the State' is one of which every actual state falls short. The precise nature and degree of its shortcomings are obscured by the transcendental vision of the ideal, and so, consequently, are the ideas which might give shape to effective or at least practicable political reforms.

But the broadsheets of the White Rose are important in an altogether different sense. They provide evidence, which is not as rare as has been made out, that there was no *effective* conspiracy of silence, that knowledge of the genocide of Jews and Poles in the east was not at all hard to come by, and that this knowledge was available to any one of the three million German soldiers on the Eastern Front. In the second of these broadsheets, composed in the summer of 1942, Hans Scholl and Alexander Schmorell write:

> We do not intend to say anything about the Jewish question, nor to enter a plea for the defence [of the Jews]; we only want to cite as an example the fact that since the conquest of Poland 300,000 Jews have been murdered in that country in the most bestial manner. In this we see the most terrible crime against human dignity, a crime not to be compared to any similar ones in the history of mankind. The Jews are human too, whatever one's attitude to the Jewish question ...

Then, having mentioned the killing, imprisonment and deportation of the entire Polish aristocracy, the two authors continue (the first set of italics is mine):

> Why do we tell you all this, *since you yourselves know of these or other, similarly grave crimes* committed by these terrible, subhuman people? Because a question is at issue here which concerns us all very deeply and which *must* give us all pause to think. Why does the German people behave so apathetically in the face of these most dreadful and unworthy crimes?

Hans Scholl and Alexander Schmorell (it will be recalled) served as orderly sergeants in the Army Medical Corps, and had no access to any special source of information.

I have stressed the lack of an adequate political motivation, the political amateurishness, of the White Rose, yet this is not to minimize the moral value of their act. For, although it is true that political action can never be wholly divorced from the precepts of morality, the converse does not hold true – the moral value of an individual act cannot be judged by its political effectiveness of or appropriateness, or by its implications in the sphere of politics. Though the Idealist tradition disabled them for effective political resistance, it made their moral opposition possible. Their political failure is one thing; their moral triumph another.

6

As the winter of 1942–3 wore on, the conspirators became more and more daring. Sophie Scholl, who for several months had lived in their midst without knowing that her brother and friends were the authors of the broadsheets she read, became now as active as the rest. They painted slogans ('Down with Hitler!') in the Ludwigstrasse and on public buildings, they dropped their leaflets through letter-boxes and sent them through the mail. Yet even at this time they never became fanatical, they never allowed their own great act of courage to obscure the reality of small acts of considerateness:

> Lest you should be alarmed by receiving this broadsheet [they wrote], we wish to add that the addresses of the readers of the White Rose do not appear in any written list. These addresses have been selected at random from postal directories.

The end came very quickly. The secret police began an extended search; a price was put on the heads of the anonymous authors, the evidence available to the police pointed to Munich; and on the morning of Thursday 18 February 1943 (it was later said) an unnamed friend came to warn Hans and Sophie Scholl that they were being watched by agents of the police. Whatever the facts, the warning came too late. They had left early that morning and had gone, with a suitcase full of leaflets, to the main university building. They arrived long before the first lectures began; the building was still empty. They first distributed their leaflets along the corridors and then, taking the open staircase in the centre of the building, they mounted to the second floor and showered what remained in their case into the entrance below. The head porter, whose suspicions may have been aroused on previous occasions, observed them and, having locked the main doors of the building, called the secret police. (According to another source it was the rector of the University who personally summoned the Gestapo.) Hans and Sophie Scholl were arrested in the building a few minutes later and confessed to the authorship of the broadsheets after some twenty hours of examination and torture. Willy Graf was arrested in the afternoon of the same day. A hand-written draft for a new broadsheet, by Christoph Probst, was found in Hans Scholl's pocket. And Christoph Probst, probably still ignorant of the Scholls' fate, was arrested on Saturday morning, 20 February 1943, while applying at his company office for a weekend pass to Innsbruck, to visit his wife, who was expecting a child. On hearing of these arrests, Alex Schmorell fled into the mountains, intending perhaps to escape into Switzerland. But he returned to Munich, was recognized and denounced by people in an air-raid shelter, and was arrested on the 24th. A day after his arrest the 'Gaustudentenführer' (the local party official in charge of university students) gave an address in the University, in which he (quite correctly) dissociated the German students from the activities of the

White Rose; the audience applauded his declaration of loyalty to the regime. Two days later, on 27 February, Professor Huber was arrested; immediately, before his trial had even begun, the university authorities deprived him of his post and of all academic honours.

The Scholls' examination lasted from Thursday till Saturday; on Sunday afternoon at 3 o'clock they were given the typescript of their indictment, and on Monday morning they were tried by one of the notorious 'People's Courts', specially convened for the occasion. What tortures they suffered we do not know; according to one witness, Sophie Scholl appeared before the judge on crutches. The court itself is not easy to describe; the atmosphere of it eludes one. It was presided over by Roland Freisler, Hitler's chief hanging judge. Its legal maxim had been expounded by Freisler himself, in his account of National Socialist jurisprudence published in 1938; it is that 'there is no other authority and ultimate source of law except the conscience of the Nation itself'; and elsewhere in that book he speaks of 'sound national feeling' ('das gesunde Volksempfinden') as overriding, in the case of legal doubt, all existing laws. It is the Fichtean argument again (invoked this time by Freisler), but no metaphysical axiom is provided to decide which is the true Germany, which is the true realization of German nationhood; there is only the simple, 'a-metaphysical' criterion of force. In the confidential report to the Berlin Ministry of Justice which Freisler wrote after the trial he cuts the Gordian knot, the intricate metaphysical argument: by their actions (he writes) the accused had forfeited their right and privilege to be regarded as Germans.

Two remarks of Freisler's may perhaps help us to understand the atmosphere in which these six were tried: 'Der Angeklagte faselte etwas davon, daß . . .' ('The accused drivelled on, something to the effect that . . .'), he writes in his report; and when, at the end of the trial, Hans Scholl pleaded for mercy on behalf of his fellow-accused Christoph Probst (who, it will be recalled, was married and had two small sons), Freisler interrupted him: 'If you have nothing to say for yourself, kindly shut up.' Professor Huber prepared a statement of his beliefs (in which occurs the poem I quoted), and intended to deliver it in court. The speech has been preserved by his widow, but it is not certain whether he was allowed to read it.

The trial – the first of three – was brief, the evidence overwhelming. Hans and Sophie Scholl and Christoph Probst were condemned to death and beheaded in the early afternoon of the fourth day after their arrest, on Monday, 22 February 1943. Alexander Schmorell and Professor Kurt Huber were executed on 13 July and Willy Graf on 10 October 1943. From one of the shorthand clerks present we know that throughout their trial the Scholls refused to give incriminating evidence against their friends. And the testimonies of the prison chaplain and of the warders bear witness to the courage and exaltation they showed in their last hours. Hans Scholl died with the word 'Freiheit' on his lips. Frau Scholl's last words to her daughter were, 'Gelt, Sophie, Jesus!' and the girl replied, 'Ja, aber du auch.' ('Remember, Sophie, Jesus.' 'Yes, but you too.')

7

The moral precepts of the Categorical Imperative have often been criticized – especially outside Germany – as excessively theoretical and 'abstract'. They are frequently indicted as being all very well on paper but 'unreal', that is, lacking the kind of direct appeal to living experience that informs the arguments of, say, the last Socratic dialogues. Such criticism questions not so much the logical cogency of the philosophical argument as rather the possibility, not beyond the vision of moral philosophers, of putting the theoretical precepts into practical action. Existentialist philosophy in particular, in the wake of Kierkegaard, has frequently argued that the generalizing of the particular into an abstract system of universals fails to meet the demand for authenticity, must fail to commit the self to its chosen task. The pragmatist, on the other hand, contemplating the story of the White Rose, may point to the futility, in practical terms, of what he would call 'this gesture of defiance'. ('What does it matter that we should die', Sophie Scholl is reported to have said to a fellow-prisoner, 'if thousands are stirred and awakened by what we have done? The students are bound to revolt.' Neither the students nor anyone else in Germany did; there was no response whatever.) Yet the act and its moral motivation remain. It is the particular glory of the life and death of the Scholls and of their friends that they accepted and acted on the maxims of this 'abstruse' moral doctrine, that to them it had no taint of unreality or excessive generality, that for them it was as living as the Sermon on the Mount. The quality of this belief, the fact that (though they did not seek death) they were prepared to die in upholding the doctrine as they understood it, is no proof of its truth. Again, both French and German Existentialists have gone too far in arguing for the truth of a given belief (as opposed to the truthfulness of the believer) from the degree and quality of the personal commitment involved in the defence of that belief. But the Scholls' and their friends' deaths do bear witness to the livingness of the precepts they upheld and propagated in their broadsheets – or rather, they give the measure of a man's or woman's capacity to live by ideas, to integrate theoretical and practical elements alike in decisions and actions, to make a coherent whole of experience and to act on it. As we try to picture to ourselves what sort of a person Hans Scholl was, the outstanding thing about him seems to be his simplicity. There seem to have been no thoughts in his mind that were at odds with his warm and feeling heart, and no feelings in excess of his capacity to act. He was no abstruse moralist. His conscience had been stirred into action by his recognition of the moral problem of his time and place, he had made the traditional moral doctrine his own and he showed himself capable of acting upon it in complete and conscious disregard of the consequences, and with the vigour of an infinitely courageous young man.

Yet the question may be asked whether an exclusively moral motivation adequately explains the action of this little group; and their intimate contact with Catholic thinkers makes it relevant to consider the question of religious motives.

In the case of Willy Graf, the Saarlander, the answer leaves no room for doubt. Willy Graf's whole cast of mind, his upbringing and his outlook, were clearly religious. In the thoughts he jotted down during his army service in Russia he returns again and again to the themes of Christian contemplation, and his letters of the last months express not sudden discoveries so much as thoughts matured during long periods of intense faith. He too speaks of the Invisible Church, and in turning to the contemporary situation he is acutely conscious of the abyss that lies between the ways of God and the ways of the world. In a diary entry of 14 January 1943 (a few weeks before his friends' and his own arrest) he confesses to some misgivings about the leaflet action, mainly, it appears, because he sees it, after all, as capable of a political interpretation. Yet when we read in Freisler's report that in the course of the trial Willy Graf accepted full responsibility for his action, stressing himself that what he had done was quite 'unpardonable', we recognize that he spoke as one possessed by a steady religious purpose, as a man secure in his faith.

As for Hans Scholl, both in the reminiscences of his friends and in the diary entries that have been published, there is a clear indication of a change in outlook in the last year of his life. The conviction grew in his mind that the evil that surrounded him could not be remedied but only redeemed, that only a religious vantage-point could provide him with an adequate view of the terrible events of his time: 'If Christ had not lived and died,' he wrote towards the end of his active service in the front line, 'then truly there would be no way out. Then all the tears would be horribly meaningless. Then you would have to batter your head against the nearest wall. But not if he did [*So aber nicht*].' Nevertheless, what he actually appeals to in the broadsheets is a moral point of view, not a religious one. The apparent contradiction is resolved if we distinguish between the conscious, overt motivation of his act on the one hand and, on the other, the sanction under which his act may be seen to stand and under which it yields its fullest meaning. If we consider his action in this light, no contradiction arises between an immanent morality and transcendent faith. In the sphere of conscious motivation it was a noble pride that informed Hans Scholl's act – the pride to do from within himself and by his own strength that which he believed all decent men should do. Yet as such it was an act which, though it sought no support from faith, was, by virtue of the serenity and joyfulness that accompanied it, related to faith. In an essay on this very theme of the heroic in the world, a Cambridge theologian, the late Baron von Hügel, writes:

The Supernatural should not be identified by the amount of its conscious, explicit reference to Christ or even simply to God, but by certain qualities ... of which heroism, with a keen sense of givenness and of 'I could not do otherwise', appears to be the chief. Thus [von Hügel continues] a man may ... be in a truly supernatural condition of soul, and may yet

possess, at the time or even generally, only the most dim and confused
– a quite inadequate – theology.

Was Hans Scholl in such a condition as is here suggested? It is not only the
courage and single-mindedness of the act which intimate the condition, but
also the singular absence of any moral rigorism or cold severity or harsh
fanaticism. The calm assurance with which they went out, in the small hours
of the morning, into the hostile streets of Munich, the serenity with which
they faced mortal danger, intimates that they acted under a sanction which,
for the believer, transcends that of the moral law.

The members of the White Rose did not seek death for its own sake. There
is no trace of suicidal despair in any of their utterances or actions, and not
until their last days did they reckon with death as a certainty. Overtaken by
catastrophe, they fought for their lives; they threw themselves into the battle
of wits against their judges with all the vitality and intelligence they possessed.
To save their friends became for them their last intellectual task. Thus Sophie
Scholl was full of joy when, reading the hurriedly contrived indictment, she
found that her confession had been accepted and that none of her friends
were mentioned as accomplices. (In his notes on the second trial – that of
Professor Huber, Alex Schmorell and Willy Graf – Freisler admits that Sophie
Scholl, 'a common hussy', had pleaded guilty to, and been convicted of, a
number of charges of which she was later proved to have been innocent.)
Since they never betrayed the beliefs for which they were tried their action
remained meaningful for them to the very end. It is this meaningfulness which
distinguishes the White Rose from several other, similar German groups. The
purity of their motive was unblemished; their action remained linked with that
motive in a direct and simple nexus more commonly praised in ethics than
met with in actual conduct.

8

Looking back over the spiritual journey of Hans Scholl, who had once, in the
1930s, been a typical young German, we may perhaps see it in three distinct
stages. In the first, representative stage, he belonged to the world of his day,
he was ensconced in a false universal. The second is the stage of his maturing
decision, in which, with his few friends, he lived in the particular; feeling
himself to be the exception, he lived by his own laws and not by the laws of
the world around him. It is at this point that, for the Existentialist, the choice
of conscience, the *acte gratuit*, is said to take place. Yet since such a decision
is said to be accompanied by loneliness, despair and a somewhat inhuman
moral rigorism, the theory of the *acte gratuit* does not seem to describe Hans
Scholl's outlook at all correctly; the tone of the description does not accord
with his final state of mind. There is nothing superhuman about him. There
were moments, witnessed by one of his friends who survived the war in prison,

when Hans, aware of his responsibility, especially for the fate of his younger sister, was overwhelmed by despair. But these were moments only – throughout his life and to its very end he remained in communion with his friends. And in that way, I think, he reached a third stage, that of the true universal, in which he found himself at one with the spiritual-moral law, at one (if we take all significant acts to be ensconced in a continuity) with the perennial human tradition of sacrifice for the truth.

What meaning can we discern in those last words which the anguished father called to his children as they were being taken to the block, 'You will go down in history'? His intention, very probably, was to restate, in our contemporary, intellectualized form, men's age-old desire to be made immortal on this earth, to live on for ever in the memory of their fellow men. In the political history of their own country the place of the members of the White Rose is marginal, the notional continuity which we call 'German history' remains unaltered by their ineffective act. The tradition to which these six belong is of all time and all places; but it has few participants and only occasionally practical results. Among those who belong to it are the students of Prague who in 1941 were executed on the ramparts of their city and the students of Budapest in 1956. And, recently, the students of Tiananmen Square. If it is in the language of German Idealist philosophy that the Munich students described the notion of freedom for which they died, this language was, ultimately, contingent to a decision which belongs to no nation and no supra-national state, to no body politic whatever. Perhaps theirs was that 'reasonable service' of which St Paul speaks in the Epistle to the Romans (12:1): 'I beseech you therefore, brethren, . . . that ye present your bodies a living sacrifice, holy, acceptable unto God, which is your reasonable service.'

1958 (1990)

14

A Man without Ideology*

1 The Celebration

Seen from afar, the picture seemed quite clear.

A small town in southern Germany – in that strangely independent-minded province of Swabia, to be exact – had come to a corporate decision to celebrate, on 9 November 1979, the fortieth anniversary of the attempt on Hitler's life by a working-class man who had been one of its citizens. Everyone in Heidenheim knew about the journeyman carpenter Johann Georg Elser, but very few ever expected to find him being commemorated with solemnities, like a real hero. For some years past the local branch of the DKP (the new German Communist Party) had annually laid a wreath on the memorial to him set up in a small park in the suburb where Elser had lived for a time (the tablet is a good deal smaller and less conspicuous than the memorial on a hill above the town commemorating the only other prominent Heidenheimer – Field-Marshal Erwin Rommel). It was obviously with a good deal of amazement that some of the townspeople had come across a book of mine, entitled *Hitler: der Führer und das Volk* (first published in English), a long chapter of which was devoted to Georg Elser. Based on the oppressively complete Gestapo files of the case, the chapter attempted to characterize Elser as 'Hitler's true antagonist', by showing how the initially similar social situations of the two men merely emphasized the absolute contrast in their moral attitudes. This contrast formed the background to an analysis of the motives that led Elser to his attempt on Hitler's life, and to the central question of what had sustained him in the total solitude of his twelve months of careful preparation.

Together, a Protestant clergyman and a Catholic priest who were on friendly terms and had collaborated in various ecumenical experiments came to the conclusion that Elser's was a case overdue for municipal and ecclesiastical attention. As a result of their joint lobbying an invitation came from the town

---

* The first part of this essay was written together with Sheila Stern.

of Heidenheim to the author of the book and his wife, to join in a three-part programme consisting of a documentary play (originally composed, from the book, for the BBC), a public discussion, and a Sunday morning memorial celebration with an address, flowers and a brass band, a solemn offering of wreaths at the memorial stone closing the proceedings.

All this was clear enough, yet as we flew to Stuttgart a number of uneasy questions occupied our minds. For example, were the three planned occasions not too many, and would the civic junketing not be overcast by gloom? After all, Elser's attempt was frustrated by the merest chance through Hitler's leaving his Bürgerbräukeller meeting on 9 November 1939 thirteen minutes earlier than planned. Elser's bomb had killed and injured innocent people, and he himself was shot in Dachau a few days before the war ended, when Hitler and his myrmidons had to recognize the improbability of their being able to stage a show trial in London and to produce him there as an agent of the British secret service.

It was Elser's peculiar fate to be constantly assigned, by his contemporaries and later by misguided journalists and historians, to groups and allegiances with which he had in fact no connection. Apart from a complicated British-secret-service story, there were rumours, after the war, to the effect that he had really been hired by the Gestapo, or the SS or the dissident National Socialist Otto Strasser, either to kill Hitler or to stage a scenario of Hitler's providential escape (this version is taken over by Alan Bullock in his Hitler biography). The entirely accidental survival of the verbatim Gestapo transcript of Elser's depositions, some of them made under torture, leaves no reasonable doubt that all these hypotheses parading as facts are wrong. The Gestapo officials who cross-examined Elser were the only ones who were immediately convinced of the truth of what he said. Would we when attending the proceedings in Heidenheim be faced by people who still doubted the evidence because (like the National Socialist leaders) they would not believe that a single German working-class man was capable of acting thus, independently and on his own initiative? Would we succeed in convincing our audience that here was a man whom no group or party or 'ism' was entitled to claim for its own? That he represented a phenomenon not often known in German history – a true non-conformist with *Zivilcourage*, Heidenheim's Robert Kett? That he, a perfectly ordinary man who was a highly skilful carpenter, played the double-bass and accordion and had a number of love-affairs, acted, when the time came, without thought of personal gain, from (one blushes to admit it) the highest moral and spiritual motives? And, since the portrayal of Elser as 'a man without ideology' was bound to be hotly disputed by the communists, who were claiming to see in him a Marxistically motivated working-class hero, would we therefore find ourselves overwhelmed by the not exactly disinterested assent of the Right? And, finally, in praising an essentially political act of violence, would we be taken to be advocating political violence generally? Would we be taken to be sanctioning the actions of the terrorists then prominent on the West German scene?

These were some of our anticipatory thoughts as the municipal Mercedes drove us over the darkening Schwäbische Alb to Heidenheim and deposited us at the local theatre, where an amateur group performed an adaptation of my radio play to an overwhelmingly full house. On us, at least, the impact was tremendous. Sitting near us in the audience, with his wife, was Leonhard Elser (a carpenter too), Georg's brother. Having shaken hands with them, to be plunged into darkness and to hear the well-simulated voice of Hitler summoning the German people to follow him to perdition robbed us of our serene objectivity in a few seconds. The subject of Elser's life and motivation, which we had discussed so often, seemed suddenly to have reached out and drawn us in to where it was still a matter of personal memories, affections, habits and passionate involvement – not 'history' at all. The heavy local accent in which the main character was played was of course Elser's own; the man who took the part, a workman in a Heidenheim factory, brought us closer to Elser than we had ever expected to be.

This, generally and repeatedly, was the most important thing that happened during the three-and-a-half days of our visit: to see this slow-moving community – a true 'home town' of the social historian's theorizing – coming to terms with its past through one of their lot; to see it being forcibly brought face to face with what every other such community in Germany has categorically denied – the possibility of political resistance.

Talking to Leonhard Elser and his wife in their home, we became aware of the unexpected openness and warmth of their attitude to us. We came from far away, yet as strangers who understood their past and its anguish we were not going to be treated as strangers – we were indeed closer than some of the town's rich industrialists who preferred to ignore the occasion.

We were initiated into the tensions and resentments inseparable from the possession of a local hero. 'Why all the fuss?' one lady had asked at the end of the play. 'He killed those people – nobody praises the quiet citizens who did no harm to anyone.' It was not possible, nor would it have been right, to tell her that being a quiet citizen was all very well, but that being millions of quiet citizens had turned out to be disastrous.

Another revelation was the fragmentation of small places into tiny places. It is there as a major theme in nineteenth-century German literature – most perfectly in the work of the Swiss writer Gottfried Keller – but that it should have survived into present-day Germany in such fierce integrity could only be appreciated in direct contact with the *Bürger* of a town which had no tourist attractions, no foreign visitors, no university, and hence no detached view of its own status. Some opposition to the Heidenheim celebrations had been voiced on the ground that Elser was actually born in Hermaringen, a minuscule village some miles away, that he had lived in another small village, called Königsbronn (as his brother still did), and that even when he lived in Heidenheim he really lived in the working-class suburb called Schnaitheim – which was only incorporated in 1907 and has its own dialect, its own cuisine, its own Communist Party, and even its own small town hall and its own deputy mayor, a courtesy title for an official utterly devoted to the small world of Schnaitheim.

But it was the splendours of the immense, brand-new *Bürgerhaus* of Heidenheim, with its elaborate air-conditoning, split-level labyrinths and vistas, exhibition areas and luxurious leather seating that were the setting for the public discussion held in its roomy auditorium on the Saturday evening. Once more the sheer size of the audience was astonishing. The involvement and tension that had been latent in the audience at the play were manifest during this curious session. The chairman allowed each of the platform speakers to make a brief statement, but most of the three-and-a-half hours was occupied in contributions from the floor. These made it perfectly plain that the occasion had become one for letting off a considerable amount of steam. Speaker after speaker pointed out to the Heidenheim gentlemen on the platform that but for the interest of the visitor from England, Elser, as a working man, would never have received any attention in his own place. There was a brief shouting-match between a well-known young communist (super-salesman, we heard afterwards, for Rank-Xerox) and the Mayor of Heidenheim. But apart from this exciting incident, during which old scores and new sores were made public while the PR-conscious mayor watched us in an agony of embarrassment, the platform took its medicine like several very honest men.

The most surprising effect of the discussion, and its most moving moments, were produced by two elderly speakers, both close friends and workmates of Elser's, who spoke up in public for the first time since the events of forty years ago.

The first described with apparently total recall ('It was that summer of '39, when there were so many raspberries') his unexpected meeting with Elser in the nearby hills, and Elser's determination to keep aloof from everyone who knew him as the moment approached for his attempt on Hitler's life – everyone, it transpired, except perhaps his father, with whom he had been on bad terms for many years, but whom (it seems) he trusted in his anguish and solitude.

The other old man, a life-long communist, testified to Elser's refusal to join or work for the local party, and ended by saying, 'The professor from England is right. Elser was a great idealist, but he was no communist. I tried to get him to join the Party, but he wouldn't hear of it. He was, like the professor said, a man without ... ideology.' No praise the professor ever received was so sweet.

They say England is the land of class distinctions, and it is certainly true that the immense and visibly general prosperity of a small industrial town like Heidenheim is based on a conscious identification of working people with the interests of factory owners and management. But this is a functional alliance, and the class division, manifest in working-class feelings of shyness and inferiority which have no parallel in England, remains as strong as it has ever been. There was no end to the kindness and thoughtfulness we met from everyone, so it may seem churlish to record that Elser's brother and sister-in-law were never included in the numerous occasions when we sat down to a convivial meal or drinks with our hosts from town hall, presbytery and vicarage – and yet the two clerics, who had after all thought the whole thing up, were on the warmest personal terms with their working-class parishioners and spoke with them as with intimate friends. When we visited the Elsers, they shared an excellent bottle of Franconian burgundy with us and gave us presents. If Georg Elser was there in spirit at this most surprising of civic celebrations, he must have been ruefully aware that, as a member of the town-hall audience pointed out, it makes a great deal of difference whether your hero is a field-marshal or a carpenter, even long after he is dead.

The Sunday morning celebration was a solemn blend of the various elements we had seen at work. Somewhat pale still from the unwinding-sessions we had participated in at a restaurant after the discussion the night before, we gathered in the crowded assembly hall of the Schnaitheim school and I gave the brief memorial address printed below, surrounded by magnificent flower arrangements and a passable brass band.

Afterwards, in pale sunshine, wreaths were placed on Elser's modest memorial in the tiny Schnaitheim park named after him. 'Have you many revolutionaries in England?' we were asked by an elderly communist widow-lady of the neighbourhood. It was a difficult question to answer. The circumstances, we attempted to suggest, were different in England. Did she mean revolutionaries like Hitler? Or like the Baader-Meinhof group? Or . . . She went off without shaking hands; a bit of a slap in the face, really.

2 A Tribute

Formal acts of commemoration are not always the best occasions for arriving at historical truth, for they often serve to create myths. However, as anyone must who belongs to a university, I see my task primarily as the search for rational explanations of human actions and motives. To pay proper tribute to Johann Georg Elser we must not allow false piety to distract us from interpreting and understanding his deed as faithfully as we can on the basis of the documentary material we have.

Are we right to pay tribute to Georg Elser at all? Today there is no need for me to spend time in refuting the various suspicions and rumours that surrounded his name in the early post-war years. This has been done at length, first in 1950, by the Munich public prosecutor's office, and secondly, in 1969, in a very fully documented article, by Anton Hoch; anyone not convinced by these arguments can go to the Federal Archives at Koblenz and inspect the record of Georg Elser's interrogation in Berlin by the Gestapo, which was forwarded to Himmler and initialled by him; and I wonder what kind of evidence will convince anyone not convinced by that. (To this, though, I must add with what astonishment I learned, from the documents I was shown by an official at your town hall after the public discussion yesterday, that Georg Elser's mother's request for compensation was turned down by the Munich court to which she applied.)

Quite apart from any unfounded suspicions, Elser's deed presents certain dubious aspects, and they need to be fairly stated. Let me enumerate them.

Georg Elser attempted an assassination. His unsuccessful act of violence led to the deaths of eight innocent people and inflicted injury on more than sixty others. Our daily lives teach us all to believe that in some circumstances the end justifies the means, or at least excuses it, but here the end was not achieved. The killing and injuring of these people remains – and remained for him too, as long as he lived – an unqualified evil, and it is clear, even through the bureaucratic phraseology of the Gestapo record, that Elser expressed deep sorrow and remorse for the unintended but foreseeable consequences of what he did.

Even the self-sacrifice that he consciously determined on – for he knew exactly what would happen to him if he were caught – is not in itself something we should praise. The capacity for self-sacrifice in itself seems to me valueless; to ascribe value to it is one of the major superstitions of our century. Elser lived in an age when sacrifice as an absolute value, sacrifice without any 'reason why', was incessantly being proclaimed – by National Socialism. Indeed, I believe that this appeal to the potentiality for absolute and indiscriminate self-sacrifice in the population as a whole was a part of the essence and attraction of the National Socialist ideology.

It must also be said that this picture of a would-be assassin is deeply horrifying to us. It is the picture of a man who carried the thought of this assassination about with him for a whole year; that is, from the time of the Munich agreement in the autumn of 1938 until the date we are commemorating, almost exactly forty years ago today. Throughout that year all his daily care and deliberations were concentrated on preparing and installing his instrument of death.

Finally, it should be added that Georg Elser's attachment to the Christian Church was extremely vague; even the non-denominational Pietism of Swabia had no hold upon him. The chief personal statement of his life is the very detailed transcript of his second interrogation by the Gestapo (in Berlin) – a statement which not only is convincing in form, but has, in spite of the circumstances, an inner authenticity about it. As far as we can tell from this record it was not Christian faith that motivated him in what he did, but the other way round – his deed drove him back to faith; that is to say, it was fear, of a kind hardly imaginable to us, which impelled him to go into churches in the search for support and consolation, and, as he says: '. . . to say the Lord's Prayer there. To my mind it doesn't matter', he goes on, 'whether you do it in a Catholic church or a Protestant one . . . anyway the fact is that after praying I always felt calmer.' Expressions like 'anyway the fact is' ('es ist schon so') are among the phrases that leave us in no doubt as to the genuineness of this evidence.

So much for what is questionable about the man and his deed. I believe we are nevertheless right to pay tribute to Georg Elser, and indeed that these very circumstances are what justify our doing so. Elser was not one of the martyrs of the Church. As far as we can judge, he was not inspired by that absolute faith for which we know many others went to their deaths. What he did was determined by political motives and aimed at political effects. His project displays the imperfections all human action has. It is just these flaws that constitute the human appeal and human limitations of the deed that was to cost him his life, and give this deed its likeness to a tangle of many-coloured strands. The deed owes its character also to its time, one in which purity and freedom from evil could perhaps be found only in passive suffering and the will to save others, not in any deed aiming at political effectiveness.

Georg Elser stands before us as a free, active and rational man, and his life and death derive their meaning from these three aspects of his nature.

He was a free man. His freedom showed itself in, and was founded upon, his unassuming life-style, his skill as a craftsman and his nonconformism or independence of mind. The first two of these attributes or conditions were common to many others, but the third makes him stand out from the broad mass of his compatriots, who saw – or claimed to see – the highest virtue in toeing the line, in thinking and feeling in conformity with a deliberately mythologized national community, the *Volksgemeinschaft*.

Understanding him as a free, independent man, we recognize him as the almost total opposite of the man he wished to do away with. There was probably not too much difference between the modest home of a customs official's family 150 miles east of here at Braunau in Upper Austria, and the equally modest home of a Swabian timber merchant; and when Georg Elser in his interrogation describes his father's material worries and excessive drinking, this reminds us of very similar descriptions in *Mein Kampf*, which may likewise be autobiographical in origin. The contrast between the two men lies, rather, in the sphere where human freedom prevails. Here, self-restraint and modesty stand opposed to a boundless craving for power and self-assertion, while the conscientiousness of a craftsman is set against bungling and dilettantism; a rhetorically inflated fanaticism, self-deluding and deluding others, against an independence of mind articulated in faltering, unpractised words; a roarer and ranter against a man who quietly thinks for himself.

Thinking for oneself is never popular. Forty years ago in Germany, it meant isolation from all public affairs and confinement to a purely private sphere of friends and family. In the early years of the Third Reich, Elser may not have found this hard, for though he had friends he was not a very gregarious man. But later, as his assassination plan took shape, he must have come to feel the terrible loneliness of his position. Unlike the aristocratic conspirators of 20 July 1944, he could not count on any class solidarity or appeal to any mystically tinged class consciousness. Unlike his comrades in the Communist Party, he had no dialectical, tactically adjustable explanation for the Hitler phenomenon. And unlike those victims of National Socialism whose motives were above all religious, he was pursuing a very clearly conceived political goal.

He was a man alone. And if, perhaps, there was after all someone who shared his secret, either here in Elser's home district or in Munich – for this is the one point where his recorded testimony may not be entirely trustworthy, and a friend of his has told me that Elser's father, at all events, was in his confidence – then we can only admire his constancy under interrogation, when he refused despite severe physical maltreatment to disclose the names of any accomplices or persons in the know.

I mention the solitude in which he lived – which to us, though we live in a free society, is unfortunately by no means unimaginable – simply because the few historians who mention Elser at all draw a false conclusion from it. His loneliness was the consequence of his deed, not its reason or cause. Several historians call him an eccentric and a loner. Nothing in his life suggests that he was an eccentric, and he was a loner only because he thought, surely with very good reason, that he could trust nobody. He was alone like a Jew among hostile Aryans. His aloofness stigmatizes not him but the 'national community' of fellow-travellers and potential informers among whom he lived.

He stands before us not only as a free man but as one who acted rationally, that is, one who was prepared to translate his inner conviction into action by using the possibilities available to him. If he ever asked himself 'Why me? Why should *I* be the one to face the risk, the deadly danger?', his answer would have had nothing to do with any ideological reflections, much less any calculation of personal advantage. There was a very concrete answer to that question, and it lay in his hands, in his manual skill. We may regard it as significant and fitting that his deed depended on the exercise of his craft as a carpenter; and also as tragic, that this craftsmanship had to serve him for an assassination attempt – that by means of the best thing he had, the skill which was a part of his identity, he was compelled to seek his own liberation and that of his compatriots through an act of destruction. The few words of explanation he was allowed during his interrogation show clearly that he understood the tragedy of this situation well enough. What we should view as exemplary is not the execution of his deed, but the spirit in which he performed it.

He certainly lacked a capacity for theoretical political argument – he was a man without ideology – and what led him to do what he did were very simple considerations such as any one of us might conceive. It was that modest decency of ordinary people (of those 'masses' despised by the philosophers of his time) which can express itself in phrases of no great originality but of great clarity and forcefulness. 'By my deed I wanted to prevent even more bloodshed' he tells his tormentors. But this thorough decency that has something of the old-fashioned ideal of the gentleman about it is to be found in his daily life too, long before he decided to act. We find it in his being generally known, especially here in Heidenheim, for helpfulness and kindness, but also in his refusal to give the Hitler salute, in the unease, the almost physical nausea, that overcame him whenever he had to listen to a speech by Hitler on the radio in a public house.

To be sure, he was a practical man, a craftsman. But let us not make a naïve enthusiast of him, or exaggerate his simplicity – he was an intelligent Swabian capable of arriving at his own conclusions about the world. His lack of interest in ideological discussions does not indicate that he lacked the ability to theorize. On the contrary, the one moment in the course of his interrogation when he shows personal pride is when he begins to describe the mechanism of his home-made time bomb: only in the initial stage of the work, he points out, did he carry out experiments with various detonators in his father's garden; everything else – that is, the technically complex arrangement of the timing and detonating devices – he solved 'at the drawing board', in other words theoretically. Again we may wish that his gifts could have found a different fulfilment, yet clearly for this man at this historical moment this was the one course he could freely choose.

What he lacked, then, was not intellectual capacity, but any interest in ideologies. In the Gestapo record, we read: 'Some concepts from the National Socialist world view are explained to the accused. He alleges that these processes of thought are unknown to him.' And we can hardly hold this lack of interest against him. But again, this is not to say that he was politically uninterested or ignorant. (It is the peculiarly arrogant notion of many intellectuals that there is no political insight without ideological commitment.) Without taking any notice of the communists' revolutionary plans or their philosophical casuistry, Elser voted for them, he said, for the same reason that he joined the timber-workers' trade union and read its periodical – simply because both organizations promised to improve pay and working conditions. (Even today it is not well known that the price of economic success in the first few years of National Socialism was a drastic lowering of wages and a no less drastic curtailment of workers' rights.) When Elser says that his observations have led him to conclude 'that the German government wants to abolish the Churches that exist in Germany, that is, the religions', 'that conditions in Germany can only be changed by removing the present leadership', 'that on the removal of these three men' – meaning Hitler, Göring and Goebbels – 'the government will be taken over by others who will not make unacceptable demands on foreign countries or wish to incorporate them, and who will take care to improve the workers' social conditions', and 'that the Munich agreement will not be the end of it all, that Germany will make still more demands on other countries and still more annexations of territory, and that war is inevitable – that is, I had the feeling it would turn out that way' – when Elser states all this, circumstantially, including the caveat at the end, indeed with almost pedantic precision, to be recorded in the protocol, these thoughts reveal not only much accurate insight into the position of Germany in the late 1930s, but also a surprising understanding of the developments that were imminent in Europe. If you suppose that all he says is obvious and hardly a matter for surprise at that time, it must, I think, be added that neither the German generals nor the French and British prime ministers possessed such an understanding.

The tone of these political reflections is highly characteristic. We detect in them neither the apolitical idealism of the heroic Munich group around Hans and Sophie Scholl, which in the contemporary context was also unrealistic, nor yet that fatal calculation of tactical possibilities and territorial demands familiar to us, for example, from the memorandum of the Lord Mayor of Leipzig, Carl Goerdeler, and his entourage. Elser's concern was not to justify his class and its ethos to posterity – to make the concept of a 'sacred Germany' shine forth one last time; in fact, he probably had no very definite conception even of parliamentary democracy. His knowledge and motives were of a concrete, immediate kind: they came from his experience of an infamous regime and of the dynamics of the National Socialist state, in home and foreign policy alike.

Once again we must try to envisage, from our present-day standpoint, the character of the epoch in which Elser lived and yet found the intelligence and courage for such insights. Terror brutalizes and corrupts; but, while in most people it also dulls the intelligence, there are a few whom it makes brave and cunning, and whose power to distinguish between good and evil – the faculty Immanuel Kant called practical reason – is made more acute by it. Georg Elser was such a man.

If, to the philosophers, this form of reason seems sharply separated from and opposed to religious faith, that separation and opposition does not correspond to Georg Elser's experience. He says: 'I believe in the continued life of the soul after death, and I also believed that one day I should go to heaven, if I had had the chance to prove by my later life that my intention was good.' These words express his belief in the validity of good works for the salvation of the human soul, his belief that human efforts can be transcended.

It seems especially important here to guard against any pious misunderstandings. I do not believe that Elser thought of himself as religiously motivated. In religion as in other matters, he had no distinct self-consciousness; in religion too, he was as it were a man without ideology. Like Job in Kant's interpretation of the Book of Job, Elser disdains to seek consolation in any theodicy, that is, he has no notion of trying to explain the evils in the world as the workings of divine justice, as 'so many punishments for sins committed' (to quote Kant).

I would like to remind you of the ironic story of Job. When those who claim to be his friends besiege him with questions about his sinful life and God's just dealings, Job can only declare his innocence and his obedience to God. Beyond that, all he knows is that he knows nothing: 'But he is in one mind, and who can turn him? and what his soul desireth, even that he doeth' (Job 23:13). Elser's confession is similar. He too has been harried by his interrogators with questions about his attitude to God (we can hardly suppose they are concerned about his soul: they hope he will betray accomplices and confidants). Elser answers them very clearly and directly:

I believe that the whole world and human life too were created by God.
I believe that nothing happens in the world without God's knowledge.

People are probably free to do as they will, but God can intervene whenever he wants to.

He has left me too to do as I wish. Whether he intervened in my actions and caused the Führer to leave earlier, I just don't know.

Where Elser can see events reflecting the operation of choices or individual decisions, he neither excludes nor pretends to understand the workings of divine providence; while the claim to stand under its protection, which is Hitler's claim, is as alien to Elser as any other form of self-assertion.

'Whether he intervened in my action ... I just don't know': the reason which informs these words is not the adversary of faith. The religious motivation which to me seems the most convincing explanation for Elser's resolve to act is to be taken not as an alternative to the moral motive, but as its complement. It identifies the moment at which his essential decency and reasonableness, in their extremity, find strength in faith. Perhaps this is the meaning of St Paul's words in the Epistle to the Romans (12:1) which may serve as the right text for our commemoration of Georg Elser. Paul demands, not the bloody sacrificial death on the altar – sacrifice *per se* – but the reasonable resolve to place one's life in the service of God: 'I beseech you therefore, brethren, by the mercies of God, that ye present your bodies a living sacrifice, holy, acceptable unto God, which is your reasonable service.'

We are ultimately forced to a disturbing conclusion: we must assess a political killing as reasonable, and yet approve of it as part of a life which, at least at its end, sought and found help and consolation in a religion that assesses it as evil. Since from all we know of Elser there can be no question of either a self-interested or a pathological motive for what he did, he must himself have been confronted with this harsh paradox. I can see no solution for us here except to face the full tragedy of his decision.

The aim was to prevent, or terminate, the war. It was a rational aim, which, as far as was humanly foreseeable, could have been attained by killing Hitler. What makes this aim rational is, among other things, the fact that in evaluating it Elser took account of Hitler's role and authority as leader – in other words, Elser acted rationally in assessing the political probability that the war might be ended by the assassination. The fact that this aim, both rational and moral, was not achieved, should not affect the way we judge the value of his decision to act. And even if the means used – the assassination – is not justified by the purpose intended, it is at least excused and explained by it. This paradox bears the imprint of its time. Georg Elser shouldered the burden of it freely and consciously – and that is why we ought to honour his memory today and in the future. His deed was conditioned by the age in which it took place. The spirit that inspired it remains exemplary and free.

1979

15

The Gypsies

How poignant newspaper headlines can be! Like this one: 'Rabbi NN shares a feeling of permanent exile with the refugee poet'. And yet, I find this a strange bit of information, because the last time I saw the rabbi on the box, laying down the law on some matter of profound moral concern – well frankly, it wasn't a permanent feeling of exile she conveyed to me, but a permanent feeling of having a jolly good time, and of being so much at home in the TV studio, you could hardly tell where the rabbi ended and the studio began. 'As German unification becomes a certainty, there is growing disquiet among Jews,' the rabbi's article begins; and it goes on: 'Perhaps most strongly affected are those who are refugees, such as my mother, and children of refugees, who have seen the problems of rootlessness and question their own "identity" as a result of early memories.' Well, I'm sure that's true of many people, but NN's mother's daughter doesn't seem to me to suffer from 'problems of rootlessness', and if she questions her own 'identity', I daresay she will take good care to do it at peak viewing time. Could it be that, like many professional agonizers, NN is a bit of a humbug?

I have been wondering about the people who have never heard of 'problems of identity', who live a life of 'rootlessness' without having the nous, the time or the education to fasten on to that word, or indeed on to any other words, who have never heard of *PR* or 'personality problems' or 'the guilt of survival' ... the people who were murdered, in the same way as were the Jews, in their tens and hundreds of thousands, the people whose deaths are not recorded in any memorials or statistics, who have no names, who have had almost nothing written about them, who were gassed, killed with phenol injections, tortured to death, experimented on, sterilized and castrated, and maimed for life. What is this monstrous competition of suffering that makes a serious historian write: 'It was the Jews alone who were marked out to be destroyed in their entirety'?

There were others. Two of their kind stood by the garden gate, with a silent girl behind the younger one. They were graceful; their brown crinkly hair just like the Jews' but with strands of different colours, bleached by the sun. Would the lady like to buy some lace, the elder one asked, proffering a wicker basket full of coarse cotton edging-lace. Then, in a gentle voice, she added: were they going the right way into town? They'd come on the train, from Lincolnshire, had walked from the station, and had lost their way. But now they were on the edge of the town, having almost gone past it.

They came in for a cup of coffee, and the silent little girl drank a glass of lemonade. 'Is this your home, lady?' they asked. And 'Oh, doesn't it smell lovely!' They had left their husbands in the caravans. She couldn't bring the boy, said the younger one, he had burned his foot, her husband was looking after him while they were away. Had they taken the boy to the doctor, the lady asked. No, they couldn't do that, the younger one replied: you had to be registered, you had to have a home address to do that, and they hadn't got a home address. They had their herbs, though. They did a lot of travelling about, she said, but they'd never been in this town. Oh yes, they'd heard about it. As they were leaving, they enquired once more the way into town. You turn right, said the lady, and at the next corner you take the first on the left. Then the elder one stretched out an arm and said: 'Is this the right, lady?'

Around the time this happened – in the mid-1980s – the government of the Czechoslovak Socialist Republic was sterilizing some of the Gypsies who were living on its territory, and removing the children from their families. This practice seems still to be going on in many parts of Central and Eastern Europe (though not in President Havel's Czechoslovakia). In 1980 the government of the People's Republic of Poland forcibly deported groups of Gypsies by boat, after having confiscated documents which would have allowed them to return. Nobody seems to be much interested in what is happening further east.

For the Gypsies, the war did not end in 1945. In 1950 the Ministry of the Interior of Land Württemberg issued a circular in which West German judges were quoted as saying that 'Gypsies were persecuted under the National Socialist regime not for racial reasons but because of [their] asocial and criminal record'; this ruling excluded 'almost the entire Gypsy population [of Germany] from compensation'. Subsequently, West German officials rejected the citizenship applications of several thousand Gypsy survivors of the war, in spite of the fact that their families had lived in Germany for several generations. In the 1970s a West German government spokesman called Gypsy demands for war-crimes reparations 'unreasonable and slanderous'. In 1985 the Mayor of Darmstadt told the Central Council of German Sinti and Roma that they had 'insulted the honour' of the memory of the Jewish genocide by wishing to be associated with it. What strange hubris does suffering breed: two years later a Jewish Nobel laureate defended the claim that 'the Jews were the only group singled out for total systematic annihilation by the Nazis.' In that year, too, the US Holocaust Memorial Council organized a conference on 'The Other Victims', explaining that it had done so 'without wishing to diminish the uniqueness of the Jewish tragedy'; no Gypsies were invited to participate in organizing the conference. And in 1988 a rabbi in Pennsylvania wrote, 'Please keep the Holocaust Memorial just that, a memorial to the unique Shoah which consumed six million Jews', for otherwise 'the US Holocaust Memorial Council will be lobbied by Gypsies and Armenians, Native Americans and Palestinians, ad infinitum. Surely that is not what we want.' However, it's not only American Jewish zealots and Central European racists whose pronouncements continue the war on the Gypsies: in 1984 a Bradford councillor was reported to have called for their extermination.

Most of this information comes from an article by Ian Hancock, a professor of linguistics at the University of Texas at Austin, where he also teaches Romani and Yiddish. His article contains abundant acknowledgement of the work of several scholars, among them Jews, whose researches have kept alive the memory of the Gypsies who were victims of Hitler's Germany, alongside the memory of the Jews who perished. Though Hancock also quotes a Jewish writer who refers to 'a certain paradoxical envy on the part of non-Jewish groups directed at the Jewish experience of the Holocaust' – an envy which 'would seem to be an unconscious reflection of anti-Semitic attitudes.'

Why the Jewish claim to uniqueness? Why the misprision – the monstrous catachresis – of 'the Holocaust'? In what conceivable way was this a 'sacrifice of burnt offering'? By what believers and to what god? Where, above all, was the freedom which is entailed in every meaningful notion of sacrifice? There were the tens of thousands of Germans diagnosed as incurable or congenitally insane, tens of thousands of Jehovah's Witnesses, and of homosexuals, and hundreds or thousands of ordinary criminals, too – why were their deaths less monstrous? 'No cry of torment can be greater than the cry of *one* human being', Wittgenstein wrote; and '*no* torment can be greater than that which a single human being can suffer.' There is something indecent about trying to account for the murders by way of a competition to decide who suffered the most, and about politicizing the suffering.

The Gypsies, of course, have little by way of organizations which would politicize their cause. They cannot compete. They have no lobbies, hardly any records, no libraries of books listing those killed. We don't even know whether their dead were numbered in hundreds of thousands or in millions; some of them don't even know their left hand from their right. Perhaps it doesn't matter. It was Heidegger's Jewish colleague, the phenomenologist Edmund Husserl, who wrote that 'the Gypsies don't belong to Europe ... they are forever travelling around in Europe [... *die dauernd in Europa herumvagabundieren*]'. So now there are fewer of them travelling.

1990

16

Notes on the German Army

It all began during a sherry party in the pretty eighteenth-century drawing-room of the German Embassy in Belgravia. 'So – you have written *a book* about Ernst Jünger in the Great War, yes?' I could hear from the tone of the military attaché's voice that this wasn't just small talk. 'Have you ever *served* in the German Army?' Well no, I had to admit I hadn't. How then, lacking all 'close contact' (the word he used, '*Tuchfühlung*', is itself a military term), could I undertake such a thing; where was my sense of responsibility? He, the colonel, claimed no authority as 'a scientific expert in matters of literary history', but it stands to reason, doesn't it, that '*real* experience' (*wirkliche Erfahrung*) is 'closer to reality' than book knowledge . . . ? The terminology is deeply, eerily familiar. Would I like to see what it was *really* like, this new Bundeswehr?

Koblenz, 31 March 1964 Train. As we approach Koblenz, more and more soldiers enter the carriage. Civilian youths in the compartment – aged seventeen to twenty – are at first hostile to them ('They didn't get *me*, I've got a good reserved job!'), relent only when football results are mentioned. Exit from Koblenz Hauptbahnhof, vast throng of adolescents, some in uniform, some in uniform suede jackets, piling towards the exit, back from their weekend leave.

Major Martelli, the press officer: a greyish, long, ascetic face, big grey eyes, the expression a little gloomy, anxious, changing suddenly, perhaps dutifully, to a welcoming smile. Enormous courtesy, bows, handshakes, after-you's, luggage taken. The bewilderment (mutual) at total civilian meeting total soldier? In his careful mufti he is entirely distinct from the flushed, jolly crowd, my first impression is of something like monastic severity. He introduces himself with his full title, 'Major Doktor . . . ', then 'Koblenz is the greatest garrison town, you know . . .' – I nod – 'of Europe' – I didn't know; did he mean 'largest'? I don't really think so.

1 April 8.35 a.m., five minutes late, for which fact apologies were tendered,

I was fetched from my hotel by Major Martelli and we drove off, a lance-corporal at the wheel, after chits and meal tickets for the driver were collected and cross-checked, to the Scharnhorst Lager at Giessen, where we arrived at 12.10. Sitting in the back of the car we talked in German – I did most of the questioning. First about barrack-square drill, which has now been very greatly eased, and is confined to two hours a week for recruits. Why was there ever such a thing as Prussian drill? Answer: because it was generally held that total outward discipline – physical – led to inward discipline and 'spiritual' loyalty. Was loyalty not to be had in any other way? A host of inferences hovers in the air, the question is not pursued. How were the officers recruited in 1956 (the first year of the new army)? The smallest number came from the Grenzschutz, the West German guard on the eastern frontier of the Federal Republic, whose members had been carefully screened; then came the members of the Wehrmacht (the army up to 1945), without loss of rank, including people in the Waffen-SS up to Sturmführer (field rank, major), after some political investigation. All officers from colonel up had to be interviewed by a semi-military, semi-civilian panel, which included members of parliament and parliamentary secretaries of both main parties.

Martelli's way of talking: very complex and fully worded, eloquent, elaborate sentences, a good deal of it sounds as though he had learned phrases by heart but had wholly appropriated them, like: 'The purpose of army discipline: *one*, defence against the enemy, *two*, personal resoluteness [= the old "moral fibre"], *three*, strengthening of body politic.'

He stresses: *one*, freedom of soldiers to complain at various levels, including ultimately the Wehrbeauftragter (a sort of Ombudsman, appointed by Parliament and responsible to the defence committee), whose office has some 600 cases to deal with in a year; *two*, triviality of most complaints. All this sounds a bit like concessions to new-fangled ideas; the way he stresses the change of tone in the army does not.

One function of the Bundeswehr, I realize, is to put some cohesion – the 'ideals' of patriotism – into the aimless juveniles, the 'Halbstarken'. Clearly the same problem as the Hitler-Jugend faced in the early 1930s, yet from totally different material presuppositions: *then*, social disaffection in a slump, *now* social disaffection in an age of plenty. Is the army out to teach them how to dispose of the burden of freedom?

Martelli's own career: called up in 1940, disabled (frost-bite) on the Russian front, service in Norway, again Russia, finally taken prisoner of war in Norway, but, enormously lucky, released after two months. He became a professional officer in 1943. Why? He had never intended to, but: 'This was the time – well, we all – still believed in the victory of Germany, and my company commander took me aside and said to me: "When we win, there must be some people in the Officer Corps who will be able to take *the whole thing* out of the hands of the Party and make it into a decent State. I know your religious leanings [Martelli is a church-going Roman Catholic], we'll need people like you. Discuss it with your father, I'm sure it's the right thing for you."' He did, the father – at that time an active air force officer – agreed. I ask: 'The whole thing?' 'No,' he hastens to correct himself, 'what my CO meant was not of course the political sphere.' When he came back from the war, Martelli studied at Mainz – the condition of being admitted as a student in those days was sixty hours of rubble-clearing per month – took a degree in history, enlisted, and was called up again in 1956, now press officer. Married in 1947; his wife was also a history student.

More questions: political education. This is conceived exclusively in legal and constitutional terms. The army manual says: party politics may and should be discussed, but nobody may 'influence his partner in discussion' towards any one party. Don't members of parliament take an interest in the army? Yes – with great verve Martelli throws himself into a description of the legalities and technicalities of the defence committee of the Lower House. (This wasn't of course what I meant.) What about the trade unions? Again he misunderstands my question: 'Yes, there is something like that for the officers – my wife keeps on telling me we should join it, but I don't like the idea. After all, what it really comes down to is getting cheaper baby cots and buying at cut rates – all rather trivial considerations, don't you think? I don't like trade unions.' What he actually says is: 'I can't arrive at a satisfactory relation *vis-à-vis* the trade-union phenomenon.'

On arrival in the mess of the Scharnhorst Lager at 12.10, lunch is in progress, the CO, a lieutenant-colonel, presiding. Neatly groomed (most officers wear signet rings with large stones, like American officers, besides wedding-rings), ribbons; controlled, agreeably friendly manner, slightly precious. Major Martelli reports, stiff salute but no clicking of heels, the mess rises. Apologies for our lateness – apologies for their having begun to eat; they thought the signal 'Major Martelli + journalist Stern' (there is a German illustrated magazine of that name) was an April-Fool's Day joke. Great and spontaneous hilarity – chairs are rearranged – I sit next to the CO. The food is frugal – thick pea soup with an immense sausage looming through the khaki bog, then each receives a bar of chocolate; coffee after elaborate counting up. Mess waiter? Homely middle-aged woman with white apron. The large room has a brilliant blue lino floor and yellow timbered walls, metal chairs, the CO's and guests' chairs are covered with woollen rugs, the rest is bare; a bar at one end – beer, coca-cola and a few bottles of wine. Pictures on the wall: Scharnhorst, Speidel, the late colonel.

Lengthy conversation with the CO. Shortage first of officers, now of NCOs. Why? Because of all the abuse that was heaped on the Officer Corps after the war . . . : 'We were the scapegoats, nothing was bad enough when it came to doing us down. I myself was sent to Dachau.' Why? For the simple reason that he had his family in the Eastern Zone, yet wouldn't go east himself . . . No mention either of any personal antecedents or of the fact that Dachau in October 1945 was not what it had been in April 1945.

How did people get back into the army after 'the white years' (1945–55)? The typically 'efficient' German solution: whoever had 'shown his mettle' in the ten years of life in civvy-street was accepted, in some cases with advancement of rank. How do you judge (I asked) what constituted success? Well, take the example of a man who in '45 started as a bricklayer – if in '55 he was still a bricklayer . . . etc. My first reaction: the old story of survival of the fittest. Reply: 'But how else should we prove that we are really competent? That we're not military dinosaurs?' Unanswerable? Later it occurred to me that success in that period must often have depended on connections, help from colleagues in influential positions. But even though that is true, the repeated stories show that these men *did* prove their worth – as worth is proved in our societies, East *or* West – and that (as in West German post-war life generally) the defeat, demolition, dismissals, dismantlings and all the other d's were turned to good account.

Other officers join in. Views of their status fluctuate between 'They [the civilians] are slowly realizing that it's a job like any other job' and 'There are not many who understand that ours is a very special calling, that the leadership of men, service to the nation, and the acceptance of responsibility for men's entire lives are not like any other job, that they require a very special kind of selflessness and energy and integrity.' To deflate the mounting solemnity, I ask how many war-commissioned professional officers have not gone back into the army. Estimate: no more than 50 per cent.

At 4 p.m. through drizzle and fog patches, we arrived in the Hessian hills, near Schönborn, where a group of three supply battalions are on exercises. Introduction by Major Martelli to the CO, Lieutenant-Colonel Freiherr von Charpentier, who is to be my host. Here things are less formal. Battalion HQ in a country inn overlooking a courtyard, farmhouses with black timbering, byres steaming next to brand-new Mercedes 190s (all officers drive about in modest but efficient DKWs). The room is divided into a dining space and an area of typewriters and company telephones; toing and froing, route marches are issued, pay-day is in progress, an orderly reporting.

Most of the afternoon with Captain Schneider, Thuringian, who left 'the Zone' (= GDR) in 1959, where he was burgomaster and farmer in his native village. He professes respect for Russian officers, amused amazement at the 'Gypsy-like quality' of the Russian troops with their little panye horses – all these are the usual clichés. He had to leave, he says, after rows and threats; 'halfway through the harvest', he adds – and only then do you feel that he is conveying a personal experience, an immediate truth.

Men's dormitories in the village-school hall. Quilted nylon sleeping-bags on clean, ruffled-up straw. Rifles and MG-equipment gleaming in corners, the rest dark shapeless bundles.

At supper in the 'mess' (the orderly-room in the inn) the lieutenant-colonel cuts up his food and spreads his margarine with the neat, skilful movements of an old campaigner. Our table is shared by a young lieutenant, tongue-tied and awkward but clearly very keen, overalls and open shirt with white T-shirt *à l'américaine*. Another lieutenant, reservist, on field exercises during his vacation from Frankfurt University, historian, reels off a long list of history professors, eyes on the CO at every name, dries up thereafter.

Curiosities of equipment: track suits, blue, come from the Eastern Zone via Austria, the rifles are manufactured in Israel, ammunition from Turkey, mortars ex-US Army; long discussion about the advantage of old V-sight over the new ring-sight with numbers. Goodwill towards the conscripts is patent everywhere, criticism of old NCOs as unadaptable and too rigid.

I'm driven to my billet, a small pension in the neighbouring village of Neukirchen, where the lieutenant-colonel lives too; the other officers are lodged in farmhouses, the young lieutenants with the men. At 7.45 p.m. the company commanders assemble for a drink in a pub in the village – two glasses of wine each. Again the frugality is impressive. Talk of money – the monthly pay of a captain is about £62 – an extra two or three marks on the bill raises an anxious but brief discussion, then 'Let's talk of more pleasant things.'

Litanies: Captain Kröner recites stanzas from the medieval poets who come from his part of Saxony, caps it with a string of towns famous in the Reformation, the lieutenant-colonel adds a string of names from Luther's entourage (the regiment is predominantly RC), then another officer chimes in with a list of German dialects and their locations, draws a linguistic map in the air: this is East, this is East, this is East . . . No sooner has he finished than the first takes it up again, with a recital of customs at Christmas festivals, wax candles with coloured transfers of the Christ child, St Catherine, St Anthony, St Theresa on each candle, Martinmas with fat goose for the Protestants – all is East, is East, is East . . .

The battalion Medical Officer comes in and is treated as something of a special guest. Bright small-boy's face, quick intelligent eyes, a bit too fat; in his olive anorak he looks like an Eskimo. He sits down beside me – his conversation is full of abrupt changes of direction and pace. A long historico-moral confession to me. Aged forty-three, five years of war-service in the army, then four years in Russia as a prisoner of war – 'a time when I could think at leisure about my own and my nation's past'. Then repatriated to the Eastern Zone, Dresden, began medicine at Rostock University, in some danger of arrest by the Volkspolizei, so he left for the West, finishing his medical studies at Hamburg. 'Well, you may ask why I went into the army.' The reasons are a plausible mixture: moral – 'I want to look after men and see to it that their spirit is not ignored when their body is in need' – and material – 'I came from the East and found all good civilian jobs already taken': the authentic voice of the German middle-brow intellectual.

I tell him that in a book of prize essays on topical questions by young lieutenants, published by the army, I found references to the last war couched exclusively in technical terms: 'We were defeated because this [AA defence] went wrong, because that was badly organized, because this [radar] discovery wasn't taken up, etc.' Why, I ask, this insistence on technicalities? His instant reply: 'Evasion, abstraction.' This of course is an entirely truthful answer, and his offering it at this point, and so promptly, means that I shall take anything he says in good faith. The discussion turns to films, TV: '*Selbstzerfleischung*: we can't go on forever devouring each other and ourselves.' The Auschwitz trials which are now proceeding? . . . 'After all I've said, you will believe me that I speak without nationalistic bias when I say, let's put an end to it. Every one of the people involved must surely have gone through such a hell of self-reproach that no prison sentence can make much difference to him. But let them be deprived of every penny they own over and above the meanest subsistence level – that'll hit them hard enough. And let there be no more mental agony for the witnesses who have to go through it all again and again.' All this is said very quickly, he mops his brow throughout, a great emotional effort, a strange smile, contrite rather than apologetic, flits across his pale face, a look drawing reassurance from me, his listener. 'After all I've said, you will believe me . . . '

We part at 10.30, I walk with the CO, von Charpentier, to our common billet. Through the dark comes his voice, haltingly, with tales of the battles in which his ancestors fought: Jena, Austerlitz, Sadowa, then: Verdun, Somme, Langemarck. And there we stop and say good night.

2 April Woken by the CO at 7.00, we breakfast together in the pension – two hard-boiled army eggs emerge from his pocket, we share them to save my expenses. In his early fifties, he is altogether more formal than the others, comes from Baden (I fancy I can discern French blood in his features), small sharp eyes, nutcracker chin and mouth, highly-coloured cheeks, careful speaker, not over-decisive, consistently even-tempered. He likes to emphasize the importance of 'our mixture of formality and informality', himself exemplifies it: to English or American eyes his manner would of course err on the side of the former, in the German popular idea of a lieutenant-colonel on the side of the latter. Everything about him is neat and carefully ordered (though later in the day he did lose the spectacles he brings out to study the maps).

I spent the morning travelling about with him. His companies are dispersed at various shooting-ranges in the beautiful Hessian woods within a circle of some ten miles. Weather around freezing-point, snow patches still line the roads. All weapons are anti-tank, a small flame-thrower in cardboard casing operated from the hip turns out a flop: nine out of ten charges fizzle out without properly exploding, the one exception occurs of course when the CO himself fires, hitting the wrecked plates of an old tank with a smoking cascade of small flames. Apologetic smile, 'We have to economize on targets.' At this point – when he operates one of these absurd tubes – all informality goes by the board, and he goes through the drill with the self-possessed physical precision of a professional.

My next stop is the medical room and field-hospital in the camp, surrounded by pine forests, in charge Major Reznitzek, the Dresden MO I met last night. While von Charpentier moves about on his own, the MO tells me of overwork and of difficulties in keeping up with scientific literature. His main care is for the older NCOs and officers; complains of his own lack of wider experience, since his cases are confined to fairly light ones, 'and my civilian colleagues get a better view of things – they're gaining on me all the time.' One or two of his colleagues have left the army again: 'Surely such changes of mind are irresponsible. When I first contemplated joining up, I spent three sleepless nights, discussing the matter with my wife. But now I've battled my way through to my conviction and I am committed to it.' Reznitzek spends his leaves standing-in for a civilian doctor of his acquaintance in Bavaria. 'I never tell my – his – patients that I'm in the army.' The bombing of Dresden figures, and his Catholic school ('the last *Gymnasium* where Jewish pupils were allowed ... we all defended them, even after we joined the Hitler-Jugend'), there is an appeal in his unconsciously hushed conversation; little dark eyes in a pale fat face glistening with sweat which he carefully wipes away with a folded white handkerchief.

I'm becoming more familiar with them. A heated argument between Second Lieutenant Kästner (professional, about twenty-three, pale and sharp-lined, tunic buttoned to the chin, normally he volunteers only technical information) and First Lieutenant Braun (the history-student reservist) on the *Spiegel* affair: the manner is more important than the substance. Braun begins with a strong and reasonably well-argued condemnation of the way the ministry conducted the case, Kästner doesn't like the attack and proceeds by way of dark hints behind which lies, suppressed, a deep hostility towards the press, towards the meddling of civilians in army affairs, and towards the civil service. He is badly routed by Braun for mixing up the *Spiegel* affair with an earlier bribery scandal, so he begins to invent evidence by hinting at 'the fact known to us all' that there really *is* a sinister connection; the discussion breaks up when news comes that the colonel has arrived.

Colonel Gebhardt got his promotion last Friday and is touring his companies to thank them for their congratulations. On his arrival – with civilian driver in brown Opel – the tension mounts; the parking lot lies just beneath our windows, his progress is watched, von Charpentier receives him in the yard. Aged fifty-five, clipped grey hair, colourful ribbons including the Iron Cross (the only actual medal), bronzed face, short, somewhat the sporting type, quick, energetic, slightly exaggerated movements; his double-breasted greatcoat (wide collar and lapels with silver oakleaves and three stars) is off before anybody can assist him. Has his lunch alone, round him a circle of officers whom he occasionally addresses, he is clearly much elated by his promotion. A celebration at a country inn famous for its trout is arranged for the evening.

After lunch we all go over to a nearby farmhouse where the farmer – tough and small and bow-legged, with a good flow of talk – has laid out his family's costumes for inspection in the icy-cold Sunday parlour. Proudly and with detailed comments he displays a dozen garments, magnificently embroidered on homespun and -woven linen, gaudy reds, greens and dark purples on hard white or black canvas. His simple but shrewd talk is translated by the officers into 'their' folkish language of 'Brauchtum' and 'Sitte', known in the old Party slang as 'Brausi', meaning something like 'mores' and 'customs'. This is National Socialist terminology which has come to stay, all the more rigidly since the things it describes are mostly dead and gone. Not here, though: all the girls and women in the village wear four skirts on top of each other, their hair combed into a hideous little cylindrical pile on top of their heads, and thick white stockings, while forking the middens and driving the tractors – the men are in town in various commercial or municipal jobs. The farmer regrets the passing of the weaving craft; why doesn't it go on, asks the colonel. The splendid, gaudy silks used to come from England, says the farmer (they're Indian silks), it's the Jews who used to sell them (Schneider glances involuntarily towards me), and now the Jews are no more ... (It's the only time, except in the conversation with the MO, that Jews are mentioned.) The farmer tells of his escape from the Czechs north of Prague, which he effected by means of following exactly the old army manual's instructions for such contingencies (or so he claims). We eventually leave – the general verdict is, 'a decent fellow' – they liked his story. An English ex-soldier, it occurs to me, would probably boast of the opposite – of having improvised his escape in defiance of all rules and regulations.

Invitations for tonight are issued. The MO accepts reluctantly, claiming that he isn't interested in trout. Orders are taken for either 'blue' (boiled) or baked for fourteen – baked is regarded as not quite the thing. Captain Schneider, the Thuringian farmer, asks outright what it will cost, and is somewhat coldly put right by the CO; however, no offence is taken, and finally the cost of the meal – 5 DM per trout – is fixed.

We all assemble at the inn at 16.00 hours, the CO obviously pleased at the efficiency and tactical success of 'Operation Trout'. Beginning with a glass of sweet sherry, we stand in a circle and drink the colonel's health. All very quiet, a short speech – 'It's a public place, we mustn't have an address, otherwise the press will be full of articles about officers' secret meetings in village hide-outs.' The only other guests at the inn are three or four villagers who watch us with some interest. Then, very formally and according to rank, we sit down at the T-shaped table, the newly promoted colonel at the head, I on his right. Regimental gossip: he tells them who congratulated him and when. No love is lost between the military and the ministry: 'he [der Herr Staatssekretär] only spoke of his own worries, and said he deliberately left his office every day after the shops closed, so that on his way home he should not be tempted to spend any money.' Ironical laughter without much sympathy, but without malice either.

Having read a brief biography of the colonel in the local press, I remark that he was there described as having begun his career in the police. Brief hesitation, then his 'correction': yes, he joined the police force in East Prussia in 1930 but in 1935 his section was taken over into the army, 'you see, they didn't want us to be independent ... *Gleichschaltung* ... I had joined the police from conviction – it was a call [*eine Berufung*], I was sceptical about service in the army and, to be honest – I think I can speak openly and in confidence to you – I remain sceptical to this day. The point was that the Führer – that is Hitler, you understand – betrayed us unhesitatingly – he never really intended [*er dachte garnicht daran*] to keep to the law, legality was his least worry. And then, after the war ... '

I'm coming to understand that the hiatus ('. . . and then, after the war . . . ') can only be filled with personal anecdotes which are essentially apologetic: the abrupt changes in narrative pace and manner are always remarkable, always the same. With the new colonel it is different, for here, in spite of his saying that he can speak to me, a stranger, 'in confidence', the war is omitted. The slightly harsh, clipped voice has an overtone of cordiality which doesn't go with the man or with his slightly embarrassed occasional laugh: 'And then, after the war ... I wasn't unemployed, not for a single day. As soon as I had rejoined my family in Hessen I began working for a farmer. That got us enough potatoes and milk to see us through the first winter. Then, as I had an instructor's certificate, I hired a small swimming-pool and made a go of that. With my savings I built a sauna bath, then another two, and I was undecided what to do when they asked me to join the Frontier Guards – indeed, my wife was none too pleased when I first came to her with the idea.'

Healths are drunk – I make a little speech thanking them all for their friendliness and hospitality. The drink – which the colonel has brought as a present to the battalion – is 'Türkenkopf', a half-and-half mixture of German Bordeaux and Sekt served in a large glass jug, we all have a good deal of it; it is a light, unheady drink. The elaborate toasting proceeds always from the higher rank to the lower, and with each glass anew; the proposer (the colonel) calls out a name, the glass is held with the right hand against the heart, a deep meaningful stab of a glance is exchanged, a long drink, then both parties carry the glass to the heart once more, and another deep eyeful concludes the ritual. I ask about the origin of the ceremony, embarrassed silence. What ceremony? There is no ceremony ...

At last the civilians have left the room and the colonel, remaining in his chair, addresses his 'few words to the gentlemen', ending with a not very funny pun on 'die Fahne hoch', the opening of the 'Horst Wessel Song'. Then the colonel is gone, we each pay our 5 DM for the trout (mine was enormous and not very tasty) and, the time now being 8 p.m., are off to the gunnery range for the night exercise.

A strong half-moon over ghostly grey fields; at a distance of 120 metres black targets of the enemy ('Pappkameraden' – 'cardboard comrades') rise up; six men at a time fire five rounds each from a prone position, rifles resting on little mounds of turf. There is something weird about the way each man is taken to his place by the NCO in charge of safety arrangements, as though to his execution. The CO is enormously painstaking about safety, but even when he reprimands men for not standing sufficiently far back from the firing line he does it calmly and without much fuss. My presence is obliterated by the darkness – it is obvious that whatever other reasons there are for the occasional artificiality of the atmosphere, it is *not* due to anybody's behaving differently or being under a strain because of me. The salvoes echo round the hillside, target scores are called across the field, a soldier who has scored zero stands before the lieutenant-colonel, a wretched mixture of confusion and fright. A friendly but firm discourse on marksmanship is as far off the target as were the soldier's five shots – von Charpentier notices the man's state, stops and lets him depart, remarking to me that 'when one of them is in such a funk there's no point in talking to him.' Just before we leave the two platoons, the CO suggests that the targets don't show up enough in the waning moonlight. Captain Kröner replies that the conditions of the exercise are close enough to the real thing – or would so reply were he English. What he actually says is: 'Bitte Herr Oberstleutnant, jedes Verhältnis ist wirklichkeitsnah' – that is, every set of circumstances is close to, is like, reality ... Shades of Rilke and T. S. Eliot stalk across the dark field, and Henry James's beast waiting in the jungle. Perhaps the good captain has unwittingly put his finger on it. 'Wirklichkeits*nah*': is not this the temper of the German life around me? As though 'reality', 'the real thing', were always just around the corner, as though all experience were veiled by the conditional, by an 'as if'? Is the violence of Germany not a heedless attempt to tear through that veil?

Abstraction (or what sounds like it from outside) is built into this language system – into this mode of experience. 'Time', 'world', 'reality', 'fate' – these are the pivots of ordinary conversation, regardless of the intellectual sophistication or social standing of the participants; 'fatherland' used to be another.

At 11.30 the CO decides to call it a day and we drive back. A last look at the shooting-range from a hilltop – curved silver lines of tracer-shot flow down into the dark sea of sky. We finish the day with a brandy in the lounge of our inn. Von Charpentier talks about a family chronicle, kept by successive generations since the time they left France in the 1750s. Battles and battle honours, an unbroken and, *pace* Hitler and the Bomb, unbreakable tradition?

3 April It appears that part of last night's exercise (Lieutenant Braun's) was 'sabotaged' by a deliberate mix-up of instructions posted on trees and near wells in various outlying places: the result was chaos and long delays; some of Braun's men didn't come back till 3 a.m. and were up again at 5. He is indignant, suspects Schneider (the Thuringian Humphrey Bogart), who denies it point-blank, but later confesses to us. Schneider is the least 'military' of them all, most of the time informal and easygoing, though when inspecting his men at roll-call he has an oddly tough, almost brutal stance, with a slight slouch and a somewhat dark expression in his rugged face – then, but only then, he looks the *Landsknecht* type – which soon changes to a rather charming, friendly small smile. The official expression, with him and most of the others, comes on with the grey kid gloves without which no officer is seen out of doors, or, oddly, when talking to his men. Schneider's skill in deceiving Braun is surprising to me, because I had taken him to be wholly guileless and, for whatever reason, perhaps indifference, incapable of dissimulation. Braun insists on a full inquiry, thinks the whole thing is past a joke. The lieutenant-colonel, who only now hears of the ruse, good-naturedly and then a little impatiently refuses to take the matter up.

Braun begins a discussion with me about Mayor Willy Brandt's war-service as a major in the Norwegian Army; in his view, this makes it impossible for Brandt to become chancellor. I argue that, whatever the relevance of Brandt's wartime past, it's not likely to affect his political acumen. Furthermore, that it's only possible to see his service as a treasonable act if you identify Hitler with Germany (which is what most Germans accuse Churchill of having done). Clearly, Braun wishes to appeal to some deeply inward, absolute, 'völkisch' criterion, but doesn't quite dare to be explicit. His 'rationalizations' are more complex in the next topic of conversation: the officers' conspiracy round von Stauffenberg. The crux here is the concept of the army oath (with which the Army School for Leadership and Morale also operates a good deal): a man who doesn't 'believe in' the oath can have no moral standards; 'der Fahneneid' is 'beyond all discussion'. The argument that follows is clearly intended to rationalize the underlying emotion of disapproval and suspicion of von Stauffenberg's conspiratorial act: but why should Braun feel that way? Because his father was killed in Libya and he thinks that his father's memory as an officer was slighted by the surviving Allied conquerors? But Braun knows all this only at second hand, he himself is too young to have any extensive memories of 1945–8, the anti-army years. I can't really guess further at the reasons for his hostility, I simply know too little about him. Yes, he says, von Stauffenberg had the moral *right* to kill Hitler, because (again, the same formal, legalistic argument) Hitler had broken his part of the oath and therefore von Stauffenberg was no longer bound by *his*. But, Braun continues, von Stauffenberg's *right* to assassinate Hitler was conditional on the duty to sacrifice his own life in the act, that is, *not* to leave the attaché-case with the bomb behind him in the staff room but to remain with it himself in Hitler's immediate presence until it went off. (Stauffenberg placed it near the map-table Hitler was using; after he left, the case was moved against a wall by an adjutant, and thus the damage the bomb wrought was much reduced; Stauffenberg was later shot without trial.) Clearly, to Braun the hallmark of the genuineness of the act is *self-sacrifice*, not the risking of life – self-immolation is what the legalism invokes.

A brief discussion, in the yard, with Company Sergeant-Major Baumann, an old-time NCO. Short and tough, with slightly blood-shot eyes, a loud and rasping voice and unchanging gruff manner, neither what he says nor to whom he says it makes any difference to his voice and manner. Precise, automatic movements, the only one with really tough language and bearing. He describes Hitler as 'ganz große Scheiße' ('a whole lot of crap'), his politics ditto, but the army was OK, 'da gibt's nichts zu sagen'. (This phrase, 'you can't say a thing against it', crops up again and again, as if 'to say' equalled 'to find fault with, to criticize'; I note that all such phrases are impersonal – the abstraction again?) Then, after Hitler, Baumann proceeds, there were 'changes for the sake of changes. Boots, webbing, salute, position of hands at "attention" – all *had* to be changed, yet *they* [= NATO] need us again, to pull the chestnuts out of the fire for them ... *You* know what it's like, you've been a soldier ...' Clearly, it is difficult to draw Baumann into a real discussion, but the gruff monotone is a good deal friendlier than it sounds; it goes on and finishes with his war injury, and 'their' (= the nation's) ingratitude; when at last 'das Volk' is mentioned, it is as a separate entity whom he has 'served'.

Second Lieutenant Jungius, reservist, doing his four weeks on vacation from the University of Berlin. Very tall and good looking in an entirely English way, reddish hair and slightly loose mouth, forceful in argument, age twenty-three. 'On duty', for example when talking to the CO, he has a very smart, slightly tough manner, probably hiding inexperience, in marked contrast to his habitually carefree, almost slapdash way; with the professional officers the contrast between the two manners is less noticeable. He shows me the mechanism of a light MG during an exercise we watch, which involves firing from a prepared position at *Pappkameraden* at 300 metres: running – shooting from a standing position – again running – etc. He gets stuck over spring and swivel arrangements (memories of similar balls-ups with Browning and Lewis guns float through my mind), the CO suggests, ironically, 'How about taking your gloves off?' Oil and grease ooze on to Jungius's smart tunic, all of which doesn't endear me to him, the CO is impatient – tells me afterwards how the reservists have to be broken in every time they come back. The shooting exercise is slow and the lumbering-on of men irregular and untidy. Meanwhile the weather has cleared, the sun shines brightly from a colourless high spring sky through groups of birches and maple trees, the frozen ground thaws a little, those who have finished firing lie in starfish patterns in the grey short grass between pyramids of rifles: dark khaki shapes, arms crossed under heads, forage-caps over sleeping faces, immemorial pattern of soldiers resting.

The exercise finishes with a demonstration of rifle attack under cover of MG-fire with live ammunition, this time by NCOs, co-ordinated by Staff Sergeant-Major Jerzabek (a Sudeten German from Znojmo, Moravia): whistle, MG-fire, rifle-fire, advance, whistle, MG-fire, rifle-fire, advance ... The whole thing is done brilliantly, with no noticeable pauses between the different phases, the CO seems impressed, the difference between this concluding exercise and the earlier ones, which were done by the conscripts, is enormous.

After lunch I'm taken by 'jeep' (in fact a DKW, a tossing and lurching wreck with four-wheel drive) by Lieutenant Jungius to a battalion in a neighbouring village. During the drive it is he who plies me with questions, more firmly – indeed aggressively – than anyone else. Do I know anything about the British Army? 'What is your qualification for undertaking this "inspection" ?' (No more than an interest in modern German literature and a deep dislike of Arnold Wesker's *Chips with Everything*, based on wartime service in the RAF – an institution mercifully as different as can be from this or, I suspect, any other German army. I tell him about Ernst Jünger and my conversation with the German military attaché in London, but obviously he doesn't believe a word I say.)

This afternoon I am to meet some NCOs, and as soon as we arrive at the inn which again serves as headquarters, Lieutenant Jungius has the good sense to make off, but alas Captains Kröner and Schneider stay with us, and of course dominate the conversation. It's not so much that the NCOs are deferential to the officers present, but since they speak less quickly and coherently (where don't they?) they are less ready to launch out beyond war stories. General agreement that the old 'Kommiß' ('bull') was absurd, that you can get as much out of the soldiers by way of rational argument as by an appeal to 'Kadavergehorsam' ('corpse-like obedience'? 'obedience unto death'?). The absence of rifle drill – except for guards battalions – is commended; unblancoed webbing (the old German 'Koppel'), soldier's paybook and soft boots halfway up the leg, all these mementoes of ancient lore are praised. From that, a jump to mechanization: each man must be something of a technician, 'the age of heroism is over. They [the rookies] come as an anonymous mass and must be made into responsible [*selbstbewußte*] individuals.' No, says the staff sergeant, 'into individualists'; no, says Captain Schneider, 'they *are* individualists, that's the trouble, they're self-centred, civvy-street has taught them to fight for themselves – the small car, the motor-bike . . . and the wages!' But then, Staff Sergeant-Major Wawra says, the career they offer to an NCO can't compete with civvy-street; when he leaves after ten or twelve years, his time in the army will be a dead loss to him. They laugh, a little bitterly, when I ask about the social advantage of having been in the army. I point to the army training schools whose courses an NCO can attend before discharge, and the lump sum with which he leaves; the case of a top sergeant who left after twelve years of Wehrmacht and seven years of Bundeswehr with a gratuity of £900 is mentioned. No, they say, that's no real compensation. Industry is so bureaucraticized that what counts is the loss of seniority. And then (memories of the 1930s? these men are all in their middle and upper forties) 'when unemployment comes, you know what happens then: those who came last are the first to be fired . . . ' And back to the litanies: Monte Cassino – Livorno – Rimini – days of Christmas truce and exchange of cigarettes with the English on the Via Emilia . . . Monte Cassino: well, what can you expect of the American? He doesn't have any medieval monasteries at home – 'ist eben doch kein Kulturvolk', 'not a cultured nation when all is said and done', the 'doch' said apologetically, with good-natured regret. The English on the other hand, chivalrous enemies . . . that was the old war, the real war . . . Prisoner-of-war cage in the market-place in Pisa, uncertainty of what happened to you if you *did* go over to the Partisans, and then 'die Kettenhunde' – military police – 'who always shot their way through the thick of it, and no sooner had we got on decent terms with the Partisans than they mucked it up again, small wonder the Partisans didn't trust us . . . But then, they didn't trust the English either.' Switch: Vosges mountains, contacts with the Maquis

in the last days of the war, sunny spring days with clear views into France –
'ah yes, France is beautiful, *da gibt's nichts*.' 'It was all a horrible mistake, yes,
we know that well enough *now*, but the suffering and sacrifice our men went
through – is all that to be wasted? devoured by oblivion?'

These are NCOs, simple, ill-educated men, who read the *Bild-Zeitung*, the
popular tabloid, and spend their evenings playing skat; they drink beer and
schnapps (no more than two or three rounds in the course of our discussion),
roll their own cigarettes, they never put pen to paper except on an official
form, economics for them means pay-day and allowances for married quarters,
politics little or nothing, though they know about 'the soldier's legal right of
appeal' and all that. In resorting to the 'sacrifice' argument, are they exonerat-
ing their own past? Is it their Germanness that speaks in them, or their national
defeat? This powerful need to *make something* of their own past, so often the
source of that ghastly tactlessness which rightly offends all surviving victims
– where does this need come from, this inability to let go, *to shut up*, the
compulsion to return (like a criminal?) to the thought and the place and the
time of the deed? They are getting old, and the despairing thought that their
lives were wasted in the service of an evil cause is a frequent companion of
their days. There is no one to forgive them and they cannot forget. In the
course of their journeys into the dubious past they search for what clean things
they can find there to bring with them into the present: and all they find are
their silent dead. Those they brush down, blow the dust and rubble away
from them – ah, *these* you mustn't touch, you can't accuse and sully these, *our*
dead: are they not, then, like us, flesh of our flesh, ourselves?

These are ill-educated men: which, in our age, means that their conversation
proceeds, haltingly, from one cliché to another, often regardless of contradictions. Thus: 'The age of nationalism is over' *and*, in the next breath, 'The
Italian, you know, is utterly unreliable, always after his own advantage'; or:
'Why, the American army is more Prussian than we ever were' *and* 'With the
American you have a chance of a commission, he hates all bull' *and* 'The
army *is* a bit too soft now, you know'; or: 'The idea he [Hitler] had, that he
could win the war on both fronts – how could we possibly expect the West
to trust us?!' *and* 'Great man, Churchill, no doubt, but we could have settled
the Russian hash together if he had been ready to negotiate with us . . . ' *and*
'The Russian war was a different story – you people don't know the first thing
about it'; or: 'They're Asiatics, they're simply not like us' *and* 'It was a clean
war in the east too, until the moment when all our plumed Party officials ["the
pheasants"] moved in – well, what could you expect after that, I ask you?'; or:
'I was stationed within 100 kilometres of Auschwitz and I swear to you, I and
my lot had no idea . . . ' *and* 'Of course one knew what the game was [*was
gespielt wurde*] – I mean, not in detail but you had only to look round a bit
when you came home on leave, but what could any one of us do?'; or (young
Jungius): 'We are quite unburdened by the past [*in jeder Hinsicht unbelastet*]'
and (the MO, mopping the drops of sweat from his brow): 'Anybody in his

senses knows that what has happened will not be expunged from the German consciousness in a thousand years, and that the name of Germany . . . '

Above all, these are talkative men, men who, artlessly and unselfconsciously, weave endless patterns of stories, straining to join things together into a meaningful life, a meaning of life. Are they also trying to implicate their listener? Perhaps. They aren't exactly trusting, trust is not a precondition of their telling but its product. Occasionally, they seem irritated by their own telling. These may well be the moments when they wonder whether the trust is really there, whether, driven by some inner compulsion, they haven't assumed too much, given away too much. The more I listen to them the more certain I become that when they – three million of them – came home on leave from Poland and the Ukraine, the Baltic and Russia itself, no oath of secrecy and no threat of punishment could have stopped them talking, talking about what they had heard and seen – and done. The more I move among them (a stranger: not completely trusted, perhaps occasionally lied to, yet how much more trusted than a stranger would be in a comparable English unit!), the less I believe there ever was, ever could have been, public ignorance about what happened in the east.

Are these men now 'democratic'? They are certainly not a politically conscious electorate; politics is to them, still, largely alien. (Here again the clichés operate, mainly along the lines that, in around 1957–8 'the SPD changed its mind about us – so you see, even *they* agree that we need a German army' – remarkably enough, it never for a moment occurs to the NCOs to associate their own interests with those of the social-democratic working classes.) No, they are not 'democratic' in that sense but, rather more simply, in the sense of being more thoughtful, more open to argument and pros and cons than they've ever been in their lives, than the 'average' lower–middle-class Germans have been at any time during this century.

The clerical NCO, Wawra, had dropped out of the conversation; at the end he says, quite suddenly: 'I always go with my family for a holiday to the Czech border, so I can show my children the way I used to go to school, just the other side of the frontier. I used to like that path. It's still lined with wild chicory and lady's slipper.'

The favourite type At the battalion HQ, 10.15 p.m., we've been sitting over our beers in desultory talk. The CO is away, the older captains have already turned in, everybody is ready for bed, but we are awaiting the return of recruits from a night cross-country march over 15 kilometres. When suddenly the door flies open and in bursts a staggeringly young-looking major: square hard shoulders sloping to narrow waist, tanned sallow face almost unlined, eyes slightly slanting over sharp cheekbones, whip-crack north-German voice from somewhere between Berlin and Hamburg; noise of chairs and banging doors, a humbly bespectacled sergeant brings up the rear, basking in the light that goes before him – an enormously effective entry. We all rise – 'Where the hell are you all, chaps?!' – cap and gloves and webbing belt come off: Major Hoffmann, recently promoted and now posted with a transport company in Cologne. He had three years in our battalion, and soon something of their old intimacy (when he was captain like the rest of them) is re-established; but it doesn't impair the authority of his new rank. All officers and one or two senior sergeants are roused in the billets by telephone (no reason given: a great joke), Captain Schneider glowers disapproval but says nothing, and we sit down again, after some more hurried arrivals, in an enlarged circle, to new beers. With his sharp vitality, quick, elegant (though self-conscious) movements, superbly tailored uniform with two rows of medal ribbons, large onyx ring and golden watchband, the looks of a man in his late twenties (he is at least forty-five: 'In 1937, when I was a young slogger . . .'), Hoffmann totally dominates the table, the room, each man's words and attention – even the peasants round the bar in the next room crane their necks to peer through the half-open partition and (shades of Bruegel, and Brecht's seventeenth-century tales) actually stare open-mouthed. Hoffmann is puzzled by my presence, once or twice throws a suspicious frown in my direction, but his brisk talk cascades unceasingly.

More beer, Hoffmann is getting into his stride. The first story concerns a jeepful of bouncy Feldjäger (present-day military police) to whom he gave a dressing down; this is instantly capped by a story about the Kettenhunde in a round-up in Paris in 1943, then some gossip about promotion; the captains listen eagerly, anxiously – they are all in their late forties and have been more than once disappointed in their hopes. While young Braun is out of the room, Kröner in a hushed voice repeats the 'sabotage' story and his fears for Schneider's future promotion, whereupon Hoffmann, exasperated at my witnessing such anxious confidences, strikes up another story about exercises in the woods near Helmstedt which (he explains to me) is 'still on German soil'. All his stories are accompanied by vivid hand movements – as when, his flattened palm and fingertips with carefully trimmed nails slightly bending backwards, he follows the progress of a dispatch rider's bike through a cambered bend. All things make their impact upon his essentially child-like mind in terms of efficiency and daring certain semi-technical words like 'Schneise' ('ride' in a forest) serve as bearing-points in his brisk talk, like precious jewels in a watch; every now and then phrases like 'bei Nacht und Nebel' ('in the dead of night') and 'Kimme und Korn' (sighting devices) loom up, serving as leitmotifs and stage directions rather than as descriptions of actual circumstances: unconsciously he calls up the age-old magic – or at least reassurance – of German alliterations . . . How strange that the totemistic function of words should survive in unsophisticated German conversation but not in English.

It is not hard to see that, with his elegant energy and vital narrow intelligence, Hoffmann is the hero of the popular German imagination; this – not Goebbels's and Jünger's 'hard-as-Krupp-steel, tough-as-shoe-leather', nor 'the blond beast' – is the German image of the officer. (The Luftwaffe in the war was dominated by such aces.) There is none of the English officer's naïvety about him, none of the long-limbed ease of movement of his American counterpart. He clearly does his duty with a good deal of gusto, and all his talk turns on his job, or moves round the exhilarating adventurous edge of it; he prefers to describe situations which he and his lot got the better of with difficulty and cunning, perhaps against great odds, but the cunnning is intended to imply not personal ingenuity and improvisation but rather the opportune application of military skills – thus various army manuals and instructions are mentioned verbatim every now and then. He doesn't understand his own ethos (his self-consciousness concerns not his thinking but his physical person – the way he takes out a cigarette from his silver case, giving his neighbour just enough time to light it for him); would it be fair to sum that ethos up as 'Pride, but not class bigotry' as von Charpentier did the other evening? Hoffmann's relationship with his lot has always been good, so he needed little 're-education' in that respect; and 'democratic politics' means as little to him as academic learning or literature. So (you will say) he is unreliable? He will no more *make* policy than his English or American colleagues, and a good deal less than some French majors. My literary training is in the way: I have to accept the fact that here set phrases do, in this military context, represent *somebody's* genuine opinions and convictions, if not necessarily the speaker's; clichés, in this set-up, don't necessarily connote insincerity or falsehood.

After midnight the corporal in charge of the first platoon reports back from the night march. Then, five minutes later, the entire second platoon of young conscripts piles in – flushed faces covered with grime and sweat under wads of matted hair, eyes blinking in the sudden light, one or two men speechless with fatigue. It turns out that they were without their NCOs and tried to beat the first lot 'just to show 'em', although they had left half an hour later. Once the embarrassed surprise at the intrusion of the horde of perspiring bodies has passed, the pleasure at this spontaneous effort suffuses our circle and draws it together.

Yet when, around 1.30 a.m., Hoffmann and I drive back to my inn, the atmosphere in his sports car is uneasy, he seems irritated, almost sullen. Is it because his adventure stories are flanked in his memory by other, less exhilarating stories?

5 April Snatches of talk behind the firing lines. I'm joined by Reznitzek (the MO), who takes up our conversation from the other night as though it had not been interrupted – as though he had this one occasion in his life to unburden himself. Yet every episode or observation leads him into isolation, exception, disclaimer. Of course he adored the Hitler-Jugend when, after the disbanding of his own Catholic young group, he was pushed into it: camp-fires and ancient songs – *but* ... Of course he served in the army from the first day of the war, *but* very soon he saw ... No ante-datings, no dramatic conversions are asserted. The cliché, 'unbewältigte Vergangenheit' – 'the undigested past' – comes up again (I've heard it half a dozen times in these few days), and again the truthfulness hiding behind the set phrase strikes me. I'm overwhelmed by confidences, close relationships spring up after an hour's talk, as though the past could be dissolved in words, as though I had the power of absolution.

Farewells all round – handshakes in order of rank – 'Don't forget us,' says the MO. 'Don't forget us,' says Captain Schneider.

We drive to the garrison town, the battalion will follow later in the afternoon. The roads are bad from the winter's hard frosts, we have to ask our way at a diversion. The car stops, von Charpentier (the CO) lowers the window and calls to a road-mender working in a hole a few yards away. Instantly, at the sight of the silver braid on the lieutenant-colonel's cap, the road-mender jumps out of the pit, a second later (the new democratic spirit) the lieutenant-colonel throws open the car door and rushes towards the man to talk to him, they almost collide in their eagerness; meanwhile the driver grins, and winks at me silently in the mirror. Rain and mud on the roads.

With the driver, Corporal Haller, back to Koblenz, in the afternoon I rejoin the press officer, Major Martelli, in the mess of a pioneer battalion. CO plus twenty-five officers, aged between twenty-two and fifty-odd, makes twenty-six handshakes. Question-time. Only three of them join in very readily, all Bavarian. I try to address myself to the young, not always very successfully: the CO – high polish, good-natured perhaps, ironical certainly – likes to take over. The complaint I've heard (I say) is that there is too much talk of the horrors of the Hitler era, and that the young are sick of it. Silence. The CO comes out with a long and precise sentence to the effect that 'To be fully informed about the past is the duty of every officer . . . ' Silence. I glance round the circle of young faces, hopefully. At last Schmitz, a young lieutenant from Berchtesgaden, taking no issue with the CO's statement, answers me: 'I think you've got it wrong. The point is not that we don't want to hear about the past, but the way it's thrown at us by TV and films, just in bits and pieces, one sensational thing after another, without any connected explanations – that's what we object to.' 'Besides,' says another, 'we're still too close to that era to be able to form a correct judgement of it – at least, a scientific [*wissenschaftliches*] judgement . . . ' I suppress impatience. Schmitz: 'No, I don't think that's true. The main lines of events and the main connections [*Kausalzusammenhänge*] are clear enough.' I: 'They're clear to most people outside Germany.' Middle-aged major: 'You can't expect us to accept the verdict of foreign historians.' The CO is irritated. Gruber (another Bavarian) grins good-naturedly: 'Well, we're only simple officers and haven't much time for bookwork. Besides, we don't really need all that *wissenschaftlich* analysis . . . ' Another lieutenant: 'But if you read two different books on the same topic you find all sorts of historical contradictions . . . ' Several others agree with this. I: 'Such as? An example would help.' No example is offered.

I briefly repeat to them an anti-Brandt argument (Brandt's wartime service in the Norwegian Army) – will this stop *them* from voting for him? Middle-

aged major: 'Well, you know, there *are* certain things, a certain attitude ...'
Schmitz interrupts, with animation: 'But that's completely beside the point.
In a democracy you surely don't give your vote to a *man* but to a party
programme, and you judge a politician by what he is worth in a concrete
situation.' Major: 'Well, it's a big jump from being Lord Mayor of Berlin to
the chancellorship.' I: 'No bigger than from being Lord Mayor of Cologne.
Though Adenauer's progress was halted, as you know, by a British major who
fired him for inefficiency.' Roars of laughter. Other SPD names are mentioned,
mainly by the young lieutenant; it all turns into an easy political conversation,
uncommitted to any strong views and reasonably well informed, such as might
take place anywhere in Western Europe. We return to Brandt. 'All right,' I
say, 'you don't consider it an act of treason. But don't you think it was an act
of German patriotism?' No comment from anybody. Clearly, they can't go
'that far', any of them. Someone offers an opinion about 'tragic compromises',
and the conversation threatens to move into those misty regions in which
words like 'catastrophe', 'tragic guilt' and 'historical forces' replace actual
thinking. Schmitz has now remembered an example of 'historical contradictions': Stalingrad. I'm puzzled. What 'contradictions' are there, I ask; perhaps
there are strategic, technical questions which have so far not been answered
satisfactorily, I wouldn't know. No, that's not the point, says Schmitz. 'What
we can't solve is the problem whether our defeat was due to guilt or fate
[*Schuld oder Schicksal*].' The question – another ancient alliteration – is absolutely serious and honest, and to me at first totally incomprehensible. In trying
to explain, Schmitz, puzzled at my incomprehension, can do no more than
repeat: 'Guilt or fate.' I try to show that it makes no sense; that it is not a
rational question; and that it is absurd to expect any answer to it to contain a
moral of any kind. I quote Napoleon's saying at Erfurt in 1808, 'Politics, *that*
is our fate nowadays' – but how can a single argument dispel the superstition
behind which a whole culture is ensconced?

Evening at my hotel in Koblenz: discussion among a group of three men at
the table behind me. Why is there again an army in Germany, in both
Germanies? The official explanations mention only 'the post-war German
situation ... in which ... new German Armed Forces had to be built up
within NATO'. (Actually, the NATO requirements weren't formulated until
1958, two years *after* the army was reconstituted.) From there the argument
continues on familiar lines: 'We don't expect the Americans and the French
– oh, and the British – to carry the burden of our defence alone ...' Or
again, the GDR Army, established even earlier, is mentioned (by the CO of
the Pioneers): 'Our frontier guards were simply not strong enough to meet
the threat.' All these are arguments from an *external* need. There still remains
the internal, specifically German readiness to respond to that need. It *is* there:
this readiness, to put it no higher, has been a constant factor in German
history from the time of Frederick the Great onwards. The problem that
Weimar botched and the new Federal Republic has successfully tackled was

Scharnhorst's problem in the 1810s: the problem is never whether or not to
have an army, but how to make the army into a decent instrument in the
hands of the government, how to make it non-exclusive and relatively non-
autocratic, and how to subordinate it to the needs of the State. (How decent
was it under Hitler? Subordinated, after 1939, it certainly was.) The question
remains: why the readiness?

Is not the need to interpose a screen of formality between self and world
a part of life everywhere? An army, any army, is such a screen. But *how strongly*
the threat of chaos – think of Lieutenant Schmitz's 'guilt or fate' – makes
itself felt through the screen, *that* is specifically German. The German screen
. . . : in behaviour it is politeness (rather than easy good manners); in intellectual matters it is the passion for system; in politics, the insistence on explicit
ideology and overt declaration; in learning, literal-mindedness. And the army,
a remarkable amalgam of all these, is the most formal way, the firmest screen
of all. Since the Wars of Liberation the German Army has always drawn its
ethos from Kantian rigour and, above all, from its objective, 'scientific', wholly
impersonal mode of operation. The conscious efforts of the men in command
today are directed (as far as I've seen) against the impersonal and ultimately
inhuman operation of this morality, but always on the premise that its 'positive'
side must be salvaged. And the result, it seems to me, is as decent and humane
an army as Germany has ever had, as perhaps any country is likely to have.
In its modesty, frugality, ironical resignation and unpretentiousness it is the
most *sympathisch* social group I've come across anywhere in Germany. I think
of the joyless evasiveness of Redakteur X, addressing a university audience
on the subject of the German press; of the blustering Herr Y, explaining to
me complacently the McCarthy–Hitler parallel; of the Zs, in their opulent
villa above the Neckar, telling me that, whatever else was wrong with Hitler's
war, there were no servant problems; of Professor Q's culture patter about
Germany's mission in the New Occident; I think of a midnight conversation
overheard in a mountain hut where a history master was explaining to a few
of his pupils the 'historical justification' of Hitler's annexation of the Sudeten-
land; I think of the dozens of people who have embarrassed me by their
unsolicited avowals of 'I was always against the regime', and I find that the
men I've met this week compare favourably with any of them.

When, in the Pioneer mess, Lieutenant Schmitz asked me whether a British
Labour Government would acknowledge Ulbricht, I countered this by saying
that this may well depend on whether the Federal Government acknowledges
the Oder–Neisse line as a border with Poland. Silence ensued. I drove home
the point to suggest that no new transfer of populations is 'diskutabel'. The
middle-aged major then started a lengthy count of the 'number of victims on
both sides', the obscene figures filling the room. Schmitz exploded: 'That's
the sort of argument that makes us look so impossible in the eyes of the rest
of the world! These "accounts" [*Abrechnungen*] won't get us anywhere. We're
suffering from the effects of a chain reaction, but *we* started it off, *we* were
the first agent. If the acceptance of the Oder–Neisse line is the price of

unification and if the politicians tell us so, we've got to accept it.' Major: 'Ah well – I quite agree, it's up to the politicians.' Schmitz: 'Yes, but we've all got the vote now.' The slogan 'Citizens in uniform' has penetrated; but it was Schmitz, too, who spoke of 'Stalingrad – guilt or fate . . . '

6 April, Democratic Indoctrination   What I've seen of the Army School for Leadership and Morale was unthrilling. It's a co-operative enterprise, run by the Bundeswehr together with a staff of middling university teachers and civil servants. It conducts courses, lasting some six weeks, for senior NCOs and officers, and has had some 10,000 course members since it began in 1956; I spent the morning with two of its permanent senior officers. One of the university lecturers was laid on, gave me ten minutes on methodology, ten minutes on 'Didaktik', reams of bumph, 'morale . . . responsibility . . . histori-cal introduction . . . the New Occident . . . supra-national comradeship . . . psychological – actually, you know, we prefer the term 'geistig' – insight into the 'Problematik' of leadership . . . sociological understanding . . . initiation into totalitarian ideologies . . . the problem of the oath, the problem of command, the problem of technological and ideological warfare, the problem of political consciousness, the problem of opposition without hatred . . . ' – the jargon makes one wilt.

'We aim at no stereotype.' Yet this is what the CO, Colonel von Kralik, sounded like, even at his most plausible. And it was the plausibility, the suavity and quickness of the man that I disliked. For instance: in his office, 'simply but tastefully furnished', on a hill overlooking Koblenz and the Rhine, he began by asking me why I was interested in the German Army; in response to which I trotted out my story about Ernst Jünger, and so on. 'Ah, Jünger . . . of course, my entire generation was most deeply inspired by his *Storm of Steel*.' However, no sooner had the colonel said this than he corrected himself: 'No, not my *generation* – I mean that *I* was most deeply inspired . . . ', the point of the correction being that he has got the idea that it is 'undemocratic' to generalize. Or again: 'Of course, you know, democracy isn't learned in a trice, in fact it isn't *learned* at all, is it? It takes a bit of time, doesn't it, for some of our officers to enter into the spirit of it. And, to be quite honest with you, I'd have no respect for them if it were otherwise – well, one wouldn't, surely. The thing [democracy?] must really be firmly established [*das Ding muß eben sitzen*], it must become second nature [like rifle drill?], well, and that takes time . . . ' His capacity for the sort of 'self-criticism' that he showed on the subject of Jünger is presumably among the reasons why he holds this important job. Enlightened arguments about the 'citizens-in-uniform army' abound, praiseworthy opinions are exchanged in a self-consciously 'easy' atmosphere. Yet a curious film of abstruseness lies over it all: this meeting-place of army and academe seems to bring out the worst in both – not the moral but the intellectual worst. For the lowest common denominator of both is legalism – the appeal to the letter of the law, to the literal and thus often misleading facts of the past: another screen.

Afternoon   A 'discussion' which consists in a mere question-and-answer drill, and the gap between legal theory and actual application is filled by anecdotes which are sometimes relevant and sometimes not; and from the anecdotes the 'discussion' is jerked back to the letter of the law.

The forests of legalism thicken as the afternoon proceeds. The lecturer, a retired senior officer turned academic lawyer, points out that the code of honour which until 1945 governed the conduct of an officer had no foundation either in the civil or in the military law of the land. (Obvious reply: so what?) Again: he mentions the *present* right of every soldier to refuse to obey an order the execution of which offends against common humanity, and adds, 'As a matter of fact the old regulations (pre-1945) also contained this proviso.' I: 'But we haven't heard much about its being put into practice during the war?' He: 'I think you will find that the British *Queen's Regulations* contain no such reservations.' (I don't suppose they do.) Later we all get down to verbal definitions: What is an officer? What is theft? What is the 'principle of guilt'? We establish by means of verbal drill that 'no man may be denied the right to his proper legal judge.' But nobody hints that the judiciary is still the least reformed public institution of Federal Germany. (Later, in a private discussion, one of the colonels gives it as his opinion that the civilian judges are too severe in their sentences on soldiers.) The way these dead formulae were actually applied in the past is not discussed. Yet these are not deliberately disingenuous arguments. These legalistic conundrums, and the litanies of place-names, and the litanies of anecdotes, and the appeals to the dead – they *are* their troubled attempts to come to terms with the past, and to defend those parts of it which appear to be defensible.

Perhaps this is what the German Army itself – or at least the ethos of its middle-aged officers and NCOs – amounts to: an honourable attempt to hand down the least dishonourable parts of the past. The knowledge that this is a difficult task distinguishes them from most of their civilian contemporaries. Hence there is here no bluster, there are no 'dialectal' skills, little of the *et tu quoque* stuff; there are no easy assumptions of false familiarity alternating with moments of gross unease. Instead, there is a good-humoured resignation, an unfanatical sense of duty and pride, and even (goodness knows it comes hard to admit it) a certain charm. Is all this a little quixotic, a little unreal? But then: 'every condition is like reality . . .'

1966

17

Bitburg

On 5 May 1985, President Reagan, in the company of Chancellor Kohl, visited Bitburg in the Palatinate (a town known mainly for its brewery), to honour 2,000 German soldiers buried at the nearby cemetery. Forty years after the end of the war in Europe, the visit was intended as an act of reconciliation of the USA with Germany. It evoked protests following the disclosure that forty-nine members of the Waffen-SS were buried at the same site, but it also raised wider questions: Should the dead not be allowed to bury the dead? Was this farce, played out over the graves of Bitburg in the full light of the media, not a legitimate part of the democratic process of vote-catching? All this must be distressing to the Federal Republic's friends abroad, who will feel a deep distaste at the spectacle of *all* the parties concerned turning homage to the dead into a political issue. Yet the occasion was no more than a particularly telling reminder that the past is not dead; that even so many years after the end of the Third Reich, the continuities established by Hitler and his henchmen have not been forgotten and, in free societies which do not exercise any control over the study of the past, cannot be forgotten. Those who are most ignorant of history's ghosts are most likely to conjure them up.

Continuities? One doesn't have to subscribe to the pseudo-religious doctrine of collective guilt (or to the ghastly rabbinical injunction, 'Never forgive!') to recall that the war which ended forty years ago was not waged by Hitler's National Socialist Party but by the armed forces of the Greater German Reich, sworn to the leader of that Party. The troops which occupied Prague in the blizzard of an early morning in March 1939 were not 'Nazis' but ordinary German infantry, and it was on these troops that the Gestapo officials who followed in their wake relied for their protection. The SS-men who committed the massacres at Oradour five years later lie side by side with those ordinary German soldiers and, though one may do homage to the individual dead, there is no way of honouring the one group without honouring the other. When Himmler claimed the status of front-line soldiers for his SS murderers, he was exaggerating but not inventing the continuity which the regime had succeeded in establishing between its leadership on the one hand and the armed forces on the other, with the Waffen-SS acting as a convenient liaison.

To say all this is not to say that every member of the German forces was equally guilty – or that every member of the German public was equally aware – of the crimes perpetrated in their name. But it is to remind ourselves of what our West German friends know anyhow, and the East Germans strenuously deny: that the war which modern Germany's most popular leader unleashed and directed was itself an immensely popular affair almost to the end. The question is not how 'genuine' these sentiments (or indeed any other public sentiments in the Third Reich) really were, but how effective. No doubt a steadily increasing number of troops felt increasingly disillusioned about German war aims, and worried about the identification of Party interests with national loyalties at which they were conniving. The Prussian officers' attempted *coup d'état* of 20 July 1944 was a desperate last-minute protest against that identification. But the narrow social base of that conspiracy makes it all too plain that the *coup* was never intended to be the opening move of a popular revolt. There is no reason for refusing credence to the regime on this point: Germany's aggressive war was as patriotic an affair as was the defensive war waged by Stalin's Russia.

But this popular war – popular, at all events, as long as the going was good – was also the paradigm of an unjust war. Why then should those who fought and died in it be honoured – honoured, that is, not for their individual lives and deaths but collectively? Seeing that one cannot honour soldiers collectively without honouring the cause for which they fought (for there is no soldierly collective without a cause), this ceremony at Bitburg was an occasion, not for paying homage or for the grandiloquent talk of 'tragedy', but for sorrow and sadness. It was Stefan George who, in the course of another war (1917), had the dignity to write of 'the unseemliness of triumph' and of 'death undignified' and unredeemed by talk of sacrifice:

Zu jubeln ziemt nicht: kein triumf wird sein.
Nur viele untergänge ohne würde . . .

The aggressive, warlike disposition of the Germans, which the National Socialist regime fostered but did not invent, has been described and argued over in countless historical, sociological and psychological investigations, and has been the theme of countless novels, poems and plays. The predominance, in that disposition, of the authoritarian personality with its 'non-political', anti-libertarian outlook; the conspiracy of fear in the face of modern adversarial democracy (Ralf Dahrendorf's 'Kartell der Ängste'); the perverted religious values to which the regime appealed as well as the longing for destruction, sacrifice of others and of self – these are some of the hallmarks which set the Third Reich apart – largely but not wholly apart – from other countries and from Germany's own history.

In this complex of attitudes, war and the prospect and memory of war played a special role. War was glorified by the National Socialist regime and its public as a veritable feast of sacrifice and self-sacrifice; and in so doing the regime was reaping the harvest the literary men of the Great War generation had sown. For it was not only the third-rate hacks who had contributed to the penitential kitsch. It was Rainer Maria Rilke who, in three hymnic poems of August 1914, had invoked the war-god's gifts of suffering and pain as the means whereby modern man might achieve a new, full-blooded 'reality'; Thomas Mann who spoke of the carnage as a holy sacrifice the Germans were called upon to make on behalf of European culture; Stefan George who, in the very poem from which I have quoted, demanded (in a hideous periphrastic imperative) the extermination of inferior races; Ernst Jünger who, in a series of fictionalized diaries, made 'das Fronterlebnis' ('the front-line experience') the touchstone of human authenticity.

This is part of the story of how war, regardless of victory or defeat but especially in defeat, came to be seen as bestowing on the Germans a seriousness and weightiness of experience others did not possess; how men shamelessly bared their injured minds, calling for a spiritualization and redemption beyond the individual, on a national scale; and how literature and philosophy were turned into an instrument drawing meaning and value from defeat like poison from a corpse.

One of the facts unlikely to be subverted by latter-day 'revisionism' is that those who joined Germany's cause in that war were recruited from the scum of Europe; another, that only on the German side were there men who, in the last two years of that war, were determined on their own and everyone else's destruction. Albert Camus's 'Letter to a German Friend' of July 1944 explains and bears witness to that determination:

> You never did believe in the meaning of this world, the idea you derived from it was that . . . good and evil are to be defined at will. You assumed that in the absence of all human or divine morality the only values were those that ruled the animal world, that is, violence and cunning. From this you concluded that human beings were nothing and that one could kill their souls, and that, since history is meaningless, the individual's task could only be the adventure of power, and his morality the realism of conquest. And, to tell the truth, believing my own ideas were the same as yours, I could find no arguments against you except a headstrong attachment to justice, which ultimately seemed to me as unreasonable as a sudden caprice of passion.
>
> The difference between us was that you readily accepted despair, and I never submitted to it. It was that you were so convinced of the injustice we are born to that you were prepared to add to it, while to me it seemed we must assert justice to fight eternal injustice, create happiness in protest against the universe of unhappiness. Because you were drunk on your despair, because you rid yourself of it by setting it up as a principle, you were ready to destroy the works of man and fight against humanity

to perfect its essential misery; whereas, rejecting this despair and this world of torture, I only wanted men to recover their solidarity and take on the struggle against their hateful destiny.

As you see, we started from the same principle and arrived at different moralities. This came about when you abandoned lucidity on the way, deciding it was more convenient (or unimportant, you would say) if another person did the thinking for you and for millions of Germans. Because you wearied of battling against the heavens, you found repose in an exhausting adventure, this task of mutilating souls and destroying the earth. In a word, you chose injustice, you took sides with the gods. Your logic was a sham.

In a later preface Camus makes it clear that he meant, not 'you Germans' but 'you Nazis', and one might no doubt add that the 'friend' he was addressing is likely to have been one of those who spelled out the ideological background of their allegiance, perhaps a member of the 'intellectual elite' of the SS. The army, however, never did dissociate itself from those whom Camus has in mind.

We come at a different time. The commemoration of war had and still has something of a special place in the German memory, but that penitential syndrome of values derived from the warlike experience is no longer a part of it. There are, among German post-war writers of any significance, no extollers of the value of suffering. Post-war German literature abounds with attempts at coping with the past and these attempts may not always produce great writing, but they are not morally the worse for occasionally congealing into clichés of *Vergangenheitsbewältigung*; qualms about the meaning of patriotism and the value of nationhood have brought about a much publicized 'crisis of identity' (essay 20), but it is of wholly manageable proportions; and for one hideous monument to the Luftwaffe's past glory left standing in a village on the island of Crete there are now two generations of Germans to express their embarrassment at this tactlessness.

And literature? Instead of trotting out the great and famous names, let me pay homage to one Corporal Felix Hartlaub, an art historian aged thirty-two, last seen at the eastern gates of Berlin exactly forty years ago. He didn't leave much to posterity. Apart from some letters and poems, a play, several *Novellen* and his PhD dissertation (on Don Juan d'Austria and the Battle of Lepanto), there is only his war diary, *Von unten gesehen (Seen From Below)*, (1950). These are the notes of a humble army clerk – a very mouse of a clerk – who has found a safe funkhole in the 'historical section' of the Führer's special train. Typing away at the official history of the war (under the direction of the eminent Professor Percy Schramm), Corporal Hartlaub comments on the grotesque landscapes that race by, country after country, occupied and again abandoned, month after month of victory and defeat, past the windows of that ghostly *Führerzug* with its blue velvet upholstery, where the day starts with real coffee and English marmalade – a haven of privilege and comfort at the precise moment when what for years on end was the cushiest and safest of jobs anywhere in Europe is about to turn into a deadly mousetrap. Exquisitely pedantic descriptions of things and people, ironically distanced observations stylizing the momentous 'historic' situation of this trainload of monstrous data filed away in a subtle lacework of bureaucratic slang, Felix Hartlaub's 'notes and impressions' commemorate nothing. Yet, being the first post-war book to offer a wholly new glimpse of that period, they provide the kind of permanent record without which learned reconstructions of the past remain arid and void.

And Bitburg? One's heart goes out, not to the visiting dignitaries, but to the relatives who go there to mourn their dear ones, regardless of who they were and what they did. The Germans no longer think that inflicting suffering on others and on themselves is an ennobling experience. They remember the past and don't need reminding of it, least of all by buffoonery among its graves.

1985

18

In Praise of Integrity

1 Paul Anton Roubiczek

Born into a German-Jewish family in Prague on 28 September 1898, Paul Roubiczek spent the inter-war years as a freelance writer and publisher in Berlin (where he first went to study philosophy), Vienna and Paris, coming to England as a refugee in 1939. From the end of the war until his retirement in 1965 he taught German literature and philosophy at Cambridge; he retired to Gmund in Bavaria, where he died on 26 July 1972. His college teaching (eventually as a fellow of Clare College) and his enormously popular lectures on the history of philosophy (for the Board of Extra-Mural Studies) as well as the books he wrote made him one of the most influential teachers in the subject – almost in spite of himself, for he was an intensely private person: it is the evenings of conversation with him and his wife Hjördis that will remain memorable to many generations of students who were their guests; his friends and pupils throughout many lands in many walks of life will be delighted to hear his voice again in his moving book *Across the Abyss*, and those who did not know him will find in it a record of spiritual strength that neither ignores nor succumbs to the terrors of an adverse time.

Across the Abyss is Paul Roubiczek's Cambridge diary from 1 September 1939 to 1 September 1940. The book is what the man was: of one mind. The point of view is unremittingly personal, yet this is in no sense an intimate diary. Roubiczek did not share his contempories' enthusiasm for psychological inquiry, nor did he believe that the uncovering of motives explains all human actions. Rich in ideas and insights, the book is free from labyrinthine introspection. The events of daily life – together with other refugees he spent some months on agricultural work in Cambridgeshire – merely provide occasions for reflection, and so do his observations on literary topics, his evocations of Cambridge architecture, or again the strangely poignant day-dreams of a meeting with Shakespeare in the autumnal court of Queen's. And reflection – the quiet yet unabating activity of a mind determined not to engage in airy speculation but to remain in close contact with the world, to see things through and to see them coherently – is the dominant passion of his life.

The main structure of the book consists of day-to-day and later week-by-week meditations on the outbreak and progress of the war as it appears to a continental intellectual who had followed the disastrous course of European politics throughout the 1930s with deep forebodings. Now, in the face of what he has come to accept as a just war against Germany and its allies, he sets out to revise his longstanding pacifist commitment, and to inquire into the meaning of Christ's life and message to a world at war and into the role of the Church in making that message accessible. This in turn leads him to evaluate the part played by religion in moral and ethical thinking, the relation of such thinking to the experimental and quantifying procedures of the natural sciences, and hence to the central preoccupation of his own philosophy.

A full account of that is to be found in Roubiczek's book *Thinking in Opposites* (1952). Its leading idea, expounded here in a non-systematic form, derives from the attempt to hold together two aspects of experience which he calls 'inner reality' and 'outer reality'; these (he points out) roughly correspond to that duality of 'the starry sky above me and the moral law within me' of which Kant speaks in his *Critique of Practical Reason*. In this diary Roubiczek shows how this idea of a dynamic dichotomy came to him in the course of reflecting on his own experiences as a front-line soldier in the last months of the First World War, and he also shows the relevance of the idea to the events of the first year of the Second World War recorded here.

For three terrible days and nights the nineteen-year-old Austrian officer cadet was in command of a diminishing platoon of infantrymen caught in the cross-fire between the Austrian and Italian lines on the Isonzo River in the Alto Adige.

> Then, late on the evening of the third day, there was ... one of those incomprehensible miracles – two men managed to fetch water. We threw ourselves upon it, and only when I had drained the second bottle did I notice that what I was drinking was thick brown mud. It was this miracle probably that gave me the courage to try to get back to my regiment ... The other one-year volunteer was ready to come with me ... So off we set into the pitch dark night. I would have liked to avoid the road by the village. The water-carriers claimed that it was still under a creeping barrage, and that was highly likely. But I was confused by the firing from our own lines in our rear – and when we came to a couple of men lying in a tiny trench and asked the way, they answered in Italian. I don't know if they guessed what was up – we just took blindly to our heels. I dimly remember the grenades falling incessantly, practically on top of us. Times without number another step left or right, one second earlier or later, would have meant certain death. Again and again we were hurled to the ground, but again and again we managed to get up unhurt. Our lives were definitely saved by our following, with

mathematical precision, the way which we could neither choose nor determine – that of blind chance.

From Roubiczek's deeply-felt need to reflect on this experience and to give himself a true account of it two possible explanations emerged. On the one hand, it became clear to him that a full scientific – causal – description of the event, accounting for each shell fired in the barrage and each conscious and unconscious movement of his, could be made to yield an explanation of his survival; but so, on the other hand, could a belief in God or fate. He saw that both explanations were flawed. The scientific one, a mere abstract hypothesis of complete knowledge in the future-perfect mode, patently failed to convey anything like the full force of the feeling of the experience itself, while the 'religious' explanation failed to justify the survival of this one man in the face of the deaths of so many around him. It then came to him that 'there is nothing for it but to let the two thoughts stand side by side', and instead of attempting 'feverishly and vainly to reconcile them', to apply different criteria of knowledge and experience to each:

> I now saw that I must not read fate into the external – this external was relatively comprehensible with the aid of causality, and causality alone, but this knowledge was, after all, relative; within us, on the other hand, lives and speaks the Absolute that no absolute external knowledge can impart but which nevertheless imposes on our lives compelling moral laws. As long as we struggle for absolute unified knowledge we shall always get into hopeless confusion and become helpless and at a loss – we must let the opposition stand, recognize the reality and follow the moral laws nevertheless, then we achieve harmony with that compelling feeling which opposites engender in us, thereby obtaining a certainty that extends beyond all knowledge. We have an externally needful fate that is internally coincidental – we must recognize external necessity, but live in the essential, then we shall make fate our fate, and live off that essence which makes external compulsion our servant.

Metaphysical thinking on the Continent during Roubiczek's formative years was centred on two often closely connected notions. The first, called 'reality', was given various meanings, some of them contradictory, and had to do service in various metaphysical, quasi-religious and political contexts. Roubiczek's two kinds of 'reality' derive from this contemporary source on the borderline between philosophy and ideology; to examine their cogency the reader must go to Roubiczek's later books. But continental thought was also heavily pre-occupied with the exaltation of suffering, self-sacrifice and strenuousness as 'absolutes' by means of which to validate and redeem the existence of modern man: Roubiczek's resolute rejection of these false absolutes is perhaps the greatest single achievement of *Across the Abyss*. Certainly, he is intent on finding an appropriate place for the warlike experience and on contrasting it with experience that has no more than the bits and pieces of humdrum daily life to fall back on; but he is even more concerned to show up the corrupting nature of heroism when seen as an end in itself and – again in quasi-religious contexts – as a redemptive value. Contrasting it with the heroism that is a by-product of moral action, he comes to recognize the warlike situation in which his own philosophy was born as merely contingent. Acknowledging the value of courage in adversity, he exalts neither courage nor adversity at the expense of life. And the conception of life he strives for is a synthesis of a religious, Christian faith that does not denigrate the world, and a worldly reasonableness that does not impair the belief in Christ as the supreme, and supremely concrete, embodiment of morality. Again and again he turns to the work of Dostoevsky, to rebut its then fashionable 'catastrophic' interpretations as gnostic misreadings, and to emphasize its wisdom as well as its positive spirituality.

The reader will find here little of that critical analysis of linguistic usage which dominated Cambridge philosophy in Roubiczek's time. (It is one of the less exhilarating ironies accompanying the quarrels of philosophers that Ludwig Wittgenstein, his comrade-in-arms on the Isonzo Front and professor of philosophy at Cambridge when Roubiczek arrived there, showed no interest in the man or in his philosophy; indeed, anyone who knew them both had to face the paradox that the greater philosopher showed no sign of being possessed of greater integrity.) The philosophical thinking which is recorded in Roubiczek's book belongs to the tradition of German Idealism modified by Kierkegaard. Dispensing with the distinction between 'practical' and 'theoretical' reasoning, it was conceived not as an abstract pursuit, but as a full mode of life: 'the important thing', Roubiczek writes, 'is that the feeling which has forced me to keep this diary should not be lost in fantasies that do not stand firm against life, but that it should receive a clear content capable of being lived.' *Quod erat demonstrandum*.

2 Johann Wolfgang Bruegel

Johann Wolfgang Bruegel was born on 3 July 1905 in Hustopeč (Auspitz), a small town in Southern Moravia where his father was a judge. He was educated at the famous Deutsches Staatsgymnasium in Brno, the capital of Moravia, and he graduated as a doctor of law in the German University of Prague. At the age of nineteen he became a member of the German Social Democratic Party and remained faithful to the spirit and ideals of that party throughout his life. In January 1929 he joined the civil service of the First Czechoslovak Republic – the republic without a hyphen and without the 'Socialist' in its name. When, at the end of 1929, the German Social Democrats entered the Czechoslovak government for the first time, their leader, Dr Ludwig Czech, became minister of social welfare, and Bruegel became his private secretary and served him in several ministries for eight years. Throughout this time he

also wrote a great deal of political journalism, most of it for the German Social
Democratic press, and also his first book, a biography of Dr Czech.

An episode from that era is characteristic. Bruegel was a lifelong admirer
of the satirical work of Karl Kraus, and yet he was at all times his own master,
guided by his own social, political and moral conscience. And so when in
1934, after the murder of Chancellor Dollfuss, Kraus pinned his remaining
hopes for Austria on the right-wing establishment of Major Fey and Prince
Starhemberg and attacked the Social Democrats in terms he might have done
better to reserve for the German and Austrian National Socialists, Bruegel
did not hesitate to challenge Kraus's views in a polemical 'Reply' ('Antwort
an Karl Kraus'); the analysis of the malaise and disaffection in the last years
of the First Austrian Republic which is contained in this 'Reply' is as valid
today as it was when he wrote it all those many years ago.

A few months before Munich, the French and British governments forced
Prague into negotiations with Konrad Henlein, leader of the Sudetendeutsche
Partei, who was now as eager to declare his allegiance to Hitler as he had
previously been anxious to deny it. In this situation a man with Bruegel's
background and convictions was bound to be increasingly isolated, yet he
continued his work as a legal officer in the Czechoslovak ministry of social
welfare – a ministry of which, perhaps more than of any other, the country
was justly proud – until the German invasion of 15 March 1939. It is not my
task to dwell on the personal suffering these events brought him. But it is
clear that with his abundant experience of the affairs of the State on the one
hand and the increasingly embattled situation of the Social Democratic Party
in the midst of Sudeten German nationalism and Czech suspicions on the
other, Bruegel was acquiring a uniquely intimate knowledge of the events and
of the social and political atmosphere which he would be recapturing in his
later work as a historian.

In April 1939 Wolfgang Bruegel fled to Paris, where he worked for the
International Federation of Trade Unions, and in June 1940 he was evacuated,
with parts of the Czechoslovak army, to England. Throughout the rest of the
War he worked as an official of the Czechoslovak government in exile under
President Beneš. In 1945, at the request of the Czech Social Democratic
minister Bohumil Laušman, Bruegel briefly returned to Prague, where the
wholesale expulsion of the Sudeten Germans was in full swing. His position
there soon became impossible, and what had begun in November 1946 as a
temporary posting to London turned into permanent exile. During the few
months in Prague he was increasingly isolated and had hardly any friends who
understood the dilemma in which he was placed – these were the crucial
months of his life, crucial for his further development as a historian. He had
devoted his working life as a civil servant, politician and writer to the experiment of making his own kith and kin, the Sudeten German population of
Czechoslovakia, into an integral part of the democratic state, and this experiment had failed. It was his unwavering conviction that there was a proper
place for that population in the State and, unlike the leader of the Sudeten

German Social Democrats, Wenzel Jaksch, he had declared his adherence and loyalty to Beneš's London government unconditionally and without hesitation. He believed that but for Hitler that experiment would have been successful, that the two nations had a great and vital need of each other, and that as a consequence of the policy of retribution – a policy as much of anarchy and lawlessness as of planned expulsion – the Czechs lost in the long run more than the Germans did. Bruegel had warned of the danger of Czech retribution in a memorandum he wrote before the fall of France in 1940, and he fully foresaw its dire consequences. When we look back at the recent history suffered by that faraway country of whose peoples, at one time, the English knew nothing – those milestones of defeat dated 1938, 1948, 1968 – we must, I think, add those fifteen months in 1945–6 when the Czechs inflicted a defeat – a moral defeat, but by no means only that – on themselves.

Among the many fates cast up by the last war, Bruegel's fate has a special poignancy. Divided by his convictions from his native country and the government he had served for so long, divided from the representatives of the two cultures – the German and the Czech – to which he owed his allegiance, divided, finally, from the mainstream of his own political party, Bruegel wrote his two-volume history, *Tschechen und Deutsche* (1967, 1974) (and a revised English version of the first volume in 1973) as an explanatory account of the divisions, betrayals and shortsighted compromises he witnessed taking place around him. He died in London on 15 November 1986.

In writing his books Bruegel was able to make very full use of the files of the Czechoslovak government in London, and he was among the first scholars to have access to the pre-1945 files of the German Foreign Office that were captured by the Allies. Drawing on these and numerous other sources, he was able to visualize that history from the angles in which each phase presented itself to all the parties involved. The insights one reader has gleaned from his perspectival account may be summed up as follows:

1   Evidence relating to its last phase is assembled to substantiate the claim that the Habsburg Empire was not 'reformfähig' in terms of the prevailing ideology of the day – that it was not capable of such reforms as would have adequately accommodated the political, cultural and economic aspirations of Czech nationalism before August 1914, let alone in the deteriorating conditions of the war years that followed.

2   The bulk of Bruegel's first volume contains evidence to show that the Czechs saw themselves as the governing nation in the new state, and committed many of the follies and petty actions characteristic of a nation in the first throes of its newly-found freedom; yet it also shows that they did not at any time attempt to repress or disadvantage their German fellow-citizens in the manner in which they – the Czechs themselves – had been repressed and disadvantaged in the old empire. Bruegel shows the areas of anti-German discrimination, he details the grounds of justified

complaints (and also quotes abundant statistics to show where the complaints were unjustified). But Bruegel demonstrates equally convincingly that Czech policy after 1919, and especially after 1928, was one not of static oppression but of gradual improvements in all the aspects of life of the state the Germans shared with the Czechs and the other nations and tribes that composed the First Republic; that the economic hardships suffered by the highly industrialized western and northern Bohemian districts were the result not of Czech discrimination but of the world recession of 1929; and, above all, that this state provided more than one democratic forum in which all kinds of complaints, including national complaints, could be aired and were being remedied.

3 All this came to a sudden end with the rise of Hitler. As a result, both the great majority of the Germans as well as the Czechs could claim that the experiment of a symbiosis of the two peoples in an independent Czechoslovak state had totally failed. In both cases the claim was retrospective, for the Czechs it assumed the further function of justifying the expulsions of 1945–6 by means of the further claim that even if their policy toward the three and a half million Germans had been more tactful, more concilatory and more sympathetic, the destruction of the state could not have been prevented.

4 Bruegel places the responsibility for the Munich agreement squarely on the French and British governments' inability and/or unwillingness to honour their explicit or implicit undertakings to the Czechoslovak state; he rejects the notorious communist claim that Stalin's Russia was ready and eager to come to its rescue, and (here I feel less convinced) he assesses as suicidal the argument that the Czechoslovak state should have repudiated the Munich agreement and defended itself against its dismantling and eventual occupation.

5 He argues that by legalizing the policy of indiscriminate expulsions in 1945–6, Beneš's government, by then installed in Prague, was violating the very principles it had repeatedly proclaimed in its opposition to German policy. Moreover, by violating these principles – principles which repudiated the barbaric doctrine of collective national responsibility and guilt – Beneš and his government were violating also the laws and the spirit of the First Republic. Bruegel interprets the policy of Beneš's government above all in inner-political Czech terms, documenting the repeated changes in communist tactics – including those of the London Czech communists – towards the Sudeten German problem. With a degree of fairness I have not found in any other account, he shows how German policy in the years before and throughout the war was designed to make conciliation between the two nations all but impossible; and he also shows that there were very few Czech politicians – though, again with characteristic fairness, he shows that there were some – who were honest and courageous enough to offer critical objections to the indiscriminate expulsion of virtually the whole Sudeten German population. For more than thirty years the Czechs have

regarded the largest population transfer of modern times as a taboo topic. The discussion which has recently begun among Czech dissidents at home as well as those who chose exile abroad is based to a large extent on Bruegel's account of the events of 1945–6.

6 Lastly, and most poignantly, Bruegel tells the individual stories of many of the German liberals and Social Democrats to whom his volumes are dedicated and who suffered persecution and violent death at the hands of the National Socialist regime and its Sudeten German henchmen.

The special virtues of Bruegel's work were impartiality and accuracy, its main theme the defence of the State against the nations. Inevitably, since so much of the history of the Sudeten Germans among the Czechs is a history of opportunities either improvidently lost or violently destroyed, some of Bruegel's most interesting arguments are of the 'What would have happened if . . . ?' variety; and such arguments are bound to derive the validity of their hypothetical conclusions from the accuracy of the factual premises on which they rest. It is therefore particularly important and helpful that in his articles, in his letters to journals and above all in his books Bruegel always made sure that his quotations were extensive and verbatim, that facts should wherever possible be verified and always distinguished from conjectures and gossip, that where opinions and convictions change, those changes should be not fudged but acknowledged, and that in any given argument what is said for the contrary point of view should be as strong and as convincing as possible. Practised consistently, with great energy and skill, and some gusto, these procedures were bound to land him in controversies in which he had to disregard personal considerations. His controversies with A. J. P. Taylor on the subject of the communist claims about what the Soviets would or would not have done at Munich, and on the subject of Ernst Bevin's observations on the virtues of the Habsburg Empire, are cases in point. And many of us lesser luminaries have had our inaccuracies exposed, our 'Schlampereien' corrected and the errors of our ways demonstrated. Yet on those occasions with which I am familiar I found that Bruegel did not disregard personal feelings lightly, and that he was intent on making his point without hurting. Accuracy, in writing about an age full of passionate lies, is not a minor virtue.

The lies were largely those of virulent nationalisms. Looking to the democratic state as an arbiter between conflicting nations, J. W. Bruegel has a secure place as a chronicler of his country's past. In that, however sad this past may be, there is ground for satisfaction and delight.

1983, 1986

19

The End of the Prague Spring

Two kinds of voices can be heard from the Czechoslovak radio stations. The first is the one that has been heard for twenty years now. It is monotonous, impersonal, an automaton voice going through phrases like 'normalization of conditions' or 'activation of imperialism's machinations against socialist countries' as though they belonged to the vocabulary of a strange tongue. It pronounces a sentence like 'The talks passed in an atmosphere of frankness, comradeship and friendship' with a tired indifference to its meaning: an atheist reeling off a litany.

The other kind of voice has an intimacy, a calm and informal directness of address quite unlike that heard anywhere else. Its sentences are unstudied and impromptu, colloquial and unfaltering. Again and again it returns to the words 'reason', 'realism' and 'truth'. Not fanatically, not as though these words were a magic formula of propitiation. The words are proffered with a slight didactic edge, as an invitation to consider a case the right and justice of which will surely be established and implemented.

The national motto, 'Truth will prevail', is not quoted nowadays; it has become a cliché. The Czechs and Slovaks know from bitter experience that there is no reason to assume that, in some mysterious way, it necessarily will prevail. They also know that the appeal to their reasonable and legal rights, 'under our constitution', has a limited chance of success – limited, that is, by the exercise of a might which, in the last resort, is irresistible. But after twenty years of bondage, some of it self-imposed, the country has found its own soul. Reason, realism and a strenuous determination to find out the truth are part of its very own vocabulary.

'A nation in which everyone is guided by reason and conscience will not perish', thus Dubček ended his speech to the nation on 27 August this year; 'While there is still time we want to assure our listeners that we will never knowingly tell you lies', said an English-language broadcast from Prague. The task which the intellectuals, the writers and broadcasters have taken up is the task of enlightenment and plain speaking. Whatever concrete measures of suppression are about to be taken to implement the equivocal and abstruse wording of the Moscow *Diktat*, the understanding which has grown up between the writers and their public in the past few months is so close that the process of liberalization has at least some chance of continuing – at least for a little time. The nation, in its present agony, has become a family. The wonder of it is that, after twenty years of lies, the middle-aged intellectuals have not lost the capacity for truthfulness (as had so many of their German contemporaries after 1945). The wonder, equally great, is that the young generation have acquired it in the few months since last January. This part of the message of Prague is simple. It is: *1984 does not happen.*

Prague in 1968 is not Budapest in 1956. The Czech predilection for realism includes a good deal of rational calculation – as precise an appraisal of risks and chances as the situation will allow. But beyond the careful appraisal it also includes a major act of courage – the step into disciplined resistance. To have taken this step alone, without an appeal to help from the West (an appeal which could only compromise the cause of reform without substantially aiding it), is a piece of political wisdom learnt in the bitter school of Munich 1938.

The Czechs have been called a nation of schoolmasters. They have never resented the designation. The three greatest figures in their national Pantheon – John Hus, John Amos Comenius and Thomas Garrigue Masaryk – all belong to a tradition of scholarship and enlightenment by means of rational inquiry and teaching. The word, in that tradition, is no high mystical concept. It was, and is, the carrier of nationhood first and foremost. Word and language, for the Czechs, are, above all, media of information and instruction, source and repository of national identity; and their poetry, too, is the creator of a national intimacy.

John Hus, like Martin Luther after him, stood for religious reform in the vernacular; unlike Luther, he remained faithful to the cause of the common people from whom he sprang. In his lectures as rector of the University of Prague (from 1402), and in his sermons at the Bethlehem Chapel, Hus combined theological, social and national concerns in an unbroken unity. The German Protestant notion of an enmity between the spiritual and secular spheres was alien to him. And during his trial at the Council of Constance (1414–15) Hus's anxious thoughts turned again and again to that small group of disciples whom he had left behind in Bohemia, enjoining them to remain steadfast not only in their faith but also in the written word for which he went to the stake. There are no religious overtones in the broadcasts of the free radio stations of Budějovice and Brno. Yet the astonishing calmness of tone, the appeal to reasonable argument, to the constitution and the law of the land – to the very letter of that law – must remind English listeners of Sir Thomas More's image of 'the Forest of the Law'. To the Czechs they echo the gentleness, the sweet reasonableness of Hus's missives.

John Amos Comenius, Bishop of the Moravian Brethren, was an exile from his country when, in 1641, he was invited by the parliament at Westminster to help in reforming the system of public instruction in England. In his writings the didactic element, the unfanatical faith in learning, becomes central. Theologian and theoretical linguist, educationist and 'ardent pansophist' (the phrase is Sir Ernest Barker's), Comenius wrote a number of allegorical treatises that occasionally stray into extravagant baroque speculation. Like Leibniz after him, he laid elaborate plans for a permanent European settlement on Christian lines, but insisting at the same time on the preservation and (Bohemia and Moravia having been by that time annexed by Austria) restoration of national sovereignty: 'I too believe before God that when the storms of wrath have passed, to thee shall return the rule over thine own things, O Czech people!' – every Czech schoolboy used to know these words of his by heart. But above all, and most characteristically, Comenius's writings contain an appeal to the idea of learning and culture as the essence of nationhood and humanity itself.

Small nations face their predicament in different ways. The Czechs did not invent the cuckoo-clock, though they are industrious and ingenious technicians. Their love of learning is not a disinterested thing. (Last week the department of psychology at Prague earnestly announced that 'the moral state of the nation was sound', and that 'collaborators were likely to be in a state of mental imbalance'.) Some of the theoretical work – one thinks of the more abstruse aspects of Czech linguistics – gets lost in the clouds. But there is a dogged, no-nonsense pragmatism about Czech thinking which, at its best, is intuitively related to the needs of its time and place. It was so related in the life-work of Thomas Masaryk, founder and president of the First Czechoslovak Republic.

Masaryk was the nearest thing to a philosopher-ruler that modern European history has to show. He began his career as a sociologist at the University of Vienna and later (in 1882) as a professor of philosophy at the reconstituted Czech University of Prague. He was not a profound or original philosopher, and his various attempts to provide a conceptual basis for the 'realism' he professed were not successful. But then, what he meant by realism was simple enough: hoist yourself up by your own bootstraps – the educational motif again – but make sure that while you do this you do not confuse your own aspirations with reality.

Almost the first action in which he was involved on his arrival in Prague was a bitter dispute over manuscripts which purported to testify to the maturity of Czech culture in the late thirteenth century. His patriotism was never 'My country – right or wrong'. Denouncing the manuscripts as forgeries, he alienated influential Czech politicians who were less scrupulous in their choice of weapons in the fight against Austrian and German cultural domination. The dispute left Masaryk with a taste for the truth to which his 'Conversations' with Karel Čapek bear eloquent testimony. Written down in the course of many informal meetings with the president during the last years of his life, Čapek's book remains the best guide to Czech social and political thinking.

Masaryk's moral seriousness and unsophisticated good humour, his utter lack of pomposity and fanaticism, his conviction that a small country has nothing to fall back on for its survival save its integrity, industry and intellectual acumen – all these are qualities which have been reawakened since last January.

While acknowledging the Slav element in Czech history, Masaryk stripped it of those starry-eyed romantic pretensions it had acquired after 1848. (It is one of the grotesque turns of Czech history that 100 years later Panslav sentiments could still be invoked to secure popular support for the *coup d'état* of February 1948). Problematic as 'philosophy of history', Masaryk's *Spirit of Russia* (1913) shows a profound and original understanding of the interdependence of Russian literature and social thought, and of the Slavophile and Orthodox tradition. Yet he was forthright in rejecting Russian mysticism and absolutism as precepts for his own country, and he had a clear appreciation of Russia's century-old tyrannical attitude towards her 'brother Slavs'. For him there was no question of a choice between East and West. Unambiguously he directed the political life of the state over which he presided for seventeen years towards the West. If, after the tragedy of Munich, some Czech intellectuals – narodniks and communists alike – questioned the wisdom of his and his successor's policy, the events of August 1968 have shown that from the East no light shines on Czechoslovakia.

The West, to Masaryk, meant democracy. And democracy he defined as 'discussion': by which he meant not Hegelian or Marxist dialectics with its dogmatic predetermined conclusions but a free, informed and vigorous exchange of ideas.

The extent to which Masaryk accepted Marxist thinking in social matters is difficult to determine. The fact that in the course of his stay in Russia during the Revolution he steered the Czechoslovak legions clear of the civil war was enough to cause the Stalinists to revile him. Yet in recent months articles have appeared in Czech periodicals, suggesting that his idea of a 'practical Christian socialism' is not so very far removed from the aims of today's reformers. His notions of Christian morality, which were those of a nineteenth-century liberal, were largely secularized. On the other hand, he would not have accepted the idea of public ownership, to which the regime remains committed.

But for the reformers, too, democracy means discussion and the freedom to seek and speak the truth. And Alexander Dubček's valiant attempt to combine democracy and socialism, though it is at odds with the *données* of the contemporary political world, is a logical development of that tradition to which Masaryk's First Republic also belonged. For twenty years and more Masaryk's name and achievement were vilified or ignored in the Czech history books. For twenty years the tradition for which he stood has lived underground.

Today it has emerged to a new life. It informs a nation which, in dire adversity, is united as never before in its history.

It was not so at the time of Munich. Perhaps there is a common denominator to the mistakes of the First Republic. Perhaps one may define it as a certain political dogmatism and self-righteousness, a complacency and self-assurance unwarranted by the facts of Central Europe. 'My to máme na beton' was the Czech equivalent of the 'I'm all right, Jack' attitude. Self-righteousness goes with the schoolmaster mentality. When the Munich *Diktat* came, the entire foundation of the national life – all that 'beton' – collapsed overnight.

Here again a lesson has been learnt. From the very beginning of their campaign the new leaders have stressed the precariousness of their undertaking, emphasizing that they were setting out on untried ways, asking the advice and consent of all. During a television discussion last April a Viennese journalist asked whether the politicians in Prague and Bratislava could be sure that democratization would be successful. 'No, of course we cannot be sure', one of the Czech writers present replied: 'None of us can be sure of what the future will bring. But even if we are buried under the debris of a new cataclysm, the history of the future will never be the same. The meaning and the value of our experiment cannot be lost.' And when, in May, a group of journalists asked for official guidance on how to present government policy, Dubček said to them, 'Gentlemen, there are no directives. You must know what to write – you are the publicity experts.' These words would not have been uttered in the First Republic, except perhaps by Masaryk himself.

The call 'We want to know the truth', which now echoes through the streets of Prague, is both a moral and a political call. The people who voice it have learnt that knowledge of the truth of their situation is a necessary condition of their unity, and thus of their national life. No such life was possible under the Germans; but for reasons which reflect no credit on them it may well be possible under a partial occupation by the Russians.

Not all the models of Czech national life are paragons of highmindedness. There is, after all, the good soldier Švejk and the vital sense of humour he stands for. He too is based on a realistic and democratic view of life. Now, it seems quite possible that a permanent Russian occupation might provide conditions under which the Švejk ploy (*švejkovina*) could work. But let us not think that this would be anything other than a national disaster.

It would mean a return to something like the situation under the Habsburgs. Czech history since 1621 – the defeat on the White Mountain – has been a story of bondage, with hardly more than twenty years, from Versailles to Munich, of freedom and national independence. The Czechs have thus had a long lesson in living on their wits, exploiting the small occasion and cultivating the small private life. For the past twenty years all manifestations of public life were hostile to the private individual, all political life was discredited. In ruining what was once the most highly industrialized and prosperous economy of Central Europe, (and the Czech countryside) the Old Guard all but succeeded in obliterating the vestiges of a common national concern. The hideous paradox of a 'socialist' society in which practically everybody – certainly everybody outside the *aparát*, and almost everybody inside it – cares only for his own livelihood was all but accomplished.

But again: the wonder of the last eight months is that the new leadership succeeded in carrying the country beyond *švejkovina*, that a genuine concern for the common weal was being re-established. This common concern (this is the point of these reflections) is anchored in the Czech past, it is germane to the life of the nation. It hibernated in the year after Munich and throughout the last war. Whether it will survive now depends on the severity, the closeness and the length of the Russian oppression. But it depends in equal measure on the political and intellectual leadership and on its ability, in the face of the Švejk mentality, to preserve the popular confidence it has so recently acquired.

In a sense that should no longer be hard to imagine in the West, the intellectuals matter and are vital to Czech and Slovak national life. Their rapport with the public is by now close enough for it to surive *some* degree of interference and censorship. 'I come before you with deep emotion, to thank you for the trust you have expressed in the government . . . '; 'We must work with resolve and with necessary prudence and circumspection . . . '; 'Concrete steps for strengthening the socialist system are our exclusive concern, *but you will understand* that this is now influenced by our extraordinary situation . . .': the most significant parts of Prime Minister Oldřich Černík's address of 28 August are those in which he appealed to the closeness, almost the intimacy, of that rapport. How long will such appeals be effective? The national morale can outlast the present mood of the Kremlin for *some* time to come, but not for very long. In the long run it is bound to break, and life will once more return into the terrible isolation of 'normality' and oppressed privacy.

Is this the lesson of Czech history? Is there nothing the West can do to save one of its own? Will it heed the voice of the Free Radio Prague: 'When we are no longer headline news, when the present crisis is over, do not forget us!'

1968

20

A Crisis of Identity

In the modest little town of A. in the German province of B., C., a professor of media studies, let it be known by an announcement in the newspapers that he was issuing invitations to a platform discussion in which he hoped a wide public audience would participate; it was to be on the well-tried subject of 'the German crisis of identity'. And the author was surprised as well as flattered to receive, in London, a separate invitation of his own to what seemed, after all, an internal German affair.

The discussion began with a youngish Frenchman with a bow-tie and a largish pocket-handkerchief, who spoke very fluently of our responsibility towards the unhappy past. First, with great candour, he explained about *la résistance*, and then, after a slightly coarse interpellation from somewhere in the back of the crowded auditorium, he spoke with the same lucid honesty and conviction about *la collaboration*. No, he was not a believer in collective guilt. But the fact that a people we must all admit to 'ave, er, relatively speaking, such a very 'igh culture as the Germans 'ave ... et cetera, did certainly give one to think. Ze *paradigmes* of national be'aviour, after all ...

The newspaperman G. spoke next. Of course, at the start of the whole unfortunate story things had been very far from clear. For one thing there were the materials of the binding and the tassel and the plastic – I ask you! the plastic lettering – and *the glue*, above all *the glue*! – all these were invented much much later and indeed they were products of very complex chemical processes which of course no layman ... *But*: they all ought to have been asked to give an undertaking *in writing*, they all ought to have been literally *obliged* to sign on the dotted line that until the thing had been officially authenticated they wouldn't mention a syllable of it to the Press, and the press, you know, really, they have enough on their plate as it is, I mean serious matters ... Anyone not prepared to sign simply shouldn't have been let in on it, that would have been the only way. In addition to which, a distinguished English historian, if you please, a world-famous expert on A. H. in fact, had, at the time, been ready to swear that the stupid thing was absolutely genuine – and anyway it was totally unimportant, the scribblings of a naïve little provincial con-man. And later on? Well of course, later *on*! Anybody can be wise after the event and pretend to have known about its being a forgery all along. Historians – ha!

'Naturally,' said the province's vice Pooh Bah, F., 'my friends the historians – not to speak of the sociologists – the historians have always known everything all along. But what I'm asking you, ladies and gentlemen, is this: who was actually there at the time? Of course I don't mean actually *there*, we know how everything was kept secret in those days, and I do mean *everything*. No, what I mean is this: who is entitled to speak about how it *really* was, who are the true, reliable witnesses – our learned colleagues here, from the University, who were sitting tight all through, or the likes of us, we who *lived* through it and *went* through it all and *suffered* the way we did? The indisputable fact is that the Wehrmacht was the first to stand up and resist. It was Colonel von Reichenau, even as early as '32, yes, at the end of '32, who saw to it that the Wehrmacht, standing to arms, the grey granite rock, was raised above the brown Nazi flood, and the honour of an officer remained untarnished. Oh yes, later *on*. Later on of course we had the Concordat, the wheeling and dealing with all those foreign politicians who loved being dined and wined in Berlin (who wouldn't?) and by that time how could we – well, what could *we* have done, that is my question tonight, ladies and gentlemen? And as for the historians, who were sitting on their arses in their universities as they still do to this day . . . ' (*Chorus on the right*: 'Hear hear, so they are!' *Chorus on the left*: 'Rubbish! I ask you! What sort of an argument is that?')

'And what's more,' the vice Pooh Bah continued, raising his voice somewhat, 'our country's flag – we may as well say it frankly, it comes from the heart, I suppose that's one of the things we're still allowed to say, I hope – is not just some black, red and yellow rag, after all, our flag is black, red and *gold*, we are surely allowed to take pride in that, as it says in the Constitution. And as for the Wehrmacht and the Fleet, there too we may feel some pardonable – well, I won't say *pride*, but at least God knows we need not feel ashamed either.'

Here he paused for a while. From somewhere in the back rows came brief, isolated clapping, a bit shy, but while he waited a little longer to let it swell into applause, it suddenly stopped, and only the humming of the television cameras was heard in the silence. The vice Pooh Bah gave it another try: 'With sober courage we went about our duty, hard as it was, *non sine gloria* as they say, from Murmansk to Salonika', but there was nothing doing, the clapping still didn't come to anything.

That's where you were lucky, old chap, said the author to himself. And remembered the butterflies he had whenever he climbed into the kite. And when they crossed Switzerland at twenty-one thousand feet on the Milan raids, he always looked down from his turret with a little envy at the dimly-lit neutral streets – there was Geneva, and up on the right Lausanne, where he'd spent a year at boarding-school. You had it really cushy, old chap, *non sine gloria*, he thought (without fear or envy now), there was always the chance of a spot of engine trouble, preferably not over the Alps of course, but in that right-hand corner of the map, that triangle of Geneva – Lausanne – Montreux.

A short pause was meant to follow, but the chairman, elegant, trying rather hard not to be embarrassed, very determined, intervened almost at once. 'Well now, ladies and gentlemen, to come to our actual subject. What we're after of course is a fair, honest, unsparing understanding of the past. Because without this fair, unsparing understanding we shan't get down to our real theme, the German crisis of identity. Yes, that young lady in the blue pullover, please.'

She stood up, her likeable, excited face turned to the platform. With a nervous movement of her right hand she pushed the hair back from her forehead. Her words came haltingly but clearly. 'This crisis of identitity.' A slight giggle, not unkind, rose from the ranks of students but was quickly silenced. 'This identity crisis,' she repeated, sounding more confident. 'We've all got friends, young French and young English people. How do they see us? And we want to understand history, but how can we feel we were responsible? I mean us, we weren't there, were we? And what can we do about it now? Last summer I was on an exchange in Clermont-Ferrand and we helped with the grape harvest. We got up at five, and the grapejuice, it made your hands all black, you couldn't get them clean, and the people were all so friendly, the older ones too. Well, I didn't have this feeling at all, I mean about the identity crisis like they always told us at school . . . ' She looked around smiling and a little at a loss, as though she might find some more words in the air of the hall.

'Of course we've all seen the Holocaust, that was terrible, all ordinary people like us, how shall I put it – citizens like us. But we don't know any real . . . I mean any Jew*ish* people. I don't think there are any here in our town, and so it's very difficult to imagine how things were then and what we would have done. And then they tell us we ought to take responsibility for our national past. But we're just the children and children's children . . . *die Kinder und Kindeskinder . . .* '

'Professor Joachim E., professor of current affairs at the University of Z.,' the chairman intoned. 'May I ask you . . . oh, and I'd like to thank the young lady for her down-to-earth testimony, her really fine personal statement. Professor E., now can I ask you to present to us your esteemed point of view?'

'Yes, certainly, now on our actual subject, the theme of the crisis of identitity.' He stumbled, but only for a moment, smiled, corrected himself immediately, his words followed each other rapidly and precisely, ready to print, yet with a suggestion of easy, relaxed discursiveness. 'Human identity in our age. That indeed is the problem we must all of us try to help solve. We historians,' he said, bending slightly in the direction of the vice Pooh Bah, with an intensified smile, 'we historians who always know everything better, can perhaps shed *a little light* here after all. I would refer you to the historical foundations of our social dialogue, our communicability, our *Kommunikationswille* – foundations which are not as outdated as many people think. In our society with its high standards of living *and* its immense psycho-spiritual expectations, each of us hopes for security within the community. The community has a past of its own. So the individual can't just write off that past. Nor can he divide it into two, the good past and the bad past. I am speaking of the German ideal of humanity, the liberal spirit, recognized by the whole world as a model throughout the nineteenth century, and yes, even in *this* century. It must not make us proud, certainly not, but it does put us under an obligation to strive for honour and for the intellectual achievement we owe the world.

'I come back now to the admirable personal statement the young lady made just now. You see, the country we live in, the country we are at home in, *that* is what gives us the strength and the joy to face the harsh demands of daily life, it's like a family. And we know that in every family there's always a black sheep, some old uncle who somewhere once upon a time behaved very badly. Are we to reject him, to cast him out of the family? Surely not. We have to stand by him, don't we, make him understand where he went wrong, how he misbehaved?'

Uncle Arnošt on his farm in northern Bohemia near the Moravian border? But he wasn't all that old. How old could he have been, on 15 March 1939? About forty? There had been a hard frost in the night, and early in the morning with the gale came the snow. The meadow path with its deep cart-ruts, that led from the farm through the straggly wood down to the little river, more like a brook really, must have been frozen hard that morning. Perhaps there was a slight mist. Of course I wasn't there, thought the author, when they set out, the three of them – my uncle and aunt, and the black-and-brown Alsatian, Rolf. Perhaps it is only memory that makes the scene rather blurred and a bit misty; I wasn't there of course, and the bailiff who told me about it wasn't there either. And they, they went down the icy path, uncle carrying the old hunting-rifle that belonged to grandfather from the time they had that farm in Kolozoruky, with the wood full of pheasants. I wonder if Uncle Arnošt was wearing his beautiful brown leather leggings? The path led to the big old oak-tree on the riverbank. And that's where they were found a few hours afterwards, late in the forenoon. Some days went by before the German troops marched into the courtyard, requisitioned the horses and interrogated the bailiff. By then they'd been buried, not under the oak-tree but properly, in the churchyard, on the eastern side, next to the wall – the priest had insisted that that's where they belonged, regardless.

'The country where we have our roots has its own eminent history,' Professor E., the eminent historian, went on, 'which is like the history of a family – no, it's like the family itself. The family name, the familiar language, family property and customs – whether they're old or new – like the dealings with our neighbours, that's all part of the identity shared by the individual members of the family, good and bad alike. And this *identity*' – the eloquent historian was in full spate now, the word caused him not the slightest difficulty – 'may very well be not unproblematic, in this day and age it certainly isn't a thing to take for granted. I know it's not fashionable to quote our dear old Goethe.

Please bear with me. I would ask you to consider his words, the words of the
old Faust –

Freedom is earned, as is the right to life,
Only by winning it in daily strife ...

– because the freedom he was talking about all those years ago ... '

All those years ago ... The villagers (it must have been them) had put up
a little monument on the spot next to the little river where they died, just a
rough piece of granite; somehow I had heard of it but it took half a century
before we could go and see it, actually see it. I didn't really believe it existed,
but there (on that exquisite Sunday morning in May) it was; you could just
read the inscription, though it was a bit defaced by the weather after all those
years: their names and the date, '16 March A.D. 1939.' Then we crossed the
white country road and walked up to the little churchyard that was rising
gently above it, and there was their grave, alongside the eastern wall, really
quite well kept. As we were about to leave, the old man (I had noticed him
watching us out of the corner of his eye while he was tending a plot nearby)
at last made up his mind and came up to us: 'The gentleman will excuse,
please? Perhaps you knew Mr Arnošt? And perhaps the old gentleman too?
Ah yes, all those years ago. Me? Of course I worked for them, the whole
village got work on the manor farm in those days. Not like afterwards.' He
crossed his wrists and looked down on them, as if they were still manacled.
'Better not talk about afterwards. First the Germans, then the communists.
Your uncle, was he? And the old gentleman, your grandfather? It's the one
time the farm was really prosperous; they knew what to plant, and when;
though of course when the price of sugar went down and the exports to France
came to an end, the beet didn't do so well either. Perhaps you remember the
fields?' he pointed beyond the western edge of the churchyard. Looking up,
I saw a solitary bird inscribing circles deep into the cloudless blue of the sky.
I said: 'That's where the mustard grew, wasn't it? And beyond that they
planted poppy seed.' He looked at me and nodded. 'Ah yes, you remember
well, don't you? It's all just grass nowadays, they don't care what they do with
the land. But the old gentleman, *he* died peacefully, in his bed in Prague,
didn't he?' No he didn't. He died in Theresienstadt. 'We didn't think they'd
take him, he was so very old.' He accompanied us down to the little wooden
gate then: 'And here, maybe you'd care to see what it was like in those days.
Here is another grave.' The granite headstone was polished, but there were
no names on it, only letters – 'D', 'F', 'H' – and numbers. 'You see the railway
down there', he pointed beyond the straggly trees, the little river. 'It must
have been in '43. My father was coming home from the next village, and he
saw some kites circling above that railway line. He made me go with him,
down to the tracks. That's the line to Silesia and beyond. And there they
were, lying in the grass along the line, the corpses, that had been thrown out

of the cattle trucks. They had no names, no identity, only "D" for "Deutschland" and "F" for "Frankreich" and "H" for "Holland", and the numbers
tattooed on their wrists. So we buried them all together, in one grave – what
else could we have done? – and the priest said Mass for them all, regardless.'
And there, in the cloudless, blue sky, the solitary kite went on, drawing its
circle ever deeper into the blue and sunny sky above the churchyard.

' . . . because the freedom Goethe was talking about all those years ago,'
the eminent historian concluded, 'is the very core and substance of identity
as nothing else is, even today, even in our so very difficult times.'

Now at last there was real applause (the broomsticks with their microphone
heads shot upwards, startled) and it was applause from all sides, though of
course the platform decently refrained. 'That's the sort of thing he's really
good at,' said the newspaperman in a half-whisper to his neighbour, the
chairman, who however was off again. 'Thank you, Professor E. The past, as
you see, ladies and gentlemen, the good past. How *much* it has to offer us –
even the *youngest* among us – how much that is *genuine*, great, helpful! I would
now like to ask our honoured guest from abroad to say a few words. May I
introduce – Herr Stern, a Jew from Prague?'

'Why on earth are you going there?' a sceptical friend had asked the author
before he left home. 'I suppose it's all because of their bloody money.' Serves
you absolutely right, the author thought, being shown off like that performing
horse in Büchner: 'Yes indeed, this is no brute beast, this is a person, a man,
a human animal. (*The horse misbehaves.*)' Of course he isn't going to misbehave.
On the contrary, he has diligently prepared some thoughts on this and that,
and now he's going to trot it all out nice and neatly. (Economic miracle,
democracy *and* tact? It was a bit too much to expect.) He had intended to say
something about the English nostalgia for war-stories, understated heroism
and the loss of Empire. About the Second World War as the Falklands writ
large, how the media are dominated by it, right down to the base pornography
of violence. Then he meant to talk about British punks, their cult of swastikas
and death's-heads, as representative of what the down-and-out are deprived
of by a society that still, in spite of everything, is rolling in money. He had
thought up a particularly cunning little connection there between the violence
of National Socialism and the violence of the modern mass media, and how
those media, come victory or defeat, through thick and thin, through dictatorship and democracy, seek to dominate the world, and, 'in the swampy areas
of consciousness' (he liked that), more or less succeed in doing so. He meant
to show how the English vocabulary of speech-acts joins the vocabulary of the
emotions and turns into the rigid patterns of clichés (or was it clichés of rigid
patterns?) as it is sloshed about the ether waves. How in Germany 'crisis of
identity' and 'conquest of the past', 'work of mourning' and 'acting under
superiors' orders' all merge into a brew that is past warming up. The past is
dead, he had meant to say, the dead have buried their dead; now somebody
had better look after the living. The generation problem has not been solved

either, only buried, though the old chaps are dying out – and the mourning? 'The German people at their *Trauerarbeit*'? Does sound rather funny. No, another Jew from Prague had put it better:

The gods grew weary, the eagles grew weary, the wound closed wearily
. . .

– what more is there to say? Young people must feel safe and be as nice to each other as they can, even without conducted tours through concentration camps which have been scrubbed clean, out of all recognition. And the performing horses ought to stay at home, he wanted to add. But then he remembered the very pretty girl in the blue pullover, who was now smiling nervously across at him. She and her identitity crisis, he thought. That's the way it is. People with tact can't get a grip on anything, not even a word.

He had intended to speak about the para-myths, the myths of the modern poets, and Herder's recognition of how they are designed to bring 'consolation and words of comfort', and how, since it is impossible to do without them, it is better to create life-enhancing myths than those that are heavy with death. Rather the Brechtian myth of vulnerability than Schopenhauer's myth of the inexorable Will. 'A bit of fun on doomsday morning' was the way a not impartial German observer had described the atmosphere in England, and what he meant by that was yet another offshoot of the National Socialist death-wish, this time for a war – the Second World War – that had been won and yet not won: perhaps it was possible to save the younger generation from that. Was this why he had come, this J. from P., to A., a modest little town in the province of B.? Father Beránek in his cassock covered with chalk dust would certainly have understood, approved. Him too they had . . . in 1941, or was it 1942? Gone, vanished, forgotten. Memory, you can't snatch anything back.

'And on the subject of National Socialism, we'd like to ask our honoured guest, a traffic accident of German history, yes?'

Neither an accident nor an incident nor a blow of fate, he was going to reply, nor a destiny either, but a part of German history. No ramshackle notions of 'historical necessity' or that fatuous 'direct line from Martin Luther to A. H.', but gallantry, discipline and service, the true, genuine, authentic experience, self-sacrifice (they said for life and they meant for death) – the will to obedience and the will to power, the longing for a nation and a community and the dread of the alien: wasn't that what all Europe between the wars had been about, and what on earth could any of it possibly have to do with that girl in the blue pullover? To will nothingness had seemed better than not to will at all, freedom existed only in the fulfilment of duty: how could she understand any of this patter, why on earth should she? There is no need to burden her with the heirloom of an identity whose least terrible part was alienation from its own self, whose least inauthentic part was fear of its own past, and whose least inappropriate comment on that past was silence.

A crisis of identity – but whose, he was about to ask himself, and why should *he* assist at its resolution? But now, thank goodness, there was no time left, and the hotel dinner was probably getting spoiled, the media researcher still had his summing-up to make, so the J. from P. added a few amiable remarks about *l'Europe des patries* and a message of greeting from his students in London and so on, and that was the end of it. The cameras had long since ceased whirring, and the camels who had to lug them away had begun their long weary trek through the night.

As the platform speakers moved towards the exit through the audience, who had suddenly metamorphosed into Bruegelian peasants and now gazed at him with immense interest and kindly curiosity, a more intimate note was struck:

'Really, you know, I thought you were genuine English, you know, no idea you came from Prague ... '

'A beautiful, splendid city, a great place! I was there in 1941, no, must have been 1942. God knows what the communists have been ... '

'Just wanted to tell you, one of my best friends comes from Prague too, half-Jewish actually. Perhaps you know the family.'

There was no sign of the girl in the blue pullover, and it was starting to snow again.

1984, 1991

21

Revising the German Past?

The 'white years' of German history – the period between the end of the Second World War and Adenauer's first government of 1949 – were notable for two blank spaces in the national consciousness. The first was the space left by the demise of community spirit: in the material circumstances that followed on the bombing of Germany's cities and the unconditional surrender of the German armed forces, *Volksgemeinschaft*, the centrepiece of National Socialist ideology and propaganda, gave way to individual interest, to the spirit of 'everyone for himself'. But this in turn was part of a larger blank, a kind of national amnesia. With Hitler's disappearance, his and his movement's tenets, their 'faith' and goals, seemed forgotten, their actions beyond recall. It wasn't merely that individual men and women were unwilling to speak of their own immediate political past: the ideology, indeed the very substance of that past, had become unavailable. Reinhart Koselleck in a recent essay recalls 'the speechlessness of the Germans when, in 1945, they were faced with the catastrophe into which they had drawn countless people and countries. And to this day,' he writes, 'every attempt to find a language adequate to the mass annihilation seems to fail. Every effort to stabilize recollection by means of language comes too late – too late for those who were its victims, too late for the event itself.' How does one stabilize such a recollection? Even today, fifty years later, the historian's question can hardly be separated from the travails of the national identity.

There is, then, a seemingly inevitable chasm between the event and the description of the event which any tolerable historian of that intolerable past must face, if its history is not to become a recital of insensate clichés, and the deaths of millions a series of mere technicalities: if, in other words, the history is not to be trivialized. Given the self-protective limits of our capacity to understand a phenomenon such as the attempted annihilation of whole peoples – a capacity which our mass media are designed further to impair – some trivialization is inevitable. And since this is a past which won't go away, and which has continued to haunt the national conscience of the Federal Republic throughout its history, it seems equally inevitable that the manner of its recollection has become a political factor, to an extent unequalled in the life of other countries. And it is inevitable that the bitter quarrel of historians and publicists, the *Historikerstreit* which erupted in the German press and academic life some three years ago, should have assumed a political dimension. The memory of 'the German Catastrophe', writes one of the participants in the debate, has faded less than the memory of the founding years of the Second Republic.

Generating more heat than light, these battling academics and journalists (not a woman on either side of the dispute) present a spectacle which is anything but exhilarating. And yet, for all its repetitious and clumsy polemics, its *ad personam* insinuations and its evasions, the row is not without a grain of virtue. The Austrians have not faced their past as members of the Third Reich with comparable concern, nor have the East German party bosses. By November 1989 – as momentous a date as any in European history – it had become clear that by suppressing any proper discussion of the past and by making the Federal Republic alone responsible for the crimes of the Third Reich, the rulers of the German 'Democratic' Republic had perpetuated the iniquities of totalitarianism. The fall of the Berlin Wall and the migration of 200,000 working people to the West amount to a popular uprising. They show that doctrinaire Marxism is the last obstacle on Germany's road to democracy.

2

An American scholar, Charles Maier of Harvard, has followed the historians' dispute and written a commentary on it, *The Unmasterable Past: History, Holocaust and German National Identity*. The nonce word in his title raises expectations of originality which the book doesn't fulfil. His summaries of the main contributions are useful, fair and almost as lengthy as Piper Verlag's *Historikerstreit*, on which he draws. He shows how the attempt by the 'revisionists' to 'relativize' the Final Solution has become part of a concerted effort to provide the country with a 'usable past'. He has buttressed the whole controversy with an intellectual background, and with inconclusive comments of an on-the-one-hand-and-on-the-other kind; and he tells a hilarious story of how a recent Austrian foreign minister asked the country's historians to pull their socks up and refute their British colleagues' calumnies on the Austrian resistance; but he has done little else.

Another account of the controversy – Richard Evans's *In Hitler's Shadow* – is better informed, and more perceptive. Evans shows in abundantly documented detail how the arguments that some of the embattled historians are advancing 'are derived, consciously or unconsciously, from the propaganda of the Nazis themselves'; and, exceptionally, he gives intelligent thought to the political significance of the current controversy: 'How people regard the Third Reich and its crimes provides an important key to how they would use political power in the present or future. That is why the neo-conservatives' interpretation of the German past is so disturbing.' Evans seems unnecessarily worried: the way his 'neo-conservatives' have used political power so far isn't all that disturbing.

Among the topics at issue in the Federal Republic are the role of the conspirators of July 1944 (patriots or traitors?); the 'desperate war in defence of the German Reich's autonomous independence and position as a great power', cited as a patriotic reason for prolonging the war after the breakdown of the eastern fronts; and above all the question of whether 'the Germans . . . were justified in fulfilling their warlike duties punctiliously, correctly, efficiently and bravely', or whether they should have 'betrayed their country because of its regime'. All these questions, however, and the dispute as a whole, focus on the 'revision' undertaken by Ernst Nolte, a historian in the Free University of Berlin, concerning the annihilation of the Jews.

Nolte's paper was first published in English under the title 'Between Myth and Revisionism? The Third Reich in the Perspective of the 1980s', in *Aspects of the Third Reich* (1985), an anthology edited by one H. W. Koch, a historian whose attitude to the Third Reich I find too obscure and distasteful to unravel; it was not until the paper appeared as an article in the *Frankfurter Allgemeine Zeitung*, and was attacked by Jürgen Habermas, that it created a stir.

In spite of a style of periphrastic longwindedness, Nolte's main purpose seems fairly clear: it is to lighten German guilt by placing responsibility for the annihilation of the Jews entirely on Hitler's shoulders, and to present his policy of genocide as in no sense unprecedented or unique. (*Et tu quoque* joins 'It's all old hat.') The roots of this policy (Nolte argues) are to be found in Hitler's – justified – fear of 'the Red Terror' and of 'the Asiatic deed', by which Nolte means the torture in rat-infested cellars which George Orwell mentions in *1984* and with which Hitler said German officers were threatened after their capture at Stalingrad. (Nolte seems unaware that Hitler knew nothing of this threat in 1941, when he began to put the policy of the systematic annihilation of the Jews into practice.) 'Auschwitz is not primarily the result of traditional anti-Semitism', Nolte writes, 'and was in its essence no mere "genocide", but it was first and foremost a reaction born of the fear of the Russian Revolution's process of annihilation'; and, he continues, 'the so-called destruction of the Jews during the Third Reich was a reaction or distorted copy, not a primary act or original.' Nolte's strategy is to support this thesis with an all but impenetrable jungle of episodes and persons which are said to display genocidal tendencies; then to concede that these episodes and persons are only partly relevant, yet to let them stand on the page, not (like the Russian Revolution) as causes but as signposts pointing the way to Auschwitz. They include the French Revolution and Napoleon, Malthusianism and an assortment of French and English social reformers, but also the author of a pamphlet published in London in 1940 called 'Germany Must Perish', the leaders of the National Front of Cambodia as well as 'the clique around Pol Pot', the President of the Jewish Agency (whose letter to Neville Chamberlain, published in *The Times* of 5 September 1939, promising Jewish support of the Allied cause 'amounts to something like a declaration of war'), and an assortment of Russian and other communists. (In a public discussion with me Nolte added 'the English in eighteenth-century Ireland'.)

To return to the historians' quarrel: Nolte's opponents then proceeded to refute his (and his allies') 'revisionism' by examining the formidable array of anachronisms, special pleas and eclectic readings of German history with which he had supported his argument; though it must be added that the opposition's opening move by Jürgen Habermas was itself flawed by misreadings and indignant political insinuations; only the ancient historian Christian Meier on the conservative side of the argument and the twentieth-century historian Eberhard Jäckel on the social-democratic side come out well from the protracted and heated controversy.

However, Nolte's aim is somewhat more complicated than I have made out. What really troubles him (he says) is that the history of the Third Reich has been presented as 'wholly negative' (at least, that is the nearest I can get to his 'Die Lebendigkeit des Dritten Reiches ist also eine durch und durch negative'); and since this 'negative life of a historical phenomenon represents a great, indeed a deadly danger for the science [of history]', some sort of a 'revision of that negativity' is urgently required. That, illustrated with a hypothesis concerning the Palestinian–Israeli conflict and a parallel between the bad name that historians have given to the Third Reich and the bad name the Southern States acquired after the end of the American Civil War, is all that Nolte says about the ultimate purpose of his revision.

Across this entire argument, unobserved by any of the participants, falls the shadow of the young Nietzsche. In the second of his *Untimely Meditations* Neitzsche pleads for 'a history in the service of life'. There are occasions, he writes, when history can best serve these mysterious interests either by abolishing itself entirely – hence his praise of 'the art and power of forgetting' whenever recollection of the past militates against the interests of 'life' – or, at least partly, 'by the as it were *a posteriori* attempt to give oneself the past from which one would prefer to be descended, as opposed to the past from which one does descend.' There is always something risky about such attempts, Nietzsche adds a little ruefully, 'because it is difficult to find a limit to the negating of the past.' Clearly Nolte is one of several German conservative historians who do not consider that the attempt to cook the past carries any risks.

3

Strangely enough, Nolte's 'revisionist' thesis has some striking affinities with a book whose intentions are very different. Arno Mayer, Professor of European History at Princeton University, takes his title, *Why Did the Heavens Not Darken?*, from Solomon bar Simson's chronicle of the massacres of the Jews of Mainz in 1096: but the book's motto could well be Ernst Bloch's *ubi Lenin, ibi Jerusalem* (essay 26).

Three aims, Mayer tells us, inform his thinking in this book: to abandon the vantage-point of the Cold War; 'to place the Judeocide in its pertinent historical setting'; and 'to use an overarching interpretative construct to explain the horrors both of the Jewish catastrophe and of the historical circumstances in which it occurred'. These guidelines, however, direct one's attention to the grave flaws of the book: Mayer does not mention a single previous account of the Final Solution that is coloured by the McCarthyite politics he wishes to refute; his presentation of a 'pertinent historical setting' ignores the ground rules of the historical scholarship he invokes; and the explanation he offers doesn't fit what actually happened.

Unlike Nolte, Mayer doesn't claim that the German campaign of annihilation was a 'reaction' to or a 'distorted copy' of the Red Terror, but he is nonetheless determined on a novel interpretation (the book in which elements of a similar interpretation were considered, Uwe Dietrich Adam's *Judenpolitik im Dritten Reich*, published in 1979, is not mentioned in Mayer's bibliography). His 'overarching interpretative construct', which partly overlaps with Nolte's, goes as follows: Hitler's campaign of destruction was aimed not against the Jews but against the Bolsheviks, who were at all times his principal foe. While his eastern campaign was going according to plan, the 'Nazi policy' against the Jews was casual, barely co-ordinated, not very different from the traditional 'wild' pogroms the Jews had endured under the Tsars and in the period after 1918; but 'when its eastern campaign bogged down in the late fall of 1941, Nazi Germany radicalized the conduct of the war against the Soviets and the crusade within it, fixing on the Jews for slaughter as the most hated and accessible member of the "common enemy" – "Judeobolshevism".'

Although Mayer is far from consistent in asserting this central thesis of his, I can see nothing else that is original about the book – certainly, most of its inaccuracies are intended to support this 'construct'. Shorn of its rhetoric, Mayer's view is that the Final Solution was a by-product of the failure of Operation Barbarossa. This of course is manifestly untrue. The systematic annihilation of the Jews began in co-ordination with the Polish campaign. It was conducted not only in the wake of the Wehrmacht, but with its now tacit, now explicit agreement, and occasionally with its co-operation (numerous writers, most recently Richard Evans, offer abundant evidence of this). The Final Solution was thus dependent on the military campaign only in the obvious sense that the more territories the German armies occupied, the larger the number of Jews that fell into German hands. Mayer's contention that it was the anti-Bolshevik 'crusade within the war that generated the destructive fury which became so singularly fatal for the Jews' is not so much a surmise as a complicated fabrication.

As D. G. Goldhagen (a mere research student in this professorial *galère*) has shown in a meticulously documented review of Mayer's book, a large number of witnesses and participants have testified to the concerted nature of the murders, and their accounts were verified, first at Nuremberg, then in numerous trials before the German courts. Goldhagen quotes from the testimony of a member of one of the SS killing-gangs, talking about the murder of some 1,100 Jews twelve days after the start of the undeclared war on the Soviet Union:

> The Jews were killed because they were Jews, and because the so-called Führer Order demanded it. To my knowledge the first instruction about the tasks of the Einsatzkommando was given by [its commander] at the first stop in Russia [on 3 July 1941]. I do not remember [his] exact words, but their gist was that the Jews were a useless, bad people, and must therefore be annihilated.

As we have seen in an earlier essay (13), this knowledge was not confined to the murderers. In the second of the anti-war broadsheets written by Hans Scholl and his friends, we read: 'We ... cite as an example [of German atrocities against the Jews] the fact that since the conquest of Poland 300,000 Jews have been murdered in that country in the most bestial manner.' Seeing that the broadsheets also mention the killing, deportation and imprisonment of the Polish intelligentsia and aristocracy, one might expect them to refer also to 'Judeobolshevism': but they don't; nor, for that matter, does Julius Streicher in the most notorious of his attacks on Jews, in *Der Stürmer* of May 1939.

Although Arno Mayer is not generally choosy in his use of words, treating us to the same empty phrases throughout the book, he does insist on distinguishing between 'anti-Semitism' as a broad ideological attitude, and 'Judeocide' as the more accurate designation of the events; and he rejects the term 'Holocaust' (as Walter Laqueur did before him), a word that has petrified into an empty cliché since it was given currency by an American television show. What was done to the Jews, Mayer rightly observes, had nothing to do with the word's traditional meaning: they were not 'a sacrificial offering, wholly consumed by fire in exaltation of God'.

One of the sources of anti-Semitism in Central and Eastern Europe (and in eastern France) is the local populations' view of Jews as Germans or Germanizers. Their very language, Yiddish, has as its basis the German dialect which the Rhenish Jews brought with them when they migrated to Poland after the ravages of the Black Death of 1348. ('I would like to tell you, ladies and gentlemen,' Franz Kafka told a German-speaking audience in Prague before a recital of visiting Yiddish poets, 'how much more of the jargon you will understand than you think.') This kinship was the reason why the Slavs, and the Hungarians too, denounced their Jews as propagators of the enemy language. From the age of the Enlightenment, the Jewish love-affair with German thought and literature, though sometimes reciprocated, was more often scorned and ridiculed by the writers in whose culture they sought their secular salvation. Of the monstrous irony of this predicament (which has nothing to do with 'anti-Bolshevism') Mayer says not a word – it doesn't fit his 'construct'. In the perspective he attributes to the populations among whom the Final Solution was enacted, the Jews are 'unassimilable aliens in the service of Judeobolshevism' (the fact that they were simultaneously accused of trying to subvert Bolshevism is not mentioned).

Mayer offers a Stalinist apologia for the Soviet failure to assist the Warsaw rising, and relieve the siege of the city, in the summer of 1944 (Katyn is not mentioned). Of the notorious Wannsee Conference of 20 January 1942, at which the Final Solution was the only item on the agenda, we read that 'there could be no doubt for any [of its participants] that they were assembled to increase, not alleviate, the torment of the Jews,' though 'there was nothing definitive' about the action on which the conference decided. (When Eichmann was asked what was meant by the euphemisms used by those present, and what Heydrich in particular had meant by saying that the surviving Jews 'must be treated accordingly', he replied: 'Killed. Killed, undoubtedly.') Mayer's book distinguishes between those prisoners in the camps who died a 'normal' or 'natural' death – meaning death from exhaustion, starvation, dysentery and other epidemics – and those who were murdered by asphyxiation, phenol injections, shooting and other 'unnatural' forms of violence. The point of the distinction seems to be that, although Mayer has doubts about the precise number of those killed at Auschwitz, he is quite certain that the number of those who died there of so-called 'natural causes' exceeded the number of those who were killed by 'unnatural means'. In this way he creates the impression that the mass annihilation was adventitious and improvised; and the annihilation appears a matter of sheer carelessness when he informs us that 'the Nazi leaders decided to transport frail and sick Jews, and Gypsies, to Auschwitz in full awareness of the perils they would face, and they continued to do so once there was no ignoring or denying the deadly conditions there, including the endemic danger of epidemics.' Any historian of the Final Solution is bound to consider the many recorded occasions when a conflict arose between Hitler's anti-Jewish policy and the German war effort; as, for instance, in December 1944, when all half-Jewish serving officers and men were ordered to be dismissed from active service while boys of fourteen and old men in their sixties were pressed into the Volkssturm; or when, in that last winter of the war, German rolling-stock desperately needed to move troops from the collapsing Eastern Front to the defence of the Reich was in fact used for the transport of Jews to the camps in Poland. In all these cases, the policy of annihilation had priority over the pursuit of the war. Mayer mentions none of this – to do so would leave his 'interpretative construct' in tatters.

4

Harold James is a recent export to Princeton from Peterhouse, Cambridge, and his book *A German Identity, 1770–1990* has solid, old-fashioned fare to offer. It is inspired by Ralf Dahrendorf's *Society and Democracy in Germany* (1965) but James lacks Dahrendorf's width and intellectual stamina; the book's argument works, above all, from the data of socio-economic history. Perhaps this explains why there is so little on Prussia's role in the formation of a German national state, and nothing on German militarism and its mystique. The book gets better as it goes along, however, mainly because German history after 1945 is easier to cope with in the traditional manner of English social history. As James convincingly demonstrates in his last two chapters, the growth of parliamentary democracy in the Federal Republic means the dismantling of *Weltanschauungspolitik* – that is, the displacement of nationalistic ideologies by the ideology of a modern industrial and consumerist society. This, as James shows, is not a wholly new development. As German nationalism after 1848 'became more anti-intellectual, the case about a German superiority in the things of the mind (*Geist*) was replaced by a doctrine about a German ascendancy justified by the material facts of economics.' These 'things of the mind', as well as Germany's 'very extensive and unusually literate culture', are briefly spoken of. But concentrating instead on the notorious absence of stable national institutions, James ignores the centrality of language as a social and political institution: its reification, in the wake of Herder, was a major political force. What is so exceptional about subsequent German history is its mixture of commercialism and spiritual high-mindedness, the extent to which literature and philosophy determined the German self-image: materialism with a bad conscience. James discusses in some detail the foreign influences on German architecture, but far more striking are the claims made by German intellectuals on behalf of *heilige deutsche Musik* (meaning sometimes 'sacred German music' and at other times 'German sacred music') and the philosophical and ideological aspirations of German literature, which are both a major source of its interest and the reason it has so often been appropriated by nationalist sentiment.

James steers clear of these metaphysical riddles – his rundown of 220 years of German history is cast in the perspective of the last forty-five. Concentration on economic success within the framework of consensus politics has been the making of the Federal Republic, its pride as well as the relief-cum-envy of its neighbours. It sounds like tempting providence to complain, but over it all looms the *Third Man*'s image of Switzerland – the civilization of the cuckoo-clock, at a time when what is needed in the heart of Europe is both economic success and political leadership. Harold James has built the contemporary bonanza as a teleology into the German past, but that past was both better and worse than he makes out.

Only an attack of academic hubris can explain why, in 1989, James chose '1770–1990' as his sub-title. In his summing-up he ignores not only the inhumanity but also the incompetence of the East German regime. When he writes, 'The GDR is without doubt the most successful of the Eastern bloc economies', without a word of comment on the wretchedness and precariousness of that success, his entire 'economic' approach becomes questionable. Nor, however, does he help us to understand the much-reported emergence on the German political scene of the Republikaner (REPs), whose founder and leader, Franz Schönhuber, will sue you if you get his name wrong. He at all events can testify that there weren't two wars (as Mayer implies), but that (as Richard Evans puts it) 'all the German troops were fighting for the same cause. They were not fighting to preserve Europe from Communism. Almost to the end, they believed they were fighting for Hitler and fighting for Germany.'

<h1 style="text-align:center">5</h1>

It isn't altogether easy to be serious about Franz Schönhuber, whose political career is described as a 'phantom image of the New Right'. Though he is not as funny as Josef Švejk (perhaps Schönhuber's best part in his brief post-war career as a cabaret artist and actor), he does resemble the Good Soldier in other ways. *I Was There* is the title of his autobiography, but its point is that he was but that nothing much happened, at least not *while* he was there. In 1941, a mere lad of eighteen from Upper Bavaria, he volunteered for service in the Waffen-SS. He knew there was something fishy about their tattooing his blood group on his upper arm (the time he had getting it removed by a doctor after it was all over!), but he is quite emphatic, at least *some* of the time, that there was no *real* connection between the military elite of the Waffen-SS and the criminals who were in charge of the concentration camps. He was lucky, and he thanks providence more than once: it so happened that *he* saw no atrocities (except in photographs 'the Tommies' showed him); he was on a training course *near* Warsaw in the spring of 1944 but took no part in the fighting; almost the only warlike action in which he participated was the evacuation of Corsica, and he was hospitalized suffering from . . . well, never mind, while his battalion was in the thick of battle.

To this day he deeply mourns the execution of a battalion of French volunteers on the Eastern Front, though he recognizes that 'our *Zeitgeist* doesn't allow for a decent fascist' – in other words, the National Socialists have given fascism a bad name. While he is in favour of providing a home to the *Volksdeutsche* from Eastern Europe and the Soviet Union, he fears that with them will come a lot of alien riff-raff who must be kept out. Of course he is not anti-Semitic – how could he be, seeing that his first wife was Jewish and some of his best friends etc. Nor is he hostile to the *Gastarbeiter* as such: after all, he has a villa in Turkey! After a brief but profitable time as a prisoner of war in British hands, a career in acting, and a few years in journalism, he ran a popular chat-show on Bavarian television, which was cut short by what he calls 'a campaign of character assassination'. On being dismissed from his post, with a decent pension, he soon found that his literary genre, a mixture of autobiography and political day-dreaming, was a little goldmine. In November 1983 he and six of his friends founded 'a democratically-legitimated, authentic right-wing party', the REP. (The literary genre, like the appeal to the lucky number, is not without its precedent in the Munich of an earlier era: 'And so I applied to join the German Workers' Party, and received a provisional membership card which bore the number 7', we read in *Mein Kampf*.) Schönhuber's loyalty to the Waffen-SS remains unshaken. Though he disclaims any heroism for himself, he quotes Nolte: 'They were the last genuine sons of the god of war.' The aim is to legitimate today's fatty culture by grafting National Socialist sentimentalities on to it.

What, then, is the programme of his party, and where does his electoral success come from? The party programme of 1984 mentions unemployment, loss of national identity, lack of historical consciousness ('the usable past'), and the environment. His electoral success is highly localized: in the Berlin state elections, where he polled 10 per cent, the programme was reduced to three points: Drug dealers and Turks go home! We are proud to be German! And the division of Germany must not be thought of as permanent. 'The most important thing is to keep alive the faith and hope and the will' for a united Germany. To his contemporaries ('I am sixty-six and will probably not live to see the reunification') the terminology of 'faith and hope and the will' must be familiar. He was reluctant to let his party contest the Berlin state elections, and thought at first that his success there was a fluke. The 17 per cent he polled in his own constituency of Rosenheim in Upper Bavaria was based on his personal popularity. There at all events he seems to be looked on as the heir to Franz Josef Strauss; and it is the Bavarian vote, rather than any socially-determined factor, which is reflected in the 7.1 per cent he polled in the European parliamentary elections of 1989. He is no less anti-EEC than his farmer constituents, and occasionally speaks of German autarky. 'I can not only move the masses, but think them,' he boasts of his speeches on the Munich Oktoberwiese, where he has scored his greatest successes, adding: 'Once I've left the tent, I say: anti-Americanism will not be tolerated.' Reports of his political meetings in Bavaria don't suggest Hitlerian hysteria, even though, what with guards in black breeches and white shirts complete with shoulder straps, these meetings are rough. In short, there is (as *Der Spiegel* has it) a 'Dr Jekyll–Mr Hyde quality' about him. His party (with a membership of over 8,000) offers a political home to the Far Right, which both the Christian Democratic Union and its Bavarian equivalent, the Christian Social Union, have been intent on keeping out, though not always successfully. Half the paid-up REP members are civil servants, junior officers and policemen (in Berlin, Schönhuber has claimed, four out of five policemen voted for him), and all these, he insists, being 'sworn on the constitution . . . , can't be neo-Nazis'. In addition, he counts on the votes of those who consider themselves social failures – *das no-future-Milieu* from which he himself made his escape – while looking hopefully to members of the Freie Demokratische Partei, the German Liberals, a party which he thinks is finished. Will this rag-bag of discontented voters provide him at the next national election with the 5 per

cent needed for parliamentary representation? There is no doubt that only a
major economic crisis, of which there is no sign, could so weaken German
democracy as to force a future government to accept the REPs as coalition
partners.

6

Why do none of the books I have mentioned contain the slightest intimation
of the events of November 1989? Imperception, even when it afflicts historians,
is not beyond explanation. One reason for the failure of imagination among
Western intellectuals, including those of the Federal Republic, is their lingering
distrust of that state and especially of the strength of its democratic spirit.
This distrust is expressed by Richard Evans when, contemplating the prospects
for German unification, he writes that the seventeen million East Germans
have no guarantee that a majority of electors among the sixty million West
Germans would not dismantle the East German welfare state and its social
security, as though the Federal Republic were an outpost of Thatcherism.
The fact is that the overwhelming majority of East Germans, brought to the
verge of economic ruin, know that their 'welfare state' is corrupt and doesn't
work. But there is a further reason why hardly anybody in the West foresaw
these momentous events. The old anxiety about what the Germans are up to
is accompanied not only by a consistently apologetic attitude towards the
government of the GDR, but also by ignorance, or an underestimation, of
Central Europe's deep longing for liberty, and a blasé attitude to what the
West has to offer its populations.

Well – what has contemporary Western Germany to offer the recently
liberated rest of Central Europe? Clearly, it must be something the country
itself has attained, however imperfectly, as part of its identity. In the conclusion
to his book Harold James attempts an answer: 'We may . . . speak of a cycle
of answers to the problem which Germans so insistently posed themselves:
what constituted national identity? It moved from cultural, to political, to
economic, and then back to a series of cultural claims. This is the peculiar
cycle that justifies a German claim to uniqueness.'

James's description of the peculiar German cycle is accurate enough, but
he fails to identify the point at which Western Germany since Adenauer has
broken it. The country's immense economic success is not in doubt, and one
hopes it will be accompanied by the recognition that only by sharing it with
its neighbours is that success likely to help maintain a lasting peace. But what
determines the country's identity, and what it has to offer, over and above the
economic bonanza – not uniquely at all but for the first time in its history –
is its by now ingrained constitutionalism; by which I mean the habit of its
citizens, both as individuals and as members of its institutions, of successfully
appealing to a system of laws as part and parcel of the country's constitutional
ideology.

The revolution, almost entirely bloodless so far, has only just begun. The ghosts of warring nationalisms have not been laid, and it will require many acts of statesmanship to allay the deep fears of the battered peoples who make up that 'torso that is forever being eroded by the waves of history.' All the same, a vigorous west wind is blowing. What are we witnessing is an unprecedented consensus in which Poland, Hungary, the old dismantled Prussia and now Czechoslovakia are all borne along by the same fervent hope. This hour, though, belongs not to the historians but to the poet who wrote, 'Bliss was it in that dawn to be alive.'

1989

22

The End of German Communism

1

The East Germans, whose armies occupied Bohemia and Moravia twenty-one years ago, and who, in the eyes of ordinary Czechs and Poles, combine the human warmth of Prussia and the tolerance of communism – the despised East Germans have now, in 1989, in less than two weeks achieved liberties and promises of democratic rights far beyond any that their eastern neighbours would have dreamed possible. Some of the sickeningly bland double-talk of the discredited officials of the Sozialistische Einheitspartei Deutschlands (the communists' whale's-belly party) goes on. The army and the police – the two sources of state power – show no signs of disobeying government orders. But the government itself is in flux, its orders are more conciliatory by the day – and there is no anarchy. The great 'experts' on the conduct of 'the masses', from Le Bon and Freud to Ortega y Gasset and Canetti (essay 25), have been put utterly to shame; many of their 'laws of mass behaviour' turn out to be arrant (and arrogant) nonsense. For this is a non-violent, good-tempered and – so help us – gentle revolution, the very thing Lenin ridiculed when he observed that the German workers couldn't occupy a railway station without first queuing up for platform tickets.

What is happening in the eastern half of Berlin has its precedent in the Berlin not of Dr Goebbels but of Theodor Fontane's novel *Before the Storm*. The year in which the novel is mainly set, 1813, was the year when, forced by a series of popular uprisings, the King of Prussia declared war on Napoleon's France: paradoxically, these patriotic German rebellions were inspired by the French Revolution. 'And where does all this come from?' asks Fontane's ultra-conservative hero, and he answers himself: 'From over yonder, borne on the west wind.' For 1813 represents the beginning of the horrendously long-drawn-out process of the Westernization of Germany; and with the knocking down of the Berlin Wall on 9 November 1989 (the fifty-first anniversary of *Kristallnacht*) the last stage of that Westernization has begun. The liberty which the seventeen million Eastern Germans aspire to, and which is now within their reach, doesn't come as a gift from President Gorbachev, though without the discrediting of the Communist Party's *Apparat* that his reforms have brought about this orderly revolution could not have begun; nor does it come from Lech Walesa, though one fervently hopes that a comparable figure will arise in Eastern Germany, to consolidate the gains already achieved and make possible a peaceful transition to full democratic government.

What inspires the tens of thousands who are moving westward and the millions who don't want to move but will no longer put up with the material, moral and intellectual restraints of an inefficient and corrupt bureaucracy can hardly be described in terms of an 'ism'. Even 'socialism' has for them become an empty word, merely another bit of ideological patter. Nor does one hear much of individual freedom of conscience and of 'the spirit' (which the German philosophers have so often extolled and theorized over). No doubt we shall in due course invent a new 'ism' to describe what motivates these cheerful thousands. For the present, at all events, their goal is political liberty within the bounds of a welfare state of the Western European dispensation. 'If modern Germany has a historic patron,' Edward Pearce wrote recently, 'it is not Marx, nor Bismarck, nor the Frederick the Great celebrated by East Germans' – or at least by the Party hacks who were dictating *Kulturpolitik* as relentlessly as the National Socialists had done – 'but Walther Rathenau, the industrialist-statesman murdered [in 1922] by the proto-Nazi *Freikorps*,' not least because he was a liberal-minded Jew.

With a mere eleven years to go, the last bit of Germany is moving into the twentieth century, the century in which ordinary men and women, reasonably well-fed at last, have obtained a voice in the political arrangements which guarantee them liberty under a tolerable constitution. Such arrangements (Michael Oakeshott once observed) don't make for human felicity, but at least they 'make felicity not impossible'.

This – something like this – is what the Western Allies helped to initiate in their three 'zones', and what the inhabitants of the fourth zone are achieving by their own resolve: with no help from those Western fellow-travellers who used to speak of 'the tragically misunderstood Wall', though with abundant, not at all disinterested assistance from beyond the crumbling divide. The welcome the Federal Germans are giving to those 'from over there' is warm and generous. Lübeck and Hamburg may have said, 'Enough is enough', but even the mafiosi Bavarians, with their traditional hatred of everything Prussian and Protestant, for whom 'socialism' and 'atheism' are synonymous, got schools, town halls and *Ratskeller* ready to receive the masses pouring over the frontier which runs through the Bohemian Forest. Of course, this Sunday mood will not last. Jealousies and distrust sprang up when the post-war immigrants from the east arrived, with no more of their possessions than they could carry, and it took time to integrate them into the communities in which they settled. Indeed, some members of the associations they formed in the late 1940s, as well as some of their descendants, remain irredentist to this day; and it is they who have been trying to use the present exodus as an excuse for 're-opening the question of Germany's eastern border'. They may not be without political influence – should things go wrong on a national scale. But of course just now things aren't going wrong, and Helmut Kohl – tirelessly energetic and hard-working, on the obese side and a little short of tact but full of optimism and good will – represents the country's buoyant mood. The new immigrants – the bulk of them young skilled workers: the very people whom the Party sought to attract and hold – are quickly finding jobs, and most of them will settle down. No doubt some, perhaps a quarter, will want to return; many of them because the working pace in the West is too fast for them. But it is clearly inconceivable that they will be returning to the country they left: to the same constraints and lies, the same monotonous speechifying by self-regarding functionaries; the same 'critical works discussions'; the same pretend-democracy.

While English children love 'playing shops', German children play at being postal workers: weighing parcels, franking letters, issuing postal orders and registering mail. To follow the proceedings of the East German deputies on West German television is to see a lot of grown-up men and women playing at being democratic parliamentarians with the eagerness and earnestness of children engaged in a game of make-believe.

'Democracy is discussion': I have quoted this well-intentioned tag of T. G. Masaryk's before. And the Czechs, who believed him, have been paying the price of that mistake ever since. Democracy is of course more than the ironing out of conflicts of interests within the framework of a consensus, more than parliamentary 'discussion'. To survive, the democratic process must include readiness, and the means, for action in its defence – the sort of action the Czechs (let alone the Slovaks) were not ready to take in 1938, or 1948, or in 1968. In the present instance it includes a people's readiness 'to vote with their feet': to leave behind all they have (and what that means for *German* working people with their deep emotional attachment to possessions it is not easy to assess) and to move into an uncertain future in a land full of promise but full of unknown hazards, too. The wonder of this uprising, which has no close parallel in history, is its lack of that ghastly 'Germanic' earnestness which in the past has so often spilled over into aggressiveness, fanaticism and violence; and its rehabilitation of that once terrible term, 'das Volk'. Of all the slogans I have seen on television (and surely this is the first historical movement in which television has played an important positive role, if only because most of Eastern Germany is within range of Western transmissions) the one that best summed up the people's mood was the motto on an East Berliner's T-shirt: 'Last one out switch off the light!'

Could this be the end of the tyranny of 'das Tragische' over Germany? Ever since the days of Heinrich Heine, German intellectuals and writers have been on the side of gloom, *et pour cause*. Not one of my many German friends had foreseen these developments, no writer I know of (except Fontane) has given an inkling of them. On the contrary: the more German and Western intellectuals analysed the status quo in the east, the more they affirmed it and the less they believed in the possibility of change.

A complicated mixture of historical factors has made this moment possible, among them that 'cunning of reason' of which Hegel wrote. However eager conservative German historians have been to 'revise' the past, a consensus in the Federal Republic has accepted responsibility for it in its unrevised version – in fact and deed if not always in word. From this acceptance springs the fear of repeating its horrors, and this profit from the lessons of history has enabled the politicians of the Federal Republic to provide a democratic framework for the advances in technology and management which the Weimar Republic failed to achieve, and which Hitler achieved only at the monstrous cost of his dictatorship. Repudiating all responsibility for the National Socialist past, the rulers of Eastern Germany never tired of accusing the Federal Republic – its officials, its politicians and its wealthy establishment – of following in the steps of Hitlerite imperialism, and like Hitler himself they may have believed in the nonsense of their own propaganda. No wonder that they failed to understand the political conditions of the Federal Republic's economic success. The open and articulate repudiation by the East German people of every one of the old gang who offers to stand again for office, as well as the suicides among the middle ranks of party leaders, indicate the gravity of the regime's human and political failure.

The communists were oppressive, but not oppressive enough to prevent people from acting on the knowledge and experience of their daily lives: the knowledge and the experience that (to quote Brecht) 'the measures taken' to secure the workers' paradise did not work. In the face of endless indoctrination to the contrary, people conceived the uncertain hope that the benefits of the welfare state can be separated from the paralysing pressures of single-party rule. In this hope too they were strengthened by the example of the Federal Republic and by the economic aid, unashamedly political in its intention, which was given to them throughout the last decade.

They were also supported by their churches – mainly by the Lutheran clergy, the only section of East German society that accepted its share of responsibility for the horrendous past. 'For seven days Joshua marched round Jericho with his people,' the pastor of St Nikolai's in Leipzig preached on Monday, 13 November, 'and on the seventh day they blew their trumpets, and the Walls of Jericho fell down. For seven days we have prayed in this church, and now this great wall has fallen down.' The old story conveyed a better message to the people than did the assorted ideologies from Rosa Luxemburg to Herbert Marcuse.

Deep worries remain. What will be the national and international consequences of the unification of the two Germanies? When Chancellor Kohl declaimed, 'Wir sind ein Volk', ('We are one nation') could most of his audience fail to recall the rest of that slogan: 'ein Reich, ein Führer'? This of course is what Conor Cruise O'Brien meant when (in an article reported in the German press with astonishment) he warned of a Fourth Reich with a statue to Hitler in every town. (It is no thanks to O'Brien's country that there isn't one in every British town.) He is unlikely to be reassured, but when unification does become a live issue, it will not be within the context of the sovereign ultra-nationalist states of the 1930s, but within a European context; and President Mitterrand is right to argue that the more fully contained Germany is within such a context, the greater the advantages to Europe as a whole. Wisely, Willy Brandt spoke not of 'unification' but of 'a greater degree of unity, in whatever form'. That form nobody can foresee at present; perhaps German–Austrian relations since the last war offer at least an approximate parallel. However that may be, the need for free elections in the East overshadows all other considerations. For the conceivable future, O'Brien's 'Fourth Reich' is a chimera.

The Poles and the Czechs, on the other hand, are bound to be frightened. For a long time to come they will go on recalling their wartime suffering. This is the memory that keeps the communists in Prague in power (in spite of incompetence and corruption on the East German scale), and this, too, is the subtext of all Polish–German negotiations; nor can the few Jews who, victims of the victims, have survived in Eastern Europe be expected to view the German development with anything but fear. Yet the Europe that may arise as the old Iron Curtain goes up should assuage all those fears and at last rise to the grand occasion.

Thinking about Berlin in November 1989, I recall Bertolt Brecht's finicking his way through the tragic uprising of the workers of Berlin in the summer of 1953. In nothing he wrote did he foresee what is happening today. On the contrary: the chances are that, hating capitalism more than he loved the workers, he would have sided with the oppressors – for the sake of 'the cause' to which he committed his poetry and his plays. But poetry, like reason, has its strange cunning. He is, after all, among the three or four greatest poets German literature has to show in this century. We must therefore accept the fact that, although his expectation of the nature of the liberation to come was mistaken, he described the circumstances in which it would come with unequalled poignancy:

> Ach wir
> Die wir den Boden bereiten wollten für Freundlichkeit
> Konnten selber nicht freundlich sein.
>
> Ihr aber, wenn es so weit sein wird
> Daß der Mensch dem Menschen ein Helfer ist
> Gedenkt unser
> Mit Nachsicht.

(Oh, we/Who wanted to prepare the ground for friendliness/Could not ourselves be friendly.//But you, when the time comes at last/And man is a helper to man/Think of us/With forbearance.)

2

Two States – One Nation? is the title of a recent collection of essays by Günter Grass, Germany's most distinguished man of letters. All except the last essay in the collection consist of gripes and sour grapes. Grass's 'case against German reunification' is that the Federal Republic has nothing of real value to offer to the people of what was once the GDR. Grass's case is Nicholas Ridley's intemperate outburst ('I'm not against giving up [Great Britain's] sovereignty in principle, but not to this lot. You might just as well give it to Adolf Hitler, frankly') spelled out less crudely and in detail: the political culture of the Federal Republic is still poisoned by nationalism, its aspirations are still imperialist and aggressive, the strength of a united Germany, now sustained by a buoyant currency, is not to be trusted. Moreover (Grass adds) there was something – a sort of Biedermeier sociability and honesty – about life in the GDR, which was worth preserving but which will be destroyed by big business and its heedless rapacity. He rails against the injustice that the GDR – the Soviet zone of occupation – should have been saddled with a disproportionately greater share of reparations than the west, refusing to recognize that it is this circumstance, an outcome of the Cold War, which has sharpened many western German politicians' sense of responsibility for their fellow-countrymen on the other side of the Wall. Since Grass says almost nothing about the real conditions of life in the east, one might wonder why thousands of men and women risked their lives to escape from it.

There is no need to idealize the causes of the collapse of Honecker's corrupt and inefficient regime; the promise of material welfare in the west was no doubt the first of them, but the yearning for individual freedom and political liberty ran a close second. The desire for unification – 'Wir sind ein Volk' ('We are one nation'), the slogan accompanying the breaching of the Wall on 9 November 1989 – came only at the point when 'the people' – 'Wir sind das Volk' ('We are the people') – realized that they were victorious. After almost sixty years of indoctrination, tyranny and the vilification of all liberal thought and all democratic politics, first by Hitler's National Socialists, then by the bosses of the 'Socialist Unity Party', the East Germans realized that the emperor really had no clothes. Hobbes's famous maxim, 'Reputation of power is power', was proved wrong. The revolution was organized not by intellectuals but by leaders who rose spontaneously from among the much-despised masses. A few clergymen were among them; Grass's literary colleagues – pampered mediocrities of the state publishing houses of Leipzig and East Berlin – were not. The East German uprising that Europe and indeed the world witnessed was not preceded by years of civil strife, some of it bloody, such as took place in Poland. Nor was it purposefully and consistently prepared for by years of clandestine deliberations – a whole library of samizdats – such as were produced and disseminated by the leaders of the Czech and Slovak Charter 77. It was, to revert to the old ethnic cliché, an un-German, untheoretical revolt, guided not by ideology but by exasperation, a simple 'Enough is enough!' There are great moments in the history of humankind, and this was one of them: it seems astounding that Germany's greatest writer should not be among those who rejoice. But is it? Does he perhaps miss the gore? It seems that Grass in his rejection of western peace and prosperity is perpetuating that love-affair with tragic destiny which settled like a blight on German politics and life in the first half of our century. (Here, incidentally, is a lesson that Critical Theory may learn: great literary themes don't necessarily make for tolerable politics.)

The last chapter of Grass's unhappy book contains his address of February 1990, entitled 'Writing after Auschwitz'. Here at last he lets go of special pleas in a hopeless case, and instead traces with unsparing candour (and only a little relevance to the rest of the book) his own development as an artist. The account begins with his return in 1945 from an American POW camp:

> In response to the overwhelming number of photographs showing piles of shoes here, piles of hair there, and again and again bodies piled on top of each other, captioned with numerals I could not grasp and foreign-sounding place names – Treblinka, Sobibor, Auschwitz – there was one ready answer, spoken or unspoken, but always firm, whenever American educational zeal forced us seventeen- and eighteen-year-olds to look at the documentary photos: Germans never could have done that, never did do a thing like that.

The shock when Grass found out that they did is with him still: it makes him the honourable man he is, but it also forms the tenor of his remarkable style (essay 11). And so he comes to tell the story of his writings as a series of quests to find a language and a mode of fiction that would move on, beyond Germany's past crimes, without forgetting their horror, without offering excuses for them or allowing the passage of time to obliterate them. In this, though, Grass is not (as he claims) an outsider on the West German scene. The country he so often condemns has undergone a development not all that different from his own. German governments too, in the west though not in the east, beginning with Konrad Adenauer's (whom he vehemently despises), have been guided by an acknowledgement of the terrible past. True, this acknowledgement has been neither as frank nor as consistent as his own; it is hard to see how, coming not from an individual but from representatives of individuals in the body politic, it could be. But, within the framework of the Federal Republic's remarkable constitution, the acknowledgement of the past has, I think, been frank and consistent enough to offer a measure of reasonable reassurance to the rest of Europe.

Is Günter Grass really not aware of what hope the disintegration – a sort of spontaneous combustion – of the GDR has created in the minds of millions of people and of the improved conditions it has created in their lives? That the improvement in the natural environment, for which he cares so passionately, could not possibly come about without western aid? Grass's book is ill-considered, and yet I think his attitude evokes sympathy. Not because the German scene can afford a few voices which protest against the national euphoria; dissent, after all, was expressed by the clergy who, on the day of national unity, would not allow the churchbells to be rung, in spite of Chancellor Kohl's displeasure. One's sympathy is with the author's sour grapes, his deep and (to use that word again) honourable disappointment. His is, after all, a literary not a political awareness. The chief target of his satire has been the opulence, the self-indulgent prosperity of the west. His hope, on the other hand, has been 'socialism with a human face'. He has spoken with admiration of his fellow-writer Václav Havel, but he has had no experience of the conditions of life in which Havel's character and political stand were formed. Grass's intermittent delusion has been the belief that a decent and equitable socialism was perhaps about to be achieved in the east, that given time and generous help short of radical political change it really might be achieved in the state of the 'workers with hand and brain'. We can see that this was a delusion – intermittent because every now and then (as when he speaks of the worker's suppressed uprising of June 1953) he is aware of the futility of such hopes.

The Europe of which Germany has now become an integral part is not, and will not be for many years to come, a 'federation of states', but, rather, in Charles de Gaulle's phrase, *'l'Europe des patries'*. 'What is at stake', the late Geoffrey Barraclough wrote, 'is not the fate of Germany alone, but the fate of Europe; for there can be no lasting settlement in Europe without the settlement of the German question which, removing the age-old bars to German unity and German democracy, permits the German people to take its place as an equal partner in the comity of European nations.' The historian's statement is a bit too orotund for our taste, but it is truer all the same than Ridley's outburst or Grass's jeremiad. It was written in 1946: the era of Germany in ruins, of the 8-mark cigarette, hoarding peasants, brick-laying academics and all. It was not, in spite of Grass's misgivings about 'Vorsprung durch Technik', a happier time.

1989, 1990

23

What is German?

The highly intellectualized German nationalism of the recent past and its terrible consequences are among the reasons why nowadays we regard all talk of national character with suspicion and even distaste. Certainly, we don't believe in a 'national spirit' which every true German (or whoever) breathes or which flows in his veins like an elixir of ethnic or racial purity. Yet we live – still – in a *Europe des patries*, and not every attempt to describe the character of one of these *patries* is necessarily disreputable. Might not the fact that English has no unembarrassed equivalent term provide a first step toward such a description?

National identity, folk-soul, national community (*Volksgemeinschaft*) or whatever more or less neutral or awkward words we choose – all these expressions are part of various cultural vocabularies, they denote the arrangements of a cultural consensus and derive their meanings from it. Such expressions don't lend themselves to the setting up of the kind of definitions that Aristotle bequeathed to Western philosophies: like labels on boxes, his 'categorical' definitions denote fixed entities, whereas cultural expressions refer to fluid, variable states of affairs and overlapping functions, to values which are relative to their time and place. This is, but was not always, a commonplace: the denial of this variability, coupled with the assertion of absolute cultural superiority, was a part of the German nationalist creed after 1870; and though they made less fuss about it, the English believed much the same sort of thing.

Not definitions but descriptions are relevant to our purpose, and descriptions of a particular kind: the kind presented in Wittgenstein's method of family resemblances. (To this method many arguments in these essays are deeply indebted, and I discuss it more fully in the last of them.) The method appeals to one of our simplest experiences. We may ascertain the family to which a person belongs, and that family's characteristics, by observing overlapping similarities: it is not only that some of its members have the same nose, some the same eyes, and so on, but also that some (though not necessarily all) have the same name, others (again, not all) speak the same language, while yet others have the same way of speaking that language. (Similarly, there is no hard and fast line between describing and defining.) Here again the German domination of Central Europe has foregrounded a categorical generalization at the expense of variety: when people called themselves German and spoke the same language, that was enough to settle the question of nationhood and to legitimate the claims to national territory; and (as we have seen in the Bolzano essay (2)) the German example was followed by the 'ultra-patriots' of other nations.

What the Wittgensteinian method teaches us is that there is no need to abstract one similarity, one 'essence' or 'spirit' of the nation from the cultural multiplicity of attributes (no need which the method of family resemblances wouldn't satisfy), as if its various members represented more or less faithful embodiments of that single essence. And if the objection is raised (as it often is) that only definitions are *exact*, and that the method of family resemblances is a mere empirical insipidity leading to inaccurate conclusions, the obvious reply is that 'accuracy' too is a collective term deriving its meaning from similarities of usage, and that *in this context* (and there always *is* a context; not even the dictionary can get very far by way of 'contextless definitions') the method meets the demands of accuracy better than any other.

National identity, then, is a collective name for a group of similarities possessed by people who all call themselves by the same name; and who become recognizable to each other and to their neighbours by these similarities. Calling yourself by a national name doesn't provide adequate or incontestable grounds for membership, but it does provide the necessary grounds, the *sine qua non*, of such claims, as indeed 'being human' applies to all members of a family. It is because national names have traditionally received this absolute status (as the one constant among the varied attributes admitted under those names) that the giving or denying of such names is apt to excite enormous passions. And again, the more one lot of people are made to admit that they share certain qualities with another lot, the more passionately they attack those who claim that the remaining differences don't matter. Since the nations we know don't live on the moon or in isolation from each other, the all-too-obvious fact that many of these resemblances can be found in more than one place and more than one national community – albeit in different combinations and degrees – enhances the usefulness of our procedure. The same applies to the time-span to which the following observations refer. To change the metaphor: cultural concepts of time, such as an epoch or era, contemporaneity as well as non-contemporaneity, the spirit or temper of an age, *Zeitgeist* – all these denote bundles of biographies (bundles of individual as well as collective experience) of varying length and historical range: collective names and dates for configurations of attitudes and value-judgements, which offer useful characterizations of segments of time.

These notes about 'What is German?' don't pretend to be comprehensive, but confine themselves to five overlapping topics: national self-assertion; mythologies; abstraction; order and work; and war. What determines the choice of these topics is the hope that they might illuminate some of the

changes in temper that have come about on the German scene since the end
of the Second World War.

1 National Self-assertion

The greatest of these changes undoubtedly occurred in the forms of German
national consciousness and self-assertion, by which I mean variations on the
theme of 'I am a German.' Chief among these forms were the traditional
feelings of superiority over Germany's eastern neighbours, which became an
important element of German political life from 1848 onwards, beginning in
the Frankfurt Parliament of that year. Hitler's pronouncements in *Mein Kampf*
(1925–6) have their more discreet forerunners in the novels of Gustav Freytag
and in the manifestos of the ideologues and clerics of the Wilhelmine era.
These claims were matched by feelings of social and cultural inferiority toward
the West, which found their ambivalent confirmation in, say, Richard Wagner's
novella 'An End in Paris' (1844), but also in Nietzsche's critique of Wagner.
Thomas Mann in his wartime *Reflections of a Nonpolitical Man* (essay 6) was
determined to treat these national complexes ironically (they became the theme
of his polemics against his elder brother Heinrich), but his ironies provided
no safeguard against the nationalism he hastily contrived for belligerent uses.
It was a particular piece of good fortune that Konrad Adenauer and Willy
Brandt, two chancellors from opposite political camps, were able to bring to
an end the old hostilities, against France and against the Slavonic East
respectively. Adenauer was the luckier of the two: the pacification of
Franco–German relations was indeed one of the great achievements of post-
war European politics. Unfortunately it is unlikely to serve as a pattern for
Germany's relations with its eastern neighbours. As long as those countries'
bitter memories remain unrelieved by prosperity and political progress, the
'historical' memories of past terrors will continue to determine their attitude
toward their powerful neighbour. (Only a civil servant quarantined in the
fastness of Washington could have conceived of the notion that 'history is
dead'.)
    As though German resentments and humiliations after the debacle of 1918
weren't enough, the new ideology that sprang up in the 1920s received its
boost from the fabrication of internal enemies, a fabrication which reached its
peak in the racial policies of the Third Reich. In this process certain physical
and mental qualities were attributed to various groups like the Jews and
Gypsies, homosexuals and Jehovah's Witnesses; or, rather, groups were formed
by means of these attributions, and then declared inferior and proscribed. As
for the Gypsies and Jews, the qualities singled out and ascribed to them were
abstracted from their social contexts and made absolute by being declared
innate and natural. The preference for 'natural' over other forms of origin
remains an ingrained heritage of German Romanticism to the present day.
Although it is not only in Germany that power (political or some other form)

determines what counts as 'natural', it is there that power was eked out with claims to metaphysical sanction. These procedures were not confined to party politics. Early remarks about the 'historically necessary' extirpation of inferior races or peoples (usually Slavs of one kind or another) can be found in the writings of Friedrich Engels and Karl Marx; and the disdain many German Jews, especially those close to the Wilhelmine establishment, felt for their eastern co-religionists belongs among the tragic aspects of their effort at assimilation. As for the story of the happy symbiosis of Germans and Jews in the decades before 1933, in proof of which the same old list of distinguished names is trotted out, starting with Albert Einstein and Lise Meitner and ending with Franz Werfel and Carl Zuckmayer – it is largely a sentimental post-1945 legend. The assimilation was largely a one-sided affair of high culture and upper-class status; it took place in the civil service, in business and in the professions, but much less in intimate personal or family contacts. This is shown by the speed with which events unfolded after Hitler came to power: 'It appears [writes a recent critic] that while the German population at large witnessed rather unwillingly such violent actions as the boycott of 1933, yet the measures which were given formal legal status (such as the Nuremberg Laws of 1935) were readily accepted even though their sole purpose was to carry through a programme of racial anti-Semitism of the most brutal kind.' These were the measures which led to the monstrous farce of state and party officials complaining that they had no adequate instructions on how to sort out the Jews from the Aryans, in view of which 'terrible mistakes might occur' . . .

Some nationalistic attitudes, as forms of xenophobia, persist toward foreign workers in Germany today, and it may be that some of the anti-Polish feelings (of a traditional, racist kind) common throughout the defunct GDR will survive in a united Germany. Apart from indicating the strength of the economy, the permanent presence of 1.6 million foreign workers on German soil conjures up among some of its critics the spectre of the millions of wartime 'slave labourers', whose living and working conditions were for the most part tolerable as long as they were French and employed in agriculture, but inhuman and mercilessly exploitative when the labourers came from the Slavonic countries and did forced work in industry, usually in munitions factories. These comparisons with wartime conditions are unjustified and as often as not politically motivated. But they indicate how strong is the memory of the Third Reich, if not in the national consciousness, then in the consciousness of a range of people which includes but is much wider than the intelligentsia. It is a moot point whether the social unrest created by the new immigrant minorities could have been foreseen (though the failure of 'the Republicans' (essay 21) and other extreme right-wing parties to exploit these difficulties suggests that, once they are perceived, there is good will enough to solve them). But to one side of party politics, it is the attitude of the population at large which confirms and perpetuates the otherness of the *Gastarbeiter*; however, this otherness is not legitimized by the State and its regulations, as it is in Switzerland. This should not surprise us. Quite often in recent European history the notion of 'good ordinary people' being misrepresented by 'evil rulers' has turned out to be a sentimental fallacy.

The greatest achievement of Austrian *Public Relations*, the Germans often claim, is to have presented Beethoven to the world as an Austrian and Hitler as a German. Yet the related practice of *Kulturpolitik*, whereby literature, music, art and philosophy are converted into instruments of national self-assertion in support of domestic and foreign policy, was a German accomplishment to start with. Born in the defeats of the Napoleonic Wars, *Kulturpolitik* became a political force during the decades after 1870, especially in support of eastward expansion. Today the notion in its old aggressiveness survives only in the propaganda of a few associations of exiles from the eastern territories; for the rest the Goethe Institut (chief dispenser of German *Kultur* abroad) is about as nationalistic as the British Council, the Institut Français or the Amerikahaus (which is, not very much), except that it and other such German organizations are better endowed.

In all, the sense of national identity is less strong in Germany today than at any time in its recent history, and is strongest in those who deplore its absence; even the revolution of 1989 proceeded with very little national self-assertion. Controversy flourishes, but largely within the bounds of a national consensus and the prevailing, relatively novel, temper of thoughtfulness. Almost half a century after Hitler, this is still a society whose public life at all events is dominated by the fear of its own past.

2 Mythologies

Can a modern society and the state that encompasses it exist and prosper without myths of some kind? In *The Birth of Tragedy* and then again in the second of his *Untimely Meditations*, 'The Uses and Disadvantages of History for Life' (from which I have quoted before), Nietzsche argued that myths are indispensable to the ecology and survival of a community, for they form 'the horizon of its imagination', the measure of its ethical standards and the scale of its moral judgements. Basing his view on the function of myth in the life of pre-Socratic Athens (or rather on his own interpretation of that life), the young Nietzsche became an ardent advocate of the Wagnerian mythopoeia. He deplored the disenchantment that followed in the wake of Socratic scientism, but failed to make clear how a myth is to fulfil its social function once it has been perceived ('unmasked') as a myth. It was the great poets of German Modernism, with Stefan George at their head, who tried to give poetic substance to the Nietzschean postulate, but they were wholly out of touch with popular culture and its feelings (and proud of it). More realistically conceived because more relevant to German life in a post-heroic era (and of course *infra dig*, in the poets' view) are such old mythic figures as 'der deutsche Michel' (the plain, honest and slightly stupid German peasant, nowadays no longer the victim of Jewish cunning), the Bavarian figure of 'der Saupreuße' ('Prussian swine'), the myth of 'Nibelungentreue' ('the troth of the Nibelungen', the meaning of which is somewhat obscured by the fact that any notion of loyalty is plainly contradicted by the story itself) and the myth of 'das arme Frontschwein' ('the front-line crock'), which came Hitler's way during his wartime service in the Flanders trenches, and which he used to good effect in his 'table talk' more than twenty years later. In the writings of 'theorists' like Houston Stewart Chamberlain, Alfred Rosenberg and a whole lot of National Socialist Party hacks a veritable bestiary of mythical figures was resuscitated, some of them legitimized by the Zurich patrician psychologist C. G. Jung – figures which today strike any German as both comical and embarrassing.

What of this survives? The attempt to heroicize the German army has had a mixed reception. It was viewed a little more favourably than such an undertaking would be in most other European countries, but the inclusion of the dead of the Waffen-SS in the commemoration (essay 17) led to a bitter debate in the Bundestag and in the country. During the Falklands War only those Germans who remembered the Second World War showed any understanding for Mrs Thatcher's attempts to mythologize the military undertaking, and even they understood without approving, while the younger generations were invariably shocked by the Iron Lady's rhetoric. When Helmut Schmidt observed during a speech in Bonn that 'We must have a foreign policy that is transparent to everybody', he was clearly addressing a society which he believed can manage without myths. The German attitudes to the war in the Persian Gulf were as varied as may be expected in a parliamentary democracy with a vociferous and articulate Protestant pacifist intelligentsia which is still haunted by its memory of silent conformism throughout the Third Reich. Some of Germany's friends in the Anglo-Saxon West found that their efforts at 're-educating the Germans' half a century ago had been rewarded with success that now turned out to be inconvenient; and when Germans, to justify their staying out of Operation Desert Storm, quoted their 1949 constitution, which, they claimed, allows for participation in an armed conflict only if NATO is threatened, this was interpreted abroad as legalistic finicking and evasion. More sympathy for Germany's quandary would be proper. It isn't only that 're-education' has been effective; so has the terrible lesson of Dresden. And for the Germans the Constitution has become what the constitution of 1788 is for the Americans, and what emblems like the flag or the German eagle used to be: the most powerful symbol of nationhood. All the same, sympathy with German feelings cannot silence the question of how long the economic giant at the heart of Europe can avoid its share of European political responsibility.

From Goethe's time onwards it has been in the figure of Hamlet that German writers have seen the truest pattern of their national characteristics. 'Hamlet has no way, no direction, no manner,' wrote Ludwig Börne in 1829, 'I would not be surprised if a German had written *Hamlet*. All a German needs is a good, legible handwriting – he just copies himself, and Hamlet is done.' Thus the German vacillations about the Gulf War have been likened to Hamlet's hesitations and uncertainties of purpose in a parallelism of illuminating details, which brings us back to our earlier argument: has the disposition of fear created a political vacuum, a situation in which the country proves incapable of any independent action that cannot be reduced to economic considerations? The Gulf War was the first occasion since the Second World War when a wholly independent war-related decision – as a form of national self-assertion – was expected from a German government; and this government, guessing that the feeling in the country was 'We have had our wars, let them get on with theirs!', responded to the Allies' appeal with a resolute 'Yes – well, no, but . . . ' Yet Hamlet's indecisiveness does not survive him – it is Fortinbras's 'Go, bid the soldiers shoot!' that ends the play.

On 20 July 1984 there appeared a leading article in *The Times* which could have been inspired by Nietzsche's observations on the uses of the real or fictive past. A people (the article said) needs 'a myth like that of 20 July 1944' in order to strengthen its sense of identity with consolations and reassurances derived from its own past, for thus it safeguards its own historical continuity. What *The Times* meant by the 'myth of 20 July 1944' was not entirely clear; at all events, it cannot have been the incontrovertible facts of the attempt on Hitler's life. The only thing that may qualify as 'mythical' are the plans the courageous and honourable conspirators had prepared in case their attempt succeeded. Their notion that the Reich they envisaged would be acceptable to the rest of Europe and could possibly form the basis of a future German republic shows what kind of Cloud-cuckoo-land most of them lived in. It is clear that the German public are, or are expected by some of their rulers to be, less troubled by right-wing patriotic celebrations than by reminders of the martyrdom of men and women on the Left; which is why in Western Germany the fact is hardly ever mentioned that of all the active opponents of the National Socialist regime it was the German communists who made some of the bloodiest sacrifices, and why there were so few protests when the rector of Munich University in 1974 forbade the commemoration of Hans and Sophie Scholl on the anniversary of their execution (essay 13) because he feared that it would be exploited by students with subversive (left-wing) views.

The British Legion, Anciens combattants, Frontsoldatenverbände – none of these, nor ancient Greece for that matter, provide the myths of our world. The names of the modern mythopoeia are not *Das Nibelungenlied* but *Dallas* and *Coronation Street*. Yet neither of these has had the power and popular appeal of the two German mega-serials *Heimat* (1985) and *Holocaust* (1979). These two 'epic achievements' of television offer very different but complementary accounts of the recent German past. *Heimat* says: 'It was the way all life is – it wasn't so very bad', and *Holocaust*: 'Whatever you may think of the past, it was much, much worse.'

These serials are efficient, readily identifiable reconstructions, which have also proved to be what modern art-works so rarely are: necessary reconstructions. They do what Nietzsche said myths should do: re-enacting the past, they set up the imaginative horizon of a society's present. But *Holocaust* also does what Nietzsche says historical recollection should not do: it offends against his postulate of a 'critical history', which (as he disastrously argued) should aim at eliminating those parts of the past the recollection of which is likely to disturb the present (I have called it the Katyn Syndrome history). The history Nietzsche enjoins us to forget, *Holocaust* urges us to remember. It is an American commercial product first and foremost – an irony Nietzsche would not have enjoyed. It was heavily criticized by historians of every stripe, and received with raised eyebrows and a good deal of sarcastic comment by the media critics, while many fastidious viewers thought it intolerable. Yet it achieved what no other product of fiction or scholarship or well-intentioned 're-education' achieved: it placed the persecution of the Jews squarely and for a time irremovably at the centre of the German popular consciousness, and by doing so unearthed for one generation and created for another a collective memory of their common past. It too was an instrument – the most powerful single instrument – for modifying national self-assertion through the nation's fear of its own past.

For Nietzsche the proposition that effective myths are great art would have been a tautology: in this too, as in his notion of 'critical history', he was wrong. Like *The Good Soldier Švejk*, the *Holocaust* serial proves that there is a disjunction betwen works of art and their consequences, between the aesthetic and its ethics: whereas *The Good Soldier Švejk* demonstrates the problematic consequences of great literature, *Holocaust* demonstrates the positive effects of a product which, inaccurate in some details, apt to follow old clichés and create new ones, is close to kitsch. For *Holocaust* has done more in Germany to stop the psychological repression by the public mind of past evil and thus to encourage some collective understanding of it than any serious work of art or scholarship or philosophical reflection.

3   Abstraction

In §27 of *Being and Time* (1927), from which I have already quoted (essay 10), Martin Heidegger attacks 'the daily business of being together in the world that surrounds us' as the source of our inauthentic existence. It is characteristic of this modern togetherness that it reduces 'every other person' to 'being just like another' and not himself. Inauthenticity (he tells us) is the avoidance of *my* choices, *my* decisions, *my* responsibilities, it is hiding behind the choices, decisions and responsibilities of some more or less anonymous collective. Heidegger himself of course dissociates himself from this mode of being – this is one of several passages in the book which take the form of an impersonation conducted in free indirect style:

Dieses Miteinandersein löst das eigene Dasein völlig in die Seinsart 'der Anderen' auf, so zwar, daß die Anderen in ihrer Unterschiedlichkeit und Ausdrücklichkeit noch mehr verschwinden. In dieser Unauffälligkeit und Nichtfeststellbarkeit entfaltet das Man seine eigentliche Diktatur. Wir genießen und vergnügen uns, wie *man* genießt; wir lesen, leben und urteilen über Literatur und Kunst, wie *man* sieht und urteilt; wir ziehen uns aber auch vom 'großen Haufen' zurück, wie *man* sich zuruckzieht; wir finden 'empörend' was *man* empörend findet. Das Man, das kein bestimmtes ist und das Alle, obzwar nicht als Summe, sind, schreibt die Seinsart der Alltäglichkeit vor.

It is relevant to my argument that the pivotal terms of this text will have to be paraphrased rather than translated:

This togetherness entirely dissolves one's own being into the mode of 'the others', so that the others in their distinctness and explicitness disappear even more completely [than one's own self]. In this inconspicuousness and unascertainability [the mode of] *one* develops its proper dictatorship. We enjoy ourselves and take pleasure in things the way *one* enjoys them, we read, see and judge literature and art the way *one* sees and judges; but we also distance ourselves 'from the crowd' the way *one* distances *oneself*; we find 'shocking' what *one* finds shocking. The *One* [or, the *They*] which is indeterminate and which is what all are, though not as their sum, prescribes the mode of everyday being.

It could certainly not be said that this is 'ordinary' written or spoken German: transforming '*man*' into a noun, a transformation on which the entire passage depends, is an idiosyncratic Heideggerian turn, satirized by many authors (chief among them Günter Grass). However, it must also be said that the entire passage with all its oddities is made up of elements of everyday German, and that these elements and the language to which they belong lend themselves to such a transformation into a philosophical ideolect much more readily than, say, English. Whether this ease makes the language especially (or even uniquely) suitable for conveying philosophical insights, as Heidegger claimed, or whether, on the contrary, it discredits philosophy by making it all too easy to assume that where more or less intelligible words are compounded, there more or less precise meanings are sure to follow, need not concern us. The point at issue is that the passage proceeds by way of a treble abstraction: it reports on the manner in which people abstract from their everyday experience, it then abstracts from the report, and it does all this in a language which, although tied to the elements of the vernacular (for example, 'Nicht-fest-stell-barkeit' = 'non-ascertain-ability'), recasts these elements in its own highly abstract way. But (it will be objected) is this procedure more than one of those strange games that philosophers play?

In 1978 Walter Kempowski, a best-selling middlebrow novelist of the post-war wave of Social (not Socialist) Realism, published a book called *Haben Sie davon gewußt? (Did You know About It?)*, in which 300 contemporaries of the Third Reich, chosen at random in various parts of Western Germany, give their answers to the question of complicity, 'How much did you know about what was happening in the Reich, about the atrocities perpetuated in the last years of the war?' Apart from a brief introduction, Kempowski reprints the answers without comment. Assured of anonymity, the people questioned had no obvious reason to answer other than truthfully about their past knowledge, or, rather, as truthfully as their memory permitted, yet the substance of their recollections is less interesting than their form. In an overwhelming number of cases the answers go something like this: 'Man ist in ein Haus eingebrochen, das einem nicht gehörte' ('One [or, You] would break into a house that didn't belong to one'), or 'Und dann ging das Erschießen los. Das durfte man nicht wissen' ('Then the executions by shooting started. One wasn't supposed to know about it'). This simple pattern confirms Heidegger's claim that 'one's own being dissolves into the mode of "the others"': the self, fearing the charge of complicity in guilt, hides in the anonymity of 'one'. But another pattern, less simple and still more revealing, also occurs:

Das sind Mißstände, hat man gesagt, aber der Führer weiß das nicht. Ich war damals sehr nahe daran, ihm zu schreiben. [Those are evils, it was said, but the Führer doesn't know about them. At that time I came very close to writing to him.]

Ich erwähne das auch nur, um darzustellen, wie man als harmloser Volksgenosse etwas davon hörte. [I mention this just to illustrate how one came to hear something about it as an ordinary innocent citizen.]

Ich weiß, daß mir das sehr peinlich war, wenn da einer mit'm Judenstern ging. Man wollte nichts davon wissen und sehen. Ich fuhr da mit'm Fahrrad und sah da einen gehn. Man hatte keine feste Wertskala. [I know I found it very embarrassing to meet a person who wore the star of David. One didn't want to know anything about it or see it. I was riding on my bicycle and saw a man walking. One had no firm scale of values.]

These statements (typical of many) confirm Heidegger's analysis, but they do more than that: they locate it within a contrasting context of ignorance and self-exculpation. In all of them a good '*ich*' 'distances itself from' an evil '*man*' that the '*ich*' will have nothing to do with: the entirely concrete and present 'I' in which the speaker has invested his identity is abstracted from the anonymous 'one' and its historical situation, in an unconscious attempt, which only the linguistic device betrays, to keep the 'I' uninvolved in the past and thus exonerate it. Only at the point where (less typically) a 'scale of values' is mentioned does the answer become a conscious ploy to preserve the self from being damaged by guilt, though in the event the opposite occurs, and the device shows the 'I' rejecting its own past, and with it a part of itself.

Here then are two overlapping uses of abstraction: the one, Heidegger's, is the opening move in a discussion of inauthentic being; the other is a Gallup poll of everyday examples of such being, in which linguistic usage encourages the form they take in a way it wouldn't in English. They happen to be negative uses of a device of language and thought which in itself is value-free; and the fact that the examples quoted happen to belong to the past doesn't of course mean that they relate to an outdated form of language or mode of being. Revolutions, reforms and defeats may change frontiers, dynasties or constitutions, but they make very little difference to the verbal habits of the survivors of those defeats, reforms and revolutions: verbal habits change but (in spite of Roland Barthes's claim to the contrary) they do so remarkably slowly.

Designations of what is and what is not 'felt to be abstract' are 'culture specific'. Take the suspicion that all abstractions might turn out to be negative (in the way that those I have quoted involved lies and evasions and denials of the past). To recognize this attitude for the peculiarly English superstition it is, is to recognize the relative nature of a device more often censured in a neighbouring culture than acknowledged in one's own. For of course abstractions aren't only 'negative'. There is no system of justice that doesn't require abstracting from the individual case; no social institution can function without setting up a roster of classes, or trades, or professions which doesn't merely generalize but also abstracts from individual interests; and the same is true of the sciences, which press for the setting up of laws and regularities and the elimination of exceptions. And Germany's enormous technological advances are made possible by much the same talent for abstraction as that which turns so many 'theoretical discussions' in the humanities into paradigms of tedium.

Of course there is abstraction's other side, the danger of 'the contemptuous attitude towards the particular case', and hardly any continental philosopher – except Wittgenstein, whose phrase this is, and Nietzsche – has taken much notice of that danger. Max Weber speaks of it, but it can hardly be said that he heeds it. And one of the comic aspects of the present intellectual scene is the spectacle of a *bien-pensant* social democrat like Jürgen Habermas turning out tomes of all but impenetrably abstract *Zeitgeschichte* – 'unascertainabilities' indeed – while Nietzsche, an anti-democratic elitist if ever there was one (and whom Habermas quotes abundantly), is incapable of producing an abstruse sentence or argument; and when a German writer (Peter Sloterdijk is a case in point) deliberately sets out to avoid the pitfalls of abstract diction, obscenity is the main device he resorts to.

In this untidy area between rhetoric, psychology and philosophizing lies one of the most interesting paradoxes at the heart of German culture and civilization. Thus, on the one hand, abstraction – in political schemes as well as in philosophical speculation, in social blueprints as well as in technological advances, in the legal domain as well as in literary criticism – dominates the

German scene in a way and to an extent that it dominates no other, and yet, on the other, this state of affairs has not prevented the German mark becoming the strongest currency in the western hemisphere, while German exports continue undiminished through one international recession after another, the German welfare state offers benefits second to none, and scholarship and research at their most abstruse are more richly funded in Germany than anywhere else.

What then is abstraction? (One might as well ask, 'What is German?') It is a device in the economy of both life and letters. A defection from living experience, it can mar poetry and prose alike – but then again it can protect the sentient soul from an excess of suffering. It is an element in the constitution of both our courage and cowardice, now the source of craven comfort, now again the price of survival. And it is not only the source of contempt towards the particular case, but the process that made the most monstrous measures of cruelty and destruction an acceptable part of everyday life – it is all these things as well as one of the indispensable ways of presenting the individual case to the mind. It is the gift that makes thoughtfulness – the philosophical disposition – possible, and the curse that turns that disposition into evasion – the source of some of the best and worst things on the German scene.

4   Order and Work

If there is one theme which German poets of the last three centuries have made peculiarly and poignantly their own, it is their concern with the world as a place of insecurity and impermanence, a provisional state – a feeling for life as a mere option liable to be revoked. Among those who have contributed to this theme are Johann Christian Günther, Hölderlin and Kleist, Georg Trakl, Rilke and Paul Celan. Unlike Plato's Cave or the Christian's images of the after-life, many of the poems (and, in Kleist's case, the stories and plays) which belong to this tradition imply no expectation of a redeeming reward in another world, nor indeed of any other kind of life. If we think of this feeling and the literary works which embody it as specifically German, this is because before the end of the nineteenth century this was not a theme often found in other literatures, and perhaps only Leopardi and Laforgue convey it with comparable poetic intensity – apart, of course, from *Hamlet*, which, from Goethe's *Wilhelm Meisters Lehrjahre* onwards, has been far and away the first and most fully considered play in German literature's canon of Shakespearean and world literature.

The theme dominates Rilke's cycle of *Duino Elegies*, written in the ten years before 1922 and conveying more accurate insight into its epoch than Rilke's critics have credited him with. The First Elegy especially, composed in a flurry of inspiration in the castle of Duino above the Adriatic near Trieste in January 1912, focuses on images which convey modern man's feelings about his world with wonderful clarity: we seek help, succour and strength in many different places (the Elegy opens), but we do so in vain, for the strength of the angelic beings to whom we wish to turn for support (in the hope that they might intercede on our behalf, though we don't know with whom) is too much for us, it would be our undoing. All this is cast in conditional, tentative terms, and our uncertainties are underlined by an ironic contrast:

> Ach, wen vermögen
> wir denn zu brauchen? Engel nicht, Menschen nicht,
> und die findigen Tiere merken es schon,
> daß wir nicht sehr verläßlich zu Haus sind
> in der gedeuteten Welt.

(Alas, who is there/whom we can use? Not angels, not men,/and even the canny animals are sure to notice/that we are not very securely at home/in the interpreted world.)

And here is Rilke's contemporary, Max Weber, the greatest and most realistic of German social philosophers: 'As in my life I have "dreamed" more than one ought to permit oneself, so I am nowhere *entirely* reliably at home' – 'so bin ich auch nirgends *ganz* verläßlich daheim.'

'Living and partly living', T. S. Eliot wrote. Again and again the *Duino Elegies* return to this feeling that our 'being' and 'dwelling' are not in the 'real' world at all but only in an intellectualized, uncertain, somehow provisional world at second remove – a mere interpretation of the real thing. Here the basic metaphysical theme of Plato's *Republic* is taken up, though not as a perennial philosophical insight but as an actual experience within a concrete historical context. The numerous compounds from 'Leben-' and 'Welt-' have few if any counterparts in other languages: a problematic 'view of the world' (*Weltanschauung*), an unassuaged 'feeling for life' (*Lebensgefühl*) – these are the kinds of experience which such words are intended to express. The remarkable rise of the word 'Wirklichkeit' to fashion and dominant usage in the second half of the nineteenth century (remarkable because, as noted above, the word comes to stand for at least two divergent states: one of the boring everyday, the other of the moment of exceptional, 'existential' intensity on the margins of experience) – the rise of this 'reality' points to the same cluster of doubts and velleities. In the wake of Schopenhauer and the young Nietzsche's *Birth of Tragedy* (1872), German society harboured feelings of spiritual deprivation and dissatisfaction and cultivated its literary and intellectual spokesmen to voice them, at the same time as it prided itself on the material progress and growing political power for which most of those philosophers had little more than contempt.

Where, then, asked generations of German poets, novelists and story-writers, but also the influential profession of pamphleteers and literary ideologues, are assurance and the old *centrum securitatis* to be found? The famous or notorious love of order, industriousness now greatly praised or envied, now again mocked or despised – these characteristic phenomena of Wilhelmine society provide answers to the question, responses to this *Lebensgefühl*. This often imperious longing for order and certainties is perhaps best described by way of a contrast: it is the polar opposite of Keats's temper of '*Negative Capability*', that is, when a man is capable of being in uncertainties, mysteries, doubts, without any irritable reaching after fact and reason' – except that the 'irritable reaching' was less often after fact and reason than after such assurance as was once provided by religious faith and in the modern age is expected from all manner of ideological and metaphysical placebos. My argument points in the direction of Max Weber's famous essay on the Protestant work-ethic: work and order become an anchor in a sea of uncertainties. The German state and society that arose after 1945 on the ruins of the Third Reich link up not with the Weimar Republic but with the work-ethos of the Kaiserreich before 1914: pride in the remarkable economic success in the decades following the currency reform of 1948 – pride in German work – does more to shape Germany's self-image and national identity than any of the old notions of aggressive nationalism. 'Außenwelt', 'Umwelt', 'Lebenswelt', 'Mitwelt' – all these are common terms of the everyday vernacular which aren't readily translatable into other languages: all of them refer to aspects of that 'world' which was so recently subject to one interpretation and will soon be subject to another ... And if that world is so 'unreal', a scene of mere shadowy interpretations, what then is there to hold on to, other than a substantial or palpable achievement, a massive product of undoubted value, like a six-cylinder BMW ... ? *Wissenschaft* itself becomes the sheet-anchor of dreams. This is assurance, and who is to doubt that it works. But alas, it is a good deal less inspiring of great literature and art than were the chaos and disaffection of the 1920s.

In Max Weber's view all order and discipline of work are military in origin, and by 'military' he means a rationally (that is, bureaucratically) regulated threat of violence. (We shall return to Weber's views on war and the meaning of war.) Ernst Jünger takes up and in a sense caricatures Weber's argument in *Der Arbeiter* (1932) by identifying 'the warrior' with 'the worker-technocrat' and setting up a romantic-brutalist continuity between warlike action and the industrial productive process – between 'the stutter of the machine-guns of Flanders' and 'the rattle of the textile mills of Manchester'. In the event, both Weber and Jünger are generalizing from a specifically German analysis to societies rather differently disposed. All the same, even though Weber (who died in 1920) collected his insights in the heyday of the *bürgerlich* era, while Jünger (still with us, hale and hearty at ninety-six) stridently exploited its decline, both have an intuitive understanding for the sense of legitimated violence at the heart, not indeed of 'Germany' or *Deutschtum*, but of the Germany of their time.

Another consequence of the search for certainties is a strong resistance to all forms of nonconformism, even where it is harmless. Mockery of German obedience goes back at least as far as Kant, who said that of all European peoples the Germans were furthest removed from the spirit of opposition. Hence also the acute fear of anarchy, the desire to avoid civil war at all costs, which was one of the factors in Hitler's successful calculation in 1932–3. With the conqueror's effrontery he later professed to envy Mussolini the 'battles' that fascism had to fight in order to gain supreme power – the Germans, he boasted, offered no resistance; his boast uncannily prefigures the fact that while it was the Italians themselves who got rid of Mussolini, it was the Allies (not the Germans) who got rid of Hitler. When they instituted their horrific measures against the homosexuals, the National Socialists were appealing less to the German public's sense of moral disapproval than to their fear that what was generally regarded as nonconformist behaviour would lead to 'Volkszersetzung' – a 'disintegration of the nation'.

There is, of course, nothing particularly German about the fear of national disintegration. It was this fear that gave rise to Hobbes's *Leviathan* in the era of the English Civil War; General Pétain invoked it in his call for national unity after the French defeat in 1940, and so did Senator McCarthy in America in the 1950s. But because the history of the German states after the lasting trauma of the Thirty Years' War was punctuated by many episodes of revolutionary turmoil, the patriotic appeals to unity there had a very particular fervour, and suspicions of noncomformity were particularly prone to turn into fear of anarchy. It is the literariness of these episodes – the verbal violence that informed them – that is so striking. The first was the Storm and Stress movement – revolutionary in literary and ideological terms but hardly serious politics – which in the 1780s and 1790s challenged the ethos of the German Enlightenment, even before fear of the French Revolution stifled any effective political discussion; both the liberal students' movement of 1819 and the echo of the Paris revolution of 1830 were too localized to offer a real challenge to Metternich's rule; the literati of the *Vormärz* anticipated 1848, the revolution that failed, this time not so much because of its literariness as because of dissensions among the revolutionaries (though some of these dissensions, too, arose over bookish projects); next, Expressionism offered a literary and Utopian challenge to the Wilhelmine establishment in the two decades before and during the Great War, again with political aspirations and again without political results; the abortive communist revolution of 1918–19 was suppressed by a pact between the army and a social-democratic government frightened of some of its own supporters, a pact which led to a permanent split among the left-wing parties from which Hitler eventually profited; and Hitler's own revolution succeeded partly because inept politicians thought mistakenly that they could use him and his party for their own ends, and partly because he promised a 'national rebirth' and 'an awakening of Germany' to an electorate which was looking for a charismatic leader who would redeem it from the conflicts of ordinary politics; the students' rebellion of the 1960s (like Expressionism, but more violently) mobilized the forces of protest in the name of yet another new beginning and new 'image of man' and ended by having to defend itself against its own radical anarchists and their fringe of terrorists; and finally, in contradistinction to the previous episodes of revolt, the East German uprising of November 1989 succeeded not only without violence but also without an ideological blueprint, and it did so not only without the co-operation of intellectuals of East or West, but mostly against their views and expectations.

Most of these revolutionary episodes failed because they were undertaken in ignorance of the forces of order arrayed against them, by intellectuals who weren't very clear about the difference between literary protests and effective social and political action. For 200 years or so, the phrase 'The country cannot afford ... ' became the motto of every political establishment getting ready to suppress calls for reform.

Why was the November 1989 uprising different and why did it succeed? The reason – to one side of the after-effects of the end of Stalinism – lies partly in the sheer inability of the incompetent GDR rulers to suppress it without bloodshed; for however ill-informed the party officials were about the contemporary world (to meet them was to be vividly reminded of what the arrogance and ignorance of the National Socialists had been like), they did at least acknowledge that as long as the Western Allies were in Berlin, the bloody suppression of an uprising in the heart of Europe was ruled out. But the reason for the difference of this revolution and for its success lies also in the fact that the ideology that was on offer in the West was the local – German – variant of the Western liberal-democratic ideology, propagated not by blue-prints or the *ukazy* of authorities (such as 'the Classics of Socialism'), but by the daily Western fare shown on the West German television network. In turning to that ideology, the East Germans were belatedly adopting what in many other parts of Europe was commonplace. Unification with the Federal Republic offered prosperity and welfare, political liberty and freedom of choice. The choice was not just of this or that party, but of politics – the politics of capitalism modified by protection from its worst consequences, in exchange for a social order and material conditions which for the vast majority of the East German population were dreary but not intolerable, with many accepting the propagandists' claim that things were improving. Unification also offered a fair rule of law, though it is doubtful whether to a population that knew only a politicized judiciary this can have meant as much as those other, more concrete benefits. And, finally, unification satisfied nationalist aspirations, though in a surprisingly peaceful, unaggressive and orderly way. In the course of the revolution one German public, living in circumstances which were far from desperate, was prepared to turn its back on an accepted order. To be sure, this public's motives were mixed, though none of them was disreputable; their rhetoric was relatively mild, occasionally biblical; and the initial risk of failure was real enough, though not daunting. None of this would have availed had not another German public been ready to help in this venture, again from mixed motives, motives which were neither wholly disinterested nor sordid, nor designed to inspire fear abroad – and of course, none of *that* would have availed without Gorbachev's abandonment of the Honecker regime. It is not often that a country is visited by such good fortune in the conjunction of circumstances, motives and the possibility of acting. As to the politicians – all *they* had to do was to let it happen.

5   War

Hobbes, Durkheim and Weber all see social integration as 'the violent subduing of human quarrelsomeness': Ralf Dahrendorf's summing up expresses a fundamental social theorem. In the portrait I am attempting there is no need to decide whether the warlike disposition is a 'more fundamental' component than the nervous search for security and certainties on which I focused earlier. From the time of the Franco-Prussian War (through which German unity was achieved) the combination of a sense of order with work-consciousness and its ethic was reflected in the army as an institution and in militarism as its consistent ideology, and dominated the public life and foreign policy of the country; and it was not the secretly unconceded defeat of 1918 (with not an Allied soldier on German soil) but only the unquestionable defeat in the field in 1945 and the subsequent dissolution of Prussia that turned the armed forces into unequivocal servants of parliamentary democracy – for the first time in German history. This was not a simple process. I have already referred (essay 16) to that colonel in charge of the Army School for Leadership and Morale and his difficulties with 'democracy'.

Writing in 1915, Max Weber summed up his thoughts on war and its function in modern society in a memorable way:

War, which is the threat of force made reality, creates an emotional heightening and a communal feeling in modern polities, thus releasing in the combatants a community of devotion and of unconditioned sacrifice, while in the mass of the population the effect is an active compassion and love for the needy which breaks through all barriers of natural association. Generally speaking, religions have nothing comparable to show except in heroic communities practising the ethic of fraternal love. Moreover, war provides the warrior with something that is unique in its specific significance: it is the awareness of a sacramental meaning in death which belongs peculiarly to death in war. The community of the army in the field, in our own day as in feudal times, feels itself to be a community unto death – indeed the greatest of its kind. And the death which is only the common lot of human kind and which overtakes each of us with no hope of an answer to the questions 'Why me? Why now?', which makes an end when, with all our immeasurable developments and refinements of culture, it is only a beginnning that seems to make any sense – from that unavoidable death the death of a soldier in battle is distinguished by his being able to *believe*, as nobody else can on this mass scale, that he knows that he is dying 'for' something. The fact that he has to face death, with its whys and wherefores, must be so clear to him – and to nobody else except to those who die 'at work' – that for him the very presuppositions are absent in which the problem of the meaning of death, in that most general sense in which religions of salvation concern themselves with it, would arise.

This translation has sought to preserve as many of the long German sentences with their anacolutha and piled-up clauses as seemed tolerable in order to show what the 'official' English translation fails to show: a mind tensed to unburden itself of its rich stock of ideas quickly, somehow, anyhow. From this complex structure three leading ideas emerge. In the first, the *social* function of war, integrative for the military and civilians alike, is insisted on; the second emphasizes the *sacramental* meaning of death in war, though the religious dogma (or whatever) to which this evaluation might belong is not indicated; and the third and most interesting throws a light on the *existential* character of the warlike situation, a character which doesn't allow the problematic religious question of the meaning of death to arise. None of these insights is presented in a 'value-free' manner; the reader, bludgeoned into agreement by the rush of the argument, is told how to evaluate what has been put before him. First: you are wrong to think that modern wars fail to create communities, Weber insists, repeating '*Gemeinschaft*' four times in the first sentence alone. Then: the 'meaningfulness' (*Sinnhaftigkeit*) of death in war for the soldier (actually, like Jünger, Weber uses the somewhat archaic term 'Krieger', that is, warrior) is something quite different from that of mere everyday dying (Heidegger no doubt would call it 'der Tod des Man') – this death is something unique, utterly concrete, and capable of a sacramental heightening, as it was in the days of old. However, before the end of that sentence Weber retreats from accepting the religious claim in his own person and merely reports that this is a situation in which such a 'belief' is possible. Only in the third part of the argument is the threat of death in war presented in psychological terms: so complete or (as a later lexis would put it) so authentic is the soldier's commitment to his warlike task that the question of what it is all 'for' – the question of meaningfulness – ceases to have any meaning for him ('*daß das Problem des "Sinnes" des Todes . . . gar keine Voraussetzungen seiner Entstehung findet*').

(The reader who has got this far might like to know that although Max Weber was very proud of his commission as a Prussian lieutenant, he never actually served in the field; and that the patriotic exhortation the passage contains was not intended for the front-line military only, who in any event were quite likely to miss the odd number of the *Archiv für Sozialwissenschaft und Sozialpolitik*, where Weber's meditation first appeared: the factory workers were not to be excluded from sacrificial death, as long as it occurred 'at work'.)

War and the meaning of death in war: why should trying to find answers to the questions this raises be thought of as a German preoccupation? Weber is not denying that at some point in time and at some level of clarity and articulateness, any soldier in the field and any civilian involved in the war may have given some thought to these questions. What he is saying is that in the dire press of the moment the question of the meaningfulness of war is answered intuitively and positively – the soldier under threat of death knows what he may have to die for. And yet he, Weber, doesn't tell us what it is, beyond saying that the meaning discerned by a soldier in his imminent death in war is 'sacramental'; which means that in some way or other a positive answer has been 'internalized' by upbringing, social pressure or regimental drill, 'until it really sticks'. And again, I can see no good reason why the notorious British practice of the giving of the white feather should have been less effective in the indoctrination of those who had their doubts about the meaning of death in war than comparable signs of public obloquy in Imperial Germany. What, if anything, then, is specifically German about Weber's passage, why have I quoted it?

First, and most obviously, because I think that no English social philosopher of comparable brilliance and genius would have written about the problem in such a relatively uncritical way; I cannot think that someone of Bertrand Russell's standing (to one side of his pacifism) would have given so much complex and subtle thought to the matter and then placed it within an unconsidered, dogmatic framework, implying that all this argument is being conducted in a situation in which 'one cannot afford' any critical doubt (except the little doubt expressed in Weber's dissociating himself from the belief about knowing what it's all for).

Moreover – and more directly relevant to the change in national consciousness which is the main theme of this essay – nobody writing seriously on these matters in Germany today would, I think, be prepared to accept Weber's argument as anything other than a sign of his time. But the argument isn't only of his time – it prefigures the grounds of the bitter *ressentiments* and hatreds of the 1920s. The soldier's blind belief (Weber had written) is conditional on his being involved in the battle. Once he returns from the war he no longer believes that he knows 'what it had been for'; but defeat does not stop the question being asked – on the contrary, it continues to be asked not just irritably but with growing violence. And indeed there was an answer to this insistent search for a meaning of the lost war, its cost in deaths and sacrifices, in hopes, illusions and betrayals: it was the nationalists and eventually Hitler who offered that answer.

Max Weber lived to see the defeat which, ironically enough, he had expected from the summer of 1914, as soon as war broke out. (He died of pneumonia on 14 June 1920 – I have no doubt the Weimar Republic would have turned out quite different had he lived to guide it.) Yet it was not he but Friedrich Nietzsche who anticipated the answer and noted its consequences: 'Nihilism as a psychological condition', Nietzsche wrote in the winter of 1887–8, 'is bound to arise when we seek a "meaning" in all that has happened – a meaning which isn't there, so that at last the seeker loses all courage' – and, we might add, accepts whatever ersatz meaning happens to be on offer.

And this (to return to our comparative inquiry) is perhaps the greatest change of all in the national consciousness: that search for meaning characteristic of the German situation in the century before 1945 is no longer violent, if indeed it has survived at all. The point was recently made that the 'economic miracle' and its consequences have transformed a once belligerent nation into a nation of hypochondriacs, crunchers of pills and drinkers of medicinal waters. However, things are not as bad as that; and, in any event, it is less than equitable to blame the Germans whenever it suits us, when, having learned the lesson of their past, they not only have ceased to believe in the sacramental meaning of death in war, but, given the choice, would rather claim their medical insurance, in order to pay for a stay at a French or Austrian watering-place, than go to war.

1985 (1991)

24

Havel's Castle

1

The social memory of small countries is punctuated by dates which, as often as not, recall national defeats. When the students of Prague assembled in the late afternoon of Friday, 17 November 1989, to march into the city's main thoroughfare, the Národní Street, the purpose of their officially sanctioned demonstration was to commemorate the fiftieth anniversary of the death of Jan Opletal, a student murdered by the Germans on 17 November 1939; but at the same time they were remembering the death of Jan Palach, another student who, on 16 January 1969, burned himself to death beneath the statue of the country's patron saint, Václav, known as the Good King Wenceslas, in protest against the invasion of Czechoslovakia by the armies of the Soviet Union and three other countries of the Communist Bloc. Now, for the first time in twenty years, 'the grown-ups' were taking the students, and the actors who soon joined them, seriously: 'our children shamed us into action.' By 9 p.m. a crowd of some 50,000 people were moving toward Wenceslas Square. The violence which the police (white helmets, riot-shields and truncheons) and anti-terrorist units (in red berets) used to disperse the crowd led to some broken limbs and numerous concussions, but there were no deaths. This is how Czechoslovakia's 'kind of peaceable revolution' began, and it was over, without any further violence, some twenty-four days later. It was not, to begin with, a nation-wide uprising. Both television and radio were slow to begin giving up-to-date news; people had to rely on West German broadcasting stations, and on Radio Free Europe in Munich. In the provinces they suspected that these were the cavortings of a few crackpot intellectuals in Prague, most of whom had been in gaol anyway.

Václav Havel was not in the city when the uprising started; he was staying in northern Bohemia, at his country cottage, called 'Hrádeček', which means 'Little Castle'. On his return to Prague (probably on Saturday morning), he took charge of events from his headquarters in the basement dressing-room of the Laterna Magica Theatre. His leadership seems never to have been in dispute. The size of the popular support for the students and actors took him by surprise, and he instantly made their cause his own. His next, indeed decisive step was to call a two-hour general strike for Monday the 27th at noon. The call-out, which included the most critical section of the population, the workers in heavy industry and in the mines, was a complete success. By a strange coincidence, the city happened to be full of people from the countryside who had come to attend High Mass to celebrate the canonization two weeks or so earlier, in Rome, of Princess Agnes (1205–82), the daughter of yet another King Wenceslas. (An old lady whose house lies on the steep way to St Vitus's Cathedral put a notice in her window: 'Pilgrims are welcome to a night's lodging, but I have only two beds, two eiderdowns and four blankets.') This was the first Czech uprising fully supported by the Catholic Church: a year earlier a petition for religious freedom, drawn up by Augustin Navrátil, a dispossessed Moravian farmer, and endorsed by the ninety-year-old František Cardinal Tomášek, was signed by more than half a million people; and an hour after his election as president of the Republic, on 29 December 1989, Havel (no longer in his habitual jeans and pullover but in a neat three-piece suit) attended High Mass celebrated by the cardinal in the cathedral. In a little over a month he had moved from the Little Castle to the big one overlooking the city – 'z Hrádečku . . . na Hrad', seven months after his last term in gaol.

The Czechs are a cautious people; they have taken a long time to emerge from the traumas of national defeat. Few of them have been ready to face the fact that, to one side of the 'betrayal of Munich' of 1938 by the French (and less directly by the British), the Czechoslovak government's acceptance of Hitler's *Diktat* meant a collapse of everything the country had stood for throughout twenty years of democratic freedom and self-determination. Munich represented the generals' readiness to surrender a highly equipped modern 'people's army', without resistance and on the first occasion when that army was called upon to fight; it represented a total collapse of what Havel (among the few who saw the past undistorted by apologies and lies) has called 'the spurious realism' of Edvard Beneš, the then president, who, though not consulted, accepted the terms of the surrender. The demoralization which followed that defeat and the harshness and untold humiliations of the German wartime occupation of Bohemia and Moravia (Slovakia chose to become an 'ally' of the Germans) explain at least partly the next defeat – this time a moral one: the vengeful fury unleashed by the Czechs on the Sudeten German population after May 1945 (with Beneš's government looking the other way); but they also explain the lack of any effective democratic resistance to the communist *coup d'état* of 1948, and the failure of the Prague Spring of 1968. Jaroslav Hašek's good soldier Švejk has often been praised for his resilience and cunning, and his ability to survive under adverse conditions (essay 7): astonishingly enough, in November 1989 the Czechs succeeded (and the

Slovaks took their cue from them) precisely because they did not behave like the Good Soldier but chanced their arm; because they behaved like Václav Havel.

Moreover, the Czechs were willing to learn the lesson of their three neighbours, Poland, Hungary and Eastern Germany, that the Soviet Union under Gorbachev was in no mood and in no position to turn Wenceslas Square into Tiananmen Square. This too is astonishing – after all, Czechoslovakia had had bitter territorial quarrels with all three countries since the peace settlements of Versailles and Saint-Germain, and its relations with them went from bad to worse when all three sent their military forces to take part in the occupation that followed the Prague Spring. For Czechoslovakia with its respectable democratic past to be willing to follow on the road to democracy countries with very different political records suggests a commonality of political spirit unprecedented in the annals of Central Europe.

The self-liberation came because there were enough people to follow the students and actors who formed its spearhead – enough people with the courage, perseverance, perspicacity and imprudence of the man whom they later had the good sense to elect as their president. It would be nice to be able to say that in his utter decency, good humour and honesty Havel is 'a true representative of the Czech people'. So he is. But in all representation there is an element of fiction – a fiction which, in the event, encouraged 'the people' to rise to the ethical demands of a charismatic maker of fictions.

2

Václav Havel was born into a bourgeois family in 1936, the year before Thomas Garrigue Masaryk died, and two years before the death of Masaryk's creation, the First Czechoslovak Republic. Havel's grandfather, an enterprising builder, came to Prague from the Moravian town where Havel's friend Tom Stoppard was born; his father, a civil engineer turned architect and speculative builder, got into debt in the course of putting up one of Prague's prettiest residential suburbs, above the River Vltava, and he was popular enough with his workforce to retain a managerial job in the theatre and leisure complex he had built in town, even after the communist takeover. The cosseted 'master's son' grew up, first in Prague, then in Moravia, with a feeling of undeserved privilege: 'It may seem paradoxical,' he writes in one of his letters from prison to his wife Olga, 'but I think that because of those early experiences I have always had a heightened sensitivity and aversion to various manifestations of social inequality, and to privilege in general.' This, together with his chubbiness ('I was just a well-fed piglet'), gave him a feeling of 'being a bit outside the order of things', which in turn made him prey to uncertainties about his place in the world, to the fear that there might be a fatal flaw in his character which justified his exclusion from the company of his less privileged schoolmates. But at the point where this self-portrait looks like becoming pure Oblomov, the 'Czech' element in his character prevails: his 'oddness' (he adds) is not only the source of his self-doubts, but also 'a lifelong wellspring of energies directed at continually improving my self-definition, . . . it is also a decisive force behind everything worthwhile I have managed to accomplish.' After forty years spent in the shadow of 'isms' – called now 'communism' or 'Marxism', then again 'socialism with a human face' or 'reálný socialismus' – he acknowledges in himself 'that traditional quality of the bourgeoisie [*měšt'-anstvo*], particularly in the era of liberalism, which is the ability to take risks, the courage to start all over again from nothing, the ever vital hope and *élan* to begin new enterprises.'

Because of his family's 'political profile', the formal schooling of 'the millionaire's son ended abruptly when he was fifteen. For the next four years he attended evening classes while working as a technician in a chemistry lab. In 1955 he published his first article and appeared for the first time as a public speaker, at a government-sponsored young writers' club. His applications for a place at the University of Prague and on a film course were turned down. Called up for military service, he was not allowed to finish an economics degree at the Technical High School. But in the army he wrote together with a friend a satirical play which turned out an embarrassing success. In 1959 he was taken on as a stagehand by Jan Werich, by then the Grand Old Man of the Czech theatre. When Werich died in October 1980, 'an isolated, sad, bitter and disaffected man, without faith and hope', Havel wrote to his wife Olga that he owed to him his first practical experience of the theatre as a socially and politically conscious institution; Werich's death 'was the definitive end of an era in Czech intellectual history'.

From the early nineteenth century onwards, the small popular theatres in Prague and in the provinces expressed the patriotic aspirations of the Czech people; in these theatres (often with amateur casts) the Czech language was cultivated in defiance of Austrian censorship; national pride and its historic roots were asserted in opposition to the Habsburg rule. By 1927, when Werich, together with his partner Jan Voskovec, took over the Liberated Theatre, the patriotic themes could be guyed and replaced by a mildly left-wing, anarchic form of humour: Voskovec's and Werich's energy and talent created what was probably the most influential and certainly the most popular of the many small theatres of the First Republic. They wrote, directed and staged their musical revues, acting the main parts stereotyped as chalk-faced surrealist pierrots, with Voskovec as the romantic, occasionally melancholy Don Quixote and Werich as Sancho Panza, romping through closely rhymed, topical dialogues and songs. All this came to an end in 1938, by decree not of the Germans but of their own government. After the war the Voskovec and Werich collaborative enterprise didn't have a real comeback, though their lyrics, set to superb jazz music by their own composer, Jaroslav Ježek, are alive in Prague to this day. Through Werich, Havel caught a glimpse of the ribald end of the intellectual life of the First Republic, and a little of this heritage has remained alive in the plays he wrote throughout the long years of single-party rule.

Government during those years was far from monolithic: conditions were determined by Soviet pressure, Western homiletics and 'dissident' protests – the only stable factor was the dreariness of everything affected by the mutual back-scratching ideology which ruled all. Havel joined neither the communists nor any other party. He remained his own man, yet he did so without retiring into privacy; he never seriously contemplated emigrating, as did many of the best writers around him. In 1960 he joined the Theatre on the Balustrade, initially as a stagehand. For that miniscule theatre and its sixty serried faithful attenders he wrote his first plays, beginning with *The Garden Party* (1963), which remains one of his best works. He soon acquired a reputation for speaking out on behalf of the anti-ideological 'view from below', in opposition to those who see the world 'from the balcony of official ideology.' In Olga Šplíchalová, whom he married in 1964, he found intelligent criticism and courageous support for his views, and much practical help in the theatre. In March 1968 – the Dubček era had just begun – he was elected chairman of a 'Circle of Independent Writers' within the official writers' union, and from that time onward 'the theme of opposition' (the title of his first major essay, of April 1968) has dominated his thinking. He seems to have been active in every group that protested against the violation of justice, appealing at all times to the country's own constitution and, after December 1977, to the Helsinki Agreement. In May–June 1968 he spent some weeks in the West, visiting a large number of Czech *émigré* writers; he returned to Prague at the height of the Dubček crisis. In the course of a 'long distance interview' he gave in 1985, he spoke with singular accuracy and lack of illusion of the mood and attitudes that led to the ignominious ending of the Prague Spring: this understanding informed his work as a 'dissident' and its culmination in the uprising of November 1989. During the first week of the Soviet-led invasion (21–7 August 1968), he contributed daily commentaries to the 'Free Radio' broadcasts from northern Bohemia, and a year later was charged with 'subversion of the Republic'. Now began his 'prohibited years.'

The judges who were obliged to try him were as conscious of the ludicrous nature of the charges against him as they were anxious to acquit him without inflicting too much loss of face on their political masters, and on several occasions Havel with great courtesy told them so. Among these tragicomical occasions was the 1976 trial of a pop group called 'The Plastic People of the Universe', whose crime consisted in their being a part of the illegal 'musical underground'. (One of them, a young Canadian called Paul Wilson, who had come to Prague to teach English, is the translator of *Letters to Olga*.) In January 1977, Havel, together with the philosopher Jan Patočka and Jiří Hajek, foreign minister in Dubček's cabinet, was arrested after founding Charter 77, the group whose members formed the core of the opposition throughout the years leading to the November uprising. In March 1978 Havel submitted a letter (signed by some 300 citizens) asking for the abolition of the death penalty; and in April of that year he was arrested as one of the founders of VONS, the Committee in Defence of the Unjustly Prosecuted (life of sorts imitating art, this contiguity of Inauguration and Liquidation is prefigured in *The Garden Party*).

Among the qualities Havel shares with Gandhi are a fascination with the law and an occasionally mischievous delight in telling the truth. Whenever he appeared in court he was defended by counsel, often with some skill, yet he took great pains to acquaint himself with the legalities of the indictment; and some of the best and most closely argued writings of this well-organized playwright are the texts of his speeches before the various courts he had to face. His bourgeois good manners were not the least effective of his weapons: 'Beware', wrote his friend, the late Heinrich Böll, 'here speaks a rebel, one of the dangerous kind, the gentle and courteous kind.' He rarely used invective. 'The Trial', a *feuilleton* addressed to the chief prosecutor, contains a passage aimed, characteristically, not at the court but at the *je-m'en-foutisme* of those who happen to be unaffected by it. On his way from the Plastic People trial he meets a friend, a film director, and tells him where he has been. Were they up on a drugs charge, the director asks. No, Havel replies, 'no drugs were involved, and then I tried to explain briefly what the trial was about. When I finished he shook his head and asked, "Well, and what else is happening?" Perhaps I am doing him an injustice, but at that moment I was seized by a feeling that this dear man belonged to a world with which I wish to have nothing in common ever again, a world – now listen carefully, Mr Prosecutor Kovařík, what's coming is a vulgarism! – of cocked-up life.'

Havel spent altogether almost six years in gaol, two of them doing hard labour, and with several months in solitary confinement. He was never tortured or under threat of execution; but, especially during his first period of imprisonment (1977), he lived under great psychic pressure. His resilience and self-discipline were remarkable. At first he thought life in gaol would provide him with copy for his plays, but he soon found that preserving his own equanimity and making the best of things for those around him took up most of his time and energy at the end of a gruelling day. Two of his friends were in the same gaol and occasionally he and they were able to talk to one another, but his daily contacts were with criminals and 'asocial elements' (he and Jiří Dienstbier, now foreign minister in Havel's cabinet, were given a week in solitary for helping an illiterate Gypsy to write a letter home). For three years his wife's and brother's letters and their visits – one hour every four months – were his only contacts with the outside world. But instead of falling prey to self-pity, he came to see his situation as a challenge to do what none of the characters in his plays succeeds in doing – to make his condition meaningful to himself, and help others to do likewise.

This is what the letters he wrote to his wife between June 1979 and September 1982 are about. He was allowed one letter a week, 'strictly confined to family affairs', its exact form prescribed: four pages, no underlinings or deletions, no descriptions of conditions in gaol, no foreign words or quotation marks, and no jokes (punishment is a serious matter!). Couched in an abstract and occasionally abstruse language ('If for instance I wanted to say "regime",

I would have to write "the socially manifest focus of non-self" or some such rubbish'), these letters are 'a cry for fidelity and constancy', they are his attempts 'to prevent a breakdown of [my] identity and continuity'.

3

As a boy of sixteen Havel discovered for himself the banned writings of the philosopher Jan Patočka (1907–77), a disciple and friend of Edmund Husserl and a student of Heidegger; later Havel came to know him personally. In December 1976, Patočka joined Havel and Jiří Hajek in founding Charter 77 as 'an association of real social tolerance, not merely an agreement for the exclusion of others.' Havel's last meeting with Patočka, a meeting which provided the theme of one of Havel's most moving essays, took place in Ruzyně prison while they were waiting to be cross-examined; two months later, after further interrogations, Patočka died of a cerebral stroke. Patočka conceived of human identity as constituted by 'a responsibility which is ours, at all times and everywhere', and which surrounds us, like the world, with an 'absolute horizon', and whose only real test is in adversity: this, it seems, is the main concept Havel took from his Socratic mentor.

Havel disclaims all authority as a philosopher; his speculations, he says, are no more than 'the testimony of one man in a particular situation, his inner murmurings'. Yet he is irresistibly drawn to the philosophical reflections that came his way in Patočka's 'unofficial seminars'. In one of his letters to his wife he tries to discover why a visit from her and his brother didn't go well. Each visit has its own special atmosphere (he writes), made up of the three people's moods, the events that came before and after the visit, their 'individual wills' and their 'collective will'. But all this is merely a 'physical preamble' to a 'higher order', an order determined by a 'collective spirit' with its own identity, integrity, continuity and mood. And this 'order of spirit' in turn is part of a higher order still, 'an order of Being', which transcends 'epochs, cultures, civilizations . . .' Will he (the reader, and perhaps Olga Havlová too, ask) never come down to earth? 'Every work of the spirit', he continues, 'is a small re-enactment of the miracle of Being, a small re-creation of the world', and this is especially true of those two spheres of collectivity that are peculiarly Havel's own, the theatre and politics. Moreover (the speculation, now turned metaphysical, continues), no work of the spirit is ever wholly lost, each is registered for ever in the memory of Being; so that every political act, grounded as it is in responsibility acknowledged or denied, is, like every artistic creation, registered in the spiritual experience of mankind as well as in the totality of Being of which mankind is a part. And though he adds, 'Our lives are known about', he is reluctant to call on a religious authority in support of that claim; moreover, his liberality of outlook allows him to recognize that most of his friends don't share 'the metaphysics' of that conviction.

The greatest challenge to his search for meaning didn't come from the powers-that-be, that increasingly absurd amalgam of Moscow, the Party and its police force, and the army. It came from his friends, who wondered whether his suffering (though he never called it that) was worthwhile, whether he would not be better advised to renege on his beliefs. Embarrassed by the publicity his imprisonment aroused in the West, 'the regime' (in effect the president, Husák) was eagerly looking for the least damaging way of releasing him. Would he like to go to America 'on a course of study of the New York theatre?' they asked. He knew that the slightest sign of recantation on his part would do the trick, and they almost succeeded. During the interview of 1985 (*Long Distance Interview*) he recalls his first short imprisonment eight years earlier:

> I didn't know what was happening outside; it was only by reading the [government-controlled] newspapers that I could follow the frenzied campaign waged against the Charter. I was disappointed in my investigators and even in my defence counsel. I was in a strange, almost psychotic turmoil of mind and feelings. I had the impression that, being one of the initiators of the Charter, I had injured a lot of people and brought terrible misfortune on them. I was taking upon myself an excessive responsibility, as though the others didn't know what they were doing, as though I alone were to blame. In this very unwholesome psychic disposition it gradually dawned on me at the end of my prison sentence that a trap was being set for me. Certain relatively harmless statements of mine – at least I thought them innocent at the time – in one of my appeals for remission were to be published in a corrupted form in order to discredit me.

In one of the last of these letters to his wife (25 July 1982), from his third and longest period in gaol, he comments unsparingly on this appeal for remission which he had written during his first imprisonment:

> Of course, I knew that whether or not I'd be released would be decided by things which had nothing to do with whether or not I wrote the appropriate request. Well – the interrogation was getting nowhere, and it seemed proper to use the opportunity and let myself be heard. I wrote my request in a way that at the time seemed very tactical and cunning: while saying nothing that I didn't think or that wasn't true, I simply 'overlooked' the fact that truth lies not only in what is said but also in who says it, and to whom, why and how and under what circumstances it is expressed. Thanks to this minor 'oversight' (more accurately: this minor self-deception), what I said came – as it were by chance – dangerously close to what the addressee wanted to hear. What was particularly absurd was my motive in this manœuvre, at least my conscious and admitted motive. It was not the hope that it would lead to anything, but merely a kind of professionally intellectual and somewhat

perverse delight in what I thought of as my 'honourable cleverness'. (To complete the picture I should add that, when I re-read it some years later, the 'honour' in that cleverness made my hair stand on end.)

This episode and his understanding of it as an act of betrayal formed one of the fundamental experiences of Havel's life. The experience is incorporated in at least two of his plays, *Largo Desolato* (1985) and in the Faust play, *Temptation* (1986). But his self-understanding is also relevant to his political tactics. Here lies the source of his tolerance – particularly striking among Central European intellectuals – toward those who have succumbed to such temptations; and this tolerance (so different from the attitude of his persecutors, but also of the 'reformists' of Eastern Germany) would in due course be recognized by 'the people' as legitimating his authority to lead them. From its very beginning, Charter 77 insisted that, as Professor Patočka put it with unwonted succinctness, 'This is not a battle, this is a war!' The Chartists' aims were not single 'demos' and isolated 'actions', but the continuous unrelenting work of enlightening people about their rights and duties; and from this enlightenment nobody willing to participate was to be excluded.

This is Havel's 'Post-Modernism': in an age still governed by Manichaean politics, he refused to accept the Western view that the country was divided into 'dissidents' – people concerned to secure freedom primarily for themselves – and the rest of the population, which was waiting to see how things would turn out for 'the dissidents' before venturing out into the streets – those streets of Prague 'in which [Havel writes] on a Saturday night the only people you met were five secret policemen, five illegal currency dealers and three drunks'. (The rest of the population sat at home, watching West German television.)

Here is the element of fiction I mentioned earlier: Havel had no illusions about how things were, yet he acted and wrote (for instance in his letter of May 1975, addressed to 'Dear Dr Husák') as though the public were waiting to be won over to the side of justice and freedom; as though the 'dissidents' and 'the people' were one. Conscious of the film of lies that had covered national life throughout four decades, he didn't play the moral simpleton. Yet his quiet, unhysterical indictment of the regime was undertaken on behalf of 'the people' no less than on behalf of his fellow-dissidents, and it was founded on the belief that people who lie can be made to recognize the truth and speak it. There was that week in August 1968 (essay 19) when he took an active part in the resistance against the invasion in one of the few towns that had stood out and for a while at least had remained unoccupied. The experience taught him that 'we never know what possibilities are dormant in the soul of the populace. A whole nation, acting out Švejkian tactics at one time, can bravely oppose a foreign power a year later . . . and another twelvemonth after that can plunge into an abyss of demoralization with the speed of lightning.' He didn't and doesn't delude himself into thinking that there aren't worse crimes than lies, or that die-hard ideologists and power-seekers can be turned into liberal democrats. But all the rest, including the trimmers and the

Vicars of Bray, can be reclaimed for the common weal. This belief is his strength; and one's fervent hope is that a situation will not arise in which it turns out to be his weakness.

This is a philosophy in which 'the lightness of Being' is anything but 'unbearable'. It is the heavy, bloodstained theory behind Marxist revolutionary politics (the politics of *Darkness at Noon*) that is shown up for the self-seeking farce it really was (and in some parts of our world still is). Once the great heroic invasion of 1968 was completed and Husák's tough new regime installed, the protesting writers met for a last time and decided to publish a last proclamation, 'a sort of solemn testament addressed to the nation', and Havel was chosen to draft it. A tiny room was found for him at the Prague Film Club, and he set to work. However, unfortunately, at that very hour he was meant to open a painter friend's exhibition,

> not with a serious address, you know, but just with some verses and songs. It was my friend's dadaist wish, because he loved my out-of-tune singing of patriotic songs and my heartfelt recitation of our national classics ... And, believe it or not, I actually managed to do both: pretending I had to go to the lavatory, I fled from the room where I was composing the historic manifesto of Czech artists, got to the exhibition, did my songs and recitation in front of a shocked public, instantly dashed back to the Film Club and managed to write the last paragraph ... Don't you think it's characteristic that in this country the gloomy historic events which are our lot and which we try to stand up to honourably, at a price of sacrifices others find hard to understand, are organically linked with our traditional irony and self-irony, with our sense for the absurd, or with a sense of humour that looks for no purpose outside itself or, contrariwise, our black humour?

The playwright Václav Havel provides some of these links.

4

'Co se stalo?' 'What's happened?' Time and again, one of Havel's plays or the peripateia of a scene is introduced by that question. It marks the moment when the life of an individual or of a family has been disrupted by a sudden *ukaz* from above, an order that is pointless yet unignorable. And even though 'what happens' hardly ever takes the form of what has been expected, and occasionally the answer to the question is, 'Nothing, nothing at all', from that moment on everything is senselessly different. In the flat of a 'dissident', the secret police are expected, and instead friends come, or a couple of political sympathizers, and their importunate arrival, encouraging patter and well-intended demands, brings with it disruptions which seem worse than any havoc the police may wreak (*Largo Desolato*). In *The Garden Party* a friend who is well in with the authorities, and has promised to fix things for the son of the family, is expected but doesn't come, and instead his secretary arrives, and reads out a series of telegrams interlarded with her plans for a weekend excursion with friends. Some time later the son, Hugo, turns up after all, but now that he has got the job the family friend promised (having meanwhile ousted the family friend from his place in the nomenklatura), the father thinks he will be too grand to talk to them – and indeed, Hugo is so grand that he isn't their son any more but someone quite different, and of course the garden party where the deal was struck wasn't a garden party at all but an anxious get-together where everybody watched everybody else, hoping for preferment or fearing demotion. The job Hugo has secured in the Inauguration Service involves him in the ceremonial opening of the Department of Liquidation – and *its* first job is to liquidate the Inauguration Service, while its *next* job is to liquidate itself, all under Hugo's direction. 'How suicidal our happiness can be!' says Kafka's official – the Inaugurator about to liquidate the case against K. – at the end of *The Castle*.

Life in this society is governed by the mutual back-scratching ideology I have mentioned, the simplest version of which is shown in *The Audience* (1975). The play was occasioned by Havel's own time as an unskilled labourer in a provincial brewery, a job he took mainly because it was a convenient and uncompromising way of making a living. The characters have it all worked out to a T: the working-class Head Maltster will help Vaněk (a playwright doing his punitive stint in the brewery) to secure a cushy job in the dispatch office, in return for which Vaněk will help the Maltster to write the weekly report on his (Vaněk's) doings, by means of which the Maltster will placate his friend, Tonda Mašek, who stood by him when he was about to be tried for theft, whereas Mašek needs the report in order to keep the authorities sweet, because . . . Alas, this perfect mechanism fails to work, because Vaněk won't co-operate, *because* he has 'principles'. This is the cue for the Maltster's Great Speech, and in the whole of Bertolt Brecht's work there is nothing like it. Here speaks the anger and pain of the working man who feels himself condemned to perpetual inferiority by his lack of education and by his very language. He must do without the intellectual's la-di-da words, but even so he knows how to ram home his point:

> Now you wouldn't mind my getting you a warm spot in the storeroom, would you? But when it comes to taking on a bit of this muck I have to wade in every day – no sir! You're all very clever, you've got it all figured out, haven't you? You really know how to take care of your own lot! *Principles!* Of course you've got to protect them, those principles of yours – because you know how to cash in on them, because you're sure to get a good price for them, they're your bread and butter, those principles – but what about me? . . . Nobody's ever going to look after me, nobody's afraid of me, nobody's going to write about me . . . You'll go back to your actresses one day – you're going to show off to them how you

rolled out the barrels – you'll be a hero – but what about me? What do you think I've got to go back to? Who's ever going to appreciate what I've done? What have I got out of life? What's in store for me?

Isn't that a speech to tear a hole in the motley, a genuine, even moving challenge to the 'master's son' by one of the underprivileged? So it is, except that no sooner has the speech been delivered than it is drowned in a crate of lager and forgotten – and the play can begin all over again.

In *The Conspirators* (1971), Havel's only dramatic reference to anti-Semitism and the Slánský trials of 1952, it's not a cushy job in the warm storeroom that is at stake but the Fate of a Nation. When the conspirators meet (the attorney-general is named after the man who prosecuted Havel in what one hesitates to call 'real life', and there is an illiterate censor), each of the four men hopes he will lead the nation in the coming revolution, and the woman (who is or has been the mistress of three of them) encourages each in turn; then each pretends that he thinks one of the others is better qualified for the great task, and again the caballing leads nowhere: it is as though it had never been, and the play ends where it began. What fascinates Havel here is not the 'political problem' – these are not Shavian or Brechtian 'problem plays' – but the self-generated movement of human relations (Act 1: A:B = C:D, Act 2: A:D = B:C, etc.). This sounds a pretty arid formula, yet the plays work, because the problem-parodies they contain are pushed to a point of 'absurdity compounded by absurdity' (the phrase is Tom Stoppard's), involving both assertions and losses of identity so complete and so contradictory as to be comic. *The Mountain Resort* (1976) takes this idea as far as it will go (and perhaps a little further). Not just Rosencrantz and Guildenstern, but nine characters with interchangeable indentities are presented, whose Pavlovian reaction (every time the train passes they glance at their wrist-watches) is the only thing they have in common with each other and with what they were an hour or two before. As two more people – the hotel manager and his assistant – are introduced, the scenes get shorter and shorter, dialects, saws and memories float freely from one 'character' to the next, answers precede questions, convictions are swapped, identities melt and collapse – the ending is like Madame Tussaud's wax-works on fire.

The loss of personal identity – Havel's central theme with numerous variations – works particularly well when characters are placed in the service of some cause nobody is allowed to reveal as pointless, or of some expectation everybody knows to be absurd. 'Ptydepe', the artificial language constructed on the principle of maximum redundancy, which is the subject of *The Memorandum* (1966), doesn't work, not only because it is absurdly cumbersome, but also because, however idiotically abstract its words, they acquire, as they were bound to, emotive connotations and contextual undertones, just like any 'unscientific', ordinary language. So the *ukaz* which made Ptydepe the compulsory medium of inter-departmental communication is revoked, and everybody who was involved in teaching it – a whole bureaucratic 'machinery' – is discredited and demoted. But no sooner does this happen than 'Chorukor', another artificial language, constructed on the opposite principle of minimal redundancy, is introduced. Why? As an assertion of bureaucratic power? But whose power?

The machinery that is at work here is of course that of 'the Party', which (a little like the authorities that are said to be at work in the Castle in Kafka's novel) is everywhere and nowhere, and the metamorphosis that goes with power is total: the office boy who becomes the director of a nationalized enterprise assumes the outlook and the jargon of the director he has displaced, at least while he is lording it over everybody. But unlike the powers ascribed to the bureaucrats of Kafka's Castle, this power isn't in the least mysterious: instead it is negotiable, and most of the characters know it to be so. The mimesis of these tragicomedies is perfect: the 'Party' (and other self-propelling, self-purposive constructs like it) is the most convenient because the most readily available representative of social entropy or (to use Havel's own, simpler term), of 'the world of cocked-up life'. As to the relevance of this entropic construct to our national and multinational institutions, the reader or member of the audience is left to draw his own conclusions.

In some ways these characters resemble the figurines of bar football; they all look alike, but if you get close you will see that they are all a little different, each knocked about and damaged in a different place. Nobody is wholly truthful, though almost everybody has a moment of weakness which is also his or her moment of truth. Time and again one of these figures delivers the Great Speech which is meant to sum it all up, like Hamlet's 'To be, or not to be', or Lucky's 'Given the existence as uttered forth in the public works of Puncher and Wattmann', or the Professional Orator's platitudes in *The Chairs* by Ionesco. And as often as not these speeches turn out to be replicas of the weighty pronouncements of the Great Socialist Panjandrums, the Marxes and Engelses, the Blochs and Lukácses, full of veiled threats and abstract promises, signifying very little. Is there then in the world of Havel's plays nothing that is to be taken seriously? Sex? When not in the service of distraction or professional advancement, it leads to ludicrous disappointment or disaster. True community? The only place where you can find it is in the queue outside the office canteen, whose themes of discourse range from roast goose to goulash.

As Marketa Goetz-Stankiewicz has shown in her splendid study *The Silenced Theatre* (1979), 'Vašek' Havel has kept company with a whole bevy of playwrights with similar aims and similar dramatic resources. What is original about his tragicomedies is the single-mindedness with which he places all human relations inside socio-political brackets. Outside these brackets there is a sign saying, 'Beware, farce!', and around them there is another set of brackets and another sign, which says, 'This is serious, because, though it shouldn't be, this is how life passes here.' But as you read that last sentence it grows more faint, until it becomes (to use a word for which Havel has a special penchant) 'metaphysical'. Cheerfulness is always breaking in: absurdity is an absence of meaning, an absence which, in this theatre, is 'inseparable from the experience of meaning'. And the only way to escape all those brackets is to escape life; though that happens only once, in Havel's latest play, *Restoration* (1988), in the Oblomov character who takes his own life.

5

What does the future hold? Will the good-tempered new life last? Havel's relative lack of a historical background may limit him as a playwright, but in the context of the country's social memory it is a blessing in disguise. Of course, he *knows* the national mythopoeia well enough (the liturgy of the great national names, from John Hus through John Amos Comenius to T. G. Masaryk) but, unlike Milan Kundera, he rejects the *kitschig* notion that appeals to myth as a substitute for political action. He rejects the 'small country syndrome' that has led the Czechs and Slovaks more than once into deep unhappiness, into an abrogation of the communal spirit, fear inviting oppression, oppression inviting revenge. Public misery and withdrawal into timid privacy have been the hallmarks of their history on many occasions throughout the last four centuries. Can a country free itself from its traumatic past by a single act of self-liberation? Possibly. After all, history is 'us' as well as 'them'. There is no law of history that condemns a people to perpetual darkness. In the dark years following the destruction of the First Republic, the grave mistakes which preceded that destruction dropped out of the national memory; the monstrosity of the Third Reich obscured the fact that long before Hitler came on the scene Czechoslovakia had no adequate German policy; and the long nightmare of communism created the myth of an unblemished haven of liberty and fairness. Yet the image of a decent democracy, unique in a region of Europe unpropitious to such things, wasn't all *PR*: enough of Masaryk's democratic heritage survives for the new republic to build on, and its beginnings are encouraging enough. On his first official visit abroad President Havel went to both parts of Germany, and he wasn't exactly courting popularity in his homeland when, in the course of that visit, he announced the formation of a commission of inquiry into the expulsion of the Sudeten Germans: true, it was an act of surprising political skill and self-assurance; but more than that, it reflected his great moral courage. Together with complete and partial amnesties for all prisoners except murderers and rapists, the proposal to establish diplomatic relations with Israel, an invitation to the Pope to visit the country, an invitation to Frank Zappa to make a film in Prague (presumably in the Barrandov studios in the suburb, the building of which once nearly bankrupted Havel's father) and plans for a sort of Central European summit meeting with the Hungarians and the Poles in Bratislava, the Slovak capital – this is not a bad record for a presidency in its first flush. A single man, however charismatic, cannot ensure that the decencies of a single moment can be perpetuated into an era. Still, Václav Havel, helped by his fiction, can do a lot.

1990

25

Canetti's Later Work

1

A remarkable air of self-confidence informs the work of Elias Canetti. Long before the old men of Stockholm bestowed their accolade on him (in 1981), he wrote with the authority of one determined to make his readers take him at his own valuation: he saw himself as a major German author of his time, which is the half-century since 1935, when *Die Blendung* (*Auto da Fé*), his only novel, appeared. Whether or not it is justified, such overt self-confidence is unusual among his contemporaries. Some of the best of them, in Central Europe at all events, were beset by profound doubts about themselves, their calling and its relevance in an age which saw the rise of the Third Reich, the defeat of European humanism, the Second World War and its aftermath. Even Bertolt Brecht, little given to public self-doubt or literary self-deprecation, questions (in the most famous of the *Svendborg Poems* of 1939) any man's right to equanimity in an age when

> A talk about trees is almost a crime
> Because it implies silence about
> So many horrors.

Canetti understands and occasionally shares such doubts. In *The Conscience of Words* (a collection of fifteen mainly literary essays and addresses written between 1964 and 1975, published in English in 1986), there is an essay, 'The Poet's Profession', on the question of what justifies our contemporaries in devoting their life to literature. It cannot be the sheer love of writing – 'formulation as an end in itself' – which he rejects as 'mere literary vanity'. It must be something more weighty, 'for, in reality, no man can today be a writer, a *Dichter*, if he does not seriously doubt his right to be one'; and Canetti goes on to quote an anonymous diarist (it may have been the Berlin poet Oskar Loerke) who wrote ten days before the outbreak of the Second World War: 'But everything is over. If I were really a poet, I would have to be able to prevent the war.' Paying homage to the sense of responsibility that makes a poet commit himself to such a noble illusion, Canetti offers an interpretation of those moving words: 'It is precisely this irrational claim to responsibility that gives me pause to think and captivates me. One would also have to add that words, deliberate and used over and over again, misused words, led to the situation in which the war became inevitable.' The original lament – 'Es ist aber alles vorüber' – contained no such explanation. Setting up a causal connection between 'misused words' and 'war', Canetti is following in the footsteps of Karl Kraus, to whom he devotes two of the essays in *The Conscience of Words*. The claim that words are the causes of deeds – and the only causes the satirist is interested in – provides the theoretical foundation for the satirical element in Kraus's work, and satire, unlike the anonymous *cri de coeur*, is involved in fiction. But if the causality set up between words and deeds is at least partly fictitious (a truth plus a vast exaggeration of what happens in the world), the conception of 'responsibility', too, becomes a fiction, a metaphor rather than a literal truth, leaving the writer's – Kraus's *or* Canetti's – self-confidence unimpaired.

The point of these remarks is not to question the seriousness of Canetti's ambitious literary undertaking, but to introduce the thought that it is cast in arguments, and that the majority of these arguments – in his essays and reflections and even more so in his *magnum opus* – live just such uneasy lives in the uncharted territory between extended metaphor and literal truth, between fiction and fact. The complex and fascinating edifice of *Masse und Macht (Crowds and Power)* (1960), which Canetti regards as his most important contribution to twentieth-century thought, reminds one of the complex and fascinating edifices of M. C. Escher. The first impression one receives from either *œuvre* is of a detailed, painstaking realism, but this impression soon gives way to the recognition that nothing here works quite the way it does in ordinary life: perspectives deceive, clouds turn into birds, leaves into frogs, embryos into corpses, spheres into hollows. But whereas in Escher all this happens through the deliberations of irony, sophisticated parody and wit, Canetti's constructs defy realism not by design but by inadvertency.

2

Crowds and Power is a huge and, after its own fashion, systematic inquiry into human conduct, its biological, zoological and anthropological origins and/or parallels, its psychopathological oubliettes, the social and moral values it exhibits and the catastrophic consequences it entails – and all this astonishing collection of true insights and oddities is both sustained and vitiated by its mixed status on the borderline between the fictional-metaphorical and the literal-empirical. Conversely, Canetti's novel *Auto da Fé* contains scenes in which the fictional guise is torn asunder by an authorial loathing that reveals moments of horrifying, matter-of-fact cruelty. The book may well be, as John

Bayley has called it, an 'attempt at an intellectual imagination of the true nature of the twentieth century', though it is very far from being 'the most remarkable' of such attempts. But to speak of it as 'an apotheosis of the immensely weighty and serious Faust tradition of German letters' is to mistake Goethe's *Faust* for one of those latter-day 'Faustian' abstractions – among them, Spengler's *Decline of the West* – which may have influenced Canetti. Almost thirty years after *Auto da Fé*, in the essay 'Power and Survival' (1962), included in *The Conscience of the Words*, Canetti wrote: 'Among the most sinister phenomena in intellectual history is the avoidance of the concrete.' *Auto da Fé* is a book about life 'lived in the head' – it was Canetti's friend, Hermann Broch, who saved him from the vulgarity of calling its hero 'Kant' – and abstraction may not be its dominant mode. But the book does pose the question by what margin it succumbs to the dangers it describes.

In a morning newspaper of 15 July 1927 Canetti, then a twenty-two year-old student of chemistry in Vienna, read of the acquittal, by a Viennese jury, of a number of right-wing thugs who had attacked working-class demonstrators, killing a disabled war veteran and a child. In protest against this acquittal, the workers of Vienna downed tools and converged on the Palace of Justice in the Ringstrasse. Despite attempts by a few social-democratic leaders to pacify the crowd, extremists entered the building and set fire to it, while other demonstrators prevented the firemen from getting at the flames. Police opened fire and in the ensuing massacre, which lasted until the evening, they killed eighty-eight people, including children and passers-by; and, forcing their way into the hospitals, they manhandled some of the doctors who were tending the wounded. Canetti followed the crowd on his bicycle. The burning of the Justizpalast was the seminal experience of his life, and he has presented it as such more than once. In its two aspects – the fire and the crowd – it is the biographical occasion and literary source of *Auto da Fé* and *Crowds and Power* respectively. The event was the provider of Canetti's central imagery – the connection between crowd and fire is one of his recurrent themes:

Of all means of destruction, *fire* is the most impressive. It can be seen from afar and it attracts ever more people. It destroys irrevocably; nothing after a fire is as it was before. A crowd setting fire to something feels irresistible. So long as the fire spreads, everyone will join it. Everything hostile will be destroyed. The fire is the strongest symbol we have of the crowd. After the destruction, crowd and fire die away.

The principal interest and strength of *Crowds and Power* derive from the book's precise analyses of the physical phenomenon – the very feel – of human crowds. (The German word, *die Massen*, is more expressive and carries the connotation of anonymity and evil more surely than does the English.) What we are given here is a series of functional descriptions – a sort of phenomenology – of the human condition under the aspect of crowds: their density or looseness, whether they are moving or at rest, aimless or directed by a leader, led by a pack or driven on by it, surrounded or surrounding, organized or thronging in chaos, festive or lamenting, intent on increase or on destruction, calm and patiently waiting or spreading panic like wildfire: the variations seem almost endless, the only kind that is not mentioned is the happy, carefree crowd. Of 'the method' Canetti uses in elaborating his central insight it can be said that it enables him to present *die Massen* without deciding on their actual status, as an archetypal phenomenon from which an astonishing variety of human activities are to be inferred or extrapolated: indeed, the tacit implication is at hand that the totality of human conduct is to be accounted for in this way.

3

Even though the writings of Gustave Le Bon and especially of Ortega y Gasset on the function of crowds in modern Europe were very much part of the mid-European intellectual atmosphere (though they are not mentioned in Canetti's book), the decision to choose what may be called the phenomenological method and to apply it to his central image or concept is largely original. The method itself, however, places the book squarely in the context of that philosophical anthropology which, in the wake of Herder, of Kant's *Anthropology with a Pragmatic Intent* and of Husserl, formed one of the major schools on the German philosophical scene between the wars. (Again, no acknowledgement of this is made in Canetti's book.) Mercifully undramatic, not given to startling vatic pronouncements and free from political influences or consequences, 'philosophical anthropology' is a movement which has not, as far as I know, had much of a following outside Germany. It aims to answer the question 'What is man?' by considering the actual ways in which our organism as well as our intentions and drives relate to the human environment; or, attempting to bridge the Cartesian gulf between body and soul, philosophical anthropology relates our states of mind to our vital powers and through them to our being in the world; or again, it investigates the ways in which man in his status of 'defective creature' compensates for his vulnerability and 'openness to the world'. All such inquiries proceed by reflecting on data which derive from our concrete and sensuous experience of the 'life-world' that surrounds us and of which we are a part. Kurt Stavenhagen's seminar in Göttingen in 1947 on 'the phenomenon of physical revulsion', known among his students as 'das Ekelseminar', is a case in point: the aim was to show how our feelings of revulsion in the presence of mud, serried crowds of people or herds of animals and some invertebrates arise at the point where we expect to touch or see hard and firmly delimited single things, but instead come into contact with a soft, inchoate, indistinct mass or mess of things.

Canetti's section on man's postures, repeated in a slightly shortened form in the essay 'Power and Survival', provides a vivid example of the fascination the method yields, as well as the limitations of his use of it. Each of our postures – standing, sitting, lying, squatting and kneeling – is seen in terms of its vulnerability: that is, in its relationship to the threat of death. 'Man's pride in standing consists in being free and needing no support,' we read, and: 'A man lying is a man disarmed . . . [so much so] that it is impossible to understand how human kind has managed *to survive* sleep' (Canetti's italics); 'Squatting expresses an absence of needs, a turning in on oneself'; and 'kneeling is a gesture of supplication for mercy . . . [It] is always a rehearsing of a last moment, even if in reality something quite different is involved.' The claim that man is the most vulnerable of creatures, a claim which is elaborated in many parts of Canetti's book, is central to the writings of the 'philosophical anthropologists'.

The trouble with these picturesque arguments is that the reduction of such postures to an 'essential' or 'fundamental' meaning which is then generalized simply doesn't work (for example, there is no 'fundamental' sense in which the accused who is made to stand facing the court is 'free', or superior to the sitting judge). Their meanings, like the meanings of most other phenomena assembled in *Crowds and Power*, are bound to be determined by the contexts – social, moral or whatever – in which they occur, that is, by something other than the 'inherent' or 'natural' qualities of the postures themselves: but Canetti's arguments leave no room for such contexts. Thus when he repeatedly expresses his conviction that any man's 'real' or 'true' or 'essential' first reaction in the presence of another's death is a feeling of satisfaction and relief (a view which in any less serious writer one would take to be a piece of smart-alec cynicism), this is, in this scheme of things, not a disconnected opinion. On the contrary, it is an illustration of Canetti's view that the act of standing is a sign of strength entailing satisfaction, and that, in the presence of a body lying prone *and therefore* defenceless on the ground, satisfaction is joined by a feeling of relief – relief at not being the body on the ground. But why, to one side of such 'anthropological' inferences, should satisfaction and relief in the presence of the dead be a truer or more fundamental attitude than sorrow? Why should sorrow always be 'fundamentally' an expression of fear of not being 'the survivor'? And how is one to decide what meaning to give to the claim that one view rather than the other is right?

To conclude that Canetti's use of the method of philosophical anthropology is uncritical – that is, unphilosophical – is to advert to the fact that at no point in the book does he (or indeed, more surprisingly, Iris Murdoch in her enthusiastic review of 1962) show any interest in providing a validation for his insights and claims. Relying (presumably) on the evidence of a certain kind of robust and aggressive common sense, the book contains no truth-criteria by which to assess its arguments. It was Kant – not Kien, the central character of *Auto da Fé* – who observed that there is nothing wrong with the appeal to common sense so long as that appeal is not challenged.

Our common-sense perception that in a crowd men are apt to behave differently from the way they behave when on their own – Canetti's experience at the burning of the Justizpalast – is radicalized to the point where *die Masse* is seen as the normal condition of existence. The reaction against Freudian psychology, seen as the analysis of individuals, is obvious. More interestingly, it is the European experience of crowd-manipulation, in Mussolini's Italy and especially in the Third Reich, that provides the undertone of the entire book, and becomes explicit in two essays, 'Hitler, According to Speer' and 'The Arch of Triumph' (1971), in *The Conscience of Words*. The two essays offer powerful illumination of and insight into aspects of Hitler's personality and rule, aspects which many historians and sociologists have ignored. However, the Hitlerian experience as Canetti describes it does not provide a political paradigm. Crowds function in a politically effective manner only when they have intuited some values and goals. And those intuited by politically effective crowds in Germany at that time, though they were appropriated by National Socialism, were accepted largely because they belonged to a traditionally legitimated German and European ethos. Of those values and goals and of that ethos we hear nothing in Canetti's account, so that we get the impression that crowds form spontaneously, without a common belief, without any purpose other than conquest and its complement, destruction. This was not true even of Hitler's Germany, where other motives too were at work; in almost any other political situation Canetti's account offers even less illumination. Political parties are always seen as warring 'double crowds'. 'The Essence of the Parliamentary System' is defined as the immunity of the House of Commons from the violent death which such crowds aim to inflict on each other: a remote historical origin is identified with 'the essence' or 'true nature' of a complex modern practice. But origins and essences of such remoteness 'explain' everything in general and nothing in particular. 'A simile that has been absorbed into the forms of our language,' writes Wittgenstein, 'produces a false appearance, and this disquiets us. "But *this* isn't how it is!" – we say.'

4

Why is 'the crowd' as Canetti presents it always evil, potentially destructive, threatening death or suffering it? What precisely is the relationship between all those many, often very lengthy episodes and myths he quotes from the papers and journals of anthropologists and explorers, on the one hand, and our modern Western experience, on the other? Are these episodes to serve as parallels to and illustrations of our conduct, or as accounts of its origins, or again as rudimentary prefigurations of it? Why is power seen always in its relationship to the crowd? Why is all power whatever seen as evil, concerned only with dealing death to others in order to ensure survival of the self? Why is survival always an outliving that entails the death of others? And what is the ontological status of Canetti's *Masse* – when does it cease to be an actual crowd and become a metaphor?

These are Hobbesian themes and questions. Indeed, Thomas Hobbes is almost the only philosopher mentioned by name, and the only one spoken of with modified approval, in *The Human Province* (first published in 1973), a collection of aphorisms and reflections from Canetti's notebooks, most of them written while he was working on *Crowds and Power*. (It is mainly Hobbes's longevity that Canetti admires.) Yet Hobbes's criticism of writers who use 'metaphors, tropes and other rhetorical figures, instead of words proper', has left no trace in Canetti's writings; and it is one of the lacunae of this idiosyncratic author that although he spent his formative years in the Vienna of the 1920s, he shows no interest whatever in the critical linguistic philosophy that was going on there throughout that time. Iris Murdoch writes, 'Canetti has done what philosophers ought to do, and what they used to do: he has provided us with new concepts', yet she never asks what need these new concepts are intended to supply. She never asks whether phrases like 'the fundamental nature of power', or 'a man's *true* reaction', or 'the essential feeling' – phrases which tend to be used when disclosures of a disagreeable or humanly discreditable kind are introduced – amount to more than strong personal opinions energetically expressed. Given his great skill in making up a terminology that will serve his obsession, and the facility of German for the expression of such a skill, the absence of truth-criteria gives free play to the erstwhile novelist's imagination.

Among the unnumbered sections of *Crowds and Power* there is one entitled 'The Forms of Survival', which I take to typify Canetti's procedure. The scientific statement with which the section opens is immediately framed with an evaluative hypothesis and followed by one of his insistent claims to originality:

> The earliest event in every man's life, occurring long before birth and surely of greater importance, is his conception; and this process has never yet been considered under the important aspect of survival. We already know a great deal – indeed pretty well everything – about what happens once the spermatozoon has penetrated into the egg cell. Scarcely any thought, however, has been given to the fact that there are an overwhelming number of spermatazoa *which do not reach their goal*, even though they play an active part in the process of generation as a whole.

I have italicized the anthropomorphic part of the argument, which, taken literally, leads on to the analogy upon which this entire excursus into genetics is based. The passage continues:

> It is not a single spermatozoon which sets out for the egg cell. It is about 200 million. All of them are expelled together in a single ejaculation and then in a single mass they move together toward one goal. Thus their number is immense. Since they come into existence through partition, they are all equal; their density could hardly be greater, and they all have one and the same goal. It will be remembered that these four traits [partition, equality, great density and singleness of goal] have been described as the essential attributes of the crowd.

And then, with some unease, the methodology is invoked: 'It is unnecessary to point out that a crowd consisting of spermatozoa cannot be the same as a crowd of people. But an analogy between the two phenomena, *and perhaps more* than a mere analogy, is *undoubtedly* given.' It is hard to know how seriously to take an arguement which relies for conviction on the ambiguities I have emphasized, or its sequel:

> All these spermatozoa perish, either on the way to the goal or in its immediate vicinity. One single seed alone penetrates the egg cell, and this seed may very well be described as a survivor. It is, so to speak, their leader, who has succeeded in achieving what every leader, either secretly or openly, hopes for: which is to survive all those he leads. To such a survivor, one out of 200,000,000, every human being owes its 'existence'.

By now the free-floating analogy has moved into the centre of the argument and starts pretending it has become a proof.

Such passages make it difficult to avoid an obvious association with the 'genetic' metaphors in Hitler's *Mein Kampf*, with that leader's penchant for phoney analogies and relish for loaded images of doom. Whatever their overt purpose, all naturalistic arguments derived from *Sozialdarwinismus* end up offering 'scientific' grounds for 'inevitable' destruction and thereby reducing the area of human responsibility in favour of the operations of some biological mechanism. This is a matter not only of retrospective criticism but of contemporary concern. Can we really rest content with designating Freud or Lévi-Strauss – or Nietzsche, for that matter – as mythopœicists? The uncritical use of 'anthropological' fictions, our heritage from the troubled 1920s and 1930s, has acquired a new academic respectability: now as then we are surrounded by enquiries in which metaphors replace theory and analogies explanation. Anyone intent on doing away with distinctions between fiction and philosophy should read *Crowds and Power* to see what discord follows.

5

In a notebook entry for 1948, included in *The Human Province*, Canetti writes:

> How many credible utterances of hope and goodness we would have to find, to balance those of bitterness and doubt we have thrown around so generously! Who can dare think of death knowing he has only increased the sum of bitterness, albeit from the best motives? Had one always kept silent, one could at least die. But one wanted to be heard and one shouted out loud. Now it's time to say the other thing and yet be heard, for it cannot be shouted.

And again, in an entry for 1952: 'he thinks in amazement of that period in his life when he dashed off his characters with hatred and bitterness.' This is one of many reflections which suggest a change in Canetti's attitude. Throughout his career he has been deeply concerned with death. *Auto da Fé* and *Crowds and Power* (and two minor satirical plays *à la* Karl Kraus) are dominated by a spirit of obsession; in the later writings a spirit of reconciliation prevails.

Reconciliation to what? At no point does Canetti reconcile himself to death. Throughout he upholds a spirit of protest: unlike Freud, for instance, he regards death, not as 'natural, inevitable, the necessary conclusion of all life', but in the manner of the Psalmist and the Gospels, as an abomination.

The reconciliation in Canetti's writings from the end of the war onwards is not with death but with humanity that must suffer it: protesting against the idea of its unavoidability makes us ashamed of our death-dealing sentiments, and brings to the fore some that are less shameful. His formulation of what, in these mortal circumstances of ours, will stand the test of experience and remain valuable is careful, and is worth careful attention, because it takes into consideration much that might be said *against* all affirmations of value:

> With the growing awareness that we are perched on a heap of corpses, human and animal, that our self-confidence actually feeds on the sum of those we have survived – with this rapidly spreading awareness we find it harder and harder to reach any solution we would not be ashamed of. It is impossible to turn away from life, whose value and expectation we always feel. But it is equally impossible not to live on the death of other creatures, whose value and expectation are no less than ours . . .
>
> The good fortune of relating to a remoteness, on which all traditional religions feed, can no longer be ours . . .
>
> The Beyond is within us; a grave piece of knowledge, this, but it is trapped inside us. This is the great and unbridgeable chasm in modern man; for the mass grave of creatures is within us too.

Unlike the fee-fi-fo-fumming of the Existentialists, such reflections take no pride in our predicament. Canetti fully understands the pitfalls of the 'death-where-is-thy-sting-aling-aling' mentality, of the Rilkean transformation of lament into praise. Yet there are, in *The Human Province*, surprising affinities with Rilke's thinking.

The only positive value mentioned in *Crowds and Power* was the human capacity for 'transformation' or 'metamorphosis'. Here again one may point to the philosophical anthropologists, who, in Gladys Bryson's words, insist that for man alone 'it is natural to make an order of life different from that in which the race was nurtured earlier.' Under this heading of 'transformation' Canetti includes, not only the poetic and artistic creation of shapes and meanings different from those that surround us in our daily lives, but also man's ability to change himself into another, to empathize with another, and to think in metaphors; and in the context of our crowd-existence, he describes 'metamorphosis' as the mechanism men adopt to enable them to flee from the pursuing pack. Less was made of the positive aspect of our capacity for transformation in *Crowds and Power* than of its abuses and evil consequences: creativity, in our world of 'increase crowds', was shown to turn into pointless, senseless productivity, the human capacity for change into dissimulation and deceit, masks of protection and play into masks of terror.

But Canetti's later work *is* different. Even though the positive concept of 'transformation' is not worked out nearly as fully as the negative concepts of crowd and power, for it is in the nature of the aphorisms and reflections in *The Human Province* that a systematic elaboration of that concept is not attempted (his unstinting praise of Lichtenberg provides good reasons why such an attempt is not made), enough of an outline is given to indicate its closeness to Rilke's images of *Wandel* and *Verwandlung*. Exemplified by Canetti's own later work, these variations on 'metamorphosis' in Rilke's rather than Kafka's sense leave us less at the mercy of the evil and violence that are in us than did Canetti's earlier, more self-confident writings.

1986

26

Marxism on Stilts

1

Hegel's *Zeitgeist* is a vengeful spirit. There is ghostly poetic justice in the fact that the intellectual life of Western Germany was dominated, in its first thirty years at all events, by the Jewish Marxist outcasts of the Third Reich – Ernst Bloch (1885–1977), Georg Lukács (1885–1971), Max Horkheimer (1895–1973), Herbert Marcuse (1898–1979) and T. W. Adorno (1903–69), and by the enigmatic heritage of Walter Benjamin (1892–1940). It was they who inspired the students' rebellion of 1968, and even today the socio-political disputes in the West German universities take place in an area staked out by their writings.

Still, the laugh is not on the Germans alone. Anyone old-fashioned enough to believe that tolerance is a Jewish virtue will be in for a surprise: the one thing these intellectuals had in common with each other (and indeed with the Germany they so precipitately left in the 1930s) was their deep, undisguised contempt for the liberal mind. Western liberal democracy in particular they regarded as a 'post-' or 'crypto-Fascist' makeshift compromise. The fact that those who returned to post-war Germany were greatly acclaimed and given the highest academic positions seems to have made little difference to their views. After the trauma of exile, they turned out to be valiant biters of the hand that fed them.

Like all his revolutionary colleagues, Ernst Bloch was brought up in the comfortable security of a middle-class home, his father being a senior official of the Imperial Railways. Proletarian Ludwigshafen in the Rhineland-Palatinate, where Bloch was born in 1885, with its heavy chemical industry, contrasted starkly with Mannheim, its twin city – a model of eighteenth-century town planning, with residential palace, famous Jesuit church, and superb library – where he went to school.

The daily walk across the Rhine, past working-class tenements to the quarters of the mercantile bourgeoisie, provided the boy with the adversarial theme of a lifetime. The Dutch sailors in the harbour bars filled his imagination with exotic tales. Furtwängler, Weingartner and Kleiber were among the conductors whose performances he attended at the Mannheim theatre. An unimpressive school record gives little idea of the boy's real interests. From the age of seventeen, when Bloch was exchanging letters with Ernst Mach and other leading philosophers of the day, he was obsessed with the idea of a philosophical system, a total account of the world which would accommodate all experience, actual and visionary alike, within a single mode of discourse.

An early glimpse of his future task is recorded in a note that speaks of 'my discovery of the "Not-Yet-Conscious" [*des Noch-Nicht-Bewußten*], the kinship of its content with what is similarly latent in the world. In creative work especially, writes the twenty-two year-old university student,

> an impressive boundary is crossed, which I call the point of the transition of the Not-Yet-Conscious. Strenuous effort, cracking ice, becalmed sea and happy voyage are gathered around this point. Here, when the breakthrough succeeds, rises the land where no one has been, the land that has never been. That needs man the wanderer, compass, depth in the landscape . . .

The hyphenation, the eccentric punctuation, the rousing yet adventitious mixture of concepts and metaphors – all these will be the stock-in-trade of Bloch's philosophical style over the next seven decades. What is to be added to this half discursive, half poetic Expressionist notion of 'the Not-Yet' is its politicization in terms of a Romantic, fictionalized Marxism. *That* is to be 'the land where no one has been'.

In his wide-ranging university studies (which included music and some physics) at Würzburg, Munich and Berlin, Bloch focused on the history of the philosophy of matter from Aristotle through Lucretius to Karl Marx. Here again Brecht's ironical remark about the abstruseness of German 'materialism' is relevant. For Bloch was concerned to extend materialism as an account of the human and natural world, so as to include in it the dreams and constructions of scientific, religious and political Utopias of all ages. The year 1918 saw the publication of his first major book, *The Spirit of Utopia*, which contains Bloch's first attempt to conjoin socialism with the messianic spirit of the Bible, Marx with the biblical Apocalypse. This was followed in 1921 by his reconstruction of the chiliastic beliefs of Thomas Münzer, a revolutionary follower and antagonist of Martin Luther. In presenting Münzer as a 'theurgic' theologian, Bloch is prefiguring a major theme of the third volume of *Das Prinzip Hoffnung (The Principle of Hope)*, his *magnum opus* – the theme of the connectedness and interaction of earthly Utopian aspirations with Christian doctrine, the ardour ('boiling') of human freedom under divine equanimity.

Apart from participating in the German liberal-patriotic youth movement, Bloch seems never to have engaged in any public political activity. The bulk of his *œuvre* was written in the 1920s and early 1930s in Southern Germany and Switzerland, and made little impact outside the coteries of Marxist intellectuals. What the metaphysician of materialism actually lived on is not clear. In 1913 he married Else von Stritzky, a sculptress from Riga; on her death in 1921 and after a brief marriage to a painter from Frankfurt he lived with Karola Piotrkowska, a young Polish student of architecture, whom he married in 1934. These were the years of his friendship with Brecht, Walter Benjamin, Theodor Adorno and, above all, Georg Lukács (whose influential *History and Class Consciousness* was published in 1923). Lukács's dogmatic Marxism and his rejection of German Expressionism, which he was later to associate with National Socialism, led to a break with Bloch lasting many years.

2

A month after Hitler came to power Ernst Bloch left Germany, moving from Switzerland to Vienna and then to Paris, living a hand-to-mouth existence as a collaborator on several exile publications. He never visited the Soviet Union, preferring to write his apologia for the Moscow trials of 1936–7 in Prague. He arrived in New York in 1938, and settled first in New Hampshire, then in Cambridge, Massachusetts, where, between 1942 and 1947, *The Principle of Hope* was completed. Like Walter Benjamin (who in September 1940 committed suicide on his flight from German-occupied France) Bloch received no financial support from Max Horkheimer's well-heeled Institute for Social Research in New York, and indeed suffered great hardship. The household (which now included two children) was supported by Karola Bloch, who worked first as a waitress, then as an architect's assistant in Boston.

Though he had never been a Communist Party member, he experienced some difficulty and delay in acquiring American citizenship. However, the claim made by his translators (*The Principle of Hope*, p. xxiv) that he was forced to undergo an oral examination on the American Constitution only demonstrates their ignorance of US immigration procedures, and is not a confirmation of Bloch's belief that there is really no difference between 'the American way of life' and 'the Fascist *Volksgemeinschaft*' (p. 442). In brief (and Bloch is never brief), his eleven years in America left him with the impression of 'a society stripped of any will to truth' (p. 276).

In 1949, now sixty-four, Bloch took up his first teaching post, an East German professorship of philosophy at the Karl Marx University of Leipzig. The vigorous old man with the heavy shock of grey hair and thick spectacles soon proved to be a charismatic teacher and a fearless, brilliantly articulate debater, drawing large and enthusiastic student audiences. But, alas, his time in the German Democratic Republic overlapped with the confused period of 'the Thaw' and 'de-Stalinization' leading up to and following the Twentieth Party Congress, the Hungarian uprising and the consolidation of Tito's power in Yugoslavia – all contributing to an ideological retrenchment of the embattled Ulbricht regime.

The publication in East Berlin of the first two volumes of *The Principle of*

Hope and Bloch's seventieth birthday were still accompanied by official celebrations and honours; but soon the predictable 'criticisms' began to make his position difficult. Academic stooges of the government accused him of 'subjectivism', revisionism and excessive emphasis on 'the Hegelian heritage in Marxism', and – gravest indictment of all – of bourgeois 'mysticism'. Finally, Walter Ulbricht himself joined the attack with a few simple home truths about 'inadequate practical concern for the working classes . . . ' Bloch's closest disciples were jailed, and he himself pensioned off.

On 13 August 1961 the Berlin Wall went up, and Bloch, who had been staying with Wieland Wagner in Bayreuth, decided not to return to Leipzig, preferring 'the many lights of the many wholly rotten West Berlins'. The letter in which he announced his decision to the president of the East German Academy is couched in the simple, not exactly original terms of that 'bourgeois liberalism' – the appeal to the freedom of expression – which is denounced in *The Principle of Hope*. Friends secured him a visiting professorship at Tübingen, and there he continued teaching and arguing the views that had brought about his isolation and enforced silence. It speaks well for the West German academics that, in the face of considerable hostility from the conservative press and politicians, they had enough confidence in their own brand of democracy to give him a safe and secure berth.

Among the friends Bloch made in those last years in Tübingen was the student leader Rudi Dutschke, who had left East Germany at the same time as Bloch. Separated by fifty-five years, the two men were bound by surprisingly close affinities of temperament and mind. Both were immensely gifted speakers, and both were deeply troubled by the division between philosophical theory and social and political practice. Yet while Bloch was content to fudge the difference by devising the weasel word 'theory-practice' (*Theorie-Praxis*), Dutschke entered the political scene and paid for it with his life. Both read the Gospels as the charter of an ethical and social revolution, the initial impetus of which Bloch placed in the Mosaic Exodus. Dutschke's statement (made six years before he met Bloch), 'I take Jesus's words, "My Kingdom is not of this world" only in an immanent sense', is identical with Bloch's claim (p. 500, Bloch's italics), *à propos* the same text (John 18:36), that

'This world' is synonymous with that which now exists, the 'present aeon', whereas 'the other world' is synonymous with the 'future aeon'; [and this] is not a geographical division between this world and the beyond, but *a chronologically successive division in the same arena, situated here below.*

Although his eyesight was rapidly failing, Bloch was able to finish the revision of his *œuvre* for a complete edition (amounting to eighteen volumes). He died in Tübingen in August 1977, aged ninety-two.

All in all, it was not a bad life. Combining great intellectual energy and single-mindedness with the barging temperament of an ideologue, he lived through the disasters of the 1930s yet never had to take political responsibility for his views. The key of a prison door never turned behind him; he never heard a shot fired in anger. Compared with the overwhelming majority of his European contemporaries, he could surely look back on a life of good fortune; for however peculiar his chosen task, he never had to work at any other.

When considering its politics, a reader of *The Principle of Hope* should bear in mind that none of it was written under duress. American readers especially may be in for a shock. So hostile is Bloch to the American scene that it comes across as a huge, undifferentiated, industrial swamp with bits of barbed wire sticking out into the poisonous gases hovering above it. 'It goes without saying' (to use one of his favourite turns) that he denies its contribution to 'the theory-practice' of democratic government, though (p. 962) 'the young American states' are credited obscurely with 'cut-price freedom'. His model democracy is the USSR.

However, if his interest in US institutions is perfunctory, his praise of the Soviet Union is equally unencumbered by any detailed knowledge of its life and social arrangements. Most of the quotations from Stalin have been omitted from the West German (Suhrkamp) edition on which the English translation (1986) is based. Bloch's main source of information on the Soviet Union seems to have been Lenin, who died in 1924. Apart from some purple patches and conventional references to the nineteenth century classics, a quotation from Chernyshevsky (whose famous novel *What is to be Done?* was all the rage in pre-1905 Russia), and the usual Marxist attacks on the anarchist Bakunin, Bloch's knowledge of Russia is confined to lyrical guff, presumably at second hand, about Russian folk-dancing (as opposed to American 'vomit', pp 393–4); about the unique stoicism and courage of 'the Red Heroes', and the upright posture of 'Soviet Man'. Of Stalin's liquidation of the Ukrainian and Russian peasantry, the Gulags or the murders at Katyn we hear not a word. In an interview of 1965, he explains his earlier silence by the manifest untruth that 'one did not know much about Stalin's *Schrecklichkeiten*'; but then, perhaps because he has a reputation for ideological sophisms to uphold, he falls back on the two predictable claims which intellectual Stalinist apologists were reduced to throughout the 1930s. First, that 'capitalist historiography is so partial, and Stalin's horrors fitted its scheme so hideously well, that there were scientifically methodological reasons why one could not take [the news of those horrors] at face value.' His second excuse is that he and his like had no choice and could not afford not to side with Stalin's Soviet Union. But that was the motto of fellow-travellers on both the Left and (in regard to the Third Reich) the Right in the years between the wars.

To his less than illuminating observations on the great Tocquevillean theme of America and Russia one must add Bloch's equally perfunctory treatment of German history. Thus the Third Reich figures as no more than a mistake 'which fails to further the dialectics of history' (p. 310); Hitler is a pawn of international capitalism; and about the enthusiasm with which the German munitions workers acclaimed their *Führer* all the way to the end of 1944, Bloch maintains a dignified silence. The reason is much the same as for his evasion of the truth about Soviet Russia: like many other Marxists he seems never to have acknowledged the fact of Hitler's unparalleled popularity among all classes, including the German 'proletariat' – again, I surmise, because he felt that this was a fact of such momentous consequence for his own beliefs and 'scientific' convictions that, in the good fight on behalf of that 'proletariat', he and his like could not afford to admit to it. Add to this some snide remarks about Israeli bankers, 'Tel Aviv capitalism', and his unfortunate manner of quoting anti-Semitic remarks without doing much to dissociate himself from them (known in literary theory as 'free indirect style'), and you get the pattern from which the Baader-Meinhof group drew their picture of the world. All this suggests that, whatever may be the merit of Bloch's work, it does not lie in its political insights.

3

In all its straggling, messy immensity, *The Principle of Hope* is another of those all-about-everything books characteristic of German culture over the last 150 years. However, unlike its direct predecessor, Oswald Spengler's *Decline of the West* (essay 8), whose panoramic perspective it adopts, Bloch's *magnum opus* is ruthlessly optimistic. What it does is to reverse Spengler's world-historical scheme by turning 'Weltangst' – the source, for Spengler, of all creativeness – into 'hope'. In this placing of 'hope' at the very centre of a history, anthropology and phenomenology of mankind lies the originality of Bloch's undertaking.

The principle which guides the five sections (arranged in fifty-five chapters) is simple enough. All history and the entire contemporary world are divided along the lines of a chiliastic Marxism. 'Hope' resides in every scientific, artistic, political or religious event that can be interpreted, however doubtfully, as a guide to or promise of a 'Marxist' Utopia. The rest is irredeemably condemned.

After a rather jolly opening section on the value of day-dreams of a better future (contrasted with nocturnal dreams, which are seen as retrospective and therefore regressive), the argument settles down to an extended quasi-Freudian discussion of the unconscious. The motto cited, somewhat dubiously, by Bloch, supposedly an inscription on the walls of the 'bourgeois *déclassé*' Viennese clinics – 'Economic and Social questions cannot be treated here' (p. 66) – is rejected. The motor of the unconscious is hunger, for it is hunger alone (not Freud's libido) which 'transforms itself .... into an explosive force against the prison of deprivation'. A section on anticipating consciousness – the discovery and notation 'of the forward-looking Not-Yet-Conscious or of Forward Dawning [*der Dämmerung nach vorwärts*]' as the essence of 'reality as process' – is followed by a pious exegetic exercise on Marx's 'Theses on

Feuerbach', and by another long section on the trivial but redeemable hopes of the everyday. This includes a fairy-tale-like discussion of fairy-tales; reflections on travel and on the theatre seen not as an 'illusion' but as 'pre-appearance of the ideal' ('Every great drama is great because it is transparent to the future', p. 428); and a defence of 'the Happy Ending' against its usurpation and corruption by Hollywood.

Since the Utopia Bloch is advocating is not a state of 'being' but of 'becoming', it is never described in detail—to do so, he argues, would be to foreclose its possibilities. Similarly, any attempt to abolish authority is rejected as 'putschism' since (in Engels's phrase) 'the State will wither away' of its own accord. The reign of Utopia will come when the threefold division which is the cause of all evil in our world – the division of classes, the division of labour, and the immanence/transcendence division of Christian belief – is abolished.

A section on the history of social Utopias, from Plato through St Augustine, Joachim di Fiore and Thomas More to Francis Bacon, Saint-Simon, Moses Hess and William Morris, shows which aspects of these earlier Utopias prefigure Bloch's future state. Evgeny Zamyatin's and Orwell's dystopias are not mentioned. Seeing that here the higher flights of Bloch's fanciful style are largely avoided, this turns out to be one of the most illuminating sections of the book. But then, in the chapters that follow – on the role of nature, of non-mathematical science and of music in the building of that Utopia – the characteristic jumble of reified images and metaphorized concepts gradually takes over once more.

Mere verbal litter is spread over the thinnest bits of the system, especially where the oblique suggestion is made that the true socialist (or perhaps communist?) is a physiologically different type from the pathetic *petit-bourgeois* (the Goebbels-like passage on page 956 is not the only one that is much softened in the translation), and that disease and death itself may 'perhaps . . . possibly . . . one day' be abolished along with the class system. Nothing much else is said about death, presumably because the death of individual persons doesn't matter; while the universal Marxist scheme of history is immortal. Bloch does not say in so many words that capitalist wickedness is the cause of cancer, but he does the next best thing by calling the growth of cancer cells 'imperialist' (p. 465). Many passages in the book, including much amateurish patter on medicine, sport and technology, and a painful chapter on humour as 'the smile of pre-appearance', do no more than fill in vacant spots in the system. They remind me of Lucky's contribution to the wisdom of mankind in that famous monologue beginning with 'Given the existence as uttered forth in the public works of Puncher and Wattmann . . . ' But no Pozzo intervenes, to stop the flow of words.

In the last section of Bloch's mega-tome the famous images of the privileged moment are invoked in terms of Faust's wager with Mephistopheles. That moment in time and out of time of which Faust will be willing to say, 'Stay a while, though art so fair', is offered as the nearest thing that words can convey to the content of Bloch's Utopia. Finally, Don Quixote and Don Juan, Faust and *Fidelio*, Christ and Karl Marx provide the central images (or are they 'concepts'?) of a narrative that has by now abandoned most of its claim to being analytical and become largely a recital of archetypal scenes and persons lyrically evoked.

4

True 'hope' is only hope for the right and possible thing. Central to the first volume, and one of the most interesting theoretical parts of the book, is Bloch's analysis (pp. 224–8) of the two meanings of the word 'possible'.

In traditional philosophical discussions of possibility, he claims, knowing or not knowing what was the case in the past was confused with knowing or not knowing the conditions under which something is certain to be the case in the future. To avoid this confusion, we must distinguish between possibility that is confined to 'the singularity and immediacy of an accident or a stroke of luck', and possibility that is 'a capability of being an other', which implies purposeful and informed change. But since all 'true' or 'real' change is seen here as change in the direction of the greatest good, this second 'possibility' soon shrinks into and becomes identical with 'certain hope'. And for this reason, too – since for Bloch, if not for the rest of us, all 'true' change is toward classless Utopia – the philosophers of feudal and early capitalist times had a vested interest in perpetuating the traditional confusion. What is missing in Bloch's entire discussion of possibility and hope alike – *et pour cause* – is the recognition that, in any ordinary view of them, both are distinct from certainty.

Hitler's rule was a mistake, representing change only in the wrong sense of the word. By reducing 'change' to 'change for the better', Bloch is proposing to eat his cake and have it too. The notion of 'hope' which he asserts, illustrates, and supports by endless quotations (some of them disingenuous) is characterized in the following ways. It must be hope for a possible better future in the second of the two meanings of the word. It must be grounded in the present, in what we know now, but directed toward a better thing. It must have the fervour and seriousness of religious faith but, transcending what we are, it must not aim at 'transcendence'. Yet the sense in which it is to be not a vague but a certain hope must not be a religious sense, but the way that propositions of science are certain. It is not a passing mood but a clear programme and consistent goal, involving all that is positive in our moods and feelings ('premonition' is identical with 'utopian certainty', p. 826); and it must bear the stimulus toward its attainment within itself.

This hope will be entertained by some of mankind, called unblushingly 'the People' or 'the Proletariat', but it is absolutely beyond the reach of the rest. In this hope all that is valid in all theory and practice is united. There can be nothing squeamish about the way it is to be realized – bloody revolution is the most likely way of attaining it, since the entire Western world is not just hope*less* but actively opposed to that attainment. All good and great art either shows the way toward the fulfilment of that hope or offers examples of it. His treatment of Brecht's work is characteristic of his ruthless attempt to subordinate whatever is within reach to his do-it-yourself ideology. He concludes a discussion of Brechtian dramatic theory with the claim that 'Brecht's theatre seeks a mode of action in which there is only Communist conclusiveness of conduct .. ' (pp. 413f.). The opposite is the case. The dilemma – between justice and mercy, or again between accommodation and truth – of the great plays of Brecht's maturity remains unresolved: non-resolution is Brecht's great theatrical discovery.

In sum: hope, as Bloch presents it, is not just a concept or a feeling or the content of a man's imagination – it is all these things and more. It is one of the forms of our perception, on a par with the Kantian forms of space, time and causality (pp. 241 ff). *Our* perception? Well – not really ours, but rather the perception of the Marxist part of the world, in which Utopia 'has started to begin' being fulfilled (p. 582, etc.).

This list of what Bloch subsumes under 'hope' is problematic enough, but it is only one part of his total assertion. Most of the characteristics I have enumerated are in turn qualified. The certainty with which hope is to be endowed cannot be like the certainties of our natural sciences because they are the products of capitalism. The 'facts' of capitalist science are tainted by the purpose for which they were discovered; in the West all discoveries, let alone inventions, we are told, are determined by a social purpose of one kind or another – that purpose is the maintenance of the capitalist status quo and the intimidation of those who oppose and wish to alter it.

Hope must be grounded in the present – but only in those parts of the present which are harbingers of the good future, the Utopia of a non-adversarial society in which the three divisions I have mentioned (of classes, of labour and of immanence/transcendence) have been abolished. True hope must bear the stimulus toward its attainment within itself – but not to the extent that it becomes an end-in-itself and thus loses its quality of being a means toward the good end.

The present, Bloch reluctantly concedes, is grounded in the past. But the past is its true ground only in those of its aspects (Bloch here conflates the consciously tainted practice of Marxist historiography with Nietzsche's guileless but equally unacceptable theory of 'critical history') which offer an 'extended line' toward the Utopian future. (Thus the Hitler – Stalin friendship pact of August 1939 is not a part of the historical past.) Moreover, the present is, for Bloch, a 'dark' region, less knowable than either the past or the future. The task of selecting those aspects of the past and present which are to be the proper grounds for hope is simple enough: it is outlined in Bloch's unquestioning acceptance of Marxist-Leninist party dogma. When Jürgen Habermas writes of his disappointment 'that Bloch does not ground the Marxist method epistemologically', he understates Bloch's dogmatism. It is not just 'the method' but the very premise of the Marxist argument, the class theory, that is left unexamined. And criticism of that theory, or any suggestion that it may have been invalidated by the course of technological development which separates us from Marx, is swept aside as hostile propaganda and part of the Cold War. (The idea that centralized planning might be economically disastrous never enters his mind.)

Where recent French and (in its wake) American philosophical thought has offered to take the drama out of human experience by reducing all life and history to a set of contingent metaphors, Bloch proceeds in the opposite direction. He rejects those metaphors that do not fit his scheme as 'illusions', and hypostatizes the rest in a mystique and mist of literalness. By-passing the two major critiques – Kant's and Wittgenstein's – of reason and language, of reasonable utterance, he is trying to set up and sustain a mystical view of human destiny by means of a 'scientific' argument (p. 1,367). He re-enacts the old dream of German Romanticism and, in order to make it 'real', he politicizes it.

5

What – if anything – can be salvaged from such a convolute? Does anything of importance emerge from this chaotic combination of dogma, self-indulgence and Expressionist rhetoric? Neither Bloch's procedure nor his conclusions qualify as reasonable utterance. The importance and interest of the work lie in the questions it asks, in Bloch's remarkable ability to raise some of the problems that disturb us because we need to find new solutions to them, or at least improve on the solutions we have relied on so far. From our discussion of that oxymoron, 'certain hope', two such problems emerge: one concerns the role of nature in our scientific age; the other relates to the religious foundation of our ethics.

The first of these problems Bloch subsumes under Marx's heading of 'the humanization of nature'. His revision of the natural sciences follows Goethe's well-known distaste for Newtonian physics. Bloch reformulates this by attacking Kant's observation that an inquiry is scientific to the extent that it is amenable to quantification and mathematical procedures. Mathematics is seen as the descendant of the profit-and-loss calculations of clever merchants and traders (p. 1,348). So radical is Bloch's rejection of mathematics that it leads him to argue against its connections with music (in the tradition based on the Pythagorean 'music of the spheres' and in Kepler's 'harmonia mundi'), because it leads (p. 1,073) to the anti-human conception of modern music. Of course, one may sympathize with Ulrich, the hero of Robert Musil's all-about-every-thing novel, when he proclaims that he likes mathematics because of the people who don't. Apart from that though, any reader who is unbefuddled by Bloch's style will rightly think that a mere liking for or dislike of mathematics is, to one side of biographical considerations, a blatant irrelevance.

Bloch's rejection, however, is based on an ethical argument. It is the 'abstractness' of mathematical procedures, their being unavailable to sense perception, which intimidates us and allows these procedures and their application to follow ethically indifferent paths to unforeseen and unintended ends. Uncontrolled and apparently uncontrollable, this is 'capitalist science' – and, as such, a reflection of the chaotic society that has created it.

In this criticism of our science Bloch retraces an anxiety with which we, or at least most of the non-scientists among us, are entirely familiar. We are (as the saying goes) 'overwhelmed by science', intimidated and overawed by what we do not understand. The remedy he proposes (with some help from a misreading of Bacon) is hardly less abstract. 'Nature' is no longer to be the object of scientific inquiry, but to be itself the subject (the mystical 'natura naturans') from which scientific and human insights and progress will originate. Hence Bloch's apparently serious concern with alchemy and astrology as 'sciences' of phenomena which are supposed to teach man not through what he learns from observation and experiment, but by 'speaking' to him 'directly' and disclosing their own laws.

In other words: quantification is to give way to hermeneutics, the 'science' of interpreting difficult signs—the science of 'tongues in trees, books in the running brooks, / Sermons in stones, and good in everything . . . ' which (alas) is unlikely to flourish outside the Forest of Arden. Bloch makes a 'progressive' plea on behalf of this 'science'; yet it does not seem particularly 'reactionary' for Socrates to be telling us that we can learn a lot from people in the market square but nothing from trees; or for St Augustine (in a passage not quoted by Bloch) to ridicule such anthropomorphizing as absurd heresy.

Even though the anachronistic remedy Bloch proposes will not find many takers at the Massachusetts Institute of Technology, whose Press published his book, the problem to which he draws our attention is real enough. We do indeed treat nature as a mere object of experiment and exploitation; and the dangers inherent in the uncontrolled course of our scientific investigations go largely unheeded.

What emerges at the end of Bloch's 'scientific' discussion is a natural world from which all contingency is excluded, and a human world without mistakes and without any freedom of individual choice in anything we do. In this perfect world there is no room for the spontaneous, single-minded pursuit of discrete, partial knowledge. The 'mystical' philosopher who speaks to us from these pages will not admit, and seems to have no understanding of, an activity that bears its own *telos* within itself. He roundly condemns every philosopher and artist, every scientist and inventor, who is intent on less than the total view. There is no room in his scheme for all those who follow their freely chosen, self-imposed task, who may not even be conscious of (because they are not particularly interested in) a use beyond that which they aim at, a purpose beyond that which they pursue. Such gifted persons may hope that the eventual uses of what they have understood or invented will be good uses; but their achievements are purchased at the price of intentness on one goal, and disinterestedness in respect of all other goals. Where the division of labour and the unexpected, unplanned uses of the products of labour are seen as evils (pp. 970–1), creativity is surely at an end. That, in the West at all events, is what the history of art, science and technology teaches us – *any* history that is not falsified by a millennial perspective.

The choice that *The Principle of Hope* enables us to see, more clearly perhaps than any other book I know, is not a choice that Bloch offers. It is this: recognizing that such self-propelled activities may lead to evil ends, are the ends to be prevented by proscribing them, or by proscribing the activities that lead to them?

The former – the prevention of evil ends, as in the destruction of our natural environment – must be the aim of our laws. The latter – the suppression of such activities before they have got under way – presupposes a dictatorship, not indeed of 'the proletariat' but of the Lenins and Stalins, and of the Blochs and Marcuses too: the dictatorship of the guardians of the public good, whose authority rests on the claim that they know all – and, knowing all, know best.

However odd Bloch's discussion of 'nature as subject' may be, it does vouchsafe us a piece of knowledge about ourselves and our place in the natural world – a knowledge we recognize as woefully incomplete. From this admission of incomplete knowledge Bloch does not exempt himself. His claims on behalf of 'natura naturans' are, for once, not stentorian but tentative. But this only makes his claims of having a solution to every one of our social and political problems all the more damaging. *There* he admits to no possible ignorance, *there* all problems have already been 'potentially and latently' solved, and all non-Marxist solutions are rejected: 'Where only one flag is the right one, choosing ceases . . . .'

Democratic pluralism, however, is based on the admission of ignorance. We simply do not know how our neighbours will behave in new, unprecedented situations (or even in those situations that have well-known precedents). We must face the consequences of unforeseen, spontaneous behaviour; and where these consequences are destructive we must devise laws whose delay will not be too long in catching up with those consequences. All this is no more than the opening move in a discussion which Bloch never enters. Indeed he cannot enter it without abandoning his central Utopian claim to 'certain hope', the oxymoron on which his entire argument rests. Without that claim, his 'hope' would be no more than hope is for all of us – an uncertain prospect, open to a variety of possible fulfilments, or to none at all.

6

The other lesson this book offers to the reader who has the stamina to persevere to its end, concerns the religious foundation of our ethical beliefs. Here, again, it is the question Bloch poses that matters. Is our predominantly atheist world capable of salvaging, if not the objects of religious belief, at least its ardour and seriousness? Is the 'humanization of the divine' he proposes any more meaningful than his notion of 'certain hope'?

The argument opens with the claim (a half-truth, at best) that every religion and every prophetic or messianic figure arises in response to a specific social need, to the 'order' (*Auftrag*) given by society. The 'Urkommunismus' of the nomadic tribes of the Old Testament and the 'exodus religion' of Moses are continued in Christianity's communal faith – *Liebeskommunismus* – in succour of the underprivileged and oppressed. This view is just about compatible with orthodox Marxism, but Bloch's speculation does not stop here. Taking his cue from Revelation 21:5 – 'Behold, I make all things new' – he constructs (p. 1,270) 'a new God, who [is] absolutely strange' at the meeting-place of the human and the divine. Where the Gospels contradict such a view, Bloch draws on his considerable biblical learning to reject 'the eschatology of the two kingdoms' as a part of Christ's 'real' teaching (p. 580). Christ is, thus, presented as living proof of man's ability to 'transcend' his own human condition without intervention from 'transcendence'.

Bloch's 'humanization of the gods' takes some pretty fantastic forms. It includes such memorable pronouncements as 'The end of the tunnel [that is of anti-Semitism] is in sight, certainly not from Palestine but from Moscow – *ubi Lenin, ibi Jerusalem*' (p. 610), and that 'the Bolshevist fulfilment of Communism' is part of the 'age-old fight for God'. I wonder whether the German Protestant parsons who have been set agog by Ernst Bloch's 'theology' remember Hitler's claim to be acting on orders from the Almighty. The Catholic theologian Josef Pieper is more critical. He argues that whereas Christian hope is hope for salvation beyond death and beyond the Apocalypse, the hope-without-death Bloch offers is meaningless to mortal men. To which it might be added that Bloch does no more than follow in Nietzsche's foootsteps by invoking Christian ardour on behalf of a godless theology.

In this realm of fantasy it does not, in the end, matter greatly what qualities Bloch attributes to 'the greatest good' of that classless society we are certain to enjoy at the victorious conclusion of Marxism's Holy War. Nor does it make much difference whether or not he succeeds in giving his notion of that meeting-place of the human and the divine a modicum of coherence. The excuse for – or, at least, the explanation of – his wildly politicized and socialized interpretation of Christ and the Gospels lies not in his Utopia, but in our sins of omission.

Throughout the work, and especially in its last section, there are passages where Bloch's ruthless optimism gives way to its obverse – to a reprise of Marx's searing indictment of the conditions in which man becomes 'a debased ... an enslaved ... a forlorn ... a contemptible being' (pp. 265, 622, 1, 355–9). Bloch accepts Marx's diagnosis and the accusation that issues from it, but then turns the tables both on Marxism and on liberal democracy, by showing up the incoherence in both. Unlike any other Marxist I know, Bloch acknowledges that Marx's accusation derives its strength from its appeal to 'traditional Christian values' – the values of a biblical faith which Marxism seeks to extirpate.

Our attitude, of course, is more tolerant. We neither bother to deny nor proscribe 'the *novum*' in the teaching of the New Testament, but we acknowledge the Gospels' insistence on the value and dignity of the individual, 'the metaphysical single soul' (p. 623) in our rhetoric, leaving the rest (if there is a rest) to our sense of charity. But: 'How can we be just in a world that needs mercy and merciful in a world that needs justice?' asks the poet. As long as that question goes unheeded in our world, *ollas podridas* like Bloch's work will be written to remind us of it.

1988

27

The Commissar, the Student and the Blackout

1

He was born György Bernát Löwinger on 13 April 1885 into one of the richest Budapest families. His father, the son of a quilt-maker from southern Hungary, left school at thirteen, was made branch manager of the Anglo-Austrian Bank at twenty-four, and changed the family name to Lukács when the boy was five; in 1901 he bought the title of minor nobility, and in 1906 was appointed director of one of the largest credit institutions in the Austro-Hungarian Monarchy. Georg dropped the 'gentry-bureaucratic' designation 'von' only on his conversion to communism in 1918. The mother came from an ancient family of rabbis and licensed moneylenders to the Habsburg emperors, and remained contemptuous of her self-made financier husband. She had been brought up in Vienna, a city for which, like many similarly placed ladies from the provinces, she yearned throughout her life. To annoy her and as a sign of protest against her attempts to cultivate a Viennese salon in Budapest, Georg, her second eldest son, insisted on addressing her in Hungarian, which she spoke with difficulty. It seems that throughout his adolescence the boy couldn't make up his mind which of his parents he loathed more. If Arpad Kadarkay, the author of *Georg Lukács: Life, Thought and Politics* (the immediate source of most of these facts about Lukács's life), is to be believed, there was only Georg's sister 'Mici' to negotiate ceasefires in the family, and only long village holidays with friends to provide periods in which the boy could enjoy something like a carefree life.

Lukács attended the Budapest Evangelical Gymnasium (where Theodor Herzl had been a pupil), and in 1907 converted to the Augsburg Confession; he doesn't seem to have taken his baptism very seriously. Well read in contemporary Hungarian and Western literature and immensely ambitious to contribute to the fashionable area of literary and cultural history in the footsteps of Wilhelm Dilthey, the young man was active in a circle around Endre Ady, the greatest Hungarian poet of the age. Jószef von Lukács's great wealth allowed his son to take a good many friends on journeys abroad, mainly to

Italy, and to support a number of literary and theatrical ventures. Ill-favoured in his looks, Georg seems to have been frightened of attractive women and given to hiding his shyness behind huge metaphysical statements about the 'nature' of this, the 'essence' of that and the 'fundamental concept' of the other. He acquired a doctorate in political science at the University of Kolozsvár without, apparently, submitting a dissertation, and another, in philosophy, from Budapest, but his plans to submit a *Habilitationsschrift* – to the philosopher Georg Simmel in Berlin, then to Max Weber in Heidelberg – never came to anything. Precocious drama critic and co-founder of a small privately financed theatre where Ibsen and Strindberg had their Hungarian premières, frequent visitor to Florence and Paris, Lukács acquired a somewhat esoteric reputation as the author of two slim volumes of literary essays in a high metaphysical mode, without showing much interest in politics. Repudiation and denial of his origins and background were the tenor of the first thirty-three years of his life; and it is interesting to note that Kadarkay, who seems to have been one of his assistants, doesn't report a single statement of his on the fate of the Jews in his time.

Throughout Kadarkay's biography the reader is importuned with all sorts of ingenious but irrelevant comparisons of Lukács with the great heroes of Western intellectual history; yet what is not said is that much of this story is set in the most nationalistic and politically aggressive province of the Habsburg Monarchy. Many characterizations of the hero are given – he is 'fundamentally lonely', a saviour of Western culture; an ascetic, a stoic *and* a voluptuary, a lofty spirit *and* a Dostoevskyan super-sinner. But actually it is nothing very esoteric, only good old-fashioned Magyar nationalism, that informs large parts of the book. Thus, both Lukács *père* and Karl Mannheim, his son's friend, figure as English Hungarians (patron saints: Ramsay MacDonald, Lord Keynes and Philip Snowden), the revolutionary Endre Ady is a French Hungarian (patron saint: Baudelaire), while Lukács figures as a German, then a Russian, then briefly a Jewish and finally once more a German Hungarian (patron saints: Goethe, Nietzsche, Martin Buber, Dostoevsky and Marx, in that order).

The Budapest world that Kadarkay presents is not wholly unfamiliar. When one of Lukács's women friends commits suicide by jumping into the Danube, the man who fails to rescue her because he isn't allowed to use a private telephone to call the police turns out to be none other than Alexander Korda's friend Lajos Biró, the scriptwriter of *The Scarlet Pimpernel* and *The Thief of Baghdad*. And when Lukács feels guilty about the woman's death, he tries 'to translate his own inadequacies in love into a philosophy. Hence the Socratic irony and drama that pervade these [early] essays'. Why 'Socratic'? Well – 'Lukács once said that Socrates had no philosophy, he was it. Hungary lacked a philosophy or philosophic culture, Lukács was it' (p. 142). At this point, though, where 'guilt' turns into 'philosophy', we enter an altogether more sinister world: 'Hunting for female flesh in Paris in 1911', the biographer observes, Lukács's closest friend, Béla Balázs, met Ljena Grabenko, 'ugly, emaciated, and neglected', a half-crazed survivor of the 1905 Russian revolution who had once carried a baby borrowed for the occasion to hide a bomb in its blanket (p. 160). Having induced Lukács to marry her, the Russian girl, together with her lover, moved into Lukács's house in Heidelberg and proceeded to turn it into 'a brothel of shame' and him into a nervous wreck. Whatever may have been Lukács's need for self-punishment, expiation and redemption, it was this weird experience, typical of the Dostoevsky-dominated decade of the Great War, which brought him into contact with revolutionary politics. As to the disastrous affair itself, Lukács was rescued from it in 1917 by Gertrud Bortstieber, the daughter of a rabbi from the Slovak region of Hungary, a Catholic convert. 'Ever since I met Gertrud', he wrote many years later, 'it became the central concern of my life that she approved and seconded me' (p. 184). Ljena Grabenko eventually disappeared into the Gulag, and Lukács's second marriage lasted until Gertrud's death. The family included two boys from her previous marriage as well as their daughter, and it provided him with all the equanimity and serenity he was ever to know. Its delightful memorial is his study of Lessing's *Minna von Barnhelm*, in which he identifies Gertrud with Minna and himself with the maligned but honourable Major von Tellheim.

2

The process that led him to revolutionary Marxism took some time. When war broke out (he was living in Heidelberg at the time) Lukács, unlike practically all the literati and savants around him, did not greet it as a liberation – this (it seems to me) marks the only unambiguously positive moment in his political life; and on his return to Budapest he used his father's influence to secure exemption from military service, though he worked briefly as a 'military mail-censor'. By 1917 Lukács's friends had formed an eclectic aesthetic grouping, the 'Sunday Circle', and in that year formed the 'Free School of Humanities' to propagate in Hungary a 'new culture' of idealism. His conversion to communism only took place in November or December 1918, in circumstances every bit as macabre as his later political moves. It was effected by Ernö Seidler, the brother of the woman who had drowned herself in the Danube. Seidler had been trained as a political commissar while a prisoner of war in Russia and seems to have appealed to Lukács's feelings of guilt about Irma Seidler's death as well as to his urge to 'kneel' before an absolute (p. 203). By the time the first Hungarian revolution began, in March 1919, Lukács was a member (no. 52) of the party under Béla Kun's leadership, serving throughout the 133 days of the revolution as deputy (though in practice actual) commissar responsible for education as well as, for some of the time, as a political commissar in a Red Army division.

His view of Marxism resembles the Grand Inquisitor's view of Christian morality – a doctrine to be upheld for the good of the simple believers, an eudemonism which hides the true, tragic nature of human experience for the believers' own good. He shared the fashionable misreading of the age: Dostoevsky's novels were important because they focused on 'the interesting sinner', on personal salvation turning into political action through criminality, excess, confession and punishment. This sensational reading was a simple matter of identifying the meaning of the novels with the most extreme views held by their characters. Thus Lukács can write, 'Bolshevism rests on the metaphysical notion that good can come from evil. That it is possible, as Razumikhin says in *Crime and Punishment*, to lie our way to truth' (p. 200), without ever dissociating character from narrator, parts of the text from authorial opinion, literature from ideology – ignoring all the while 'the fictional totality' of the work, even though it was he, more than any other critic, who prosed on about the importance of 'totality' in the world of the novel. Viewed less and less disinterestedly, Dostoevsky's œuvre became for the literary-savant-turned-revolutionary the catalyst that produced from sexual failure and a deep hatred of the bourgeoisie a chilling readiness to discard (once he got the chance) the restraints of bourgeois or indeed any other form of morality. Of his fellow-revolutionaries Brecht, Ernst Bloch and Herbert Marcuse it can be said that, with bourgeois institutions of one kind or another to fall back on, their nerve in turning more or less fantastic theory into revolutionary practice was never really tested. Of Lukács this was only partly true.

Were it not for the loss of lives, the looting and the lawlessness, Béla Kun's revolution and the prominent role Lukács played in it might figure as one of those farcical moments in the history of Central Europe so exquisitely staged in the comedies of Johann Nestroy. The confiscation of paintings and 'reaction-ary' books, the closure of all bookshops and the establishing of mobile libraries to supply remote villages and farms with party propaganda, the destruction of all legal documents relating to banking and private property, the proscription of 'all dilettantism in art', the setting up of seminars to instruct workers in the anti-modernist aesthetics of 'healthy art', censorship and the licensing of press, theatre and concert hall – these are some of the measures which the 'earnest little professor' with the 'red Nietzsche moustache' was introducing in the first weeks of this feverish commotion. Of all these measures, it might be said that they carry one man's parricidal urge inordinately far (the debauching of the currency by printing bank notes nobody wanted was not done on his orders). But before the farce was over it turned bloody.

There are no indications that Lukács had the slightest notion of military matters. In an outfit of plus-fours, green stockings and heavy walking-shoes he visited the trenches of the Red Army's fifth division (which was defending the Hungarian frontier against Czech troops), and addressed the lice-ridden troops on the subject of sacrifice, in a speech that must have brought the dugouts down:

The youth [?] desires terror. Terror *an sich*. This is what you long for and that's what you will bring to pass ... If blood can be shed, and who would deny that it can be, then we are permitted to shed it. But

we can't allow others to do it for us. We must take full responsibility
for the blood that is shed. We must also provide an opportunity for our
blood to be shed . . . In short, terror and bloodshed are a moral duty,
or, more plainly, our virtue. (p. 222)

Most astounding of all, the author of *Soul and Form* personally ordered the
summary court martial of eight soldiers of the twelfth Red Army battalion,
which had deserted its post, and had six of them executed. A month after it
was over, Lukács was safe and sound in Vienna, which he reached after his
father had bribed a British officer to smuggle him out of the country as his
chauffeur; though of course, unable to drive a car, he had to pretend his arm
was injured and the officer had to do the driving. Having mostly fled to Vienna
on a special, diplomatically immune train (which Kun had prevented Lukács
from boarding), the exiled revolutionaries were charged by the Horthy government with, among other crimes, 236 murders and 19 robberies; in addition,
Lukács personally was charged with the murder of a medical student, Béla
Madarász, who had failed to observe the blackout. All these events are
meticulously recorded in Kadarkay's biography, but this does not prevent him
from comparing his subject to Socrates and Christ, Montaigne, Goethe and
T. S. Eliot, nor T. Eagleton, one of Marxism's latter-day saints, from giving
the book his imprimatur as a 'magisterial study [which] . . . will surely restore
[Lukács] to his true political status'. There cannot be many scholars in the
history of humanist learning who have ordered executions and been proud of
it.

The years of Lukács's exile in Vienna – 1920–9 – were penurious but not
intolerable. Although he and his fellow-exiles had undertaken to abstain from
illegal political activity, and though the Austrian government was besieged by
the Horthy government with requests for their extradition, they continued a
more or less clandestine existence of intrigues and factional strife, of spying and
counter-spying. To prevent Lukács's extradition, now pressure was brought to
bear on the Austrian Chancellor, Karl Renner, from some committee abroad,
now again Viennese officials were bribed, the money and string-pulling that
saved Lukács from Horthy's gallows being provided by his father. The minuscule Hungarian Communist Party was still led by Béla Kun, while Lukács,
on ever-worsening terms with him, was put in charge of the party finances
and sent on the rounds of the Vienna cafés to collect subscriptions and search
for missing funds. In 1928 he published an attack on Kun's policy, the 'Blum
Theses', in which he advocated collaboration with the social democrats (the
Comintern was in one of its optimistic phases, certain of capitalism's imminent
collapse, accusing the social democrats of being fascists), whereupon he was
promptly ordered to Moscow, there to be 'Cominterned' for the next fifteen
years.

3

Lukács's best-known political tract, the eight essays assembled in *History and Class Consciousness*, was published during his Viennese exile early in 1923. 'In so far as I am able to recall those years', he writes in the apologetic preface of 1967 (almost invariably his prefaces were exercises in 'self-criticism'), 'I, at least, find that my ideas hovered between the acquisition of Marxism and political activism on the one hand; and the constant intensification of my purely idealistic ethical preoccupations on the other.' In other words, Lukács's motive in producing the book in those months and years of licking recent wounds was to legitimate his yen for political power, of which he had just had a first taste, while at the same time increasing the Hegelian – that is, the abstract – component of Marxism. Even in such a devious structure as the Comintern, this doesn't look like the most direct road to power; but then, sooner or later the commissar-turned-theoretician must have recognized that it was not only power that was at stake, but survival – or, as that hated 'modernist' Rainer Maria Rilke had written, 'Wer spricht von Siegen? Überstehn ist alles.'

The process of 'idealization' is exemplified by the book's central concept of 'consciousness', to the analysis of which its most accessible essay is devoted: 'The unique function of consciousness in the class struggle of the proletariat has consistently been overlooked by the vulgar Marxists who have substituted a petty "Realpolitik" for the great battle of principle . . . ', Lukács writes. His aim is to specify that function: (1) 'consciousness' is to be identified with 'class consciousness' and correspondingly all other forms of consciousness are to be disregarded: what is at issue is not 'actual' or 'psychological' but 'imputed' ('zugerechnet') consciousness, imputed to a class because it is said to be 'logically' appropriate to the 'objective situation' of that class; (2) the object of 'true' class consciousness is the 'social totality', outside which there is nothing, and any partial view of which is a form of 'false consciousness'; (3) there is only one class that will achieve this 'objective consciousness', the modern industrial proletariat; (4) the realization, both theoretical and practical, of such total class consciousness, in which 'object' becomes identical with 'subject', will dispose of the proletariat's feeling of powerlessness in the face of what had once been feared as fate, and thus of the trammels of 'reification'; (5) finally, history itself turns out to be the path toward the realization of that consciousness – a path at the end of which that consciousness annihilates and 'transcends' itself by 'creating the classless society'. Meanwhile, however, the Communist Party 'must exist as an independent organization so that the proletariat may be able to see its own class consciousness given historical shape.' The one place where Lukács's scheme manifestly deviates from its Hegelian origins is in substituting 'class' for Hegel's 'country' or 'nation', thus leading to that underestimation of national consciousness which proved a major factor in communism's undoing.

Luckily for Lukács, the book appeared when Lenin was on his deathbed; even so, unsurprisingly, it did nothing for Lukács's political prospects. Its influence seems to have been proportionate to its *aficionados'* distance from Moscow, and thus inversely proportionate to their political importance.

4

There is a gap between Lukács's political philosophy in *History and Class Consciousness* and his writings on literature. Given his activation of consciousness – his insistence on its being not a passive 'reflection' of the historical and political world but a dynamic part of it – one might expect him to attribute the same active character to literature; to present literature not merely as a 'mirror' or 'passive reflection' of the world, not merely as a repository, but as a source of experience as well. And so, again and again, he does, all the way to the claim that literature is good and great to the extent that it contributes to the attainment of the hallowed goals of revolutionary Marxism. (In this way the *faux-naif* jollities of Socialist Realism come to qualify as great literature.) However, another parallel to the activation of consciousness, and a no less important one, would be an understanding of the active or 'performative' function of language. (Such an understanding of language as 'a form of life' would have helped Lukács to fulfil one of his last ambitions – to delineate what makes literature the distinct thing it is.) In fact, his literary studies – even the best-known of them in *The Historical Novel*, written in Moscow in the grim winter of 1936–7 – relate the Marxist scheme invariably to the crude story-content of fiction: 'Novels are approved because their content is approved and the content is the more approved the more it portrays the larger conflicts of society', writes Richard Humphrey of Lukács's critical procedure. And since the size of the conflicts in history or society is assessed by the same critic who assesses them in literature, and according to the same criteria, the circular argument allows for no real critical view. Only rarely, as in his observations on the essential fragmentariness of Goethe's *Faust* (which closely follow Schiller's comments), or again when Lukács speaks of 'the light and floating lyrical laconicism' of much of Goethe's poetry, does he convey the kind of insight which only literary criticism can provide.

An interest in the language authors use would have made the heedless ideologizing and politicizing of literature difficult. However, Lukács's panegyrics on Stalin's 'theory of language', like his primitive diatribes against Wittgenstein, suggest that this was a matter on which he was less than well-informed (The Great Russian Formalists are not, as far as one can discover from Kadarkay's book, even mentioned by Lukács – no wonder: they were imprisoned, exiled or murdered, most of them.)

And yet Lukács's entire critical edifice is based on a 'formal' critical misprision as grave and absurd as his insistence on telling authors past and present where they have gone wrong and how to do better. His campaign

against 'photographic realism', 'straightforward mimesis', and in favour of its
'energetic abandoning' amounts to no more than a series of otiose *obiter dicta*
– for the obvious reason that in literature (whether good, bad or indifferent,
'socialist', 'bourgeois' or 'Laputan') there is no such thing as the 'simple
copying of reality'. Literature, to the extent that it is the business of translating
experience (or whatever) from one place or one time to another, and from
one medium to another, whether by way of 'description' or by way of 'narration'
('*Beschreiben*' or '*Erzählen*'), involves creative choices. And this is so, whether
the translation is 'simple' or 'mechanical', or commendably sophisticated
because instinct with a consciousness of 'historical forces'.

5

The 'shabbiest and most humiliating period of his life', Daniel Bell has called
Lukács's years – 1930–45 – in the Soviet Union. Lukács himself called them
the most 'harmonious' – they were certainly the years of his most sustained
propaganda on behalf of Marxism-Leninism and Stalinism. During them, he
achieved the singular distinction of becoming an authority on Russian literature, from Lomonosov to Ehrenburg, excluding Ossip Mandelshtam, without
ever managing to learn the language properly; now he laboured at the antithesis
of 'degenerate Modernism' (Rilke and Kafka, Joyce and Beckett, etc.)
vs. Progressive Realism, which is analogous to the National Socialist antithesis
of 'entartete Kunst' vs. true German folk art, claiming that 'Modernism leads
to the death of literature as such'. (Most things, with him, are 'as such'.) The
vast majority of his Hungarian fellow-communists in exile in the Soviet Union
met their death in Stalin's labour-camps, he himself was imprisoned for a few
months (Kadarkay doesn't bother to explain why), and he broke with most of
his old friends. However, he not only survived those years, but employed them
in writing a large number of literary-political essays (and was even able to
publish some of them), as well as his major study *Der junge Hegel*, which
appeared in 1948 after his return to Budapest. Kadarkay makes it clear that
in everything Lukács wrote then he had to exercise the utmost care not to fall
foul of the party line and its varying interpretations by his minders. The point
bears emphasizing. It is no thanks to him that present-day readers may not
find it easy to envisage a situation in which a few misplaced or mistimed words
of supposedly literary appreciation could lead to a loss of favour, employment,
freedom and life. It was in those years that his criticism became prescriptive,
his assessments normative, his norms ideological, and his ideology a weather
vane.

Lukács did not leave the Soviet Union for 'liberated' Budapest until August
1945 (some months after most of the other surviving 'Hungarian Muscovites'),
after mediation by one of Beria's bridge partners during a game had led to
the freeing of Ferenc Jánossy, one of Lukács's stepsons, who had attempted
suicide in one of Stalin's camps and whose incarceration there would have

been an embarrassment to Lukács on his return to Hungary. His life over the next twenty years was shaped by a series of ever more desperate accommodations to the politics of Stalin's Hungarian satellite. And again, from one perilous episode to the next, he not only survived but, frequently travelling to the West, took his bow as the spokesman of a regime which kept him guessing as to the importance it would attach to what he said or didn't say. In this as in some other ways he resembled the fellow-travelling writers of the Third Reich, though the periods men like Carl Schmitt, Gottfried Benn and Martin Heidegger spent currying favour with National Socialism seem mere episodes in comparison; they at all events signed no death warrants.

Having been appointed to the Chair of aesthetics and 'cultural policy' at Budapest University in the autumn of 1945, Lukács was acquiring a following among his students and fame on the international conference circuit when the purges began. In May 1949 László Rajk, the minister of the interior, was arrested on Stalin's orders for conspiring with Tito against Stalin, and after a brief trial executed; in Paris Julien Benda wrote in approval of the death sentence. Lukács, as always lower down on the vultures' pecking-order, was charged, in a public indictment, with 'idealism, cosmopolitanism and blasphemy against Lenin' and accused of inadequate appreciation of Soviet literary and cultural achievements; whereupon he wrote the by then customary litany of self-denigration, following it up with a piece in praise of a Soviet novel by Alexander Fadeyev, his old enemy of Moscow days. Lukács's 'confession' was concocted with the help of Mátyás Rákosi, the party chief himself; 'not even Stalin had the audacity to "help" Bukharin draft his self-indictment' (p. 406), Kadarkay notes.

And although what Lukács called his 'relentless struggle against decadent Western philosophy and art' continued (p. 410), it didn't save him from the next round of humiliations. When the second Hungarian revolution broke out in October 1956, Lukács, though highly critical of its leaders, nevertheless accepted the post of minister of culture in Imre Nagy's government, resigning on the day Nagy announced the end of the one-party system. The reason Lukács gave for his resignation – 'This party's composition is not consistent with my conscience' (p. 429) – reminds one more of Groucho than of Karl Marx; anyway, Kadarkay isn't convinced that it was the real reason. Nor, however, is there certain evidence that, as has been speculated, Lukács was tipped off about Khruschchev's decision to crush the revolution with tanks. But since Lukács was regarded in Budapest as 'our great Marxist thinker . . . [who] knows everything and sees the future' (p. 430), Kadarkay thinks it quite possible that he was not deceived by Moscow's offer to withdraw its troops, recognized it for the ruse it was and got out of the firing-line before the firing started. In any case, together with other members of the government, Lukács took refuge in the Yugoslav embassy. Once there, however, he not only distanced himself from Nagy (possibly on the advice of one of his old friends in the Kremlin), but advocated reconciliation with János Kadár, the new head of government. Unlike his minister of culture, Imre Nagy did not

The Commissar, the Student and the Blackout

survive for very long. Forced by the Soviets to witness the execution of two of his friends, as Rákosi had forced him to witness the execution of László Rajk in 1949, Imre Nagy was hanged in June 1958.

As for Lukács (who refused to testify against Nagy), his habit of public 'confessions' having by this time become second nature, he was comfortably interned in what later became one of the Ceausescus' favourite residences. Never one to miss an occasion for a bit of sententious kitsch, he claimed that his stay at Snagov Castle convinced him that Kafka was a realist writer after all. He was released and returned to Budapest in April 1957, partly on the intervention of the philosopher of whom he had written, 'For people like Bertrand Russell, the demise of humanity is more bearable than the prospect of a socialist victory' (p. 439).

The controversies of the last years of Lukács's life, when he was visited by more than one Western busybody, were less violent and less momentous. Forever on the literary *qui vive*, he found a niche for Solzhenitsyn's *One Day in the Life of Ivan Denisovich*, greeting it as a 'good example' of Marxist writing. Gertrud's death in April 1963 robbed him of the one companion whom he utterly trusted. In the essay on Lessing's comedy mentioned earlier he praised her, through praising Minna, for possessing, 'not wisdom at all, just a real human being's unbroken longing for a sensible existence that is possible only in companionship and love' (p. 449). The main work that occupied him in his last years was an attempt to formulate a systematic Marxist aesthetics, *Die Eigenart des Ästhetischen (The Specificity of the Aesthetic)*, parts of which were projected as prolegomena to an ethical *summa*. This attempt is seen by Kadarkay as his 'strategic response to communism, which had been distorted and uglified by Stalinist practices. Works of art – those which Lukács admired all his life – were to redeem and rescue communism from its fallen grace' (p. 453). How he does that in the two volumes of this *magnum opus* of his old age I confess I have failed to find out.

Lukács protested against the Soviet-led invasion of Czechoslovakia in the summer of 1968 (planning of course 'to publish a special paper to express my views on the central question ... of democratization today' (p. 461)), and shortly before his death circulated, without much success, an appeal on behalf of Angela Davis, a 'black militant communist' academic accused in the USA of murder and kidnapping. He died of cancer of the lung on 4 June 1971, intellectually active to the end of his long life; his last notes, or perhaps just underlinings, were made in his copy of an edition of Freud's works.

6

Lukács's life was rent by a dilemma unusual in its intensity but not (it seems to me) in its kind. It arose from his refusal to make up his mind: did he want to be a politician whose revolutionary ends justified any or almost any means (as he repeatedly claimed), or would he content himself with being a literary scholar, whose *métier* he came to see in much the same light? It may be that, taking seriously one of the more extravagant Marxist tenets fashionable in his time, the critique of 'alienation through the division of labour', he felt justified in not making up his mind, intent not merely on furthering the Marxist cause as he understood it, but on wielding political power through his scholarship. If so, his ambition was disappointed. His political influence seems to have been minimal, most of it having to be expended on protecting himself and his family from the lawlessness he at other times supported; while his scholarship became so ism-infected that most of his insights are distorted by considerations which have almost nothing to do with literature and undermine its 'specificity'. Kadarkay does his best to elevate Lukács into the ranks of such as Montaigne and Machiavelli, Kierkegaard and Nietzsche, not to mention Achilles, Faust and several Shakespearean heroes. More relevant by far would be a comparison with Lukács's contemporaries Benedetto Croce, Ernst Robert Curtius, Erich Auerbach and Arnoldo Momigliano, who did more for the survival of the cultural values to which he paid lip-service than it was in his power to do. There is a brief reference to Croce in Kadarkay's book, the other names are not mentioned; which is just as well.

28

Wittgenstein in Context

1

To place Ludwig Wittgenstein's philosophical writings in the history of European thought is an undertaking beset by difficulties. The first and most obvious of these derives from the fact that Wittgenstein himself published only one book, *Logisch-philosophische Abhandlung* (1921), better known as the *Tractatus Logico-Philosophicus*, the title G. E. Moore suggested for the first English edition of the book, which appeared in London in 1922, with an introduction by Bertrand Russell and a parallel English translation by F. P. Ramsey and C. K. Ogden. After Wittgenstein's death in Cambridge in 1951, all his other works, beginning with *Philosophical Investigations* (Oxford, 1953), the manuscript of which is said to be lost, were published from a *Nachlass* of at least 13,000 pages of brief notes, reflections and diary entries. In the posthumous editions, these writings are arranged in accordance with the philosopher's own intentions when these intentions are known; at other times the editors have had to rely on their own sense of the work, their task being made difficult by Wittgenstein's own doubts about the usefulness of any conventional arrangement:

> If I am thinking about a topic just for myself and not with a view to writing a book, I jump about all round it; that is the only way of thinking that comes naturally to me. Forcing my thoughts into an ordered sequence is a torment to me. Is it even worth attempting?
>
> I *squander* an unspeakable amount of effort making an arrangement of my thoughts, which may have no value at all.

To complicate matters further, there are several volumes of lecture notes taken by Wittgenstein's students, in one of which (1933–4) the question of a systematic approach is raised:

There is a truth in Schopenhauer's view that philosophy is an organism, and that a book on philosophy, with a beginning and an end, is a sort of contradiction. One difficulty with philosophy is that we lack a synoptic view. We encounter the kind of difficulty we should have with the geography of a country for which we had no map, or else a map of isolated bits. The country we are talking about is language, and the geography is grammar. We can walk about the country quite well, but when forced to make a map, we go wrong. A map will show different roads through the same country, any one of which we can take, though not two, just as in philosophy we must take up problems one by one, though in fact each problem leads to a multitude of others. We must wait until we come round to the starting point before we can proceed to another section, that is, before we can either treat the problem we first attacked or proceed to another. In philosophy matters are not simple enough for us to say, 'Let's get a rough idea', for we do not know the country except by knowing the connections between the roads. So I suggest repetition as a means of surveying the connections.

Overlaps, repetitions and rearrangements are, thus, integral parts of 'a new conception of the way to do philosophy', whereas a book (such as the *Tractatus*) is, in David Pears's words,

> an artificial break in a continuous development, like a still excerpted from a film. It must be remembered that [Wittgenstein] always found great difficulty in putting his thoughts in linear order to make the kind of treatise that is expected from a philosopher. They are interrelated in too many ways for the usual two-dimensional linear arrangement. That is one reason why he always had to struggle to make a book the natural expression of his thoughts. But there is also another, connected reason: his thoughts live in his notebooks, and form their relations with one another slowly over many years. A work published by him is, therefore, an artificial cut in a continuous process of growth, and, instead of treating either of his two great books [that is, the *Tractatus* and *Philosophical Investigations*] as a definitive revelation, we ought to trace their ideas back to their points of germination and then move forward again, following the gradual process of growth in their own ecosystem (p. 192).

Similar considerations apply to Nietzsche's large posthumously published *œuvre*: its fate demonstrates not only the need to make connections between disconnected notes, but also the danger of getting some of these connections wrong. In spite of some delays in the editing of Wittgenstein's *Nachlass* one fervently hopes that the dubious editorial practices which Nietzsche's work suffered for more than half a century will not be repeated.

A second difficulty relates to the dual 'background' of Wittgenstein's thinking. For many years we were presented with two Wittgensteins: a rigorously 'scientific' Anglo-Saxon logician, and an Austrian or continental philosopher with 'mystical' leanings. Of the 'Cambridge' or 'scientific' philosopher, it has been said that he was concerned with questions involving the relationship between facts and ideas and their representation in everyday language, with inquiries into the rules according to which we form pictures of the world and with the difference between 'saying' things and 'showing' them or 'making them manifest'. This procedure involved above all determinations of the *logical* limits of language, for at the centre of the *Tractatus* lies the view that 'language cannot contain an analysis of the conditions of its own application' (Pears, p. 11). The 'mystical' thinker, on the other hand, was said to be concerned with how to live the good life, what to do in the face of temptation and sin, how to endure solitude and (more difficult) how to endure company; what it is to have faith in God, and what it is to lack such faith. In this version much was made of the *ineffable* limits of language. Such questions are briefly touched on in the last pages of the *Tractatus*, but, of course, once you concentrate your reading entirely on 'mysticism' and ignore the rest (as most recent Austrian interpreters have done), anything goes.

But there is a third difficulty. Wittgenstein wrote within a highly history-conscious culture, and in a massively politicized age. Yet the very few political reflections he confided to his letters and diaries are quirky rather than illuminating, and, compared with everything else he wrote, unremarkable. And what he says about history (again mainly in the diaries, and in the prefaces to some of his works) are little more than expressions of a heartfelt regret for the passing of more dignified and more *decent* ages. Kristóf Nyíri is not the first interpreter to call these views conservative, Viennese and Austrian, and this makes them representative, though not necessarily original or profound. The task of a historian of Wittgenstein's ideas (such as Nyíri) is to provide a political context and historical continuity for the life and work of a man who had little more than contempt for the world in which he lived. Both original and profound, however, are Wittgenstein's methodological observations, which, without necessarily mentioning history, are relevant to it as well as to cultural inquiries of every kind.

What I have in mind is, above all, the method of family resemblances which Wittgenstein devised in order to do away with Procrustean generalizations (those which rely on the lowest common denominator or an invariable set of defining qualities). He replaces such generalizations by what has recently been called 'sporadic resemblances', or again by the 'polythetic method', a method in which the members of a group or class are taken to share 'a number of common characteristics, without any of these being essential for membership of the group or class in question'. Wittgenstein offers several models of classification by family resemblances; I have mentioned the procedure in several of the essays in this volume and followed it in almost all of them. A version of the same principle occurs in *Philosophical Investigations*, § 67: 'the strength of [a] thread does not reside in the fact that some one fibre runs through its whole length, but in the overlapping of many fibres,' and, as noted earlier, in § 71 of the same book, where Wittgenstein writes of the advantages, *for a specific purpose*, of 'a concept with blurred edges' and then asks, 'Is it even always an advantage to replace an indistinct picture by a sharp one? Isn't the indistinct one often exactly what we need?'

These are some of the models Wittgenstein uses in applying his discovery to a variety of problems which had previously been dealt with by 'categorical' or 'monothetic' definitions. The method has been traced back to eighteenth-century taxonomy, and examples of it may be found in Nietzsche and Benedetto Croce, and, no doubt, in many others. Yet the convincing way Wittgenstein sets out the advantages of this procedure, along 'different roads through the same country' of language, the detailed way we can trace its development in his reflections, and the significance it has for his entire later philosophy – all these make me think that it will always, and justly, be associated with his name. Surprisingly, Nyíri virtually ignores it; even more surprisingly, so does Ray Monk, Wittgenstein's latest biographer. Its importance for every kind of synchronic or diachronic inquiry is obvious: in an age bludgeoned by mass phenomena and statistics, it alone offers the means of preserving the significance of the single phenomenon. Avoiding what Wittgenstein calls 'the contemptuous attitude towards the particular case', it gives the particular case its meaning as an element in a coherent and perspicuous, surveyable (*übersichtlich*) picture. In other words: the method offers a remedy against avoidable abstraction; which is what *Geistesgeschichte* – a history of ideas constructed from trends and movements and 'isms' – so often fails to do.

2

The first aim of Kristóf Nyíri's book *On the Margins of Europe* is to describe, document and illustrate the Austrian or Central European alternative to German (or Prussian, or Kantian) Idealism. This alternative arises at the end of the Enlightenment because (as Nyíri observes in the first of the five essays which make up his book) 'for the Austrian citizen the very abstract form of Kantian Idealism does not represent a natural direction of his thinking' (p. 178); and from this perception Nyíri proceeds to a confrontation of an Austrian Catholicism of good works with Luther's 'solifidianist' Protestantism. Abstraction is an important aspect of categorical or 'monothetic' generalizations. At this point Nyíri offers an outstandingly clear example of an argument conducted along 'polythetic' lines in a quotation from one of his heroes, the 'progressive Conservative' Hungarian Graf Stephan Széchenyi, who (writing in 1830) discusses four different kinds of 'understanding' which overlap and are perfectly compatible with each other, and accepts each kind as 'rational' because (Széchenyi writes) each meaning 'corresponds to its [appropriate] circumstances'. However, seeing that the quotation is tucked away in a footnote (p. 180), one cannot be sure whether Nyíri appreciates its relevance to Wittgenstein's method, or its philosophical importance as an example of concrete thinking.

No other method is likely to do justice to the structure of a tradition (which is what Nyíri sets out to describe): consciously or not, he shows us the time and place in which the method provides the structure of a richly variegated 'anthropological conservatism'. Founded in hallowed custom and a religious order of things, this is an inherently anti-ideological, Burkean tradition. And – this is the second aim of Nyíri's book – it is in this tradition that Wittgenstein's writings are to be placed, even though (as I have suggested) Wittgenstein himself is never directly concerned with either politics or history (or at least not more than any contemporary of Stalin and Hitler had to be).

Nyíri begins with a brief history of 'Austrian conservative thinking' about man in society from the end of the eighteenth century through five generations to the second half of Wittgenstein's work, and to the writings of his cousin, F. A. Hayek (said by some to have been Mrs Thatcher's guru). This, not counting an unconvincing attempt to make Freud an honorary member of a Viennese Primrose League, is one of the best chapters in the book. It includes an illuminating outline of the differences between Western and Eastern European feudalism, of the economic and social consequences of different forms of land tenure and of the different political functions of religious reformers; and in his succinct accounts of the writings of two eminent Hungarian social critics, Graf Stephan Széchenyi (1791–1860) and Joseph Eötvös (1813–71), Nyíri presents Central European political thinking at its best: progressive aristocrats throughout the Habsburg Empire were in love with the British constitution, as long as it was love at a distance. The following chapter is less convincing. Its main subject is an improbable compound of Wagnerian dramatist, Professor of Philosophy and prophet of a new 'Eastern' Protestantism, called Christian von Ehrenfels (1859–1932): a figure somewhat dwarfed by being provided with a background of 1,000 years of socio-economic and political history. Next, T. G. Masaryk's first study, on suicide in the modern world (1879), is convincingly related to his speculations on 'the spirit of Russia' and 'the spirit of the Czech nation', and Nyíri justly criticizes the moralizing and normative purpose of these speculations. The chapter on Ludwig Wittgenstein's father, presented as the most influential figure in the history of heavy industry in Central Europe, seems to belong to the unattractive history of *laissez-faire* capitalism, but it provides a family background for the topic of the next (fourth) chapter, Wittgenstein's 'conservative anthropology', to which I shall return. The working notes towards a book on Dostoevsky which the young Georg (still: von) Lukács sent to Paul Ernst (*c.*1914) form the subject of Nyíri's last chapter. Lukács's book was never written, and the notes illustrate the rigidity and aridness of his literary criticism as well as the perceptiveness of his political understanding, even before he placed both in the service of Marxism.

It will be readily seen from this outline that whatever went by the name of 'philosophy' in *this* Austrian tradition has very little in common with what Wittgenstein wrote. It is not only that the genre called 'philosophy of history' which came into being in Central Europe in the wake of Herder (and of which the Czech historian František Palacký and Masaryk are the most famous practitioners) makes for tendentious history and unsubstantiated speculative philosophy alike. (Nyíri quotes on page 24 a spirited attack by the young Franz Grillparzer on Hegelianism, which ends with a lament for the loss of philosophical sobriety and wit: 'O Lichtenberg, Lichtenberg, why wert thou reft so early from our native land?') The point that needs making is that philosophy in this Central European tradition is less concerned with 'everything that is the case' than with what should be and (with that philosophy's help) very soon will be the case in the world.

Wittgenstein's programme is very different: 'In philosophy it is always a question of applying a series of extremely simple principles which are known to every child, and the only – albeit enormous – difficulty is to apply them amidst the confusion created by our language.' This, too, is the way Bernard Bolzano (essay 2), the first and only important 'Austrian' philosopher of his age, saw his task: 'to discover the objective ground of that which we already know with the greatest certainty and concreteness'. But Bolzano is not mentioned in Nyíri's book.

3

The first volume of Brian McGuinness's *Wittgenstein* contains the most detailed and by far the most reliable portrayal we have of the philosopher's life up to the publication of the first, German edition of the *Tractatus* in 1921, the only work of his to appear during his lifetime. It is written in a less flowing style than the other recent biography, Ray Monk's *Ludwig Wittgenstein* (which in its early parts relies on McGuinness's volume in some respects), but that is not necessarily to its disadvantage.

The greatest merit of McGuinness's long-awaited book is that it firmly focuses on the connection between Wittgenstein's early philosophy and his life. Instead of the lurid gossip purveyed by at least one of his predecessors, McGuinness has written a philosopher's biography, at the centre of which lies the cardinal achievement of the first half of Wittgenstein's life, the *Tractatus*: mentioned only briefly by Nyíri, it is seen by McGuinness as the answer to its author's philosophical and existential problems. The 'logic' of that work is presented as the form and content of a philosophy. Abstract, schematic and aphoristic it may be but, for the reader who learns how to read it (and even for one who skips the middle, mathematical sections), it is rich in insight, and comprehensive. Its author's life was a difficult one (the biographer is saying), it was difficult to live and it is difficult to describe, but there is nothing scurrilous about it.

It is, indeed, difficult to present convincingly a life cast in superlatives. The Wittgensteins, German and three-quarters Jewish by origin but Protestant by declared allegiance, were among the three or four wealthiest families in the Austro-Hungarian Monarchy. Karl Wittgenstein, the philosopher's father, was outstandingly successful both as an engineer and as an entrepreneur. The family houses in Vienna and Lower Austria were among the most lavishly appointed and fashionably designed of *fin-de-siècle* Vienna. Here Brahms and the Joachim Quartet 'made music', and some of Vienna's greatest artists were frequent guests. The acquisition by Wittgenstein of his share of the vast family fortune (described also by Nyíri) was as dramatic as his repeated renunciations of it, his periods of ascetic withdrawal as untoward as his generosity to friends and his anonymous gifts. Momentous family conflicts, assertions of independence and suicides abound. His father's choice of the Technische Hochschule in Berlin–Charlottenburg and of the University of Manchester for young Wittgenstein's engineering studies is as unusual as the student's approach to Gottlob Frege (1848–1925), then a largely unknown professor of mathematical logic at the University of Jena, but whose posthumous fame places him among the greatest logicians since Aristotle; and the willingness of the old and reclusive Frege to discuss his own work with a young man 'whose mathematical education and sophistication barely qualified him to discuss mathematics' (McGuinness, p. 76) is as surprising as Frege's advice to the young man to go to study under Bertrand Russell at Cambridge. There is something superlative, too, about the bravery Wittgenstein showed and the deprivations he endured throughout four years of the First World War, and the subsequent months as a prisoner of war in Northern Italy and at Monte Cassino. Among the most moving passages in McGuinness's book are his descriptions of the hardships Wittgenstein bore on the Russian Front, hardships which 'gave him the sunken face that was to mark him for the rest of his life'; at the age of twenty-six he appeared 'no longer as a serious young man but as one who had suffered deeply' (p. 238). His mental suffering during that war was heightened by his awareness that most of the troops among whom he served were recruited from the Slavonic parts of the Empire, and were, therefore, hostile to the cause for which they were supposed to be ready to lay down their lives; and his deep unhappiness was further increased by his early conviction, born of his knowledge of England, that the Austrians were fighting a war they could not win. Wittgenstein's war diaries, in which he records some of the horrendous events around him side by side with his philosophical ideas, reflect the greatest exaction of all: these years of mortal danger and all but annihilating doubt were the years, too, when the notes for the *Tractatus* and most of the book itself were written. Monk too relates the war experience to the philosophy. After quoting Schopenhauer's observation that 'it is the knowledge of death, and therewith the consideration of the suffering and misery of life, that give the strongest impulse to philosophical reflection and metaphysical explanations of the world', he comments:

> If Wittgenstein had spent the entire war behind the lines [as he did during its first two years], the *Tractatus* would have remained what it almost certainly was in its first inception of 1915: a treatise on the nature of logic. The remarks in it about ethics, aesthetics, the soul and the

meaning of life have their origin in precisely the 'impulse to philosophical reflection' that Schopenhauer describes, an impulse that has as its stimulus a knowledge of death, suffering and misery. (p. 137)

This of course leaves open the question of whether these 'remarks' are connected with the main body of the *Tractatus*.

In all this – Wittgenstein is thirty-two at the end of McGuinness's first volume – are there no scandalous love-affairs, no homosexual liaisons, no occasions for Freudian disclosures, not even a night out in a Viennese brothel? The answer is that, since McGuinness does not choose to entertain us with unfounded conjectures, we do not know; he is, as things go, an unfashionable biographer. He acknowledges much help from friends and members of the Wittgenstein family, and tells us that he has had full access to documents of every kind; how fully he has utilized the available sources will become clear when his second volume is completed. Both he and Monk have to admit that the scandalous stories about Wittgenstein casually picking up homosexuals in the Vienna Prater (told by an earlier biographer) are impossible to disprove; though, being based on unattributable 'evidence' collected sixty years later, they seem highly improbable (McGuinness; p. 294; Monk, pp. 581–6).

4

To return to the two Wittgensteins – the severe logician and the 'mystic'. It is a part of McGuinness's argument that such a dichotomy is bound to be misleading, but we can think of instances where it may be justified. Detaching the philosophy from the life, we can picture a logician whose biography has nothing to do with his professional achievement. Gottlob Frege's was one of the two most powerful influences the young Wittgenstein encountered in his search for a meaningful vocation. Yet Frege's paramount discovery of a reliable common notation for logic and mathematics, together with his later work on the foundations of both, seems to be wholly unrelated to what we know of his biography; his immense achievements receive no added illumination from a knowledge of his sad and dispiriting personal circumstances, or from his anti-Catholic and anti-Semitic prejudices. Bertrand Russell (the other major influence on Wittgenstein) wrote a number of popular books which reflect his pacifist stand in the First World War, his marital problems, his experiments as an educator and his politics. But in a 'Reply to My Critics' of 1944 Russell writes that he sees 'no necessary connection between my views on social questions and my views on logic and epistemology': the work which formed the basis of Russell's close friendship with Wittgenstein and which made him think of Wittgenstein as his successor is unrelated to what he called 'my shilling shockers' (McGuinness, p. 107). In another essay (10) I have examined Martin Heidegger's wholly reprehensible involvement in, and compromises with, National Socialism, and his subsequent refusal to retract or to give a truthful account of them; and there is a very obvious sense in which one may say that his political views and his personal actions in the twelve years of the Third Reich were wholly unbecoming his calling as a philosopher. Yet Heidegger's philosophy contains profound (and it may be unparalleled) insights into the technological impasse of our time, and the validity of these insights is unaffected not only by his personal conduct but also by those of his philosophical views which must now be read as attempts at justifying his own peculiar version of National Socialism.

The dichotomy is plausible in another sense, too. Focusing our attention on the life, we shall find that detaching it from the philosophical work is a way of making it available to literature. Thus, the sheer interest of Wittgenstein's strenuous life, with its rejections and self-imposed severities, resembling in some ways the life of Adrian Leverkühn, the hero of Thomas Mann's *Doctor Faustus*, may sustain the narrative of a novel that need not take issue with the philosopher's 'professional' work. (At least two such fictions of the life have, in fact, been written; and the late Thomas Bernhard has written a weird play, *Ritter, Dene, Voss* (1986), which conveys not a single philosophical idea of Wittgenstein's while presenting his passionate commitment as a form of certified insanity.) Moreover, there is a literariness about Wittgenstein's philosophical undertaking which McGuinness notes but does not fully explore.

To speak of Wittgenstein's philosophical passion is only another way of saying that he was not a 'professional' philosopher in that restricted sense of the word; of this sort of professionalism he was deeply contemptuous. The act of will by which he committed his life to the work is manifest on almost every page of McGuinness's book, which is guided throughout by the recognition that the biographer cannot be content to present the man as distinct from the philosopher. Without recourse to fiction or scandal, though not of course without reasonable conjectures clearly marked as such, McGuinness pursues his argument to the points where the man and the philosopher meet, and where he can show that such a division would go, not indeed against the arguments of the *Tractatus*, but against the spirit and ultimate intention of Wittgenstein himself. The biographer's intention is to take the writing of the *Tractatus* out of the realm of contingency at least to the extent of demonstrating that this man with this life was uniquely fitted to write this book.

Does McGuinness succeed? In a general sense he does. Working hard not to lose the reader who is not a philosopher, he shows how the *Tractatus* really fulfils the promise implied in its first sentence, by being about 'everything that is the case' – that is, the world seen in the mode of its logical relations. And this 'everything' will, of course, include the logical structure of the propositions of 'factual language' (the phrase is David Pears's) made in, and in part constituting, the life of the author of the *Tractatus*. But to acknowledge this general sense in which McGuinness is successful is not the same as acknowledging that there is a necessary relationship between the life and the work.

Did Wittgenstein want his biography to be written? McGuinness conjectures – convincingly, I think – that he did (does this explain why Wittgenstein went to enormous lengths to preserve all he wrote, even the most embarrassingly private observations?), and my guess is that he might have approved of McGuinness as its author. But what is clear, beyond conjecture, are the serious obstacles the author of the *Tractatus* puts in any biographer's way. For one of the things the *Tractatus* is about, especially in its second half, is the limits of our language: Wittgenstein's book reflects his abundantly reasoned insistence that the kind of language whose logical relations it explores is not available for the discussion of the problems of our existence whenever these are formulated as ethical, aesthetic, or religious problems; is not, therefore, available for substantial parts of McGuinness's undertaking. And this insistence on the limits of what can be clearly said, which is argued ever more strongly as the *Tractatus* moves towards its concluding negations, issues in the claim that, apart from the kind of language examined in the book, there is no other – there is only waffle (in his diaries Wittgenstein uses the homely Austrian term, 'Schwefeln') or silence. McGuinness neither waffles nor is silent. But in his endeavour to connect the life and the work, and to be as accurate as possible about both, he is bound to write against the grain of the *Tractatus*.

5

Ray Monk for his part has certainly made use of every manuscript, diary note and letter that came his way, and the resulting story is told with great competence and skill, and some empathy. The English tradition of biography flourishes at the present time, and Monk's book belongs to that tradition. It tells the story of a quest for what used to be called the good life. For a time in the 1920s Wittgenstein, like many of his contemporaries, thought he could find it in a rural setting, among the poorest peasants in Lower Austria. He was to be deeply disappointed, and the experiment of teaching in village schools ended in disaster; Wittgenstein narrowly avoided prosecution for ill-treating one of his pupils. A plan to settle in the Soviet Union (perhaps the last bit of Tolstoyan romanticism) came to nothing, and his return to Cambridge in 1929, though it turned out to be the decisive turning-point in his philosophical development, must at times have seemed like defeat – a failure, at least, to free himself, as Nietzsche had done, from institutional pressures and obligations. Like Nietzsche, he was forever seeking solitude and unable to endure it, seeking ideal conditions and places of work – in a log cabin built to his design on a Norwegian fjord, in Ireland, with friends in Birmingham, in Swansea. By the time war broke out in 1939 he had become a British subject and had managed to use, on behalf of the family, some of their immense fortune to bribe the authorities in Berlin (in much-needed dollars) to certify that the regulations (the 'Nuremberg Laws') relating to 'persons of mixed blood' did not apply to those of his family who had remained in Vienna (a humiliating process which Monk is the first biographer to record in detail). Finding wartime Cambridge unendurable, Wittgenstein left it in 1941 for service at Guy's Hospital as a dispensary porter, moving two years or so later to Newcastle, where he worked as laboratory assistant; yet by the time he had become a useful member of a medical team investigating the effects of injury (there being much heated argument on the usefulness or otherwise of the term 'shock conditions'), he was impatient to return to Cambridge, to his friends there, and to philosophy.

Writing on Wittgenstein's friendships – three of his closest friends, David Pinsent, Frank Ramsay and Francis Skinner, died in their twenties – Monk sums up:

> In writing this book . . . I have chosen to quote virtually all the remarks [cast in a very simple code] that are in any way revealing of Wittgenstein's emotional, spiritual and sexual life . . . have left nothing out that would lend support to the popular notion that Wittgenstein was tormented by his homosexuality, although I myself believe this to be a simplification that seriously misrepresents the truth.
>
> What the coded remarks reveal is that Wittgenstein was uneasy, not about homosexuality, but about sexuality itself. Love, whether of a man or a woman, was something he treasured. He regarded it as a gift, almost as a divine gift. But, together with Weininger (whose *Sex and Character* spells out, I believe, many attitudes towards love and sex that are implicit in much Wittgenstein said, wrote and did), he sharply differentiated love from sex. Sexual arousal, both homo- and heterosexual, troubled him enormously. He seemed to regard it as incompatible with the sort of person he wanted to be. (p. 585)

I have quoted these observations at length because they illustrate not only Monk's fairness and straightforwardness, but also the lack of perception which characterizes all those parts of the book in which Wittgenstein's religiousness is at issue.

What sort of man *did* Wittgenstein want to be? The 'unease' which Monk mentions in this passage from the very end of the book (it seems to me) is essentially the expression of a troubled religious conscience. The intellectual climate in which English biography flourishes is not propitious to what I take to be the central problem of *this* biography: it seems difficult to make out what sort of perception Monk brings to bear on the complex fabric of a Christian mind in our age – a religious or would-be religious mind with its strengths and doubts, its humilities and brief moments of assurance, its deliberations on what is and what is not permitted, its sloughs of despond. Monk quotes from one of Wittgenstein's diaries –

> Christianity is not a doctrine, not, I mean, a theory about what has happened and will happen to the human soul, but a description of something that actually takes place in human life. For 'consciousness of

sin' is a real event and so are despair and salvation through faith. Those who speak of such things (Bunyan for instance) are simply describing what has happened to them ... (p. 376).

– and there are numerous similar remarks ('if Christianity is the truth, then all the philosophy that is written about it is false', is another) which go uncommented. Their poignancy lies in Wittgenstein's awareness that he is not one of those who are 'simply describing what has happened', that philosophy itself prevents him from being one of them. The conflict between 'love and sex' is subsumed by Wittgenstein under the uncertainty whether his entire life, including his 'duties as a philosopher', can indeed be interpreted 'religiously'. An occasional air of bemused wonder draws the limits of the biographer's insights. St Augustine *and* the ghastly Otto Weininger, Kierkegaard *and* Maynard Keynes, assistant gardener at the monastery of Klosterneuburg *and* Cambridge Apostle ... the strangeness of it all seems a little overwhelming.

6

Thinking about the limits of language – as opposed to the rigorous logical grounding of such thinking – is not original to Wittgenstein. Philosophy in Austria (I have suggested) began almost precisely at the time of the dissolution of the Holy Roman Empire, with the work of the Bohemian priest Bernard Bolzano. In this first phase it was, as Nyíri observes (p. 178), a reaction against German Idealism in general and the Kantian critique in particular. Bolzano's effort (in his *Wissenschaftslehre* of 1837) had been directed towards replacing Kant's concept of an unknowable 'Ding an sich' by arguing for our ability to conceive of 'truths in themselves'. But in many of his popular writings and sermons Bolzano was concerned with language – language seen not as an abstract philosophical problem, but as a social and political phenomenon. After Bolzano, philosophy as written, taught and discussed in Vienna became increasingly an inquiry into what German Idealism had ignored – it became a philosophical inquiry into the role played by language in experience. At much the same time, however, this inquiry, in *fin-de-siècle* Vienna and only there, ceased to be confined to philosophy and theoretical thinking about the natural sciences and technology, and was taken up in journalism and fiction, and in polemical writings on the borderline between the two. This is the background which offers a partial but very specific answer to one of the questions asked in McGuinness's book: the question, 'Why should this man write a philosophical treatise, the central claim of which is that philosophy is nothing other than a critique of language?' Because at some point he came to feel the need to make all this talk (some of it mere chatter) about language and its limits more precise. McGuinness is right to distinguish (pp. 251 f.) between contemporary Viennese polemics against the abuses of language

conducted by the literati and politicians (essay 3), and Wittgenstein's fundamental critique of it. The difference is, roughly, between seeing language as
the source of evil and seeing it as the source of nonsense. But there is a family
resemblance between these different kinds of critical language consciousness. McGuinness's reference to the question of Viennese language consciousness is one way of converting contingent biographical facts into necessary
aspects of the philosophy. Still, the broader question remains: if, for Wittgenstein, logic is such a fundamental and all-embracing preoccupation as the
Tractatus demonstrates (not only a formal concern, but the content of the
philosophy), can biography account for that? The short answer is that in
Wittgenstein's preoccupation with logic a personal passion and a sense of duty
are combined. The fuller answer, which is implied in the subtitle of Monk's
book, 'The Duty of Genius', but only partly spelled out there, goes something
like this:

(1)   Here is a thinker who is at almost every point in his life visited by a
sense of moral duties imposed on him, accepted and (judged by his own
uncompromising standards) inadequately discharged. It is this sense which
dominates both McGuinness's and Monk's accounts of Wittgenstein's relations
with his family and friends, and especially their portraits of the philosopher's
energetic, unconventional and ambitious father. Such portraits, in our day and
age, can hardly be drawn without some help from Freud, but they are
mercifully free from Freudian stereotype, jargon and theory.

(2)   Closely connected with this sense of moral duties perceived and
accepted are several extended references, based on his diaries and letters, to
Wittgenstein's religious sense, which was perhaps awakened and certainly
intensified by the war experience. And just as Wittgenstein's acknowledgement
of his moral duties was almost always accompanied by a sense of moral
inadequacy, so his religious sense was almost always accompanied by a consciousness of sin. Though Wittgenstein rejected any institutional religious
framework (remaining a stranger to institutions of any kind), his reading of
Tolstoy and, perhaps more directly, of Dostoevsky and Kierkegaard, leaves
one in no doubt that this religious sense was Christian.

(3)   At some point, probably during his time as a student at the Technische
Hochschule in Berlin (October 1906 – May 1908), but certainly during his
time as a research engineer at Manchester (1908, with interruptions, until
1911), a powerful philosophical ambition was awakened. Exactly how this
happened is not clear. All we know is that the move away from engineering
was not caused by mathematical difficulties Wittgenstein encountered while
experimenting (somewhat haphazardly, it appears) with kites and aeroplanes
(McGuinness, p. 76). The interest in the connections between mathematics
and logic had already been kindled during his time at Charlottenburg, where
Wittgenstein read books by Russell and Frege, and it was intensified at

Manchester. It was this interest that took Wittgenstein, in the autumn of 1911, to Cambridge. These influences are not presented as sufficient reasons for his finding a vocation, yet without them the philosophical achievement of a lifetime is unthinkable.

These three aspects of the young Wittgenstein's life and mind, including the religious one, all point in the same direction. They offer different reasons why he conceived of his duty as a philosopher – his duty towards logic – 'religiously', that is, in the most rigorous and exacting manner. That this view of the philosopher's task did not change is confirmed by what Wittgenstein wrote in the 1940 Preface to *Philosophical Remarks* (not, it will be noted, in the book itself): 'I would like to say that "this book was written in honour of God"', but then he adds, with the bitterness with which he came to view Western civilization, that 'this would nowadays be an infamy, i.e. it would not be understood correctly'.

(4)   But a further aspect of this mind, mentioned by either biographer only in passing, must be considered. To some readers, especially to those who, like the present writer, are not philosophers, the most admirable and stimulating aspect of Wittgenstein's work is his capacity to muster a rich array of analogies and images, to see one set of ideas under the aspect of another: 'What I invent are new *metaphors [Gleichnisse]*'; and again, in a letter to G. E. Moore: 'You see, I still make beautiful similes' (Monk, p. 363). Often such images are not merely illustrations, but form the coda of the argument. (This capacity for lateral thinking he shared with Lichtenberg, though he gave one little thanks for pointing this out; and it is a matter of regret that McGuinness's remarks on Lichtenberg are perfunctory and Monk's conspicuously absent.) This gift, which is one of the main sources of Wittgenstein's philosophical achievement, was fully developed by the time the *Tractatus* received its final shape. After all, the core of the book is formed by the insight (or, to use Lichtenberg's word, *Einfall*) that sentences are pictures of the world; that the relationship between language and the world becomes clearer and ceases to be mystifying as soon as we see language as having a structure in some significant ways similar to the structure of the world; as soon as we see propositions in the same light as facts: 'A gramophone record, the musical idea, the written notes, and the sound-waves, all stand to one another in the same internal relation of depicting that holds between language and the world. They are all constructed according to a common logical pattern.' The criticism of this view, as well as of the book as a whole, McGuinness leaves for his second volume.

7

If that gift for metaphor and analogy was as central to Wittgenstein's genius as I have suggested, the question arises how intrinsically it is related to the moral and religious elements in his thinking. And the answer must surely be that it is not, at least not in any discernible or determinable way; that the imagination (the gift for metaphor and analogy) is, in all of us, a free-floating, *wertfrei*, amoral gift. Its origin is akin to the origin of poetry: to paraphrase T. S. Eliot's famous formulation, it lies in an expectation being both disrupted and enriched by an individual talent. It can be placed in the service of ethical thinking and need not be indifferent to it, but it is unpredictable and indeterminable in its effects on it. Some pictures which the imagination conjures up mislead, others do not; beauty and ugliness and truth and lies are permutable. This may well be a truth about life and ourselves to which Wittgenstein felt incapable of reconciling himself, which he felt it his duty to deny.

Such a view of the imagination and of the aesthetic, its product, seems to run counter to Wittgenstein's later philosophy of 'social contextualism'. This is Nyíri's term (p. 131) to indicate Wittgenstein's central insight that 'language games' of all kinds are to be understood neither as mainly, or purely, mental acts, nor as mainly, or purely, physical events, but as events which belong to the rich and varied whole contexts of socially embedded and institutionalized individual lives. (This insight, incidentally, is not all that distant from Heidegger's anti-mentalist phenomenology of skills and crafts and work.) But why (one might object to this notion of the value-indifferent and free-floating nature of metaphors) should the imagination be exempt from this 'social contextualism'? Because metaphors are by their nature only tenuously connected with common situations. They are minute sorties which the imagination conducts against accepted rules, traditions and social contexts and their laws in order to illuminate these rules and contexts and laws, or in order to modify them and make them more precise, or in order to show them up in their absurdity: metaphors help our understanding by illuminating all 'forms of life', of which language is one. Often they are tied to one language and are untranslatable into another (in *PI* § 83 Wittgenstein writes 'die Analogie . . . steckt uns ein Licht auf', which is a far cry from its nearest English translation, 'analogy throws a light' – and what is 'a far cry' in German?). And often the promised illumination may not come, or may be much delayed, to delight another generation of readers or audiences; today's surrealism may become tomorrow's realism, a promise unredeemed is still a promise. The delight metaphors and the imagination yield is immediate, but this does not exempt them *finally* from the order of the contexts in which they appear, and which their appearance disrupts and may eventually alter. Hence, Wittgenstein's unease with Shakespeare: the reluctant admirer seems to trust neither the moments of instant delight nor the achievement of order deferred (least of all when these are described by 'a thousand professors of literature'). Any help from literary criticism – that is, from a discursive, non-aphoristic account of what happens when we read a text – is dismissed.

This mention of the imagination takes our argument to the frontier between philosophy and literature. It places in the foreground the figure of Karl Kraus, the Viennese satirist whose entire *œuvre* constantly reiterates its author's conviction that the imagination is an absolute value in itself; that it is inseparably bound up with morality; or, in terms of the *Tractatus*, that 'ethics and aesthetics are one and the same' (6.421), or rather, could be said to be one and the same if there were a meaningful way of discussing them.

Both biographers mention Wittgenstein's pre-war reading of Kraus's satirical periodical *Die Fackel*, and McGuinness mentions his disastrous meeting with the satirist himself (p. 281). In the course of that meeting – there was probably only one, and it probably took place in 1919, after Wittgenstein's return from Italian captivity – Wittgenstein is reported as having accused Kraus of 'repulsive vanity', while Kraus is said to have taken Wittgenstein for a madman. Kraus certainly had no inkling of Wittgenstein's philosophical undertaking, and little understanding for the distaste Wittgenstein felt towards the coterie around the embattled satirist. As for Wittgenstein, what had changed his favourable pre-war view of Kraus's writing – his admiration of 'the man and his style' (p. 37), that is, the unity of 'ethics and aesthetics' – was his own traumatic war experience. Did he now feel that Kraus's 'repulsive vanity' was proof that he (Kraus) had not suffered as much? This was the kind of accusation Kraus was all too ready to launch against others. Embarrassingly, the post-war years in Austria and Germany abounded with flauntings of suffering and self-sacrifice. It was a period in which many (like Joseph Roth) could not reconcile themselves to the new Central Europe that arose on the ruins of the defeated Empire, while others (like Kraus in the aftermath of the war) looked back on that Empire as a rotten state and its defeat as the deserved outcome of its history of iniquities and ineptitudes. It is very unlikely that Wittgenstein shared either of these views, and it is certain that he would have found the appeal to 'the supreme sacrifice' and to 'das Fronterlebnis' (the main plank of Hitler's and his contemporaries' political platform) both morally and aesthetically repulsive, an experience it would not be proper to talk about: 'If you make a sacrifice and pride yourself on it, then both you and your sacrifice will be damned.'

McGuinness sees Kraus's satirical undertaking as 'something very Austrian, and something, we can now see, very Wittgensteinian – to achieve a kind of moral reform of life and thought without attempting to alter the conditions of life' (pp. 205f.). Too little troubled by what he calls its 'unworldliness', McGuinness describes this attempt at reform as 'an important discovery that the revolution needed (however impossible it might be) was not one in institutions but in the thinking and sensibility – Kraus would say in the language – of men'. I doubt whether this is really 'an important discovery', it looks more like a chimera. Distrust of institutions and lack of positive interest in them were a feature of both Kraus's and Wittgenstein's thinking for the rest of their lives. This means that the 'social contextualism' which Nyíri postulates as the central insight of Wittgenstein's later philosophy needs to be qualified: Wittgenstein is more often concerned with emphasizing the need for setting up such contexts beyond the reach of all psycho-physical dualisms than with discussing them in concrete detail. To this lack of 'enargeia' ('concreteness'), however, there is an important exception: the discovery of language as an institution (recognized as such by Bolzano, but not by Frege), a discovery which would not become a philosophical issue until the second half of Wittgenstein's *œuvre*. Kraus's satire is built from the converse of the 'truth=beauty' equation. The cliché – the main butt of Kraus's satire – is seen not merely as ugly, but as the unfailing linguistic indication of moral turpitude; the satirist need do no more than show up the cliché for what it is, deconstruct it, to reveal the truth – always the ugly truth – about its author-perpetrator. Paul Engelmann, Wittgenstein's closest wartime friend, saw Wittgenstein's analysis of language as the philosophical analogue of Kraus's satirical sorties (McGuinness, p. 251). However that may be, by the time Wittgenstein returned from the war, Kraus's procedure had ceased to be of interest to him; in later years he thought it tediously repetitious.

8

The 'idea of the unutterable truth that makes itself manifest', Monk writes, is 'the central thread that links the logic and the mysticism' (p. 150); to which we should add that the belief in the inadequacy of language and the search for the unsayable, 'the mystical', was *the* fashionable topic in the literature of the time. We find it in Rilke's poetry, in Hofmannsthal and in Robert Musil's prose. The paradox of Rilke's poetic variations on 'das Unsägliche' (in the Ninth Duino Elegy) is adumbrated in a comment of Wittgenstein's on a very different poem, by Ludwig Uhland (1787–1862): 'If only you do not try to utter what is unutterable, then *nothing* gets lost. But the unutterable will be – unutterably – *contained* in what has been uttered!' McGuinness relates this statement directly to the concept of 'showing' in the *Tractatus*:

> 4.12 Propositions can represent the whole of reality, but they cannot represent what they must have in common with reality in order to be able to represent it – logical form . . .
> 4.121 Propositions cannot represent logical form: it is mirrored in them.
>   What finds its reflection in language, language cannot represent.
>   What expresses *itself* in language, *we* cannot express by means of language.
>   Propositions *show* the logical form of reality.
>   They display it.

Now McGuinness's point, supported by quotations from the diaries and letters, is that these central passages of the *Tractatus* are 'wedded' to Wittgenstein's feeling for literature (p. 251); and this may well be true in a general sense. But the concern with the limits of language expressed in this quotation is surely of a very different kind, and it is not at all clear how it might be related to a 'feeling for literature'.

Uhland's ballad, 'Count Eberhard's Hawthorn' (the poem Wittgenstein loved well enough to recite thirty years later), tells the story of a German knight who, on his pilgrimage to the Holy Land, cut a spray of hawthorn and stuck it in his helmet. On his return he planted the spray in the soil of his native Württemberg and watched it grow into a majestic tree. Sitting beneath the tree, the old man would dream and remember his pilgrimage of long ago.

True, my prosy retelling of the story does little to re-create the charm of this typical conceit poem. Attempting to indicate what is 'unutterably contained' in it, one would wish to say something about the way the life of the tree retraces and encompasses the passage of years, symbolizes a lifetime. In such an analysis, too, something would be lost, though the loss would be diminished by one's pointing to that part of the poem which shows that the old count himself is reminded by the tree's arching branches of the past ('Die Wölbung, hoch und breit,/Mit sanftem Rauschen mahnt/Ihn an die alte Zeit/Und an das ferne Land'); in other words, the critical account would show that the poem itself explicitly initiates its symbolic interpretation by using a part of its narrative to hint at what we would call the interpreter's 'meta-language'. And though the loss entailed by the prosy version would still remain, a renewed reading of the poem would be enriched by what has been said about its symbolic meaning. I am not suggesting that critical analysis can replace the poem; but in the course of it 'the unutterable' becomes relative – relative to the skill and tact of the analysis – and thus what remains unsaid is quite different from what remains unsaid because it is impossible for propositions to represent the 'logical form' that is 'mirrored in them'.

What is involved, then, are two very different kinds of 'the unutterable', two different concerns with the limits of language. One is grounded in the logic of the *Tractatus*; and the notion of a philosophical 'meta-language', considered but not named at the end of Bertrand Russell's introduction to the book, will eventually serve as a refutation of that part of its logic. Whereas the second concern – this alone we may call literary – though ruled out of court in the *Tractatus*, is not subject to the same refutation.

An observation of Nietzsche's will help us to see more clearly what is involved in this 'literary' concern. Placing his argument on that borderline between ethics and aesthetics on which Wittgenstein will place Kraus's pre-war satire, Nietzsche writes:

We no longer esteem ourselves sufficiently when we communicate ourselves. Our real experiences [*unsere eigentlichen Erlebnisse*] are not at all garrulous. They could not communicate themselves even if they tried. That is because they lack the right word. Whatever we have words for, we have already outgrown. In all talk [*in allem Reden*] there is a grain of contempt. Language, it seems, was invented only for the average, for the middling and communicable. With language the speaker *vulgarizes* himself.

Nietzsche's reflection illuminates some of the ground of the aphoristic – that is, elegant *and* peremptory – style of the *Tractatus* (and of Wittgenstein's later writings). This style may not be a matter of deliberate choice but reflect a necessity; it certainly derives its force from the sheer abundance and magnitude of a philosophic vision which its author feels cannot be presented in a more discursive fashion. This vision is reflected in the style in many ways. It is a part of David Pears's argument that the aphoristic style reflects the author's concession to the necessity of that linear, *nacheinander* presentation that goes with printed language. But what the style also shows is something more than impatience and less than arrogance – impatience with the reader who expects to be spoon-fed, but should either work out and supply by himself the connections that are not provided by the author, or else stay away. (All these remarks apply, *mutatis mutandis*, to those of Nietzsche's own writings which are cast in a similar mode.)

But (it will be objected) what has this to do with 'what cannot be said', with Wittgenstein's concern with the limits of language? Beyond the impatience, and connected with what may appear as arrogance, the style is governed by something like a personal categorical imperative. I mean Wittgenstein's deep (and surprisingly English) conviction that it is neither right nor proper, that it is not decent, to talk of the 'last', the most important and fundamental things in life; or perhaps it is right to talk about them, with a friend, or rather to a friend, but not to write about them, and by writing to 'vulgarize them', to make them available to any Tom, Dick, or Harry. Because . . . ? Because. Something like an aesthetic limit or interdict is imposed on explanation. Here, from Wittgenstein's discussions with Friedrich Waismann, is another example: challenging the view that 'God wills the good because it is the good' is more profound than 'the good is good because God wills it', Wittgenstein commends the latter view because 'it cuts short every explanation "why" it is good, whereas [the former] is the shallow, rationalist view, which proceeds "as if" that which is good could be given a further reason.' Of course, the phrase 'the shallow, rationalist view' is invective rather than argument, a mere expression of distaste – it might be Nietzsche speaking, or Heidegger.

Thus, the limits of language are set not only by what David Pears calls 'the mystery of the world beneath the surface skimmed by factual language' (p. 5), but also by the rules of what is done and what is not done. Or rather: if the rules of what is done and what is not are what we call ethics and aesthetics, and if they are traced deeply enough, then they, too, belong to 'the mystery of the world beneath the surface'.

To speak of a 'personal categorical imperative' is to use the sort of language the *Tractatus* is designed to proscribe (McGuinness, for one, does not use the term). It is to speak oxymoronically; at least in the sense that this is an imperative which is not explicitly universalized. The term is convenient because it describes at least approximately the strength and seriousness of that conviction from which one of the two strands of Wittgenstein's investigation into the limits of language proceeds – the strand which legitimates the biographer's work on a portrait of the author of the *Tractatus*.

In this imperative, the unity of ethics and aesthetics reappears in the implied claim that what is in bad taste is morally wrong. True, this imperative renders the idea of the limits of language contingent upon the person of the philosopher; makes it contingent upon what McGuinness calls 'the helpless and hopeless situation of an Austrian officer' at the end of a war which brought with it the end of his world (p. 313). (When the *Tractatus* at last found a publisher and made its appearance – in a periodical – before an almost wholly incurious public, Wittgenstein was in the throes of a profound depression; he saw nothing that would take the place of the ruins around him.) But the contingency receives its philosophical sanction in the view of the world towards which the logic of the book has been advancing: *'The limits of my language* mean the limits of my world' (5.6).

As the *Tractatus* nears its end, it turns repeatedly to the problems of 'life', of 'God, freedom and morality' (the phrase is McGuinness's) – towards the things that, we were told, cannot be said. These sanctions contain 'the real message of the book' (McGuinness, p. 312). The message that (as Wittgenstein would have it) there is no message? Surely not. Truth, in this biography, is achieved against the grain. If one relates the *Tractatus* and its writing as closely to the life and personality of its author as McGuinness does, one's conclusion is bound to be different from the conclusion explictly argued and then transcended by Wittgenstein himself. Setting out to show the limits of language, the *Tractatus* neither shows the non-existence of the problems raised by 'life . . . God, freedom and morality', nor shows them to be inexpressible. As for Wittgenstein's philosophy 'after the turn' – that is, after his return to Cambridge in 1929 – we shall no longer be able to presuppose that there is a procedure 'for the whole of logic', 'a logic [for the whole] of language, a logic of all thought' (McGuinness, p. 313). Or, as Franz Kafka puts it at the end of *his* book, *The Trial*: 'Logic is doubtless unshakeable, but it does not resist a man who wants to live.'

9

There is at least one major point of agreement between Nyíri's and McGuinness's views: for both, the end of the world in which Wittgenstein grew up – the dissolution of the Habsburg Empire at the end of the last and most disastrous of the many wars in which Franz Joseph led his country to defeat – was also the end of Wittgenstein's systematic metaphysics. This is where Nyíri's Wittgenstein chapter begins and McGuinness's first volume ends, but Nyíri's interpretation proceeds very differently. His aim is to place Wittgenstein's later philosophy in a Conservative tradition. This is supported in several ways: by extended references to Wittgenstein's love of such writers as Grillparzer, Dostoevsky, Paul Ernst and Oswald Spengler; by quoting numerous examples of his hostility to 'the classical bourgeois image of man' generally (p. 107), and to the liberal ideal of progress in particular; and by arguing that Wittgenstein's analyses of 'ordinary language', and his many objections to theoretical speculations unrelated to 'actual usage' (*PI* § 124), are all signs of an 'essentially' Conservative attitude. Even though none of the definitions of Conservatism quoted comes from Wittgenstein's own writings, Nyíri does not hesitate to press an unequivocally political claim. It is not merely that concepts such as 'following' or 'obeying' a rule of our actual language (p. 199), or again Wittgenstein's (disastrous) pedagogic views, connote a vaguely conservative attitude – the Conservatism Nyíri has in mind is a fully-fledged political attitude too.

The main interest of Nyíri's chapter lies in the many previously unpublished reflections he quotes from the Wittgenstein archives, but some of them strike me as only biographically interesting; showing, quite simply, that though the passion and the intensity are always there, they are sometimes misapplied. None of Wittgenstein's 'political' observations can be adduced to support more than a distaste for revolution and an air of tetchiness in respect of reforms individually initiated. ('The sickness of a time is cured by an alteration in the mode of life of human beings ... not through a medicine invented by a single person.') Some of these remarks are strikingly similar to Michael Oakeshott's writings on 'rationalism in politics', but seen in this perspective they are merely casual: they lack the understanding that comes from a historian's extended consideration of actual social and political contexts. The only apparent exception is the well-known observations on *The Decline of the West*, a book which interested Wittgenstein not for its nationalist politics but for its comparative method. Apart from his comments on Spengler, no evidence is offered to suggest that Wittgenstein showed any interest in the German 'Conservative Revolution', that he read any of the writings from which Nyíri quotes in support of his claim that Wittgenstein '*must have been deeply interested in*' the neo-Conservative views and literature of the 1920s (p. 115). The telltale phrase I have italicized indicates how little the chronicler and analyst of Wittgenstein's philosophy seems to have taken to heart its injunction to avoid all *must have beens*, and instead *to look* for what was the case (§ 66). (What Wittgenstein was undoubtedly interested in was the Soviet experiment; though his brief stay in Russia with the intention of settling there – in autumn 1935 – came to nothing.)

The problem, then, is to place Wittgenstein's *œuvre* in its context without giving it the kind of historical dimension it doesn't possess. To resume an earlier argument: his philosophy has of course its place in history; it contains profound insights into *the structure* of historical situations as well as into reports on such structures; and it is especially original and illuminating about the relationship between the two, and between deeds and words generally. But it takes no issue with historical structures as such, as (say) Locke's or Hegel's or Marx's philosophy does. 'Existentialists' are frequently scandalized by this omission, others think it regrettable – it may be that Nyíri did, and then constructed the 'Conservative' argument to supply it.

There are no signs that Wittgenstein was *au fait* either with the day-to-day events of the 1930s, or with its ideologies and practices, new and old. It is one of the truisms of the monstrous history of that age that the 'neo-Conservative circles' Nyíri mentions helped to bring about the dissolution of the Weimar Republic and the rise of National Socialism; again, we are offered no evidence (either by Monk or by Nyíri) that Wittgenstein paid any significant attention to this process. The glimpses one gets of his concern with politics – above all his summary condemnation of ' . . . the fascism and socialism of our time' – suggest that in such matters he was ready to let himself be seduced by 'the terminology in common currency' – that is, by contemporary clichés. And this, I take it, must also apply to Wittgenstein's anti-Jewish remarks, many of them made in connection with Otto Weininger's *Sex and Character* (a book which, to me, reads in parts like a high-class edition of *Der Stürmer*). Nyíri sees these remarks in a different light, and makes a valiant but, I think, vain effort to give them some sort of respectable meaning. McGuinness's comment seems a little more convincing: 'Today, after Hitler, most families with Jewish blood have a different attitude towards their origin and see it as the source of their energy and intelligence, but Ludwig belonged to an earlier way of thinking' (p. 2). At least, McGuinness follows the Wittgensteinian paradigm: to understand what was said at another time you have to understand more than – that is, the context of – what was said. Monk (p. 314) goes further than McGuinness. He shows very clearly the self-destructive nature of these remarks, and he is surely right to conclude that 'were [it] not written by Wittgenstein', 'this whole litany of lamentable nonsense' would be rejected as anti-Semitic rantings. Yet these remarks too belong to the theme of 'Wittgenstein in Context': they are one more example of the views of one who bore witness to 'the sickness of his time' because he shared it, and to the time's 'contemptuous attitude towards the particular case' because, occasionally, he shared that too. It must be added, though, that (as far as I can tell) none of these remarks occur after 1931.

10

Is Nyíri saying that a philosopher of a different political persuasion would have produced a different philosophy? Or that Wittgenstein's philosophy invalidates, say, socialism and its reformist ideology? If he comes close to implying such a conclusion, this is because at the centre of his argument there is something like an inadvertent metonymy.

The 'conservative' attitude that is basic to the philosophy is exemplified by Wittgenstein's insistence that certainty, understanding, agreement and disagreement among human beings are possible only within a shared institutional framework; not that reforms are impossible, or undesirable, but that what is being reformed (the status quo) is bound to be reflected in the outcome, for 'I cannot start from anywhere except where I happen to be.' In support of Wittgenstein's supposed Conservatism, Nyíri quotes (p. 107) from *Philosophical Investigations* (§ 18): 'Our language can be seen as an ancient city: a maze of little streets and squares, of old and new houses, and of houses with additions from various periods; and this surrounded by a multitude of new suburbs with straight regular streets and uniform houses.' But the metaphor says more than Nyíri takes from it: comparing our language to an ancient city, it 'speaks of the straight new avenues in the suburbs as well as of the twisted streets in the old centre'.

How are towns planned and built? People's agreement and disagreement about what should be left as it is and what should be changed and made straight, which is agreement and disagreement in their 'opinions', is possible not in spite of but because of their agreement on the language they have in common, that is, in their 'form of life' (§ 241). In setting out the implications of this seminal view of the way things actually are, Nyíri's argument is at its best: here, to one side of its *kaisertreu* apologia, lies its great value. But this 'conservative' disposition has nothing to do with party politics – seen in *that* perspective the argument, indeed the philosophy itself, turns out to be non-political, whereas the Conservative attitude that Nyíri also attributes to Wittgenstein is concerned with affirming one particular arrangement within a shared institutional framework, and denying not just the value but the possibility of other arrangements within the same framework. The misprision here is between a whole and one of its parts, or again between the language people use and the opinions they express in that language. We end where (in this book's first essay) we began: at this point Wittgenstein's map of our language resembles Saussure's: the difference between the two meanings of 'c/Conservative' resembles the difference between *langue* and *parole*.

If then, Wittgenstein was not a conservative philosopher in the sense claimed by Nyíri, his place as an 'Austrian' philosopher (one of the stations mentioned at the end of the Bolzano essay (2)) is equally problematic. As we have seen, the name may help to pinpoint certain aspects of his philosophy, but it offers no fundamental or final insight; it is *not* as though one could say, 'He has learned from, and argued with, Frege and Russell, he has taught and thought in Cambridge, in his writings Western critical philosophy reaches its summit, but *really*, you know, he is an Austrian at heart.'

Reflecting on 'the good Austrian' element in Grillparzer, Lenau, Anton Bruckner and the composer Josef Labor (a Bohemian friend who lived in the family house in Vienna), Wittgenstein says that whatever is characteristically Austrian – *das gute Österreichische* – is 'particularly hard to understand. There is a sense in which it is *subtler* than anything else, and the truth it expresses never inclines towards plausibility.' In this sense, his name must be added to the list. But other things are Austrian too, among them a propensity for myth which readily turns into chatter, and which, for more than a century, has been a mainstay of the country's search for a national identity. After years when his very name was ignored in Austria, a 'Wittgenstein myth' is now in the making. And, seeing that the truth of his life 'never inclines towards plausibility', this is hardly surprising. At a time when Europe was divided, his life and writings reflected the tensions of some of its contrary elements – against the time when the divisions might start to heal.

1991

Notes, References and Acknowledgements

Abbreviations

GW   Franz Kafka, *Gesammelte Werke*, ed. Max Brod (7 vols, Frankfurt/M, 1976)

HFP   J. P. Stern, *Hitler: The Führer and the People*, 3rd edn. (London, 1990)

LRB   *London Review of Books*

PI   Ludwig Wittgenstein, *Philosophical Investigations*, tr. G. E. M. Anscombe (Oxford, 1953)

TLS   *The Times Literary Supplement*

Introduction

The Wittgenstein quotations come from *PI*, I, §§ 71, 65 and 241; the translations are almost entirely by G. E. M. Anscombe. Sir Michael Howard writes of 'the old lands of Western Christendom' and of the Imperial-Royal bureaucracy in 'Impressions from a journey in Central Europe' in *LRB*, 25 October 1990, pp. 3, 5. For the quotations from 'Josef K.', whose real name I now find is Josef Kroutvor, see 'Střední Evropa; torzo omílané historií', *Svědectví*, 16, 63 (Paris, 1981) 443–66. For Marlow's observation, see Joseph Conrad, *Youth, Heart of Darkness, The End of the Tether* (London, 1989), p. 96. The remarks about the 'neat timetable' of the revolutions are quoted from a review of mine in the *Observer* of 23 December 1990. Bruno Schulz's portrait of the Emperor is taken from his *Sanatorium pod klepsydra kometa* (Cracow, 1957), pp. 199–200; I have used and slightly amended Celina Wieniewska's translation in *Sanatorium under the Hourglass* (London, 1978), pp. 54f. For the 'crass' Czech humorist, see Robert Pynsent's 'Jaroslav Hašek: 1883–1923', in *European Writers: the Twentieth Century* ed. George Stade (New York, 1981), pp. 1,091–118. Karl Kraus's sketch is taken from his famous 'Nachruf' ('Obituary' of Austria), in *Die Fackel* no. 501, January 1919, pp. 54f.; on 'the banality of evil' see 'ein Dämon der Mittelmäßigkeit', in *Die letzten Tage der Menschheit*, Act IV, sc. xxix (Zurich, 1945) p. 485. For the discussion about 'Košice', see Misha Glenny, *The Rebirth of History* (London, 1990), p. 86. The remark on grammarians comes from Michael Oakeshott, *On Human Conduct* (Oxford, 1975), p. 78. For what I have called the 'panlogistic idyll', see Richard Rorty, *Contingency, Irony, and Solidarity* (Cambridge, 1989), pp. 34f., 173, 176, 29. For the comment on 'theory', see Odo Marquard, *Abschied vom Prinzipiellen* (Stuttgart 1981), p. 79. My colleague Irving Dworetzsky drew my attention to F. D. Matthieson's *From the Heart of Europe* (New York, 1948); I quote from pp. 83, 186.

1 Literature and ideology

This is a revised version of *Über Literatur und Ideologie* (Veröffentlichung der Joachim-Jungius Gesellschaft der Wissenschaften, no. 30) (Göttingen, 1977); English translation by Sheila Stern 'Literature and Ideology', in *Comparative Criticism*, 3 (1981), 31–70. I am very grateful to Ursula Riniker for some critical observations on the original German lecture.

References to Goethe: *Faust* I. 2092–3 ('a horrid song'); *Die natürliche Tochter*, IV. 1; *Werther*, the narrative following Werther's letter of 20 December; the poem 'Eins und alles' of 1821 ('arm itself into rigidity'). For the biographical background of *Die natürliche Tochter*, see *Tag- und Jahreshefte* for 1899; also E. Staiger, *Goethe* (3 vols, Zurich, 1956), I, 373.

References to Nietzsche: *The Twilight of the Idols*, § 26 (on the 'commonness' of language); *The Birth of Tragedy*, §§ 5, 24, and preface of 1886; 'Die Philosophie im tragischen Zeitalter der Griechen' (1873), beginning of § 7 (for the 'metaphysic of play'); the second essay in *Untimely Meditations* (for 'historical horizon'); the final essay (IV) in *Untimely Meditations*, 'Richard Wagner in Bayreuth', end of § 1 (for 'When on that May day . . .'). For Nietzsche's 'philosophy of strenuousness', see J. P. Stern, 'Living in the Metaphor of Fiction', *Comparative Criticism*, 1 (1979), 3–16; also J. P. Stern, *A Study of Nietzsche* (Cambridge, 1979). On the question of influence, see Bruno Hillebrand (ed.) *Nietzsche und die deutsche Literatur* (3 vols, Tübingen, 1978).

References to G. C. Lichtenberg: *Schriften und Briefe*, ed. W. Promies (6 vols; Munich, 1968–71), I, B22, B159, etc. (for *Gesinnungsystem*), B365, C148; *Physikalische und mathematische Schriften* (4 vols, Göttingen, 1803–6), IV, 145–6 ('at close quarters none of it is true').

The poem by Matthias Claudius was first published in J. H. Voss's *Musen-Almanach auf 1779*. For 'aspectival' criticism, see Peter Jones, *Philosophy and the Novel* (Oxford, 1975), ch. 5. For Wittgenstein's chess metaphor, see *PI*, I, § 108, and compare Ferdinand de Saussure, *Course in General Linguistics* [held *c.*1906–11], 3rd edn. (New York, 1966), pp. 88–9. For 'methodological fictions', see also J. Culler, *Saussure* (London, 1976), e.g., pp. 37–8. Quotation from *Der Stechlin* (1898), see ch. 29; from *The Glass-Bead Game* (1943), see the last chapter ('Die Legende') of the main part (Suhrkamp edition, *Das Glasperlenspiel*, Frankfurt/M 1973, pp. 434–5), and compare 'Der Regenmacher' (pp. 503–4). The concept of 'reality' is criticized in Johannes Kleinstück, *Wirklichkeit und Realität* (Stuttgart, 1971), pp. 61, 66. 'The Dear Purchase' is in *German Quarterly*, 41 (1968), 317–37; for the title, compare Andreas Gryphius, *Lyrische Gedichte*, 'Sonn- und Feiertags-Sonette', ed. H. Palm (Tübingen, 1884), pp. 22–3. For the relation of the 'dear purchase' to National Socialist ideology, see *HFP*, *passim*. For 'family resemblance', see Ludwig Wittgenstein, *The Blue and Brown Books* (Oxford, 1964), pp. 17–18. Brecht's poem 'An die Nachgekommenen' is in *Gesammelte Gedichte* (4 vols, Frankfurt/M, 1967), II, 722–5; I quote from *Poems 1913–1956*, eds

John Willett and Ralph Manheim, rev. edn. (London and New York, 1987), p. 320. The quotations 'Him – what a performance . . .' and 'And I ask myself . . .' are from Siegfried Lenz, *Deutschstunde* (Hamburg, 1968), pp. 92, 292, 395. For the quotation from St Augustine, see *Confessiones*, bk. vii, ch. 15.

2 Bolzano's Bohemia

First published as 'Language Consciousness and Nationalism in the Age of Bernard Bolzano', *Journal of European Studies*, 19 (1989), 169–89. Reproduced by kind permission of Alpha Academic.

Bolzano's views on the nature of philosophy and mathematics are quoted from Bolzano, *Vermischte philosophische und physikalische Schriften, 1832–1848*, eds Jan Berg and Jaromír Loužil (Stuttgart – Bad Canstatt, 1978), III, 15, 33 (see also pp. 83–5 for his criticism of the concept of 'the organic'); and from the editor's introduction to Bolzano, *Theory of Science*, ed. and tr. Rolf George (Oxford, 1972), pp. xxix–xxxii. See also *Bolzano, Grundlegung der Logik: ausgewählte Paragraphen aus der 'Wissenschaftslehre'*, ed. F. Kambartel (Hamburg, 1963); and Karel Berka, *Bernard Bolzano* (Prague, 1981). For Bolzano's criticism of Kantian ethics, see Jaromír Loužil, 'Bernard Bolzanos Sitten- und Gesellschaftslehre', in *Bernard Bolzano: Leben und Wirkung*, ed. Curt Christian (Vienna, 1981), pp. 12–16; for the attacks on anti-Semitism, see Irena Seidlerová, *Politické a sociální názory Bernard Bolzano* (Prague, 1963), pp. 96–7. Biographical data and further quotations are from Eduard Winter, *Die Sozial- und Ethnoethik Bernard Bolzanos* (Vienna, 1977), especially pp. 71–2 ('people take the teachings of religion in their literal sense . . .'), 97–8 (' . . . an empire ruled by God himself'); from Winter, *Bernard Bolzano: ein Lebensbild* (Stuttgart – Bad Canstatt, 1969), especially pp. 52–71 ('Der Bolzano-Prozeß'), 80–1 (Husserl's tribute), 145 ('But the worst is this . . .'); from Winter, *Bernard Bolzano und sein Kreis* (Leipzig, 1933), especially p. 136 (résumé of *Theory of Science*); from Marie Červinková-Riegrová, *Bernard Bolzano* (Prague, 1st edn. 1881, 2nd edn. 1893); and Eduard and Marie Winter (eds) *Der Bolzanokreis: 1824–1833* (Vienna, 1970).

On the history of nationalism in Bohemia, see Jörg Hoensch, *Geschichte Böhmens* (Munich, 1987). For Jungmann's 'national programme', see the résumé in Jan Patočka, *O smysl dneška* (Purley/Surrey, 1987), especially pp. 88–104 ('Dilema v našem národním programu: Jungmann a Bolzano'); Patočka's tribute to Bolzano is quoted from p. 107. In František Palacký, *Dějiny národu v Čechách i na Moravě* (Prague, 1939), III, see especially pp. 10–12, 235ff. Further quotations are from Milan Machovec, *František Palacký a česká filosofie* (Prague, 1961), pp. 5, 116. Compare also J. F. Žáček, *Palacký: the Historian as Scholar and Nationalist* (The Hague and Paris, 1970); R. G. Plaschka, *Von Palacký bis Pekař: Geschichtswissenschaft und Nationalbewußtsein bei den Tschechen* (Graz and Cologne, 1959); Constant von Würzbach, *Biographisches Lexicon des Kaiserthums Österreich* (Vienna, 1870), XXI 179–93; and T. G. Masaryk, *Palackýs Idee des böhmischen Volkes* (Prague, 1898). On Masaryk at Prague University, see Emil Brix, 'Mentalität ist gut – die Teilung der Prager Universität 1882', *Österreichische Osthefte*, 20 (1988), 371–82; Masaryk speaks of the 'newly founded Czech University' in K[arel] Č[apek], *Hovory s T. G. Masarykem* (Prague, 1937), p. 88.

The quotation from Herder is from his *Ideen zur Philosophie der Geschichte der Menschheit* ed. Erich Schmidt (Leipzig, 1869), II, 110–15 (Herder's emphasis). For references to Wittgenstein, see *PI*, I, §§ 19, 546; *The Blue and Brown Books* (Oxford, 1964), p. 17; and *Remarks on the Foundations of Mathematics*, eds G. H. von Wright, R. Rhees and G. E. M. Anscombe (Oxford, 1956), p. 65 (I have added the phrases within square brackets to G. E. M. Anscombe's translation). See also Joachim Schulte, 'Chor und Gesetz: zur "morphologischen Methode" bei Goethe und Wittgenstein', *Grazer philosophische Studien*, 21 (1984), 28–9. Michael Dummett is quoted from his *Ursprünge der analytischen Philosophie*, tr. Joachim Schulte (Frankfurt/M, 1988), pp. 22, 33, 167. Hermann Hesse is quoted from *Das Glasperlenspiel* (Frankfurt/M, 1973), p. 15. The reference to Kant ('Bezeichnungsvermögen') is to 'Anthropologie in pragmatischer Absicht', in *Kant's Werke* (Berlin, 1907), IV, 191–4.

3 'Words are also deeds'

First published in *New Literary History*, 12 (1980–1), pp. 509–25. Reproduced by kind permission of Johns Hopkins University Press. An earlier version appeared in *Studies in Modern Austrian Literature*, ed. B. O. Murdoch and M. G. Ward (Glasgow, 1980), pp. 104–22. Josef Weinheber is quoted from *Sämtliche Werke*, eds. Josef Nadler and Hedwig Weinheber (Salzburg, 1954), II, 468–9, and V, 199. An appraisal of Weinheber's poetry is given by Walter Muschg in *Die Zerstörung der deutschen Literatur* (Berne, 1956), pp. 71–92. The soliloquy of the lawyer's clerk is in the fragmentary 'Papiere des Teufels', in *Johann Nestroys Komödien*, ed. Franz H. Mautner (Wiesbaden, 1979), VI, 296. Karl Kraus's poem 'Bekenntnis' is in *Worte in Versen* (1917; repr. Munich, 1959), II, 79. The passage on the Press is in *Das Weltgericht* (Vienna, 1919), I, 21. See also *Werke*, ed. Heinrich Fischer (Munich, 1962), II: *Die Sprache*, 436. The autobiographical quotation from Fritz Mauthner is in *Erinnerungen: I Prager Jugendjahre* (Munich, 1919), pp. 32f.; compare Hans Weigel, *Karl Kraus oder die Macht der Ohnmacht* (Vienna, Frankfurt and Zurich, 1968), p. 18. The *Antony and Cleopatra* quotation is from Act II, sc. v. The remarks on the unreliability of language are in Allan Janik and Stephen Toulmin, *Wittgenstein's Vienna* (London, 1973), pp. 118, 126; see also p. 86 for the remark on Nestroy's word-creations. Kafka's 'Rede über die jiddische Sprache' is in *GW*, VII 306–9; compare pp. 113–17, 'Vom jüdischen Theater', and the letter to Max Brod from Matljary of June 1921. For the German–Jewish language problem, see Kafka's diary entry for 24 October 1911, in *Tagebücher 1910–23*, ed. Max Brod (New York, 1949). Rilke's letters to August Sauer and Gräfin Margot Sizzo-Noris Crouy are in *Briefe*, ed. Karl Altheim (Wiesbaden, 1950), I, 472–3, and II, 340; the italics in quotations from Rilke are his own. For an earlier discussion of Rilke's language consciousness, see Peter Demetz, *René Rilkes Prager Jahre* (Düsseldorf, 1953), pp. 201–5. For further details of the Rilke–Kafka comparison and contrast, see the introduction to *The World of Franz Kafka*, ed. J. P. Stern (New York and London, 1980), pp. 2–5. For Paul Celan's linguistic dilemma, see Israel Chalfen, *Celan: eine Biographie seiner Jugend* (Frankfurt, 1979), p. 148. For Nietzsche's ideas on language, see J. P. Stern, *A Study of Nietzsche* (Cambridge, 1979), ch. 10. Robert Musil is quoted from *Der Mann ohne Eigenschaften*, ed. Adolf Frisé (Hamburg, 1952), ch. 37. For Wittgenstein, see *Tractatus Logico-Philosophicus* (London, 1922), §6.41 (Wittgenstein's italics), and *PI*, I, §§19, 241, 546 (again, Wittgenstein's italics).

4 On Prague German literature

'Begegnung mit dem Fremden' ('Encounter with the Strange(r)') was the theme of a conference of the world's *Germanisten* held in Tokyo in July–August 1990. Commissioned by its president, Professor Eijiro Iwasaki, this essay started out as a contribution to that conference, was published in *Merkur* no. 502 (January 1991), 1–10, translated by John Sugden, and expanded for the present book. It is reproduced by kind permission of *Merkur*.

The following works by Prague writers are discussed: Gustav Meyrink, *Der Golem: ein Roman* (Munich, 1915); Alfred Kubin, *Die andere Seite: ein phantastischer Roman* (Munich and Leipzig, 1909); Leo Perutz, *Nachts unter der steinernen Brücke: ein Roman aus dem alten Prag* (Frankfurt, 1953); Max Brod, *Tycho Brahes Weg zu Gott* (Leipzig, 1916); Ludwig Winder, *Der Thronfolger: ein Franz Ferdinand Roman* (Zurich, 1939) (pp. 324–5 quoted); Franz Werfel, *Die vierzig Tage des Musa Dagh: Roman* (Frankfurt, 1933); H[ans] G[ünter] Adler, *Eine Reise: Erzählung* (Bonn, 1962); Josef Mühlberger, *Der Galgen im Weinberg: Erzählungen* (Munich, 1960) (p. 167 quoted). Egon Erwin Kisch is quoted from *Gesammelte Werke in Einzelausgaben* (Berlin and Weimar, 1983), VIII, 421. For the quotation from Kafka, see 'Das Stadtwappen', in *GW*, V, 71. For the Morris Rosenfeld anecdote I am indebted to my friend the late Erich Heller.

Ernst Jünger is quoted from *Strahlungen* (Tübingen, 1949). For 'Mozart auf der Reise nach Prag', see Eduard Mörike, *Sämtliche Werke* (Munich, 1981), III, 1,024–81. The following critical works are relevant. Mohammed Qasim, *Gustav Meyrink: eine monographische Untersuchung* (Stuttgart, 1981). Margarita Pazi (ed.) *Max Brod 1884–1984* (Berne, 1987); see especially the contribution by Walter Schamschula, 'Max Brod und die tschechische Literatur'. P. S. Jungk, *Franz Werfel: A Life Torn by History* (London, 1990); on *Musa Dagh*, see, e.g., pp. 144–5 (the novel was finished at Christmas 1933, after Werfel had applied to join Goebbels' Association of German Writers; the book was later suppressed in Germany as a result of Turkish protests). For Kubin (*et al.*), see Peter Cersowsky, *Phantastische Literatur im ersten Viertel des zwanzigsten Jahrhunderts* (Munich, 1983). For the portrait of the archetypal Prague writer, see Hartmut Binder, 'Jan Gerke: Soziogramm eines Prager Musensohns', in *Prager deutschsprachige Literatur zur Zeit Kafkas* (Schriftenreihe der österreichischen Kafka-Gesellschaft 3) (Vienna, 1989), pp. 1–36. Jürgen Serke's *Böhmische Dörfer* (Vienna and Hamburg, 1987) is unimpaired by some melodramatic formulations and extreme judgements prompted by the tragic fate of most of the writers discussed; for Mühlberger (one of the few non-Jewish authors included), see pp. 415–20, 463f. For F. X. Šalda's triptych, see *Boje o zítřek* (written 1904; new edn., Prague 1941), pp. 249–51, and compare J. P. Stern, 'Das Wien der Jahrhundertwende aus tschechischer Sicht', *Österreichische Osthefte*, 28 (Vienna, 1986), 18–19. Šalda's reference to Kafka is in *Kritické glosy k nové poesii české* (Prague, 1939), p. 399; for his discussion of Brod's novel, see 'Židovský román staropražský', in Šalda, *Časové i nadčasové* (Prague, 1936), pp. 494–7. Josef Nadler refers to Rilke's 'Jewish mother' in *Literaturgeschichte der deutschen Stämme und Landschaften*, 1st and 2nd edn. (Regensburg, 1928), IV, 891; compare this with the anti-Semitic passages in the 3rd edn. (1932), I, 9, and IV, 891–2; compare these in turn with the postscript to *Geschichte der deutschen Literatur* (Vienna, 1951), p. 1,007. For the concept of *Alterität*, see Alois Wierlacher, 'Mit fremden Augen, oder: Fremdheit als Ferment', in *Das Fremde und das Eigene*, ed. A. Wierlacher (Munich, 1985), pp. vii–xv, 1–27. 'Alterity' ('the state of being other or different; diversity, "otherness"' – *OED*) occurs, e.g., in Coleridge's *Table Talk*, 8 July 1827.

Die böhmische Zitadelle is the title of the history of Bohemia (Vienna and Munich, 1965) by 'Christian Willars' (i.e., Oswald Kostrba-Skalický). On the history of the Jews, see *Die Juden in Böhmen und Mähren: ein historisches Lesebuch*, ed. Wilma Iggers (Munich, 1986). On Rudolf II, see Jörg Hoensch, *Geschichte Böhmens* (Munich, 1987), pp. 202–13; for the expulsion of the Sudeten Germans in 1945–6, see, e.g., p. 436, where the number of Sudeten German victims is estimated: 'After the 215,000 killed [in the war], a further 225,000 people died as a direct or indirect result of Czech retributive measures.' (These figures are supported by several sources from both sides.)

5 The education of the master race

A shorter version of this essay appeared in *Teaching the Text*, eds Susanne Kappeler and Norman Bryson (London, 1983), pp. 35–55. Reproduced here by kind permission of Routledge.

Page numbers in the text refer to *Young Törless*, tr. Eithne Wilkins and Ernst Kaiser (London, 1971); my quotations are adapted from this edition. References to Musil's diaries and essays are to *Tagebücher, Aphorismen, Essays und Reden*, ed. A. Frisé (Hamburg, 1955), pp. 201, 441, 776. Critical studies include Elisabeth Stopp, 'Musil's *Törless*: Content and Form', *Modern Language Review*, 63 (1968), 94–118; Gerhart Baumann, *Robert Musil: zur Erkenntnis der Dichtung* (Berne and Munich, 1965); F. G. Peters, *Robert Musil: Master of the Hovering Life* (New York, 1978). For biographical and bibliographical data, see Helmut Arntzen, *Musil-Kommentar* (Munich, 1980), I, 95–105. The historicity of the novel is neglected by Arntzen and is insufficiently treated by David Turner, 'The Evasions of the Aesthete Törless', *Forum for Modern Language Studies*, 10 (1974), 19–44. For the importance of a historical reading, see Paul de Man, *Allegories of Reading* (New Haven and London; 1979), p. 79. See also Friedbert Aspetsberger, '"Der andere Zustand" in its Contemporary Context', in *Musil in Focus*, eds Lothar Huber and J. J. White (London, 1982); and Josef Strutz, 'Politik und Literatur in Musils *Mann ohne Eigenschaften*', in *Literatur in der Geschichte – Geschichte in der Literatur*, 6 (Königstein, 1981). The quotations from T. S. Eliot are from 'East Coker' § 5 and 'Burnt Norton' § 1. For Himmler's speech, see *HFP*, p. 196.

6 The ideas of 1914

First published in *LRB*, 3 April 1986, p. 7 and reproduced here by kind permission of the London Review of Books. The article, entitled 'Deutschtum', reviewed Thomas Mann, *Reflections of a Nonpolitical Man*, tr. Walter D. Morris (New York, 1983). My translations are adapted from this edition. See p. 155 for the quotations 'A good part of my patriotism . . .' etc.

G. C. Lichtenberg is quoted from *Schriften und Briefe*, ed. W. Promies (Munich, 1968–71), I, D 272, and *Lichtenbergs Briefe*, eds A. Leitzmann and C. Schüddekopf (Leipzig, 1901–4), II, 282. The reference to Herbert Marcuse is to *One-Dimensional*

Man (London, 1964), p. 163. Johan Galtung is quoted from *Struktur, Kultur und intellektueller Stil*, tr. Bernd Samland (Berlin, 1982), p. 22. For Golo Mann's memoir of his father, see his *Erinnerungen und Gedanken: Eine Jugend in Deutschland* (Frankfurt/M, 1983), p. 41.

7 War and the comic muse

First published in *Comparative Literature*, 20 (1968), 193–216 and reproduced here by kind permission of *Comparative Literature*, revised. A slightly longer version of the material on Hašek was published as 'On the Integrity of the Good Soldier Schweik', *Forum for Modern Language Studies*, 2, 1 (January 1966), 14–24. The Penguin edition of *The Good Soldier Švejk and his Fortunes in the World War*, tr. Cecil Parrott (Harmondsworth, 1974), is referred to in the text by page number. My translations are adapted from this edition. The Dell Paperback edition of *Catch-22* is referred to by chapter and page number. (For the remark by the Red Indian Chief from Oklahoma, see ch. 5, p. 45.) *The Posthumous Papers of the Pickwick Club* is referred to by chapter number.

A facsimile of Hašek's note of June 1911 is in J. Kalaš, *Jaroslav Hašek ve fotografii* (Prague, 1959), p. 42. The same volume contains photographs of the real counterparts of several characters (the model for Lt. Dub is said to have been F. Trávníček). The sketch 'Klub českých Pickwicků' is reprinted in J. Křížek, *Jaroslav Hašek v revolučním Rusku* (Prague, 1957), pp. 92ff. Bibliographical information is in R. Pytlík and M. Laiske, *Bibliografie Jaroslava Haška* (Prague, 1960). Hašek's reference to Franz Joseph's *Manifesto to my Peoples* may be compared with Karl Kraus, *Das Weltgericht*, (Vienna, 1919), vol. I, ch. 1. On Hašek's 'natural', unliterary imagination, see the anonymous article in *TLS*, 7 September 1962, pp. 665–7, in which the writer Josef Kodíček is quoted describing a scene in the office of the Prague weekly *Tribuna*: 'I myself induced [Hašek] to write two volumes of stories, by the simple device of withholding payment until he had written them down in my presence. He would sit down at my desk and, without a pause, and mostly without a single correction, write each story in the neatest of scripts with extreme rapidity.' For Arne Novák's view of *The Good Soldier Švejk*, see *Dějiny české literatury*, part 7 (Prague, 1933); on pp. 191–2 Novák comments on Hašek's linguistic devices. For the claim that Hašek's reproduction of Czech vernacular is naturalistic, see, e.g., F. Daneš, 'Příspěvek k poznání jazyka a slohu Haškových Osudů ...', *Naše řeč* (1954), 124–9; also M. Jankovič, 'Umělecká pravdivost Haškova Švejka', *Rozpravy Československé akademie věd a umění*, 10 (1960), 27. Julius Fučík is quoted from Jankovič, pp. 60ff. Hašek's indebtedness to Dickens is mentioned by Pavel Petr in *Hašeks Schwejk in Deutschland* (Berlin, 1963), pp. 189f.; Petr also refers to an article by M. Shaginian in *Oktyabr*, 4 (Moscow, 1968), 208. Brecht's diary note is quoted from Petr, p. 143. F. X. Šalda is quoted from *Zápisník*, 7 (Prague, 1934), 127. Milan Kundera's article 'The Czech Wager' is in *New York Review of Books*, 22 January 1981; see also my reply in *New York Review of Books*, 16 April 1981. The dictionary entry for 'švejkovina' is in *Příruční slovník jazyka českého* (Prague, 1948–51), V, 1,208. For the 'leeward life of the nation' ('im Windschatten Wiens'), see Oswald Kostrba-Skalický, 'Vom Sinn der böhmischen Geschichte', in *Bohemia: Jahrbuch des Collegium Carolinum* (Munich, 1975), p. 36. See also Christian Willars, *Die böhmische Zitadelle* (Vienna and Munich; 1965), p. 145.

In an 'Impolite Interview' with the editor in *The Realist* no. 39 (New York, November

1962), Joseph Heller mentions his debt to Louis-Ferdinand Céline [i.e., Louis-Ferdinand Destouches], *Voyage au bout de la nuit* (Paris, 1932). On Yossarian's principle of self-protection, see R. Brustein's excellent review, 'The Logic of Survival in a Lunatic World', *The New Republic*, no. 145 (13 November 1961), pp. 11–13. For a prolixly hostile review of *Catch-22*, see the anonymous article in *Daedalus*, 92 (1963), 155–65. I wish to acknowledge the friendly and helpful discussion I had with Mr Heller on the subject of his book. On *Tristram Shandy* and Locke, see Wolfgang Iser, *Laurence Sterne: Tristram Shandy* (Landmarks of World Literature) (Cambridge, 1988), pp. 11–17.

8 The rise and fall of random persons

Published for the first time in this book, this is the expanded text of a lecture delivered at the Institute of Germanic Studies in London, and at Northwestern University in Evanston, Illinois.

Oswald Spengler, *Der Untergang des Abendlandes: Umrisse einer Morphologie der Weltgeschichte* (2 vols, Munich, 1927), is referred to in the text by volume and page number. Erich Auerbach, *Mimesis: Dargestellte Wirklichkeit in der abendländischen Literatur*, 2nd edn. (Berne, 1959), is referred to by page number. I have used and freely modified C. F. Atkinson's translation, *The Decline of the West*, (2 vols London, 1926–8), and Willard Trask's, *Mimesis: the Representation of Reality in Western Literature* (New York, 1953). The reference to 'our spontaneous ability . . . to understand one another' is to Erich Auerbach, *Literatursprache und Publikum in der lateinischen Spätantike und im Mittelalter* (Berne, 1957), p. 11.

For biographical data on Spengler, see A. M. Koktanek, *Oswald Spengler in seiner Zeit* (Munich, 1968). The most influential of Spengler's sources, particularly for the Egyptian material in vol. II, may have been Sir Flinders Petrie, *The Revolutions of Civilisation* (London, 1911), with its periodization of world history and its analogies between Egyptian and modern European civilization. For biographical data on Auerbach, see U. Knoke, 'Erich Auerbach: eine erkenntnis- und methodenkritische Betrachtung', *Zeitschrift für Literaturwissenschaft und Linguistik*, 5, 17 (1957), 74ff.; and Harry Levin, 'Two *Romanisten* in America: Spitzer and Auerbach', in Levin, *Grounds for Comparison* (Cambridge, Mass., 1972), which includes an account of Auerbach's stay in Istanbul (pp. 112f.). I have analysed Auerbach's opening chapters in 'In Praise of Erich Auerbach's *Mimesis*', in *London German Studies III* (London; 1986); pp. 194–211; there I have also offered some critical remarks on Auerbach's uncritical use of the concept of *Wirklichkeit*, and enumerated the literary-critical premises mentioned here on pp.132–3.

Schiller's lecture 'Was heißt und zu welchem Ende studiert man Universalgeschichte?' is in *Sämtliche Werke*, Säkular-Ausgabe (Berlin and Stuttgart, n.d.), XIII, 3–24. On Goethe's concept of *Urphänomene*, see H. B. Nisbet, *Goethe and the Scientific Tradition* (London, 1972), p. 42. For the quotations from St Augustine I have used Henry Chadwick's annotated translation of the *Confessions* (Oxford, 1991), p. 101.

9 Freud by a Freudian

A shorter version of this was first published in *LRB*, 4 August 1988, pp. 9–10. The original article, entitled 'All about Freud', reviewed Peter Gay, *Freud: a Life for Our Time* (London, 1988), to which the page numbers in the text refer. Reproduced here by kind permission of the London Review of Books.

Carl Schorske's essay 'Politics and Patricide in Freud's *Interpretation of Dreams*' (1973) is reprinted in Schorske, *Fin-de-Siècle Vienna: Politics and Culture* (New York, 1980), pp. 181–207. The quotations from Richard Rorty, *Contingency, Irony, and Solidarity* (Cambridge, 1989), are from pp. 31, 33–4, 52; For Rorty's remarks on 'the contingent' and 'the adventitious', see p. 99. Burke's aphorism is quoted from 'Thoughts on the Causes of the Present Discontents', in *Works* (London, 1932), II, 269. My criticism of Freud's attitude to politics is in *HFP*, pp. 89–90. The quotation from Kafka (November, 1919) is from *GW*, VI, 162.

10 Inauthenticity: theory and practice

Parts of this essay appeared in 'Heil Heidegger', *LRB*, 20 April 1989, reviewing Hugo Ott, *Martin Heidegger: Unterwegs zu seiner Biographie* (Frankfurt/M and New York, 1988): Reproduced here by kind permission of the *London Review of Books*.

The passage on 'das Existential des Man' is in *Sein und Zeit*, 5th edn. (Halle/Saale, 1941), I, § 27, pp. 126f. (This edition is identical with the original edition of 1927; the second volume was never written.) Other relevant passages are §§ 15–17 (pp. 66–80) and §§ 54–62 (pp. 267–300), especially § 58 (p. 285). A still-helpful introduction to *Sein und Zeit* is Heidegger, *Existence and Being*, with an introduction by Werner Brock (London, 1949). For Heidegger's inaugural address, see *Die Selbstbehauptung der deutschen Universität* (Breslau, 1934). The proclamation before the referendum of 12 November 1933 is in *Bekenntnis der Professoren an den deutschen Universitäten zu Adolf Hitler und dem nationalsozialistischen Staat* (Dresden, 1934), pp. 13–14. For the reference to the Nietzsche lectures, see Heidegger, *Nietzsche* (Pfullingen, 1961), I, 578. For 'the House of Being', see Heidegger, *Über den Humanismus* (Frankfurt/M, 1946), p. 5. *Gelassenheit* is the title of a short piece (4th edn., Pfullingen, 1959) which takes the form of a discussion around the meaning of the term 'equanimity'. Part of the discussion focuses on words reminiscent of those of Stefan George's invention. The discussion ends with a prose-ode on a single-word fragment of Heraclitus, *anchibasin*, 'to come close to'. Compare Ott, *Martin Heidegger*, pp. 185–6. The quotation ' . . . the truth and greatness of National Socialism . . . ' is from Heidegger, *Einführung in die Metaphysik* [the text of lectures delivered in the summer semester of 1935], 4th edn. (Tübingen, 1976), p. 208. For the altered version, see the 5th edn. (1987), p. 12; exceptionally, the emendation is not acknowledged. For other references to the 5th edn., see pp. 112–13, 117, 152.

On the subject of Heidegger's attitude to contemporary politics and history, I have found Alexander Schwan's two contributions particularly helpful: *Politische Philosophie im Denken Heideggers*, 2nd edn. (Opladen, 1989) (this edition contains a useful appendix); and 'Vorbild oder Verführer? Über den politischen Einfluß von Philosophie: Martin Heidegger', *Die Zeit*, 30 September 1969, p. 9. Additional material on the early 1930s is from Guido Schneeberger, *Nachlese zu Heidegger: Dokumente zu seinem Leben und Denken* (Berne, 1962). See also the interview of 23 September 1966, published in *Der Spiegel*, 31 May 1976, pp. 193–219. For Jaspers's view of Heidegger's relation to National Socialism, and his characterization of Heidegger's thought as 'diktatorisch, communikationslos', see Ott, *Martin Heidegger*, pp. 315–17. Hubert Dreyfus's essay 'Husserl, Heidegger and Modern Existentialism' is in Bryan Magee, *The Great Philosophers: an Introduction to Western Philosophy* (London, 1987), pp. 252–77.

The phrases 'Schwarzwald redneck', 'resentful, petty, squint-eyed', etc., are quoted from Richard Rorty, *Contingency, Irony, and Solidarity* (Cambridge, 1989), pp. 111, 120. For the concept of *enargeia*, see Carlo Ginzburg, 'Veranschaulichung und Zitat: Die Wahrheit der Geschichte', in Ferdinand Braudel, *et al.* (eds), *Der Historiker als Menschenfresser: Über den Beruf des Geschichtsschreibers* (Berlin, 1990), pp 85–102, p. 91. Plato's *Cratylus* offers a full discussion of the 'seduction of names' – see Anne Barton, *The Names of Comedy* (Oxford, 1990).

For the reaction of German journalists (e.g., Friedrich Sieburg) to the defeat of France, see Franz Schonauer, *Deutsche Literatur im Dritten Reich* (Olten and Freiburg im Br., 1961), pp. 168–75. For the quotation from Thomas Mann, see *Doctor Faustus*, 3rd part of ch. 34. The Hölderlin poem is in *Werke und Briefe*, eds F. Beissner and J. Schmidt (Frankfurt/M, 1969), I, 50; translation by Sheila Stern.

11 Günter Grass's uniqueness

First published in *LRB*, 5 February 1981, pp. 11–14 and reproduced here by kind permission; reprinted in *Critical Essays on Günter Grass*, ed. Patrick O'Neill (Boston, Mass., 1987), pp. 69–82.

I quote from the Luchterhand paperback edition of *Danziger Trilogie* (Neuwied and Darmstadt, 1974); and from the English translations by Ralph Manheim: *The Tin Drum* (London, 1962) and *Dog Years* (New York, 1965) (referred to by page numbers in the text). Biographical material is from Heinrich Vormweg, *Günter Grass mit Selbstzeugnissen und Bilddokumenten* (Reinbek bei Hamburg, 1986). See also John Reddick, *The 'Danzig Trilogy' of Günter Grass* (London, 1975). (Oddly, the theme of Danzig at war is not central to Reddick's book.)

Moby Dick is quoted from the Everyman edn. (London, 1986), p. 179. *Tristram Shandy* is quoted from the Penguin edn., introduced by Christopher Ricks (1978), p. 403; see also pp. 16–17 of that introduction.

12 The Matljary Diary

First published in *The World of Franz Kafka*, ed. J. P. Stern (New York and London, 1980), pp. 238–50.

For the quotations from 'Josefine, die Sängerin oder Das Volk der Mäuse', the story which Kafka proof-read on his death-bed, see *GW*, IV, 202, 206–7. His 'conversation slips' are quoted from *Letters to Friends, Family and Editors*, tr. Richard and Clara Winston (London 1978), pp. 417–22. (Kafka used these slips as a means of communication during his final illness – tuberculosis of the larynx – in the sanatorium at Kierling near Vienna where he died.)

13 The White Rose

First published in *German Life and Letters*, NS 11, 2 (January, 1958), 81–101; a shortened version appeared in H. Siefken (ed.), *Die Weiße Rose: Student Resistance to National Socialism, 1942/3*, a Nottingham University symposium (Nottingham, 1991), pp. 11–36. The essay has been extensively revised for this volume in the light of some of the recent publications listed below.

Biographical data are contained in three essays by the late Ricarda Huch, 'Die Aktion der Münchner Studenten', *N. Schweizer Rundschau*, 16 (September and October, 1948), and 'Alexander Schmorell', *Hamburger akad. Rundschau*, 3 (1949), 193ff.; in Clara Huber, *Kurt Huber zum Gedächtnis* (Regensburg 1947); in the account of a surviving sister, Inge Scholl, *Die weiße Rose* (Frankfurt/M, 1952), now available as no. 88 of the Fischer Bücherei (English translation, *Six Against Tyranny*, by Cyrus Brooks, London, 1955); and in an article by H. Hirzel (a close friend of the Scholls), 'Es waren ihrer sechs', *Studentische Blätter* no. 2 (Tübingen, February 1948). Details of the first trial will be found in G. Weisenborn, *Der lautlose Aufstand* (Hamburg, 1953), pp. 95–101, 267–75; for the 'theory' of Germanic justice, see R. Freisler, *Nationalsozialistisches Recht und Rechtsdenken* (Berlin, 1938). For quotations from the contemporary German press, including the indictment in *Münchner neueste Nachrichten*, 23 February 1943, see K. Z., 'Der 18. Februar, Umriß einer deutschen Widerstandsbewegung', *Die Gegenwart*, nos. 20–1 (Freiburg im Br., October 1946), pp. 9–13. The students' last days in prison are described in the reminiscences of their prison chaplain, K. Alt, *Die Todeskandidaten* (Munich, 1946), pp. 85–94. Relevant letters are in the collection by Annedore Leber, *Das Gewissen steht auf* (Berlin, 1954), pp. 22–3, 44–5; for the same collection of material in English, with an introduction by Robert Birley, see *Conscience in Revolt* (London, 1957). Further references to the conspiracy are in E. Zeller, *Geist der Freiheit* (Munich, n.d.), p. 126; R. Pechel, *Deutscher Widerstand* (Zurich, 1947), p. 98; and K. O. Paetel, *Deutsche innere Emigration* (New York, 1946), *passim*. For contemporary reaction in Berlin, see Ulrich von Hassell, *Vom andern Deutschland* (Zurich, 1946), p. 302; and R. Andreas-Friedrich, *Der Schattenmann* (Berlin, 1947), pp. 112–14. The position of the Catholic Church is described by Father J. Neuhäusler in *Kreuz und Hakenkreuz* (Munich, 1946), especially vol. II, pp. 26ff.; and also by Michael von Faulhaber, *Judentum, Christentum, Germanentum* (Munich, 1934). Commemorative addresses were delivered by Karl Vossler, *Gedenkrede für die Opfer* ... (Munich, 1947), and Romano Guardini, *Die Waage des Lebens* (Tübingen, 1947). A useful analysis of German underground activities is Michael Vyvyan, 'The German "Opposition" and Nazi Morale', *The Cambridge Journal*, 2 (1948), 148–68.

The following friends of the Scholls were kind enough to answer questions about them: Alfred von Martin, Max Stefl, Josef Furtmeier and, during the symposium at Nottingham University, Hans Hirzel; and I am indebted to my friend the late Reinhold Regensburger for help in obtaining some of the above sources. For the quotation from Luther, see 'Von der Freiheit eines Christenmenschen' (1520), in *Werke* (Erlangen,

1839), XXVII, 117ff.; from Fichte, see especially the postscript to his *Wissenschaftslehre*, in *Werke* (Berlin, 1846), III, 573, and VII, 546; from Theodor Haecker, see *Tag- und Nachtbücher* (Heidelberg, 1947), *passim*; and from F. von Hügel, see *Essays and Addresses on the Philosophy of Religion* (London, 1941), pp. 280, 282ff.

For recent publications, see Willy Graf, *Briefe und Aufzeichnungen*, eds Anneliese Knoop-Graf and Inge Jens (Frankfurt/M, 1988); Hans and Sophie Scholl, *Briefe und Aufzeichnungen*, ed. Inge Jens, 2nd edn. (Frankfurt/M, 1989); Michael Verhoeren and Marion Krebs' commentary to the film *Die weiße Rose* (Frankfurt/M, 1988); and for an attempted apologia of their judge, see H. W. Koch, *In the Name of 'Das Volk'* (London, 1988).

14 A man without ideology

The first part of the essay 'The Celebration', was published (in a slightly longer version) as 'The troublemaker from Heidenheim', *New Statesman*, 21–8 December 1979, pp. 986–7. Reproduced with permission of *New Statesman and Society*. The second part, 'A Tribute', is the text of an address delivered in German at Elser's memorial celebration in Heidenheim on 11 November 1979. It was published as a pamphlet, *Georg Elser zu Ehren* (Heidenheim, 1989), by Martin Wahl, with an introduction by Hermann Pretsch.

The Gestapo record of Elser's interrogation is quoted partly from the Bundesarchiv Koblenz (file R22/3100), partly from *Autobiographie eines Attentäters: Johann Georg Elser*, ed. Lothar Gruchmann (Stuttgart, 1970). See also Anton Hoch, 'Das Attentat auf Adolf Hitler im Münchner Bürgerbräukeller 1939', *Vierteljahrshefte für Zeitgeschichte*, 17 (1969), 383–413, and my account of Elser and his deed in *HFP*, ch. 17. Alan Bullock's misleading account is in *Hitler: a Study in Tyranny*, 2nd edn. (Harmondsworth, 1962), pp. 566–7. For Kant's interpretation of Job, see 'Über das Mißlingen aller philosophischen Versuche in der Theodizee' (1791), in *Kant's Werke* (Berlin, 1912), VI, 253–71.

15 The Gypsies

First published as 'Is This Right?', *LRB*, 19 April 1990, p. 14. Reproduced by kind permission of the *London Review of Books*.

Ian Hancock's article '"Uniqueness" of the Victims: Gypsies, Jews and the Holocaust' is in *Without Prejudice: International Review of Racial Discrimination*, 1, 2 (1988), 45–67; see also Martin Gilbert, *The Holocaust: The Jewish Tragedy* (London, 1986). 'Problems of rootlessness . . .' is quoted from *The Observer*, 11 March 1990. For the Wittgenstein quotation, see *Culture and Value*, ed. G. H. von Wright, tr. Peter Winch (Oxford, 1980), p. 45. Husserl is quoted from *Gesammelte Werke*, ed. Walter Biemel (The Hague, 1962), VI: *Die Krisis der europäischen Wissenschaften und die transzendentale Phänomenologie*, 239–40.

16 Notes on the German Army

First published as 'Notes on the West German Army', *German Life and Letters*, NS 19 (1966), 89–115. The present version is slightly expanded. Names of persons (but not their national connotations) are invented.

For the implications of the oath ('der Fahneneid'), see *Handbuch der inneren Führung*, 2nd edn. (Bonn, 1960), pp. 9, 12. Fritz Erler's essay is in the officers' handbook, *Schicksalsfragen der Gegenwart* (Tübingen, 1958), III, 223–56. The explanation of the need for a West German army is quoted from the official pamphlet of the school: *Schule der Bundeswehr für innere Führung* (Koblenz, 1961), p. 1.

17 Bitburg

First published (in a shorter form) in *TLS*, 18 May 1985. Reproduced by kind permission of the *Times Literary Supplement*.

The quotation from Stefan George is from his long narrative poem 'Der Krieg' (1917), published in his last collection, *Das neue Reich* (1928). The quotation from Camus comes from his *Lettres à un ami allemand* (Paris, 1948), pp. 71–3.

18 In praise of integrity

Section 1 was first published as 'Within and Without', *The Times Higher Education Supplement*, 7 January 1983, p. 13 and is reproduced here by kind permission. The article reviewed Paul Roubiczek, *Across the Abyss: Diary Entries for the Year 1939–1940*, tr. George Bird (Cambridge, 1982); my quotations (some of which were added for the present volume) are from pp. 237–8, 244–5. Section 2 was first published as 'Defending the State against the Nations: the Work of J. W. Bruegel', *Historical Journal*, 28, 4 (1985), pp. 1,023–7.

The main systematic exposition of Roubiczek's philosophy is *Thinking in Opposites: an Investigation of the Nature of Man as Revealed by the Nature of Thinking* (London, 1952). The works by J. W. Bruegel to which I refer are *Ludwig Czech: Arbeiterführer und Staatsmann* (Vienna, 1960); *Tschechen und Deutsche: 1918–1938* (Munich, 1967), *Tschechen und Deutsche: 1939–1946* (Munich, 1974); *Czechoslovakia before Munich: the German Minority Problem and British Appeasement Policy* (Cambridge, 1973). Bruegel is also the editor of *Friedrich Adler vor dem Ausnahmegericht* (Vienna, 1967) and *Stalin und Hitler: Pakt gegen Europa* (Vienna, 1973).

19 The end of the Prague spring

First published as 'Czechoslovakia and the Common Weal', *TLS*, 5 September 1968, p. 939. Reproduced by kind permission of the *Times Literary Supplement*.

Čapek's conversations with Masaryk in the period 1926–35 are recorded in K[arel] Č[apek], *Hovory s T.G. Masarykem* (Prague, 1937). Other quotations are taken from contemporary newspapers.

20 A crisis of identity

Parts of this essay were published as 'Die "Identitätskrise" der Deutschen', *Merkur*, 38 (June 1984), 458–63, and were translated by Sheila Stern. Reproduced here by kind permission of *Merkur*.

The Goethe quotation, 'Nur der verdient sich Freiheit wie das Leben, / Der täglich sie erobern muß', comes from *Faust* II. 11575–6. For the misbehaving horse, see Georg Büchner, *Woyzeck*, sc. 6. 'The gods grew weary . . .' ('Die Götter wurden müde, die Adler wurden müde, die Wunde schloß sich müde') is a quotation from Franz Kafka's 'Prometheus', in *GW*, VI, 74. For 'A bit of fun on doomsday morning', see Karl Heinz Bohrer, *Ein bißchen Lust am Untergang* (Munich, 1979).

21 Revising the German past?

First published as 'Germans and the German Past', *LRB*, 21 December 1989, pp. 7–9 and reproduced here by kind permission of the *London Review of Books*. The following are the books reviewed: Charles Maier, *The Unmasterable Past: History, Holocaust and German National Identity* (Cambridge, Mass., and London, 1988); *Historikerstreit* (Munich and Zurich, 1987); Richard Evans, *In Hitler's Shadow: West German Historians and the Attempt to Escape from the Nazi Past* (London, 1989) (pp: 62, 138 quoted); Arno Mayer, *Why Did the Heavens Not Darken?* (New York, 1988) (pp. xii, 16, 31, 69, 226, 302, 365 quoted); Harold James, *A German Identity, 1770–1990* (London, 1989) (pp. 54, 214, 217–8 quoted); Claus Leggewie, *Die Republikaner: Phantombild der neuen Rechten* (Berlin, 1989); Franz Schönhuber, *Ich war dabei* (Munich, 1989).

Reinhart Koselleck is quoted from 'Sprachwandel und Ereignisgeschichte', *Merkur*, 43 (1989), pp. 657–73 (p. 660). Nolte's essay 'Zwischen Geschichtslegende und Revisionismus?' is reprinted in *Historikerstreit*, pp. 13–35; I quote from pp. 24–5, 32–3. Habermas's reply, 'Eine Art Schadensabwicklung', is in *Historikerstreit*, pp. 62–76. Arno Mayer's book is reviewed by Daniel Goldhagen, 'False Witness', *The New Republic*, 17 April 1989, pp. 39–44; I quote from p. 43. The reference to *Mein Kampf* is to the 17th edn. (Munich, 1943), p. 244.

For the quotation from Nietzsche's *Untimely Meditations*, see the second essay, end of § 3. Kafka is quoted from *GW*, VI, 306.

22 The end of German Communism

Section 1 was first published in *LRB*, 7 December 1989, p. 25 and is reproduced here by kind permission of the *London Review of Books*. A slightly longer version of section 2 appeared as 'Grass on the Other Side of the Wall', in *The Observer*, 14 October

1990, p. 64, reviewing Günter Grass, *Two States – One Nation? The Case Against German Reunification*, tr. Krishna Winston with A. S. Wensinger (London, 1990) (pp. 95–6 quoted).
Conor Cruise O'Brien's warning of the 'Fourth Reich' is in *The Times*, 31 October 1989. Nicholas Ridley's outburst is recorded in an interview with Dominic Lawson in *The Spectator*, 14 July 1990, p. 8. Lothar Kettenacker ('Zum Tag der deutschen Einheit: 3. Oktober 1990', typescript) quotes Sir Alec Cairncross's estimate of German reparations to the Soviet Union from the Soviet zone as amounting to 7.5 milliard dollars, while the Western allies exacted 500 million, plus 400 million in Germany's foreign assets, sums which were compensated for by Western aid amounting to almost ten times that figure. For the quotation from Geoffrey Barraclough, see his *Origins of Modern Germany* (Oxford, 1946), p. 465.
Thomas Hobbes's maxim is in part 1, ch. 10 of *Leviathan*, ed. Michael Oakeshott (Oxford, n.d.), p. 56; see also p. lxvi of Oakeshott's introduction: 'civil society . . . offers the removal of some of the circumstances that, if they are not removed, must frustrate Felicity. It is a negative gift, merely making not impossible that which is desirable.' For the 'cunning of reason', see, e.g., G. W. F. Hegel, *Philosophie der Geschichte* (Stuttgart, 1961), p. 78 (Section II, b of the introduction).
For the quotation from Theodor Fontane, see *Vor dem Sturm* (1878), ch. 81. For Brecht, see *Poems 1913–1956*, eds John Willett and Ralph Manheim, rev. edn. (London and New York, 1987), p. 320.

23 What is German?

In October 1984 I was asked by a somewhat mysterious body called 'Landeszentrale für politische Bildung' to contribute to a symposium for the civil servants of Nordrhein-Westfalen held at Bad Meindorf; the topic was 'Die Frage nach der deutschen Identität'. My paper was printed as a pamphlet by the 'Landeszentrale' under the title of the symposium; in the present essay I have used the structure and some of the arguments of that paper.

For the quotation about the fate of the German Jews after 1933, see Wolfgang Benz, 'Deutsch-jüdische Symbiose – eine Legende', *Merkur* no. 503 (February 1991), 170ff. For the Hamlet parallel, see Jürgen Manthey, 'Glossa continua (X)', *Merkur*, no. 507 (June 1991), 642–6. Heidegger is quoted from *Sein und Zeit* 5th edn. (Halle/Saale, 1941), I, § 27, pp. 126f. ('Das alltägliche Selbstsein und das Man'). For the 'contemptuous attitude towards the particular case', see Ludwig Wittgenstein, *The Blue and Brown Books* (Oxford, 1964), p. 18. For Max Weber's criticism of 'generic terms . . . : the wider their general validity, the less content and value they have', see *Max Weber* (Reinbek bei Hamburg, 1985), p. 78. For the relevance of 'military discipline' to industrial conditions, see Weber, *Wirtschaft und Gesellschaft*, ed. J. Winckelmann (Tübingen, 1976); p. 123; for the State as an industrial enterprise, see pp. 825–6. Weber's view of the meaning of war is quoted from an excursus to part 3 of 'Die Wirtschaftsethik der Weltreligionen: Zwischenbetrachtung', *Archiv für Sozialwissenschaft und Sozialpolitik*, 41 (1916), 398; for the English version, see *From Max Weber: Essays in Sociology*, tr. and ed. by H. H. Gerth and C. Wright Mills, 7th edn. (London, 1970), p. 335. Weber's remark 'As in my life I have "dreamed" . . .' is reported by his wife, Marianne Weber; I quote from Gerhard Hufnagel, *Kritik als Beruf: der kritische Gehalt im Werk Max Webers* (Frankfurt/M, Berlin and Vienna, 1971), p. 304. Ralf Dahrendorf is quoted from Hufnagel, p. 267. For the views on discipline, cf. Dahrendorf, *Gesellschaft und Demokratie in Deutschland* (Munich, 1965), p. 67. For a discussion of the history of 'Wirklichkeit', see J. P. Stern, '"Reality" in Early Twentieth-Century German Literature', in *Philosophy and Literature* ed. A. Phillips Griffiths, Royal Institute of Philosophy Lecture Series (Cambridge, 1984). For Kant's view of the Germans, see his 'Beantwortung der Frage: Was ist Aufklärung?' (1784). Brecht is quoted from *Kleines Organon für das Theater* (Frankfurt/M, 1961), p. 43: For the quotation from Rilke, I have adapted the translation by J. B. Leishman and Stephen Spender of the *Duino Elegies* (London, 1952). 'Negative Capability' is defined by Keats in his letter of 22 December 1817 to his brothers George and Tom. For Ernst Jünger's comparison between the Flanders battlefield of Langemarck and Manchester, see J. P. Stern, 'Ernst Jüngers Zwischenkrieg', in *Die in dem alten Haus der Sprache wohnen*, ed. Eckehard Czucka (Münster, 1991), p. 470. For the resort to obscenities, see Peter Sloterdijk, *Kritik der zynischen Vernunft* (2 vols, Frankfurt/M, 1983). For the Nietzsche quote ('Nihilism as a psychological condition'), see *Sämtliche Werke: Kritische Studienausgabe*, eds Giorgio Colli and Mazzino Montinari (Berlin, 1980), XIII, 46.

24 Havel's Castle

First published in *LRB*, 22 February 1990, pp. 5–8 and reproduced here by kind permission of the *London Review of Books*.

Havel's letters to his wife are published as *Dopisy Olze* (Toronto, 1985); see also *Letters to Olga, June 1979 – September 1982*, tr. Paul Wilson (London, 1990), pp. 75, 177, 181, 271–3. The last sixteen letters were published separately as *Výzva k transcendenci* (London, 1984), with a commentary by 'Sidonius' and the text of Havel's speech (not delivered in person since he was in gaol at the time) accepting the honorary doctorate of Toulouse University. For a collection of Havel's essays, addresses and interviews of the period 1969–79, see *O lidskou identitu*, eds Vilém Prečan and Alexander Tomský (London, 1984); I quote from pp. 6, 151. For Havel's December 1968 exchange with Kundera, see pp. 187–200. For the 'long distance interview' with Karel Hvížd'ala in 1985, see *Dálkový výslech* (Hamburg, 1989); I quote from pp. 8ff., 61, 78, 95, 125, 129, 155, 169. Wherever possible, throughout this essay I have checked my own translations against published ones.

The quotation from *The Audience* is from *Hry 1970–1976: Audience* (Toronto, 1977), p. 265. For *The Garden Party*, see *Ztížené možnosti: Zahradní slavnost* (Purley, 1986), especially p. 55. In connection with 'Ptydepe' in *The Memorandum*, Havel has acknowledged advice from his brother, Jiří Havel, a mathematician.

The uprising of November 1989 is the subject of a brilliant report by Timothy Garton Ash, 'Magical Prague', *New York Review of Books*, 18 January 1990, pp. 42–51. The notice 'Pilgrims are welcome . . .' is quoted from *Mladý svět*, 36, 51 (1 December 1989), 21. See also Timothy Garton Ash, *The Uses of Adversity* (London, 1989), pp. 193–5, for the petition for religious freedom of 1988.

25 Canetti's Later Work

First published in *LRB*, 3 July 1986, pp. 13–15, as a review of two books by Elias Canetti (both translated by Joachim Neugroschel): *The Human Province* (London, 1985) and *The Conscience of Words* (London, 1986). Reproduced here by kind permission of the *London Review of Books*. Both books contain material published in previous works, and the second contains a slightly different collection of material from that of the German version *Das Gewissen der Worte* (Munich and Vienna, 1975). For the quotation 'With the growing awareness . . .', see *Die Provinz des Menschen* (Frankfurt/M, 1976), p. 183. The quotations from *Masse und Macht* (Frankfurt/M, 1980) are from pp. 273–4; I have amended the English translation by Carol Stewart, *Crowds and Power* (London, 1962), wherever it alters or omits part of the original text. For Iris Murdoch's review, see 'Mass, Might and Myth', in *The Spectator*, 7 September 1962; John Bayley is quoted from 'Canetti and Power', *LRB*, 17 December 1981.

A very clear account of 'philosophical anthropology' is given in the last chapter of Herbert Schnädelbach, *Philosophy in Germany, 1831–1933*, tr. Eric Matthews (Cambridge, 1984). The relevant authors discussed are Max Scheler, Arnold Gehlen and Helmuth Plessner, to whom I would add Kurt Stavenhagen.

Brecht is quoted from *Poems 1913–1956*, eds John Willett and Ralph Manheim, rev. edn. (London and New York, 1987), p. 318. For the quotation from Wittgenstein, see *PI*, I, § 112. Hobbes is quoted from part 1, ch. 5 of *Leviathan*, ed. Michael Oakeshott (Oxford, n.d.), p. 19; Freud from 'Zeitgemäßes über Krieg und Tod' (1915), in vol. IX of *Studienausgabe* (Frankfurt/M, 1982), p. 49.

26 Marxism on stilts: Ernst Bloch

First published in *Encounter*, July/August 1988, pp. 27–33. A shorter version appeared in *The New Republic*, March 1987.

Page references in the text are to Ernst Bloch, *The Principle of Hope*, translated and introduced by Neville Plaice, Stephen Plaice and Paul Knight (3 vols, Cambridge, Mass., and Oxford, 1986). In addition to Spengler, a list of comparable 'all-about-everything' books written in this century would include Ludwig Klages, *Spirit as Adversary of the Soul* (1929–33); Robert Musil, *The Man Without Qualities* (uncompleted at Musil's death in 1942); Alfred Weber, *Farewell to Recent History* (1946); Hans Freyer, *Theory of the Present Age* (1956); and Elias Canetti, *Crowds and Power* (1960).

Biographical data are from Silvia Markun, *Ernst Bloch* (Reinbek bei Hamburg, 1977). The story of Bloch's friendship with Dutschke is taken from Jürgen Miermeister, *Rudi Dutschke* (Reinbek bei Hamburg, 1986). For Bloch's alleged ignorance of Stalin's atrocities, see Ernst Bloch and Fritz Vilmar, 'Ein Gespräch über ungelöste Aufgaben der sozialistischen Theorie', in *Über Ernst Bloch*, ed. Renate Kübler (Frankfurt/M, 1968). Jürgen Habermas is quoted from 'Ein marxistischer Schelling', in *Über Ernst Bloch*; the suppression of quotations from Stalin, not mentioned by the translators of *The Principle of Hope*, is noted by Habermas on p. 77.

Bacon writes that 'Natural magic . . ., containing certain credulous and superstitious conceits . . .' is 'as far differing in the truth of nature from such a knowledge as we require, as the story of King Arthur ... differs from Caesar's Commentaries in truth of story': see *The Advancement of Learning*, ed. G. W. Kitchin (London, 1973), p. 100. Bloch 'quotes' Bacon as saying: 'When magic is united with science, then this *natural magic* will accomplish deeds as different from earlier superstitious experiments as are the real deeds of Caesar from the imaginary Arthurs of the Round Table': see *Das Prinzip Hoffnung* [written 1938–47] (Frankfurt/M, 1985), p. 759; my translation. Instead of tranlating Bloch's 'quotation', the translators surmise that he must have used 'an inferior translation'. Bacon's actual argument is diametrically opposed to Bloch's.

The remark by Brecht is in *Kleines Organon für das Theater* (Frankfurt/M, 1961), § 75. The reference to St Augustine is to his *enarratio* of the 144th Psalm; see *Opera omnia*, ed. Migne (Petit Montrouge, 1844), IV, 1,887ff. The reference to Josef Pieper is to his *Hope and History*, tr. Richard and Clara Winston (London, 1969). 'How can we be just ...' is quoted from Robert Frost's last letter (dictated in January 1963); see his *Poetry and Prose*, eds E. C. Lathem and L. Thompson (New York, 1972), pp. 462–3.

27 The commissar, the student and the blackout

This is a slightly altered version of my review of Arpad Kadarkay's *Georg Lukács: Life, Thought, and Politics* (Basil Blackwell: Oxford and Cambridge, MA, 1991), which appeared in *LRB*, 26 Sept. 1991, volume 13, no. 18. Reproduced by kind permission of the *London Review of Books*. The page numbers in the text refer to the book under review.

I quote from Rodney Livingstone's excellent translation of *History and Class Consciousness: Studies in Marxist Dialectics* (London, 1971), from Richard Humphrey's *Historical Novel as Philosophy of History* (Institute of Germanic Studies, London, 1986), p. 63, and from Daniel Bell's review of Kadarkay, 'After the Age of Sinfulness', *TLS*, 26 July 1991, p. 7; for Lukács's remarks on Goethe, see his *Goethe and His Age*, tr. Robert Anchor (London, 1968), pp. 235, 246; for his praise of Stalin's linguistic genius, see his introduction to G. W. F. Hegel's *Ästhetik* (Berlin, 1955), pp. 43–5.

28 Wittgenstein in Context

A shorter version of this essay appeared in *Austrian Studies*, eds Edward Timms and Ritchie Robertson (Edinburgh, 1990), pp. 149–70. It incorporated material from a review of McGuinness's *Wittgenstein*, in *Philosophy*, 64, 294 (July, 1989), 409–19.

The following works are referred to by page numbers in the text: Ray Monk, *Ludwig Wittgenstein: the Duty of Genius* (London, 1990); J. C. Nyíri, *Am Rande Europas: Studien zur österreichisch-ungarischen Philosophiegeschichte* (Vienna, Graz and Cologne, 1988); David Pears, *The False Prison: a Study of the Development of Wittgenstein's Philosophy*, vol. I (Oxford, 1987); and Brian McGuinness, *Wittgenstein: a Life* (London, 1988), vol. I: *Young Ludwig (1889–1921)*. The German edition of McGuinness's biography, *Wittgensteins frühe Jahre*, tr. Joachim Schulte (Frankfurt/M, 1988), contains a number of quotations from Wittgenstein's diaries and letters not included in the English version.

The quotation 'A gramophone record ...' is from *Tractatus Logico-Philosophicus*, tr.

D. F. Pears and Brian McGuinness (London, 1961), § 4.014. For 'There is a truth
in Schopenhauer's view ...', see *Wittgenstein's Lectures: Cambridge, 1932–1935*, ed.
Alice Ambrose (Totowa, NJ, 1979), p. 43. 'If only you do not try to utter ...' is
quoted from Wittgenstein's letter to Engelmann, 9 April 1912; see McGuinness, p.
251, and Monk, p. 151. For 'In philosophy it is always a question ...', see Nyíri, p.
110, and Wittgenstein, *Philosophische Bemerkungen*, ed. Rush Rhees (Frankfurt/M,
1964), p. 153, § 133. For 'God wills the good ... a further reason', see Friedrich
Waismann, *Wittgenstein und der Wiener Kreis*, ed. B. F. McGuinness (Frankfurt, 1967),
p. 115 (the same kind of argument is used by Kant in defence of Job, in 'Über das
Mißlingen aller philosophischen Versuche in der Theodizee' (1791), in *Kant's Werke*
(Berlin, 1912), VI, 253–71, but there – Job claims – the interdict is decreed by God).
The quotations 'If I am thinking about a topic ...' and 'the good Austrian ...' are
from Wittgenstein, *Culture and Value*, ed. G. H. von Wright, with parallel translations
by Peter Winch (Oxford, 1980), pp. 3, 28 (Wittgenstein's italics); for further quotations,
see pp. 6, 19, 36, 49, 74, 86. Selected by the editor in collaboration with Heikki
Nyman from Wittgenstein's diaries and manuscript notes, these reflections are identical
with *Vermischte Bemerkungen* (Frankfurt/M, 1977). Neither title is Wittgenstein's. The
estimate of at least 13,000 pages of posthumous material is from Nyíri, p. 206.
    On the 'family resemblance' method, see Wittgenstein, *The Blue and Brown Books*
(Oxford, 1964), pp. 17–18. For 'sporadic resemblances', see Rodney Needham, *Against
the Tranquility of Axioms* (Berkeley, 1983), p. 38. On p. 43, Needham mentions the
French botanist Michel Adanson (1727–1806); see also p. 37, and Nietzsche, *Beyond
Good and Evil* (1886), § 20: 'the singular family resemblance of all Indian, Greek and
German philosophizing ...' Benedetto Croce, in *Aesthetic as Science and General
Linguistics* (London, 1967), p. 73, deplores the fact that 'family likenesses ... derived
from the historical conditions in which the various works [of literature] arise and from
the relationship of souls among artists ... can never be rendered with abstract
determinations.' For the 'polythetic method', see *OED*, 1982 supplement, and Needham, ch. 3. For 'The sickness of a time ...', see Wittgenstein, *Remarks on the
Foundations of Mathematics*, eds G. H. von Wright, Rush Rhees and G. E. M. Anscombe
(Oxford, 1967), p. 65.
    Russell is quoted from *The Philosophy of Bertrand Russell*, ed. P. A. Schilpp (Evanston
and Chicago, 1944), p. 727. For the references to Bolzano, see his *Vermischte philosophische und physikalische Schriften, 1832–1848*, eds Jan Berg and Jaromír Loužil (Stuttgart
– Bad Canstatt, 1978), pp. iii, 83–5. For 'truths in themselves', see 'Bolzano's Bohemia',
p. 33 above. For 'language as an institution', see Michael Dummett, *Ursprünge der
analytischen Philosophie*, tr. Joachim Schulte (Frankfurt/M, 1988), p. 22. The quotation
from Nietzsche is from *Twilight of the Idols* (1888), 'Expeditions of an Untimely Man',
§ 26. For Heidegger's phenomenology of crafts and work, see *Sein und Zeit*, § 15,
'Hermeneutik der Faktizität'. For the concept of *enargeia*, see 'Inauthenticity: Theory
and Practice', p. 163 above. For accounts of the 'family resemblances' between Wittgenstein and Lichtenberg, see G. H. von Wright, 'Lichtenberg als Philosoph', in *Theoria*,
8, 3 (Gøteborg, 1942), 201ff.; and J. P. Stern, *G. C. Lichtenberg: a Doctrine of Scattered
Occasions* (Bloomington, 1959), *passim*.
    The reference to Michael Oakeshott is to *Rationalism in Politics and Other Essays*
(London, 1962); though Wittgenstein and Oakeshott were Cambridge contemporaries,
they do not seem to have met. In his discussion of Wittgenstein's 'conservatism', Nyíri
does not mention Marx's (and Engels's) anti-metaphysical remarks (mainly in *Deutsche
Ideologie* of 1845–6), which several writers have compared with Wittgenstein's; see A.

R. Manser, *The End of Philosophy: Marx and Wittgenstein* (Southampton, 1973); and David Rubinstein, *Marx and Wittgenstein: Social Praxis and Social Explanation* (London, 1981), especially ch. 9. My point is not that the parallels are close, but that they bring out the 'revolutionary' aspect of Wittgenstein's thinking. See also Renford Bambrough, 'Roots and branches', *The Listener*, January 1966, p. 126 ('I cannot start from anywhere . . .'); and Bambrough, 'Conflict and the scope of reason'; *Ratio*, 20, 2 (1978), 86 ('speaks of the straight new avenues. . .')

Index